Critical Concepts in Media and Cultural Studies

Other titles in this series:

Television
Edited with a new introduction by Toby Miller
4 volume set

Film Theory
Edited with a new introduction by Philip Simpson, Andrew Utterson
and K. J. Shepherdson
4 volume set

HOLLYWOOD

Critical Concepts in Media and Cultural Studies

Edited by
Thomas Schatz

Volume I

**Historical dimensions:
the development of the
American film industry**

Routledge
Taylor & Francis Group

LONDON AND NEW YORK

First published 2004
by Routledge
11 New Fetter Lane, London EC4P 4EE

Simultaneously published in the USA and Canada
by Routledge
29 West 35th Street, New York, NY 10001

Routledge is an imprint of the Taylor & Francis Group

Typeset in Times by RefineCatch Ltd, Bungay, Suffolk
Printed and bound in Great Britain by TJ International Ltd,
Padstow, Cornwall

British Library Cataloguing in Publication Data
A catalogue record for this book is available from the British Library

Library of Congress Cataloging in Publication Data
A catalog record for this book has been requested

ISBN 0–415–28131–8 (Set)
ISBN 0–415–28132–6 (Volume I)

Publisher's Note
References within each chapter are as they appear in the original
complete work

CONTENTS

CONTENTS

CONTENTS

CONTENTS

CONTENTS

VOLUME III SOCIAL DIMENSIONS: TECHNOLOGY, REGULATION AND AUDIENCE

CONTENTS

CONTENTS

VOLUME IV   CULTURAL DIMENSIONS: IDEOLOGY, IDENTITY AND CULTURE INDUSTRY STUDIES

xi

CONTENTS

ACKNOWLEDGEMENTS

The author would like to thank Caroline Frick and Jennifer Holt for their invaluable editorial assistance, which included not only the 'dirty work' of tracking down countless articles, references, and the like, but also providing excellent advice on the organization and contents of this massive anthology. Like so many of my students, Caroline and Jennifer taught me a lot.

The publishers would like to thank the following for permission to reprint their material:

The University of Wisconsin Press for permission to reprint Russell Merritt, 'Nickelodeon Theaters, 1905–1914: Building an Audience for the Movies' in Tino Balio (ed.) *The American Film Industry*, Madison, Wisc.: University of Wisconsin Press, 1976, pp. 83–102. Copyright © 1976. Reprinted by permission of The University of Wisconsin Press.

The Gale Group for permission to reprint Richard Koszarski, 'Making Movies' in Richard Koszarski (ed.) *History of the American Cinema, Volume 3: An Evening's Entertainment: The Age of the Silent Feature Picture, 1915–1928*, New York, Oxford: Charles Scribner's Sons, 1990, pp. 95–137, 335–339. Copyright © 1990 Charles Scribner's Sons. Reprinted by permission of The Gale Group.

The University of Wisconsin Press for permission to reprint Tino Balio, 'Stars in Business: The Founding of United Artists' in Tino Balio (ed.) *The American Film Industry*, Madison, Wisc.: University of Wisconsin Press, 1976, pp. 135–152. Copyright © 1976. Reprinted by permission of The University of Wisconsin Press.

Taylor & Francis for permission to reprint Robert C. Allen, 'William Fox Presents *Sunrise*', *Quarterly Review of Film Studies* 2(2) (1977): 327–338. Copyright © 1977 *Quarterly Review of Film Studies*.

St Martin's Press for permission to reprint Douglas Gomery, 'The Hollywood Studio System: 1930–49' in Douglas Gomery, *The Hollywood Studio System*, New York: St Martin's Press, 1986, pp. 1–25.

Screen for permission to reprint Edward Buscombe, 'Notes on Columbia Pictures Corporation 1926–41', *Screen* 16(3) (Autumn 1975): 65–82.

Screen for permission to reprint Lea Jacobs, 'The B Film and the Problem of Cultural Distinction', *Screen* 33(1) (Spring 1992): 1–13.

The University of Texas Press for permission to reprint Eric Schaefer, 'Of Hygiene and Hollywood: Origins of the Exploitation Film', *The Velvet Light Trap* 30 (Fall 1992): 34–47.

The University of Texas Press for permission to reprint Matthew Bernstein, 'Hollywood's Semi-Independent Production', *Cinema Journal* 32(3) (Spring 1993): 41–54.

Little, Brown & Co. for permission to reprint Garth Jowett, 'The Decline of an Institution' in *Film: The Democratic Art*, Boston: Little, Brown & Co., 1976, pp. 333–363. Copyright © 1976 Little, Brown & Co.

The Gale Group for permission to reprint Christopher Anderson, 'Television and Hollywood in the 1940s' in Thomas Schatz (ed.) *History of the American Cinema, Volume 6: Boom and Bust: American Cinema in the 1940s*, New York, Oxford: Charles Scribner's Sons, 1997, pp. 422–444, 521–524. Copyright © 1997 Charles Scribner's Sons.

The University of Texas Press for permission to reprint William Boddy, 'The Studios Move into Prime Time: Hollywood and the Television Industry in the 1950s', *Cinema Journal* 24(4) (Summer 1985): 23–37.

Oxford University Press for permission to reprint Robert Phillip Kolker, 'Introduction' in *A Cinema of Loneliness: Penn, Kubrick, Scorsese, Spielberg, Altman*, New York: Oxford University Press, 1980, pp. 3–16, 407–408. Copyright © 1988 Oxford University Press, Inc.

Taylor & Francis for permission to reprint Thomas Schatz, 'The New Hollywood' in Jim Collins, Hillary Radner and Ava Preacher Collins (eds) *Film Theory Goes to the Movies*, New York: Routledge, 1993, pp. 8–36, 265–268. Copyright © 1993 Routledge, Inc., part of the Taylor & Francis Group.

The American Film Institute for permission to reprint J. Hoberman, '1975–1985: Ten Years that Shook the World', *American Film* (June 1985): 34–59.

Unwin Hyman for permission to reprint Michele Hilmes, 'Pay Television: Breaking the Broadcast Bottleneck' in Tino Balio (ed.) *Hollywood in the Age of Television*, Boston, Mass.: Unwin Hyman, 1990, pp. 297–318.

Helen Dwight Reid Educational Foundation for permission to reprint Gary Edgerton, 'The Multiplex: The Modern American Motion Picture Theater as Message', *Journal of Popular Film and Television* IX(4) (1982): 158–165. Published by Heldref Publications, 1319 Eighteenth St., NW, Washington, DC 20036-1802. Copyright © 1982.

Critical Studies in Mass Communication for permission to reprint Frederick Wasser, 'Is Hollywood America? The Trans-Nationalization of the American Film Industry', *Critical Studies in Mass Communication* 12(4) (1995): 423–437.

University of California Press for permission to reprint Alisa Perren, 'Sex, Lies and Marketing: Miramax and the Development of the Quality Indie Blockbuster', *Film Quarterly* 55(2) (2001): 30–39. Copyright © 2001 The Regents of the University of California.

Disclaimer

Chronological Table of Reprinted Articles and Chapters

Date	Author	Article/Chapter	References	Vol.	Chap.
1953	Dwight Macdonald	A theory of mass culture	*Diogenes* 3 (Summer): 1–17.	IV	61
1967	Francois Truffaut	Introduction to *Hitchcock*	Francois Truffaut, *Hitchcock*, New York: Simon and Schuster, pp. 7–15.	II	33
1968	Andrew Sarris	Toward a theory of film history	Andrew Sarris, *The American Cinema: Directors and Directions, 1929–1968*, New York: Dutton, pp. 19–37.	II	20
1968	Andrew Sarris	Alfred Hitchcock (1899–)	Andrew Sarris, *The American Cinema: Directors and Directions, 1929–1968*, New York: Dutton, pp. 56–61.	II	34
1968	Richard Corliss	The legion of decency	*Film Comment* 4 (Summer): 25–61.	III	47
1970	Jim Kitses	Authorship and genre: notes on the western	Jim Kitses, *Horizons West—Anthony Mann, Budd Boetticher, Sam Peckinpah: Studies of Authorship within the Western*, Bloomington, Ind.: Indiana University Press, pp. 7–27	II	21
1972	T. W. Adorno and Max Horkheimer	The culture industry: enlightenment and mass deception	T. W. Adorno and Max Horkheimer (eds), *Dialectic of Enlightenment*, trans. By John Cumming, New York: Herder & Herder, pp. 94–137 [120–164?]. First published in 1943.	IV	60
1975	Edward Buscombe	Notes on Columbia Pictures Corporation 1926–1941	*Screen* 16(3) (Autumn): 65–82.	I	6
1976	Russell Merritt	Nickelodeon theaters, 1905–1914: building an audience for the movies	Tino Balio (ed.), *The American Film Industry*, Madison, Wisc.: University of Wisconsin Press, pp. 83–102.	I	1
1976	Tino Balio	Stars in the business: the founding of United Artists	Tino Balio (ed.), *The American Film Industry*, Madison, Wisc.: University of Wisconsin Press, pp. 135–152.	I	3
1976	Garth Jowett	The decline of an institution	Garth Jowett, *Film: The Democratic Art*, Boston, Mass.: Little, Brown & Co., pp. 333–363.	I	10

Chronological Table of Reprinted Articles and Chapters – *continued*

Date	Author	Article/Chapter	References	Vol.	Chap.
1982	Gary Edgerton	The multiplex: The modern American motion picture theater as message	*Journal of Popular Film and Television* IX(4): 158–165.	I	17
1982	Michael Conant	The Paramount decrees reconsidered	*Law and Contemporary Problems* 44(4): 79–107.	III	52
1982	Judith Mayne	Immigrants and spectators	*Wide Angle* 5(2): 32–41.	III	56
1982	Jane Feuer	Mass art as folk art	Jane Feuer, *The Hollywood Musical*, Bloomington, Ind.: Indiana University Press, pp. 1–22.	IV	62
1982	Mary Anne Doane	Film and the masquerade: theorising the female spectator	*Screen* 23(3–4) (September–October): 74–87.	IV	64
1983	William Rothman	*North by Northwest*: Hitchcock's monument to the Hitchcock film	*North Dakota Quarterly* 51(3) (Summer): 11–23.	II	36
1983	Steve Neale	Masculinity as spectacle: reflections on men in mainstream cinema	*Screen* 24(6): 2–16.	IV	66
1984	Rick Altman	Toward a theory of the history of representational technologies	*Iris* 2(2): 111–125.	III	40
1985	William Boddy	The studios move into prime time: Hollywood and the television industry in the 1950s	*Cinema Journal* 24(4) (Summer): 23–37.	I	12
1985	J. Hoberman	1975–1985: ten years that shook the world	*American Film* (June): 34–59.	I	15
1985	Richard deCordova	The emergence of the star system in America	*Wide Angle* (Spring): 4–13.	II	27
1985	Philip Beck	Technology as commodity and representation: cinema stereo in the fifties	*Wide Angle* 7(3): 62–73.	III	44

Year	Author	Title	Citation	Part	No.
1985	Richard S. Randall	Censorship: from *The Miracle* to *Deep Throat*	Tina Balio (ed.), *The American Film Industry*, Madison, Wisc.: University of Wisconsin Press, pp. 432–457.	III	49
1986	Douglas Gomery	The Hollywood studio system: 1930–49	Douglas Gomery, *The Hollywood Studio System*, New York: St Martin's Press, pp. 1–25.	I	5
1986	Matthew Bernstein	Fritz Lang, incorporated	*The Velvet Light Trap* 22: 33–52.	II	22
1986	Richard Dyer	Introduction to *Heavenly Bodies*	Richard Dyer, *Heavenly Bodies: Film Stars and Society*, New York: St Martins Press, pp. 1–18.	II	28
1987	Robert E. Kapsis	Hitchcock's *The Birds*: Hollywood filmmaking and reputation building	*Journal of Popular Film and Television* 15(1) (Spring): 5–15.	II	37
1987	Clayton R. Koppes and Gregory D. Black	Will this picture help win the war?	Clayton R. Koppes and Gregory D. Black, *Hollywood Goes to War: How Politics, Profits and Propoganda Shaped World War II Movies*, New York: Free Press, pp. 48–81, 334–338.	III	51
1988	James Naremore	Marlon Brando in *On the Waterfront* (1954)	James Naremore, *Acting and Performance in the American Cinema*, Berkeley, Calif.: University of California Press, pp. 193–212.	II	30
1988	Thomas Schatz	Selznick and Hitchcock: balance of power	Thomas Schatz, *The Genius of the System: Hollywood Filmmaking in the Studio Era*, New York: Pantheon, pp. 271–294, 503.	II	35
1988	Tania Modleski	Introduction: Hitchcock, feminism, and the patriarchal unconscious	Tania Modleski, *The Women Who Knew Too Much: Hitchcock and Feminist Film Theory*, New York: Routledge, pp. 1–15.	II	39
1988	John Belton	CinemaScope and historical methodology	*Cinema Journal* 28(1) (Fall): 22–44.	III	42
1988	Richard Dyer	White	*Screen* 29(4): 44–64.	IV	71
1988	Jane Gaines	White privilege and looking relations: race and gender in feminist theory	*Screen* 29(4): 12–27.	IV	72

Chronological Table of Reprinted Articles and Chapters – *continued*

Date	Author	Article/Chapter	References	Vol.	Chap.
1989	Tino Balio	"007": a license to print money	Tino Balio, *United Artists: The Company That Changed the Film Industry*, Madison, Wisc.: University of Wisconsin Press, pp. 253–274.	IV	76
1990	Michele Hilmes	Pay television: breaking the broadcast bottleneck	Tina Balio (ed.), *Hollywood in the Age of Television*, Boston, Mass.: Unwin Hyman, pp. 297–318.	I	16
1990	Robert C. Allen	From exhibition to reception: reflections on the audience in film history	*Screen* 31(4) (Winter): 347–356.	III	55
1990	Mark Crispin Miller	Hollywood: the ad	*Atlantic Monthly* (April): 41–68.	IV	74
1991	Douglas Kellner	Film, politics, and ideology: reflections on Hollywood film in the age of Reagan	*The Velvet Light Trap* 27 (Spring): 9–24.	IV	63
1991	Linda Williams	Film bodies: gender, genre and excess	*Film Quarterly* 44(4): 2–13.	IV	65
1991	Steven Cohan	Masquerading as the American male in the fifties: *Picnic*, William Holden and the spectacle of masculinity in Hollywood film	*Camera Obscura* 25–26: 43–72.	IV	67
1991	Eileen R. Meehan	"Holy commodity fetish, Batman!": the political economy of the commercial intertext	Roberta E. Pearson and William Uricchio (eds), *The Many Lives of Batman*, New York: BFI-Routledge, pp. 47–65.	IV	75
1992	Lea Jacobs	The B film and the problem of cultural distinction	*Screen* 33(1): 1–13.	I	7
1992	Eric Schaefer	Of hygiene and Hollywood: origins of the exploitation film	*The Velvet Light Trap* 30 (Fall): 34–47.	I	8

Year	Author	Title	Source	Part	Chapter
1992	John G. Cawelti	*Chinatown* and generic transformation in recent American films	Gerald Mast, Marshall Cohen and Leo Braudy (eds), *Film Theory and Criticism: Introductory Readings*, New York: Oxford University Press, pp. 227–254.	II	24
1992	bell hooks	The oppositional gaze: black female spectators	bell hooks, *Black Looks: Race and Representation*, Boston, Mass.: South End Press, pp. 115–131, 195–200.	IV	68
1992	Charles Ramirez Berg	A crash course on Hollywood's Latino imagery	Charles Ramirez Berg, *Cinema of Solitude: A Critical Study of Mexican Film, 1697–1983*, Austin, Tex.: University of Texas Press, pp. 66–86, 282.	IV	70
1993	Matthew Bernstein	Hollywood's semi-independent production	*Cinema Journal* 32(3) (Spring): 41–54.	I	9
1993	Thomas Schatz	The New Hollywood	Jim Collins, Hillary Radner and Ava Preacher Collins (eds), *Film Theory Goes to the Movies*, New York: Routledge, pp. 8–36, 265–268.	I	14
1994	Richard Koszarski	Making movies	Richard Koszarski (ed.), *History of the American Cinema, Volume 3: An Evening's Entertainment: The Age of the Silent Feature Picture, 1915–1928*, Berkeley, Calif.: University of California Press, pp. 95–137, 335–339.	I	2
1994	Dennis Bingham	Introduction: I'm not really a man, but I play one in the movies	Dennis Bingham, *Acting Male: Masculinities in the Films of James Stewart, Jack Nicholson, and Clint Eastwood*, New Brunswick: Rutgers University Press, pp. 1–19, 253–263.	II	31
1994	Justin Wyatt	A critical redefinition: the concept of high concept	Justin Wyatt, *High Concept: Movies and Marketing in Hollywood*, Austin, Tex.: University of Texas Press, pp. 1–22.	IV	78
1995	Frederick Wasser	Is Hollywood America? The trans-nationalization of the American film industry	*Critical Studies in Mass Communication* 12(4): 423–437.	I	18

Chronological Table of Reprinted Articles and Chapters – *continued*

Date	Author	Article/Chapter	References	Vol.	Chap.
1995	Jon Lewis	Francis Coppola and the new New Hollywood	Jon Lewis, *Whom God Wishes to Destroy: Francis Coppola and the New Hollywood*, Durham, NC: Duke University Press, pp. 143–164.	II	26
1995	Richard Maltby	The genesis of the production code	*Quarterly Review of Film and Video* 15(4): 5–32.	III	45
1995	Ruth Vasey	Beyond sex and violence: "industry policy" and the regulation of Hollywood movies, 1922–1939	*Quarterly Review of Film and Video* 15(4): 65–85.	III	48
1997	Christopher Anderson	Television and Hollywood in the 1940s	Thomas Schatz (ed.), *History of the American Cinema, Volume 6: Boom and Bust: American Cinema in the 1940s*, Berkeley, Calif.: University of California Press, pp. 42 521–524.	I	11
1997	Martin Scorsese	DeNiro and me	*Projections* 7: 36–59.	II	32
1997	Josh Stenger	Consuming the planet: Planet Hollywood, stars, and the global consumer culture	*The Velvet Light Trap* 40 (Fall): 42–65.	IV	77
1998	Barbara Klinger	The new media aristocrats: home theater and the domestic film experience	*The Velvet Light Trap* 42 (Fall): 4–19.	III	58
1998	Craig Watkins	Black cinema and the changing landscape of industrial image making	Craig Watkins, *Representing: Hip Hop Culture and the Production of Black Cinema*, Chicago Ill.: The University of Chicago Press, pp. 77–103, 258–264, 283–303.	IV	69
1999	Thomas Doherty	Classical Hollywood cinema: the world according to Joseph I. Breen	Thomas Doherty, *Pre-Code Hollywood: Sex, Immorality, and Insurrection in American Cinema, 1930–1934*, New York: Columbia University Press, pp. 319–346.	III	46

Year	Author	Title	Publication	Vol.	No.
1999	Donald Crafton	Enticing the audience: Warner Bros. And Vitaphone	Donald Crafton (ed.), *History of the American Cinema, Volume 4: Talkies: American Cinema's Transition to Sound, 1926–1931*, Berkeley, Calif.: University of California Press, pp. 101–126, 568–570.	III	57
2001	Alisa Perren	Sex, lies and marketing: Miramax and the development of the quality indie blockbuster	*Film Quarterly* 55(2): 30–39.	I	19
2001	James Naremore	Hitchcock and humor	*Strategies* 14(1): 13–25.	II	38
2001	Jennifer Holt	In deregulation we trust: the synergy of politics and industry in Reagan-era Hollywood	*Film Quarterly* 55(2): 22–29.	III	54
2001	Toby Miller and Richard Maxwell	Audiences	Toby Miller and Richard Maxwell, *Global Hollywood*, London: BFI Publishing, pp. 171–194, 220–271.	III	59

GENERAL INTRODUCTION
Hollywood as 'critical concept'

Perhaps a logical starting point for the introduction to this particular collection is to note that, from its very beginnings, 'Hollywood' has existed not only as an actual place but also as a collective idea, a conceptual construct that was created and shaped by an array of forces. Chief among those forces were the movies themselves, of course, along with the deluge of promotional and journalistic discourse that fuelled the rise of cinema as the signal entertainment form of early twentieth-century America. Although previous entertainment forms, from dime novels to vaudeville, had been designed for mass consumption, none captured the public imagination on such a massive scale and in such a systematic, efficient fashion as 'the movies'. One might argue, in fact, that in the 1910s and 1920s Hollywood and the vast American public – or the vast legions of movie-going Americans at any rate – effectively invented modern mass culture, preparing the way for commercial broadcasting (radio), national advertising and various other forms of expressive mass culture. In the process, the movie industry and the popular press fashioned an elaborate narrative, at once a massive promotional enterprise and a lightweight journalistic exercise, that paralleled the movies themselves in formulating Hollywood as the wellspring of America's collective imagination.

As movies, movie stars and the movie colony itself captured the public imagination, Hollywood also generated a considerable amount of 'criticism' in the form of journalistic film reviews as well as intellectual and, in some cases, scholarly critique. Early film reviewers and critics were scarcely consistent or systematic in their appraisals and thus did little to refine an aesthetic of cinema or a coherent analysis of industry practices. But various scholars and intellectuals deemed Hollywood a significant social and cultural force, even in its earliest era, and they examined it as such, thus laying the groundwork for 'film studies' as a distinct academic discipline. These scholarly and intellectual analyses were few and far between, however, and in fact a governing irony in the development of film studies as a field is that it coalesced in the postwar era, only after its primary object of study – i.e. classical Hollywood cinema (and the 'studio system' that generated it) – was

1

pronounced dead and ready for an autopsy. Rumours of Hollywood's demise would prove to be greatly exaggerated, although Hollywood did suffer a severe decline due to the postwar rise of commercial television and a general shift to independent film production. Thus the steady emergence of film studies occurred in an odd symbiosis with the recovery and eventual resurgence of Hollywood.

Indeed, film studies came into its own in the 1970s and 1980s, just as the so-called 'New Hollywood' gained ascendance and re-established cinema as a driving force not only in American culture but in an ever-expanding, international entertainment marketplace. Whereas film studies and the New Hollywood developed concurrently, however, there was a curious 'disconnect between them at the time due to several factors. One factor was the continued scholarly emphasis on classical Hollywood and a preoccupation with canon formation and with questions of style, genre and authorship. Another was the inevitable influence of intellectual and academic fashion on a new field that was seeking legitimacy, as the burgeoning ranks of film scholars waded headlong into the churning waters of 'critical theory' when many of the strongest conceptual currents – semiotics, structuralism, cultural studies, postmodernism, etc. – seemed ideally suited to media studies. Yet another reason for this disconnection was what might be termed the New Hollywood's betrayal of the very principals of directorial authorship and 'art cinema' that governed postwar cinema – and not just in Hollywood – which also informed the critical values and aesthetic sensibilities of that first generation of America film scholars. Film studies devoted to Hollywood gradually overcame this disconnect and, by the 1990s, began dealing more directly and effectively with the New Hollywood. In fact, this was unavoidable for any scholar dealing with media, given the hegemony of a new breed of global media conglomerates whose key assets are Hollywood studios and movie-spawned entertainment franchises.

This introduction charts the century-long interplay of Hollywood cinema and the systematic study of it, concentrating primarily on the postwar emergence of film studies as a discipline and the concurrent transformation of Hollywood as a culture industry and an art form. These parallel histories have been in and out of sync at various times but, as I argue here, their interrelationship has been crucial to the development of both film industry and the academic and scholarly community. In tracing these parallel histories, I hope to provide a rationale for the organisation of this four-volume collection and to trace the growth of film studies from an academic sideline and intellectual diversion to a mature scholarly and academic discipline.

Classical Hollywood and the prospect of film studies

The first serious writing about American film actually predates 'Hollywood', appearing in stage, vaudeville and entertainment industry trade papers such as *Variety* and the *New York Dramatic Mirror* just after the turn of the century, when the nickelodeon craze swept through the major urban centres in the eastern United States. The first trade papers devoted directly to cinema appeared before 1910, with *Motion Picture World* (1907–1920) by far the most significant. A few years later the earliest fan magazines appeared, notably *Motion Picture Story* and *Photoplay* (both 1911).[1] The earliest scholarly treatments appeared in the mid-1910s, when the colonisation of Hollywood was in full swing and the 'moving picture' was coming of age as a viable commercial industry and as an art form. The most significant of these early scholarly studies focused less on the industrial than on the aesthetic aspects of the new medium, examining narrative cinema as a new, unique art form. The most important of these were poet Vachel Lindsay's *The Art of the Moving Picture* (1915), an insightful analysis of film and its relation to the established arts, and *The Photoplay: A Psychological Study*, a 1916 mono-graph written by Harvard professor Hugo Munsterberg, a pioneer in the field of human psychology. At about the same time, various screenplay man-uals began to appear, including several written by prominent drama scholars and theorists such as Victor Freeburg, whose *The Art of Photoplay Making* appeared in 1918.[2]

It was during the mid-1910s that the 'colonisation' of Hollywood and the development of a West Coast movie production centre began in earnest. The first full-blown 'modern' movie studio operation was University City, which began construction in 1913 and opened in 1915. That same year, Adolph Zukor began to assemble the various elements of what would become Paramount Pictures, the first vertically-integrated film production–distribution–exhibition corporation. The centralisation of film production in the environs of Los Angeles and the standardisation of film style and narrative technique were further spurred by the development of a nationwide film distribution system, as well as the rapid growth of film exhibition well beyond its storefront and nickelodeon phase. By the late 1910s, lavish motion picture 'palaces' were springing up in major urban centres across the US and the upstart movie industry was fast becoming big business.[3]

As the American movie industry matured and the Hollywood studio sys-tem stabilised into a vertically-integrated business enterprise during the 1920s, the amount of scholarly work devoted to Hollywood increased con-siderably. The first significant history of the medium, *A Million and One Nights*, by film journalist Terry Ramsaye was published in 1926 (commis-sioned by *Photoplay*) and remains one of the best surveys of the nascent US film industry.[4] Bankers, economists and business scholars examined the industry as well, most notably banker (and would-be Hollywood mogul) Joseph P. Kennedy, who organised a series of lectures at the Harvard Busi-ness School that were published in 1927 under the title, *The Story of Films*.[5] By the early 1930s, social scientists and behavioural psychologists, along with market research pioneers like George Gallup, were studying Hollywood films

3

and their 'effects' on movie audiences. These ranged from solid, scholarly analyses, like the Payne Fund's *Motion Pictures and Youth*, to shrill indictments, like Henry James Forman's *Our Movie-Made Children* (both published in 1933).[6] As Hollywood reached the height of its Golden Age in the late 1930s, two important scholarly analyses were conducted: the best-selling *Hollywood: The Movie Colony* by sociologist (and later screenwriter) Leo Rosten, researched and written in 1939 and published in 1941, and Mae Huettig's *Economic Control of the Motion Picture Industry*, initially a PhD thesis at the University of Pennsylvania in the late 1930s and eventually published by the University of Pennsylvania Press in 1944.

Hollywood's Golden Age peaked in the immediate prewar years, with the years 1939 to 1941 seeing an output of classics ranging from *Gone With the Wind* (1939) to *Citizen Kane* (1941) – there are far too many films to list here, evincing the remarkable equilibrium that had been struck at the time between Hollywood commercial, artistic and popular imperatives. The war years brought dramatic change to the movie industry due to the combined effects of politics and commerce. President Roosevelt, recognising the importance of Hollywood movies as both diversion and propaganda-by-indirection, allowed the industry to continue commercial operations on the condition that it support the 'war effort' both onscreen and off, which it did. Hollywood also enjoyed the benefits of the 'war economy', which put money in Americans' pockets for the first time since before the Depression, while depriving them of anything to spend it on with very few exceptions – most notably the movies. Thus, Hollywood reaped enormous dividends from the war economy, with the studios enjoying one record-breaking year after another in terms of revenues and profits, culminating in 1946 when returning servicemen and renewed courtship rituals generated profits for the studios that would not be seen again until a half-century later.[7]

World War Two had a pronounced impact on the study of Hollywood as well. One key reason was the displacement of European artists and intellectuals, which began with the rise of Nazism during the 1930s and accelerated during the War, bringing thousands of cultured émigrés to Southern California. This included top filmmakers like Fritz Lang, Billy Wilder and Alfred Hitchcock, along with many renowned composers, painters, novelists and playwrights, many of whom had direct contact with Hollywood. Among the intellectual émigrés, interestingly enough, were German Marxist Max Horkheimer and his protégé, Theodor Adorno, who in 1943 wrote their scathing critique of mass culture, 'The Culture Industry: Enlightenment as Mass Deception' (Horkheimer and Adorno, 1943), with Hollywood among the prime offenders. Another reason for the War's impact was the growing concern among academics and intellectuals about propaganda and media persuasion, as the national film industries in most of the Axis countries were converted to state propaganda agencies, while Hollywood continued its 'commercial' operation (extremely successfully, thanks to the war economy) while actively supporting the war effort. These various intellectual currents coalesced after the War in the mass-culture debates, with Hollywood as a conceptual flashpoint for writers such as Dwight Macdonald (1961), Gilbert Seldes (1978) and Robert Warshow (1962). By now even anthropologists were examining Hollywood, most notably Hortense Powdermaker in *The Hollywood Dream Factory* (1960).

The 'factory' itself was in severe decline at the time, however, as Hollywood fell victim to various social, economic and regulatory developments – notably suburban migration, the rise of commercial television and antitrust rulings that forced the studio powers to radically modify the economic practices that had enabled them to control the movie business for decades. The classical era that coalesced in the 1920s had been geared to the vertically-integrated 'studio system' in which a cadre of corporate giants dominated and effectively controlled the production, distribution and exhibition of movies in the US. The most powerful of these were the 'Big Five' major studios – MGM, Paramount, Warner Bros., 20th Century Fox and RKO – who not only produced films and released them via a nationwide distribution system but also owned their own theatre chains which included most of the large downtown theatres where Hollywood did the lion's share of its business. These theatre chains put the Big Five at the top of the Hollywood power structure but they actively shared that power with three other studios – Universal, Columbia and United Artists – who also produced top feature films and had their own distribution divisions but did not own theatre chains.

These eight studios constituted a 'mature oligopoly' in economic terms which, from the viewpoint of the Justice Department, also constituted a collusive system giving the studios monopolistic control of the US motion picture industry. This control was challenged in a landmark antitrust suit that was filed in 1938, suspended during the War and resumed with a vengeance in the postwar era, culminating in a 1948 Supreme Court ruling that forced the Big Five to sell their theatre chains and forced all eight studio-distributors to cease the marketing practices (block booking, blind bidding and so forth) that solidified their collective control. Thus the studio system was effectively disintegrated just as commercial television was sweeping the newly suburbanised American landscape, signalling the wholesale transformation of Hollywood – and of the US media industries generally – during the postwar era. This period also saw the emergence of 'film studies' as a serious intellectual pursuit and, eventually, as a distinct academic discipline. As suggested above, these industrial and intellectual developments were not unrelated and in fact the postwar upheaval in Hollywood was a key contributing factor in the emergence of film studies in the US and in Europe.

The decline of Hollywood and the rise of film studies

The serious study of American cinema, and particularly of Hollywood films and filmmaking, was compelled in large part by a 'critical concept' formulated during the 1950s by a group of young French critics, including Francois Truffaut, Jean-Luc Godard, Eric Rohmer and Jacques Rivette, writing under the tutelage of Andre Bazin for *Cahiers de cinema*, a relatively obscure film journal in Paris. This particular origin of Hollywood film studies was the 'politique des auteurs', an aggressively polemical approach that treated commercial cinema as a form of personal, artistic expression and singled out certain directors, from silent era masters, like D. W. Griffith and Buster Keaton, to current filmmakers, like John Ford, Howard Hawks and Alfred Hitchcock, as distinctive stylists and storytellers, mature popular artists and, thus, as the individual 'authors' of their films. This authorial status was assigned despite the commercial constraints, executive control and collaborative nature of Hollywood filmmaking, and despite the 'popular' and genre-based orientation of its films. Indeed, the *Cahiers* critics valorised directors like Hawks and Hitchcock who had been written off by most American critics as popular entertainers and commercial hacks.

The auteur policy quickly caught on in England, primarily via critics writing for the film journal *Movie*, and eventually in the US. Its transatlantic passage was effected by American critic (and Columbia University film professor) Andrew Sarris in his provocative essay, 'Notes on the Auteur Theory in 1962', which appeared in *Film Culture*. This essay generated heated debate, the liveliest involving Sarris and Pauline Kael, and their wrangling led to two of the most significant book-length analyses in the burgeoning film studies field of the time. In 1969, Sarris published *The American Cinema: Directors and Directions, 1929–1968*, in which auteurism was posited not simply as an analytic model but as a 'theory of film history', effectively reducing that history to the biographies of a few dozen filmmakers. In 1971, Kael's *The Citizen Kane Book* appeared, expanding an earlier essay, 'Raising Kane', into a sustained refutation of auteurism through a case study that undercut, in her own engaging and combative style, the notion that Orson Welles was the sole author of *Citizen Kane*.

Welles' career provided an obvious bone of auteurist contention, as did that of Alfred Hitchcock, a director who was (and remains) the object of serious critical debate and one of the very few members of the Hollywood 'old guard' who actively fuelled the critical discourse. Ever the master of self-promotion (as well as cinematic suspense), Hitchcock was an ardent and outspoken advocate of the *Cahiers* critics' efforts to rehabilitate his critical reputation. He readily collaborated with Truffaut in a series of interviews in the early 1960s, which were eventually published in a 1965 book-length version. Hitchcock was also the subject of the first credible, in-depth auteur study, *Hitchcock's Films* (Wood, 1965), which opened, aptly enough, with the question, 'Why should we take Alfred Hitchcock seriously?'. Wood spends the rest of the book eloquently explaining why, thereby validating not only Hitchcock's career but the auteur approach as well. And, despite the opposition of Kael and others, auteur analysis was embraced and refined throughout the 1960s and early 1970s by the growing ranks of American scholars and intellectuals writing about Hollywood film.[8]

Critics and scholars applied the 'auteur theory' primarily to Hollywood directors from the classical era, assessing their entire body of work (their 'oeuvre', in auteurist parlance), but important changes in the American (and international) movie industry at the time provided crucial support for an auteur approach. Whereas the title of Sarris's 1969 book, *Notes on the Auteur Theory in 1962*, indicated a certain continuity in Hollywood cinema dating back to the dawn of the sound era in the late 1920s and, although a few celebrated auteurs like Hawks and Hitchcock were still working, the American cinema of the late 1960s scarcely resembled that of the classical era. The Hollywood studios had survived the postwar travails but only after completely revamping their motion picture operations and coming to terms with the upstart TV industry. On the feature film front, the studios gradually abandoned their factory-based, mass-production system, concentrating instead on producing fewer, 'bigger' pictures while providing financing and distribution to the growing ranks of independent producers. In television, the studios in the mid-1950s began producing 'telefilm' series programmes and opening their vaults of old feature films to TV syndication companies. Thus began a number of key trends – the diversification of production, for instance, and the bifurcation of film product into studio-produced 'blockbusters' and low-budget independent films – that still prevail today.

The studios' production cutbacks created a demand for product that was filled by an unprecedented influx of imports and art films from the growing ranks of international auteurs – filmmakers like Ikira Kurosawa, Ingmar Bergman and Federico Fellini. By the early 1960s, the French 'New Wave' was cresting, as Truffaut, Godard, Rivette and the other perpetrators of the *politique* became celebrated auteurs in their own right. Film imports enjoyed widespread circulation in the US and had tremendous impact, not only on American filmmakers and the growing ranks of American cinephiles, but on the general movie-going public as well. Remarkably enough, imports like Michelangelo Antonioni's *Blowup* (1966) and even foreign-language films like Fellini's *La Dolce Vita* (1960) and Claude Lelouch's *A Man and a Woman* (1966) were top box-office hits in the US.

This director-driven 'art cinema' had a significant US contingent, although for much of the 1960s it was relegated to the marginal realm of experimental and avant-garde venues. That changed rather dramatically in the late 1960s with the release of *Bonnie and Clyde* (Arthur Penn, 1967), *The Graduate* (Mike Nichols, 1967), *2001: A Space Odyssey* (Stanley Kubrick, 1968), *Faces* (John Cassavetes, 1968), *Easy Rider* (Dennis Hopper, 1969),

Midnight Cowboy (John Schlesinger, 1969), *The Wild Bunch* (Sam Peckinpah, 1969) and *M*A*S*H* (Robert Altman, 1970). These films amongst others marked the concurrent emergence both of a 'director's cinema' unlike anything seen in Hollywood before (or since) and also a 'youth market' comprised of a cinematically sophisticated and politically rebellious movie-going constituency. Together, this new generation of cineastes and cinephiles ushered in a veritable renaissance in American filmmaking – a period that film historians have dubbed, in retrospect, the 'New American Cinema', the 'American New Wave' and, inevitably, 'the New Hollywood'. This movement was further impelled in the early 1970s by the first generation of 'film school' graduates, like Francis Ford Coppola, Martin Scorsese, George Lucas, Brian DePalma, etc., whose auteurist convictions were nurtured in academia and practised in earnest in films like Coppola's *The Godfather* (1972) and Scorsese's *Mean Streets* (1973).

Signs and meaning in the New American Cinema

In retrospect, the period of the late 1960s through to the 1970s represents a unique and important juncture in America film history, an interval of extraordinary creative freedom and innovation. It was a period when American film culture, like the culture at large, underwent enormous turmoil and change; a period when anything seemed possible. It was a period when a new generation of filmmakers and a new generation of movie-goers dominated the industry, shaping its development and signalling an end to the commercial imperatives and stylistic conventions that had ruled Hollywood for decades. It was a period chronicled by Peter Biskind in his recent bestselling account *Easy Riders, Raging Bulls: How the Sex, Drugs and Rock 'n' Roll Generation Saved Hollywood*. His title speaks volumes, indicating the general time span of the Hollywood renaissance – from the late 1960s to the 1980 release of Scorsese's *Raging Bull* – as well as the anger, rebellion and generally spaced-out disposition of the cohort that dominated and defined the era.

This was an important era not only in Hollywood filmmaking but in America film studies as well, in that it bred the first generation of scholars who actually studied cinema in academic programmes, obtained advanced degrees in the subject and published in film journals and university presses; in other words, a legion of cinephiles and critics that effectively created and defined the field of film studies. And whereas all too many of that generation's renegade auteurs would fade or fail to find work after the 1970s, this first generation of film scholars would dominate film studies for decades to come. This included European as well as American scholars and in fact much of the important writing about Hollywood during that period came from Britain and France (with British scholars enjoying an obvious advantage because their work did not require translation). The 'Cinema One series' of film monographs, co-published by the British Film Institute and its film journal, *Sight and Sound*, and the University of Indiana Press, produced some of the most influential scholarship on Hollywood, most of which had a strong emphasis on authorship or genre or both, as was the case with Jim Kitses' *Horizons West* (1970) and Peter Wollen's *Signs and Meaning in the Cinema* (1972), two of the most influential books in the series. This period also saw the British journal *Screen* emerge, along with *Sight and Sound*, as the most important English-language film periodical. The University of California Press also published a number of important books that proved to be vital to the emerging field, notably translations of the early film theory of Andre Bazin (see Bazin, 1968).

Important film-related work continued to be written and published in France, much of it focused squarely on Hollywood. This ranged from the theoretical writings of Bazin and Jean Mitry to the more current – and far more radical – writing of the *Cahiers* critics. Some of the most important and influential work regarding film studies came out of other fields however, notably the emergence of semiology (or semiotics) and structuralism in linguistics and anthropology. The key figures here were the Swiss linguist Ferdinand de Saussure and the French anthropologist Claude Levi-Strauss. Saussure (1960), a half a century earlier, had proposed semiology as the study of 'the life of signs in a society', and posited language as the 'master pattern' (deep structure) of all such signifying (meaningful, meaning-making) systems. Saussure's ideas proved massively influential and, by the 1950s, were being applied to an array of other fields by various scholars – Levi-Strauss (1963) in anthropology, Jacques Lacan (1977) in psychology (and psychoanalysis), Roland Barthes (1972) and Umberto Eco (1994) in literary analysis and popular culture, Louis Althusser (1984) in Marxist theory and so on. Barthes and Eco extended their structural and semiological analysis of literature and popular fiction into film, television and advertising, and their work in turn proved highly influential to American film scholars. Equally important in terms of film studies *per se*, and particularly Hollywood cinema, was the early work of Christian Metz, in *Language and Cinema* (1974) and *Film Language: A Semiotics of the Cinema* (1974).

The impact of structuralism and semiotics on America film studies and the study of Hollywood cinema was considerable, to say the least. Its influence emerged in several distinct areas. First and foremost, it radically reformulated the notion of film style which came to be regarded not only as the expression of individual personality or genius but also – and perhaps more so – as the manifestation of cinematic codes and signifying practices. Additionally, analytic forces shifted from individual films (regarded as masterpieces or great works) to textual and intertextual systems. Thus, there was a growing interest at the time in film genre as well as 'classical film narration', as commercial cinema was treated less as a manifestation of individual authorship than of the mass culture's collective 'way of seeing'. Given the central role of human psychology in both the organisation of film imagery (i.e. camera work and editing) and the spectator's corresponding interpretation of that imagery (i.e. reception), film studies was eminently suited to the poststructuralist analysis developed by Lacan, Jacques Derrida (1976, 1978) and Michel Foucault (1971, 1978, 1979). This approach shifted the structuralist emphasis from the codes that inform and structure as text to the process of encoding and decoding involved in any text-producing (and consuming) process. The key figure here, once again, was Christian Metz, who famously shifted his theoretical paradigm from semiotics to Lacanian psychoanalysis and thus from structuralism to poststructuralism with the publication of *The Imaginary Signifier* (1982). Subsequent poststructuralist theory cross-fertilised with literary reception studies, focusing not only on individual spectators but also on social groups and cultural constituencies ('interpretive communities') as well.

As structuralism pushed film theory well beyond the elitism and naïve romanticism of auteur analysis, film historians were moving beyond the 'Great Man' postulations and masterpiece-driven, canon-formation mentality that dominated the field until the 1970s. Two general histories of American cinema appeared in 1975–1976 that marked important advances in film studies: Robert Sklar's *Movie-Made America* (1994), a 'cultural history' of American cinema, and Garth Jowett's *Film: The Democratic Art* (1976), commissioned by the American Film Institute and subtitled 'A Social History of American Film'. Two other important books appeared in 1976 that further signalled the coming-of-age of American film history as a scholarly enterprise. One was Tino Balio's *United Artists*, an in-depth portrait of a single studio, based primarily on archival documents (i.e. production and business records, inter-office memoranda, etc.) and trade paper coverage of the company. The other was *The American Film Industry* (1976), an anthology edited by Balio of scholarly and trade-press articles about the structure and economics of Hollywood and the workings of the studio system. Another important work of film history that appeared at this time was Dudley Andrew's *The Major Film Theories* (1976), which provided an illuminating schema and analysis of the ways cinema had been conceptualised by theorists ranging from Hugo Munsterberg and Sergei Eisenstein to Andre Bazin and Siegfried Kracauer. Andrew concluded his study with a nod to Christian Metz and semiology, which he deemed a significant break with the 'realist tradition' that preceded it. But Andrew did not convey – nor could he have seen at that time – the enormous impact that structuralist and poststructuralist theory would have on the development of film studies in the next few years.

Others in that first generation of film scholars (myself included) failed to comprehend the enormous changes under way in the industry itself. A few academic studies in the 1970s did begin to describe and assess the emergence of the New Hollywood – most notably James Monaco in *American Film Now* (1979) (a follow-up, in fact, to his excellent book on film semiotics, *How to*

Read a Film). What scholars and critics in the late 1970s did not realise, however, was that the Hollywood renaissance sparked by *Bonnie and Clyde*, *The Graduate* and the other late-1960s breakthrough films was in rapid decline. The late 1970s did see the release of a succession of truly remarkable cinematic achievements, culminating with Coppola's *Apocalypse Now* and Bob Fosse's *All That Jazz* in 1979 and Scorsese's *Raging Bull* in 1980. The release of Scorsese's film in late 1980 coincided with the catastrophic preview and non-release of Michael Cimino's *Heaven's Gate* – a director's film that took down its studio-distributor, United Artists, and in many ways signalled the end of Hollywood's decade-long development of a director's cinema. But, in fact, the industry already had begun moving from renaissance to retrenchment with the release of films like *Jaws* (1975), *Rocky* (1976) and *Star Wars* (1977), commercial blockbusters that demonstrated that the industry had been relying too long and too heavily on a body of modernist cineastes and an ageing youth market. Thus, Hollywood was ripe for a change long before *Heaven's Gate*, which proved to be more of a 'last straw' than a motivating force in the emergence of a 'new' New Hollywood.

Into the New Hollywood: high concept and high theory

What we now think of as the New Hollywood scarcely emerged full-blown, of course, but underwent a decade-long gestation from the mid-1970s to the mid-1980s that might best be understood in terms of three successive stages. Stage one saw the seeds of the New Hollywood planted with three seemingly distinct events, all occurring in 1975: the release of *Jaws*, which spawned a new breed of movie blockbuster; the birth of the pay-cable movie channel with HBO's decision to begin utilising nationwide satellite transmission and Sony's introduction (in the US) of the Betamax video cassette recorder (VCR), which signalled the birth of the home-video industry. Stage two saw the seeds take root in the late 1970s, as these new technologies coalesced into motion picture 'delivery systems' and Hollywood began to systematically reproduce the kind of high-cost, high-speed, high-concept blockbuster augured by *Jaws*.

The Spielberg-directed mega-hit marked not only a breakthrough for the filmmaker (it was his second feature film) but also a watershed for the industry on several counts. It was the first major Hollywood feature to be released in the summer in a nationwide 'saturation' marketing and release campaign. It was the first film ever to return over $100 million in film rentals (the proportion of the box-office revenue returned to the distributor), which is still the benchmark of a blockbuster hit. And it marked a canny return to audience-friendly filmmaking, blending familiar genres and a kinetic audio-visual style into an utterly classical and relentlessly linear narrative. By 1977–1978, the impact of *Jaws* was readily evident in a spate of blockbuster hits – *Star Wars*, *Saturday Night Fever*, *Animal House*, *Superman*, *Smokey and the Bandit* and so on – that fuelled Hollywood's stunning resurgence and radically redirected the development of the American cinema.

The New Hollywood hit its stride in the 1980s, stage three, as the block-buster mentality came to rule the industry and the home-video and pay-cable industries went into high gear, proving to be as blockbuster-driven as the movie industry and surpassing the domestic theatrical market (i.e. theatres in the US and Canada) as the primary source of revenue for the studio-distributors that rule the resurgent industry.

Hollywood's remarkable resurgence was scarcely noted, let alone closely studied, by film scholars. Indeed, the disconnect between film theory and filmmaking practice alluded to above became painfully acute at the time. This was understandable, perhaps, in light of the fact that the scholars of that era had refined their cinematic sensibilities and formulated the field of film studies under very different industrial and aesthetic circumstances, in an era dominated by international auteurs and New American cineastes. And, as film imports all but disappeared from American movie screens, and film-makers like Robert Altman, Martin Scorsese, Hal Ashby, Paul Mazursky, Arthur Penn and Francis Coppola either struggled or failed to find work in a changing industry, Hollywood embraced what came to be termed a 'high-concept' aesthetic. This was a term often associated with Spielberg's much-quoted assertion: 'If a person can tell the idea in twenty-five words or less, it's going to make a pretty good movie. I like ideas, especially movie ideas that you can hold in your hand' (see Hoberman, 1985). And, one might add, ideas that can be captured in a single marketing image, reproduced in thirty-second TV ads and reiterated in merchandising, or, as Richard Schickel put it in a *Time* magazine review, pointing out the irony of the term, 'What the phrase really means is that the concept is so low that it can be summarized and sold on the basis of a single sentence'.[9]

While a few critics like Schickel (in *Time*) and J. Hoberman (in the *Village Voice* and *American Film*) were assessing the New Hollywood in the popular press, film scholars kept their distance as if Hollywood's resurgence marked a betrayal of the very principles – art-cinema narration, cinematic modern-ism, genre subversion and, of course, auteurism – that formed the corner-stones of academic film study. This betrayal was underscored with a vengeance by the industry's (and the press's) response to *Heaven's Gate*, which marked the end of any prospect of Hollywood as a director's cinema. Another key aspect of the disconnection between film theory and industry practice in the late 1970s and the 1980s was academic and intellectual fash-ion. As Hollywood went high concept, the academy embraced 'high theory' in the form of poststructuralism and cultural studies, turning away from films and filmmaking (especially in a contemporary context) and focusing instead on questions of spectatorship, reception and the role of media in the formation of individual and collective identity. This period saw dramatic changes in higher education and scholarship generally, due to the impact of the civil rights, feminist and gay rights movements in academia in the US during the 1970s, and the broader inroads related to 'multiculturalism' in the 1980s. Film studies, like virtually every field in the humanities and social sciences, became embroiled in identity politics and the so-called 'culture wars' that were waged during the reactionary Reagan era.

The monumental impact and sustained effect of Laura Mulvey's essay, 'Visual Pleasure and Narrative Cinema', published in *Screen* in 1977, provides a telling example of the general direction of the field and the intensity of the debates and discord at this time. Mulvey's essay presented a penetrating and provocative psychoanalytic critique of classical Hollywood's predominant visual style and narrative strategies which, in her view, were fundamentally patriarchal, phallocentric and thoroughly misogynistic. Mulvey herself was surprised at the furore caused by the essay, which set the tone and direction of feminist film theory for years to come. It also generated renewed academic interest in Alfred Hitchcock, whose work Mulvey reviled as a prime example of classical Hollywood cinema's characteristic misogyny, and the debates were further intensified by the reissue in the early 1980s of several of Hitchcock's 1950s films – notably *Rear Window* (1954), *The Man Who Knew Too Much* (1956) and *Vertigo* (1958) – which had not been available for decades.

Mulvey's essay propelled a veritable melding of feminist and psychoanalytic theory, especially in its preoccupation with the male 'gaze' and male 'agency' (in social, sexual and narrative terms); the related objectification of the female (or feminised or fetishised) Other; the coordination of the protagonist's, the filmmaker's and the spectator's desires and so on. This view also proved to be amenable to other approaches geared to distinctions between Self and Other, as well as the social 'construction' and internally conflicting nature of the individual 'subject'. These approaches included gender and gay studies, racial and ethnic studies and studies of identity formation in a range of social and political contexts. And, while poststructuralist approaches tended to focus on the individual subject, cultural studies treated reception in more collective and communal terms, gauging audiences as members of 'interpretive communities' that actively engaged with both the producers of culture and the products themselves in determining meaning. While theorists such as John Fiske (1989a, b) and Douglas Kellner (1997) were accused of assigning too much agency to spectators and audiences, their approaches did avoid the reductive determinism and logic of victimisation that often plagued poststructuralist analysis. In fact, by the late 1980s and early 1990s, a significant counter-argument had developed to reductive post-structuralism – most notably, perhaps, in Tania Modleski's *The Women Who Knew Too Much* (1988), which used psychoanalytic theory and analysis to argue for the agency of the female protagonists in Hitchcock's film and also to rationalise the prospect of the female spectator's 'pleasure' in response to the same films that Mulvey had so vehemently condemned.

13

The disconnection during the 1980s between film studies and filmmaking practice played out quite differently in terms of American film history, in that film scholars continued their retreat from naïve auteurism by considering more 'practical' aspects of film production but concentrated primarily on classical Hollywood rather than the contemporary film industry. The rapid influx of political economy theory into media studies was an important factor here, as well as the increasingly sophisticated analysis of technology and regulation. A key contribution along these lines was that of Robert C. Allen and Douglas Gomery's *Film History: Theory and Practice* (1985), a monograph on American film historiography that called for an approach to history that integrated aesthetic, technological, economic and sociological analysis. That same year, David Bordwell, Janet Staiger and Kristin Thompson published their monumental study, *The Classical Hollywood Cinema: Film Style and Mode of Production, 1917–1960* (1985), which came very close to the kind of multi-dimensional approach advocated by Allen and Gomery, although it dealt only marginally with media economics and not at all with audience, reception and exhibition. Gomery's *The Hollywood Studio System*, published a year later in 1986, provided a useful survey of the institutional and economic structure of classical Hollywood, while my own *The Genius of the System* (1988) examined the production process at four representative studios from the 1920s through to the 1950s. This latter book relied heavily on archival research as did several others from that period – Tino Balio's second volume on United Artists (1987), for instance, and Leonard Leff's study of the Hitchcock–Selznick 'collaboration' during the 1940s.

These studies, all of which appeared in the late 1980s, substantially challenged the auteurist bias against both the Hollywood studios and production executives who had been characterized as the director's essential adversaries. Other challenges came via studies of leading independent producers from the classical era, ranging from trade biographies such as A. Scott Berg's *Goldwyn: A Life* and David Thomson's *Showman: The Life of David O. Selznick*, to more scholarly treatments, like Matthew Bernstein's *Walter Wanger, Hollywood Independent*. All were heavily researched accounts of the crucial role played by a 'major independent producer' in the creative (as well as commercial) process and, thus, they serve both to complicate and illuminate issues surrounding the authorial 'agency' involved in the complex, collaborative system of Hollywood filmmaking.

These revisionist histories also encouraged (and further enabled) film scholars to turn their attention to the New Hollywood, which evoked the classical era in terms of the currency of 'the movies' as a cultural force, the studios' return to a position of collective hegemony and the resurgence of classical narrative. By now even popular critics and journalists routinely alluded to a film's 'three-act structure' and a recent mainstream Hollywood film, *Adaptation* (2002), featured a frustrated, highbrow screenwriter who discovers narrative clarity and commercial viability in a seminar with screenwriting guru Robert McKee (1997). Moreover, the steadily intensifying trend toward media globalisation, particularly the global currency of Hollywood films, effectively forced media scholars from different research traditions to broaden their conceptual and analytical perspectives.

The new New Hollywood and the prospect of convergence

By the mid-1990s, film and media scholars simply could not ignore or dismiss the obvious – that 'Hollywood' had regained the kind of national and international dominance as a social, cultural and commercial force that it had enjoyed half a century earlier. In fact, one could argue that Hollywood's power and influence as a 'cultural industry' was far greater than when Horkheimer and Adorno wrote their scathing critique in the 1940s. As German filmmaker Wim Wenders famously opined in the early 1990s, the Americans 'have colonized our consciousness', principally via Hollywood-produced entertainment that enjoyed a rapidly expanding world market, thanks not only to the size and reach of the Hollywood studios' parent companies, but also the geo-economic (and geo-political) sea change that followed the collapse of the Soviet empire in the early 1990s.[10]

Hollywood's resurgence also involved a return of sorts to the 'studio system', as Disney, Paramount, Warner Bros., etc., reasserted their collective dominion over the industry. However, the studios were scarcely integrated motion picture conglomerates unto themselves, as they once had been. In the course of the 1980s and 1990s, the cumulative impact of deregulation, technological innovation, corporate conglomeration, globalisation and an ethos of free-market capitalism utterly transformed Hollywood and the American media industries. By the mid-1990s, the resurgent studios were mere subsidiaries – albeit the 'core assets' – of vast global media conglomerates like Sony, News Corp, Viacom and Time Warner. This cartel of vertically and horizontally integrated media giants collectively dominated movies and television, cable and home video, digital and interactive media, music, publishing, theme parks, resorts, retail stores and a seemingly endless array of licensing and merchandising endeavours.

The new era of media conglomeration and convergence was ushered in by News Corp's 1985 purchase of the Twentieth Century Fox motion picture company and the creation, a short time later, of Fox Broadcasting, a fourth commercial television network in the US (along with a number of other media enterprises). This eminently successful display of 'synergy' induced other companies to follow suit and, in 1989–1990 the beginnings of a decade-long merger-and-acquisitions wave was seen with Sony's purchase of Columbia-TriStar, Matsushita's buyout of MCA-Universal and the Time-Warner merger. In the course of a decade (to mention only a few of the most significant deals), Viacom bought Paramount, Blockbuster and CBS; Disney bought Miramax and ABC; Time Warner bought Turner before closing the decade with a $150 billion merger with AOL (America OnLine). The ill-fated and vastly over-valued AOL Time Warner merger speaks volumes about the 'wildcat' mentality and the huge stakes involved in the business of global media, entertainment and information at the dawn of the new millennium. And, while the disastrous outcome was a reality check regarding the short-term prospects for synergies between old media and new – and particularly between the established 'content providers' and digital delivery giants – its failure has not discouraged the ongoing, albeit more cautious, pursuit of media conglomeration and convergence.

Thus, the New Hollywood that first took shape in the late 1970s, spawned by a new breed of blockbusters and new modes of delivery, asserted itself with a vengeance. The new era has been termed by some as the 'New' New Hollywood, not only to avoid any confusion with the 1970s renaissance but also to underscore its distinction from the resurgent 1980s. Indeed, the cumulative effects of conglomeration, globalisation and digital innovation during the 1990s did usher in an era that seemed qualitatively different from the preceding decade.

Much the same can be said for film and media studies, as Hollywood's quest for media convergence and global expansion compelled media scholars to deal more directly with the contemporary industry and to integrate the various traditions (and warring factions) that had dominated film studies for the previous quarter of a century. Although the effective integration of these traditions, especially those located in humanistic and sociological disciplines, remains an elusive goal, there have been encouraging signs of convergence. The integration of film and television studies by historians such as Michele Hilmes, in *Hollywood and Broadcasting* (1990), Christopher Anderson, in *Hollywood TV* (1994) and Tino Balio (in the 1990 anthology, *Hollywood in the Age of Television*), for instance, significantly recasts our view of the inter-relationship between the two industries. Other scholars demonstrated a similar impulse to integrate empirical (especially archival) and critical research, factoring technology, policy, economics and the institutional into a complex analytical equation. Among the most encouraging of these recent studies are Frederick Wasser's analysis of Hollywood and the home video industry; Jon Lewis's (1995) study of Francis Coppola as New Hollywood auteur; Compaign and Gomery's invaluable analyses (2000) of media economics and ownership; Justin Wyatt's assessment (1994) of the aesthetics and marketing of 'high concept' films; and the innovative treatment of 'global Hollywood' by Toby Miller, *et al.*

Miller proposes a framework for this convergence in his introduction to *Global Hollywood*, acknowledging that 'screen studies needs an overhaul' if it is to move beyond the analytic orthodoxies of subject-formation, textual analysis, and individual (directorial) authorship. Miller is encouraged by recent developments in 'critical political economy and cultural studies', particularly as they pertain to industrial, policy and 'property' issues. In this era of conglomeration and globalisation, argues Miller, 'we need to view the screen through twin theoretical prisms'. We need to understand media industries, products and production itself 'as the newest component of sovereignty' which is rapidly redefining property rights, ownership, creative capital and so forth. We also need to understand contemporary media as 'a cluster of culture industries' whose practices and protocols are crucially dependent on (and indicative of) 'liaisons between state and capital'.[11]

These 'liaisons' vary widely from nation to nation, despite the transnational nature and reach of the new class of media conglomerates. Thus, studying the cluster of culture industries that comprise the global entertainment industry at large, as well as the local entertainment options available to the individual subject/spectator/consumer/citizen, necessarily demands that the context(s) of production, distribution, consumption and meaning-making be considered. This is no small task, of course, and requires not only the blending of research traditions (with their distinctive theoretical and methodological paradigms) but also the marshalling of vast amounts of knowledge and information. This is daunting but not impossible, although it does encourage more cooperative and collaborative research – as in the case of the *Global Hollywood* project itself, which Miller conducted with three other media scholars.

Miller is not alone in espousing the need to amalgamate multiple research traditions in the study of contemporary media. In fact, this would become a mantra of sorts as 'film studies' gives way to 'media studies' and as the study of contemporary Hollywood necessarily requires far more than simply analysing films – or filmmakers or film audiences. As Marwan M. Kraidy points out in a review of *Global Hollywood* and another book on media globalisation, the study of international communication is finally coming out of a two-decade 'malaise' that set in when the 'cultural imperialism' thesis was successfully challenged by the burgeoning cultural studies movement, with its central tenets of cultural hybridity and active audiences. The rapid emergence of 'globalisation' as a field of academic inquiry, particularly within media studies, may provide a framework for integrating cultural studies and political economy – thus generating a genuinely 'critical' political economy approach – due to its focus on three central themes: the role of the state in media processes and outcomes; the dual (and self-reflexively paradoxical) conception of the media user as citizen-consumer; and the issue of cultural hybridity, which counters claims of media-induced cultural uniformity by acknowledging the activity and diversity of media audiences. The latter point invokes another crucial paradox regarding the integration and fragmentation of both the media industry and media audiences. Deregulation in the US has not only permitted but has actively encouraged media integration and, thus, the concentration of media ownership; but this has been countered by the fragmentation of markets and audiences and the diversification and multiplication of expressive forms.

This, in turn, requires a concurrent diversification and integration of media research theories and methods and it remains to be seen whether film and media scholars are up to the task. As Fred Wasser states in another review entitled 'American Film Studies Today' (2000):

> As we begin the new millennium, film continues to be one of the most hybrid of cultural artifacts. Films studies only intermittently do justice to the various intersections that film itself straddles. Should film be studied as a cultural business, an aesthetic expression, a reflection or an interpolation of the audience, or as a site where the audience itself bestows significant meaning? Of course, there are scholars who pursue each of these avenues, but has anyone found the most illuminating balance between these approaches? The quest for the Holy Grail is urgent when every instance of filmic authenticity is quickly appropriated into a New Hollywood blockbuster.[12]

Wasser, too, is struck by the paradoxical state of the industry but also encouraged by the prospects of media scholars to respond. 'Everything is in play from the conditions of viewing to the actual material base of films', he notes, even though 'the same companies that dominated world cinema in the 1920s continue to dominate today' (Wasser 2002). In the face of both radical change and enduring studio hegemony, Wasser laments that film scholars have been altogether too timid and conservative in clinging to their 'textual analysis bias'. But the books under review give him reason for optimism – just as Wasser's own work on Hollywood's international markets and on the home-video industry tend to encourage me.

Because it is not just the insatiable maw of the New Hollywood that creates a sense of urgency but also the need for media scholars to develop a more integral and thus more engaged and consequential approach to the subject. The stakes have never been higher for Hollywood – for the studios, their parent conglomerates and for the global entertainment industry at large – and thus they have never been higher for film and media scholars. The integration of cultural studies, policy studies and political economy studies may indeed signal that film studies is coming of age and that we film scholars are learning to examine and assess Hollywood's institutions and productions, its policies and protocols, its audiences and markets, in ways that truly make a difference to the development of cinema and to our collective 'critical concept' of Hollywood.

Notes

1 See Koszarski, Volume I, Chapter 2.
2 See Lindsay, 1915; Munsterberg, 1916 and Freeburg, 1918.
3 On studios see: Gomery, 1992 and Schatz, 1997; on film style, technique, BST; Bordwell, *et al.* (1985).

4 See Ramsaye, 1926; see also Koszarski, p. 193.
5 See Kennedy, 1927.
6 See Payne Fund, 1933 and Forman, 1933; see also Balio, 1993, p. 3.
7 On the 1940s, see Schatz, 1997.
8 It is worth noting that, despite her energetic denouncements of the auteur approach in the 1960s, by the 1970s Kael was sounding very much like an auteurist in her promotion (as a critic for the *New Yorker*) of directors like Robert Altman and Brian DePalma.
9 For an excellent, in-depth, historical and theoretical treatment of 'high concept', see Wyatt, 1994.
10 See Wenders, 1991, p. 98.
11 See Miller, 1998.
12 See Wasser, 2002.

References

Allen, Robert C. and Gomery, Douglas (1985) *Film History: Theory and Practice*, New York: Knopf.
Althusser, Louis (1984) *Essays in Ideology*, London: Verso.
Anderson, Christopher (1994) *Hollywood TV: The Studio System in the Fifties*, Austin, Tex.: University of Texas Press.
Balio, Tino (ed.) (1976) *The American Film Industry*, Madison: University of Wisconsin Press.
—— (1987) United Artists: *The Company that Changed the Film Industry*, Madison: University of Wisconsin Press.
—— (1976) United Artists: *The Company Built by the Stars*, Madison: University of Wisconsin Press.
Bally, Charles, Sechehaye, Albert and Riedlinger, Albert (eds) (1986) *Course in General Linguistics by Ferdinand de Saussure*, LaSalle, Ill.: Open Court.
Barthes, Roland (1972) *Critical Essays*, trans. Richard Howard, Evanston, Ill.: Northwestern University Press.
Bazin, Andre (1968) 'The Evolution of the Language of Cinema' in Hugh Gray (ed.) *What is Cinema?*, Berkeley, CA: University of California Press.
Bordwell, David, Staiger, Janet and Thompson, Kristen (1985) *The Classical Hollywood Cinema: Film Style and Mode of Production to 1960*, New York: Columbia University Press.
Browne, Nick (ed.) (1990) *Cahiers du Cinema 1969–1972: The Politics of Representation*, Cambridge, Mass.: Harvard University Press.
Cameron, Ian (ed.) (1972) *Movie Reader*, New York: Praeger.
Compaine, Benjamin M. and Gomery, Douglas (2000) *Who Owns the Media? Competition and Concentration in the Mass Media*, Mahwah, N.J.: L. Erlbaum Associates.
Eco, Umberto (1994) *The Role of the Reader: Explorations in the Semiotics of Texts*, Bloomington, Ind.: Indiana University Press.
Finler, Joel W. (1988) *The Hollywood Story*, Crown Publishers.
Freeburg, Victor O. (1918) *Art of Photoplay Making*, New York: Macmillan.
Gomery, Douglas (1986) *The Hollywood Studio System*, New York: St. Martin's Press.
—— (1992) *Shared Pleasures: A History of Movie Presentation in the United States*, Madison: University of Wisconsin Press.

19

Hilmes, Michele (1990) *Hollywood and Broadcasting: From Radio to Cable*, Urbana: University of Illinois Press.

Hoberman, J. (1985) '1975–1985: Ten Years That Shook the World', *American Film*, June: 36.

Horkheimer, Max and Adorno, T. W. (1972) *Dialectic of Enlightenment*, trans. by John Cumming, New York: Herder & Herder.

Huettig, Mae D. (1944) *Economic Control of the Motion Picture Industry: A Study in Industrial Organization*, Philadelphia: University of Pennsylvania Press.

Jowett, Garth (1976) *Film: The Democratic Art*, Boston: Little, Brown & Co.

Kellner, Douglas (1997) 'Overcoming the Divide: Cultural Studies and Political Economy' in Marjorie Ferguson and Peter Golding (eds) *Cultural Studies in Question*, London: Sage.

Kennedy, Joseph P. (ed.) (1927) *The Story of Films as Told by the Leaders of Industry to the Students of the Graduate School of Business Administration*, Chicago, Ill.: A. W. Shaw Company.

Kitses, Jim (1970) *Horizons West – Anthony Mann, Budd Boetticher, Sam Peckinpah: Studies of Authorship within the Western*, Bloomington, Ind.: Indiana University Press.

Lacan, Jacques (1977) *Écrits: A Selection*, trans. Alan Sheridan, London: Tavistock Publications.

Levi-Strauss, Claude (1963) *Structural Anthropology*, trans. Claire Jacobson and Brooke Grundfest, New York: Basic Books.

Lewis, Jon (1995) *Whom the Gods Wish to Destroy. Francis Coppola and the New Hollywood*, Durham, NC: Duke University Press.

Lewis, Justin and Miller, Toby (eds) (2002) *Critical Cultural Policy Studies: A Reader*, London: Blackwell Publishing.

Lindsay, Vachel (1915) *The Art of the Moving Picture*, New York: Macmillan.

Macdonald, Dwight (1961) *Masscult & Midcult*, New York: Random House.

Mast, Gerald, Braudy, Leo and Cohen, Marshall (eds) (1999) *Film Theory and Criticism: Introductory Readings*, New York: Oxford University Press.

McKee, Robert (1997) *Story: Substance, Structure, Style, and the Principles of Screenwriting*, New York: Regan Books.

Metz, Christian (1974) *Film Language: A Semiotics of the Cinema*, trans. Michael Taylor, New York: Oxford University Press.

—— (1982) *The Imaginary Signifier: Psychoanalysis and the Cinema*, trans. Celia Britton *et al.*, Bloomington, Ind.: Indiana University Press.

Miller, Toby (1998) *Technologies of Truth: Cultural Citizenship and the Popular Media*, Minneapolis, MA: University of Minnesota Press.

Mosco, Vincent (1996) *The Political Economy of Communication: Rethinking and Renewal*, London: Sage.

Mulvey, Laura (1975) 'Visual Pleasure and Narrative Cinema', *Screen* 16(3).

Munsterberg, Hugo (1916) *The Photoplay; A Psychological Study*, New York: D. Appleton and Company.

Powdermaker, Hortense (1960) *Hollywood: The Dream Factory*, New York: Grosset & Dunlap.

Ramsaye, Terry (1926) *A Million and One Nights*, New York: Simon & Schuster.

Rosten, Leo (1941) *Hollywood: The Movie Colony, the Movie Makers*, New York: Harcourt Brace.

Ryan, Michael and Kellner, Douglas (1988) *Camera Politica: The Politics and Ideology of Contemporary Hollywood Film*, Bloomington, Ind.: Indiana University Press.

Sarris, Andrew (1968) *The American Cinema: Directors and Directions, 1929–1968*, New York: Dutton.

Schatz, Thomas (1988) *The Genius of the System: Hollywood Filmmaking in the Studio Era*, New York: Pantheon.

—— (ed.) (1997) *History of the American Cinema, Volume 6: Boom and Bust: American Cinema in the 1940s*, New York: Scribner's.

Schickel, Richard (1984), 'Review of *Irreconcilable Differences*', Time, 8 October.

Seldes, Gilbert (1978) *Movies Come From America*, Aspects of Film, New York: Ayer.

Sklar, Robert (1994) *Movie-Made America: A Cultural History of American Movies*, New York: Vintage Books.

Warshow, Robert (1962) *The Immediate Experience; Movies, Comics, Theatre and Other Aspects of Popular Culture*, New York: Doubleday.

Wasser, Frederick (2002) 'American Film Studies Today', *Journal of Communication*, June: 459–463.

Wenders, Wim (1991) *The Logic of Images*, London: Faber & Faber.

Wollen, Peter (1972) *Signs and Meaning in the Cinema*, Bloomington, Ind.: Indiana University Press.

Wyatt, Justin (1994) *High Concept: Movies and Marketing in Hollywood*, Austin, Tex.: University of Texas Press.

Part 1

EARLY AMERICAN CINEMA AND THE EMERGENCE OF HOLLYWOOD

1

NICKELODEON THEATERS, 1905–1914

Building an audience for the movies

Russell Merritt

Source: Tino Balio (ed.), *The American Film Industry*, Madison, Wisc.: University of Wisconsin Press, 1976, pp. 83–102.

In its short heyday, the nickelodeon theater was a pioneer movie house, a get-rich-quick scheme, and a national institution that was quickly turned into a state of mind. Its golden age began in 1905 and lasted scarcely nine years, but during that time it provided the movies their first permanent home, established a durable pattern for nation-wide distribution, and—most important—built for the motion picture an audience that would continue to support it for another forty years. Even after its decline, it survived in popular legend as a monument to movies in their age of innocence: the theater primeval that showed movies to an unspoiled and uninhibited audience of children and poor people. How the nickelodeon was portrayed in movie histories, how sharply it was believed to contrast with the postwar years of the movie palace and expensive studio production, is evident in the terms used to identify it. James Agee, for example, writing from the perspective of his own childhood, turned the nickelodeon into a populist shrine, cataloguing its delights in the style of a Whitman poem. He recalled "the barefaced honky-tonk and the waltzes by Waldteufel, slammed out in a mechanical piano; the searing redolence of peanuts and demirep perfumery, tobacco and feet, and sweat; the laughter of unrespectable people having a hell of a fine time, laughter as violent and steady and deafening as standing under a waterfall."[1]

More recently, Edward Wagenknecht in *The Movies in the Age of Innocence* painted an unblemished portrait of Chicago nickelodeons as they appeared to him in his youth, a portrait more detailed than Agee's but no less affectionate. As other histories have shown, the nickelodeon era has been the epoch of film history easiest to sentimentalize.[2]

25

Few historians would claim that his nostalgic view of the nickelodeon is pure fabrication. Even those who discount the innocence of the prewar years might find it hard to resist the allure of the vintage five-cent theater. The novelty was real, the appeal obvious, the popularity undeniable. But this portrait, two-dimensional and static, is patently incomplete. The purpose of my inquiry is to define that theater more sharply and, more important, to satisfy two nagging questions. First, how did theater operators finally attract the middle-class audiences so reluctant to peer inside the early movie houses? Second, when did the industry itself, originally supported and paid for by the working class, determine to abandon that audience for the broader, more affluent white-collar trade?

No one, to my mind, has answered these questions satisfactorily, least of all those historians who suppose that the middle-class moviegoer got started with features and World War I. By 1914, the middle-class audiences were, in fact, already in the theaters waiting for the spectacles and movie stars that would follow. The seduction of the affluent occurred, I will contend, in the preceding years, between 1905 and 1912, in precisely that theater supposedly reserved for the blue-collar workers.

"Democracy's theater"

The nickelodeon itself was a small, uncomfortable makeshift theater, usually a converted dance hall, restaurant, pawnshop, or cigar store, made over to look like a vaudeville emporium. Outside, large lurid posters pasted into the theater windows announced the playbill for the day. For ten cents— nickelodeons were seldom a nickel—the early moviegoer went inside and saw a miscellany of brief adventure, comedy, or fantasy films that lasted about an hour. Movies were always the main attraction, but enterprising managers followed the formula created by William Fox and Marcus Loew in 1906, and enhanced their programs with sing-alongs, inexpensive vaudeville acts, and illustrated lectures.

The show customarily began with a song, usually one of the popular ballads of the day—"Sunbonnet Sue," "Bicycle Built for Two," "The Way of the Cross," or perhaps "Down in Jungle Town"—or else a patriotic anthem. Hand-colored magic lantern slides illustrated scenes from the song and a final slide projecting the lyrics encouraged the audience to join in the chorus. The manager might then present his first movie, or bring on a live comedian, a dog act, or perhaps a ventriloquist; or else he might go straight to his most prestigious act: the illustrated lecture. Nickelodeon lecturing became for a time a lucrative business, with increasing care taken to recruit authentic "professors," preachers, and world travelers with exotic stories to tell. For the movies, a large black projector—a Vitascope Special or a Selig Polyscope if the theater were licensed—was set up in the back, either closed off in a separate room or enclosed inside a metal booth. Potted palms and gilded marquees were less essential, but popular, ways of adding "class" to the common show.

By 1910, when the nickelodeon craze had reached its peak, more than ten thousand of these theaters had sprung up across the country, creating demands for between one hundred and two hundred reels of film every week. "On one street in Harlem," wrote a *Harper's Weekly* journalist, "there are as many as five nickelodeons to a block, each one capable of showing to one thousand people an hour. They run from early morning until midnight, and their megaphones are barking before the milkman has made his rounds."[3]

If we may believe the most conservative estimates, by 1910 nickelodeons were attracting some 26 million Americans every week, a little less than 20 percent of the national population. In New York City alone, between 1.2 and 1.6 million people (or more than 25 percent of the city's population) attended movies weekly, while in Chicago, the nickelodeon craze reached 0.9 million persons (an astonishing 43 percent of that city's population). National gross receipts for that year totaled no less than $91 million.[4]

The lion's share of that audience came from the ghetto, a fact that nickelodeon commentators never tired of discovering. The label used over and over again by journalists commenting on the five-cent movie house, usually written with a delighted air of having discovered the exact phrase, was "democracy's theater." A Russell Sage survey revealed that in 1911, 78 percent of the New York audience consisted of members "from the working class" at a time when the worker had been effectively disenfranchised from the older arts. "You cannot go to any one of the picture shows in New York," wrote Mary Vorse for the *Outlook* in 1911, "without blessing the moving picture book that has brought so much into the lives of the people who work."[5] "They will stay as long as the slums stay," wrote Joseph Medill Patterson. "For in the slums they are the fittest, and must survive."[6]

The custodians of the poor took for granted that movies were made for the immigrant, the working man, children, and the unemployed. "If Tolstoi were alive today," the *Nation* claimed, "it is not unlikely that he would find in the movies a close approximation to his ideal of art. The Russian's ultimate test of a work of art was to appeal to the untutored but unspoiled peasant . . . the man who is today the nickel theater's most faithful customer." Municipal censorship of one-reelers was under constant attack by civic groups who called it class legislation, calculated to impose harsher standards on the poor man's theater than on that of his wealthier counterpart. Many welfare agencies, seeing the nickelodeon's appeal, followed the lead of Jane Addams at Hull House and used movies as part of educational and rehabilitation programs for the poor. The United States Navy, which at that time enlisted over five thousand immigrants per year, began in September 1910 to manufacture a series of recruiting films that played in nickel theaters throughout New York and in recruiting stations across the country.[7]

27

To that audience, movies meant escape in the most literal sense. Amidst the famous horrors of overcrowded tenement barracks, sweatshop work that paid coolie wages, and continuing typhoid epidemics, movies were treated as a simple refuge—a variant of the racetrack, the lottery, the fortune-teller's, or the saloon. Movies offered the worker a chance to come in from the cold and sit in the dark.

He was not particularly interested in art—or in acculturation. When D. W. Griffith started directing at the Biograph studios in 1908, his most important competition came from heavyweight prize fights and French chase comedies. Films such as these demanded no great power of concentration; the comedy plots—if they can be called that—were simple and direct, uncomplicated by subtleties of character delineation or subplot. The fast-moving action usually rose in a straight line from one climax to another, resolving itself in a beating or an explosion. No one who leafs through the pages of *Moving Picture World* and reads the plot descriptions of new films can overlook the incredible stress on violent slapstick and knockabout humor. Vitagraph's *When Casey Joined the Lodge*, reviewed July 4, 1908, features two Irishmen at a lodge initiation fighting each other with bricks and tossing sticks of dynamite under lodge members, cops, and innocent bystanders. Three weeks later, Vitagraph followed up with *A Policeman's Dream* in which two boys awaken a daydreaming patrolman by setting him on fire.[8] Neither the policeman nor the boys are beaten, an exceptional outcome. In other comedies for July, 1908: a political candidate has dirt and paste thrown over him, then his wife beats him;[9] partygoers fall into a young man's room when a floor caves in and they are beaten;[10] a gentleman "endeavoring to be polite to all mankind" inadvertently wreaks havoc on a town through his awkwardness and receives "many an unkind blow and boost for his trouble."[11]

Later historians would claim that such films worked as part of the immigrant's acculturation to American society, entertaining guides to the values and customs of the new world. But, in fact, few movies of this period performed such a task. For all their popularity with American audiences, they revealed little about America. Indeed, the majority of them were produced in France: exports of the Pathé Frères Company, who single-handedly released more films in the United States than the major American companies combined; *film trucs* from Georges Méliès; slapsticks and travelogues from Gaumont.[12] But even when they came from the United States, one-reelers seldom worked with the particularities of American stereotypes, landscapes, or social themes. Rather, the films were offered as spectacles that induced the onlooker to marvel at the unnatural, whether in the form of a slapstick chase, a comic dream, a wondrous adventure, or a historic disaster. Those who saw them did not learn much; it was rather the act of going to the movies that mattered most. By perceiving what was general in their own situation, immigrants could identify with others who shared that situation.

Like the societies, the schools, and the press, the nickelodeon was a means through which the immigrants came to know each other.

Exhibitors aspire to the middle class

But this portrait of the nickelodeon audience, like the portrait of the nickelodeon theater, is misleading because it is drastically incomplete. The five-cent theater may have been widely regarded as the working man's pastime, but the less frequently reported fact was that the theater catered to him through necessity, not through choice. The blue-collar worker and his family may have supported the nickelodeon. The scandal was that no one connected with the movies much wanted his support—least of all the immigrant film exhibitors who were working their way out of the slums with their theaters. The exhibitors' abiding complaint against nickelodeon audiences—voiced with monotonous regularity in trade journals, personal correspondence, and in congressional testimony—was that moviegoers as a group lacked "class." A movie customer wearing a suit or an officer's military uniform was a momentous event; a car parked outside the theater was reason for a letter to *Moving Picture World*. By contrast, certain kinds of workers were discouraged and occasionally even banned from the movies. An extreme example is the case of the shantytown nickelodeons at the Portsmouth and Charlestown naval shipyards that favored military officers with reduced admission prices while they refused admittance to enlisted men. Writing sympathetically of this policy, a trade editor reasoned: "One way to keep trouble out of a theater is not to admit it in the first place. . . . The roughhouse germ is present to a greater or less extent in every squad of sailors. The manager has reason to know in advance whether they are friend or foe, and therefore one cannot blame a manager in Portsmouth or any other place for using his discretionary powers, whether it involves the livery of Uncle Sam or Johnny Bull or anybody else."[13]

Not until the secretary of the navy threatened a naval boycott of all nickelodeons in Boston and Portsmouth and Governor Eugene Foss of Massachusetts signed a bill prohibiting discrimination against military recruits in places of amusement did the operators relent and agree to take back the enlisted men. Meanwhile, big-city nickelodeon operators were cautioned against earning reputations as ethnic theaters, and given three ground rules for attracting a "mixed" house: operators should avoid booking programs heavily slanted toward any one nationality, avoid ethnic vaudeville acts, and eliminate all songs in foreign languages.[14] Embarrassed by their regulars, ambitious managers constantly sought ways to attract the larger, middle-class family trade currently the domain of vaudeville and the legitimate stage.

The thirst for affluence and respectability helps explain the curious locations of the original nickelodeons. Even when they were working-class entertainment, the most important nickelodeons were seldom built in the worker's community or in his shopping area. Instead, they customarily opened in business districts on the outer edge of the slums, fringing white-collar shopping centers, accessible to blue-collar audiences but even closer to middle-class trade.

Boston as a case study

A study of nickelodeon theaters in Boston will dramatize this phenomenon. While not necessarily a "typical" American metropolis, Boston offers a use-ful and convenient case study of a city that early established itself as a large and important East Coast film market. Thanks to its reputation as a theatri-cal crossroads (it had already become illustrious as a testing ground for New York plays, as the headquarters for B. F. Keith's vast chain of vaudeville theaters, and as the town that introduced continuous performances), its nick-elodeons were reported and analyzed in unusually full detail throughout the trade press. As a consequence of these reports and the constant attention given nickel theaters by local social workers, church groups, and the city political machine, Boston provides one of the most influential and best-documented collections of nickel theaters in the nation.

Boston's movie theaters were strung out along three strategic locations in the city's downtown shopping area. At one end seven theaters blustered around Scollay Square and Bowdoin Square—nearer expensive Beacon Hill townhouses than Italian and Irish tenements in the North End. This was Boston's original nickelodeon district, where in 1905 Mark Mitchell built Boston's first movie theater—the Theater Comique at 14 Tremont Row—and where Boston's first movie theater chain set up its main offices.

From this point, the nickelodeons were stretched out in a long line along Tremont Row and Washington Street, where they operated side by side with the downtown B. F. Keith vaudeville houses and the major legitimate theaters. Although Washington Street commanded the highest building ren-tals in the city ($30,000 per year for lots ranging from twenty-five hundred to four thousand square feet), the steady flow of business made this the most prosperous and the most fiercely competitive theater district in town. Shoppers coming out of C. F. Hovey's or Meyer Jonasson department stores could select from the Bijou Dream, the Pastime, the Gaiety, or the Park without having to cross the street. The Unique and the New Washington were one block away from the "elegantly appointed" Bradford Hotel and down two blocks from the stylish Hotel Touraine. Two nearby legitimate theaters—the Shubert at 265 Tremont and the Boston at 539 Washington—were constantly complaining to the New York *Dramatic Mirror* about the cheap competition luring away their theater regulars. To meet the threat, the Shuberts began to show ten-cent movies at their Globe Theatre during the slow 1909 summer months—an unheard-of practice among Boston's expensive legitimate houses and one that created a bitter nickelodeon price war at the Eliot Street corner of Washington Street.

Past the hotel district and Chinatown, down in the city's skid row, Boston's third group of nickel theaters were coiled around Castle Square and lower Washington Street where, run-down and poorly tended, they fit in with the gray South End landscape. Sandwiched in with local saloons, pool halls, and cheap hotels, these honky-tonk theaters were the principal targets of municipal reformers and the mayor's office. The working-class family trade avoided these theaters for the most part, hopscotching over them to attend the more remote but better-tended theaters in the north. Mainly, the Castle Square theaters were taken over by the flotsam residing in the dives along Tremont and Shawmut, or the transients from the local boardinghouses. Several of the nickelodeons were used as sleeping quarters; police raids on the Paradise and Dreamland were considered commonplace.[15]

As a location, the South End was notorious as a graveyard for nickelodeons, where, despite cheap building rates, the theaters suffered the poorest record of survival. Theaters in the district changed hands constantly; successful operators to the north regarded the area as a quarantine zone, preferring to expand their own movie empires to the suburbs and the wealthy Back Bay. The idea of constructing quality nickelodeons in the South End, if it was considered, was never tried. Even further from consideration was the possibility of building theaters further south, in the South Roxbury shopping districts or near the South End factories where the catchpenny exhibits, smaller vaudeville houses, and cheaper legitimate theaters stood. Like the North End, the South End was strictly off-limits for ambitious nickelodeon entrepreneurs.

What makes this statistic startling is that there was a group of theaters in the South End neighborhood which demonstrated that catering to the ethnic family trade was economically feasible. These were the South End's three venerable first-class theaters—the Columbia, the Castle Square, and the Grand Opera House—which started showing movies to fill in the days when they weren't presenting live melodrama and variety acts, and ended by switching over to movies altogether. All three theaters demonstrated that it was possible to cater to ethnic, working-class clienteles and maintain a successful business. The Columbia, for instance, at 978 Washington Street, the South End's largest and most elaborate melodrama house in 1895, was alternating between movies and vaudeville shows ten years later, and worked on the Irish family trade by featuring ethnic acts and Irish songs between films. The Castle Square, home of the South End's single opera company in the 1890's, became a movie house in 1907, but continued with Yiddish plays in the summer for the growing Jewish community along the Pleasant Street neighborhood and North Roxbury. These were precisely the paths the new theater operators chose not to follow. The new movie theaters were determined to crash the new neighborhoods and stay out of the old ones.

Their horizons were sharply limited: the choleric opposition to the garish common shows prevented them from entering the suburbs, nor could managers obtain licenses to build in the wealthy Back Bay area or along Boylston Street. The exclusive Back Bay shopping thoroughfares on Newbury Street or Huntington Avenue were also off-limits. But even so, the most aggressive movie managers were pushing in these directions too, and by the beginning of World War I, even these cultural havens gave in to the onslaught of the dread Philistines.[16]

The pattern was similar in New York City, Chicago, Philadelphia, and St. Louis.[17] Exhibitors and producers anxious to cover their investment made no major effort to advance the industry through the working class itself. Few if any films stressed ethnic ties, few chronicled adventures of immigrants—their arrival in the New World, life in tenements, or, until D. W. Griffith appeared, working conditions in shops or factories.[18] No one with prominent ethnic features was permitted in leading roles; the American blue-eyed, brown-haired beauty was required, whether playing an Italian street singer, a Sioux Indian maiden, a Spanish duenna, or a Gibson Girl. In the midst of a strange new audience, the industry clung to the vestiges of the safe old theatrical patterns.

The old world, in this case, meant the vaudeville theater. Vaudeville, decaying since 1900 in the wake of the nickelodeon's popularity, had in effect provided the unwilling model of exhibition for the energetic new rival. Just as, five years later, movie exhibitors would use the legitimate theater as a guide to learn how to exhibit feature films, so, in 1908, nickelodeon owners preyed on vaudeville houses for methods of exhibiting movie shorts. We have already seen one example of this: the nickelodeon locations we have described were determined less by proximity to their clientele than by proximity to the beaten path of vaudeville houses. Many nickelodeons were in fact converted vaudeville houses; others were built next door to them. When managers decided on mixing their short films with an illustrated song, a guest lecture, and variety acts, they were merely plotting variations of the vaudeville routine. Vaudeville's continuous performances and gingerbread architecture were also readily adapted to the new shows. Most important, when exhibitors imagined the ideal audience, they usually thought of the vaudeville audience—a cross section of urban and suburban American life. They preferred this old audience to the new, unfashionable audience that had discovered them. To follow the guidelines set up by vaudeville houses became the path of least resistance.

Luring the family trade

The problem was how to lure that affluent family trade, so near and yet so far. The answer, at times conscious but more frequently a matter of convenience, was through the New American Woman and her children. If few professional men would as yet, by 1908, consider taking their families to the nickelodeon, the woman on a shopping break, or children out from school, provided the ideal lifeline to the affluent bourgeoisie. Statistically, women and children numbered only 30 percent of the New York audience, even less than that during performances after 8 P.M., but they commanded the special attention of both the industry and its censors. In a trade hungry for respectability, the middle class woman was respectability incarnate. Her very presence in the theater refuted the vituperative accusations lodged against the common show's corrupting vulgarity.[19]

Theaters spared few efforts to woo her. Soon after Boston's Theatre Premier established the policy of giving free admission tickets to women for prenoon shows, the Olympic reacted by charging women and children half fare at all screenings and thereby set the precedent that virtually all the major Boston nickelodeons adopted. By the end of 1910, women and children were charged half fare in all of Philadelphia's nickelodeons while, with growing frequency, exhibitors' complaints about the movies took the form of gallant defense of the female's tender sensibilities.[20]

Women were no less venerated in the nickelodeon movies themselves. Original screenplays in particular reveal a preoccupation with women's stories. Female protagonists far outnumber males, dauntless whether combatting New York gangsters, savage Indians, oversized mashers, or "the other woman." In the best genteel tradition, audiences were spared scenes of debauchery and criminal acts; the outdated moral code of the Victorian era that required vice to be punished and virtue rewarded became an inflexible law throughout this period. "Saloons and other places of evil repute should not be shown or else shown so briefly [as] to carry small effect," warned an early screenwriter's manual. "Keep away from the atmosphere of crime and debauchery and avoid as much as possible the showing of fights, burglaries, or any other infraction of the laws. The juvenile mind is receptive and observant . . . If you write clean and decent stories, you do not have to bother about the Board of Censorship. If you want to revel in crime and bloodshed you must be careful to keep the actions of your character within the unwritten law.[21]

The pressure to keep movies "popular" was thus offset by pressure to keep them "respectable." Film producers drew heavily on the literary lions—Zola, Daudet, Poe, Tolstoi, Dumas, Hugo, Twain, de Maupassant, and Shakespeare—for film "classics." At times, the tension between the two conflicting impulses yielded bizarre results. When in 1910 Vitagraph filmed Sophocles' *Elektra* in one reel, exhibitors were told to "BILL IT LIKE A CIRCUS—IT WILL DRAW BIGGER CROWDS THAN ANY FILM YOU HAVE EVER HAD."[22] In Louis B. Mayer's Orpheum, Pathé's *Passion Play*, "the life of Christ from the Annunciation to the Ascension in twenty-seven beautiful scenes," was followed the next week by *Bluebeard, the Man with Many Wives*. Both were successful.[23]

But the more sophisticated and plausible lures came from the new blood drifting into the film production studios. Although he came from a family and circumstances profoundly different from those of the theater manager, the early director and writer of dramatic films had aspirations of his own that also worked to attract the white-collar worker to the movies. Griffith's own perspective—and in this regard he is typical of such film directors as Sidney Olcott, Allan Dwan, and Frank Powell—was one of a bourgeois, native-born theater man, proud of his old American stock, comfortably living on a family income ranging from $800 to $1,000 per month when the national average was under $600 per year.[24] Filmmakers told the stories they knew best, and inevitably, as they became articulate, their films revealed their own middle-class background. Their perpetual quest for acceptance among their own kind provided special pressure to return to figures and motives approved by the guardians of popular culture.

For better or for worse, the five-cent movie, like the theater that housed it, was effectively dropping out of the hands of its original audience. For the immigrant, movies were becoming more and more part of his assimilation into American life. Moviemakers, like the nickelodeon operators, were out to satisfy the broader, more demanding audience of their peers.

By fall 1913, the concerted effort had finally begun to pay dividends. As the comfortless thrills of watching movies on wooden chairs gave way to deluxe motion picture theaters and as movies lengthened from one to four reels, the movie clientele imperceptibly began to change. Journalists wrote continually—and critically—about the "new public" and the "quicker-minded audience" that had discovered the movies and forsaken the theater and library. Residential neighborhoods, militant in their resistance to nickelodeons in 1908, gradually softened to the pressure of aggressive entrepreneurs and permitted construction of nickelodeons on their main streets. The climax came in June 1914, when a ten-reel version of Giovanni Pastrone's *Cabiria* was shown at the White House to President Wilson, his family, and members of the cabinet. The president of the United States had gone to see a movie. Who could hope to hold out after that?

The movies did not lose the immigrant and blue-collar worker, but as new theaters invaded the suburbs and movies were shown in legitimate houses, the social stigma attached to the nickelodeon all but vanished. The most reliable estimates suggest that, in sheer numbers, movie attendance practically doubled during the nickelodeon era, increasing from twenty-six million persons per week in 1908 to at least forty-nine million in 1914.[25] Although women and children were still the most discussed groups of patrons, adult males statistically outnumbered both groups combined; Frederic C. Howe estimated that 75 percent of the national movie audience was adult male.[26] Makeup and size of audiences must have differed considerably from matinee to evening and from weekend to weekday (on Saturday afternoons, it was commonly conceded, schoolchildren reigned supreme in movie theaters everywhere). But among contemporary commentators, no one has been found to contradict the prevailing sentiment that movies were attracting "the better crowd." About the new audience, Walter P. Eaton in the *Atlantic* wrote:

> You cannot, of course, draw any hard and fast line which will not be crossed at many points. In Atlanta, Georgia, for example, you may often see automobiles parked two deep along the curb in front of the motion picture theatre, which hardly suggests an exclusively proletarian patronage.[27]

In the *Outlook* Howe wrote:

> There is scarcely a village that has not one or more motion picture houses . . . Men now take their wives and families for an evening at the movies where formerly they went alone to the nearby saloon.[28]

Boston's new theaters

This new clientele had not arrived by chance. That it was aggressively wooed by movie entrepreneurs eager to break existent social barriers may be seen by the rapidly shifting patterns of prewar movie exhibition. The Boston theater district, which in 1910 was restricted to two downtown thoroughfares, gained considerable new ground by the outbreak of World War I. New movie theaters opened in virtually every major residential neighborhood surrounding the city. By the end of 1913, Dorchester, Roxbury, Cambridge, Somerville, Newton, Belmont, and Watertown had all succumbed to the rising movie fever and had permitted construction of motion picture theaters on their main streets. *Moving Picture World* treated the steady flow of news reports like dispatches from advancing front lines. "For the first time in the history of the town," it reported on December 14, 1913, "the selectmen of Brookline, Mass., have decided to grant a license for a photoplay show." Several months earlier the same correspondent reported victory in Brighton; a nickelodeon would finally open in that wealthy suburb after three years of opposition by Mayor John F. Fitzgerald. Most remarkable of all, in Boston's exclusive Back Bay community, the city's wealthiest residential district and its cultural hub, no less than three movie houses opened during the same year. The Back Bay had been kept intact through January 1913, but within eighteen months, moviegoers were watching features at the First Spiritual Temple, which the wealthy socialite Mrs. M. S. Ayer and her friends had converted into the Exeter Street Theatre; at the St. James, one block down from Boston's Symphony Hall; and at the Potter Hall, an opera house converted to movies after its 1910 opera season had failed.[29]

Meanwhile, Boston's downtown nickelodeon district, still stretched out along Washington Street and Tremont Street, grew in another direction—

skyward. The movie cathedral was still several years away, but the trend toward bigger, more elaborate theaters was unmistakable to anyone reading the frequent theater reports made to the press. The Beacon, adorned with a gigantic spinning globe over the entrance that sparkled in the dark, opened its brass doors with *The Fall of Troy* on February 19, 1910, to a full house of eight hundred persons. Four years later, the same corporation built the Modern, a Gothic marvel with over one thousand seats, flying buttresses, and a door made to look like a cathedral portal. Nathan Gordon's Scollay Square Olympia opted for Florentine Eclectic. Passing under a golden statue of Victory, arms outstretched and belly protruding with a luminous clock, the Olympia's customer entered a vestibule decorated with Florentine murals, a ceramic tile floor, and a ticket booth resembling a Renaissance confessional. The theater claimed a seating capacity of eleven hundred, one of the largest in the city, but its special pride was the blue, gray, and gold draperies that hung from the boxes, balcony, and gallery railings, monogrammed with the letter O.[30] Not to be outdone, two Washington Street nickelodeons—the Joliette and the Park—drastically enlarged and refurbished their interiors with grandiose displays of their own.[31]

These enlarged theaters stiffened the downtown competition, but the most fearsome and far-reaching threat came from another quarter, originally indifferent to the ten-cent movies, reluctant to exhibit them, but willing to make the move when nickelodeon competition made it necessary. Driven out of the stage business by movies, several legitimate theaters had begun to show their own two- and three-reelers, and in so doing, they had diverted a considerable percentage of the audience the nickelodeons had sought for themselves. "The public," admitted a trade journalist ruefully, "evidently likes to go to a regular theatre which is playing moving pictures and vaudeville in preference to the regular photoplay theatres, even if the shows given are not better. Everyone knows that the Globe is a 'lemon' as a straight dramatic house, but reports go to state that it knocked out nearly $1,000 per week clear profit when showing the cinematographs last summer."[32]

In increasing numbers, audiences discovered that they could watch movies without going to the nickelodeon. By the end of 1913, the National Park, and Potter Hall theaters had abandoned legitimate drama altogether in favor of two- and three-reelers, while the Tremont, the Shubert, the Cort, and Opera House included occasional feature films in their regular theatrical season. The climax came on November 23, 1914, when B. F. Keith announced that the Boston, the city's oldest, largest, and most prestigious playhouse, would henceforth become a full-time movie theater. The gala premiere, by invitation only, featured William Farnum and Tom Santschi in *The Spoilers*. Even Senator Henry Cabot Lodge was there.[33]

Altogether, the number of Boston movie theaters increased more than 30 percent during the nickelodeon years, growing from thirty-one theaters in January 1907 to forty-one theaters in January 1914. In practically every case, the new theaters, with their enlarged seating capacities and more ornate decoration, were started in more prosperous and more exclusive business areas than those of their predecessors. No instance has been found of a Boston movie theater opening between 1910 and 1914 in an area that could be described as a working-class community—Castle Square, the North End, the South End, or North Roxbury. The seduction of the affluent was taking place in thoroughfares closer to home.

Prestigious trappings for movies were nothing new. For the well-to-do, private screenings at society balls were chic novelties since the 1897 Paris Charity Bazaar which caught fire and caused the famous scandal; when Nora Saltonstall threw her annual gala at Boston's Copley Plaza Hotel, the *Globe* called the five reels of silent comedies a diverting but familiar social entertainment. Schools, charity balls, churches, and civic clubs projected movies eagerly supplied by exchange men anxious to launder the nickelodeon's shabby reputation. But, of course, this was not moviegoing in its customary sense. Society and the movie operator agreed that these were special activities, exceptional performances that created goodwill without interfering with the day-to-day commercial enterprise or compromising social position.

Legitimate theaters, by contrast, were seen as places where the affluent could watch movies on a regular basis, unembarrassed, at full fare. When such theaters began screening movies, they were immediately recognized as an enemy force which Boston's most important nickelodeon owners were eager to join. Marcus Loew, B. F. Keith, Nathan Gordon, and Mark Mitchell, by 1914 Boston's four most important nickelodeon owners, started systematic raids on legitimate theaters in order to bring them into their movie chains. At the same time, smaller operators who could not afford to purchase or lease legitimate theaters revamped their nickelodeons to resemble "first-class" houses in both appearance and format. Owners went out of their way to recruit managers with background in legitimate theater management, and modified the old format borrowed from vaudeville to give their shows the new look of the legitimate stage.

One important consequence of this invasion was that a social hierarchy, nonexistent among movie theaters in 1910, was rapidly developed by World War I. Patron and exhibitor alike began to rank theaters according to size and quality, discriminating between first-class theaters and the nickelodeon. The most expensive theaters worked conscientiously to disassociate themselves from the cheap theaters even as they encouraged comparisons with legitimate playhouses, while the public quickly adopted a double standard in regard to movie houses whereby films permitted in one kind of theater were not allowed in the other. When, for instance, the five-year-old National Board of Censorship was described by its chairman, Frederic C. Howe, in 1914, its jurisdiction was limited to five- and ten-cent theaters, enabling the dollar theaters to play films—like the white slavery cycle and sex education shorts—the NBC prohibited from nickelodeons.[34] First-class theaters gained other trade advantages too, notably first-run, exclusive engagements in exchange for higher rental fees, that helped single them out from second-run, cheaper theaters which, if they played the same films, played them weeks later, frequently opposite other second-run theaters showing the same bill.

The nickelodeon's demise

When, during the war years, production companies of the Motion Picture Patents Company collapsed, they took the nickelodeon down with them. Frozen out by the new independent production companies who regarded one-reelers as outmoded, nickelodeons either enlarged, changed format, or died. As early as 1914, trade journals spoke of the five-cent theater as an endangered species. "We cannot close our eyes to the fact," wrote Stephen Bush, "that theaters with small capacity using mostly single reels are going out of business all around us."[35] Salvage efforts took many forms, but the most important operators saw the handwriting on the wall. Not until 1928, with the coming of sound, would there be another such massive effort to renovate, build, and dump movie houses as occurred in 1913 and 1914.

But, by then, the job of building an audience for the movies was about finished. Without feature films and refined theaters, it is unlikely that the middle-class audience would have long remained. But the nickelodeon and its one- and two-reelers had in fact performed the initial task generally credited to imported features, movie palaces, and World War I. Mostly, it was the work of immigrants who would go on to control production as they had exhibition. As film manufacturers their names—Zukor, Loew, Laemmle, Fox, Mayer, the Warners—would become nearly as famous as the stars they promoted. But even as anonymous nickelodeon operators they moved the industry in the direction that would remain unchanged for another generation.

Notes

1 James Agee, "Comedy's Greatest Era," *Life*, September 3, 1949, reprinted in Agee, *Agee on Film: Reviews and Comments* (New York: Mc Dowell, Obolensky, 1958) pp. 6–7.
2 See the introduction to Edward Wagenknecht, *The Movies in the Age of Innocence* (Norman: University of Oklahoma Press, 1962). Other accounts of the nickelodeon can be found in the standard film histories of the silent era: Terry Ramsaye, *A Million and One Nights* (New York: Simon and Schuster, 1926); Benjamin B. Hampton, *A History of the Movies* (New York: Covici, Friede, 1931); Lewis Jacobs, *The Rise of the American Film* (New York: Teacher's College Press, 1939); Kenneth Macgowan, *Behind the Screen* (New York: Delacorte, 1965). But these sources seldom go beyond a cursory description of nickelodeon exhibition. There is no American equivalent to the detailed study of British film exhibition found in Rachael Low, *The History of the British Film, 1906–1914* (London: Allen &

Unwin, 1949). The nickelodeon era, for the most part, has been ignored in the current literature of film history, but two important studies have recently been made available: Garth Jowett, "Media Power and Social Control: The Motion Picture in America, 1896–1936" (Ph.D. diss., University of Pennsylvania, 1972); and Joseph H. North, *The Early Development of the Motion Picture, 1887–1909* (New York: Arno, 1973), a reprint of a 1949 doctoral dissertation. Important primary documents and contemporary descriptions of nickelodeons have been collected in George Pratt, *Spellbound in Darkness* (Greenwich, Conn: New York Graphic Society, 1973).

3 Barton Currie, "The Nickel Madness," *Harper's Weekly* 51 (August 24, 1907): 1246. The theater statistic is from Hampton, *History of the Movies*, p. 58. *Moving Picture World* (hereafter to be referred to as *MPW*), December 5, 1908, p. 523, quotes an unnamed article by Glenmore Davis in *Success Magazine* claiming six thousand nickelodeon theaters in existence across the country in 1908.

4 "Moving Pictures and the National Character," *Review of Reviews* 42 (September 1910): 315–20. Michael Davis, *The Exploitation of Pleasure* (New York: Russell Sage Foundation, 1911), pp. 8–9, is slightly more conservative. He estimates that 900,000 New Yorkers attended movies weekly in 1910.

5 Mary H. Vorse, "Some Picture Show Audiences," *Outlook* 97 (June 24, 1911): 442. The Russell Sage survey is in Davis, *Exploitation of Pleasure* pp. 8–9. Garth S. Jowett, "The First Motion Picture Audiences," *Journal of Popular Film* 3 (Winter 1974): 39–54, quotes reports from social workers in Boston, Pittsburgh, and Homestead, N.Y., which also demonstrate the preponderance of working-class people in nickelodeons.

6 Joseph Medill Patterson, "The Nickelodeons: The Poor Man's Elementary Course in the Drama," *Saturday Evening Post* 180 (November 23, 1907): 38.

7 "A Democratic Art," *Nation* 97 (August 28, 1913): 193. For the anticensorship arguments, see "Un-American Innovation," *Independent* 86 (May 22, 1916): 265; "The White Slave Films," *Outlook* 106 (January 17, 1914): 121; and U.S. Congress, House Committee on Education, *Hearings, A Bill to Establish a Federal Motion Picture Commission*, 63d Cong., 2d sess., 1914, 2, pt. 2: 197–98. For navy recruiting films, see "Moving Pictures and the National Character," p. 317; and Arthur Dutton, "Where Will the Navy Get Its Men?" *Overland Monthly* 53 (March 1909): 233. The statistic for 1910 immigrant naval recruits, a figure representing 12 percent of all naval recruits, comes from "The Report of the Bureau of Navigation," *The Annual Reports of the Navy Department, 1911* (Washington, D.C.: U.S. Government Printing Office, 1911), p. 305.

8 *MPW*, July 25, 1908.

9 *The Candidate*, Pathé-Frères.

10 *Noisy Neighbors*, Pathé-Frères.

11 *Too Polite*, Gaumont.

12 Cf. "What Is An American Subject?" *MPW*, January 22, 1910, p. 82, in which an anonymous reporter counted forty films released the previous week, half of which, he noted, were produced abroad. Of those produced in the United States, he counted no more than ten with American themes, "that is, themes 'racy of the soil' and distinctly American in characterization, scenery, and surroundings. The other subjects were such as might have been made in Europe." The report concluded "that the American subject, even after a year's plugging away, does not seem to have secured a predominant part in the film program of the moving picture theaters of the United States."

13 *MPW*, June 3, 1911. The shipyard nickelodeon quarrel was reported in *MPW* June 3, 1911, p. 1246, and June 10, 1911, p. 1321.

14 *Motography* 7 (February 1912): 24.

15 The notable exception to this rule was the Idle Hour at Castle Square. For blacks living in the Kirkland Street neighborhood, the Idle Hour was virtually the only theater in town that permitted an integrated audience on the main floor. In fall 1910, a group of local black businessmen bought the theater outright and operated it (renamed the Pekin) for a year before it went out of business.

16 Theater addresses are found in the Boston *City Directory, 1910*; for remarks on the nickelodeons I have depended on the New England and Boston correspondent's report to *MPW* which began October 1, 1910, and continued more or less weekly throughout 1910 and 1911. See also Frederic E. Hayes, "Amusements," in *The City Wilderness*, ed. Robert A. Woods (Boston, 1899), for South End theaters. Donald C. King, "From Museum to Multi-Cinema," *Marquee* 6 (Third Quarter 1974): 5–22, provides a useful, lavishly illustrated history of Boston theaters from 1794 to the present.

17 For a description of New York nickelodeon locales, see Russell Merritt, "The Impact of D. W. Griffith's Moving Pictures from 1908 to 1914 on Contemporary American Culture" (Ph.D. diss., Harvard University, 1970), pp. 106–08. Contemporary accounts of nickelodeons in Philadelphia and Chicago may be found in the pages of *MPW*. Although no systematic, updated study of these theaters has yet been made, provocative essays on individual theaters and surveys of city theater history may be found in the pages of *Marquee*, the journal of the Theatre Historical Society.

18 For example, a detailed search through *MPW* film synopses published from March 9, 1907, the magazine's inaugural issue, through December 1908 revealed that of 1,056 American-produced films reviewed, a total of eight films specifically concerned the immigrant or the poor: *The Life of a Bootblack* (Essanay, 1907); *Smuggling Chinese into the U.S.A.* (Goodfellow, 1908); *The Eviction* (Selig, 1908); *The Little Match Girl* (Goodfellow, 1908); *The Rag-Picker's Christmas* (Goodfellow, 1908); *New Way to Pay Old Debts* (Lubin, 1908); *Old Isaacs, the Pawnbroker* (Biograph, 1908); and *A Mother's Crime* (Vitagraph, 1908). The two largest French companies—Pathé-Frères and Gaumont—contributed another seven films on the subject.

19 For the attendance of women and children, see Committee on Education, *Hearings* pp. 121–22. For more information on children's attendance, see *Survey* 35 (May 9, 1914).

20 Price reduction reported in *MPW*, January 21, 1911, p. 146 and March 4, 1911, p. 728. For Philadelphia's statistic, *MPW*, June 3, 1911, p. 1245.

21 Epes W. Sargent, *Technique of the Photoplay* (New York: Moving Picture World, 1913), pp. 133–34.

22 Quoted in Wagenknecht, *Movies in the Age of Innocence*, p. 64.

23 Bosley Crowther, *Hollywood Rajah: The Life and Times of Louis B. Mayer* (New York; Holt, Rinehart and Winston, 1960), pp. 30–31.

24 Linda Arvidson, *When the Movies Were Young* (New York: Dover, 1969), p. 134. By 1910, Griffith's royalty checks averaged $900 and $1,000 per month.

25 Frederic C. Howe, "What to Do with the Motion-Picture Show: Shall It Be Censored?" *Outlook* 100 (June 20, 1914): 412; Committee on Education, *Hearings*, p. 65; "Moving Pictures and the National Character," pp. 315–20.

26 Howe, "What to Do with the Motion-Picture Show," p. 413.

27 Walter P. Eaton, "Class-Consciousness and the 'Movies,'" *Atlantic Monthly* 115 (January 1915): 49–50.

28 Howe, "What to Do with the Motion-Picture Show," p. 413.

29 Henry Archer, *MPW's* New England correspondent, made steady reports on these new residential theaters throughout 1913 and 1914. See particularly his reports in issues dated March 14, 1914; May 2, 1914; May 16, 1914; and May 30, 1914.

30 *MPW*, November 26, 1910; January 17, 1914; July 25, 1914; *Boston Globe*, April 2, 1914; July 1, 1914.
31 *MPW*, June 20, 1914; December 5, 1914; *Boston Globe*, December 3, 1914.
32 *MPW*, December 17, 1910.
33 *MPW*, December 5, 1914; *Boston Evening Transcript*, November 24, 1914.
34 Howe, "What to Do with the Motion-Picture Show," p. 414.
35 W. Stephen Bush, "The Single Reel II," *MPW*, July 4, 1914, p. 36.

2

MAKING MOVIES

Richard Koszarski

Source: Richard Koszarski (ed.), *History of the American Cinema, Volume 3: An Evening's Entertainment: The Age of the Silent Feature Picture, 1915–1928*, Berkeley, Calif.: University of California Press, 1994, pp. 95–137, 335–339.

Breaking into the business

By 1915 the motion-picture industry had achieved a certain sophistication in the way it produced, marketed, and exhibited its pictures. Significant economic and industrial forces now acted to standardize these procedures, although filmmaking in the silent era could hardly be thought of as routine. What remained in a primitive and even chaotic state was the most elementary aspect of the filmmaking process: recruitment and training of new personnel. This is not to say that there was any shortage of activity in this area. Many volumes of self-instruction were published, schools abounded (some of them even legitimate), and magazine advertisements enticed men and women out to the studios. But the results of all this activity were negligible. Some actors and directors successfully came from the legitimate stage (many more were unsuccessful), and a few short-story writers and romantic novelists found new careers as photoplaywrights.

If memoirs and oral histories are to be believed, accident and bizarre coincidence seem to have been responsible for a disproportionate number of major careers. Allan Dwan, an electrical engineer, arrived to install Cooper-Hewitt lamps at the Chicago Essanay studio and stayed to write and direct. Raoul Walsh had most recently been working as a cowboy. Lois Wilson was a beauty-contest winner. Robert Flaherty was an explorer. The tremendous expansion of the industry within a single generation had created employment for thousands, but without a usable tradition there seemed no rational way to master the various professional skills involved. Relying on the theater as a model had limited application, and in the most technical areas, such as editing or cinematography, guideposts were nonexistent. Such fields soon came to be dominated by men and women who entered them just out of school and grew up with the medium, like Arthur Miller and Lee Garmes behind the camera, or Dorothy Arzner and William Hornbeck at the editing bench.[1]

Organized schooling seems to have had almost no success in preparing young hopefuls for motion-picture work, despite a surprising amount of effort. Columbia University demonstrated a commitment to film studies throughout this period but without any notable acceptance from either the industry or the academy. In 1914 Columbia introduced film as a teaching aid in the Journalism School and extended its use the following year into economics, science, history, psychology, and English-literature classes. Victor O. Freeburg (author of *Disguise Plots in Elizabethan Drama*) lectured on film at Columbia from the fall of 1915 to the spring of 1917 and eventually produced a pair of sophisticated texts, *The Art of Photoplay Making* (1918) and *Pictorial Beauty on the Screen* (1923). Frances Taylor Patterson began as "instructor of Photoplay Composition" in the summer of 1917 and continued into the talking era. While Freeburg essentially defined screen art in graphic terms, Patterson had a stronger interest in narrative, and her three books are almost completely concerned with the niceties of plot construction. The avowed purpose of her class was to help foster public appreciation of film and offer prospective screenwriters a "short cut to success."[2]

When America entered World War I, the U.S. Army Signal Corps established a training school at Columbia University to provide instruction in the making of medical and historical-record films. Among those who passed through this program, either as students or as instructors, were Josef von Sternberg, Alan Crosland, Ernest B. Schoedsack, Irvin Willat, and Lewis Milestone. These men, and others, later looked back on their Signal Corps service as a valuable shared experience, but what they might have gained directly from this schooling is unclear. Efforts to continue a course in film production after the war were defeated because Columbia refused to support it with proper equipment or facilities and because according to one faculty member, "the funds to pay competent instructors were inadequate."[3]

Other attempts to shape film as an object of university study in this period ranged from Vachel Lindsay's lectures at his alma mater, the University of Chicago, to a series conducted by Joseph P. Kennedy at Harvard's Graduate School of Business Administration. An increasingly sophisticated amateur film movement (especially after the introduction of the 16-mm Bell & Howell Filmo in 1923) did make use of many of these manuals and scenario models, but they seem to have had little effect on the industry as a whole.[4]

When established programs like the one at Columbia failed to satisfy the demand for film production courses, a rash of private technical schools arose, most derided by the industry as mere "sucker traps." Such instruction was aimed largely at four major crafts: acting, writing, cinematography, and projection. Directing, while always given lip service in the various "Breaking into the Movies" manuals, was so hard to conceptualize that little energy was devoted to promoting it as a way of making a living. For example, one 1921 manual limits its discussion of directing to this observation: "Next in line is the director, who takes the scenario and sets out to make the picture. There is a shortage of directors at present, and for that reason, salaries are particularly high in this line, but of course, direction is a profession which takes many years of study . . ."[5]

Prospective actors and actresses appear to have been the most widely victimized of these hopefuls. Relatively harmless instructional manuals like *Motion Picture Acting* (1916) offered for study "191 posed photographs of motion picture stars, showing 499 different expressions and emotions." Readers of Mae Marsh's *Screen Acting* (1921) learned that circumstance, hard work, and native talent developed before the camera were the keys to screen success—a dictum broad enough to discourage no one.[6]

Publicity regarding the "effortless" rise of many movie favorites encouraged large numbers of men and women to see themselves as potential screen material. This route was perceived as far easier than stage stardom as well as more accessible to the young and impressionable (Lillian Gish, Mary Pickford, Norma Talmadge, and others became major film stars while still in their teens). *Motion Picture* reported various "fakes and frauds" directed at such young hopefuls. In one common "scam," magazine advertisements would solicit "directory entries" (for a fee) that would be circulated to the studios. Because films were not cast in this fashion, the use of such directories by unknowns was worthless.[7]

For a time, many film studios followed the pattern of popular literary magazines in accepting unsolicited story contributions. A torrent of books on the writing and selling of photoplays was patterned after similar volumes in more established fields. For example, A. Van Buren Powell's *The Photoplay Synopsis* (1919) was the latest in one series that already included *Writing the Short Story, Writing for Vaudeville, The Technique of the Mystery Story*, and others.[8]

Organizations like the Palmer Photoplay Corporation offered a "complete Course and Service in Photoplay Writing." For a fee of ninety dollars (less for cash), students received two textbooks (including the *Photoplay Plot Encyclopedia*, which discussed the thirty-six dramatic situations in terms of motion-picture style), three sample film scripts (including Lois Weber's For Husbands Only [1918]), a subscription to the *Photoplaywright*, the right to staff criticism of five submissions, and a series of booklets or "lectures" with titles like "Photoplay Elements of Situation Comedy" by Al Christie, or "The Necessity and Value of Theme in the Photoplay" by Jeanie MacPherson. Cecil B. DeMille, Thomas H. Ince, Lois Weber, and Rob Wagner served as Palmer's "advisory board."[9]

A rival operation, the Photoplaywrights' League of America, provided no written texts but offered to act as agent for its members in the sale of scripts. Criticism of manuscript submissions and legal and financial advice were also available. Sada Cowan and J. Grubb Alexander were among the "professional members" listed in its brochure.[10]

With the availability of good 35-mm motion-picture cameras on the open market, even the once-mysterious field of cinematography became accessible to ambitious amateurs. Ernest A. Dench advised "the ambitious young man or woman determined to break into the studios as a regular Motion Picture photographer" that many local opportunities already existed. He suggested establishing a service to film weddings, children, pets, and other domestic subjects, the production of advertising or industrial films, occasional work as a newsreel stringer, or even the establishment of one's own local newsreel. Creating an "amateur photoplay society . . . is no more expensive than is dabbling at ordinary photography on a moderate scale," Dench claimed. "Those with acting ability can figure in the cast, while the member possessing the most dramatic aptitude should be made the director. The talented weaver of stories would be the right man for scenario editor, provided he studied a book on photoplay writing and mastered the technique of photoplay construction. Last, but by no means least, you should do justice to the position of camera-man."[11]

Camera skills might be acquired at the New York Institute of Photography, which offered a classroom program as well as a correspondence course. It promoted its own 35-mm cine camera, the Institute Standard, especially for such semiprofessional work, and issued various texts through its Falk Publishing Company.[12]

These were the glamorous areas of the motion-picture industry, but the ten thousand local projectionists (1920 figures) were also fair game for unscrupulous educators. Sink-or-swim training seems to have been the conventional route here, something that was not the case in cinematography or editing, where an apprenticeship system developed. It was not uncommon for the ill-trained graduates of "projection schools" to find themselves alone in a booth with no idea of how to put on the evening's show.[13] Unfortunately, these were the men ultimately responsible for the quality of the show seen by the public, the weakest link in the chain apparently being the last.

New York and Hollywood

Southern California was clearly recognized as the major American production center by 1915, although the generic use of the term "Hollywood" to describe nearly all such activity had not yet developed. With studios scattered from Santa Monica to Edendale to Pasadena (and north to San Francisco and east to Phoenix), most commentators spoke of the area "in and about Los Angeles" as the "Mecca of the Motion Picture." By 1924, however, a Hollywood mythos was clearly emerging. Perley Poore Sheehan, a popular screenwriter, issued a bizarre tract called *Hollywood as a World Center*, which combined elements of small-town boosterism, industry braggadocio, and occult transcendentalism (known locally as "new thought"). For Sheehan, "The rise of Hollywood and its parent city, Los Angeles, has world-wide significance. It is a new and striking development in the history of civilization. . . . This flooding of population to the Southwest has its origins in the dim past. It is the culmination of ages of preparatory struggle, physical, mental and spiritual. In brief, we are witnessing the last great migration of the Aryan race." Going beyond traditional American disdain for the eastern cities, Sheehan saw the birth of Hollywood as the dawn of the Aquarian age and described a New Jerusalem that would reveal to all mankind the "Universal Subconscious."[14]

In the absence of any traditional moral, intellectual, or religious framework, such philosophizing was quite popular in Hollywood in the boom years of the immediate postwar era, especially among the circle around Nazimova, Valentino, and June Mathis. Before it faded from fashion, one could see its traces in such curious films as the Mathis-Valentino YOUNG RAJAH (1922) or Sheehan's original story THE WHISPERING CHORUS (1918) for Cecil B. DeMille. But its representation in specific films is far less important than the gauge it provides to help measure the emotional and intellectual distance between Hollywood and the traditional centers of American culture. The physical isolation of the place—five days by rail from the corporate home offices—very quickly inculcated a special "Hollywood" way of looking at life that generations of audiences would instantly recognize. European films tended to be produced in and around traditional centers of national culture—Paris, London, Vienna, Rome, Berlin—but this community of desert exiles made something very different of the American cinema. Of course, such films won the contempt of American critics for many years, but audiences worldwide (and some foreign critics, such as Louis Delluc) felt otherwise. Movies from Hollywood would become the first American cultural export to conquer the world.

Equating American film production in this period with Hollywood production is, however, somewhat misleading. That colony was a factory town, producing the motion-picture industry's major product, while executive operations, newsreel production, and even much of the animation industry remained in the East. Kevin Brownlow, in *Hollywood: The Pioneers*, gives a flavorful account of early West Coast units seeking and finding "sun, space, and somnolence." The fact that Los Angeles was renowned as "the nation's leading open-shop, nonunion city" also did not hurt, keeping wages to half what they might have been in the East.[15]

The concentration of feature production in Hollywood during the teens was widely noted at the time, especially because few could have predicted the rapidity of this migration. Although visiting companies had worked in Los Angeles since 1908, much of the outlying area was still largely a wilderness in 1915, lacking equipment houses, prop and costume shops, a steady supply of professional actors, or even basic sanitation and safety. Thomas H. Ince and a group from his studio were robbed "stage-coach style" by four masked gunmen on "the lonely road near Inceville" in March 1915. Three years later, Erich von Stroheim was still carrying a revolver under the seat whenever he and his fiancée drove the dangerous Cahuenga Pass to Universal City. In this light the stories told by Cecil B. DeMille, Allan Dwan, and others, regarding the need for sidearms to protect themselves from Patents Company thugs, might conceivably have a more mundane explanation.[16]

It was generally accepted that the West Coast studios were producing 125 reels of film per week in 1915, including everything from split-reel comedies to THE BIRTH OF A NATION. Knowledgeable estimates put this figure at between 62.5 and 75 percent of total American production.[17] Despite the fact that the bulk of domestic production had already moved to the West Coast, it was only in 1914–1915 that the makeshift facilities used by most of the producers were replaced by permanent installations comparable to the eastern studios, most notably the American Studio in Santa Barbara and Carl Laemmle's Universal City.

The comparatively large segment of production remaining in the East maintained its position throughout the early feature years, when the proximity of Broadway plays and players caused firms such as Goldwyn and Famous Players to increase the output of their New York and Fort Lee studios. This situation survived until the winter of 1918–1919, when problems with coal rationing forced nearly all the companies then operating in the East to consolidate operations in their West Coast facilities. Paramount-Artcraft closed in Fort Lee but kept operating at their Fifty-sixth Street studio in Manhattan; Universal closed all their eastern studios except their Coytesville, New Jersey, operation; Goldwyn, Metro, and Fox moved everyone to the West Coast; Vitagraph kept only a small operation in the East. Only World Film remained, because "their coal is not only all purchased, but delivered."[18]

This forcible relocation was strongly resisted by many filmmakers who found California unsuitable as a production center, but not until after the Armistice could anything be done about it. As soon as wartime restrictions were lifted, a boom in studio construction swept the New York area (for various reasons this renaissance bypassed Fort Lee, which soon disappeared as a production center). D. W. Griffith, who had filmed Hollywood's most stupendous films, THE BIRTH OF A NATION and INTOLERANCE, created a new studio for himself on the Flagler estate in Mamaroneck, just north of New York City. The East was where "the money and the brains" were, he said, as he proceeded to film WAY DOWN EAST (1920), ORPHANS OF THE STORM (1922), AMERICA (1924), and other costly features in Mamaroneck.[19]

William Randolph Hearst transformed Sulzer's Harlem River Park and Casino into the vast Cosmopolitan studio, a beer-hall-to-movie-lot conversion that also occurred at the smaller Mirror studio in Glendale, Queens. At Cosmopolitan, Marion Davies starred in such lavish epics as WHEN

KNIGHTHOOD WAS IN FLOWER (1922), LITTLE OLD NEW YORK (1923), and JANICE MEREDITH (1924), an underrated Revolutionary War spectacle.[20]

Vitagraph increased the pace of its New York operations, while Goldwyn and Metro reopened their eastern studios. Fox came back as well, opening a large new studio on West Fifty-fifth Street in Manhattan, where Pearl White and Allan Dwan worked from 1920. This facility continues in operation today as the Cameramart stages. The Talmadge sisters had their studio on East Forty-eighth Street, and various rental studios abounded, hosting such New York-based stars as Richard Barthelmess. By September 1920 the *Exhibitors Trade Review* headlined "Producers Say California Has Been Filmed Out—Are Looking for New Producing Centers." The paper reported that all the major companies were now making films in the New York area and that California's weather remained its sole compelling asset.[21]

That month the most important of the new eastern studios opened, the Famous Players–Lasky studio in Astoria. Over the next seven years, this studio would produce 127 silent features, serving as home base for those Paramount stars who preferred to work in the East, such as Gloria Swanson (nine films) or Bebe Daniels (fourteen films). Such recruits from the stage as W. C. Fields and Louise Brooks began their "Hollywood" careers in Astoria, while Rudolph Valentino and D. W. Griffith saw the studio as a means of escaping the factory conditions on the West Coast. Astoria was at its most active in 1926, when the 26 features produced there constituted 40 percent of the entire Paramount program.[22]

However, by 1922 Hollywood's share of American production stood at 84 percent, with 12 percent remaining in New York and 4 percent filming elsewhere. The East Coast had several large studios and ample rental space for the smallest companies. What it lacked was a significant group of middle-level producers, an area almost completely monopolized by Hollywood. New York boosterism reached a peak soon after, when *Barron's* predicted that "the motion picture business of the next decade will be mostly in sight of the tower of the Woolworth building"—a piece of advice that its readers would have done well to ignore. Such enthusiasm on the part of New York-based industry analysts reflected the positive feelings of those East Coast stars and executives whom they encountered while dining at the Colony or "21." It ignored the efforts of the larger and more powerful West Coast branches to centralize production under their own control, the increased costs of doing business in New York (Los Angeles was still relatively free of labor unions), and continuing problems with inclement weather. While the advantages of California sunlight were no longer crucial, problems with New York's rain and snow remained an issue, especially for a system that made heavy use of large standing sets. "Weather destroyed sets on the back lot time and again," wrote Jesse Lasky of the Astoria operation, which he temporarily closed in 1927. Other New York studios had already reduced operations, and by the close of the silent era, Hollywood was unchallenged as the center of American production.[23]

But what of that 4 percent produced outside either Hollywood or New York? With 748 features released in 1922, this suggests that some 30 feature pictures (and a proportionate number of shorts) were filmed elsewhere. Even allowing for a handful of imports, the number is still significant. The bulk of these films were made by small local producers without access to national distribution. Many remained unseen. Some were sold on a states rights basis and never played in a key theater or won the attention of an urban reviewer. For historians, these regional productions are the *terra incognita* of the American film industry. Local historical societies treasure vague records of production in Ithaca, Providence, Ogden, and Augusta, for example, but so little information survives that most historians simply omit this activity altogether.[24]

Writing pictures

No matter what the location of the studio, the tremendous quantity of film generated each week required vast amounts of original (or at least semi-original) story material. The ad hoc practices of the earliest days of filmmaking had long been abandoned by most producers, although even as late as 1915 some directors could not resist a lucky opportunity. Henry Otto, directing for Flying A in Santa Barbara, noticed several hundred blackbirds sitting on telephone wires. He filmed them, then concocted a script in which the birds caused "wire trouble."[25]

In general, though, it was well understood that regular release schedules demanded a dependable flow of production and that scenario departments were needed to process scripts and synopses. A few writers, such as Ince's C. Gardner Sullivan or Thanhouser's Philip Lonergan, had steady positions generating large amounts of story material to order, but in 1915 the freelance scenario market was still quite significant. Producers solicited manuscripts in much the same fashion as literary magazines. The *New York Dramatic Mirror* carried the "For Photoplay Authors, Real and Near" column, edited by William Lord Wright. Readers of the 3 February 1915 issue were told that the Universal editorial department was giving assurances that it would read all manuscripts, so long as they were typed, carried a synopsis, and came with a stamped, self-addressed envelope. Requests for submissions were often quite specific:

World Film Corporation, Fort Lee, New Jersey, is in the market for five-reel subjects running to not less than two hundred scenes. Stories must have original plots—not necessarily with what is known as "punch," but depicting a young innocent girl in country life. No costume plays considered, nor those dealing with crime or crooks.

49

American stories preferable (William Lord Wright, "For Photoplay
Authors, Real and Near," *New York Dramatic Mirror*, 3 February
1915, p. 30).

The *Photoplay Author* was a monthly publication brimming with articles
on art and technique, profiles of photoplaywrights, and a tipsheet called
"The Photo Play Market." In one issue, the Holland Film Manufacturing
Company of Dorchester, Massachusetts, put out a call for one- and two-reel
comedies and comedy-dramas, the New York Motion Picture Company
advised authors to send their material directly to scenario editor Richard V.
Spencer, and Edison announced a contest for the most suitable conclusion to
a prospective one-reeler.[26]

Contests and similar schemes were constantly floated, in an effort to
broaden the range of available materials, but without much success. One
such contest promoted by Edison was directed at colleges across the country.
Out of 337 scenarios submitted, only 8 were judged of produceable quality
(the winner was "Jack Kennard, Coward," submitted by Harvard's William
Marston). The conclusion of the Edison editors was that a dependence on
amateur scenario writers was doomed to failure.[27]

The small amount paid for original scenarios was hardly conducive to
high-quality submissions. The *Photoplay Author* complained that writers
accepting three dollars for a two-reel script were depressing the market: "At
the present scale $35 is fair, $50 is better and $100 per reel good money. Most
of the purchases are made at $50 or less per reel."[28]

As late as 1923, Douglas Brown reported to the Society of Motion Picture
Engineers that "the completed script of a feature picture costs the producer
less than two thousand dollars." This sum did not, however, include the cost
of any story rights involved, and beginning in 1919–1920 such costs began to
soar for any property considered a sure success (essentially Broadway hits
that already seemed to work in scenario form). "Apparently a season's run in
New York automatically makes a play worth about $100,000 to the film
producers," said the *New York Times* in 1920, with only slight exaggeration.
Even before talkies, the existence of a usable Broadway playscript made a
property far more interesting to film producers. For example, F. Scott
Fitzgerald's *The Great Gatsby* reached the screen in 1926 via a 1925 stage
version by Owen Davis, not directly from the original novel.[29]

Prominent screenwriter Frances Marion reported in 1924 that the average
price for a successful play was $20,000. She offered the following list of high-
priced properties:[30]

TURN TO THE RIGHT	$225,000
WAY DOWN EAST	175,000
A TAILOR-MADE MAN	105,000
THE FIRST YEAR	100,000

TIGER ROSE	100,000
DADDIES	100,000
THE GOLD DIGGERS	100,000
MERTON OF THE MOVIES	100,000
THE VIRGINIAN	90,000
DOROTHY VERNON OF HADDON HALL	85,000

This move toward the acquisition of pretested material clearly related to the collapse of the free-lance market. Submissions had grown so heavy that no quality control could be maintained. "When manuscripts come in they are handed over to the reading department," wrote an anonymous scenario editor in the *Bookman* in 1919. "This is a room where half a dozen women at an average salary of ten dollars a week, without the competence of a stenographer or salesgirl, sit all day making first choice of the material the editor is to see." According to this source, the women all had little scenarios of their own to promote, "consciously or unconsciously" stolen, which they schemed to place with their bosses, even to the extent of suppressing incoming material.[31]

Lawsuits by disgruntled authors were another problem, although one 1914 decision by a Los Angeles court dismissed charges of scenario-stealing against Hampton Del Ruth. "I have been given to understand that scenarios cannot be copyrighted," said the judge, incorrectly. "After looking into the question of scenarios I have decided they are of no value, and therefore dismiss the case."[32]

The virtual elimination of the free-lance market was among the most significant production changes of the immediate postwar era. Writing credits went to such contract employees as Jane Murfin, Lenore Coffee, Charles Kenyon, Jeanie MacPherson, Waldemar Young, and Jules Furthman, skilled wordsmiths with backgrounds as reporters or short-fiction writers. The flood of Broadway playwrights that would engulf Hollywood in the talkie years was hardly in evidence before 1927, when dialogue skills were not a requirement.

The producer system

Janet Staiger describes the central producer system as "the order of the day" by 1914 and invokes Thomas H. Ince's operation for the New York Motion Picture Company as the traditional example. Script material was recast into continuity form, which allowed careful preplanning of all production activities. Actors needed to appear only when required; props and costumes could be scheduled on a dependable basis, and the logistics of complicated location trips (or studio shoots, for that matter) might be clearly predetermined. By closely monitoring the scripting and editing process, a central producer like Ince—or Mack Sennett—could guarantee a uniform standard of quality without having to attend personally to the filming of each scene.[33]

While this pioneering demonstration of organizational efficiency does mark Sennett and Ince as important innovators, their systems were primitive in comparison to those employed later in the silent period by more mature studios such as Paramount or MGM. In fact, the collapse of Ince's entire operation on the death of its central producer suggests that his studio was more an extended workshop than a true factory. Systems that could outlast their innovators reflected a higher level of organization and took several more years to develop.

In 1925 the new Metro-Goldwyn-Mayer studio produced a thirty-minute promotional film to demonstrate the power and scale of their factory operations. In true industrial-film fashion, they lay out the shape of their physical plant, boast of the capacity of their electrical powerhouse, and awe us with a staggering array of statistics. What is most interesting, however, is the way the film organizes and presents the studio workers. Dozens of cinematographers line up on a studio lawn, cranking away on Mitchells and Bell & Howells. They are matched by an equally formidable array of writers, directors, scenic artists, carpenters, electrical workers, cutters, even shippers packing MGM prints off to distant exchanges. Seen in control of this army of artists and technicians are three men, each busy behind a desk—Louis B. Mayer, Irving Thalberg, and Harry Rapf. Finally, we see a telegraph key that allows them to stay in constant touch with New York, where an unseen Marcus Loew and Nicholas Schenck call the ultimate shots.[34]

This little film is especially revealing because it consciously deemphasizes the glamour of the studio's employees and underscores the tight, pyramidal control exercised by the top executives. MGM's stars are reduced to a few charming close-ups. MGM's directors appear in a vast and nearly anonymous group. A title card announces, "Browning, Seastrom, Vidor, Niblo, von Stroheim, von Sternberg, . . ." but the names and faces do not really connect. All that matters is *studio and system*: clearly that is the message being communicated to the stockholders or theater owners who made up the film's original audience. To some later historians, this industrial self-consciousness must seem a simple admission of the way the business actually worked, the "real tinsel" underneath the usual phony tinsel.[35]

Production of fodder for the nation's movie screens—many hundreds of pictures annually—was clearly generated by just such a system. Yet even Staiger suggests that the leading works of the age, the product of the most powerful stars and filmmakers, remained under individual control to a great degree.[36] The most memorable work of many of the key filmmakers discussed in chapter 8, Griffith, Weber, von Stroheim, Cruze, Lubitsch, DeMille, Neilan, and Ingram in particular, was created via a simpler director-unit system, where projects were developed from script level through editing by individual creative directors and their personal staffs. In the final analysis, these were the films that created the models for new styles or genres that were then mass-produced (often more lucratively) by the factory studios. While the central-producer system certainly generated the bulk of American production in this period, those films that really mattered, to audiences of the time as well as to posterity, were often the dogged creations of an antiquated workshop system that somehow managed to survive well into the 1920s.

Just how efficient could this newer central-producer system be? One 1917 company was able to keep the costs of their five-reel features to three or four thousand dollars "by shooting players from one set to another with the speed of a Ford car assembly," but Taylorized efficiency was seldom as dramatic as this. A financial paper like *Barron's* looked for predictability as well as profitability, and here a studio like Famous Players–Lasky was at its best. "Their financial comptroller was formerly a cashier of the National Bank of Commerce. He has several young New York University statisticians associated with him," that paper reported approvingly. Of the last 164 films released by the company, only nine had failed to pay their expenses. Four of these were Arbuckle films, caught up in the scandal; one was an "English production"; and two others were only marginal failures.[37]

Richard W. Saunders, the comptroller referred to above, outlined for the *New York Times* many of the recognized industrial practices that were, by 1926, beginning to attract large numbers of investors. These practices ranged from the traditional habit of forcing theater owners to pay in advance to a relatively new method of writing off negative costs in a standardized, monthly fashion.[38]

When Saunders boasted to *Forbes* that Famous Players–Lasky had finally eliminated the seasonal peaks and slumps of production, he was making one of the manager's proudest boasts. These fits and starts had long been an embarrassment to those in the industry who had to deal with Wall Street, especially during extreme slumps, like that of the winter of 1923–1924. Then, Famous Players–Lasky stock dropped 12⅜ points when the management announced a total suspension of production, laying off nine hundred studio workers and putting contract players on half salary. Other studios cut back as well. By the end of the silent era, such economic swings no longer seemed an issue (fig. 1)).[39]

How much to make a picture?

There was great interest, both inside and outside the trade, in establishing some sort of "average cost" for a standard program feature. In July 1917 the *Motion Picture Classic* published a "conservative average" budget based on information from three different production companies. The *New York Dramatic Mirror*, a trade paper, offered its estimate for a similar production that same month (table 1).

In retrospect, the budget proposed by the *Dramatic Mirror* seems to represent less an average price than a rock-bottom one. In any case, generalizations about average picture costs in this period are of little practical use

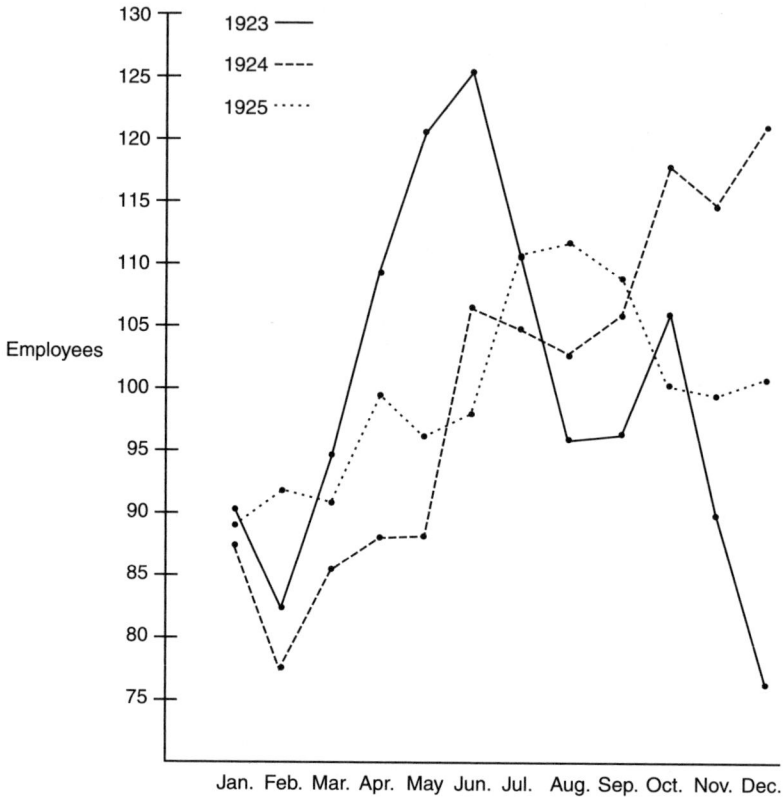

Figure 1 Studio Employment Fluctuation, 1923–1925
The graph shows the average number of workers employed by sixteen "identical" companies. Data from *Monthly Labor Review*, Feb. 1927, pp. 66–69.

because budgets rose so rapidly during the first dozen years of features, while even within a single studio or genre, costs could vary widely on different productions. As Samuel Goldwyn, who moved from Famous Players–Lasky to First National and then to United Artists during these years, told the *New York Times* in 1926, "In the old days the average negative cost of Famous Players was about $15,000. The distributors gave us an advance of $25,000. Today the average negative cost of Paramount productions is $300,000. The average negative cost of United Artists productions is from $750,000 to $800,000. The other two big companies are confronted with an average cost of between $240,000 and $260,000."[40]

The average cost of Famous Players–Lasky releases had increased twenty-fold over thirteen years, but knowing a studio's "average" production cost may not, in fact, be very revealing. In 1921, for example, Universal

Table 1 "Average Cost" Estimates, 1917

	Motion Picture Classic		New York Dramatic Mirror	
Corporate salaries	$ 5,000		$ —	
General manager	3,000		—	
Director	2,500		3,000	
Assistant directors	1,300	(two)	300	(one only)
Cameramen	1,200	(three)	300	(one only)
Assistant cameramen	600	(three)	100	(one only)
Stage carpenters	250	(three)	—	
Other employees	1,800	(twenty)	—	
Overhead expenses	900		—	
Star	12,000	(two)	6,000	(one only)
Near stars	5,000	(three)	1,200	(one leading man)
Prominent characters	2,500	(three)	1,300	("other principals")
Other salaried players	3,000	(40)	—	
Supers, etc.	1,100		300	
Transportation & location exp.	1,200		500	(transportation)
			200	(location rental)
Scenario handling	—		1,000	
Studio settings	—		1,000	
Negative stock	—		1,000	
Costumes	—		1,000	
Incidentals	—		500	
TOTAL COST	$41,350		$17,700	

Source: *Motion Picture Classic*, July 1917, p. 19; *New York Dramatic Mirror*, 7 July 1917, p. 9.

spent $34,211.79 on THE WAY BACK, a five-reel program feature. The cost of FOOLISH WIVES, an unusual "special jewel feature," made that same year, was thirty times this amount (see tables 2 and 3).

Despite the tremendous differences in scale between the production of THE WAY BACK and FOOLISH WIVES, it is clear that staff salaries were a significant part of the budget of both pictures. In 1924 *Barron's* offered the following statistics to explain where the production dollar went, figures that were generally accepted throughout the industry:[41]

Actors' salaries	25%
Director, cameraman, and assistants	10
Scenario and stories	10
Sets (manufacturing)	19
Studio overhead (including cutting, titling, etc.)	20
Costumes, gowns, etc.	3
Locations (and transportation)	8
Raw film	5

Table 2

UNIVERSAL FILM MANUFACTURING CO.			
Pacific Coast Studios			
STATEMENT OF PRODUCTION COSTS			
For Week Ending 2–1–22.			

DIRECTOR: Paton   PICTURE NO: 3723 REELS: 5

TITLE: "THE WAY BACK"   DATE STARTED: 12–23–21

FEATURING: Frank Mayo   DATE FINISHED: 1–16–22

CHARGES:	PREVIOUSLY REPORTED	THIS WEEK	TOTAL TO DATE
Stock Talent Salaries	3205.00		3205.00
Pict. Talent Salaries	1979.20		1979.20
Extra Talent Salaries	895.25		895.25
Directors Producing "	1333.30		1333.30
"Writ'g & Edit'g"	1666.70	400.00	2066.70
"Staff "	1298.75	120.45	1419.20
Continuity Writers' "	525.00		525.00
Editors' & Cutters' "	267.45	102.85	370.30
Negative Raw Stock	1450.89	118.65	1569.54
"Laboratory Chgs.	322.13	31.73	353.86
Positive Raw Stock	992.25	38.43	1030.68
"Laboratory Chgs.	321.40	14.88	336.28
Wardrobe Pur. & Mfg.	98.20		98.20
"Hire & Expense	58.54		58.54
Rent Studio Ward. Equip.	252.41		252.41
Prop Pur. & Mfg.	44.92	3.75	48.67
"Hire & Exp.—Misc.	653.47	13.64	667.11
" " & " Horses			
" " & " Special	40.00		40.00
Rent Studio & Prop. Equip.	606.90	17.09	623.99
Scenery	4744.24	256.12	5000.36
Auto Transportation	585.22		585.22
Traveling & Maintenance	330.70	2.00	332.70
Location Fees & Expense	25.00		25.00
Scenarios	2500.00	1000.00	3500.00
Light, Labor & Current	2153.31	226.90	2380.21
Rent Studio Elec. Equip.	1056.60	195.00	1251.60
Ranch Salaries & Exp.	1.00		1.00
Directors' Bonus			
Arsenal Salaries & Exp.	45.40		45.40
Misc. Unclassified Exp.	179.02		179.02
New York Title Charges			
Overhead Charges	4000.00		4000.00
Still Prints & Negatives	38.05		38.05
TOTALS, –	31670.30	2541.49	34211.79

Source: Author's collection.

Table 3

Universal Film Manufacturing Co.

Pacific Coast Studios

DAILY MEMORANDUM PICTURE COSTS

DIRECTOR <u>Von Stroheim</u> PICTURE NO. <u>3322</u> EPISODE NO. ____ DATE <u>July 7, 1921</u>

	Estimate	Amount Today	Total Amount to Date	Amount UNDER Estimate	Amount OVER Estimate
Overhead	$	$	$ 57,761.74	$	$
Stock Talent					
Picture Talent					
Extra Talent, Story and Continuity			257,283.20		
Director and Staff		167.00	101,009.10		
Film Editing			2,299.60		
Negative			19,287.85		
Sample Print			10,066.66		
Wardrobe			20,258.79		
Props (Arsenal, Drops, Props)			46,226.62		
Scenery, Sets, Etc.		4.00	351,913.53		
Transportation (Automobile)			33,178.88		
Traveling			10,469.00		
Maintenance (Lunches and Hotels)			41,209.54		
Location Fees and Expenses			1,848.11		
Lighting and Labor			77,010.23		
Ranch and Zoo			9,347.97		
Special Automobiles			814.90		
Miscellaneous Supplies		6.00	13,305.08		
TOTAL	$	$177.00	$1,053,290.80	$	$
Net Amount Under or Over Estimate _____					$

Source: Moving Picture Weekly, 30 July 1921, p. 28.

This negative cost factored into the total profit picture as follows:

Negative cost	40%
Distribution (U.S. and foreign)	30
Cost of positive prints	10
Administration and taxes	5
Profit	5

With salaries so large a part of production costs, much attention was devoted to limiting, or at least controlling, their growth.[42] A major reason for the introduction of the continuity script was to better manage personnel resources, but competition for top talent continued to force these figures higher and higher.

Photoplay reported in 1916 that salaries of $1,000 per week had recently become common, while the highest figure for a single picture had reached $40,000 (Billie Burke's fee for PEGGY). Leaving aside the well-known Chaplin and Pickford figures, they offered the following sampling of weekly star salaries:[43]

William Collier	$2,500	Keystone
Raymond Hitchcock	2,500	Keystone
Sam Bernard	2,500	Keystone
Eddie Foy	2,000	Keystone
Weber and Fields	3,000	Keystone
DeWolf Hopper	125,000/year	Keystone
	($60,000 guarantee)	
Henry B. Walthall	500	Essanay
Blanche Sweet	750	Lasky
Marguerite Clarke	1,250	Lasky
Fannie Ward	1,200	Lasky (one picture only)
Valeska Suratt	5,000	Fox
Victor Moore	500	Lasky
Frank Keenan	1,000	Ince (one picture)
William S. Hart	300	Ince
Francis X. Bushman	750 (plus a percentage of the profits)	—
Beverly Bayne	350	—

These figures reflect a relatively brief period when Broadway headliners were able to command salaries five times those of reliable film favorites such as William S. Hart. More typical of the era were weekly salary statistics offered by theater owner William Brandt following the announcement of the Famous Players–Lasky shutdown in 1923. Brandt's concern was that the exhibitors would bear the brunt of carrying these stars at half-salary while they were between pictures.[44]

Norma Talmadge	$10,000	Conway Tearle	$2,750
Dorothy Dalton	7,500	Lewis Stone	2,500
Gloria Swanson	6,500	Milton Sills	2,500
Larry Semon	5,000	James Kirkwood	2,500
Constance Talmadge	5,000	Wallace Beery	2,500
Pauline Frederick	5,000	House Peters	2,500
Lillian Gish	5,000	Elaine Hammerstein	2,500
Tom Mix	4,000	Richard Barthelmess	2,500
Betty Compson	3,500	Betty Blythe	2,500
Barbara La Marr	3,500	Florence Vidor	2,000
May McAvoy	3,000	Elliott Dexter	2,000
Mabel Normand	3,000	Viola Dana	2,000
Priscilla Dean	3,000	Lon Chaney	1,750

Brandt's figures exclude United Artists' stars, and those, like William S. Hart and Harold Lloyd, whose incomes were tied to significant participation deals. By 1926 total earning figures to date for those stars had reached truly fabulous heights:

Harold Lloyd	$1.5 million per year
Charles Chaplin	1.25 million
Douglas Fairbanks	1 million
Mary Pickford	1 million
Gloria Swanson	Refused Famous Players–Lasky's offer of $1 million to sign with United Artists

The highest-paid star then on straight salary was Tom Mix, earning $15,000 per week at Fox.[45]

Scenic art

After salaries, the highest fixed costs were those related to set construction. Wilfred Buckland, Ben Carré, and Anton Grot were already established as "art directors" by 1915, but most settings were still designed and constructed by carpenters. Cameraman Arthur Miller remembered Grot as "the first art director I ever worked with who hadn't come up from the ranks of the construction department." Grot created charcoal illustrations of the sets that displayed the scale and perspective of various motion-picture lenses. This technique enabled him to build only those segments of the set that would actually be used and resulted in substantial savings in construction costs. (He taught this skill to William Cameron Menzies.) Grot had received his training at the Akademie Sztuki in Cracow, Poland; Ben Carré came from the Paris Opera; and Wilfred Buckland was long associated with David Belasco.[46]

In his very thorough 1918 study *How Motion Pictures Are Made*, Homer Croy was still giving all of the credit for set design and construction to gangs of carpenters:

> With the scene locations determined upon, a list of the interior sets is handed the chief carpenter, who promptly starts building the necessary woodwork. The list tells him in what order they will be wanted, with the date on which the first one will be needed impressed on his mind. He is held responsible for the finishing of the scene by the time specified. . . . From a bare wooden platform the carpenters, under the direction of their chief, may start to work (Homer Croy, *How Motion Pictures Are Made* [New York: Harper and Brothers, 1918], p. 110).

It should be remembered that, in this fashion, the master carpenter Huck Wortman constructed Griffith's Babylon in INTOLERANCE, albeit under the supervision of theatrical designer Walter Hall. These two traditions—that of the graphic artist or scene painter on the one hand, and the practical carpenter on the other—remained dominant in American studios during the early feature period. But they shared an identical goal, one well articulated by Austin Lescarboura in *Behind the Motion Picture Screen:*

> Realism is one of the main stocks in trade of the screen production. Compared with the speaking stage, with its highly artificial scenery which lacks correct perspective and general impressiveness, the motion picture makes use of backgrounds both natural and artificial which have depth as well as height and breadth. . . . Realism has made the success of present photoplays; and the screen artisans have made film realism what it is (Austin Lescarboura, *Behind the Motion Picture Screen* [New York; Munn, 1922], p. 107).

Lescarboura wrote just as von Stroheim's FOOLISH WIVES appeared, with its full-scale reproduction of Monte Carlo's Casino, Hôtel de France, and Café de Paris, marking the apex of "realistic" set construction. Von Stroheim's *mise-en-scène* required such verisimilitude, but the vast majority of American films merely tried to stay one step ahead of the faultfinders. Scenic and technical accuracy became a fetish, and letters to the editors of various fan magazines prodded sloppy production teams.

But against this current, a feeble call for stylization defended that "highly artificial scenery which lacks correct perspective." As early as 1916 Edgar M. Kellar designed and produced THE YELLOW GIRL, a self-described "decorative playlet" in the style of Aubrey Beardsley. One critic casually characterized it as "Futurist," but Kellar insisted, "I see no reason why we can't have a romantic rather than a practical background." More significant yet were Maurice Tourneur's THE BLUE BIRD (1918) and PRUNELLA (1918), both designed by Ben Carré. Invoking Gordon Craig, Max Reinhardt, Konstantin Stanislavsky, and Harley Granville-Barker, Tourneur declared, "The time has come where we can no longer merely *photograph* moving and inanimate objects and call it art. . . . We must present the effect such a scene has upon the artist-director's mind, so that an audience will catch the mental reaction."[47]

Public rejection of these films was so severe that few remembered them in 1921, when THE CABINET OF DR. CALIGARI first reached the Capitol Theatre. Audiences identified the stylization in this film as "the world seen through a madman's eyes" and promptly forgot the stylistic lesson Tourneur had offered them three years earlier. Now spatial and temporal distortion became signals for lunacy and delirium (note the drug addict's visions in HUMAN WRECKAGE, 1923).[48] But even these hallucinatory exceptions were few, and three-dimensional realism ruled unchallenged.

This playground of graphic artists and carpenters lasted until around 1919, when producers began to turn to professional architects to create their settings. Robert M. Haas, who began designing for Famous Players–Lasky in New York in 1919, came to films after eight years as a practicing architect. His new position won two approving articles in the *American Architect*, which announced the fact that film design was now seen as "structural," not merely decorative, as in stage work. Haas was praised for the solidity of a town he had constructed in Elmhurst, New York, for THE COPPERHEAD (1920), where the details were aged to show the passage of time from 1846 to 1904. A rare full-card credit for the art direction on this film reads, "Robert M. Haas, Architecture; Charles O. Seesel, Decorations." His use of a ceiling "built to show" for ON WITH THE DANCE (1920) was also cited as an example of a new kind of structural realism unlike anything previously seen on the screen. Of course, this new approach to design only underscored the prevailing stylistic mode. "The men who design the 'sets' are constantly striving for the better effect of actuality," observed the *American Architect*.[49]

What Haas added to the Famous Players–Lasky art department was not just a new sense of creativity but a way of organizing the work flow that recalled the offices of top architectural firms rather than the workshops of fashionable graphic designers. In the years that followed, teams of draftsmen, sketch artists, and model-makers would set a standard for studio efficiency at Paramount, MGM, and the other great Hollywood studios.

Behind the camera

Unlike designers, cinematographers were not easily organized into hierarchical departments and in this period often contracted their services much as writers did. Some of the best were under contract to various studios on either a per-week or per-picture basis (for example, Joseph Ruttenberg with Fox from about 1915 to 1926). Some had long-term relationships, not always contractual, with the units of individual directors or stars (most notably G. W. Bitzer with D. W. Griffith from 1908 to 1928). But most drifted in and out of various jobs, hoping, especially before unionization began to offer a modicum of job security, for a decent run of steady employment.[50] Hal Mohr recalled that free-lance cameramen "used to haunt the studios" in the early 1920s, and groups of job-seekers would meet in the outer offices of production managers with work to offer. Often, the men would informally agree to demand the same salary, say $150 per week, in an effort to prevent a low bidder from depressing the wage scale. Unfortunately, someone always seemed to break the agreement, one reason for the considerable ill will and cliquishness that occasionally afflicted this particular craft.[51]

The diaries of Hal Sintzenich, a cameraman who struggled for work in the eastern studios during many production lulls, are filled with painful stories of missed paychecks and lost job opportunities. Erik Barnouw has analyzed the working records contained in these diaries:

> Most of these assignments are brief. They involve unlimited hours and intermittent pay. Two or more cameramen are often "cranking" side by side, but sometimes they work simultaneously on different scenes. A cameraman may supervise laboratory work, or edit, or even act; in one film Snitch is handed a robe and becomes a judge. His earnings rise to $175 a week but often fall much lower ("The Sintzenich Diaries," *Quarterly Journal of the Library of Congress* [Summer/Fall 1980], p. 310).

The American Society of Cinematographers (ASC), a professional organization designed to exchange useful information and promote the qualifications of its members, was chartered in Hollywood in 1919 (although earlier component organizations date from 1913). Most top cameramen quickly joined and as a group resisted the unionization they saw developing in the eastern studios. Dan Clark, ASC president in 1926, explained this anti-union position in terms of their perceived status as artists, not artisans, as well as a resistance to the fixed-wage scales they saw as detrimental to their own members. Or, as Hal Mohr remembered, "I made a pretty good reputation for myself by 1928 and I was pretty much in demand and considered a pretty fine cameraman, getting a high salary. I was getting around $350 a week then. So I figured, what the hell do I want with a union organization?" But Mohr did join, serving during a long career as president not only of the ASC but of the union local as well.[52]

Largely because of the existence of the ASC and its house organ, the *American Cinematographer*, artistic and technical problems of cameramen were given relatively sophisticated discussion in a public forum, something that was not often the case for other film workers. During this period, these problems included the use of the close-up, "soft" versus "sharp" photography, the influence of German films and filmmakers, and the use of color.

While not necessarily a photographic issue, the close-up was a matter of some controversy throughout this period and of special concern to the cameramen because one of their prime responsibilities was the lighting of glamorous star portraits. Some historians argue that nickelodeon audiences resisted the introduction of the close-up, and patrons of early features in 1915 had their doubts as well. In reviewing DAVID HARUM (1915), the *New York Dramatic Mirror* commented on one sequence of Harum at dinner, which showed only his hands and the food he was eating. This "caused a spectator behind us to say at once that it was 'a poor picture because you cannot see his face.' "[53]

Audiences soon grew sufficiently sophisticated to accept the existence of offscreen space, but various stylistic complaints continued. Extreme close-ups were so rare as to be beyond general notice. The *American Cinematographer* defined the two forms of the close-up in 1923 as the waist-to-head two-shot and the chest-to-head single figure. Full-face was clearly too rare to consider, despite its dramatic use in INTOLERANCE and other Griffith films. Welford Beaton, an otherwise perspicacious critic, waged a lengthy war against the close-up. In a review entitled "Submerging the Production Under Senseless Close-Ups," he attacked Alexander Korda's THE YELLOW LILY (1928) as a "close-up orgy" and contended, "In this picture we have elaborate sets which flit across the screen to give place to an endless parade of utterly senseless close-ups. Ordinary business sense would dictate that the sets should be shown for a longer time to justify their cost." As for von Stroheim's THE WEDDING MARCH, Beaton told readers, "I would estimate that there are between seven and eight hundred close-ups in the entire picture, proving that von Stroheim treated Griffith's discovery as wildly as he did Pat's bankroll." (The "Pat" in Beaton's review is Pat Powers, producer of THE WEDDING MARCH.) Similarly, Frank Tuttle, director of a self-described "artistic" film production unit called the Film Guild, wrote in 1922, "The close-up mania is like the drug habit. It grows upon the afflicted company at a constantly accelerating pace until the whole studio is mortally ill of it."[54]

A wide array of diffusion effects suddenly became popular after 1919, when Henrik Sartov and G. W. Bitzer filmed close-ups of Lillian Gish that recalled Photo-Secessionist portraiture. The style soon spread even to war films. "In THE FOUR HORSEMEN I made all the exteriors I could on dull days in order to use an open lens and get a softer image," explained director Rex Ingram in 1921. "I wanted to get away from the hard, crisp effect of the photograph and get something of the mellow mezzotint of the painting;

to get the fidelity of photography, but the softness of the old master; to picture not only the dramatic action, but to give it some of the merit of art."[55]

Some years later, cameraman Henry Sharp, then in New York filming THE CROWD (1928), found it useful to study Rembrandt's work in the Metropolitan Museum of Art. "Rembrandt's great strength was his use of one positive light scale. One central 'light perspective' was always used, rather than a multiplicity of attempted effects, and the results were contrasts in light and shade," he noted. The invocation of Rembrandt was used to cover a variety of pictorial effects, from Alvin Wyckoff's "smash of light from one side or the other" in DeMille's THE WARRENS OF VIRGINIA (1915) to Lee Garmes's celebrated "north light" effect. "Ever since I began, Rembrandt has been my favorite artist," Garmes told interviewer Charles Higham. "I've always used his technique of north light—of having my main source of light on a set always come from the north. . . . And of course I've always followed Rembrandt in my fondness for low key."[56]

By the close of the silent period, many of the cameramen most involved in the use of incandescent Mazda lighting, notably Lee Garmes and George Barnes, had eliminated much of the diffusion from their work, but Ernest Palmer, Karl Struss, and Oliver Marsh still continued to make heavy use of the more pictorial style.[57]

The most dramatic outside influence in silent Hollywood was certainly the importation, after 1925, of an entire generation of German filmmakers. Karl Struss, one of the American cameramen on F. W. Murnau's SUNRISE (1927), a film with a large number of Germans on the design team, saw the picture as "the fore-runner of a new type of picture-play in which thought is expressed pictorially instead of by titles."[58] Such cameramen as Gilbert Warrenton (THE CAT AND THE CANARY, 1927), Ernest Palmer (THE FOUR DEVILS, 1928), and Hal Mohr (THE LAST WARNING, 1929) were especially involved in this style which featured complicated moving camera effects, frequent use of trick shots and superimposition, and stylized, low-key lighting schemes. But the death of the most important German technicians (notably Murnau and Leni), photographic problems attendant on the introduction of sound, and a general misuse of the techniques involved muted the impact of this movement after 1929. Looking back at the period, Hal Mohr, who photographed some exceptionally "Germanic" late silent films for Michael Curtiz, Paul Fejos, and Paul Leni, remembered it simply as "the era of the goofy ideas in film":

> I'll never forget one thing we did on BROADWAY [1929; an early talkie that proved to be one of the last great examples of the style]. We had this camera swinging around during one of the musical numbers, just rotating, swinging around the camera, photographing everyone on those sets all at one time like a big merry-go-round type of thing.

If you make them dizzy enough they'll think it's a great scene, you know (quoted in Richard Koszarski, "Moving Pictures," *Film Comment*, September-October 1974, p. 48).

Film color

Until the introduction of Eastman Color multilayer negative and printing stock in 1949, color in film was largely a matter of craft. During the 1915–1928 period, color systems might be natural or artificial, with the latter by far the most commonly employed. Artificial-color systems date from the birth of cinema and involve a coloring of all or part of the image of each release print. Processes available were tinting, toning, hand-coloring, stenciling, and related variants, all of which were well established before the introduction of feature pictures.[59]

Tinting was defined by the Society of Motion Picture Engineers as "immersing the film in a solution of dye which colors the gelatine, causing the whole picture to have a uniform veil of color on the screen." Far from declining in popularity after the nickelodeon years, by 1920, according to the society's estimate, tinting was used for 80 to 90 percent of all films. Eastman Kodak began supplying pre-tinted release stock by 1921, eliminating the need for individual treatment of each release print. In toning, "a colored image [is] embedded in a layer of colorless gelatine, so that while the highlights are clear, the shadows are colored." This effect was achieved not by dying the prints but by causing a chemical change in the composition of the metallic salts that had created the black-and-white image, converting the original silver deposit into silver ferrocyanide, for example, to create a blue-and-white image. Laboratory costs were higher for toning than for tinting, and of course, no one could produce a release stock that was already toned.[60]

Combined tinting and toning allowed for complex color effects, such as "sunset and moonlight effects over water," but these were still more difficult and costly. King Vidor used a wide range of tinting and toning effects in THE SKY PILOT (1921), not only for decorative effect but as a significant element of the film's *mise-en-scène*:

> What I believe I have actually done is to "score" this photoplay for color. I have used a soft violet tint for scenes in which the earlier hours of the morning—the phantom dawn, as the orientals call the period just before sunrise—are represented. For the period after sunrise, I have used a pale yellow tint; for noon, a faint amber; for night, a blue green tone on all objects casting shadows, high lighted with a warm amber.
>
> I have tinted the moonlight scenes with carefully chosen deep blue tone, tinting the moon a faint, almost ethereal, amber, while I have used the conventional amber for interior night scenes. A delicate tint

of green is used in all scenes of virgin nature where the day is sup-posed to be warm, while in the Canadian northwest snow scenes I have used a steel blue tint. To induce certain moods, I have scientific-ally played upon the varying degrees of happiness and sorrow with varying shades of pink and green. The heights of joy are enhanced with a delicate pink glow, while the depths of grief call for a ghastly gray green tone ("Brought into Focus," *New York Times*, 27 February 1921).

Another film of the period whose use of color is well documented is von Stroheim's THE DEVIL'S PASS KEY (1920), in which the various quick cuts of a dance sequence flash green, violet, red, rose, and amber. In *The Anatomy of Motion Picture Art* (1928) Eric Elliott credited this film with "introducing colour as a psychological influence on the film scene."[61]

Highly popular in earlier years, hand-coloring of individual frames was, after the arrival of feature films, usually limited to brief sequences in a few selected prints. Gustav Brock was one of the last to offer this specialty, advertising regularly in the annual *Film Daily Yearbook*. Brock labored over FOOLISH WIVES, THE WHITE SISTER (1923), THE NAVIGATOR (1924), and a number of Marion Davies pictures, including LITTLE OLD NEW YORK (1923). He did two sequences for this film: one in which Davies, disguised as a boy, overhears a risqué story and blushes; the other, a scene of the stars and stripes being raised on Robert Fulton's *Clermont*. The eight seconds of film required thirty hours of labor. Brock never colored more than a few prints of any title, so only the prime first-run houses were likely to screen his work.[62]

The stencil coloring system introduced by Pathé Frères had mechanized this hand-coloring process to a certain degree, using a mimeograph-like system to mass-produce release prints from an original master. Although continuing in France, stencil coloring was rarely seen here after Pathé stopped American production in 1914. Its place was taken by the Handschiegl process, developed by Max Handschiegl, an engraver who had perfected a means of dye-transfer coloring of release prints, otherwise known as imbibition. Using his knowledge of printing inks and engraving technology, Handschiegl prepared as many as three printing matrices to achieve a desired color effect. Beginning in 1917, he worked on such films as JOAN THE WOMAN (1917), GREED, THE PHANTOM OF THE OPERA, SALLY (1925), and THE BIG PARADE.[63]

Natural color films, "those photographed so that the colors are selected entirely by optical and mechanical means and reproduced again in a like manner," have a history almost as long as artificially colored films. In the silent-feature era, all those systems which achieved any commercial success initially separated each image into a pair of "color records" (*i.e.*, mono-chrome images, each recording the presence of a specific primary color), one frame generally carrying the blue-green record, another the red-orange.

From these two primaries, shot on panchromatic negative stock, various methods were used to achieve a natural color screen image.[64]

Kinemacolor, the pioneer in this field, was effectively out of business by 1915. An additive system, it had projected its alternate frames through a revolving shutter that reintroduced the original colors. Commercially successful at first, it ultimately failed because of various technical liabilities and managerial problems.[65]

William Van Doren Kelley improved this system by devising a method of coloring the release prints. As a subtractive process, his Prizmacolor could be projected on standard equipment, which Kinemacolor could not. At first, Prizmacolor subtractive release prints had one frame toned red-orange, and the next toned blue-green, with the "natural color" image appearing only when the projected film was viewed onscreen. Kelley later began using duplitized stock (that is, stock with an emulsion on each side), printing the red-orange record on one side and the blue-green perfectly in register behind it. After toning each side the proper shade, he obtained a print in which every frame displayed "natural color" when viewed through transmitted light. This double-coated system was the progenitor of Trucolor and other two-color processes later marketed by Consolidated Film Industries, which acquired the patent rights.[66]

Because each color record was still recorded sequentially (not simultaneously), there was a problem with color fringes around moving objects, and as a result, Prizma had its greatest impact in relatively static travelogue films. In 1922 Prizma made and released twenty-six shorts, the only all-color regular short-subject package on the market. The process was also used for occasional inserts in such features as WAY DOWN EAST (1920), THE GILDED LILY (1921), and BROADWAY ROSE (1922). In 1921 J. Stuart Blackton directed THE GLORIOUS ADVENTURE, an all-Prizmacolor feature filmed in England.[67]

Beyond its problems with fringing, Prizmacolor had two major liabilities: excessive graininess and poor quality control. To solve these problems, Kelley joined forces with Max Handschiegl in 1926 and began to use Handschiegl's imbibition process to produce single-coated release prints under the name Kelley Color. But by this time the color film market was already dominated by the Technicolor Corporation, a situation that would continue for nearly thirty years.[68]

After experimenting with an additive system on THE GULF BETWEEN (1917), Herbert T. Kalmus and Daniel Comstock introduced subtractive two-color Technicolor with THE TOLL OF THE SEA in 1922. A beam splitter inside the camera recorded the two color records simultaneously, foot-to-foot on the original negative, thus eliminating the fringing problems of earlier systems. Skip-printing every other frame made it possible to separate the blue-green record onto one filmstrip, the red-orange onto another. Prints from these strips were then toned the proper color and cemented back-to-back to form each release print.[69]

Despite the success of TOLL OF THE SEA (produced by Technicolor and distributed by Metro), there was considerable industry resistance to any color system. Rex Ingram agreed to have Technicolor film an exterior sequence for THE PRISONER OF ZENDA (1922), but "we thought the people looked like dark colored oranges, so we took it out of the picture and threw it away," recalled his editor, Grant Whytock, years later.[70] Successful insert work on THE TEN COMMANDMENTS (1923) and CYTHEREA (1924) led to the production of such all-Technicolor films as WANDERER OF THE WASTELAND (1924) and THE BLACK PIRATE (1926), but this "process two" had inherent difficulties of its own: the cemented film strips buckled under the heat of projection, throwing the picture out of focus.

Finally, Technicolor "process three" substituted a dye-transfer imbibition system for making release prints, one similar to that employed by Kelley and Handschiegl.[71] This produced a smooth, grainless image with far greater uniformity of color than any system based on chemical toning. KING OF KINGS (1927) and THE WEDDING MARCH (1928) made use of this system, which remained in general use until 1933.

When contracting with the Technicolor Corporation to use their process, producers acquired not only the Technicolor cameras but special cameramen to operate them, at first J. Arthur Ball and later Ray Rennahan. While generally open to new technologies, the ASC at first strongly resisted Technicolor since it meant subordinating their members to a group of color technicians. Phil Rosen, one of the founders of the ASC, felt that color in film was distracting and that "true art does not necessarily mean the exact reproduction of nature." Ray Rennahan, for example, was tolerated by ASC members as a slave to his light meter who always worked by the book, a technocrat rather than an artist. Not until 1938 was he invited to join this club.[72]

Performance

The studio machinery could deliver scripts, sets, and cinematographers in an impressive and efficient manner, but no studio manager or unit producer could guarantee what might happen after the doors closed and shooting began on the stages. Soviet director Lev Kuleshov had demonstrated that traditional acting was irrelevant in silent pictures, since the editing process imposed its own structure regardless of the intentions of the original performer. This idea would not have surprised the producers of the OUR GANG comedies or the many animal films starring Rin-Tin-Tin, Rex the Wonder Horse, or the Dippy Do-Dads (a group of monkeys). Given this situation, actors and actresses needed to work with their directors to create a new style of performance directly for the silent screen, a style that had no real precedent and would change dramatically with the coming of "talkies" after 1927.[73]

Nothing better illustrates the idiosyncratic nature of silent-film performance than the use of sideline musicians on the set to inspire the cast during
filming, a practice that Kevin Brownlow dates to 1913.[74] As in a Victorian
theater piece, this underscoring of drama with music enhanced the essentially melodramatic nature of the performance, but here it was for the benefit
of the actors, not the audience. "During the making of a picture music has
become essential," wrote one accompanist in 1923. "There was a time when
the appearance of a violinist and a pianist on the set in a studio provoked
laughter. Their presence elicited ridicule, but not now."[75]

Musicians needed to command a repertoire of sad, dramatic, and joyous
arrangements and to be capable of flitting in an instant from the *Moonlight*
Sonata to "Yes, We Have No Bananas." Gounod's "Ave Maria" and the
intermezzo from *Cavalleria Rusticana* were judged most successful for tears,
while dramatic action might call for Tchaikovsky's Fourth Symphony, the
Massenet *Élégie*, or a Chopin prelude. According to the accompanist just
cited, certain stars or directors would have their own favorite pieces, regardless of the action:

> Thomas Meighan likes "Macushla," possibly because he is Irish.
> Alice Brady prefers selections from *Madame Butterfly*, and Agnes
> Ayres has a penchant for "Kiss Me Again." D. W. Griffith sometimes
> chooses dreamy Hawaiian music ("Real Inspiration," *New York
> Times*, 24 June 1923).

One special problem of silent-screen acting was the need to accommodate
the over-speeding of projection, which was the inevitable fate of every
projected "performance." Milton Sills acknowledged this in the entry on
"Motion Picture Acting" he prepared for the fourteenth edition of
the *Encyclopaedia Britannica*. Admitting that performances recorded at
60 feet per minute were typically projected at 90 feet per minute, Sills
felt it "necessary for the actor to adopt a more deliberate *tempo* than that
of the stage or real life. He must learn to time his actions in accordance
with the requirements of the camera, making it neither too fast nor too
slow."[76]

Controlling this tempo was ultimately the job of the director, who would
elicit a performance in one of two very different ways. As Gloria Swanson
put it:

> There's the director who allows the actor to give his own interpret-
> ation of a part, and becomes a conductor of an orchestra, moving it
> down or bringing it up. Then there's the other kind where the dir-
> ector is a thwarted actor, a ham as we call him, who wants to show
> the actor how to do it (quoted in Rui Nogueira, "I Am *Not* Going to
> Write My Memoirs," *Sight and Sound*, Spring 1969, p. 59).

Here, Swanson was praising her longtime collaborator Cecil B. DeMille, who would respond to actors' questions with an abrupt "I'm not running an acting school!" This approach was very much the opposite of another of Swanson's directors, Erich von Stroheim, who was notorious for indicating exactly how he wanted every gesture delivered. Von Stroheim would keep filming retakes until he saw the performance he had conceived in his mind's eye, a technique Swanson accuses Chaplin of employing as well (and with some justification, given the evidence provided in the Kevin Brownlow–David Gill Thames television series *The Unknown Chaplin*). As for D. W. Griffith, Swanson claimed:

> You could always tell when an actor had been working with Griffith, because they all had the same gestures. All of them. They'd cower like mice when they were frightened, they'd shut not their fingers but their fists, they'd turn down their mouths. . . . Lillian Gish, Dorothy Gish, all of them. Even the men had a stamp on them (Nogueira, p. 59).

The onscreen evidence indicates that von Stroheim, Chaplin, and Griffith were able to use this Svengali approach to good effect. Unfortunately, far less talented directors often employed equally intrusive techniques:

> Well do I remember watching J. Searle Dawley direct Pearl White in an intensely dramatic scene, in which he played all the parts before the rehearsal was over. . . . Mr. Dawley did everything. He reclined on the floor, as Miss White was to do, and leaned back in the villain's arms. He played the villain, and snatched her to him despite her struggles. And then, as the big red blooded hero, he burst into the room and hurled the villain back against the wall so forcibly that it shook (Inez and Helen Klumph, *Screen Acting: Its Requirements and Rewards* [New York: Falk, 1922], pp. 185–186).

By the late 1920s this technique had generally fallen out of favor, although some, including Ernst Lubitsch, continued to employ it successfully. Raoul Walsh, another of Swanson's directors, summed up the case for the DeMille approach:

> I should like to know how the silent drama is to develop great talent if the practice of curbing the players is adhered to. Granted the director must play an important part, he must supervise the players and see that they are getting the right stuff into the scene. There should, however, be a happy medium, as overdirection causes players to be self-conscious, mechanical and as colorless as dolls or marionettes on a string ("Spontaneity in Acting," *New York Times*, 27 April 1924).

Editing

As soon as filming had started, the director and editor would screen the footage processed each day ("the dailies"), make initial decisions on the best takes, and begin assembling the work print. This would be relatively easy for scenes where action was limited and only a few characters appeared, but complicated sequences presented far greater problems. Because editing was acknowledged as crucial by everyone from Griffith to Sennett, it was considered important for the director to establish an intimate working relationship with his cutter. Griffith worked for many years with Jimmy Smith, and Rex Ingram had his most successful pictures cut by Grant Whytock.

Ingram would film spectacular scenes for THE FOUR HORSEMEN OF THE APOCALYPSE with twelve or fourteen cameras grinding simultaneously. It was impossible for him to analyze so much footage each night, so he depended on Whytock to make an initial selection—something he did by ignoring all but two or three of the master cameras! The editor also assembled another original negative for foreign markets. Shots were recorded twice, either by adjacent cameras or through an additional take. Kodak duplicating stock was not available until 1926, and previous attempts at producing foreign negatives by duping the original resulted in such poor print quality that overseas audiences complained. For THE FOUR HORSEMEN OF THE APOCALYPSE, a third "original" negative was assembled by Whytock after heavy print demand wore out the primary domestic negative. Produced from third-best takes, this version lacked a few key shots and sequences, and Whytock considered himself lucky that "it all made sense."[77] (In 1971 FOOLISH WIVES was reconstructed by Arthur Lennig for the American Film Institute by wholesale interweaving of material from such foreign and domestic versions. Predictable problems with matching action resulted, especially given the film's long history of recutting and censorship.)[78]

When a film was completed, it was previewed at a local theater to gauge public reaction. Harold Lloyd, one of the most aggressive users of the preview system, remembered:

> Even back in the one-reel days, I would take a picture out to a theater when I knew the picture wasn't right. And the manager used to always have to come out and explain what was going on. When we were doing two-reelers, he came out in white tie and tails to do it, and it was quite an event for him and the audience would listen attentively ("The Serious Business of Being Funny," *Film Comment*, Fall 1969, p. 47).

By the time he moved to features, Lloyd would take "scientific" readings of audience laughter and plot them on large graphs, using the information to refine the way his comedies played.

Lloyd's rival Buster Keaton filmed a scene for THE NAVIGATOR in which, as an underwater traffic cop, he directed the movement of swarming schools of fish. Despite the fact that he was quite proud of this expensive gag, Keaton cut it from the picture when preview audiences proved too astonished to laugh.[79]

Occasionally, an already completed film would be drastically reshuffled following previews. Wrote critic Welford Beaton, months before the official premiere of THE WEDDING MARCH:

> I have seen *The Wedding March* twice, once at Anaheim and again at Long Beach. The Anaheim version had the weakness of characterizing von Stroheim as an all-good hero, a role that he has neither the appearance nor the personality to play convincingly. Nicki was made so spotless in that version that when the seduction scene was reached it gave the impression that Mitzi, his victim, had been the aggressor. In the final version Nicki is presented as the roue that he was drawn in the original story [*sic*], and all the scenes which developed that side of him were put back into the picture ("At Last One Fragment of Von's Opus Reaches Screen," *Film Spectator*, 17 March 1928, p. 7).

After the first preview of THE PHANTOM OF THE OPERA, a decision was made to put some comic relief into the film, and a considerable amount of footage with Chester Conklin was inserted. Later preview screenings led Universal to cut Conklin out of the picture entirely.[80] For modern audiences, Conklin is back in again, courtesy of a 1930 reissue and some questionable "film restoration."

Usually, of course, the preview process was far less traumatic, just another step in the production and polishing of any film. Henry King's rough cut of STELLA DALLAS (1925) was 26,000 feet, which he trimmed to 18,000 before previewing it in San Bernardino. Although nobody walked out on this 3½-hour cut, he trimmed another 3,000 feet before running it in Pasadena. At the screening of this fifteen-reel version, some 800 postcards were distributed asking for suggestions of which 420 were returned. It was discovered that Stella's dialogue titles were "resented by the public," so these were all done over. After this version was previewed in another small town, two weak sequences were excised, and the film went into general release at 10,157 feet.[81]

The director most taken with the preview idea was probably D. W. Griffith, who considered it an extension of the theatrical out-of-town tryout. Even the opening-night version was just another cut to Griffith, who continued refining his work well after the initial public showings. "As was his habit," Eileen Bowser tell us, "D. W. Griffith accompanied *Intolerance* on its first runs in the major cities, cutting the prints at the theater, striving to improve it. The result was that the print shown in Boston was not necessarily the same as that shown in New York, and it may be that neither was matched exactly by the original negative."[82]

Cameraman Hal Sintzenich's diaries show that Griffith not only recut his films after opening night but often continued shooting new footage as well. Notes Erik Barnouw:

> On February 10, 1924, Snitch mentions a [preview] showing of *America* in South Norwalk, Connecticut. On the same day he is shooting scenes for its Valley Forge sequence in nearby Westchester, impelled by the arrival of ideal blizzard weather for "the men in bare feet in the snow trying to pull the big wagon" (2/10/24). The Battle of Princeton is shot the following day, in time to be included four days later in a showing in Danbury, Connecticut, when Snitch is shooting Washington's inauguration. Two days later they are remaking "the stockade scenes." On the day of the New York premiere, February 21, Snitch is still doing close-ups of Carol Dempster, and during the following week does retakes of "Miss Dempster & Hamilton" and new "stockade scenes with 30 extras" ("The Sintzenich Diaries," p. 326).

Years later, at the Museum of Modern Art, Griffith was still eager to recut his pictures, running the now-antique prints in the Film Library's screening room, never satisfied that he had achieved a definitive version.[83]

The implications of such behavior for film scholarship are considerable. What is the authentic version of such a work? Griffith's incessant adding and subtracting of footage implies that he saw these films as essentially open texts, capable of showing one face to Boston and another to New York. Yet he copyrighted the montage of THE BIRTH OF A NATION and INTOLERANCE by submitting a frame from each shot to the United States Copyright Office. Did he see those versions as definitive? And if so, why the inevitable "improvements" that followed?

The problem goes beyond Griffith. By the late silent period, exhibitors could choose alternate endings for a number of major films. Some audiences, viewing Garbo as Anna Karenina in Clarence Brown's LOVE (1927), saw Anna throw herself under a train. Other theaters showed Anna happily reunited with Count Vronsky. King Vidor shot seven endings for THE CROWD and apparently issued it with two. Griffith's DRUMS OF LOVE (1928) still exists with a pair of different endings, and when it is screened by archives, audiences sometimes see them one after the other. Why producers suddenly lost confidence in their ability to make such basic decisions is unclear, but if they were moved to think twice about these films, later generations should be at least as careful when asserting that any version of a silent film is definitive.[84]

List of abbreviations

AC	*American Cinematographer*
ETR	*Exhibitor's Trade Review*
FDY	*Film Daily Yearbook of Motion Pictures*
MPN	*Motion Picture News*
MPW	*Moving Picture World*
NYDM	*New York Dramatic Mirror*
NYT	*New York Times*
SMPE/SMPTE	*Transactions* [later *Journal*] *of the Society of Motion Picture* [*and Television*] *Engineers*

Notes

1 Peter Bogdanovich, ed., *Allan Dwan: The Last Pioneer* (New York: Praeger, 1971), pp. 16–17; Raoul Walsh, *Each Man in His Time* (New York: Doubleday, 1974), pp. 62–67; Charles Higham, *Hollywood Cameramen* (Bloomington: Indiana University Press, 1970), pp. 35–56 (Garmes), 134–154 (Miller); Kevin Brownlow, *The Parade's Gone By ...* (New York: Alfred Knopf, 1968), pp. 308–311 (Hornbeck); "Dorothy Arzner Interview," *Cinema* (Beverly Hills) 34 (1974), p. 10.

2 J. Vorhies, "Columbia Movies," *Motion Picture Magazine*, August 1915, p. 93; Victor Freeburg, *The Art of Photoplay Making* (New York: Macmillan, 1918); *Pictorial Beauty on Screen* (New York: Macmillan, 1923); Frances Taylor Patterson, *Cinema Craftsmanship* (New York: Harcourt, Brace, 1921), p. v. See also Patterson's *Scenario and Screen* (New York: Harcourt, Brace, 1928) and *Motion Picture Continuities* (New York: Columbia University Press, 1929), perhaps the first film book published by an American university press.

3 Kevin Brownlow, *The War, the West, and the Wilderness* (New York: Knopf, 1978), pp. 119–125; Carl Louis Gregory, "Instruction in Motion Picture Photography," *SMPE* 28 (October 1926), p. 303.

4 Joseph P. Kennedy, ed., *The Story of the Film* (Boston: Shaw, 1927), contains transcripts of the fourteen lectures by various leaders of the artistic and business community of the motion-picture industry. On the amateur film movement, see, for example, Jack Bechdolt, *How to Make Your Own Motion Picture Plays* (New York: Greenberg, 1926), or Morrie Ryskind, C. F. Stevens, and James Englander, *The Home Movie Scenario Book* (New York: Anson, 1927), which offer sophisticated technical advice and sample film scenarios.

5 "Are the Motion Picture Schools Sucker Traps?" *American Projectionist*, September 1923, p. 10; John Emerson and Anita Loos, *Breaking into the Movies* (New York: McCann, 1921), p. 6.

6 Jean Bernique, *Motion Picture Acting* (Chicago: Producers Service Company, 1916); Mae Marsh, *Screen Acting* (Los Angeles: Photo-Star, 1921), p. 16.

7 Horace A. Fuld, "The Fakes and Frauds in Motion Pictures," *Motion Picture Magazine*, November 1915, p. 111.

8 A. Van Buren Powell, *The Photoplay Synopsis* (Springfield, Mass.: Home Correspondence School, 1919).

9 *The Secret of Successful Photoplay Writing* (Los Angeles: Palmer Photoplay, 1920).

10 *The Photoplaywrights' League of America: Its Object and Purposes*, promotional brochure (1921), author's collection.

11 Ernest A. Dench, "Making Money with a Motion Picture Camera," *Motion Picture Magazine*, October 1917, p. 39.

12 See, for example, Carl Louis Gregory, *Motion Picture Photography* (New York: Falk, 1927), or Herbert McKay, *Handbook of Motion Picture Photography* (New York: Falk, 1927). Gregory had been in charge of instruction for the Signal Corps during their wartime program at Columbia.

13 *Historical Statistics of the United States, Colonial Times to 1970*, part 1 (Washington, D.C.: U.S. Department of Commerce, 1975), p. 142; "Are the Motion Picture Schools Sucker Traps?" *loc. cit.*

14 George Blaisdell, "Mecca of the Motion Picture," *MPW*, 10 July 1915, p. 215; Perley Poore Sheehan, *Hollywood as a World Center* (Hollywood: Hollywood Citizens' Press, 1924), pp. 1, 102–115.

15 Kevin Brownlow and John Kobal, *Hollywood: The Pioneers* (New York: Knopf, 1979), pp. 90–107; Sklar, *Movie-Made America*, p. 68. See also Murray Ross, *Stars and Strikes* (New York: Columbia University Press, 1941).

16 *NYDM*, 24 March 1915, p. 26 (Ince; the road was probably Sunset Boulevard); Valerie von Stroheim, in an interview with the author, Los Angeles, June 1978. Actors' Equity claimed that there were only 1,200 actors in the entire state of California at the start of 1915; this number was spread among films, vaudeville, and legitimate theater (*NYDM*, 3 February 1915, p. 9).

17 The lower figure is from *MPW*, 10 July 1915, p. 216; the higher figure, *MPN*, 3 April 1915, p. 39.

18 "The Grand March," *Photoplay*, November 1918, pp. 86–87.

19 In addition to outside pressures, the city fathers also seem to have done their best to rid Fort Lee of filmmakers; see Rita Altomara, *Hollywood on the Palisades* (New York: Garland, 1983). "Sunless Temple of New York's Movies," *NYT*, 7 November 1920 (Griffith).

20 The Mirror studio was a small, independent operation typical of many scattered around the New York area. A number of Johnny Hines comedies were shot there.

21 *ETR*, 25 September 1920, p. 1822.

22 Richard Koszarski, *The Astoria Studio and Its Fabulous Films* (New York: Dover, 1983), p. 8.

23 Edward Van Zile, *That Marvel—the Movie* (New York: Putnam, 1923), p. 216; "Movies as Investments," p. 10; Lasky, *I Blow My Own Horn*, p. 195.

24 For a rare discussion, see Kathleen Karr, "Hooray for Wilkes-Barre, Saranac Lake—and Hollywood," in *The American Film Heritage* (Washington, D.C.: Acropolis, 1972), pp. 104–109. The most attention to these filmmakers can be found in locally produced documentary films such as ALL BUT FORGOTTEN: HOLMAN F. DAY, FILM MAKER, directed by Everett Foster, and WHEN YOU WORE A TULIP, about regional production in Wisconsin, directed by Steven Schaller. Florida is one of the only regional centers adequately discussed. See Richard Alan Nelson, "Florida and the American Motion Picture Industry, 1898–1930" (Ph.D. diss., Florida State University, 1980), as well as various articles by Nelson.

25 "Gossip of the Studios," *NYDM*, 3 March 1915, p. 26.

26 "The Photo Play Market," *Photoplay Author*, December 1914, p. 191.

27 "Colleges Fail in the Test," *NYDM*, 24 February 1915, p. 25. Schools competing were the University of Pennsylvania (58 entries, 2 acceptable), Columbia (32 and 1), Cornell (49 and 2), Harvard (62 and 3), and the following with no acceptable submissions: Yale (48), Princeton (15), University of Michigan (43), University of Chicago (12), University of California (9), University of Wisconsin (14).

28 Gorenflot, "Thinks and Things," *Photoplay Author*, December 1914, p. 183.

29 Douglas Brown, "The Cost Elements of a Motion Picture," *SMPE* 17 (October 1923), p. 141; "Film Rights, and What They Are Worth," *NYT*, 11 August 1920.

30 "High Price of Stories," *NYT*, 30 March 1924.
31 "The Movies: A Colossus That Totters," *Bookman*, February 1919, pp. 653–659.
32 "No Protection for Movie Scenarios," *NYT*, 13 February 1914.
33 Bordwell, Staiger, and Thompson, *The Classical Hollywood Cinema*, p. 136. See the sections on Ince and Sennett in chapter 8 of this volume.
34 "MGM Studio Tour" is available in 16 mm from the Em Gee Film Library, Reseda, Calif., which also has other such promotional reels.
35 "Take away the phoney tinsel of Hollywood and you'll find the real tinsel underneath," Oscar Levant is reported to have said.
36 Cf. Bordwell, Staiger, and Thompson, *The Classical Hollywood Cinema*, p. 137: "those with greater marketability (*e.g.*, Hart) could demand certain working conditions." United Artists, of course, was entirely based on this premise.
37 Frederick James Smith, "The Cost of a Five Reel Photoplay," *NYDM*, 7 July 1917, p. 9; "Movies as Investments," p. 10.
38 Richard W. Saunders, "Finance and Pictures," *NYT*, 7 November 1926.
39 Johnson Heywood, "How 'Movie' Industry Got on Sound Financial Basis," *Forbes*, 1 March 1927, p. 13; "High Costs Halt Production," *NYT*, 27 October 1923.
40 "Present Production Costs Contrasted with Low Figures of the Past," *NYT*, 19 December 1926.
41 "Motion Pictures and Finance," *Barron's*, 19 May 1924, p. 5. The figures are repeated by James Spearing in "A New Phase Opens in the Film Industry," *NYT*, 3 July 1927, and by *MPN* editor William A. Johnson in *SMPE* 32 (September 1927), p. 667.
42 William S. Holman, "Cost-Accounting for the Motion-Picture Industry," *Journal of Accountancy*, December 1920, p. 420.
43 Alfred A. Cohn, "What They Really Get—NOW!" *Photoplay*, March 1916, p. 27.
44 "Star Salaries," *FDY* (1924), p. 299; also "The High Cost of Film Stars," *NYT*, 4 November 1923.
45 "Harold Lloyd Heads List of Huge Earnings of Stars and Directors," *NYT*, 16 May 1926.
46 Fred Balshofer and Arthur Miller, *One Reel a Week* (Los Angeles: University of California Press, 1967), pp. 130, 134. For information on this early period, see John Hambley and Patrick Downing, *The Art of Hollywood* (London: Thames Television, 1979).
47 Mosgrove Colwell, "Something New in Pictures," *Motion Picture Magazine*, August 1916, p. 53 (Kellar); Maurice Tourneur, "Stylization in Motion Picture Direction," *Motion Picture Magazine*, September 1918, p. 101. Universal's MADAME CUBIST, a two-reeler released earlier than THE YELLOW GIRL in 1916, made specific references to the Armory Show in its advertising but used its "futurist and cubist" costumes simply as a fashion parade, unlike the integral design scheme of THE YELLOW GIRL. See *Moving Picture Weekly*, 12 February 1916, pp. 18–19.
48 Even before HUMAN WRECKAGE, a visitor to one Hollywood set wrote, "A liberal use of yellows, reds and blues assaulted the eye, and one ventured if the room was to convey a hasheesh-eaters' paradise" ("A Visit to Movieland," *Forum*, January 1920, p. 16). The requirements of orthochromatic film stock were probably responsible.
49 Leon Barsacq and Elliott Stein, *Caligari's Cabinet and Other Grand Illusions* (Boston: New York Graphic Society, 1976), p. 212; "The Architecture of Motion Picture Settings," *American Architect*, 7 July 1920, p. 1; James Hood MacFarland, "Architectural Problems in Motion Picture Production," *American Architect*,

21 July 1920, p. 65. THE COPPERHEAD is preserved in the archives of the George Eastman House/International Museum of Photography, Rochester, N.Y.

50 Other teams included John Seitz and director Rex Ingram (1920–1926), Oliver Marsh photographing Mae Murray (1922–1925), and Charles Rosher photographing Mary Pickford (1917–1927).

51 Hal Mohr, in an interview with the author, Los Angeles, 10 July 1971.

52 "A Half Century of Loyalty, Progress, Artistry," *AC*, January 1969, p. 46; "An Open Letter," *AC*, August 1926, p. 8; Hal Mohr interview.

53 *NYDM*, 3 March 1915, p. 28.

54 Stephen S. Norton, "Close-Ups," *AC*, July 1923, p. 8; Welford Beaton, "Submerging the Production Under Senseless Close-Ups," *The Film Spectator*, 12 May 1928, p. 7; idem, "Is Eric von Stroheim a Really Good Director?" *Film Spectator*, 17 March 1928, p. 8; "Now the Close-Up," *NYT*, 1 October 1922.

55 "Ideal Directors," *NYT*, 13 February 1921.

56 "Camera Expert Studies Old Masters for Effect," *NYT*, 12 June 1927; Cecil B. DeMille, "Motion Picture Directing," *SMPE* 34 (April 1928), p. 295; Higham, *Hollywood Cameramen*, p. 35.

57 See the discussion of this issue in chapter 5.

58 John Baxter, *The Hollywood Exiles* (New York: Taplinger, 1976), pp. 19–53; Karl Struss, "Dramatic Cinematography," *SMPE* 34 (April 1928), p. 317.

59 Projection through colored filters was also sometimes employed, but this was essentially an exhibitor's technique and not under the control of the filmmakers. For an excellent general discussion of the use of color in motion pictures, see Brian Coe, *The History of Movie Photography* (Westfield, N.J.: Eastview Editions, 1981), esp. pp. 112–139.

60 G. A. Blair, "The Tinting of Motion-Picture Film," *SMPE* 10 (May 1920), p. 45. L. A. Jones, "Discussion of Paper Entitled 'Transmission of Tinted Motion Picture Films,' " *SMPE* 12 (May 1921), p. 101; *Tinting and Toning of Eastman Positive Motion Picture Film* (Rochester: Eastman Kodak Company, 1927), pp. 23, 36.

61 Koszarski, *The Man You Loved to Hate*, pp. 67–70; Eric Elliott, *Anatomy of Motion Picture Art* (Dijon: Pool, 1928), p. 38.

62 "Hand Painting Films," *American Projectionist*, September 1923, p. 3. For an example of Brock's ads, see *FDY* (1927), p. K. In earlier years, other colorists, also based in New York, had also offered their services, notably G. R. Silvera (p. 80) and John Duer Scott (p. 84) in the 1922–1923 edition.

63 William V. D. Kelley, "Imbibition Coloring of Motion Picture Films," *SMPE* 28 (October 1926), p. 238.

64 William V. D. Kelley, "Natural Color Cinematography," *SMPE* 7 (November 1918), p. 38. There were some three-color systems in this period, such as Gaumont Chronochrome, which had no commercial impact and are of importance mainly in understanding later successful three-color systems. Panchromatic stock had already been offered to the trade by 1915. See, for example, the display ad for Harrison-Ramsey panchromatic negative film stock in *MPN*, 21 February 1914, p. 40.

65 D. B. Thomas, *The First Colour Motion Pictures* (London: Her Majesty's Stationery Office, 1969).

66 *Ibid.*, pp. 37–38; William T. Crespinal, "Color Photography—Past and Present," *American Projectionist*, May 1925, p. 4; "Color in the Motion Picture," *AC*, January 1969, p. 80; Kelley, "Natural Color Cinematography"; W. T. Crespinel [*sic*], "Color Photography—Yesterday, Today and Tomorrow," *AC*, March 1929, p. 4. Kelley did originally try Prizma as an additive system but soon abandoned the idea.

67 Carroll H. Dunning, "Color Photography in 1922," *FDY* (1922–1923), p. 17.
68 Kelley, "Imbibition Coloring."
69 The technology behind many of these competing systems was quite similar. Technicolor was used by Prizma in 1922 for patents infringement, but it was Prizma that soon faded from the scene (*NYT*, 26 September 1922, p. 31).
70 Grant Whytock, in an interview with the author, Los Angeles, 16 July 1971.
71 Kelley, "Imbibition Coloring."
72 Phil Rosen, "Believes Color Will Not Aid Dramatic Cinematography," *AC*, January 1923, p. 4; Ernest Palmer, who shared an Academy Award with Rennahan for BLOOD AND SAND, remembered in an interview with the author that he had had little patience with the Technicolor expert's compulsion to put adequate amounts of light under sofas and in other obscure corners. Pacific Palisades, California, January 1972.
73 For Kuleshov, see V. I. Pudovkin, *Film Technique and Film Acting* (New York: Grove Press, 1960), pp. 166–169.
74 Brownlow, *The Parade's Gone By . . .*, p. 339.
75 "Real Inspiration," *NYT*, 24 June 1923.
76 *The Theatre and Motion Pictures*, Britannica Booklet no. 7 (New York: Encyclopaedia Britannica, 1933), p. 29.
77 Whytock interview with author; "Why Some American Films Prove Failures in England," *NYT*, 27 April 1924.
78 Arthur Lennig, *Von Stroheim* (Albany: State University of New York, 1973), n.p.
79 Buster Keaton, "Why I Never Smile," *Ladies Home Journal*, June 1926, p. 20.
80 Robert E. Sherwood, "The Phantom Jinx," *Photoplay*, January 1926, p. 113.
81 "Mr. Goldwyn Describes Try-Outs of Pictures," *NYT*, 25 October 1925.
82 Eileen Bowser, *"Intolerance": The Film by David Wark Griffith. Shot by Shot Analysis* (New York: Museum of Modern Art, 1966), p. iii.
83 Robert M. Henderson, *D. W. Griffith: His Life and Work* (New York: Oxford University Press, 1972), p. 288. At the Cinémathèque Française a decade later, Erich von Stroheim not only recut THE WEDDING MARCH but inserted stock footage from MERRY-GO-ROUND which he preferred to that used in THE WEDDING MARCH. This synchronized print is now shown as the standard version (Koszarski, *The Man You Loved to Hate*, pp. 194–195).
84 *The American Film Institute Catalogue: Feature Films 1921–1930* (New York: Bowker, 1971), p. 454 (LOVE); King Vidor, *A Tree is a Tree* (New York: Harcourt, Brace, 1953), p. 152.

3

STARS IN BUSINESS

The founding of United Artists

Tino Balio

Source: Tino Balio (ed.), *The American Film Industry*, Madison, Wisc.: University of Wisconsin Press, 1976, pp. 135–152.

On January 15, 1919, five of the biggest names in motion pictures staged a revolt. Mary Pickford, Charles Chaplin, Douglas Fairbanks, D. W. Griffith, and William S. Hart issued their "Declaration of Independence" against the corporate establishment announcing their intention to form a distribution company to be owned and operated exclusively by stars for the benefit of the great motion picture public.

The declaration, which resulted in pyrotechnics unusual even for an industry that existed more or less on fireworks, read as follows:

> A new combination of motion picture stars and producers was formed yesterday, and we, the undersigned, in furtherance of the artistic welfare of the moving picture industry, believing we can better serve the great and growing industry of picture productions, have decided to unite our work into one association, and at the finish of existing contracts, which are now rapidly drawing to a close, to release our combined productions through our own organization. This new organization, to embrace the very best actors and producers in the motion picture business, is headed by the following well-known stars: Mary Pickford, Douglas Fairbanks, William S. Hart, Charlie Chaplin and D. W. Griffith productions, all of whom have proved their ability to make productions of value both artistically and financially.
>
> We believe this is necessary to protect the exhibitor and the industry itself, thus enabling the exhibitor to book only pictures that he wishes to play and not force upon him (when he is booking films to please his audience) other program films which he does not desire,

believing that as servants of the people we can thus best serve the people. We also think that this step is positively and absolutely necessary to protect the great motion picture public from threatening combinations and trusts that would force upon them mediocre productions and machine-made entertainment.[1]

Hollywood was too cynical to take the revolt seriously. "Film magnates and a number of lesser stellarites in celluloid," said *Variety*, saw Adolph Zukor behind the whole affair in just another attempt to weaken First National.[2] Others prophesied that the all-star combination would soon be riven by jealousies and never get off the ground. And then there came Richard Rowland's famous wisecrack, "So the lunatics have taken charge of the asylum." A more accurate assessment, however, comes from Arthur Mayer, who remarks, "The founders of United Artists displayed the same brand of lunacy as Rockefeller, Morgan, and du Pont."[3]

The founders

Mary Pickford

Mary Pickford's movie career began in 1909, when D. W. Griffith hired her for $5 a day at Biograph. Although only sixteen, she was a trouper with three years' experience on the stage and a position in David Belasco's eminent theatrical company. Her special appeal was soon evident on the screen. Long before her name appeared in movies, audiences began to identify her as "the girl with the curls" or as "Little Mary," the character name most often used in her films. So with a foresight that would characterize her entire career, she went to the Biograph executives to suggest that they capitalize on her drawing power by releasing her name to the public and by building her up in the press. The studio bosses refused.

But Carl Laemmle, a scurrying independent producer, had a hunch that Little Mary could be made into a star. An offer of $175 a week lured her to his Independent Motion Picture Company in December 1910, and the name Mary Pickford was revealed to the movie public. Production standards at IMP were too low for Miss Pickford's tastes, however, so she left the company within a year. After an even briefer stint with Majestic, she returned to Biograph in 1912. Finding that their stodgy mentality still prevailed, Miss Pickford resumed her stage career with Belasco in 1913. She was performing in the Broadway production of *A Good Little Devil* when she caught the attention of Adolph Zukor, who soon convinced her to join his Famous Players.

Mary quickly became Zukor's most effective box-office attraction, and her starting salary of $20,000 a year was raised to $1,000 a week. With *Tess of the Storm Country* in 1914, Mary Pickford became a household word.

Her meteoric fame and salary caused trade practices of the industry to be revamped. Famous Players had been releasing through Paramount, a distribution company that supplied theaters with two or three features a week. Theater owners contracted for the entire Paramount program, which included the Pickford pictures, in a block-booking arrangement. Although this practice was standard in the industry, it changed when Mary's mother heard that salesmen were saying, "As long as we have Mary on the program we can wrap everything around her neck"—that is, exhibitors would buy the entire Paramount output to get the Pickfords. If her daughter's neck was that strong, she reasoned, Mary was entitled to more money.

Zukor passed the problem to Paramount's president, W. W. Hodkinson. Mrs. Pickford's demands would have to be met, he decided, and Mary's weekly salary was raised to $2,000. The money would not come from the Paramount coffers, however, but from the exhibitors. Hodkinson proposed selling the Pickford pictures as a "series," and charging more for them than for the regular Paramount program. This apparently slight departure from the program system eventually broadened into a completely new method of distribution. "It made possible the high salaries that were to come to actors, the increase in admittance prices to the great theaters that were to be built, and the enthusiastic endorsement of both by the public."[4]

Hodkinson's distribution plan proved so successful that in the following year, 1916, Charlotte Pickford suggested that her daughter's salary could be boosted still further. Her logic could not be denied. To accomplish this, Mrs. Pickford proposed that Mary become an independent producer (until then she had been a contract player). Thus, in partnership with Adolph Zukor, the Mary Pickford Corporation was formed. Zukor became the president, and Mrs. Pickford, representing Mary's 50 percent interest, became treasurer with the authority of approving all expenditures. In addition to receiving half of the profits on her pictures, Mary was to earn $10,000 a week, to be paid every Monday of the year. The number of pictures she would make each year was reduced from ten to a minimum of six to enable her to improve their quality. A separate distribution company, called Artcraft, was formed to handle the Pickford features, which thereafter were to be sold individually rather than in a series. On June 24, 1916, Mary Pickford became the first star to be a producer of her own pictures and to win a considerable degree of control over her work.

The Artcraft pictures that followed marked some of the greatest achievements in Miss Pickford's career. Among these were *The Pride of the Clan* and *The Poor Little Rich Girl*, both directed by Maurice Tourneur; two Cecil B. DeMille films, *A Romance of the Redwoods* and *The Little American*; and *Rebecca of Sunnybrook Farm, A Little Princess*, and *Stella Maris*, by one of her best directors, Marshall Neilan.

Despite her popular success and enormous salary, Miss Pickford was dissatisfied. She wanted complete autonomy over her work, including script approval. Moreover, Paramount's salesmen, she discovered, were forcing exhibitors to rent other pictures in order to get hers. Knowing that Miss Pickford's contract expired in 1918, First National made an unprecedented bid for her services.

Here was the offer: First National would pay her $675,000 for three negatives plus 50 percent of the profits. To Mrs. Pickford, for her good offices, $50,000. Equally important, Mary would have complete autonomy over her productions, from the selection of the script to the final cut of the release print. First National would top Artcraft's distribution, she was told, so that her net revenue would be $1 million, perhaps even $2 million a year. This type of competition was too much even for Adolph Zukor, who regretfully bid Mary Pickford farewell.

Charlie Chaplin

Charlie Chaplin had caught the eye of Adam Kessel, a partner to Mack Sennett in the Keystone company, while touring America with Fred Karno's English pantomime company in 1913. Kessel signed him up to work in Mack Sennett's Keystone comedies at a starting salary of $150 a week, three times what he had been making as an acrobat, pantomimist, and clown in Karno's program, "A Night in a Music Hall."

In a single year's time at Keystone, Chaplin made thirty-five pictures. Popular acclaim was immediate. "Nothing like it had ever been seen before," says Edward Wagenknecht. "Chaplin swept first America then the world. This was not anything that had been expected or planned for by the motion picture industry or by Chaplin himself; both indeed were greatly surprised by it."[5]

Sennett tried to keep his star in quarantine at the studio, but, as the story goes, an agent from Essanay got to Chaplin by hiring out as a cowboy extra. Yes, Chaplin would switch—for $1,250, nearly ten times his Keystone salary, and the right to direct his pictures. "Comedians could be very serious when talking about money," as Hampton puts it.[6] Essanay promoted the pictures vigorously and the Chaplin craze intensified. After only two years in movies, he had become the top drawing-card in the business. Essanay earned well over $1 million on the Chaplin series.

Chaplin went over to Mutual on February 26, 1916. With his new salary of $670,000—$10,000 a week plus a bonus of $150,000—he had once again multiplied his earnings of the previous year by ten. Not bad for a young man of twenty-six who just three years earlier had embarked on a career in vaudeville. The twelve pictures Chaplin made for Mutual, all two-reelers, were masterpieces. Among them were *The Floorwalker*, *The Count*, and *Easy Street*. Along with increasing fame came visits from such world-famous figures as Paderewski, Leopold Godowsky, Nellie Melba, and Harry Lauder. Even the intellectuals took notice and began to write appreciations of Chaplin's art.

Mutual wanted Chaplin to make a second series of twelve pictures and offered him $1 million to stay on. This money was to be straight salary; Mutual would bear all production costs. Chaplin, however, rejected the proposition and instead signed with First National. Money was not the major consideration in this decision. The First National contract paid Chaplin $1 million plus a $15,000 bonus for the act of signing. It called for the delivery of eight pictures within eighteen months. Chaplin was to pay his own production costs from the $125,000 advanced for each negative. Since First National agreed to share the profits equally, Chaplin stood to make more money from this deal than from Mutual's. The clincher, though, was that it provided Chaplin the opportunity for going independent. As a spokesman for First National said:

> There are no conditions in that contract which permit us to inter-
> fere in the least with him as a producer. He is an independent manu-
> facturer, owning and operating his own producing company and the
> studios in which it works. He can take any length of time he feels
> is essential to quality in his releases. He is free to choose his own
> stories. He is not harassed by telegrams and long-distance telephone
> calls, urging haste in the completion of a picture to make a certain
> release date. He is entirely independent of any one or any other
> concern of any character. His contract with us provides for distri-
> bution of his output and that, to Mr. Chaplin, is First National's
> only functional part in his activities.[7]

Douglas Fairbanks

Frank Case, proprietor of the Algonquin Hotel, told the story that when Harry Aitken offered Douglas Fairbanks a chance to join his Triangle film company, Doug balked. Case noted that the $104,000 offer "was not hay," to which Doug replied, "I know, but the movies!" As a matinee idol with some fifteen years' experience, Fairbanks shared his fellow actors' disparagement of the theater's "bastard child." But Doug, like many in his profession, put his artistic principles aside and succumbed to the irresistible attraction of quick money.

Aitken's Triangle company, formed in 1915, became the industry's most spectacular scheme to capitalize on the talents of the stage. The star system was then in vogue, and Aitken and his partners conceived the plan to cap-ture the brightest theater talents and to translate their greatest plays for the screen. Triangle had three master directors, D. W. Griffith, Thomas Ince, and Mack Sennett. In addition to appealing to the upper classes, Aitken's scheme attracted Wall Street financiers, whose money he needed to engage the cream of theater, vaudeville, and musical comedy. In all, he hired nearly sixty players, among them Sir Herbert Beerbohm Tree, Mary Anderson de

Navarro, Weber and Fields, De Wolf Hopper, Billie Burke, and Dustin Farnum.

Although Doug Fairbanks was one of the less-celebrated stars, Aitken chose Fairbanks's *The Lamb* to open the first Triangle program at the Knickerbocker in New York on September 23, 1915. This theater was taken over by Aitken to be the metropolitan home of his company, and its pictures were presented there at the standard Broadway price of two dollars. Doug's debut was well received, at least by *Variety*, which said, "After viewing 'The Lamb,' it is no wonder the Triangle people signed up Fairbanks for a period of three years at any salary within reason. . . . He registers on the screen as well as any regular film actor that has ever appeared in pictures and more strongly than most of them."[8] After the picture was released, Aitken doubled his $2,000 weekly salary.

Part of *The Lamb*'s appeal lay in Doug's acrobatics and stunts; he let a rattlesnake crawl over him, tackled a mountain lion, and jujitsued a bunch of Yaqui Indians. Griffith, however, was not impressed and suggested that Doug's acting style was better suited to Sennett's comedies. With that, Griffith shunted Fairbanks to the care of Frank Woods, who "acted as a sort of cowcatcher to Griffith productions, sweeping accumulated embarrassments away from the path of the Master."[9]

As coordinator of productions, Woods guessed that the rambunctious Doug would probably have much in common with two others on the Triangle payroll, director John Emerson and scenarist Anita Loos. It was this precocious girl, still in her teens, who had the insight to realize that acrobatics were an extension of Doug's effervescent personality; if they continued to be written into his scenarios, he would develop into an immensely entertaining screen character. She was correct, for after *His Picture in the Papers*, Fairbanks's third Triangle picture, the public accepted him as a new kind of popular idol.

Fairbanks made thirteen pictures for Triangle. By the time his contract expired, Aitken was paying him the princely sum of $10,000 a week. With the exception of Doug, Aitken's high-priced stars were inglorious failures. He learned too late what Zukor had discovered at the outset of his Famous Players venture, that most actors trained for the stage could not communicate on the silent screen. Audiences stayed away from their pictures, and exhibitors refused to pay the high rentals Aitken had to ask to meet his astronomical payroll.

Sensing that Triangle was on the verge of collapse, Zukor moved to pluck its prize box-office attraction. He would help set up Doug as an independent producer and distribute his pictures under the Artcraft banner, just as he had done for Mary. No longer having qualms over making movies, Doug accepted. The Douglas Fairbanks Picture Corporation was formed at the end of 1916.

To perfect the formula developed at Triangle, Doug hired Emerson and Loos. They collaborated with him on four of the five pictures he made in

1917; in 1918 he made seven more pictures, all satires on contemporary mores. As Richard Griffith describes his output, "He spoofed Couéism, the new and growing octopus of publicity, psychoanalysis, social snobbery, pacifism, and practically anything else that came along to snatch the momentary interest of the American people."[10] By the time United Artists was formed, Douglas Fairbanks was idolized as "the ideal twentieth century American . . . a mentor, a model for growing boys, a homespun philosopher of the generation after Will Rogers."[11] He was also a millionaire.

D. W. Griffith

D. W. Griffith had the singular distinction of being the only director whose name above the title had greater drawing power than any actor in this star-crazed era. When his *The Birth of a Nation* was released in 1915, "the most important single film ever made was thus given to the public." Says Iris Barry in her appreciative essay for The Museum of Modern Art:

> The response was overwhelming: people had not realized they could be so moved by what, after all, is only a succession of photographs passed across the screen. All depends, they found, upon what is the order and manner of that passing. *The Birth of a Nation*, which had cost about $100,000 to make, grossed $18,000,000 in the next few years. Even more important, it established the motion picture once and for all as the most popular and persuasive of entertainments and compelled the acceptance of the film as art.[12]

Griffith had presented himself to Biograph as a scenario writer and actor in 1908 only because he was a thespian "at liberty." His new employment, which paid $5 a day, would be temporary, he hoped, until something, anything, became available for him in the theater. Griffith was soon asked to try his hand at directing. Biograph was in a precarious condition and needed more and better product to strengthen its competitive position. On the basis of his initial effort, *The Adventures of Dollie*, Griffith was given other movies to direct, and on August 17, 1908, he received a contract. His salary was $50 a week plus a commission of not less than $50 based on the footage he turned out. In his first year, Griffith directed 130 pictures; in his second, 100; and in his third, another 95. Biograph now owed its financial strength to Griffith's output, but his salary was still a ridiculously low $75 a week. Although royalties brought Griffith's income to about $3,000 a month, he was still essentially an employee.

For his fourth contract, Griffith insisted on receiving Biograph stock. The shrewd Jeremiah Kennedy refused and also turned down Griffith's request for 10 percent of the company's profits. By the end of 1912, Griffith had made 423 films. He complained about the commission arrangement;

nonetheless, as long as he could control his artistic destiny, he remained with the ungrateful Biograph.

But Biograph would not grant him that freedom. Griffith wanted to make longer films, even features, rather than the one-reelers that were Biograph's staple. Why tamper with success, he was told; one-reelers were earning handsome profits at the box office. Griffith replied that the length of the film should be determined by the requirements of the story rather than by arbitrary restrictions. Kennedy gave in only to the extent that if Griffith felt an urge to go over the one-reel limit, he would have to secure Kennedy's special permission.

For the first time, according to Robert Henderson, Griffith saw his directorial prerogatives threatened. "The freedom that he enjoyed at Biograph, the absolute control over his acting company, over the selection of stories to film, and the entire creation of his films, had led him to regard the Biograph executives as merely salesmen and paymasters. This assertion of administrative control was both frustrating and frightening to him."[13]

Griffith broke with Biograph in September 1913, to join Harry Aitken's Reliance-Majestic Company, which distributed through Mutual. Here, too, Griffith made program pictures, but Aitken gave him the independence of film making, including budgeting, that Biograph had denied him. Moreover, Griffith was given the opportunity of making two independent films a year. One of these was *The Birth of a Nation*. When Mutual's board of directors became increasingly distressed over the mounting costs of the picture, however, Aitken and Griffith ended up producing and distributing it on their own. Even so, after the profits from *Birth* were spread among its many investors, Griffith's cut was not as great as one might expect—about $1 million.

The sensational box-office returns of *Birth* did not vindicate Aitken in the eyes of Mutual's board, of which he was president. In a fit of jealousy, his associates ousted him from their ranks. Undaunted and riding high on the success of *Birth*, Aitken formed Triangle Film Corporation, taking with him Mutual's principal assets in the persons of Ince, Sennett, and Griffith.

Griffith soon became totally preoccupied with his most ambitious directorial project—the making of *Intolerance*. As each day this project grew in scope and expense, it began to tax even Aitken's ability as a money raiser. The result was that Griffith assumed control of the picture by forming his own companies to finance and distribute it. Griffith became the largest investor by pouring into the venture his profits from *The Birth of a Nation*; the fifty others who helped put up the $2 million for the production costs included Aitken and his brother, Roy, Lillian Gish, and Mae Marsh. *Intolerance*, as we know, became a *succès d'estime*; Griffith's prestige was enhanced, but his production venture was bankrupted.

Griffith switched to Zukor's Artcraft in 1917. Although the fate of *Intolerance* at the box office was yet to be determined, Griffith foresaw Triangle's downfall. His objective now was to own and control his own studios so that he could make his films without interference. Joining Artcraft was but a first step on the road to independence.

W. S. Hart

W. S. Hart, although in on the early planning stages of United Artists, decided that discretion was the better part of valor, and remained with Famous Players-Lasky rather than take the risks of going independent. Zukor helped him to reach this decision by offering him $200,000 per picture to stay put.

The confrontation

By 1919 an adjustment of industry conditions was clearly imminent. Richard A. Rowland, president of Metro Pictures, proclaimed that "motion pictures must cease to be a game and become a business." He wanted to supplant the star system. Metro, he said, would thenceforth decline from "competitive bidding for billion-dollar stars" and devote its energies to making big pictures based on "play value and excellence of production."[14]

Other moguls felt the same way. Production costs were rising rapidly. Negatives that before World War I cost $10,000 to $30,000 were now requiring expenditures of $50,000 to $100,000 and more. It was not just the salaries of the stars that were cutting into profits. Audiences had come to prefer feature-length pictures to the one- and two-reelers and wanted stories having more than rudimentary plots. More money was needed for plays, novels, and scenarios, for better sets and more expensive costumes. Nevertheless, the consensus in Hollywood, concurred in by supporting actors, was that too much of the gross was going to the star.

Rumors, conjectures, and guesswork about mergers filled the air: mergers that aimed to control the industry; mergers that spelled the death of the star system; mergers that eliminated the small fish of filmdom. At a convention of the First National Exhibitors Circuit in the Alexandria Hotel in Los Angeles in January 1919, A. H. Giebler of *Moving Picture World* surveyed the scene and said:

> Did Dave Griffith eat a little snack of lunch with Sam Goldwyn, a merger was seen in the offing. Did J. D. Williams stop Adolph Zukor in the lobby and say, "Dolph, this certainly beats New York for climate," the nucleus for a new combination was born.
>
> Did Winnie Sheehan shake hands with Hiram Abrams and ask him politely for news from Broadway, the name of William Fox was written large on the dope sheets . .
>
> Did those two mysterious strangers from the East, Hiram Abrams and Benny Schulberg, parade their slow and solemn way along the

length of the lobby, eyes were rolled in their direction and bated voices asked: "What have those two wise birds got up their sleeves?" . . . "The First National will control all the stars." "The First National is going to form a combination with Famous Players, Artcraft, Goldwyn, Metro, Fox, and after that they'll tell the stars just where to get off in the matter of salary."

"Doug has signed up with First National." "Doug has done no such of a thing." "Charlie's going to Europe. . . . Mary will renew her contract with First National." "Mary will not." "Mary may, but Charlie won't." "See me in the morning, and I'll give you the whole story." "Don't quote me, but here's the right dope . . ."

Thus it went on all day long, from getting up time until hay time— everywhere—all over the big hotel, upstairs and down, in parlor, bedroom and bath, lobby, grill, tearoom, candy shop and barber shop, until voices grew husky and imaginations were worn to a frazzle.[15]

The stars had reason to believe that something was afoot. Chaplin had gone before First National's board during the convention to request an increase in his production budget and had been turned down. He, Chaplin, who was earning millions for First National! He conferred with Mary Pickford and Douglas Fairbanks and found that although their contracts, with First National and Famous Players-Lasky, respectively, were about to run out, they were not receiving the customary offers from the big companies. They hired a private detective, who uncovered plans for a $40 million merger of all the producing companies, which would tie up every important exhibitor in the country in a five-year contract. The stars felt they had no choice but to form a company of their own.

The fears of the artists that a merger was brewing to deprive them of their bargaining power in the industry were subsequently borne out when the Federal Trade Commission in 1927 completed its investigation of Famous Players-Lasky for alleged infringement of antitrust laws. In one of its findings, the FTC stated that Adolph Zukor, in 1919, "endeavored to form a combination with First National by which the latter would produce no films, exhibit no films other than those produced by Famous Players-Lasky Corporation, and finally become subsidiary to, or merge with, Famous Players-Lasky Corporation."[16] The merger did not go through, as it turned out, but that did not stop Zukor. After failing to lure First National's officers to his company, he continued to struggle for control of the industry by attempting to acquire First National theater franchises. And this battle he won.

Even without this threat, the founding of United Artists was inevitable. A distribution company to market and exploit their pictures fully was but the next step for these artists in achieving autonomy over their work. Pickford, Chaplin, Fairbanks, and Griffith each started out as employees under contract. With star status came the right to form independent production units, which meant more artistic control and a share of the producer's profits. By becoming their own employers, they would now receive all the profits from their pictures. To be sure, they would have to provide their own financing, but a well-managed distribution company would certainly minimize risks.

Forming the company

The artists wanted William Gibbs McAdoo to head their company. His credentials included being head of the Federal Railroad Board during the war, Secretary of the Treasury before that, and son-in-law of President Wilson. Pickford, Fairbanks, and Chaplin had come to know McAdoo well during the Third Liberty Loan campaign when the three toured the country selling millions of dollars' worth of bonds to support the war effort.

McAdoo declined the offer, but suggested that if Oscar Price, his former assistant on the Railroad Board, were named instead, he would gladly serve as counsel for the company. This satisfied everyone; McAdoo, in the words of an editorial in *Moving Picture World*, would bring "prestige second to that of no other business man in the country. His association marks another step in the progress of the business side of the screen, and it goes without saying his voice will have large influence in many quarters where large influence sometimes is very necessary."[17] For a while, anyway, the skeptics would be silenced.

United Artists was formed on February 5, 1919, as a distribution company to promote, exploit, and market motion pictures. First and foremost, it was to provide the service of securing for its producers the highest revenues possible for their films.

This was a cooperative venture in every respect. To finance the company's operations—opening exchanges, hiring salesmen, and the like—each of the founders agreed to purchase $100,000 of preferred stock. In return for equal units of common stock, each agreed to deliver a minimum of nine pictures to the company. Griffith was required to direct his, and the others were to play the leading roles in theirs. McAdoo was issued a unit of stock in consideration of his becoming general counsel.

The common stock had cumulative voting power, enabling each of the stockholders to elect his own representative to the board of directors. Thus control of the management and policies of the company actually rested with the stockholders and not the directors. To prevent the company from slipping out of the hands of the owners, the company was given prior right to repurchase the common stock in the event that a stockholder wanted to sell his interest in UA to an outside party. To ensure complete equality among the parties, the stockholders were prevented from forming partnerships with each other. And to further stimulate the cooperative spirit of the venture and as a gesture of mutual trust, the owners decided to adopt an unwritten law stating that no proposal, policy, or decision could be effected without unanimous consent.

A key feature of the distribution contracts stipulated that each picture was to be sold and promoted individually. Block booking was out. In no way could one United Artists release be used to influence the sale of another UA picture. Merit alone would determine a picture's success or failure. The distribution fee was set at 20 percent of the gross in the United States and 30 percent elsewhere. If in the future the company gave one owner better terms, a "most favored nation" clause guaranteed similar adjustments in the other contracts. These fees were well below what Famous Players-Lasky and First National had been charging because United Artists was conceived of as a service organization rather than an investment that would return dividends. Profits would accrue to the owners as a result of the company's securing the best possible rentals for their pictures. With this in mind, the owners reserved the right to approve through their representatives in the home office all contracts with exhibitors.

On April 17, 1919, UA's certificate of incorporation was filed with the secretary of state of Delaware. The board of directors consisted of Albert Banzhaf, Nathan Burkan, Dennis O'Brien, Mrs. Charlotte Pickford, and Oscar Price, who represented the interests of Griffith, Chaplin, Fairbanks, Mary Pickford, and McAdoo, respectively. Price was named president; O'Brien, vice president; George B. Clifton, secretary and treasurer; and Hiram Abrams, the former president of Paramount, general manager.

UA's contribution to the industry

During the early years of UA's existence, its owners delivered some of the finest pictures of their careers. The première UA release was Douglas Fairbanks's *His Majesty, the American*, which was released on September 1, 1919. Fairbanks went on to produce such spectacular hits as *The Mark of Zorro* (1920), *The Three Musketeers* (1921), *Robin Hood* (1923), and *The Thief of Bagdad* (1924). Miss Pickford's best-remembered pictures were *Pollyanna* (1920), *Little Lord Fauntleroy* (1921), *Tess of the Storm Country* (1922), and *Rosita* (1923). Griffith delivered *Broken Blossoms* (1919), *Way Down East* (1921), and *Orphans of the Storm* (1922), among others. Chaplin came through with the influential *A Woman of Paris* (1923) and his acknowledged masterpiece, *The Gold Rush* (1925).

Despite this record of excellence, which earned for the company the reputation as the Tiffany of the industry, UA by 1924 was in a precarious position. The battle for the theaters was in full force. More and more of the country's most important houses were falling into the hands of a few giant concerns. These companies gave preference to their own product with the result that UA found it increasingly difficult to secure suitable exhibition outlets for its pictures. UA, moreover, faced a product crisis. It did not have the resources to finance motion pictures and could not lure other stars to go the route of independent production. An early demise for the company seemed imminent until Joseph M. Schenck was brought in as a partner and named chairman of the board.

Schenck had under contract his wife, Norma Talmadge; his sister-in-law, Constance Talmadge; and his brother-in-law, Buster Keaton. He also possessed the business acumen to stabilize the operations of the company. To solve the problem of acquiring the necessary pictures to sustain UA's operations, he formed the Art Cinema Corporation to finance and produce pictures for UA distribution. This company was owned by Schenck and his associates and was not a UA subsidiary. Art Cinema took over the Hollywood studio belonging to Pickford and Fairbanks, who were now husband and wife, named it the United Artists Studio, and went into production, delivering to UA over fifty pictures. Among them were *The Son of the Sheik* (1926), starring Rudolph Valentino; *The Beloved Rogue* (1927), starring John Barrymore; *Evangeline* (1929), starring Dolores Del Rio; and *DuBarry, Woman of Passion* (1930), starring Norma Talmadge. In addition, Schenck personally produced three Buster Keaton masterpieces, *The General* (1927), *College* (1927), and *Steamboat Bill, Jr.* (1928). To further ease the product crisis, Schenck brought in as UA partners Gloria Swanson in 1925, and Samuel Goldwyn in 1927.

To secure suitable exhibition outlets for UA's product, Schenck formed the United Artists Theatre Circuit in June 1926. This was a publicly held company, also separate from United Artists, whose purpose was to construct or acquire first-run theaters in the major metropolitan areas. This move forced the important theater chains to recognize UA as a forceful competitor with the result that these companies accommodated UA's pictures. The United Artists Theatre Circuit is still in existence today operating a nationwide chain of theaters.

Schenck wanted to bring the UA Studio, the independent production units, and the Theatre Circuit under one corporate umbrella, but his UA partners, Chaplin in particular, vetoed the idea. The thinking was that if UA became a fully integrated company involved in production, distribution, and exhibition, it would no longer foster independent production, but would adopt the mass-production techniques of the major studios. UA prided itself on the fact that independently produced pictures were handcrafted to reflect the specialized talents of their creators, as indeed they were, not always with success but at least with an imprint of individuality that set them apart from the majority of pictures produced under the studio system.

Schenck's reorganization made its impact in 1928. UA began the year with a $1 million deficit and ended it with a $1.6 million surplus. Its worldwide gross that year came to $20.5 million, $10 million more than the 1925 figure, when Schenck joined the company. Net profit for 1929 came to $1.3 million.

By 1932, UA had retired all of its preferred stock and accumulated a surplus of $2.5 million.

Despite the unsettling effects of the Depression, the motion picture industry by 1932 had stabilized. It had undergone a series of upheavals brought about by the battle for the theaters, the merger movement, and the sound revolution. The next sixteen years would be an era of oligopoly. Schenck's reorganization had created a niche in which United Artists could function successfully.

Notes

1 *Moving Picture World*, February 1, 1919, p. 619.
2 *Variety*, January 31, 1919, p. 58.
3 Arthur Mayer, "The Origins of United Artists," *Films in Review* 10 (1959): 390.
4 Benjamin B. Hampton, *A History of the Movies* (New York, 1931), p. 148.
5 Edward Wagenknecht, *The Movies in the Age of Innocence* (Norman, Okla., 1962), p. 190.
6 Hampton, *A History of the Movies*, p. 155.
7 *Variety*, November 1, 1918, p. 42.
8 *Variety*, October 1, 1915, p. 18.
9 Alistair Cooke, *Douglas Fairbanks: The Making of a Screen Character* (New York, 1940), p. 14.
10 Richard Griffith, *The Movie Stars* (Garden City, N.Y., 1970), p. 145.
11 Cooke, *Fairbanks*, pp. 20, 21.
12 Iris Barry, *D. W. Griffith: American Film Master* (New York, 1965), p. 20.
13 Robert Henderson, *D. W. Griffith: His Life and Work* (New York, 1972), p. 120.
14 *MPW*, January 4, 1919, p. 53.
15 *MPW*, February 1, 1919, pp. 607–8.
16 *In re* Famous Players-Lasky Corp., 11 F.T.C. 187 (1927).
17 *MPW*, February 15, 1919, p. 899.

4

WILLIAM FOX PRESENTS *SUNRISE*

Robert C. Allen

Source: *Quarterly Review of Film Studies* 2(2) (1977): 327–338.

To the film historian few films are more conspicuously extraordinary than *Sunrise*. Its synchronous musical and effects track makes it a curious techno-logical hybrid. It incorporates the efforts of, respectively, the most famous writer, director, and designer of the German "Golden Age," yet was made in Hollywood. Produced within the studio system, the *Sunrise* project was nevertheless given attention and freedom which, if not unique, were certainly highly unusual. Indeed, it is tempting to consider *Sunrise* that most fortunate of accidents, one of the few of many Hollywood extravagances which, more through happenstance than foresight, turned out to be a work of lasting cinematic art. But one sells short the historical importance of *Sunrise* if one attributes the fact of the film's production to the inexplicable whims of a movie mogul or simply to chance. As J. Douglas Gomery points out in his study of the innovation of sound in the American film industry, there was much more business planning and much less caprice at the highest levels of Hollywood during its heyday than we are generally led to believe.

It is the thesis of this paper that *Sunrise* can be viewed as an integral part of one of the most carefully orchestrated and ambitious bids for power and prestige in the history of the American cinema, and that in large measure *Sunrise*'s historical significance is to be found in its relation to other Fox films that were equally part of William Fox's truly grandiose scheme to con-trol the movie industry.

Production planning

Of central importance to a historical understanding of any film made within the Hollywood studio system is a basic knowledge of studio production strategies. Hollywood executives, like television programmers of today, rarely thought in terms of a single work; each film was one component of a total schedule, each production a fraction of a yearly budget.

93

The Hollywood studio of the late 1920s still organized its year around the old theatrical season, beginning in September and lasting through the spring. Production planning began in the winter, with the schedule for the coming season usually finalized by March or April. The production executive staff would begin with a production budget (based on the success of the previous year and a forecast of market conditions), breaking it down into allocations for productions or groups of productions according to properties on hand, stars, and genres.[1]

The Universal production schedule for 1927–28, for example, divided a $15,000,000 production budget among sixty-six feature films, five serials, assorted shorts, and weekly newsreels, with one-third of the amount going to the nonfeature categories. The breakdown within the feature program was divided among eleven "specials," thirty-three "features," and twenty-two "thrill dramas." The specials were the prestige pictures of Universal. The particular designation of this category changed from studio to studio (Paramount, for example, called them "New World Specials"), but the category remained the same for all the major studios. Specials (using the term to signify the most expensive productions of any studio) were often based on properties with a high public-recognition factor. Among the Universal specials for 1927–28 were five popular novels and two current plays. These films also featured the studio's biggest stars and highest paid directors and were the most expensive productions in the schedule. Next came the features which were the backbone of a studio's release schedule, utilizing contract players and directors and relying upon less expensive properties: short fiction from popular magazines and original stories contributed by the studio writing staff. The thrill dramas were the cheapest category to produce and often included the bulk of the studio's western films—in the case of Universal, a genre which composed 45 percent of the studio's total output.[2]

Following initial specification of property, star, and budget, a film would be turned over to a production executive, the actual supervisor of the project. Naturally, the studio production manager or chief production executive reserved the most important productions for himself, with those at the other end of the hierarchy being given the task of cranking out seven Hoot Gibson westerns. While the major Hollywood studios (Paramount, MGM, Fox, Universal, Warner Brothers, Producer's Distributing Organization, First National) were each producing thirty-five to seventy films annually at this time, it was the top one-fifth of their feature output—the specials—which received a lion's share of the budget allocation, attention, and advertising.

The most special of the specials would be released first as road-shows: long-term engagements at a few key theatres in large cities at top prices ($1 to $2). The Cathay Circle Theatre in Los Angeles, for example, ran only four pictures during 1927: *What Price Glory, Seventh Heaven, The Loves of Carmen,* and *Sunrise.* In New York, at the Astor Theatre, *The Big Parade* ran from January 1 to September 17.[3] Other specials, features, and thrill dramas would open in first-run theatres in large cities and then move down through the exhibition system into smaller cities and towns and subsequent runs.

It is important to keep this production hierarchy in mind in considering the place of *Sunrise* in Fox's plans, for it was the special category, the most prestigious of productions, which Fox most wanted to develop—the category into which *Sunrise* certainly falls.

Fox's position in Hollywood

In one sense William Fox is the archetypal Hollywood success: the poor son of Jewish immigrants who, through hard work and shrewd business practices, clawed his way to the top of the motion picture industry, amassing a huge personal fortune in the process. Fox's struggle is further characterized by his almost superhuman tenacity in the face of seemingly insuperable obstacles. Fox's first venture into show business came around 1905, when he was tricked into investing some $1,600, which he had saved from years of menial labor, in what he was led to believe was a prospering nickelodeon in Brooklyn but which was actually a financial disaster. Despite this most inauspicious beginning, Fox was able to build a chain of twelve vaudeville/ film theatres by 1910 and initiate his own film distribution concern. It was in January of that year that the Motion Picture Patents Company attempted to extend the near monopoly control that it had over film production to include distribution as well. Fox was the only distributor to hold out against the enormous power of the industry trust, resisting all attempts to buy and coerce him out of business. For several years he survived only through the action of a court order that forced the Motion Picture Patents Company to supply his theatres with film until his legal action against them was settled. Fox and the other independents eventually won out legally and economically against the trust, and in 1913 he added film production to his distribution and exhibition activities with the formation of Box Office Attractions.[4]

The early 1920s were, in the words of a 1930 *Fortune* article, "a time of gradual but unbroken progress which had brought Mr. Fox to a prominent, but by no means dominating position." Fox films, the article goes on to say, were "not considered of major importance," but were popular and profitable.[5] This characterization is echoed by Glendon Allvine. Fox's chief publicist in the late 1920s. The Fox output, he says, was "a steady flow of unpretentious, sentimental and folksy pictures . . . without the reaching for art and biography that occasionally varied the menu at Paramount and Warner Brothers."[6]

By 1925 Fox occupied, along with First National and Warner Bros., a middle echelon within the film industry in terms of both economic power and product prestige. In both categories Hollywood was presided over by Paramount and MGM. These were the largest and most fully vertically integrated film companies, controlling not only the production and distribution of their products but exhibition as well through the hundreds of theatres in their Publix and Loew's chains. Fox, like Warner Bros. and Universal, owned few theatres in 1925. In terms of working capital, Fox was a distant third behind MGM and Paramount—his rivals had resources of $38,000,000 and $20,000,000, respectively, while Fox had $13,000,000.[7]

Product prestige can be thought of as the extent to which the films of a studio are perceived to be of "quality" by contemporary molders of public opinion about films—commentators and critics in the trade and the general press. In determining the Fox prestige factor I have examined the annual critical poll taken by the *Film Daily Yearbook* of trade paper and newspaper film critics, a total in 1925 of 104 "best films" lists. I also consulted *Photoplay*, the most influential of the fan magazines in the late 1920s, for its monthly designation of the six best films released. In 1925, the first year of *Film Daily*'s poll, of 112 films mentioned by 104 critics, only seven were Fox productions, the highest rated being John Ford's *The Iron Horse*, which was the fourteenth most often mentioned film. It was the only Fox film to be listed by more than two critics.[8] Similarly, of the seventy-two pictures singled out by *Photoplay* in 1925, only two were Fox efforts. In both lists the films of Paramount and MGM predominate.

Parenthetically, it might be noted that there is a negative correlation between heavy emphasis on thrill drama productions and studio prestige. Universal, few of whose films were praised by critics in either source, devoted 44 percent of its production schedule to Westerns alone, while MGM's Westerns output made up only 10 percent of its releases. Fox, once again, fits neatly in the middle, with 27 percent of its release schedule composed of Westerns (mostly Tom Mix and Buck Jones).

Also, Paramount and MGM were the first of the Hollywood studios to import foreign directors and producers, particularly from Germany. In 1926, for example, MGM had under contract Victor Seastrom, Benjamin Christensen, Ludwig Berger, Marcel Del Sano, and Dmitri Buchowetzi. Paramount had hired Mauritz Stiller, German producer Erich Pommer, and Europe's hottest directorial property, E. A. Dupont, whose *Variety* was a critical and financial success in the United States. Even Universal had Paul Leni. The only foreign flavor in the Fox lineup was the release of a few films directed by Alexander Korda in Germany under contract to Fox. While I am not suggesting a causal relationship between the use of foreign talent and the critical success of a studio's output, a positive correlation does exist. The relative scarcity of Westerns among the productions of Paramount and MGM combined with their importation of "artistic" foreign talent does point to an emphasis on the "special" class of productions—the category, of course, critics would be most likely to focus upon.

The Fox move: 1925–29

Although the precise date is difficult to determine, we can say that one of the greatest expansion plans in the history of the motion picture industry was launched around June 1925. It was then that Fox Film Co. underwent reorganization, issuing common stock for the first time. In all, $6,600,000 of common stock was sold, giving William Fox the necessary capital to set up the Fox Theatre Corp. with the goal of building thirty first-run theatres of 4,000 to 5,000 seats each in key cities. A total investment of $200,000,000 was projected for theatre acquisition and construction over a four-year period.[9] These theatres would give Fox access to the crucial key markets he had not been able to control in the past and would put him in a more competitive position with Paramount and MGM. The Fox move into exhibition was stepped up in 1926–27 as he began to purchase theatres by the chain. *Moving Picture World* for April 2, 1927, announced the purchase by Fox of the premiere American picture palace, the Roxy. This acquisition on Broadway and the purchase of other Roxy theatres in the New York area was referred to in an editorial as giving Fox "a commanding position in the increasingly competitive warfare, which is the outstanding feature of this period of the film industry's development."[10] In 1927–28 Fox acquired the Poli circuit of twenty major theatres in New England, the Wesco chain of 216 theatres, one-third interest in First National Theatres, and an additional 313 theatres in New York, New Jersey, and Ohio.[11]

In 1925–26 Fox became interested in the possibilities of sound motion pictures. He supported the experiments of his engineer, Theodore Case, bought for $60,000 the rights to the Tri-Ergon sound process, and negotiated with Western Electric for the rights to its Vitaphone process.[12] In 1926 he launched the Fox Movietone News. He lost $3,000,000 for the first five years of its existence, but during this time Fox Movietone moved "so far ahead of the four other newsreels that they never caught up."[13]

At the same time, Fox production facilities were upgraded. In January 1926, Winfield Sheehan, Fox's associate since 1913, arrived in Hollywood to supervise a studio expansion program which would cost $3,000,000 and take one year to complete.[14]

Fox was certainly not alone in expansion during the late 1920s. Warner Bros. acquired the Vitagraph studios and foreign distribution network in 1925, began to buy and build theatres, and invested in the Western Electric sound process. Paramount and MGM also acquired more theatres. But the Fox move was the most dramatic of any studio expansion effort. By the end of 1928 Fox had "risen to a position of prominence among the Big Four of Cinema."[15] His greatest coup was yet to come, however. On March 3, 1929, he bought, at above market price, one-third interest in Loews Inc. (443,000 shares), paying a total of $50,000,000. On the open market he acquired 227,000 additional shares, giving him 53 percent interest in the company.

He also purchased control of British Gaumont, valuable for its distribution system and chain of important theatres in the United Kingdom. For a fleeting moment Fox was the most important and powerful film magnate in the world, controlling the production of Fox and MGM studios, Loew's Theatres, Fox's own large chain, one-third interest in First National Theatres (and its production subsidiary), British Gaumont, and assorted other holdings. The stock market crash, demands for margin payments from his bankers, and a November 1927 lawsuit against Fox for restraint of trade shattered Fox's dream. After a decade of near bankruptcy, congressional hearings, and cutthroat financial involvements, Fox wound up at Moyamensing Prison in Pennsylvania, serving a sentence of one year and a day for attempted bribery.[16]

The Fox drive for economic power in the late 1920s was paralleled by attempts to enhance the prestige of Fox productions. The first evidence of a move away from the unpretentious drama and comedy which had characterized Fox output came in the fall of 1925, when it was announced that Fox was arranging with a number of Broadway producers to finance plays with strong movie potential. For years the successful stage play had been "the most coveted of story properties to the motion picture industry." Here was a ready-made story with proven dramatic appeal and with considerable public recognition, the latter due to the advertising given a Broadway play and its usual road tours. But as the demand for successful stage properties increased during the 1920s, so did their price. *Ben Hur*, originally produced in 1899, was sold to the screen in 1921 for $1,000,000. As early as 1919, film companies began to move into theatrical finance. In return for production funds, the film company would receive the screen rights to the play.[17]

In 1925 Fox spent $150,000 in theatrical finance (a straight play could still be produced for under $10,000), a level of Hollywood involvement in Broadway which "alarmed" several observers of the American stage.[18] Fox's scheme to corner the market for film rights to Broadway successes was undone, however, in April 1926. An agreement was made between Broadway producers and playwrights that forbade film producers from securing screen rights before production of the play and required that all rights be granted on a sealed bid system, with no preference being given to the backer of the play. Fox left theatrical production after one season, the economic motivation for his move now gone.[19] But this abortive move did not by any means mark the end of Fox's attempt to bolster his special productions through the acquisition of successful stage vehicles. The January 2, 1926, issue of *Moving Picture World* contained an advertisement which set the tone for the 1926–27 Fox production plans: "For release in the new season, starting September 1926, Fox takes another great step forward through the production of the world's best stage plays and popular novels of high screen value."[20] Among the fifteen "Fox Giant Specials" for 1926–27 were four David Belasco plays (*The Auctioneer, Return of Peter Grimm, The Grand Army Man,* and *The*

Music Master); *The Cradle Snatchers*, a Broadway comedy which ran for 338 performances in 1926; *The Monkey Talks*, a stage success in London and Paris; and *What Price Glory?* the 1924 smash Broadway hit for which Fox paid $100,000.[21] In all, nine of the fifteen Fox prestige pictures for 1926–27 were adaptations of stage plays. Two others were based on novels, and the remaining four were based on short stories or were written by the Fox staff. Thus, by 1926 the strategy for the upgrading of Fox specials had begun to emerge: acquire successes in other media—stage hits, best-selling novels, etc.—rather than relying upon stars (as MGM was doing) or hiring big-name writers.

Concomitant with a new emphasis on the "Giant Specials" was a decline in importance to the Fox lineup of its "Super Westerns." As the following table shows, the portion of the Fox schedule given over to Westerns was reduced by half between 1924 and 1928.

Westerns as Percentage of Annual Output

1924	35%
1925	29%
1926	29%
1927	27%
1928	18%

In 1926 the Fox strategy began paying off. Whereas the previous year's productions had been all but ignored by critics, the 1926–27 specials fared much better, especially the stage adaptations. *What Price Glory? The Music Master, The Monkey Talks, A Holy Terror*, and *The Cradle Snatchers*, all based on Broadway hits, were among *Photoplay*'s best films of the month.

The flagship production of the 1926–27 season was *What Price Glory?* the film against which future Fox productions would be measured. Fox paid $100,000 for the rights to film *What Price Glory?* guarding its investment by having Winfield Sheehan supervise its production.[22] While *What Price Glory?* was still under production in the winter of 1926, plans were being made for the next two Fox "Giant Specials": *Seventh Heaven* and *Sunrise*. In the January 2, 1926, issue of *Moving Picture World*, Fox announced that F. W. Murnau had been hired to direct several films in Hollywood for the studio. Fox publicists attempted to depict the relationship between Fox and Murnau as one of patron/artist rather than employer/employee. Murnau had been brought to America to enable him "to put . . . subjective thought on the screen, to open up the mind, the heart, the soul."[23] Fox's decision to hire Murnau clearly indicated that he wanted the Fox Film Company to be not only the most powerful studio in Hollywood, but also the most prestigious. Fox had not merely imported another German director; he had brought to America the man he believed to be "the genius of this age," the director who, in *The Last Laugh*, had made "the greatest motion picture of all time."[24] At a gala banquet honoring "Dr. Murnau" on the eve of his journey from New York to Hollywood in July, William Fox spoke to the assembled diplomats, socialites, and literati of "the growth, by mass and class, of the entertaining power of the screen." The *Moving Picture World* correspondent covering the event remarked of Fox: "It was a proud night for him. He realizes the move on which he is embarking will have a tremendous influence on pictures as an international art."[25]

The financial and artistic freedom Murnau was given in the production of *Sunrise* indicates that Fox wanted him to make "the highly artistic picture." An editorial in *Moving Picture World* describes this genre as follows:

> Often these are made with the advance realization that their making will not be followed by a great financial return. They are made with the hope that they may gross their costs or at least represent but a small loss. They are made to satisfy the comparatively limited number who appreciate the best, and produced in the hope that they will help to give tone to the general product through satisfying the minority demand.[26]

The "highly artistic picture" served several functions for the studios. First, as the editorial points out, it was an appeal to a sophisticated minority audience. Producers were, no doubt, also sensitive to charges (particularly prevalent since the Hollywood moral scandals of 1921–23) that they were pandering to the lowest of human instincts and that the Hollywood product was nothing but pap for the masses. These prestige pictures could be trotted out by the studios as evidence that in addition to providing the populace with entertainment, they were also patrons of the highest cinematic art. There was also value in attracting critical attention to these films—giving the studio publicity which, it was hoped, would rub off on the rest of the schedule.

In May of 1927, as Fox was announcing its 1927–28 lineup, *Seventh Heaven* premiered at the Cathay Circle Theatre in Los Angeles, replacing *What Price Glory?* which had played there since November. *Seventh Heaven* followed the same formula as its predecessor. It was based on a successful stage play (704 performances on Broadway), was personally supervised by Winfield Sheehan, and was given an "unusually strong preliminary campaign." In April "Eloise," the French taxi used in the film, was driven to Chicago by a French war hero as an advertising stunt.[27] As with *What Price Glory?* much was made of the high production values of *Seventh Heaven*. A week before its premiere an article in *Moving Pictures World* announced that the film had cost $1.3 million and had taken a year to complete.[28] The next week this same trade paper predicted that *Seventh Heaven* would prove to be a popular as well as a critical success, saying the film "should make a wonderful record for itself" in the big cities *and* should do equally as well in "the lesser houses."[29]

This prophecy was indeed accurate, and with the success of *Seventh Heaven* Fox's bid for prestige began to be taken seriously. The lead article of the Hollywood section of *Moving Picture World* for May 14 notes "One does not have to travel very far in these parts to hear that not only is Fox product completed out here during the past six months many times better than it ever has been, but that Fox artistry and quality are second to no contemporary." And on June 18, in reviewing the progress of the new season's program, *Moving Picture World* says, "Recent Fox product has been surprisingly good."[30]

The situation, then, in the summer of 1927—the eve of *Sunrise*'s debut—is that Fox had attracted considerable notice both among critics and within the movie industry as a result of his effort to bolster his special productions. This attention had been directed at two films, *Seventh Heaven* and *What Price Glory?* Both were high-budget, carefully produced adaptations of successful plays—skillful, though in no way "artsy" vehicles which appealed both to cosmopolitan patrons of big city palaces (and hence to reviewers) and to rural audiences. In the midst of the production and release of these two films, Fox had brought to the United States the director he called the greatest in the world and given him carte blanche for his first American effort. E. Winthrop Sargent of *Moving Picture World* asked in July, "What's going to happen at the Fox offices after the release of *Seventh Heaven?*" After the release of *What Price Glory?* the Fox publicists had said, "Wait til you see *Seventh Heaven*." Now, Sargent said, the industry waits to see *Sunrise*—a film which, he suggested, would "have to do a powerful lot of running to outstrip *Seventh Heaven*."[31]

Anticipation began to build in March 1927 when it was announced that *Sunrise* was being titled and edited. On March 5, the Hollywood columns of *Moving Picture World* noted that "Reports and photographs filtering through from Hollywood indicate that the distinguished German director has created an unusual picture." The article gives the term "unusual" a favorable connotation by adding that John Ford, then a contract director with Fox, had declared *Sunrise* to be the greatest picture ever produced on the basis of the rushes he had seen.[32] But given the pattern of success established by *What Price Glory?* and *Seventh Heaven*, speculation began to mount that *Sunrise* might prove to be too unusual. The prospect troubled William Fox enough to cause him to issue a statement in August, one month before the premiere of *Sunrise*, denying rumors that the film was in any way bizarre or that Murnau had been unnecessarily extravagant in its production. This apologia was necessary, said Fox, "because of the exotic and sometimes freakish character of the majority of foreign films which have been shown in this country." As if to try to squeeze *Sunrise* into the Fox prestige film mold of stage and literary adaptations, Fox reminded his exhibitor-readers in *Moving Picture World* that *Sunrise* was based on Sudermann's "well-known story."[33]

Fox's statement raises the possibility that he was responding to a backlash against German films developing immediately prior to the release of *Sunrise*. In April, E. Winthrop Sargent had chastised critics who seemed to think "nothing is good, unless it be a handful of UFA's." Seven months later James Quirk, the editor of *Photoplay*, derided the "pseudo-intellectuals" who reserved their praise for foreign works while dismissing American films.[34] It is interesting to note in this regard that while Murnau's *The Last Laugh* (released in the United States in 1925) and his *Faust* (1926) were prominent among films on "ten-best" lists, *Tartuffe*, which preceded *Sunrise* by less than one month onto Broadway, is noticeably absent. *Moving Picture World* in its review of *Tartuffe* said UFA had released it in the United States "apparently for the reason that it stars Emil Jannings, for the picture itself neither measures up to the better American production standards, nor is it a type of story that appeals to the average patron in this country."[35]

The bad omen of *Tartuffe*, rumors of *Sunrise*'s "unusual" qualities, and, most important, the fact that it failed to follow the formula of *Seventh Heaven* and *What Price Glory?* in combining prestige production values with "appeal to the average patron" made *Sunrise* appear to be more of a failure to Fox than a success. Compared to the great amount of publicity given the reception of *What Price Glory?* and *Seventh Heaven*, the premieres of *Sunrise* passed almost unnoticed in the trade press. Sargent mentions the Broadway premiere only to say that the audience applauded at the Movietone newsreel of Mussolini. In October, while *The Jazz Singer* was in its second record-breaking week on Broadway, *Seventh Heaven* doing well in its third Broadway run, *Wings* drawing standing-room-only crowds in its tenth week, and *King of Kings* in its twenty-sixth week, *Moving Picture World* reported that "Thus far the Fox talking device [Movietone News] is the drag for *Sunrise*, which is supposed to be a great film, and probably is to some audiences."[36]

Sunrise and *Seventh Heaven/What Price Glory?* represent alternative routes to the prestige William Fox so dearly sought in the late 1920s: the art film, the daring stylistic tour de force, and the less ambitious though well-produced adaptation of successful theatrical and literary works. The former did not even give Fox the satisfaction of unanimous critical acclaim. The latter combined critical and commercial success. By December 1927 it was clear which path Fox had chosen. A *Moving Picture World* editorial says "From the coast comes word that Fox is going right along turning out products like *What Price Glory?* and *Seventh Heaven*." The piece describes Fox as "one of the comparatively few far-visioned men in positions such as his."[37] Far visioned, yes; a philanthropist, no.

Notes

1 "Paramount/Famous Players Lasky Corporation," *Harvard Business Reports*, 8, 1929, 182–200.

2 *Moving Picture World*, March 26, 1926, 376.
3 *The Film Daily 1928 Yearbook*, p. 844.
4 Glendon Allvine, *The Greatest Fox of Them All* (New York: Lyle Stuart, 1969), pp. 35–45.
5 "The Case of Mr. Fox," *Fortune* May 1930, 49.
6 Allvine, *The Greatest Fox*, p. 38.
7 *The Film Daily 1926 Yearbook*.
8 *The Film Daily 1926 Yearbook*, pp. 31, 417–25.
9 *The Film Daily 1927 Yearbook*, p. 741; 1928, p. 810.
10 *Moving Picture World*, April 2, 1927, 267.
11 "The Case of Mr. Fox," *Fortune* May 1930, 49.
12 Allvine, *The Greatest Fox*, p. 12.
13 Ibid., pp. 105–12.
14 *Moving Picture World*, June 25, 1927, 589.
15 "The Case of Mr. Fox," p. 49.
16 Allvine, *The Greatest Fox*, p. 157.
17 Robert McLaughlin, *Broadway and Hollywood* (New York: Arno Press, 1974), pp. 52–59.
18 Ibid., p. 67.
19 Ibid., p. 80.
20 *Moving Picture World*, January 2, 1926, 5.
21 McLaughlin, *Broadway and Hollywood*, p. 56.
22 *Moving Picture World*, April 3, 1926, 332.
23 *Moving Picture World*, January 2, 1926, 69.
24 Allvine, *The Greatest Fox*, p. 98.
25 *Moving Picture World*, July 17, 1926, 151.
26 *Moving Picture World*, April 23, 1927, 719.
27 *Moving Picture World*, May 7, 1927, 36; April 23, 1927, 734.
28 *Moving Picture World*, May 21, 1927, 192.
29 *Moving Picture World*, May 28, 1927, 289.
30 *Moving Picture World*, May 14, 1927, 92; June 18, 499.
31 *Moving Picture World*, July 23, 1927, 244.
32 *Moving Picture World*, March 5, 1927, 35.
33 *Moving Picture World*, August 6, 1927, 402.
34 *Photoplay*, November 1927, 27.
35 *Moving Picture World*, September 3, 1927, 50.
36 *Moving Picture World*, October 1, 1927; October 22, 503.
37 *Moving Picture World*, December 24, 1927, 7.

Part 2

THE CLASSICAL HOLLYWOOD ERA

5

THE HOLLYWOOD STUDIO
SYSTEM, 1930–49

Douglas Gomery

Source: Douglas Gomery, *The Hollywood Studio System*, New York: St Martin's Press, 1986, pp. 1–25.

The American film industry – Hollywood in the common parlance – has long been one of the most visible institutions in the United States, indeed the world. Before the coming of television to the US in the 1950s, no industry received more publicity. Newspapers, magazines, and radio alike continually spilled forth gossip, reviews, and advertisements. Specialized fan magazines lined news-stands. Movie houses stood in every downtown, from New York City to Augusta, Kansas to Los Angeles. But despite this presence, precious little was actually known about the handful of companies which created and marketed nearly all available feature films, newsreels, and short-subjects. Even today, with libraries brimming with surveys of film history and special-ized film journals, our accumulated knowledge of these giant corporations hardly fills one bookshelf. There are understandable reasons for this. Study of the film industry requires complex frameworks for analysis, and seemingly endless interpretations of complicated data. Economists have had a hard time with the movie business because products seem so ephemeral, not quite a manufactured good, but not a traditional service either.

In one sense the American film industry has always been like other indus-tries. All have had a common goal: making the highest possible profits. Since the turn into the twentieth century, the US film industry has striven for profits from the production, distribution and exhibition of films. Production companies create the films. Rightly, Hollywood has come to symbolize this particular industrial arena, with its cavernous sound stages, multi-acre lots and secret special-effects. The distributor wholesales films from a producer to an exhibitor. Exhibitors, in turn, present the films to paying customers. Specifically, they trade entertainment for money. In the studio era, exhibitors traded shows (in elaborately decorated, air-conditioned surroundings) for

107

fees ranging from 10¢ to $2.00. The film industry, then as now, was a collection of producers, distributors and exhibitors, all trying to make as much money as possible.

The fundamental point for understanding the studio era is that there were only eight corporations which dominated the three functions. Control of an industry by a small number of firms is termed an oligopoly (literally, control by a few). During the first three decades of the twentieth century, the American film industry evolved a complicated system for handling film production, distribution, and exhibition. This particular system guaranteed its major participants enormous profits, while maintaining effective barriers to keep potential competitors out. The so-called majors, Paramount Pictures, Loew's Inc. (parent company of its more famous production subsidiary Metro-Goldwyn-Mayer or MGM), 20th Century-Fox, Warner Bros. and Radio-Keith-Orpheum (RKO), fully integrated production, distribution and exhibition. Universal and Columbia concentrated on production and distribution. United Artists only handled distribution for independent producers, but for a time, like Universal, was affiliated with a small chain of theaters.

These eight corporations controlled the American motion picture industry throughout the 1930s and 1940s. Whether measured by volume of business, cost of films produced, or amount of invested capital, corporations aside from the aforementioned eight pale into insignificance. There were others; for example, Disney, Monogram and Republic were noted producers, but though the last two did own nationwide distribution networks, they were unable to seize a sizeable portion of the market. Instead they had to be satisfied with low returns available in specialized markets: Disney in animated shorts and features, and Monogram and Republic in cheap westerns and serials.

But it was not Hollywood production which provided the majors with the fundamental source of their power. Rather, their wordwide distribution networks afforded them enormous cost advantages, and their theater circuits provided them direct access to the box office. The five fully-integrated majors (Paramount, Loew's, Fox, Warners and RKO) did not own all the theaters in the United States, only the ones which consistently delivered three-quarters of the revenues. Affiliated theaters received the most popular films first, and for exclusive runs in any community or neighbourhood of a large city. By owning these 2600 first-run theaters (16 per cent of the total) the five fully-integrated majors skimmed off the bulk of movie revenues, allowing rivals only what was left over.

The rise of the studio system

Oligopoly control through ownership of production, distribution and exhibition represented the full-grown Hollywood studio system. This system was so profitable that throughout the studio era members were continually being sued for violation of anti-trust laws. Success, however, did not come over-night. [It took thirty years for a fairly competitive industry to turn into a tightly-held trust.] A projected motion picture show was first commercially exhibited in 1896. This initial exchange of money for filmed entertainment gave rise to an industry quite different from the studio system of the 1930s and 1940s. Even with certain corporations vying for control of basic patents, a relatively competitive situation prevailed. For the first dozen years of this new industry, it was easy to go into (and out of) business. Films, treated more or less as a novelty, were sold by the foot. There were lots of small producers. Historians have concentrated on those which survived (Biograph or Vitagraph, for example) but the records show there were hundreds, possibly thousands, of others. A like number of distributors – operating in a large city and its surrounding environs – and exhibitors also flourished. Numerous biographies of famous executives tell how easy it was to enter the industry. For example, Marcus Loew and the brothers Warner began as exhibitors and went on to give their names to two of Hollywood's five majors. Neither patent problems nor cost mounted significant long-run barriers to entry in any sector. Profits accumulated rapidly. It was the era in which to try to break into the movie business. It has not been as easy since.

This period of relative competition did not last into the second decade of the century. In 1908, ten leading equipment manufacturers banded together to form the Motion Picture Patents Company (hereafter MPPC). As a cartel, the MPPC tried to use its monopoly over equipment to extort fees from producers and exhibitors. To extract additional revenues the MPPC in 1910 formed its own distribution arm, the General Film Company. This corpor-ation, the first nationwide distributor in the United States, actively sought to acquire (or drive out of business) all possible competitors. In 1910 it looked as if one fully-integrated motion picture corporation could control filmed entertainment in the USA. But the embryonic monopoly failed. As with many other cartels, certain members, thinking they could make more profits, broke with MPPC policies. The US federal government initiated a suit for anti-trust violations. Independents flooded into the market. Scores of films from Europe – Denmark and Italy in particular – appeared on US screens. By 1914 the MPPC was finished as a formidable economic force.

As the MPPC floundered, other film industry enterprises, epitomized by Famous Players-Lasky (later Paramount), innovated a more flexible way to dominate the US movie industry. This three-part strategy enabled this one company, by 1921, to dominate as no company ever had or would. Famous Players secured its position by (i) differentiating its products, (ii) distributing on a national, then international level, and (iii) dominating exhibition through ownership of a small number of first-run theaters. Famous Players' executives did not think up the complete strategy in one day. Rather, as soon as they perceived a successful business technique, from one source or another, they took up that tool. Competitors imitated Famous Players' ploys.

In the end, Famous Players achieved the most power, not always by being first, but by being forceful enough to mold a system, and then wring out all possible extra profits.

For production, Famous Players differentiated its films using stars. Gone were the days of films being sold by the foot. Each motion picture became a unique good. Early producers (including the MPPC) did not exploit actors' and actresses' images. In contrast, Famous Players heralded certain players who seemed to guarantee high box office revenues. One of the most successful was Mary Pickford, a 'superstar' to her adoring fans, who ascended the salary ladder from $100 per week to $15,000 per week in less than one decade. By 1920, Famous Players (and its competitors) had regularized the issuance of features with stars. Famous Players, true to its name, raided the legitimate stage for potential 'kings and queens' of the screen. Other studios attempted to create indigenous stars by testing potential luminaries in cheaper productions or shorts. Studios linked stars to exclusive, long-run contracts so that the player could not seek a higher salary from a rival company. Fans may not have known they were going to see a Famous Players' product, but they would stand in line for hours to see a vehicle with Mary Pickford or Douglas Fairbanks, two of the studio's most popular attractions.

The second aspect of Famous Players' strategy focussed on national, and later, worldwide distribution. Any time operations in any business reach a certain threshold, costs level off and begin to fall. Adam Smith, the founder of modern economics, outlined more than three hundred years ago the cost savings from division and specialization of labor. In movie distribution there were savings through division and specialization in advertising, sales promotion, and service. During and immediately after the First World War, Famous Players extended its sales territory to include the entire world. By 1925 its far-reaching sales network was firmly in place, and few possible entrants into the movie business had the resources to challenge Famous Players. Only the eight oligopolists were able to construct effective world distribution networks.

Finally, Famous Players learned that it need not own all movie theaters to gain a measure of economic power in exhibition. By owning first- and some second-run picture palaces in major metropolitan areas, it could gather in the bulk of film revenue in any single region. By 1930, Famous Players (now renamed Paramount) controlled over 1000 houses, with more than two million patrons per week.

The coming of sound did not alter the fundamental strategy pioneered by Famous Players. 'Talkies' seemed to come overnight, but speed of transformation should not be taken for chaos or confusion. Warner Bros. and Fox pioneered the conversion. All corporations eventually changed over so that by 1930 the US movie industry produced sound, not silent films. Movie-going audiences of the late 1920s flocked to the new talkies. The profits of the major companies soared. The larger companies and successful innovators used their profits to buy out competitors. Warners, needing theaters, took over First National in 1929. (In 1925, Warners' assets totalled $5 million; in 1930 they topped $230 million.) Fox for a time acquired a controlling interest in Loew's. The Radio Corporation of America created a new, fully integrated firm, Radio-Keith-Orpheum (RKO). There was talk and almost agreement of a Paramount merger with Warners during the fall of 1929, but the US Department of Justice squelched the deal. So the Big Five (temporarily the Big Four) were set: Paramount, Warner Bros, RKO and Fox-Loew's. Universal and Columbia did well enough to stride into the 1930s, though well behind their rivals. United Artists, the third member of the Little Three (with Universal and Columbia) occupied a special niche in the market-place, the distribution of features for independent producers.

The coming of sound did create one new corporation, the fifth member of the Big Five, Radio-Keith-Orpheum (RKO). This firm emerged from the Radio Corporation of America's interest in talkies. In 1919, General Electric and Westinghouse Electric had created RCA to monopolize in radio broadcasting in America. Like its rival AT&T, RCA experimented with sound recording. It developed a sound-on-film recording system, but failed to secure contracts with any major company. (AT&T signed up Paramount and Loew's.) RCA reacted by forming its own movie company. First, it purchased a very small producer-distributor, the Film Booking Office. To develop a chain of theaters, RCA took over the Keith-Albee-Orpheum vaudeville circuit, and gradually wired these well-situated first-run locations. Other small companies were drawn in, and the newly titled Radio-Keith-Orpheum was established in 1928.

In 1929 the structure of the American film industry was clear. Five firms dominated: Paramount, Loew's, Warner Bros., Fox, and RKO. Each of the 'Big Five' owned substantial production facilities in Southern California, a worldwide distribution network and a sizeable theater chain. The Little Three (Universal, Columbia and United Artists) maintained only production and distribution units. A mere handful of specialized producers remained in existence. There were some 15,000 non-affiliated theaters, but collectively they took in less revenues than the 3000 owned by the Big Five, usually far less. Paramount (the former Famous Players) and its seven allies had successfully turned the US movie industry into a smooth-running, profitable trust. The 'Big Five' succeeded where the MPPC failed. Gone were the days of easy entry into the movie business. Artificial restraints loomed everywhere. Giant companies colluded to keep out the competition. And the products featured unique stars, controlled through contractual servitude to one studio. Structurally, the film industry consisted of a few firms whose conduct only served to remind all who looked closely that they were quite willing to take full advantage of their oligopolistic, vertically-integrated power.

The structure of the studio system

The US motion picture industry has never produced much in the way of real economic activity. In 1946 the industry reached its peak, yet produced only 0.5 per cent of the national income of the US. In terms of labor, the industry's employees also made up only 0.5 per cent of the US total. Following the industry's own public relations proclamations, some historians have placed the industry in the top ten (or top four) US industries in the 1930s and 1940s. But if size is measured by sales, the film industry never reached the top thirty. For 1937 it placed forty-fifth in sales, ranking with Bituminous Coal, and Life Insurance. Classic manufacturing industries like motor vehicles, iron and steel, electric power, and printing and publishing, generated sales from three to five times the amount of motion pictures. It is only when compared with other forms of recreation available at the time that the motion picture industry dominated. In 1937 movies accounted for three-quarters of America's gross income spent on amusements. It was indeed a golden age relative to the competition, much as broadcast television was in the 1960s and 1970s. But for business historians, motion pictures have always been a relatively small industry.

By one measure – profits – the motion picture industry did do exceptionally well in the studio era. In 1946 when the industry produced a little over 0.5 per cent of the US national income, and the same percentage of total wages, it was able to generate nearly 1.5 per cent of all US corporate profits. That is, the industry generated three times the expected share of profit. It is with this measure that the industry may have moved into the top ten US industries, especially during its most prosperous years, 1941–6 – the so-called Second World War boom. Still, others did far better. For example, before the Second World War restrictions, the automobile and cigarette industries generated profits at twice the rate (and many times the absolute amount) of the motion picture industry. Thus, despite all the glamour and hype, the movie industry could never be considered more than a moderately successful industry, one affected by the usual booms and busts of twentieth-century US capitalism.

With profits high, stockholders of the Big Five and Little Three did well. But these oligopolists also rewarded their executives far in excess of the normal standards of far larger corporations. Through the two decades of the studio era, corporate presidents and a few production bosses consistently earned hundreds of thousands of dollars annually. Loew's, Paramount, Warner Bros. and 20th Century-Fox, the most profitable corporations, all had elaborate management bonus systems. Indeed, throughout the studio era Loew's executives – production boss Louis B. Mayer, counsel J. Robert Rubin and president Nicholas Schenck – were ranked among the highest salaried persons in the United States. The brothers Warner, Fox's Joseph M. Schenck and Darryl F. Zanuck, and Paramount's Barney Balaban and

Y. Frank Freeman did nearly as well. These men, as a rule unknown to the general public, wielded enormous power in the industry. In contrast, stars received a large amount of publicity for their high salaries, but few earned enormous amounts for very long. Stars, producers, crafts people all came and went, while their bosses remained, guiding the profit-making destinies of the corporations which put together motion pictures for the US and most of the rest of the world.

If publicity (or even historical study) is any criterion, the bulk of the movie industry was found in the Hollywood studios. Distribution, like much of the wholesaling trade, was 'invisible'. Exhibition had a greater presence, but in most minds never matched the importance of the well-guarded, enormous California production plants. Yet in terms of invested dollars, production accounted for only 5 per cent of total assets. Speaking correctly, distribution, despite its enormous leverage, totalled even less – about 1 per cent. Throughout the 1930s and 1940s by and large most investment took place on the exhibition side – some 94 per cent. The amount of capital required for production paled when compared with the cost of financing a chain of several hundred theaters. Thus, although we know a great deal about the glories of Metro-Goldwyn-Mayer, properly that company was simply one subsidiary of a much larger theater corporation, Loew's Inc. All the highly-paid executives of the period knew where corporate revenues originated. Nearly all had started their careers in the theater end. For a clear picture of the studio era one has to characterize the Big Five as diversified theater chains, producing features, shorts, cartoons, and newsreels to fill their houses. The term 'studio' is a misnomer which has stuck. This book will use the term motion picture corporation. Studio era will be used to represent the 1930–49 era, the latter date being when the Big Five began to split off from ownership of theaters.

The five major companies in the US movie industry during the 1930s and 1940s were Loew's Inc., Radio-Keith-Orpheum, Paramount, 20th Century-Fox and Warner Bros. In terms of total assets, the Big Five corporations were about four times larger than their Little Three rivals. Paramount, Loew's, 20th Century-Fox and Warners were all about the same size. RKO, which continually struggled throughout the studio era, was 25 per cent smaller. Each mirrored the entire industry, with the bulk of invested corporate capital in theaters, not production. With most corporate assets held in, and revenues coming through, the theater division corporate decisions were aimed in that direction. For example, Paramount's vast holdings in theaters dragged the corporation into receivership in the 1930s, but then pushed the corporation to extraordinarily high profits during the boom period of the Second World War. In contrast, Loew's relatively small theater holdings assisted it in the early 1930s. By owning only one-eighth of Paramount's total, Loew's sailed through the Great Depression. But in the 1940s it could not take full advantage of the extraordinary demand for movie entertainment. During the prosperous Second World War period, Loew's was forced to continue to book its features into theaters owned by others, and thus contribute to the profits of competitors with larger chains. In poor times Loew's had, of course, booked MGM films in theaters of others, but then did not have to share in the costs of the upkeep (and mortgages). With such debts a thing of the past by 1946, whenever Loew's created a popular feature film, it only added to the profits of the owners of much larger chains of theaters, rivals Warner Bros., Fox and Paramount.

During the studio era, the Big Five created the bulk of the high budget, so-called 'A' films. Universal, Columbia, and United Artists added their share of features to bring the total of the eight oligopolists to about three-quarters of all features made. Films by marginal, small producers (Monogram or Republic, for example) consisted almost entirely of low budget features, cheap westerns and serials. Such low-cost fare played in small neighborhood theaters and houses in rural America, rarely in the first-run urban operations of the Big Five. Consequently the oligopolists' features helped generate some 90 per cent of the box-office revenues, while marginal producers had to scramble for the rest, faced with the high selling costs associated with dealing with thousands of 200-seat theaters. In addition, the Big Five controlled vital inputs into the process of production, including film processing, music publishing, sponsorship of Broadway plays (to be turned into films) and forays into television. In general, the Big Five rarely took on investments not related to film production, distribution or exhibition. The Little Three stuck to film production and distribution, making few moves into ancillary fields.

Still the majors found no totally effective way to exclude independent producers. United Artists serviced an array of independents, including Sam Goldwyn from 1926 to 1941, when RKO agreed to distribute his films. David O. Selznick created *Gone With the Wind* within his independent shop. In fact, two independent operations were able to merge with and revitalize important production units: Twentieth Century with Fox in 1935 and International with Universal in 1945. The boom in theater attendance in the Second World War plus a restricted use of stars and film stock created a profitable pull to independent entrepreneurs in the 1940s. Leading stars, producers, and directors set up production shops to make one or two films and take advantage of favorable capital gains tax rates. The rigid star system, with its binding seven year contracts, broke down in the face of this thrust. By 1945, of the 1054 members of the Screen Actors Guild who received feature billing, only 261 were under exclusive contract to a major studio. In the 1950s, nearly all important stars would form their own production companies.

A second force for creative independence in film production came with the rise of powerful Hollywood unions. As the American film industry was forming, the open-shop tradition of the Los Angeles labor market prevailed. During the First World War trade unionism began to make inroads among skilled construction crafts, but not among other motion picture workers. As was true in the United States in general during the 1920s, little progress in unionization was made before the Great Depression. The Hollywood producers, in fact, developed their own company union in the form of the Academy of Motion Picture Arts and Sciences. Effective union representation came about during the 1930s, especially under the aegis of the federal government through the National Recovery and the Wagner Acts. By the outbreak of the Second World War, most Hollywood studio labor, even the highly-paid actors and actresses, was unionized. Entrenchment took place during the Second World War; strikes after the war solidified that power. By the close of the studio era, motion picture production in Hollywood was a completely unionized operation.

With unions to support them, creative personnel of all kinds began to freelance during the 1940s. In 1945, there were 952 active members of the Screen Writers Guild, but only 174 were under long-term contract to one of the Big Five or Little Three. Of the 222 feature motion picture directors in their particular Guild, only 75 were under long-term contract. Since the majors provided employment for all the noted writers, directors, and stars, a number sought the security of a guaranteed income through a studio contract. Still, by the end of the Second World War more and more creative personnel chose to venture into independent work, seeking the best possible offer. Consequently the major film companies were able to extract less and less profit from control over stars, directors, producers and other vital creative personnel. In turn, after the Second World War the Big Five focussed an increasing amount of corporate attention on boosting their power in distribution (especially overseas) and exhibition (forcing the issue on the Paramount anti-trust case as discussed later).

For one aspect of the production process, the Big Five and Little Three openly colluded to protect their joint interests. Through their trade association, the Motion Picture Producers and Distributors of America Inc. (the MPPDA), they organized self-censorship. Originally, the MPPDA was set in motion in 1922 to fight off a rising tide of state and municipal censorship restrictions. In 1934, after twelve years of informal controls, the MPPDA set up formal enforcement machinery, complete with $25,000 fines. Member producers (the Big Five and Little Three) were obliged to submit all scripts and films for approval. Since the majors controlled the theaters in which all films sought to play, non-approved films were denied access to significant sources of revenue. Indeed, MPPDA disapproval guaranteed – in all but a few cases – box office failure. Effectively, in this manner, the Big Five and Little Three exercised prior-restraint over the entire industry. Controversial films (in terms of sex, violence, religion and politics) simply were never made, stymied early on at the script stage. The MPPDA code would gradually break down during the 1950s as the Big Five corporations spun off their theaters and relinquished a certain amount of their power in the mass entertainment business.

Far less glamorous than production, but far more important for profit-making, was distribution. Agents – in thirty-two major cities spread throughout the United States and in all countries of the world (except the USSR) – negotiated licenses and delivered films to theaters. Only the Big Five and Little Three maintained complete national and international distribution networks. The most powerful marginal producers, Monogram and Republic, had to make do with limited access to markets outside the United States. All the important producers, to ensure reasonable costs, had to work with a member of the Big Five or Little Three. If an independent producer could not negotiate such a contract, he or she stood little chance of making a profit – however promising the film might be. United Artists was set up so independent producers had at least one such outlet, and because RKO did so poorly with its own products, by the beginning of the Second World War it also regularly picked up independently-made works. In particular, Disney and Goldwyn distributed through RKO throughout the 1940s. After the Second World War the situation began to change: the remainder of the Big Five and Little Three began to handle independent deals. Universal and Columbia in particular were able to make great strides by becoming havens for independent producers.

The advantages of a national and international distribution network were considerable. Even though in 1945 it cost Loew's or Paramount about $5 million per year to operate a distribution network in the US, they could spread these costs over numerous features, shorts and newsreels, reaping *low per unit costs*. No outsider could afford to start an international organization for only a handful of films. It was far easier (and cheaper) simply to work through one of the established corporations. In addition, control over key theaters gave the Big Five the power effectively to exclude other distributors from a large share of the potential market. Theaters owned by the Big Five rarely accepted non-UA, non-RKO independent products, and in as many cases as possible independent theater-owners also gave preference to films from the major studios because they contained the most popular stars and promised to make the most money.

Distribution hegemony forced all mainstream producers to go through the Big Five and Little Three. States-rights distributors, each operating in one or two regions of the United States, handled cheap westerns, 'quickies' and exploitation films. Thus during the 1943–4 movie season, for example, the Big Five collected just about 75 per cent of all film rentals paid in the United States. The Little Three took in 20 per cent. That left only 5 per cent of the pie for everyone else. Within the Big Five relative shares did change as one year Paramount would do better, another year Loew's, but the total share taken in by the Big Five and Little Three remained remarkably consistent. The total for the Big Five and Little Three added up, year-after-year, to about 95 per cent of the US box-office takings.

116

The distribution power of the Big Five and Little Three extended to other countries. After the First World War these eight corporations completed their distribution networks throughout the world. By 1925 (and throughout the 1930s and 1940s) overseas rentals accounted for approximately one half an average feature film's takings. Hollywood dominated Britain as well as France, Italy and even Japan. The coming of sound did not hinder control. Foreign taxes, tariffs and quotas did – to a degree. The United States Department of State helped to neutralize the effects of foreign governments by working with the MPPDA to mute as much as possible foreign constraints. Problems arose during the Second World War because of the loss of markets in Axis countries. After that war the industry set up a formal equivalent of MPPDA – the Motion Picture Export Association – to handle foreign matters. There were constant battles and disagreements, but the Big Five and Little Three never lost their significant comparative advantage.

However, in the end, any consideration of the motion picture industry in the studio era has to return to exhibition. A survey of the theaters in the United States in 1945 is shown in Table 1. Although there were relatively few large theaters (picture palaces of 1200 seats or more) these few could hold more than all the other 10,000 small theaters (0–500 seats) in the US. Most of the smaller theaters were in rural towns or in neighborhood shopping areas of major cities. Larger theaters were found downtown, or in regional outlying shopping areas in the fifty largest US cities in terms of population. The Big Five concentrated their ownership in larger theaters, thereby controlling approximately 25 per cent of the total seats in US theaters. Collectively, the majors controlled more than 70 per cent of all the first-run theaters in the ninety-two largest cities in the US, those cities in 1940 with 100,000 people or more. All the statistics point to a system where the majors, through the ownership of large picture palaces in cities of 100,000 or more, were able effectively to harness the market for exhibition in the United States during the studio era. For the most part the Big Five neatly divided the US, with

Table 1 Theaters in the United States by Seating Capacity, 1945

Capacity	Theaters	Percentage of Theaters	Percentage of Seats
1500+	996	5.4	21.7
1201–1500	732	4.0	8.6
1001–1200	801	4.4	7.7
751–1000	2687	11.3	15.8
501–750	2979	16.2	16.2
351–500	4311	23.4	15.9
0–350	6507	35.3	14.1
Total	18413	100	100

Paramount dominating the South, New England, and the upper Midwest, Fox controlling the Far West, RKO and Loew's splitting New York, New Jersey, and Ohio, and Warners staking out the mid-Atlantic states. In the few areas where the Big Five 'competed', pooling arrangements and/or joint ownership were undertaken to spread the risk.

The control of key theaters by the Big Five had far-reaching consequences. The Little Three and other producer-distributors had to accede to the Big Five's marketing plan in order even to place films in first-run situations, a necessity if profits were to be made. Independent exhibitors also had to toe the line. Otherwise, the Big Five would not rent to them. Then the independent exhibitors would have to turn to poor-quality, low-profit motion pictures. In practice, in first-run houses, the need would be for 100 films per year. That would be filled from the affiliated Big Five studios plus the best from the other four. A subsequent-run house (with three different billings per week) required more than 300 features a year, and so turned to Universal, Columbia, and United Artists.

It was through the theatrical end of the industry, constituting some 90 per cent of all their assets, that the Big Five operated as a collusive unit, protecting each other, shutting out all potential competitors, and guaranteeing profits for even the worst performer, usually RKO. The relationship of the Big Five throughout the studio era was like a chronically quarrelsome but closely knit family. Theatrical inter-dependencies guaranteed that if anyone produced a popular film, all members of the Big Five benefitted. Distribution economies of scale brought forth significant cost savings. Production units corralled valuable stars, producers, directors and other creative personnel and put together variations of certain narrative forms. The Big Five and Little Three co-operated to regularize the movie business, and take out as much risk as possible. Then, subject to those rigid constraints, they competed for a small number of marginal dollars. Rarely publicized, but more forceful, was the struggle within the corporate apparatus of the Big Five. Selling at the theater level, a purely commercial process, demanded one set of skills; making films, a creative endeavour, even in Hollywood's factory days of the 1930s and 1940s, necessitated far different ones. Producers wanted to experiment and try new things to gain an edge on their competitors. If they continued with the same stories and stars, others would surge past them, but exhibitors wanted predictable box office attractions, and tended to support forms and personae that had worked best in the recent past. Consequently, the Big Five and Little Three struggled more within than without, creating a multitude of anecdotes for future biographers. Details of management decision processes will be described and analyzed in the succeeding chapters on individual corporations.

The conduct of firms within the studio system

The structure of the film industry described and analyzed above set in motion certain forms of business behavior. All companies attempted to maximize profits within a system designed to allocate the bulk of that profit to the vertically-integrated Big Five. Production decisions of the Big Five were based on information generated by their theater divisions. In general the production process began with a corporate decision establishing the number of films needed for the following season. Then, the chief executive of Big Five firm would allocate a budget for production of features (designated 'A' and 'B' by cost) and shorts (including cartoons and newsreels). At the same time, a detailed release schedule was also handed to the executives at the west coast studio. Once these decisions were made – always by the corporate president and his staff in the New York office – the Hollywood staff was relatively free to decide how to produce the most popular products. Throughout the total production process, continuing conferences and negotiation would take place between the New York and Hollywood offices concerning budgets, release schedules, wages and investments. In the end, all final decisions rested with the chief operating officer of the corporation based in New York, not Hollywood.

To produce films as efficiently as possible and still create a stream of 'new-and-different' products, Hollywood utilized a factory system of production based on extreme specialization of labor. Generally, a studio chief coordinated the desires and budgets issued by the New York office with the materials and labor at hand. Below the studio chief would be a set of producers who would each be responsible for six to eight of the necessary feature films, shorts and cartoons. (Newsreels were usually handled separately.) The producer in turn would then organize writing, shooting and editing within defined budget constraints. This form of decentralized manufacturing process was innovated during the 1920s at the General Motors Automobile Corporation. Hollywood fully adopted it by 1930. The given studio situation dictated how much relative power producers had. The process of actual film production was divided into specialized units. From finding appropriate stories to writing scripts to actual shooting to cutting, workers handled only their own tasks. Unionization solidified specific jurisdictions. Details on the practices of specific studios are outlined later in individual chapters.

To make the most from their productions and to maximize profits from their theaters, the Big Five developed a complex set of distribution practices. By manipulating trade arrangements they were able to reduce risk and ensure continuity of control. To affect bargaining relations, practices based on the economics of price discrimination were developed. Price discrimination allows the seller (or co-operating sellers) to generate larger revenues (see Figure 1). Under typical marketing conditions, the demand for a good or service is expressed by the schedule DD. That is, if the price (P) goes up,

119

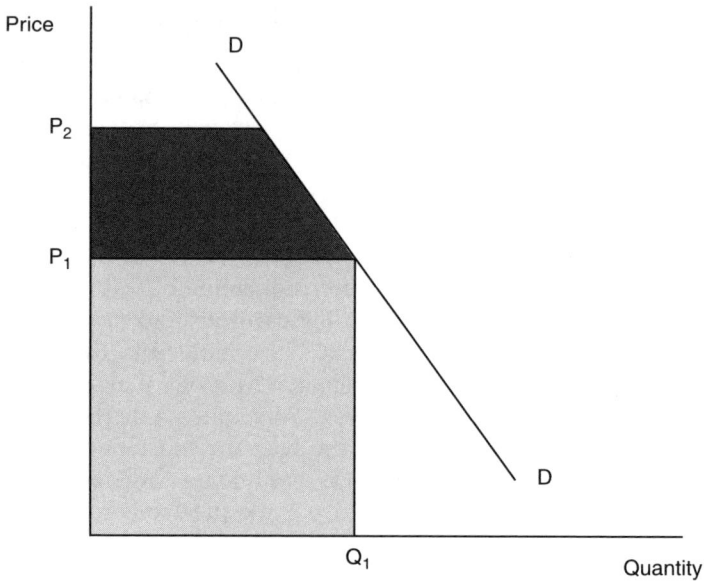

Figure 1 Admission Price Discrimination

consumers will be at a higher point on the curve (*DD*) and demand less. If the price falls, consumers demand more – all other things being equal. In most situations there is but one price offered, here P_1. Using the curve then, consumers demand Q_1. The seller makes P_1 times Q_1 in revenues. This is represented by the light gray area. However, some people may have strong preferences and be willing to pay prices higher than P_1. If somehow a seller could find those people and charge them those higher prices, additional revenues could be gained. Assuming no one is willing to pay higher than P_2, additional revenues equal to the amount shown by the dark gray area could be added to the basic revenues (light gray area). It is difficult and costly to segment consumers to charge them different prices, however. The US movie industry accomplished the task in a cost-effective straightforward fashion through the use of runs, zones and clearances (a temporal and spatial separation of markets). This pushed the Big Five away from the revenues in the light area, toward but not precisely to the light area plus darker area.

The distribution exchanges of the Big Five co-operated to establish runs, zones and clearances for all cities and towns in the US. All first-runs were followed by a period of time (the clearance) of seven to thirty days before the film could play second-run – all within certain geographical limits (the zone). Then the film would play second-run. A clearance would follow before the third-run, and so on down the line. In some large cities there might be up to eleven runs requiring more than a year to complete. In smaller communities

120

there might only be a first-run downtown and a final run at a neighborhood theater. Different admission prices were charged for each run, the highest in first-run and so on down the line. Keen movie fans paid up to a dollar to see their favorites. Casual movie-goers waited, and paid as little as 10¢. Wide-scale advertising tried to line up potential patrons to attend a first-run showing rather than some later one. Distribution executives could juggle run status, zone size, clearance time and admission price to milk the most from any market. In actual practice, through a trial-and-error method of experimentation, runs, zones, and clearances were established during the 1920s, and fixed in place for the next twenty years. With few shifts in US population during the 1930s and 1940s, the run-zone-clearance system served to maximise the revenues of the Big Five, regardless of differences in the qualities of the films produced.

Actual bargaining between distributors and exhibitors was not a compli-cated affair. Each theater had a fixed run-zone-clearance status. Contracts stipulated admission prices. A rivalry did exist among the Big Five to sell their films to the best of the non-affiliated theaters. With block-booking and blind buying the Big Five attempted to force independent theaters to take groups of films, sight unseen. These tactics kept selling costs low and helped to guarantee a base of revenues, even for the most mediocre film. In effect distributors shifted a part of their risk to powerless exhibitors, guaranteeing that even films accepted poorly in first-run houses would receive a sub-run play-off. Block-booking and blind buying helped Columbia and Universal most, enabling them to secure better rates of financing for production, and assuring a cost-effective utilization of their plant and equipment, but even at their peak use in the 1930s these two tactics affected only a small portion of total revenues of the industry.

The admission price discrimination and run-zone-clearance system had far-reaching implications for the motion picture industry. First, this system min-imized the number of theaters the Big Five needed to own to effect a measure of control. In actual practice, with approximately 15 per cent of all US theaters (but the majority of first-run) the Big Five could easily gather in 50–75 per cent of the box-office revenues. Second, it kept Big Five theaters fully utilized. Year-in and year-out, despite depressions, wars, poor films, aging stars and changes in public taste, the Big Five could count on a steady flow of revenues at its box-offices. Finally, this process of selling kept transaction costs low. With fixed agreement as to the status of run, zone, clearance and admission prices, bar-gaining and negotiation costs were minimal. Distribution staffs were small. Costs of required prints never mounted up. If all theaters showed the same film simultaneously, it would have necessitated nearly 20,000 prints. (At that time prints cost an average of $250 and lasted 200 screenings.) But with a limited number of theaters in each run, only 400 prints were needed. If prints wore out prematurely, later runs were simply canceled since striking a new print and shipping it cost more than expected revenues.

The actual practice of running large theater chains was modeled on retailing techniques developed by chain operations like Woolworths and Sears. In the 1920s Paramount's theater division, Publix Theaters, led the way. Others – Loew's, Fox, Warners and RKO – quickly imitated. Publix regularized costs, booked from a central office and made a science of national advertising. Publix carefully controlled all expenditures at its theaters. Each theater had a weekly budget detailing all costs. All figures were carefully scrutinized by accountants in the home office and any excess had to be explained in a written report. In addition local managers also recorded all non-financial aspects of their operations and forwarded such information to the New York office where experts constructed elaborate charts to serve as guides for future decision-making. For example, all assistant managers of Publix houses recorded the temperature and humidity from the orchestra floor, balcony, lobby and outside, every hour on the hour, for the complete operating day. Publix experts then used this data to issue orders concerning use of the heating and air-conditioning. Other specialists calculated traffic patterns, population densities, income distributions and recreation habits before a theater was built or purchased.

All booking was done from New York. Since Paramount did not make enough films to fill Publix screen-time, Publix bargained with and obtained favorable terms from the other major producer-distributors. Publix's central buyer relied on data from previous years, which had been compiled in massive detail, and suggestions from managers at all levels. The actual scheduling began six to eight weeks in advance. Regional managers prepared master booking sheets and then sent them down the line to be commented upon at each level. The divisional, district and local managers added the 'local' touch, eliminated regionally offensive films and returned the sheets to New York for final approval. Executive managers, recruited from the areas they supervised, visited their territories several times a year. Publix promoted experienced local managers since they had first-hand knowledge of the 'needs' of communities where Publix houses were located.

In a national market Publix could not rely on so-called 'word-of-mouth'. Advertising and publicity became vital inputs. Experts formulated numerous ambitious advertising programs in order to sell the 'Publix' name. The central slogan became '*You don't need to know what's playing at a Publix House. It's bound to be the best show in town.*' All advertising copy was prepared by specialists at the New York office and sent down the line in the form of a manual which contained sketches, model advertisements, suggestions on how to place them, descriptions of 'stunts' to promote the theater's program and even publicity stories to be planted in the newspaper. The major Hollywood producers supplied a similar press kit, but the New York office required managers to use the in-house manual. Each local manager simply selected the material appropriate to his or her market, and then executed the advertising campaign within a budget specified from New York. Since each local advertising budget was balanced only once a month, the local manager had some flexibility in advertising appropriations, but to conduct any elaborate advertising, the local manager had to secure permission from the Publix New York office.

Publix also helped make the 1920s the era of the presentation-cinema. Deluxe, ornate picture palaces served up elaborate shows made up of one-third live performance (a stage show presentation) and two-thirds motion pictures (feature, shorts, and newsreels). Ornate auditoriums housed these spectacles; lighting displays and performers turned each show into a unique theatrical event. A presentation-cinema show opened with a five-minute overture from a house orchestra of twenty-five to one hundred members. Next came the stage show, lasting from fifteen to thirty minutes. A newsreel (five to ten minutes), shorts (ten to twenty minutes), and the feature film (sixty to eighty minutes) followed. Exhibitors tried to limit the complete show to 150 minutes, sometimes cutting the feature by several minutes rather than restricting the number of shows. Big Five theaters mounted the most expensive presentation shows. Independent theaters imitated as well as costs would allow.

The coming of sound changed little. Expensive live shows were systematically replaced by vaudeville shorts. The presentation-cinema became all-movies by 1930. The Great Depression – with its attendant sharp decrease in revenues – forced exhibitors to differentiate their offerings and seek out new sources of revenues. To attract more patrons, small theater owners initiated double, even triple bills. A two-for-one policy, which had been tried as early as 1915, seemed to give the potential patron more for his or her money. In 1931, theater owners also began to tempt customers with give-aways (pillows, chinaware, bicycles, silk stockings, lamps and watches) and games (bingo, races or screeno). However, in August 1933 the US federal government's National Recovery Administration (NRA) prohibited all give-aways and games as 'unfair competition'. Consequently, more and more theater owners turned to double bills. The US Supreme Court declared the NRA unconstitutional in May 1935, and quickly exhibitors reinstituted give-aways and games. But by then the double-feature strategy had become institutionalized, and would function as the dominant US exhibition strategy well into the 1950s. Even Big Five theaters offered double bills, but not in the numbers of their non-affiliated rivals. The mix varied. Some exhibitors tendered two 'A' films, others an 'A' and 'B', still others two or three 'B's. Theater owners constantly varied combinations in order to gain an edge on nearby competitors.

Exhibitors effected other changes in order to attract more customers, the most important of which was air-conditioning, first offered in Balaban and Katz houses in Chicago in 1917. Only the Big Five could afford this sizeable investment during the 1920s. During the 1930s, with Carrier's development of a compact, relatively inexpensive apparatus, many more exhibitors installed a system for air-cooling and humidity control. Extensive use of Carrier's new inventions at the Chicago World Fair during the summers of 1933 and 1934 generated familiarity and favorable publicity. Big Five movie houses functioned as the sole institution offering such service at prices affordable to middle- and lower-income US citizens. Generally throughout the studio era Big Five theaters offered complete air conditioning – air-cooling plus dehumidification. Independent theaters more often than not only cooled the air, often with indifferent results.

Exhibitors also sought out additional sources of revenue in the 1930s, and so began to sell food directly to patrons rather than let them continue to shop at nearby confectionery stores or popcorn wagons. During the 1920s few exhibitors sold candy. Since at that time theater owners kept their auditoriums very dark and had ushers lead patrons to their seats, only a pre-packaged product could be accommodated, but in any case sales of food did not fit the 'high class' image such operations sought. With the coming of the Great Depression theater owners fired their ushers, turned up the auditorium lights and let patrons find their own seats. Nearly all added candy sales and began to experiment with the marketing of other foods. Popcorn soon emerged as the cornerstone of refreshment operations. Unlike candy, it possessed a seemingly addictive aroma which filled lobbies as customers paused before the movies and between features. Popcorn was easy to manufacture and seemed to appeal to movie-goers of all ages. To complement the salty popcorn, exhibitors introduced an array of cold, soft drinks. Soon suppliers developed beverage-dispensing equipment to solve the problem of individual glass bottles rolling and breaking in the auditorium.

Sales of refreshments skyrocketed. The Big Five purchased popcorn by the railcar load thereby obtaining substantial discounts. A box retailing at 15¢ cost only 3¢ for raw materials – container, oil and corn. Even with wages, equipment, and overhead, the profit rate usually soared past 100 per cent. Thus it was not surprising that by 1947 nearly 90 per cent of US movie houses sold popcorn. The lone Big Five holdout was the conservative Loew's Inc. During slow days, sales of refreshments often matched or exceeded box-office revenues. Popcorn soon became a major US crop. In 1920 there were 60,000 US acres devoted to popcorn; by 1948 over 300,000 US acres were planted with this movie-house favorite. Sales of soft drinks (Coca-Cola dominated here) and, after 1948, buttered popcorn added to the revenues and profits of the Big Five.

As part of this new strategy (multiple features, air-conditioning and in-house refreshments) exhibitors ritualized the intermission. The first feature would end, the house lights would go up, and the patrons would rush to the lobby to purchase popcorn, candy and colas. 'Coming attractions' would signal a return to more entertainment. The form became narrative, food, narrative in a continuous pattern. Other services, standard during the presentation era, were eliminated. Theater lobbies and auditoriums (as well as exteriors) were left to rundown. Less was spent on upkeep, most potential light sources were covered up or unused, and fewer and fewer ushers were employed. The decorative displays of Oriental, Egyptian, French or Spanish architecture gradually came to represent a bygone presentation-cinema era.

External shocks

The studio system already analyzed was so successful that only forces outside its control could significantly disrupt it. There were three such outside shocks in the studio era. The first was the decrease in demand caused by the decline in incomes during the Great Depression. Although accurate statistics are hard to come by, box office revenues seem to have declined by 25 per cent. Consumers turned to cheaper substitutes (radio) or simply cut the number of screenings attended each month. The Big Five cut wages, sought new revenues in refreshments and finessed bulging mortgages as best they could. All survived intact. The US federal government through the National Recovery Act (NRA) of 1933 helped by openly sanctioning the monopolistic behavior of the Big Five. Instead of the informal co-operation which had existed throughout the 1920s, open and explicit collusion and exploitation took place, free from any threat of anti-trust action. The Big Five immediately codified the run-zone-clearance system, and boosted revenues. The NRA, as noted above, outlawed all give-aways by exhibitors. Such a sanction helped the Big Five at the expense of independent exhibitors.

The second outside shock came in 1938 when the administration of President Franklin Roosevelt shifted gears and filed an anti-trust suit against the Big Five and Little Three. The defendants were charged with conspiring to fix distribution contract terms of runs, clearances and admission prices. In 1940 all parties signed a consent decree which set up a broad system of rules for bargaining and settling disputes similar to the pro-Big Five 'self-government' which had operated under the NRA. Little changed. In August 1944, the government reactivated the case, and pressed for divorcement of theaters of the Big Five. This solution was agreed to by the US Supreme Court on 25 July 1949, signaling the end of the twenty-year period of the studio era. Although the full force of this decision would not come about until the early 1950s, continuous pressure did exist beginning in 1938. The Big Five, logically, fought to save their valuable run-zone-clearance system, but for a variety of social and political reasons lost their case.

The final external shock felt prior to 1949 also involved the US federal government – the Second World War. As hostilities spread in Europe and the Orient during the late 1930s the Big Five and Little Three saw revenues from overseas decline. Gradually, they lost markets in Europe and the Far East, which together had accounted for 33–50 per cent of traditional revenues from abroad. When Britain declared war in September 1939 and the Germans began to bomb, some theaters closed, but once the British adjusted, revenues from the United Kingdom soared to twice pre-war levels. Britain clamped on currency restrictions. The Big Five and Little Three had great difficulty taking out all they earned, and so secured a number of investments in British studios and theater chains. Elsewhere the Second World War did what all the earlier quotas, taxes, and tariffs could not do – partially shut down the overseas distribution of Hollywood movies. To offset the loss of European and Far Eastern markets, the Big Five and Little Three turned to South and Central America. The Department of State through the Office of the Co-ordinator of Inter-American Affairs assisted their efforts. Motion pictures were a good way to promote the Good Neighbor Policy. The State Department shipped hundreds of US newsreels south, but demand for other products never followed. Hollywood had fully exploited Latin American markets prior to the war; there was little else to extract.

The market for motion pictures in the US during the Second World War offered a very different prospect. Domestically, the war period provided the best five years in movie history, and these increases more than compensated for any losses from overseas markets. As incomes rose, few durables were available for purchase. Business, especially in large cities with war-related industries, prospered as never before. Revenues in real dollars peaked in 1946; so did movie attendance. With restrictions on production, the number of features fell. No matter, revenues per film rose faster than costs. Even independent producers, usually working through RKO and United Artists, prospered. (Favorable tax benefits also helped.) The year 1946 saw the highest profits during Hollywood's studio era: Paramount – $39 million; Fox $25 million; Warners – $22 million; Loew's – $18 million; even 'poor cousin' RKO – $12 million. In real dollar terms all these were corporate records, not approached again until the 1970s. The US motion picture industry would have loved the Second World War to go on, at least on the home front, forever.

Conclusion

In sum, the studio era represented a stable twenty-year epoch in the history of American film. Eight major corporations Paramount, Loew's, 20th Century-Fox, Warner Bros., Radio-Keith-Orpheum, Universal, Columbia and United Artists – dominated all phases of industry operation. In their quest for profits, these eight regularized film production with standardized products including features, animation and live short subjects, serials and newsreels. All embraced now well-known narrative structures and then actively sought to convince potential movie patrons of the differences in their products. Through widespread advertising, all the majors heralded new stars, interesting stories and stunning special effects. In so doing, these eight corporations worked to define how Americans understood what was an acceptable (natural) use of motion picture technology.

With all the glamour and razzmatazz associated with the launching and promotion of feature films, we have come to associate the economic power of the film industry with its control over film production. Anecdote after anecdote is regularly trotted out to illustrate how movie mogul production bosses such as Louis B. Mayer, Harry Cohn and Darryl F. Zanuck controlled American movie screens. We learn how ruthlessly they dealt with the biggest stars and the smallest extras, a set of medieval lords running their manors to produce guaranteed safe mass entertainment, week after week, year after year.

But if Hollywood production was so predictable, why did others not attempt to enter film production? The answer lies with the barriers to entry created by the eight major movie corporations. Anyone during the 1930s and 1940s could have invested the necessary millions in film production, but then any new corporation would somehow have had to get the films onto theater screens. It was through these two functions – distribution and exhibition – that the eight major corporations co-operated to keep out potential competitors. In other words, it was the mundane worlds of movie wholesaling and retailing which provided the Big Five with the necessary muscle to erect and maintain barriers to entry to keep away all serious competitors for two decades.

Consequently though there were clear corporate distinctions in terms of film production (depending on stars under contract and genres utilized), there were few corporate differences in terms of distribution and exhibition. Indeed, all eight majors co-operated for the common good. There was no competition *per se*. The greatest differences lay in theater style only because, as already described, each corporation dominated one particular region of the USA. As such Paramount might publicize a film in the deep South differently from Loew's in New York City, but all corporations embraced the run-zone-clearance pattern of release, because it was in everyone's best interest to co-operate rather than compete. This constancy of distribution and exhibition made motion pictures a true national mass medium. In the end, corporate and regional differences were smoothed over in favor of the common goal of profit-maximization.

Consequently, in the chapters which follow on the individual corporations there will be little analysis of distribution and exhibition. That is not to say that these functions were not important. Indeed they were vital. My omissions underline the fact that there were few differences to note. All followed the practices described in this introductory chapter.

Also omitted from later discussion are the multitude of external problems which the industry faced through the 1930s and 1940s. The Great Depression, the Second World War, a ten-year anti-trust suit and the coming of unions and independent producers were issues with which all industry participants had to deal. However, with some historical perspective it seems fair to conclude that the studio system was able to surmount all these difficulties.

All the corporations survived the Great Depression and went on to thrive during the war years. The US federal government was held at bay for a decade. Unions were able to secure their place in the system and independent producers became commonplace by 1945. Such was the resilience and power of the studio system as a profit-making business institution.

Since the major corporations so benefitted from co-operation, it is important first to analyze them as a group, as has been done in this chapter. The following chapters take up the three-part structure set forth here. Each begins with an historical analysis of how a corporation reached its place in the industry hierarchy. The second part of each chapter then examines the structure of the corporation during the studio era, focussing on ownership, finance and composition of assets. Some corporations experienced significant changes in structure (Paramount, 20th Century-Fox, RKO, Universal); others did not (Loew's, Warner Bros., Columbia). The final part of each chapter will analyze how the corporation operated. Important changes in ownership usually precipitated changes in types of films produced, while little was varied in distribution and exhibition. New owners and managers alike recognized the source of industry power and profit. The order of the following chapters reflects the rank of the corporations in terms of profit and power, moving from strongest to weakest.

6

NOTES ON COLUMBIA PICTURES CORPORATION 1926–41

Edward Buscombe

Source: *Screen* 16(3) (Autumn 1975): 65–82.

I

'The film industry': 'the cinema'. How are these terms related in film criticism? 'The film industry' describes an economic system, a way (or ways) of organising the structure of production, distribution and consumption. Historically such organisation has, in Britain and America, conformed to the usual pattern of capitalist activity; film can be seen as an industry like any other. It has passed from the primitive stage of small-scale entrepreneurial activity to the formation of large-scale monopolies, securing their position by vertical integration, spreading from production into distribution and exhibition. Since the War the industry has, like other forms of business, developed towards diversification and the formation of multinational corporations. In other respects too film has developed like other industries. Production in particular has been based on a division of labour, of a fairly extreme kind. From early days the industry has employed the techniques of mass advertising, and it has required the injection of huge sums of capital, resulting in turn in the passing of control of the industry from its original owners and from the primary producers.

In film criticism, then, the term 'film industry' implies a way of looking at film which minimises its differences from other forms of economic activity; a way which is of course predominantly that of those who actually own the industry. Its characteristic descriptions are sufficiently indicative of a perspective: 'the trade', 'marketing', 'exploitation', a 'package', 'product'.

'The cinema' suggests something else. While the term might, notionally, encompass the industry, the pull is surely in a different direction. 'The cinema' implies film as art. As Raymond Williams has shown with convincing detail in *Culture and Society*, the opposition between art and industry has a long history in our culture. The division between the two is experienced everywhere as deep, but nowhere deeper than in film. On the one hand we are given to understand is the industry, churning out product for financial gain. On the other are artists, creating enduring works of personal expression or comment on life and society. Such an opposition has taken different forms at different times. Sometimes it has been geographical. In America there was Hollywood, the industrial system par excellence. In Europe (usually excluding Britain, apart from its documentaries) there were artists: Renoir, Dreyer, Bergman, Antonioni, etc. Later the auteur theory, as applied to American cinema, changed the emphasis. Though Hollywood was still an industry, through diligent critical work some artists could be winnowed from the chaff, artists who against the odds managed by luck, cunning or sheer genius to overcome the system, the industry. The auteur theory, whatever its 'theory' may have been, did not in practice abolish the distinction between art and industry; it merely shifted the line of demarcation.

One might suppose that a little common sense would tell us that such a distinction is nonsense, that all film is both industry *and* art, in some sense. Even the lowest, most despised products (choose your own examples) are made with some kind of art. Do they not share the same language as the acknowledged masterpieces: do they not tell a story, try to affect the spectators' emotions? They may do it more or less effectively, but isn't this a difference of degree, not of kind? Conversely, in the making of the most spiritual and sublime films grubby bank notes change hands. The film stock on which the masterpiece is recorded may come from the same batch used to shoot the potboiler on the adjoining stage.

Yet proof that the mutual exclusion of art and industry operates at a level too deep to be affected by mere common sense can be found not only in the dominant critical attitudes but in the organisation of social institutions. To give an example close to home: the British Film Institute was set up, as its Memorandum of Association states, 'to encourage the development of the art of the film'. At the same time it is stated that the BFI is not permitted 'to control nor attempt to interfere with purely trade matters'. Art not only can but must be divorced from industry. And the split is preserved even in the structure of government. Whereas the BFI is administered by the Department of Education and Science, the film industry comes under the Department of Trade and Industry. Thus the opposition art/industry has to be seen not merely as a 'mistake' in film criticism which can be easily rectified by a more careful look at the facts, but as the result of a whole practice of thinking, talking, writing and disseminating inscribed in institutions like the BFI, those parts of the education system that handle film, plus also exhibition/viewing practice – the art-house circuit and its audience(s) – the 'immaterial' thought both reflecting and being part of this apparatus; in short, as part of an ideology.

The main concern here, however, is not with the origins of such an opposition but with its consequence for film criticism. This may be baldly stated:

there has been scarcely any serious attempt to think the relationship between art and industry with regard to films produced in what have historically been for us the two most important film-making countries, namely our own and the United States. Criticism has been devoted not to relating them but to separating them out, and in practice this has meant that critics have concentrated on the beauties and mysteries of art and left the industry, presumably a tougher plant, to take care of itself. Study of the industry might require knowledge of, say, economics or of how films are actually made, knowledge which critics have not been expected to acquire. The main effort of criticism, therefore, has gone into the study of film texts viewed as autonomous, self-sufficient entities; or, occasionally, as reflections of society, but certainly not as reflections of the industry which produced them, unless they are being dismissed as rubbish. Even recent work deriving from structuralism and concerned to open up the text, to 'deconstruct' it, has tended to take the film as 'given' and has ignored questions of how the organisation of a film text might relate to the organisation of an industry or to specific working practices.

It is in respect of Hollywood, the largest field of activity in both film-making and criticism, that the lack of a history of the industry is most glaring. Of course there is a certain amount of information around. Statistics have occasionally been assembled (a number of Government and trade reports on Hollywood in the 1930's are listed in the notes of Leo C Rosten's *Hollywood: The Movie Colony, The Movie Makers*, a book which has some useful material on this period). There are one or two books, again on the 1930's, which assemble some facts about the economics of the industry (for example, F D Klingender and Stuart Legg, *The Money Behind the Screen* and Mae D Huettig, *Economic Control Of The Motion Picture Industry*). But of course they don't attempt to make any connections between the economics and the actual films produced. There is also the ragbag of publicity releases, inaccurate box-office returns and general gossip which makes up the trade press (*Film Daily, Motion Picture Herald, Variety, Hollywood Reporter*, etc). To this may be added a host of 'biographies' (or ghosted autobiographies) of prominent industry figures, of which *Hollywood Rajah* by Bosley Crowther (on Louis B Mayer) and *King Cohn* by Bob Thomas (on Harry Cohn) are representative examples. Little that is useful can be gleaned from such works, which mostly string together collections of anecdotes about the 'great men'. On such questions as the financial structures within which they were obliged to operate or the actual working methods of their studios they are for the most part silent. Of studio histories, properly speaking, there are none, with the possible exception of Richard Schickel's book *The Disney Version*, which is hampered by his failure to get any cooperation from the Disney studio itself; a fact, of course, that is not without its significance, since it indicates the difficulties of this kind of work.

Indeed, the neglect of industry history is not only a consequence of critical attitudes and priorities which have abandoned the field to those whose interest does not go beyond 'personalities'. It is also the result of very real practical problems. The fact is that the history of the American film industry is extremely difficult to write, because many of the basic materials that would be needed are simply not available. The statistics are incomplete and unreliable. The trade press presents only the acceptable face of the business, even when one can get access to it (the BFI Library, virtually the only collection of such periodicals in Britain, has no run of *Variety*, though there are plans to acquire one). The biographies, and studio histories, where they exist at all (for example Bosley Crowther's *The Lion's Share*, on MGM), are largely based on reminiscences. Concrete documented evidence in the form, say, of studio memoranda, accounts and other records, is almost totally lacking. If such records still exist they are mostly locked away in studio vaults. And the history of technological development in Hollywood has still to be written. Lastly, the films themselves; such prints as have been preserved are often impossible to see. The situation is little different from that which exists in relation to the history of the Elizabethan stage, with this exception, that infinitely less method and application has gone into researching it.

The result is that when Hollywood has been written about its industrial dimension has been ignored. Much of the writing has been based on an idea of history as one damned thing after another. Even such a prestigious work as Lewis Jacob's *The Rise Of The American Film* scarcely rises above this, most sections being simply annotated film lists. The only principle to compete has been auteurism, which leaves film history at the stage which history proper reached in the nineteenth century when Carlyle defined it as the lives of great men. Deliberate attempts to get away from auteurism, such as Colin McArthur's *Underworld USA* (on the crime film) and Jim Kitses' *Horizons West* (on the Western) are ultimately broken-backed books. Genres may be related to aspects of American history, but in the end it is the auteurs who dominate the account.

Some recent, more promising directions have been pursued. Patrick Ogle's work on deep-focus (*Screen* v 13 n 1) or that of John Ellis and Charles Barr on Ealing Studios (*Screen* v 15 nn 1–2, v 16 n 1) have from different perspectives tried to make connections between films and the nature of the industry which produced them. *The Velvet Light Trap* has brought to light valuable material on the studio system, though the use that has been made of it has often been disappointing. But the gaps in our knowledge are still enormous.

II

One consequence of the existence of such gaps has been that attempts to relate Hollywood films to the society which produced them have simply bypassed the industry altogether. The result has been a series of short circuits.

Hollywood films are seen as merely 'reflecting' society. On the one hand is society, seen as a collection of facts, attitudes, psychological patterns or whatever. On the other are the films, where one sees such facts, attitudes, etc mirrored. Though it may be conceded that the mirror sometimes distorts, in so far as there is a theory behind such a view it is a naively realist one, and indeed how could it be otherwise? If there is no conception of Hollywood as an industry with its own history, specific practices, economic relationships, technological and other material constraints, if film is seen as something that somehow mysteriously appears and having appeared is simply there, fixed and given, then how is one to understand the nature of any mediation? To confine ourselves again to the period of the 1930's, a book such as Andrew Bergman's *We're In The Money* devotes a mere four pages to 'A Note on the Movie Industry and the Depression' which ends thus: 'The preliminaries completed, we proceed to the black and white footage itself.' And in the black and white footage the social comment can simply be read off as if the films were so many sociologists' reports. Here is an admittedly rather extreme example: 'Tod Browning's 1932 MGM film, *Freaks*, had a cast made up of pinheads, human torsos, midgets, and dwarfs, like nothing ever in the movies. And what more stunted a year than 1932 for such a film?' (p 168).

One might expect that more specifically Marxist attempts to relate Hollywood to American society would display a little more rigour and subtlety. Bourgeois cultural theories, with their assumptions about the values of artistic freedom and personal expression, are obviously ill-equipped to deal with a medium so conditioned by money, technology and organisational structures. Books such as Bergman's, which dispense with most of that theory (though never completely; some auteurs, such as Capra and Vidor, make an appearance) seem to have no theory at all to replace it. Marxism, on the other hand, proposes a sophisticated understanding of the relations between society, a system of production and the actual product. Yet such Marxist models as have been put forward for understanding Hollywood have suffered from a crudity which has had the effect of deadening further thought. The crudest model of all is that encapsulated in Godard's phrase 'Nixon-Paramount'. The model implied in such a phrase has had obvious attractions for the political avant-garde and indeed contains some truth. But the truth contained in such vulgar Marxism is so vague and general as to have scarcely any use at all. Ideological products such as films are seen as directly caused by the nature of the economic base of society. A capitalist system produces capitalist films, and that is all there is to it. Alternatively, but the slight sophistication is scarcely a modification, the products of Hollywood are bourgeois and capitalist because the particular industry which produces them is capitalist. And the more specific the model becomes the more its crudity is exposed. Thus in the first section of the *Cahiers du Cinéma* text on *Young Mr Lincoln* (translated in *Screen* v 13 n 3) we are told that since Hollywood is involved with big business its ideology is not just a generally capitalist one. It supports the more reactionary wing of the political spectrum represented by the Republican Party.

The *Cahiers* text is only one example of a desire to show not only that Hollywood is a part of bourgeois ideology in general but that some Hollywood films are intended to carry a specific and reactionary message which has a direct reference to a particular political situation. Another example of such over-politicisation comes in a recent issue of *Jump Cut* n 4 Nov-Dec 1974, which contains an interpretation of *King Kong* as an anti-Roosevelt tract. The article conveniently states its premises in a footnote:

> This article is built round two suppositions. First, that all huge business corporations (such as RKO) are conservative Republican unless demonstrated otherwise, and that their products (like *King Kong*) will reinforce their interests instead of betraying them. Second, that the auteur theory in its standard application is not a germane approach when dealing with a political film, especially under the tight studio control of the 1930's. A political film would only be allowed release if its philosophy was in line with that of the studio which made it. Therefore, RKO studio will be regarded as the true "auteur" of *King Kong*, despite the innumerable personal touches of its artistic crew.

Although the phrase 'unless demonstrated otherwise' indicates that the author, Gerald Peary, is aware of the dangers of over-simple generalisations, his assumptions still seem open to two major objections. Firstly, is it not possible that even in Hollywood (not noted perhaps for its political sophistication) there were in the 1930's people who could see that the survival of capitalism (and hence of their 'huge corporations') was not necessarily synonymous with the victory of the Republican Party, especially a Republican Party so discredited as the one which had been led to electoral disaster and intellectual bankruptcy by Herbert Hoover? Secondly, what exactly *are* the interests of such corporations? In the long term, obviously, the survival of a system which allowed them to make profits. But in the short term surely it was those profits themselves. Is it to be assumed that studio executives saw the possibility of profits in attacking a leader who had so recently demonstrated his popularity at the polls (especially among the cinema-going section of the public)? Or should we assume that the political commitment of the studio executives overcame their dedication to profits?

It seems unlikely, but our ignorance about Hollywood generally and about the particular organisation of RKO is such that we cannot answer these questions. Precisely for this reason we ought to beware of assuming any answers. Even if we do assume, with the authors in *Cahiers* and *Jump Cut*, that a studio is owned by big business and that one of its products promotes the political and hence economic interests of the company (I say apparently because the actual interpretation of the films seems open to question), it does not necessarily follow that the political meaning is the direct result of who owns the studio. *Post hoc* is not *propter hoc.*

The lack of any detailed knowledge of industry history, then, suggests caution on the question of the political orientation of Hollywood in the 1930's. Firstly, is it true that the film industry was controlled by big business? And is this the same as the Republican Party (there was business influence among the Democrats too)? Secondly, if it is true can one assume a direct effect on the ideology of Hollywood films? Even the term ideology seems to pose a problem here. It is one thing to argue that, using the term in its classical Marxist sense (or as refined by Althusser) to mean a general world view or structure of thought situated primarily below the conscious level, Hollywood films are ideological expressions of bourgeois society. It is quite another to argue that they support a specific set of political attitudes. Bourgeois society is more than simply the Republican Party. And in any case Marxist theory only claims that ideological products are determined *in the last instance* by the economic relations existing at the base of society. The arguments about *Young Mr Lincoln* and *King Kong* appear to assume that facts about who controls the film industry can provide a sufficient explanation of a film's ideology, ignoring the dimension of the institutional structures which may intervene between the economic base and the final product. Without a knowledge of these structures one cannot say that these films are *not* propaganda; but if they were intended as such, as the *Cahiers* and *Jump Cut* articles imply, it is a strange sort of propaganda which requires an ingenious interpretation thirty or forty years later to make its point. Surely it would have to be demonstrated that such a reading was available to an audience at the time.

III

These problems were thrown into relief by a viewing some time ago of *American Madness*, directed for Columbia in 1932 by Frank Capra. The story of the film concerns Dickson, the manager of a small-town bank (played by Walter Huston). The directors of the bank are financiers of the old school (pre-Keynesians), dedicated to tight money policies which they pursue ruthlessly and selfishly. Dickson, however, has a different view of what the function of a bank should be. He believes that money should be put to work to create jobs and opportunities. His policy is to lend to small businessmen, trusting in his own assessment of their good intentions rather than in the security they can offer. His beliefs are put to the test when a run on the bank occurs; the run is stopped and his faith in his clients vindicated when the little people he has helped rally round to deposit money and so restore confidence in the bank.

The programme note which accompanied the screening of the film at the National Film Theatre suggested that the character of Dickson might have been based on A H Giannini, a California banker who was influential in Columbia's affairs in the 1930's. Such a suggestion raises one immediate difficulty, in that it seems to assume that the apparent, or manifest, meaning of the film is the only one, and ignores the possibility that the latent meaning may be quite different. The film might be about other things besides banking. It excludes, that is, the possibility of analysing the film along the lines of the *Young Mr Lincoln* text, which finds that despite the film's apparent project of supporting the Republican cause in the 1940 presidential election, the 'real' meaning of the film undermines this. (The problem of such readings, despite their obvious attractions, is that it is never explained how in practice the subversive meaning of the film becomes available to the people to whom it might be some use, ie the working class.) Nevertheless, the suggestion seemed worth following up because of the possibility that it might throw some light on the question of Hollywood's relation to politics in the 1930's, and on the nature of the production system generally. And this might in turn tell us something about Capra's films.

Robert Mundy, in a review of Capra's autobiography in the American *Cinema* (v 7 n 1, Fall 1971, p 56), speculates on how it was that Capra was able to make films which so closely embodied his personal ideas. He suggests two reasons: firstly, that Capra was working for a small studio where freedom was greater, and secondly, that Capra's vision 'was unusually consonant with the vision of America which Hollywood purveyed with such commercial success in the 1930's. Ideologically his films were rarely at odds with the image of life which the studios believed the public wanted to see.' Mundy avoids the facile assumption that Capra was 'in touch' with America, and that his films arise out of some special relationship to the people and the mood of the time. Instead, he suggests that his work is an expression of the point of view of his *studio*. He concludes, however, that we need to know more: 'A persuasive history of Columbia in the 1930's [is] needed before an informed critical account of Capra's work can be written.' Quite. The problem is to know where to start, given the problems of such research outlined above. Mr Giannini seemed to offer a way in.

He is referred to in a number of books about Hollywood, but as far as I know never more than in passing, as a prominent Californian banker who was involved in movie financing. In several of the references there is a curious uncertainty about his initials. Sometimes he is called A P Giannini, sometimes A H. Thus Philip French in his 'informal' history of the Hollywood tycoons *The Movie Moguls* mentions him on p 25: 'In fact the first banker to take the cinema seriously was the Californian A P Giannini, the son of an Italian immigrant, whose Bank of Italy (later renamed the Bank of America) has played an important part in movie finance since before the first world war.' On p 79 we read: 'A H Giannini, the influential movie financier whose Bank of Italy had a special claim on Hollywood consciences of whatever religious denomination.'

The mystery of A H or A P was only cleared up when I looked up Giannini in the *National Cyclopædia of American Biography*. It appears that there were two of them. (Obviously I am not the first person since Mr Giannini père to be aware of this fact, but it seems as though Philip French was not when he wrote his book. Of such confusions is film history made.) It's worth giving some details of their careers, since they are relevant to Capra's film. A H and A P (or to give them their full names, Attilio Henry and Amadeo Peter) were brothers. Both their parents were natives of Italy; their father had been a hotel keeper but had come to California to try farming. Amadeo was born in 1870 and his brother four years later. The older brother had gone to work at the age of twelve in his stepfather's firm of wholesale commission agents in San Francisco, and while still in his twenties he formed the Columbus Savings and Loan Society. In 1904 he founded the Bank of Italy. Giannini's bank was at the time of a novel kind. Branches were set up in small towns across the country to attract the savings of the man in the street and Giannini even started savings schemes in schools. His bank specialised in making loans to small businesses with minimal collateral and introduced the practice of lending money for house purchase repayable in monthly instalments. He appears to have been a man of some determination and imagination; during the great San Francisco earthquake and fire of 1906, Giannini was the first to reopen his bank, setting up his desk on the waterfront while the fire still raged. By 1930 he had built up his banking interests to the point where the holding company, the Transamerica Corporation, was the largest of its kind in the world with assets of $1,000 million. Giannini's unorthodox methods did not endear him to more conservative financiers on Wall Street; particularly deplorable was his policy of encouraging wide public ownership of his corporation and of assisting his employees to become stockholders through profit-sharing schemes.

His brother Attilio (sometimes called Dr Giannini, though he abandoned medicine when made vice-president of his brother's Bank of Italy) was involved in various movie companies between the world wars. In 1920 he lent Chaplin half a million dollars to make *The Kid*. In 1936 he became president and chairman of the Board of United Artists and though he resigned from this position in 1938 he retained an influential position in the film industry by virtue of his place on the voting trust which controlled Universal Pictures. He was also involved with several so-called independent production companies such as Selznick International Pictures and Lesser-Lubitsch. It's worth pointing out that none of these organisations possessed large chains of movie theatres. It was the tangible assets of real estate which tempted the Wall Street banks into movie finance in the 1920's. Giannini does at least seem to have been more interested in making pictures.

Giannini's main importance for present purposes is his role in Columbia. The company was originally formed in 1920 as CBC, the letters standing for the names of the three men who set it up: Harry Cohn, Joe Brandt and

Harry's brother Jack. All of them had previously worked for Carl Laemmle at Universal. Attilio Giannini lent them $100,000 to get started. In 1924 the company changed its name to Columbia Pictures Corporation (possibly an echo of the Columbus Savings and Loan Society?). Giannini continued to be closely involved. Although in 1929 the studio decided to establish their stock on the New York exchange, 96 per cent of the voting stock was concentrated in the hands of a voting trust. In 1932 Joe Brandt was bought out by Harry Cohn (after Jack Cohn had attempted to enlist Giannini's support in a coup against his brother) and thereafter the voting trust which controlled the company consisted of the two Cohns and Giannini. Unlike most studios at this time Columbia had no debts to the New York investment banks and instead was run as a family business.

Giannini's position was therefore a powerful one. Unfortunately one has no actual knowledge of how he used it. All that can be done is to suggest what his influence might have been given the kind of background from which he and his brother came. The Gianninis were quite separate from the New York banking establishment. Not only was theirs a different kind of business (deposit as opposed to investment banking), involving them with different kinds of clients; they were Catholics (unlike the Rockefellers and Morgans), they were second-generation immigrants, they came from the other side of the country, and their social attitudes were, as far as one can tell, less patrician. A P's entry in the *National Cyclopædia* says that he 'has ever been known as a friend of the poor and struggling' and if ever a banker could be so described it seems likely that he was. Not surprisingly, therefore, he supported the Banking Act introduced by Roosevelt in 1935 because, he said, he preferred a measure of government control to domination of the banks by the Wall Street establishment. In 1936 he actively supported Roosevelt's campaign for a second term, at a time when Wall Street considered FDR as no better than a Communist. It seems reasonable to assume that his brother shared his liberal views.

The Gianninis might, then, be seen as a kind of contradiction in terms: populist bankers. The populists of the nineteenth century had regarded bankers as the physical embodiment of all that was evil, and believed that the agricultural problems of the Mid-West were largely caused by a conspiracy of monopolists on Wall Street keeping interest rates up and farm prices down. (Amadeo Giannini was, we are told, greatly interested in agricultural progress.) The little man, the populists contended, stood no chance against those who commanded such resources and used them for selfish purposes. But the Gianninis believed in deliberately aiding such small businessmen and farmers who got no help from Wall Street. In this respect they are in line with the policies of the New Deal, which attempted to get big business under some kind of government control while at the same time trying to raise farm prices and help small firms and individuals by encouraging banks to make loans, by refinancing mortgages and so on.

This too is Dickson's policy in *American Madness* and it seems plausible that the character is indeed based on Dr Giannini. The question then is, what do we make of it? A simple and tempting theory might be constructed: Capra's film doesn't so much capture what 'people' were thinking at the time as represent the thinking of a New Dealer on the voting trust controlling Columbia. Such a theory certainly has its attractions. Firstly, it provides a corrective to the crude assumption that Hollywood = big business = the Republican Party. Secondly, other Capra films such as *Mr Deeds Goes To Town, Mr Smith Goes To Washington, You Can't Take It With You* also embody the populism that was a powerful element in the New Deal. Thirdly, the situation of Columbia itself, quite apart from the beliefs of those in control, might well be seen as impelling it towards the New Deal coalition of anti-establishment forces. Despite the Academy Awards Capra collected for the studio in the 1930's it never entirely freed itself from its Poverty Row origins. Although the company bought its own studio in 1926 and in 1929 set up a national distribution organisation, at the beginning of the 1930's Columbia was still producing less than thirty features a year (to MGM's forty-three) and most of these were destined for the lower half of a double bill. Output increased steadily during the decade, but the studio was never in the same league as the majors. In 1935, for example, the total volume of business of Loew's, the parent company of MGM, was $85 million; Columbia's was $16 million. Thus Loew's had nearly 22 per cent of the total volume of business of the industry, Columbia only 4 per cent. And despite the characteristically violent swings in the film industry each year from profit to loss and back again, these relative percentages did not change for the rest of the decade. The reason why Columbia was unable to increase its share of business is that, unlike the major studios, it had no chain of theatres of its own which could serve as a secure outlet for its product. All the money it made came from the sale of its own pictures to theatres owned by other studios. MGM and the other majors could, and frequently did, recoup losses on their own films by profits on the exhibition of other companies' output.

But a potential advantage of this relative weakness was that Columbia preserved its financial independence. It had not had to borrow heavily from the banks to finance the acquisition of theatre chains, and as a result the studio was still in the control of the men who founded it, the two Cohns and Giannini. Its independence of Wall Street meant that it might well become the focus of anti-establishment forces, and that if it did it had the freedom to make films which reflected that, always providing of course that it could sell them to the theatres.

But caution is necessary even before trying to test out such a thesis. Capra in his autobiography devotes several pages to recording how charmed he was by Roosevelt's personality; yet, he says, this only made him 'almost a Democrat'. One might suppose that Capra, a first generation immigrant, an Italian Catholic born in Sicily, was a natural

Democrat. But the political content of his films, while embodying support for the underdog, does not attach itself to any Party. His belief in the people goes hand in hand with a classically populist distrust of *all* their leaders. And other tendencies in his films, such as a pervasive anti-intellectualism and a hostility to central government, are certainly not characteristic of the New Deal.

Nevertheless there is a kind of radicalism in his films which would certainly not have commended itself to the fiercely Republican Louis B Mayer, for example, and it therefore seems worth pursuing the thesis that Columbia might have been a focus for Roosevelt sympathisers. Harry Cohn, who controlled the production side of the company throughout the period, appears to have had no interest in politics at all. It is true that he visited Mussolini in 1933 after Columbia had released a complimentary documentary entitled *Mussolini Speaks*. But Cohn seems to have been more impressed with the intimidating lay-out of the dictator's office than with his politics. When he returned to Hollywood he re-arranged his own office in imitation. Capra remarked in an interview at the National Film Theatre that Cohn didn't care what the politics of his studio's films were. His concern was with their money-making potential, which he estimated with a 'foolproof device. . . . If my fanny squirms it's bad. If my fanny doesn't squirm it's good. It's as simple as that' (quoted in *King Cohn*, p 142). If Giannini had wanted the studio to take a pro-New-Deal stance, then it seems as though Cohn would have had no particular objections.

The only way of testing whether there was such a policy, in default of any access to whatever records of the company may still exist, is to look at the films that Columbia made during the period and to find out what one can about the people who made them. It's at this point that the sheer physical difficulties of this kind of work intrude. Taking the period 1926–41, from just before the introduction of sound to a year or so after Capra left Columbia (an arbitrary choice, but less arbitrary than some, and one which corresponds very roughly to the period of the depression and the consequent New Deal, as far as World War II), Columbia, despite being one of the smaller studios, made on my calculations 627 feature films. (The figure may not be exact because the *Film Daily Year Book*, from which the calculation is made, lists the films of each year twice, once under each studio and once in alphabetical order for the whole industry. Titles appearing in one list don't always appear in the other.) To make those films the company employed 67 different producers, 171 directors, and 269 writers. (The figure for writers is from 1928; they are not credited in the *Year Book* before that date.) By writers is meant those credited with a screenplay. Authors of the original stories from which the films were made might amount to another two or three hundred people. There are also fifteen people whose names appear at one time or another as directors of the company, Columbia Pictures Corporation.

These are the people within the organisation whose position would have allowed them to influence the political content of the films. One might wish to argue that everyone, actors, cameramen, designers, right down to the studio policemen, had some kind of influence, however small. Melvyn Douglas, for example, who acted in many films for Columbia in the 1930's, was active in liberal causes. I have excluded these workers from consideration mainly because, given the nature of the production process, as far as one understands it, and the rigid division of labour, their control over the political content (if any) of a film would have been less. Actors didn't make up their own lines. In any case one has to stop somewhere, and it's not too easy to find out who the studio policemen were.

One is thus faced with a preliminary list of 522 people; to be precise, it is slightly less because the division of labour was not absolute and some writers directed or vice versa. But there is not much overlapping, and the total must be around 500 (this for one small studio during a mere fifteen years of its fifty-year existence). The BFI Library has a card index system which allows one to check whether the Library has entries on individuals in books, periodicals or on microfiche. I accordingly looked up everyone who worked on more than the occasional film. Very few of these names appear in the index and when they do it is often merely a reference to a tiny cutting in *Variety* recording the person's death and giving a short list of the films they worked on. (This is not a criticism of the state of the Library but of the state of film history.)

A few things do emerge. Columbia seems to have been, in the higher echelons, a tight-knit community (one precondition perhaps of a consistent policy). One of the producers was Ralph Cohn, the son of Jack. Everett Riskin, another producer, was the older brother of Robert, who wrote several of Capra's screenplays. Sam Briskin, general manager of the studio in the early 1930's and executive in charge of production from 1938 to 1942, was the brother-in-law of Abe Schneider, treasurer of the company for most of this period. Briskin's brother, Irving, was another producer at Columbia. Yet this doesn't tell us much about an industry where the pull of family relationships was always strong and where 'the son-in-law also rises' was a standard joke.

On the political affiliations of the vast majority, I found no information at all, nor even any information on their lives which would permit a guess. Some very few wrote books or had books written about them, but with the exception of Cohn and Capra their careers were peripheral to Columbia. A few more have been the subject of articles in film magazines, and from these one can glean scraps of information. Richard Maibaum, who wrote a few scripts for the studio, was the author of some anti-lynching and anti-Nazi plays before coming to Hollywood. Dore Schary, whose Democrat sympathies were well known, was also a writer at Columbia in the 1930's. So, very occasionally, were Donald Ogden Stewart, associated with left wing causes at the time, and Edward Chodorov, involved with committees for refugees from Spain and Germany and later more or less black-listed. But this scarcely amounts to much. Stewart, after all, wrote a lot of scripts for MGM.

More significant, at first sight, than the presence of 'liberals', is the fact that exactly half of the Hollywood Ten were actually employed at Columbia during the 1930's; namely Edward Dmytryk, Dalton Trumbo, Herbert Biberman, John Howard Lawson and Lester Cole. But a concerted Communist effort at the studio is hardly likely. Only Dmytryk worked there more than occasionally, and he during his time as a contract director was making routine B-feature films (musicals, horror pictures, thrillers) which, one must assume, offered little scope for the kind of social comment Dmytryk later put into *Crossfire*. There were one or two other Communists working at Columbia who testified before the House Un-American Activities Committee four years after the 1947 hearings which sent the Ten to jail. Paul Jarrico, who wrote for Columbia the screenplays of *No Time To Marry* (1938) and *The Face Behind The Mask* (1941), was called before the Committee in 1951 but refused to testify and pleaded the 5th Amendment. Another called before the Committee in 1951 was Sidney Buchman. One of Harry Cohn's favourite writers, Buchman specialised in comedy. Among his credits for Columbia are: *Whom The Gods Destroy* (1934); *I'll Love You Always, Love Me Forever, She Married Her Boss* (1935), *The King Steps Out, Theodora Goes Wild, Adventure in Manhattan, The Music Goes Round* (1936), *Holiday* (1938), *Mr Smith Goes To Washington* (1939), *The Howards of Virginia* (1940), *Here Comes Mr Jordan* (1941). Buchman admitted that he had been in the Communist Party from 1938 to 1945, but refused to supply the Committee with the list of names of other members they required and was cited for contempt. He was found guilty and given a one-year suspended sentence and a $150 fine.

Buchman clearly occupied an influential position at Columbia. He was a producer as well as a writer and was associated with some of Columbia's greatest successes in the late 1930's and early 1940's. But if *Mr Smith* is satirical about Washington life, it retains an unswerving, even touching, faith in American political institutions, and it is difficult to see that Buchman's membership of the Communist Party had any great effect on what he wrote. Indeed many of his associates appear to have been surprised to learn that he was a Communist.

It may be that a more detailed search through such records as are available would turn up some decisive evidence. But on what has been presented so far it seems unlikely that, Dr Giannini notwithstanding, there was any deliberate policy of favouritism to the New Deal or left causes. The same conclusion seems likely to follow from the films. Here again one is attempting generalisations based on woefully inadequate knowledge, because, apart from those directed by Capra, I have seen very few of the films Columbia made during the period. Nevertheless some impressions can be gained from looking at the records. In the late 1920's and early 1930's the staples of the studio's output were adventure and action films, comedies, often mildly risqué, and the occasional exposé (one of Jack Cohn's first successes at Universal was to convince Carl Laemmle of the box office potential of *Traffic In Souls*, a sensationalist feature on the white slave trade). Westerns and thrillers made up the rest of the production schedule. Of course titles can be misleading, but a list of the films produced in 1928 probably gives a fair indication of at least the type of films being made:

That Certain Thing, The Wife's Relations, Lady Raffles, So This Is Love? Woman's Way, Sporting Age, Matinee Idol, Desert Bride, Broadway Daddies, After The Storm, Golf Widows, Modern Mothers, Name The Woman, Ransom, Way Of The Strong, Beware Of Blondes, Say It with Sables, Virgin Lips, Scarlet Lady, Court Martial, Runaway Girls, Streets of Illusion, Sinners' Parade, Driftwood, Stool Pigeon, The Power Of The Press, Nothing To Wear, Submarine, The Apache, The Lone Wolf's Daughter, Restless Youth, The Sideshow.

Besides Capra, directors working regularly for Columbia at this time included the veteran director of serials George B Seitz (*The Perils of Pauline*), and Erle Kenton, another veteran who had been in pictures since 1914. The policy, one guesses, was one of efficient professionalism dedicated to getting the most out of Columbia's meagre resources. Not only did Columbia make less films; they also spent less on each production than the major studios. (Few of their films at this time ran more than seventy minutes.) This would seem to leave little room for the carefully considered personal statements of the kind Capra aspired to later in the 1930's. This is not to say that there was no possibility of social or political comment, however, as the history of Warners at the same time shows.

After Capra's astonishing success with *It Happened One Night* in 1934, which won Columbia its first Oscars and enormously increased the studio's prestige, pictures of the earlier type were supplemented by the occasional more expensive production. Though Columbia had contract players of its own (for example Jack Holt, Ralph Bellamy or, in Westerns, Buck Jones and Charles Starrett), they could not compare in box-office appeal with the stars of bigger studios. Columbia could not afford the budgets which having bigger stars would have entailed. On the other hand it could never break into the big time without them. Harry Cohn's solution to this vicious circle was to invite successful directors from other studios to make occasional pictures for Columbia, pictures which would be given larger than usual budgets and which would have stars borrowed from other studios. Careful planning permitted short production schedules and kept costs down to what Columbia could afford. Capra too was given increasingly larger budgets and outside stars. Thus a number of big-name directors came to work at Columbia during the later 1930's, often tempted by the offer of being allowed to produce their own films. Among the titles produced at Columbia during the period after *It Happened One Night* were:

1934: *20th Century* (dir Howard Hawks, with John Barrymore and Carole Lombard), *The Captain Hates The Sea* (dir Lewis Milestone, with Victor McLaglen and John Gilbert); 1935: *The Whole Town's Talking* (dir John Ford, with Edward G Robinson), *She Married Her Boss* (dir Gregory La Cava, with Claudette Colbert), *She Couldn't Take It* (dir Tay Garnett, with George Raft and Joan Bennett), *Crime and Punishment* (dir Josef von Sternberg, with Peter Lorre); 1936: *Theodora Goes Wild* (dir Richard Boleslavski, with Irene Dunne); 1937: *The Awful Truth* (dir Leo McCarey, with Cary Grant and Irene Dunne); 1938: *Holiday* (dir George Cukor, with Cary Grant, Katharine Hepburn); 1939: *Let Us Live* (dir John Brahm, with Maureen O'Sullivan and Henry Fonda), *Only Angels Have Wings* (dir Howard Hawks, with Cary Grant, Thomas Mitchell and Richard Barthelmess), *Golden Boy* (dir Rouben Mamoulian, with Barbara Stanwyck and Adolphe Menjou); 1940: *His Girl Friday* (dir Howard Hawks, with Cary Grant and Rosalind Russell), *The Howards of Virginia* (dir Frank Lloyd, with Cary Grant), *Angels Over Broadway* (dir Ben Hecht and Lee Garmes, with Douglas Fairbanks Jr), *Arizona* (dir Wesley Ruggles, with William Holden); 1941: *Penny Serenade* (dir George Stevens, with Cary Grant and Irene Dunne), *Texas* (dir George Marshall, with William Holden, Glenn Ford and Claire Trevor), *You Belong To Me* (dir Wesley Ruggles, with Barbara Stanwyck and Henry Fonda), *The Men In Her Life* (dir Gregory Ratoff, with Loretta Young).

But despite this sprinkling of prestige productions the basic recipe remained much the same as before. There were lots of low-budget Westerns (a dozen or so in 1940) directed by Lambert Hillyer, a veteran of the Columbia lot, or Joseph H Lewis, and starring Bill Elliott or Charles Starrett. The studio made several series: a number of films based on Blondie, the cartoon character, the Lone Wolf series of thrillers, an Ellery Queen mystery series and so on. There were light comedies from Alexander Hall, more light comedies and musicals from Walter Lang, and plenty of crime films (a few titles at random from 1938: *Women In Prison, When G-Men Step In, Penitentiary, Highway Patrol, Reformatory, Convicted, I Am The Law, Juvenile Court, Smashing The Spy Ring*).

What is one to conclude from what emerges of Columbia's production policy in this period? Aware that a viewing of all the films might prove one wrong, it could be said that there is no evidence of Columbia's deliberately following a line favourable to the New Deal. Of course it could be objected that a similar scanning of the titles of Warner Brothers films of the same time would fail to reveal what an actual viewing of the films shows, a detectable if not pronounced leaning towards Rooseveltian attitudes. But this much seems likely: the policy of bringing in outside stars and directors (and writers too) for big-budget productions would have worked against the continuity required for a deliberate political policy. Whereas at Warners a nucleus of stars, writers, producers and directors was built up capable of producing pictures that fused the thrills of crime with social comment, at Columbia the occasional film (such as *A Man's Castle*, directed by Frank Borzage in 1933) which took the Depression as its subject was a one-off, with the exception of Capra. And it does seem as though Capra *was* an exception. As far as one can tell the directors who did not have his freedom at the studio did not follow him in the direction of social comment, and neither did directors brought in from outside with a similar amount of freedom. And Capra's films, after all, despite his standing within the studio, are only a tiny proportion of all the films Columbia made in the 1930's.

If one can say that the presence of Giannini on the trust controlling Columbia did not lead to films predominantly favourable to the New Deal, then can one not also throw doubt on the assumption that control of a studio by interests favourable to the Republican Party led to films (such as *Young Mr Lincoln* and *King Kong*) designed to make propaganda for that party? No-one would argue that there was a total lack of correlation between ownership and the content of films. No studio in the 1930's would have tolerated outright Communist movies, or anything very close to that. (Nor for that matter would a Fascist film have stood any chance of being made.) But within these parameters considerable diversity was possible, a diversity, moreover, which it is dangerous to reduce by the simple expedient of labelling all the films as bourgeois. The difference in political attitudes between, say, *The Good Earth* (MGM, 1937) and *The Grapes of Wrath* (20th Century-Fox, 1940) – two films with not totally dissimilar subjects – are not negligible and relate to real political and social events of the time. But they cannot be explained simply in terms of who owned the studios or in terms only of social attitudes at the time. Any explanation would require that a number of factors be taken into account, and not least of these would be the exact nature of the institutions which produced them.

The history of the American film industry, then, forms a kind of missing link in attempts, Marxist and otherwise, to make connections between films and society. As we have seen, many of the materials needed to forge that link are missing, which is why the title of this essay, 'Notes on Columbia Pictures Corporation 1926–41', is intended to imply more than the customary academic modesty. The problems of producing such a history are both practical and the result of a massive ideological prejudice, and I am aware that the information I have produced on Columbia in the 1930's amounts to very little in the way of real knowledge. But this information has been the result of a few hours in the library, not of a large-scale research programme. If one considers how much has been learned, for example, about British labour history in the nineteenth century the possibilities for further research do not seem hopeless. As a subject it would appear equally as unpromising as the history of the film industry. Apart from newspapers there are few written sources and the people involved are all dead. The history therefore has to a great extent to be reconstructed from the material objects which survive: buildings, institutional structures, the customs and practices of a people. But full-time academics and research students have been working in the field for years. The study of the history of the American film industry has scarcely begun.

7

THE B FILM AND THE PROBLEM OF CULTURAL DISTINCTION

Lea Jacobs

Source: *Screen* 33(1) (1992): 1–13.

In 1934, Fred Eastman, writing in *Parent's Magazine* about how to select films for children, cautioned: 'The fine effects of a picture that meets these tests [of suitability for children] may be offset if the picture is presented on a program along with cheap and trashy pictures.'[1] Letters to the editor of the Sunday edition of the *New York Times* amusement section raised similar objections to the pairing of children's movies with inappropriate second features, one father complaining about a 1938 double bill of Deanna Durbin's *Mad About Music* and *Penitentiary*.[2] In 1939, Dr Ray Lyman Wilbur, of the Motion Picture Research Council, went on record against the double feature saying that 'diversified programs made it unlikely that both features of a double bill would be of "family" suitability'.[3]

The evaluation of the B film by parent/teacher groups as 'cheap and trashy', 'lurid', without serious intellectual or moral content, is precisely the sort of judgement which film critics like Manny Farber, and later, Todd McCarthy and Charles Flynn had to argue against in asserting the importance and interest of the Bs. My aim here is to discuss how the 'low' cultural status of the B movie was institutionalized within the film industry itself in the thirties. I am not concerned with how particular critics or reformers judged the Bs, but rather the construction of the *distinction* between A and B features, between 'quality' films and what was sometimes called 'the lower half' of the double bill.

The practice of exhibiting two features on a programme seems to have begun in the late twenties, although at this date the double bill was largely confined to theatres in the Northeast and Southwest.[4] It became widespread among independent exhibitors in the early thirties and by the middle of the decade even the first-run theatres affiliated with the major studios were forced by the pressure of competition to offer their patrons double bills (although some first-run theatres continued to programme single features augmented by shorts, newsreels and live vaudeville).[5] As Paul Seale has shown, the development of the double feature gave new impetus to the so-called Poverty Row studios, and more generally to low-budget filmmaking.[6] But the studios had always produced films in various budget ranges, and hence price ranges. For example, in the teens, Universal's feature output was divided into several series: the low-budget 'Red Feather' productions, the more costly 'Bluebird' releases, and the occasional prestige or 'Jewel' production.[7] The growth in the thirties of what *Variety* called the 'duals', however, necessitated the elaboration of new mechanisms for distinguishing between films based upon their cost.

We tend to assume that a film's position within the double bill was determined in the planning and financing of production. By this definition, a B film is one made quickly on a low budget, without major stars or expensive literary properties, in a specialized production unit – such as Lee Marcus's unit at RKO – or by a B studio like Monogram or Republic. While I certainly do not want to discount the importance of the production context for defining the B film, I would argue that its status was determined much more complexly within the system of distribution and exhibition. The pattern of a film's release, the kinds of publicity and critical attention devoted to it, even the sorts of theatres it played in, all worked to articulate and maintain the distinction between A and B pictures. Of course, these factors were not independent of film budget, but neither were they reducible to it. Relatively low-budget films were sometimes given the kind of release and publicity typical of an A. John Ford's *The Informer* (1935), for example, was produced on a budget of $243,000. While this cost more than a run-of-the-mill B, it was inexpensively produced compared to most A films which, according to Richard Jewell, ranged from $350,000–$1.5 million at RKO. Nonetheless, the film opened at the prestigious Radio City Music Hall in New York, and was widely regarded as a production of high quality, garnering Academy Awards for Ford, Dudley Nichols, Victor McLaglen and Max Steiner.[8] Even run-of-the-mill B films sometimes played as A during part of their initial run. *Pacific Liner* (1939), a B film produced by Robert Sisk at RKO, was described by *Variety* as 'filler in the duals'.[9] Yet it screened singly or on the top half of the double bill for six weeks after its release in January 1939.[10] And films moved down as well as up the spectrum – some of those financed as A productions were relegated to the lower half of the bill on their initial or subsequent run. Take the example of *Room Service* (1938). RKO spent $255,000 for the rights, the most expensive property ever purchased by the studio.[11] For three months the Marx Brothers' film either played singly with vaudeville, or on the top half of the double bills listed in the 'Picture Grosses' pages in *Variety*. After 12 December 1938, however, it was relegated to the lower half of the bill due to its poor performance at the box office. The point is that in the sphere of exhibition, the distinction between A and B was a fluid one; a function of marketing and distribution strategies which varied as distributors and exhibitors responded to box-office returns and a film's reviews during its opening run.

The redefinition of a film's status was made possible through the system of block-booking and blind-selling. Exhibitors did not contract for specific titles but rather for a block of films identified only by number and price bracket.[12] Contracts usually specified multiple price brackets, in some of which the distributor received a percentage of the gross (the A or 'quality' films), in others a flat rental (the Bs). In the Amended and Supplemental Complaint in the Paramount case, the government gives the following as a typical example of price bracketing: 'Four features at 35%; six at 30%; ten at 25%; ten at $200.00 flat rental; and ten at $100.00 flat rental.'[13] Because the contract did not stipulate titles, distributors and exhibitors could negotiate over where any particular film fitted within the overall price system. In the Paramount case, the government notes, '. . . most features are not definitely allocated to a price bracket until after their release, and the question of proper allocation is a continuous source of dispute between exhibitors and distributors'.[14] Thus, the major producer-distributors, in negotiation with their own affiliated theatres, as well as the large, independent theatre chains, made decisions concerning the length of time any given film would be in first-run release and on what terms. Based upon trade showings of completed films, and upon reports of a film's initial box-office performance in key cities like New York and Los Angeles, the most powerful exhibitors were in a position to turn down films which they thought likely to be unprofitable[15] or to extend the run of highly profitable ones. Films which were unattractive to the major first-run houses were either moved directly to less desirable subsequent-run theatres or screened on the second half of the double bill in the major cities. While relatively unprofitable A films could be relegated to the ranks of the Bs, there was also an incentive for the studios to sell attractive B films to exhibitors as As if they could. This was especially the case for so-called 'intermediates', which cost between $250,000 and $500,000.[16] The cost of the 'intermediates' precluded the studio making a profit unless some exhibitors could be persuaded (or coerced!) to pay a percentage of the gross rather than the flat rental fee usual for westerns and other B pictures.

Seeking to understand how the A/B distinction was structured at the level of distribution and exhibition, I have examined the entirety of RKO's output for the six-month period between October 1938 and April 1939. There is no particular logic to the choice of dates, aside from the fact that double bills became increasingly widespread over the decade (there are very few double bills in the major first-run theatres listed in *Variety* prior to 1935). Using the 'Picture Grosses' pages in *Variety* I have been able to determine where films played on double bills in both affiliated and independent theatres in major US cities. I have also looked at the kinds of reviews and publicity the films received when they opened in New York. These data indicate that the release pattern typical of RKO's A features differed considerably from the B features, but nonetheless that it was possible for a film's status within the system to be redefined after its initial release.

As Mae Huettig noted in her study of vertical integration in the motion-picture industry, one of the most important functions of the ownership of first-run theatres by the majors was that it permitted them to give their films a 'build-up' on their initial run.[17] A barrage of publicity and advertising, accompanied by film reviews and related stories in big-city newspapers, helped to build audience interest at the time of a film's opening. More importantly, what amounted to a national advertising campaign helped to secure successful subsequent runs in small cities and towns throughout the country. Yet the treatment of A and B features was very different in this regard. While the release of A features was calculated to maximize publicity build-up, the release of B features was often unheralded and even haphazard.

RKO's *Gunga Din*, which opened in late January of 1939, and *Love Affair*, which opened in late March, will serve as examples of the release pattern typical of an A picture. *Gunga Din* was a 'special', that is, it played singly even in theatres long accustomed to double bills. Some theatres, such as the Pantages in Los Angeles, even charged a special admission price of $2.00 at the premiere. *Love Affair* is a more 'ordinary' A, in that it generally played with a second feature or a vaudeville programme even on its opening run. Both films were released almost simultaneously in a large number of metropolitan centres. *Gunga Din* opened in Los Angeles and New York in the week ending 1 February 1938, and then within the next two weeks opened in fifteen other cities: Washington, San Francisco, Boston, Denver, Baltimore, Philadelphia, Chicago, Minneapolis, Portland, Louisville, Detroit, Indianapolis, Providence, Kansas City and Buffalo. The release pattern of *Love Affair* is similar, with the film opening in nineteen cities within three weeks (the cities are: New York, Philadelphia, Denver, Omaha, Cincinnati, Baltimore, Los Angeles, San Francisco, Indianapolis, Louisville, Chicago, Seattle, Boston, Denver, Buffalo, Portland, Washington, Cleveland and Kansas City). There are several indications that this kind of release pattern was timed to coincide with a national advertising campaign. The review of *Gunga Din* in *Variety* notes that the film 'has numerous exploitation angles and is backed by a giant bally and advertising campaign' and exhibitors in Washington (at the Keith's theatre) and Indianapolis (at the Indiana theatre) report a splurge of advertising prior to the film's release in those cities.[18] Janet Staiger's work on the history of advertising suggests that this kind of coordinated national advertising campaign, which effectively bypassed the local exhibitor, had become an industry norm by the early thirties.[19]

Quite apart from the publicity orchestrated by the studio, the openings of both *Gunga Din* and *Love Affair* were accompanied by a great deal of press coverage. *The New York Times* published four pieces related to *Gunga Din* within the space of three weeks, including a piece in the Sunday edition entitled 'Poets and the cinema' in which B. R. Crisler discussed the film in relation to Kipling's original.[20] The film and theatre magazines which reviewed *Gunga Din* include: *National Board of Review Magazine, Photoplay, Rob Wagner's Script, Sight & Sound, Stage* and *Tatler*. A large number of general interest magazines also carried material on the film including: *Commonweal, Country Life, Nation, New Masses, New Republic, New Statesman and Nation, New Yorker, Newsweek, Scholastic, Time* and *World Horizons*. The *New York Times* coverage of *Love Affair* was not as extensive as *Gunga Din*, consisting of only one review.[21] But the coverage of *Love Affair* was wide-ranging, including both film magazines – *National Board of Review Magazine, Photoplay, Sight & Sound, Stage* – and general interest magazines – *Canadian Magazine, Life, New Statesman and Nation, New Yorker, Newsweek* and *Time*.[22] Because these pieces appeared either in the week immediately preceding the opening of these films or in the following month, this kind of press coverage effectively buttressed the pattern of the film's release and the national advertising campaigns orchestrated by the studio.

Made without stars or prestigious literary properties, B features were not expected to draw audiences to theatres in the way that A features did. Moreover, since distributors received only a flat rental fee (as opposed to a percentage of the gross) for B films, it is not surprising that the studios did not devote many resources to advertising the Bs. An article in *Variety* notes the difference in the treatment of A and B features:

> Millions of box office dollars are lost in the course of a year by an industry that is too much concerned with the pushovers made to order for theatres, and too little enthused over many good films which require advertising push and bustle to get their values before the public. . . . Of course, the reason why many good films are passed up is because the major producers themselves concentrate on their biggest and best, and many a deserving but small-budget film is shot out to the exchanges without so much as a letter of introduction to its (the studio's) own salesmen and branch managers.[23]

In general, the release pattern of RKO's B features confirms the suggestion in *Variety* that the distribution of the Bs was not accompanied by a national advertising campaign. Where as the openings of A features in major cities were concentrated within several weeks, timed to coincide with publicity and promotion efforts and film reviews, the openings of B features in major cities were spread out over several months, with films seemingly slotted into first-run theatres as they were needed to fill out double bills. The releases of two B pictures, *Next Time I Marry*, a comedy starring Lucille Ball and James Ellison, and *Fisherman's Wharf*, one of a series of Bobby Breen musicals produced by Sol Lesser and distributed by RKO, are indicative of this release pattern.

Fisherman's Wharf did have a gala opening at RKO's main San Francisco theatre, the Golden Gate. The film screened singly in tandem with public appearances by child star Bobby Breen and co-stars Henry Armetta and Leo Carillo. This opening was apparently motivated by the film's setting – the exhibitor noted 'Natives are suckers for pictures with a San Francisco locale'. Despite this successful premiere, however, *Fisherman's Wharf* appeared in only five cities within the first three weeks of its opening run: San Francisco, Minneapolis, Buffalo, Omaha and Brooklyn. It reached New York only on the fourth week of its run, Chicago on the fifth and Los Angeles on the sixth. *Next Time I Marry* had a similarly restricted opening in seven cities in three weeks: New York, Providence, Baltimore, Boston, Omaha, Los Angeles and Kansas City.

The fact that B films did not receive a nationally organized advertising campaign meant that it was not necessary for the studios to coordinate a pattern of near simultaneous releases across the United States. Indeed, I suspect that one of the advantages of the Bs for distributors and exhibitors was that they could be booked in and out of theatres in a relatively flexible manner. They could be used to vary a programme from week to week when a popular A film was 'held over', or a programme of two Bs could be booked into a theatre in order to fill a few empty days in the middle of the week. For example, in March of 1939 *Gunga Din* played for two weeks in the Adams theatre in Detroit, the first week accompanied by *Next Time I Marry* and the second week by *Peck's Bad Boy at the Circus* (RKO). A similar pattern occurred at the Paramount theatre in Portland during the weeks of 15 and 22 February and the Paramount in Seattle during the weeks of 22 February and 1 March.[24] In the same period, RKO's reissue of the relatively low-budget *Lost Patrol* (originally released in 1934) with *Star of Midnight* (originally released in 1935) was often used to fill in gaps in a theatre's programme. For example, the Fulton theatre in Pittsburgh showed a double bill of *Star of Midnight* and *Lost Patrol* for four days, following the end of the run of a major A release – Shirley Temple in *The Little Princess* (20th Century-Fox).[25]

The lack of a coherent advertising and publicity campaign for B films was seconded by the paucity of national press coverage for such releases. In striking contrast with *Gunga Din* and *Love Affair*, neither *Fisherman's Wharf* nor *Next Time I Marry* were reviewed in any general interest magazines. The only film journals to discuss these films were industry trade journals such as *Variety* and *The Motion Picture Herald* which reviewed all the films in release, and hence covered the Bs. The *New York Times*, among other daily newspapers, tended to review Bs in an attempt to discuss most of what was exhibited in the city. However, much less column space was devoted to second features in a newspaper like the *Times*. For example, Brosley Crowther reviewed *Next Time I Marry* in a short 2½ inch single column space.[26] In the same issue of the *Times*, Frank Nugent's review of *Sacrifice d'Honneur* by Marcel L'Herbier spread over several columns at the top of the page and was given a headline in bold face. Moreover, some B pictures were never reviewed in the *Times* at all; Nugent and Crowther seem to have drawn the line at dog pictures like RKO's *Almost a Gentleman*.

Thus B films tended to open in many fewer theatres than A films did in the initial weeks of their run, and they came to exhibitors without the benefit of national advertising or extended press coverage. Moreover, precisely because they were not calculated to draw a large audience, they tended to appear in smaller and less prestigious venues than did A films. In New York, for example, RKO's A features premiered with a stage show at the Radio City Music Hall, a picture palace which seated 5,980 with admission prices ranging from 40 cents to $1.65. Both *Gunga Din* and *Love Affair* opened there. In contrast, B films played in one of a number of smaller venues: the Rivoli, seating 2,092 and charging 25–85 cents admission; the Palace, seating 1,700 and charging from 25–55 cents; and the Rialto, seating 750 and charging 25–55 cents. *Fisherman's Wharf* opened at the Palace, on the second half of a double bill with Warners' *Wings of the Navy*, an A film on its second run. This kind of New York opening is quite typical of RKO's B films in this period. *Next Time I Marry* also opened on the second half of a double bill, playing at the Rivoli with RKO's *The Mad Miss Manton*, an A film in second run. Even lower on the scale, action films, westerns and horror films do not seem to have played at the Rivoli or the Palace very often. These films seem to have been restricted to the small Rialto theatre: *Boy Slaves*, an RKO exploitation picture opened singly at the Rialto, as did the western *Renegade Ranger*. In the mid-forties, the films of Val Lewton's unit also premiered at this theatre.

Outside New York city, many of RKO's B films opened in small theatres which, like the Rialto, specialized almost entirely in B films and reissues of older A features. Unlike the Rialto, however, such theatres often showed two double or triple bills a week. Thus, *Next Time I Marry* opened in Minneapolis in the fifth week of its run in the Aster, a 900 seat theatre charging from 15–25 cents. During the first half of the week the Aster showed a double bill of *Tough Guys* (Universal) and *Comet Over Broadway* (Warners) and the second half of the week *Spy Ring* (Columbia) and *Next Time I Marry*. Similarly, the RKO film played in Omaha in the Avenue Dundee Military which encompassed three theatres seating 950, 810 and 650, and charged 10–25 cents admission. The programme at these theatres consisted of a double bill of *Dawn Patrol* (Warners) and *The Cowboy and the Lady* (United Artists) for the first half of the week and followed by a triple bill of *Gangster's Boy* (Monogram), *Service De Luxe* (Universal) and *Next Time I Marry*.

The system of distribution and exhibition thus functioned to promote A films much more actively than Bs through the placement of A films in larger and more expensive theatres, and the scheduling of releases to allow for a build-up of publicity and coverage in national magazines such as *Life, Time* and *Newsweek*. Not only did A films tend to make more money as a consequence of this system of distribution and exhibition, but also they were accorded marks of cultural distinction – playing in the most elegant downtown theatres, reviewed and discussed in literary magazines like *New Republic* and *Nation* as well as film magazines like *Sight & Sound* and *National Board of Review Magazine*. In this sense, the trade practices of the film industry recapitulated the same cultural hierarchy which informed the complaints of parent/teacher groups about what Fred Eastman called 'cheap and trashy' second features. The patterns of film distribution and exhibition functioned according to the assumption that B films did not merit and could not support the kind of attention which the studios routinely tried to drum up for the As.

The distinction between A and B features was thus well institutionalized within the system of distribution where it signalled both a strategic judgement about the kind of profit that could be expected from a film (an A film was worth advertising because of the greater proceeds that could be derived from it) and, perhaps more amorphously, an aesthetic judgement that the film was of a certain 'quality' (at the very least, the back projection in an A film would not embarrass the studio in front of the reviewers from *Sight & Sound* and the *New York Times*). But if the distinction between A and B films was relatively well fixed within the system of distribution, the status of any individual film within this system was open to negotiation. As I have already noted, it was possible for low-budget films to garner an A release. Such 'crossovers' are of particular interest because they reveal how both economic and aesthetic considerations were brought to bear upon the marketing and distribution of features.

The example of *A Man to Remember*, released in late November of 1938, points to the importance of notions of 'quality' and aesthetic standards in determining a feature's status. The film was planned and financed on a low budget and had no major stars. The story of a small-town doctor and his family, the doctor was played by Edward Ellis and top billing was given to the child star Anne Shirley, who played the doctor's daughter. It was the first film directed by the then unknown Garson Kanin, scripted by Dalton Trumbo. I would like to know more about how the decision-making hierarchy at the studio functioned in this instance, but apparently sometime in late October or early November it was decided that the film was 'good' enough to distribute as an A. The *Motion Picture Herald* noted that the preview of the film at the studio brought tears to the eyes of supposedly hardened 'newspaper folk'.[27] There were two reviews of the film in *Variety* (itself an unusual occurrence). The first appeared in October, when the film opened in Kansas City, and characterized it as a B, albeit an extraordinary one: 'Without any b.o. power to carry it along [i.e. stars], the picture is nevertheless a strong programmer that will go particularly well in spots where audiences appreciate a study of human nature with all the dramatic strength involved in such unfoldment.'[28] The review thus already called attention to the film's subject matter as a possible selling point with a serious and putatively discriminating audience – 'spots where audiences appreciate a study of human nature'. The second review appeared in November and by this time *Variety* was suggesting that the film could be sold by the local exhibitor as an A:

> *A Man to Remember* won't be recalled by exhibs unless it is studiously and extensively exploited. With hardly a name in the cast that will mean an extra nickel in the till and a tepid title, the picture should mean nice business if accorded showmanly treatment. This is the sort of entertainment the average American likes but it will take painstaking bally to let customers know it. This is one that the exhibitor can personally endorse in his advertisements because the picture will back up such boosting with word-of-mouth boosting. . . . This production tags Garson Kanin, newcomer from New York legit, where he was an actor and production assistant to George Abbott, as an outstanding Hollywood directorial find of the year. His crisp approach to the country doctor saga and the novel handling of nearly every situation lifts an ordinary programmer into a money feature.[29]

The release pattern of *A Man to Remember* seems to mirror *Variety*'s difficulty in characterizing the film, wavering between B and A status. In the first four weeks of its run, it screened in only eight [*sic*] cities (Kansas City, Omaha, Providence, Denver, New York, Philadelphia and Buffalo), playing the top half of the double bill in four. It opened on the second half of a double bill in Kansas City on 19 October 1938. By the next week it had top billing but opposite other RKO Bs in relatively small theatres (in one case with *Mr Doodle Kicks Off* at the Albee in Providence and in the other with *Affairs of Annabel* at the Brandeis in Omaha). When it finally opened in New York on 9 November 1938, it played at the Rivoli, a theatre of moderate size which premiered many RKO B features before it closed its doors later that same year. Yet the film clearly got excellent reviews. An exhibitor at the Aldine theatre in Philadelphia noted: 'Came in almost unheralded, but is getting plenty of belated pushing now as result of rave notices.' Frank Nugent gave it an enthusiastic review in the *Times*: 'It has a modest cast. . . . Its sets are as commonplace as the small town which is its scene. . . . In brief, it is probably one of the most uncolossal pictures of the year. But there is no real connection – although Hollywood often says so – between a big budget and a big picture.[30] The film was also picked up in a number of national magazines, although some reviews must have come too late to do it much good: *New Masses* (22 November 1938); *New Yorker* (12 November 1938); *Rob Wagner's Script* (24 December 1938); *Time* (24 October 1938); *New Statesman and Nation* (1 April 1939); *Newsweek* (17 April 1939).

The accumulation of good reviews seems to have helped to maintain the film's distribution as an A, despite some complaints in the 'Picture Grosses' pages of *Variety* of poor performance at the box office. By 14 December 1938, that is six weeks after its opening in New York, *A Man to Remember* had showed on the top half of the double bill in four out of the seven theatres in which it played (an A in Cincinnati, Washington, Chicago, Portland; a B in Los Angeles, Seattle and Indianapolis). It played singly for a run of nine weeks in Minneapolis, where the exhibitor at the World theatre offered the following advice: 'Critics have fallen all over selves in boosting this one and customers also are singing its praises. House tripled usual newspaper display advertising appropriation and went all the way in selling it.' In the long run, the distribution strategy for this film seems to have been quite advantageous for RKO, earning profits of $145,000, a performance characterized as an 'outstanding success' in one business history of the studio.[31] I should note, however, that the exhibitors in the 'Picture Grosses' pages of *Variety* complained repeatedly that their returns were below par for *A Man to Remember*. I surmise that the film made most of its money in subsequent-run theatres or in smaller cities and towns.

Clearly then, the studio was able to capitalize on the supposedly 'worthy' subject matter and ensuing critical acclaim accorded to *A Man to Remember* in planning its distribution. The studio did not hold to this strategy in all instances, however, and the case of *The Great Man Votes*, John Barrymore's last film, provides an interesting contrast. In many ways the Barrymore film resembled *A Man to Remember*. Directed by Garson Kanin, it was initially budgeted as an intermediate (it cost $265,000, which put it in a higher budget bracket than *A Man to Remember* which cost $118,000).[32] The studio evidently decided to release it as an A following the success of Kanin's previous feature. It opened in late January 1939, showing at the Radio City Music Hall in New York and twelve other cities within the first three weeks of its run (Denver, Chicago, Baltimore, Washington, Kansas City, Indianpolis, Washington, Brooklyn, Pittsburgh, Detroit, Providence and Omaha). Although the review in the *New York Times* was lukewarm, it seems to have been widely discussed in the daily press. Exhibitors in New York, Baltimore, Kansas City, Pittsburgh and Cleveland referred to 'good notices' or 'good exploitation and word of mouth'. Nonetheless, the film did not do well at the box office. The Music Hall reported a 'sorrowful 55,000' on one week. The Orpheum in Kansas City noted 'biz average at 5,000'. The Stanley in Pittsburgh complained 'flicker well received but getting no b.o. attention'. The Palace in Cleveland made a similar observation: 'Earning excellent notices but trade is off.' The Gopher in Minneapolis pulled the film early, noting 'picture out after 800 on four days.' By the week of 15 March 1939, that is six weeks after its opening in New York, *The Great Man Votes* only appeared in the B feature slot in the theatres listed in *Variety*. In Indianapolis and Seattle it screened as the second half of a double bill with *Love Affair*, which did well in both theatres. In Oklahoma City, the Barrymore film took second billing to a western, RKO's *Arizona Legion*. By late March and early April the film appeared in the smaller theatres offering split double and triple bills. In Omaha, the Avenue Dundee Military showed a double bill of *Kentucky* (20th Century) and *Zaza* (Paramount) split with an unforgettable triple bill of *The Great Man Votes, Up River* (20th Century-Fox) and *Down on the Farm* (20th Century-Fox). In comparison with *A Man to Remember*, then, *The Great Man Votes* played in many more theatres during the opening weeks of its run, and had the benefit of a premiere at the Radio City Music Hall. Yet it was demoted to B status much more quickly – after only six weeks – and in a much more definitive manner. Six weeks after it opened *A Man to Remember* was still being billed as an A in over half the theatres it played in, despite the complaints from exhibitors about its low box-office draw.

I can only account for the difference in the handling of *A Man to Remember* and *The Great Man Votes* in terms of the other RKO features they had to compete with. *A Man to Remember* was released in early October, and thus competed with two A films that did not make very much money – *Room Service* released in mid-September and *The Mad Miss Manton* released in mid-October.[33] In these circumstances the studio was clearly well advised to sell Kanin's first film as an A if it could, since it did not have much other product for the A slot in its own theatres at its disposal. The season of the release also worked in favour of the film – a sentimental 'family' picture, *A Man to Remember* was widely screened during the Christmas season (especially the weeks of 7 and 14 December). In contrast, *The Great Man Votes* opened in late January, only one week before the opening of *Gunga Din*. A very good box-office draw, *Gunga Din* was held over from two to three weeks in most of the major first-run theatres in which it played. It thus served to drive other RKO features from the A slot in RKO theatres. And just as *Gunga Din* was finishing its first run, *Love Affair* opened in mid-March, another success which was held over an average of two weeks. In these circumstances, it was clearly in the studio's interest quickly to demote *The Great Man Votes* to the lower half of the double bill, despite the presence of Barrymore, a prestigious if waning star, and generally good reviews.

The effect of RKO's distribution strategies on the definition of the B picture gives us some insight into how the classical Hollywood cinema, as opposed to other institutions, worked to perpetuate cultural hierarchies. Within the fields of literature and cultural studies, the debate over canons has given rise to great interest in the ways aesthetic hierarchies are elaborated and maintained. Writing in 1979, the sociologist Pierre Bourdieu has studied the way in which the education system produces differences in taste as a function of class.[34] More recently, there have been studies of how the distinction between 'high' and 'low' culture has been constructed within institutions such as the symphony orchestra, the legitimate theatre and the art marketplace.[35] The distinction between high and low culture can be applied to the classical Hollywood cinema only with difficulty however, since, like most forms of mass culture, it seems to have reached people of diverse classes, and ethnic and national traditions. Thus, clearly, A films were not geared solely to upper or middle-class sectors of the audience. Those patrons who could not afford to see *Gunga Din* at Radio City Music Hall at an admission price of at least 40 cents, could have waited to see it at the Albee in Brooklyn a month later for 25 cents. But while Hollywood did not make specific kinds of films for specific classes, it did mobilize cultural hierarchies in the distribution and marketing of features.

As I have noted, the distinction between A and B films established within the system of distribution was based both upon economic considerations and received notions of 'quality' and cultural importance. Bs in what were generally considered 'low' genres – animal stories, westerns, action and horror films – were much less likely to cross over into the A brackets. The horror films of Val Lewton, for example, were consistently screened as Bs, opening at the small Rialto theatre in New York and quickly relegated to split double and triple bills outside the New York metropolitan area. These films were generally dismissed by the critical establishment as well, despite the fact that critics Manny Farber and James Agee championed Lewton's work.[36]

As the case of *The Great Man Votes* suggests, however, a culturally respectable form and subject matter, even given good reviews, was not enough to protect a film's A status if the studio stood to make greater profits through distributing other features in its choice first-run theatres. The marketplace thus played a powerful role in determining what was distributed as an A, and therefore in the definitions of 'quality' and of 'cheap and trashy pictures' which Hollywood produced.

Notes

1 Fred Eastman, 'How to select movies for children', *Parent's Magazine*, March 1934, pp. 18, 67–8.
2 See letters by Marie Duff and Benjamin S. Lichtenstein, *New York Times*, 12 June 1938, section X, p. 4.
3 'Against double features', *New York Times*, 8 March 1939, p. 19 Throughout the thirties, parent/teacher groups protested about double bills and attempted to organize ways of controlling children's attendance at double features. In 1938, *Variety* reported on a bill proposed in the Nebraska legislature limiting theatre programmes to 150 minutes 'as a sock against the duals', *Variety*, 14 December

1938, p. 11. As early as 1934, *Parent's Magazine* proposed a model movie ordinance aimed at ensuring that local theatres provided at least one programme each week in which every feature would have met the approval of a community motion-picture commission (to my knowledge this ordinance was never passed). See George J. Hecht, 'A model movie law', *Parent's Magazine*, November 1933, pp. 23, 77–8; George J. Hecht, 'How to get better movies for your children', *Parent's Magazine*, September 1934, pp. 15, 54–61. Also see the article 'Mothers' aid sought in drive to elevate movie standards', *New York Times*, 26 February 1939, section II, p. 4.

4 Paul Seale, ' "A host of others": toward a nonlinear history of poverty row and the coming of sound', *Wide Angle*, vol. 13, no. 1 (1991), pp. 74–5.

5 'What to do about duals?' *Variety*, 12 October 1938, p. 1; 'Duals' here to stay for long time', *Variety*, 5 April 1939, p. 1.

6 Seale, ' "A host of others" '.

7 Clive Hirschhorn, *The Universal Story* (New York: Crown Publishers, 1983), p. 13.

8 On the cost of *The Informer* see Richard Jewell and Vernon Harbin, *The RKO Story* (New York: Crown Books, 1982), p. 84: Jewell discussed the relative costs of As, Bs, and 'intermediates' in 'B film production at RKO Radio Pictures', a paper presented at the December 1990 conference of the Mostra internazionale del nuovo cinema in Siena. In the thirties. RKO budgeted westerns at $30,000–$90,000, other Bs were budgeted at $100,000–$150,000, 'intermediates' or A/Bs at $250,000–$500,000 and an A film with major stars cost from $350,000–$1,500,000. By this scale, *The Informer* was budgeted as an 'intermediate' rather than a B. The opening of *The Informer* at the Radio City Music Hall in New York is noted in the 'Picture Grosses' pages in *Variety*, 15 May 1935.

9 *Variety*, 28 December 1938, p. 13.

10 A review of the major first-run theatres listed in the 'Picture Grosses' pages in *Variety* shows that *Pacific Liner* played the top of the bill for the weeks 11 Jan 1939 through to 8 Feb 1939. After this date, it plays the bottom half of the bill. As I show below, this is not the typical distribution pattern for B films at RKO.

11 Jewell, *The RKO Story*, p. 123.

12 Mae Dena Huettig, *Economic Control of the Motion Picture Industry. A Study in Industrial Organization* (Philadelphia: University of Pennsylvania Press, 1944; rpt Jerome Ozer, 1971), pp. 120–4.

13 'Amended and Supplemental Complaint. United States of America v Paramount. et al', published in *Film History*, vol. 4, no. 1 (1990), p. 39, note 12.

14 Ibid, p. 20.

15 Ibid, p. 25.

16 Jewell, 'B film production at RKO Radio Pictures'. I am indebted to Richard Jewell for this analysis of the problem of making a profit on so-called 'intermediates'.

17 Huettig, *Economic Control of the Motion Picture Industry*, pp. 80–1.

18 *Variety*, 25 January 1939, p. 11 and 'Picture Grosses' pages.

19 Janet Staiger, 'Announcing wares, winning patrons, voicing ideals: thinking about the history and theory of film advertising', *Cinema Journal*, vol. 29, no. 3 [1990], pp. 12–17.

20 The following appeared in the *New York Times*: a piece in advance of the premiere, 13 January 1939, p. 25; a review, 27 January 1939, p. 17; B. R. Crister's 'Poets and the cinema', 29 January 1939, section IX, p. 5, and an interview with Sam Jaffee, who played Gunga Din, 5 February 1939, section X, p. 4.

21 *New York Times*, 17 March 1939, p. 25.

22 In order to gauge the extent to which films were discussed in the contemporary press I have utilized Patricia King Hanson and Stephen L. Hanson, *Film Review Index, Volume 1 1882–1949* (Phoenix, Arizona: Orys Press, 1986).

23 John C. Flinn, 'Film showmanship', *Variety*, 8 March 1939, p. 8.
24 These are the dates that the programme changes are described in *Variety*. For similar weekly changes in the case of *Love Affair*, see the Pantages theatre in Los Angeles, *Variety*, 22 March 1939; and the Keith Memorial in Boston, *Variety*, 29 March 1939.
25 *Variety*, 29 March 1939, 'Picture Grosses' pages.
26 *New York Times*, 2 December 1938, p. 27.
27 *Motion Picture Herald*, vol. 133, no. 1 (1938), p. 39.
28 *Variety*, 5 October 1938, p. 14.
29 *Variety*, 9 November 1936, p. 16.
30 *New York Times*, 7 November 1938, p. 23.
31 Richard Jewell, 'A history of RKO Radio Pictures, Incorporated, 1928–1942', Diss. University of Southern California, 1978, pp. 445–6.
32 Richard Jewell was kind enough to share these figures with me; they are based upon his work with the RKO legal files, as well as distribution files, which are unfortunately no longer available for research.
33 In ascertaining release dates, I have looked at the date of the first review of a film in *Variety*, and its mention in the 'Picture Grosses' pages. Richard Jewell informs me that *Room Service* was the 'major disaster of the year', recorded as a $330,000 loss by the studio, while *The Mad Miss Manton* was 'an indifferent performer' which earned a profit of $85,000.
34 Pierre Bourdieu, *Distinction: A Social Critique of the Judgement of Taste*, trans. Richard Nice (Massachusetts: Harvard University Press, 1984, originally published in 1979 by Les Editions de Minuit, Paris).
35 Lawrence Levine traces the creation of this division in terms of the performance of Shakespeare, the creation of the symphony orchestra and the museum in *Highbrow-Lowbrow: The Emergence of Cultural Hierarchy in America* (Cambridge, Massachusetts: Harvard University Press, 1988). Francis Haskell refers to the elite audience for modern art and complicates what can become an all too neat equation between taste and class in 'The enemies of modern art' *in Past and Present in Art and Taste* (New Haven: Yale University Press, 1987), pp. 207–21. Andrew Ross discusses the politics of the debate on the canon in *No Respect: Intellectuals and Popular Culture* (New York: Routledge, 1989), pp. 210–12.
36 On the confinement of Lewton's films to B status in the forties see Joel Siegel, *Val Lewton: The Reality of Terror* (New York: Viking Press, 1973). The *New York Times* review of Lewton's *Walked With a Zombie* (1943) is a good example of the dismissal of his work by the critical establishment, calling the film a 'dull, disgusting exaggeration of an unhealthy, abnormal concept of life', *New York Times*, 22 April 1943, p. 31. The film is now highly regarded, characterized by J. P. Telotte, for example, as 'the masterwork of the RKO (horror) series' in *Dreams of Darkness: Fantasy and the Films of Val Lewton* (Chicago: University of Illinois Press, 1985), p. 42.

8

OF HYGIENE AND HOLLYWOOD

Origins of the exploitation film

Eric Schaefer

Source: *The Velvet Light Trap* 30 (Fall 1992): 34–47.

In 1915 the *Moving Picture World* hailed *Damaged Goods*, a film about venereal disease, claiming it was "not a problem play catering to the morbid but a genuine tragedy. As such it surely is entitled to take its place in the film literature of the day." In 1919, *Exhibitor's Trade Review*, another industry publication, ran an ad addressed "To Whom It May Concern" which stated: "This publication will hereafter accept neither advertising nor publicity concerning any picture dealing with venereal disease or sex hygiene, which is intended for commercial exploitation in the theaters of the United States before mixed audiences in the manner of dramatic productions." The ban by the trade journal was just one instance of a general backlash against sex hygiene films after World War I. Relatively common and accepted in the years leading up to the end of the war, after 1919 the sex hygiene films could only be made as exploitation movies,[1] occupying a plane somewhere between legitimate commercial cinema and the socially circumscribed world of pornography. What had occurred in the course of a few short years to precipitate this sharp change in the American motion picture industry's reaction to sex hygiene films? As we shall see, censorship efforts directed at hygiene movies not only excised the subject from the mainstream but served as a catalyst to create a separate industry that began to make films on topics which Hollywood would no longer approach.[2] As a result of such censorship, the exploitation film as an entity and an industry apart from the mainstream began to appear around 1920 and flourished in an often hostile atmosphere for some forty years.

In the pages that follow, I will identify several reasons for the suppression of early sex hygiene films and the subsequent emergence of exploitation films. Two of those reasons actually contributed to the longevity of the exploitation phenomenon. First, several of the hygiene pictures released in

1919 offered a more egalitarian view of the social hygiene problem by not identifying the lower classes as the source of venereal diseases. These films did not offer unquestioning support for the bourgeois positions on social hygiene that earlier films had. This resulted in their fall from favor with industry groups, which felt pressure from outside sources. In later years, exploitation films often gave the impression of resistant or alternative positions to mainstream films. Their very existence appeared to fly in the face of Hollywood's image of propriety and responsibility. However, while later films invariably broke with the mainstream industry's self-imposed guidelines regarding content, the moral position they took, whether regarding drug use, prostitution, or illicit sex, was invariably the dominant. Exploitation films thrived from 1919 to around 1959 by becoming the medium for telling stories of the socially marginalized—those stigmatized as disease carriers, criminals, or drug addicts, those who were forced to undergo back alley abortions, and those who chose alternative lifestyles. The average American could explore "unacceptable" topics from the safety of a seat within the socially sanctioned space of the movie theater.

The second reason for the excision of hygiene from the mainstream repertoire of "acceptable" subjects was the increasingly graphic depictions of VD in several of the films beginning in 1919. This reliance on graphic spectacle remained a crucial component in the success of the exploitation film over the next four decades. In contrast to the use of spectacle in the classical Hollywood film, exploitation spectacle often overwhelmed and obscured a film's ostensible narrative. Since audiences were primarily coming to see such spectacle, filmmakers were frequently slack with classical devices like continuity editing. The net result was to place even greater emphasis on forbidden sights. Unlike the classical Hollywood film, the exploitation film was essentially an exhibitionistic form which positioned the viewer in a fundamentally different way.

With the suppression of the hygiene film and other movies that dealt with taboo topics, the exploitation film emerged as a distinct class of motion picture, existing alongside the classical Hollywood cinema from 1917 to about 1960. The exploitation industry functioned in a symbiotic relationship with Hollywood. Exploitation filmmakers embraced many topics that the major production companies refused to deal with, short of the actual depiction of sexual activity. Until restrictions on content began to disappear in the early 1960s, the "shadow cinema" of exploitation films thrived.

Venereal disease, class, and the conspiracy of silence

In order to understand the controversy surrounding and resulting in the suppression of sex hygiene films, it is necessary to examine the social evaluation of venereal diseases and their treatments in the years prior to World War I. Allan M. Brandt's social history *No Magic Bullet* offers a solid guide to discourses around the diseases themselves. Medical progress throughout the nineteenth century had increased physicians' knowledge about the systemic threat of syphilis and the seriousness of gonorrhea. Yet the diseases were also attended by a social stigma which led many physicians to adopt the attitude that patients who suffered from the maladies were only receiving their due for moral transgressions.[3] Brandt states: "Because of misunderstandings of the pathology of the disease, as well as a desire to avoid the moral opprobrium attached to venereal infection, physicians often ascribed deaths due to syphilis to other causes" (10). Prince A. Morrow, the Progressive physician who led the fight against venereal diseases at the turn of the century, claimed in 1901 that from 5 to 18 percent of all men carried syphilitic infections (Brandt 12).

The attention accorded to sexually transmitted diseases by Morrow and other Progressive physicians largely stemmed from fears that venereal diseases were the reason for declining birth rates among the middle class, a phenomenon labeled "race suicide."[4] The gravity which Progressive physicians attached to the potential decline of the white middle-class family was related to an attendant fear of the lower classes. Brandt elaborates:

> The substantial professional interest and popular anxiety that extragenital infections generated . . . reflected concern about changes in American society during the late nineteenth century, particularly the heterogeneity and unhygienic nature of the burgeoning cities. Innocent infections promoted apprehension of the city, the working class, and the new immigrant populations, ultimately encouraging racism, and nativism. Progressive unease about hygiene, contagion, and cleanliness were evoked in the belief that in the brief contacts of everyday life—at the grocery, in the park, at the barber shop—these infections, originally obtained in "immoral" circumstances, could be passed to native, middle-class "moral" Americans . . . Venereal diseases had become, preeminently, a disease of the "other," be it the other race, the other class, the other ethnic group. (22–23)

In a 1921 booklet, *The Control of Sex Infections*, J. Bayard Clark placed much of the blame for the spread of venereal disease on modern industry and the working class. Clark wrote that professional prostitutes were not the largest source of infection since they knew how to keep themselves free from disease. Instead, he placed "three-quarters" of infections on women who worked in shops, in factories, or as servants. Where, Clark rhetorically asked his readers, does "the responsibility rest for this group of infected and oftentimes sexually ruined industrial workers who ignorantly spread the majority of sexual havoc to all classes of society?" (17). Clark blamed industrialism, which put young women to work while in "the flower of maternal possibility" (18), as the ultimate source of the spreading venereal diseases.

He identified the working class as the conduit which carried the "social evil" from the lower classes to the middle and upper classes.

Similarly, a paper delivered at the National Conference of Social Work in 1919 by Edgar Sydenstricker of the U.S. Public Health Service quoted statistics indicating that 5.5 percent of white army cadets, " 'representative of the better class of young men found in our colleges,' " suffered from venereal disease as compared to 16 percent or more for recruits "regarded as representative of 'mechanics, artisans, and untrained laborers' " (210). Sydenstricker went on to suggest that those in the lower economic strata were faced with conditions that led to "increasing sexual excitement and ... lowering self-restraint."

> There hardly will be any disagreement on the general observation that among the economically less favored group of our population these conditions are far more pronounced than among the well-to-do. These influences arise not only from the conditions which directly stimulate sexual activity but also from the conditions of living. The lack of healthful recreation and avocational opportunities, the monotony of daily life and work, the brevity of formal education— these factors which may be considered just as seriously as the more direct and positive forces that lower the standard of morality and tend towards vulgarity and grossness of thought. (210)

Whether because of social conditions or "direct and positive forces that lower the standard of morality," the upper and middle classes had located the source of venereal disease in the lower classes.

The fullest expression of this class doctrine can be found in the ideology underlying the pseudo-science known as eugenics. The eugenics movement was an effort to combat "race suicide" by encouraging the "fit" white, Anglo-Saxon, middle and upper classes to have large families while attempting to reduce the growth of the "unfit" lower classes through means ranging from immigration restrictions to sterilization. Fighting venereal disease among the middle and upper classes was an important facet of the eugenics movement, which was able to draw financial support from many wealthy bankers and businessmen. Writing about the movement, Thomas M. Shapiro notes that "by focusing on both class and racial challenges, the propertied class simultaneously united on the basis of class consolidation and segmented the working class along race and ethnic lines." He goes on to suggest that the movement gradually worked its way downward from society's upper strata to become the dominant ideology, nurturing attitudes of "racism, superiority, and outright hatred among the American people—all in the name of science" (38).

Although physicians spoke of venereal diseases among themselves, little information was available to the society at large. As Morrow claimed in 1906,

"Social sentiment holds that it is a greater violation of the properties of life publicly to mention venereal disease than privately to contract it" (quoted in Brandt 23). The "conspiracy of silence" prevented the lower classes, who were identified as the cause of venereal diseases, from receiving medical and preventive information about them. As Brandt notes, the U.S. Post Office confiscated Margaret Sanger's pamphlet "What Every Girl Should Know" in 1912 because its references to syphilis and gonorrhea were considered obscene under the Comstock Law (24). Although the "conspiracy of silence" was relieved somewhat in 1909 when Paul Erlich developed a viable treatment for syphilis, the heartening information about prophylactic measures was counter-balanced by moralists who claimed that dissemination of the knowledge would encourage sexual promiscuity.

The sex hygiene film

In this atmosphere of class tension, of new hope for sufferers of syphilis, and of lingering moral admonitions, the first play to attack directly the problem of venereal disease appeared in the United States in 1913. Although Ibsen's *Ghosts*, with its references to Osvald's "hereditary illness," had been produced in America as early as 1882, the American public heard the word "syphilis" spoken on stage for the first time in Eugene Brieux's *Damaged Goods* (Levin 1). Brieux's play about a wealthy young man who contracts the disease was staged in New York City and produced under the auspices of the *Medical Review of Reviews* in order to stave off possible public protest ("Eugenics Play"). The ploy was successful, for *Damaged Goods* encountered little opposition.[5] The play was given the endorsement of many in New York society, who engaged boxes for the initial "special" performance ("Eugenics Play"; "Brieux Play"). In a feature story, the *New York Times* noted that the play had been given "the approval of many of our leading men and women" and that a special performance had been arranged for President Woodrow Wilson and the Congress in Washington, D.C. ("Use Play"). Although most of the reviews of the production rhetorically asked if the stage were the proper place for the discussion of venereal disease, they concluded that Brieux's play served a useful purpose. A review from *Hearst's Magazine* is representative: "I would wish to take a young boy or girl of mine to see this play. If they could get harm out of it, I confess I do not understand how . . . This play puts the horrible truth in so living a way, with such clean, artistic force, that the mind is impressed as it could possibly be impressed in no other manner" (805–806). A *New York Times* editorial conceded the good that could come from dramatic treatment of "subjects generally considered too delicate for common conversation" but concluded that "it invariably causes harm, too, by its appeal to the merely curious and morbid minds" ("That Moral Play"). Nevertheless, the conspiracy of silence had been broken and venereal diseases became legitimate subject matter for drama. "*Damaged Goods*," writes Brandt, "became a symbol of a new sexual openness" (47).

It was only a short time until *Damaged Goods* and its star and driving force, Richard Bennett, made the transition from the stage to the screen. Scenarist Harry Pollard expanded Brieux's chamber play for the American Film Manufacturing Company, and the film was released by Mutual in late 1914. In a letter to the *New York Times* in 1952, Terry Ramsaye characterized the movie as a prestige production, claiming that it was "pretentiously made, for that day, at a cost, including promotional expenses, of less than $50,000, and its states' rights . . . sold for $600,000, thus indicating a box-office take of probably more than $2,000,000." Ramsaye claimed the production required special promotion and advanced prices. Reviewers for the industry trade magazines were aware of the unique nature of *Damaged Goods* and many seemed to be caught up in a Progressive fervor when they discussed the film. In the first of two reviews in *Variety*, the paper urged, "See 'Damaged Goods,' and after seeing it, tell your son or daughter to see it, and let them tell other boys and girls, and you tell other fathers and mothers, until all the world has seen 'Damaged Goods' on the picture screen." The *Moving Picture World* found the film "free from taint which inheres in most of the 'sex problem plays.' It does not parade evil in order that good may come of it."

What was being praised? For one thing, the reviews took special note of the social status of the protagonist. George Dupont was described as "a young man of excellent home," a lawyer by profession, who is set to marry "a prominent society belle." George gets syphilis from a "street walker" (reviews of *Damaged Goods*, MPW; *Variety*, 1915; *Variety*, 1914). While Kuhn notes that "VD propaganda films . . . construct sexually active women as the principal cause of venereal infection" (63), it is important to note the low social station of those women and how the disease is visited upon those of the upper classes. The social dynamics established in *Damaged Goods* (and repeated in most other hygiene films) illustrate Brandt's claim that venereal disease was seen as a malady of "the other" inflicted on the bourgeoisie. This catastrophe is brought about by a related error. In the film version of *Damaged Goods*, George is given a bachelor party by his friends. He gets drunk and spends the night with a prostitute, acquiring the disease from a momentary failing of standards. Alcohol was often cited as one of the contributing factors in the spread of venereal disease (Brandt 59, 72; Clark 39–43) and hygiene pictures assimilated this notion. In *Damaged Goods*, as well as its successors, the consumption of alcohol results in the bourgeois hero dropping his guard and engaging in social (and sexual) intercourse with the lower class. Consequently, the audience was encouraged to view drinking as wrong, not because of some innate moral doctrine or sin but because it broke down social discriminations. Lower classes then spread venereal diseases to the bourgeoisie, rendering wives sterile and babies dead or diseased, with the middle class facing "race suicide." In *Damaged Goods* George gives syphilis to his wife and their child is born with the disease. Morality becomes class doctrine rather than religious dogma in the early sex hygiene films.

Just who comprised the audience for the early sex hygiene films is difficult to determine. In any case, we can be assured that the films were successful. A 1915 article in the *Moving Picture World* spoke of *Damaged Goods'* run in Detroit: "The Grand Circus started to show 'Damaged Goods' on Monday, Oct. 18, and has placed [*sic*] to capacity every performance. The Grand Circus only seats about 650 and the total daily attendance averaged 5,000 people. In the evenings the crowd had been so large that three policemen were sent over by the police department to keep the people in line and from blocking the sidewalks. Manager Blankmeyer will run 'Damaged Goods' at least four weeks" (*Damaged Goods* Suit). The same article also indicated the willingness of distributors to capitalize on the hot topic of sex hygiene in its reference to a 1913 film, *A Victim of Sin*, released to compete with *Damaged Goods*. *A Victim of Sin* was almost identical to the Brieux work in structure and detailed the story of a rising young medical student, Albert, who falls in love with the daughter of a prominent banker. While spending an evening in Bohemia with his friends he becomes infatuated with a lower-class "demimondaine" and is infected with a venereal disease. Returning to his home town, he is overcome by "a moment of forgetfulness," resulting in the pregnancy of his fiancée. A child is born, "suffering the sins of his Father, but soon after birth, is relieved by the merciful hand of Death" (copyright records, *A Victim of Sin*). Again, a member of the bourgeoisie—a physician—suffers because of a sexual liaison with an individual from a lower class.

Following American military engagement along the Mexican border, the newly acquired freedom to discuss the topic of venereal diseases had focused national attention on conditions in cantonments along the United States' southern border, where troops had assembled to guard against raids by "Pancho" Villa in 1916. Saloons and red light districts contributed to a general air of moral laxity and fostered the concern in Progressives and politicians alike that an army suffering from the ravages of venereal diseases was, in fact, no army at all. The Commission on Training Camp Activities (CTCA) was created in 1917 to battle venereal diseases among America's armed forces through a program of planned recreation, distraction, and coercion. The Progressive philosophy that posited education as a cure for all ills was bureaucratized in the CTCA with its program of "educational prophylaxis" (Brandt 59, 62).

In 1917 *Damaged Goods* was rereleased in a "new edition," probably to capitalize on concerns over the spread of venereal diseases among U.S. fighting men. In June of the same year American Standard released *S.O.S.*, which told the story of the wealthy Drexel brothers, Harold and John. Harold, the profligate sibling, contracts a "dreaded disease" from Lorraine, a "mercenary café habituée." Harold then wins his brother's fiancée, Ruth Dixon. They marry and Ruth gives birth to a child, "a hopeless cripple and a degenerate." Like *Damaged Goods, S.O.S.* showed the greatest danger in venereal disease to be the prospect of "race suicide" among the propertied classes. Cautioning that one or two scenes were somewhat depressing, *Exhibitor's Trade Review* still praised *S.O.S.*, noting "nothing is necessarily distasteful. This picture probably will attract a big crowd to any theater" (review of *S.O.S.*). By 1919 eight new sex hygiene films—along with another rerelease of *Damaged Goods*—hit American screens in rapid succession.

At the vanguard of the postwar wave of sex hygiene features was *The Spreading Evil*, produced by James Keane and released in the last months of 1918. Though complicated by a story of wartime intrigue, the theme of venereal disease penetrating the upper strata of society from the lower classes was once again evident. The film received the enthusiastic endorsement of Josephus Daniels, secretary of the Navy. The *Moving Picture World* praised the film for its frankness, while nothing that "the production must be given credit for setting forth every phase of its story with acceptable delicacy" (McElravy). *Variety* fairly trumpeted: "We are moving rapidly in the advancement of civilization! Only a very short time ago an educational film of the undoubted value of 'The Spreading Evil' would not have been permitted by the authorities" (review of *Spreading Evil, Variety*).

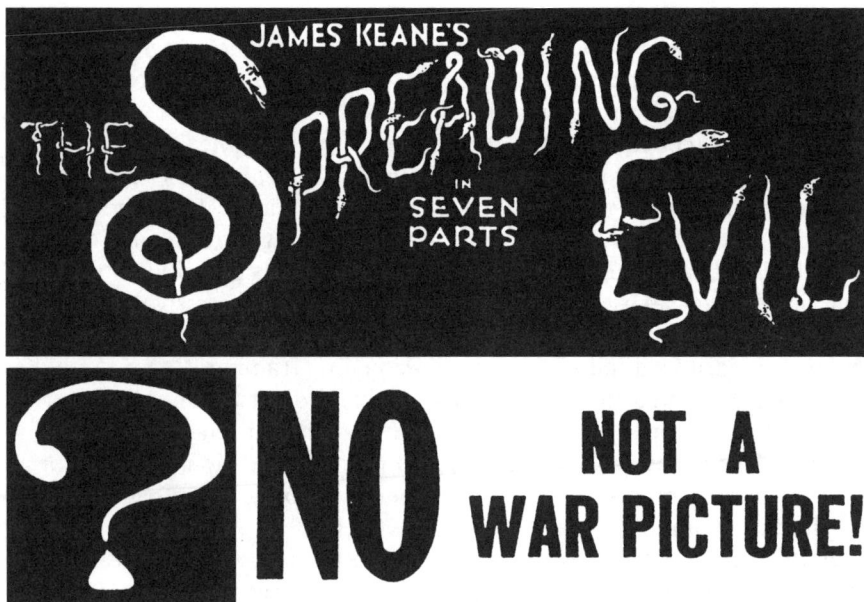

Figure 1 James Keane's *The Spreading Evil* (1918) was at the vanguard of a postwar wave of sex hygiene features. The serpentine lettering of this advertisement demonstrates the film's concern with sexual temptation and the spread of venereal disease. (From the collection of the author.)

At the beginning of 1919, *The Scarlet Trail* was added to the group of films which illustrated the effects of venereal disease on the middle class. In this film, a corrupt financier threatens the bourgeoisie with his uncontrolled avarice. Not only does Ezra Grafton head a syndicate of quack doctors who sell venereal disease nostrums, but his son Bob was born with congenital syphilis. Bob, planning to marry a debutante, learns of his fate and eventually kills himself, leaving his father "crushed by the knowledge that he is reaping of his own iniquities" (copyright records, *Scarlet Trail*). The film did not point directly to the lower classes as the breeding ground of syphilis but, like *S.O.S.*, did demonstrate the dangers inherent in the middle class letting its guard down. The threat comes from Bob, who could perpetuate his father's disease among the bourgeoisie by marrying Ethel Harding. The film was widely praised for its inoffensiveness: "A disagreeable theme has been handled carefully"; "One point in the picture's favor is the absence of suggestive scenes"; "[the director] may be criticized, in fact, for being too delicate . . ."; "the picture was made in a clean way" (review of *Scarlet Trail*, ETR; Weitzel, *Scarlet Trail*; review of *Scarlet Trail*, NYT; review of *Scarlet Trail, Variety*).

Up to and including the release of *The Scarlet Trail*, venereal disease pictures had been, above all, "clean." What offense they were able to generate seems to have been attributable to the subject itself rather than their treatment of venereal disease. Indeed, the earliest venereal disease films were evidently subjected to little pressure from censors. Perhaps this should not come as a surprise since the films had little reason to be censored: They espoused morality and continence as a middle-class defense against the threat posed by subordinate classes. Thus, the early sex hygiene films can be viewed as part of a discourse where class conflict was played out on an intimate level. Venereal disease was represented as tantamount to a revolutionary weapon for the poor, a weapon which posed a far greater threat to the middle class than bullets since it robbed the bourgeoisie of the chance to reproduce. The "educational" aim of the films was to offer morality and continence as a shield for bourgeois protection, not to offer broader solutions which would benefit the underclass as well. Trade journals, newspapers, and censors had little reason to argue with the films that cautioned against "the evils that threaten our future race unless we act now and act quickly" (ad for *Scarlet Trail*).

Yet given this, what explains a turnaround in public opinion in 1919 after the release of *The Scarlet Trail*? The backlash against the venereal disease pictures can be linked to three films produced by the CTCA as armed service training films: *Fit to Fight* (1918), *Fit to Win* (1919), and *The End of the Road* (1918). Ironically, it was these state-supported films that accelerated the suppression of the hygiene film and contributed to the institution of exploitation movies. *Fit to Fight* traced the adventures—and brushes with venereal disease—of five young men of divergent backgrounds in an army training camp. *Fit to Win* was essentially the same film, but with an added epilogue

BACKED BY THE GOVERNMENT
PUBLIC HEALTH FILMS
Announces

It has been Designated by the U. S.
Public Health Service to Distribute

"FIT TO WIN"

With SGT. RAY McKEE

as "BILLY HALE"

Personally directed by
Lieut. E. H. GRIFFITH

¶ The Motion Picture shown
to 1,500,000 Fighting Men during mobilization and now part
of the Crusade launched to
Make the World Safe for Posterity.

¶ The Film that Warns Against
Sex Disease Perils, depicting
Life Truths in startlingly Plain
Terms, with the wiles of unfit
women dramatically revealed.

PUBLIC HEALTH FILMS
1493 BROADWAY   Suite 211   Phone: Bryant 9496   NEW YORK

Figure 2 Ironically, *Fit to Win* (1919) and other films produced by the Commission
on Training Camp Activities accelerated a backlash against venereal disease
films. (From the collection of the author.)

that takes place after the war (copyright records, *Fit to Win*). *The End of the Road* was created to impart lessons about social diseases to a female audience (copyright records, *End of the Road*). The three films were turned over at war's end by the CTCA to the American Social Hygiene Association (ASHA), an organization created by the merger of two existing groups in 1913 to combat prostitution and venereal disease through education. ASHA placed the films under copyright and selected Isaac Silverman's Public Health Films to distribute them. Twenty-five percent of the profits from the pictures was to be returned to ASHA.

With the "war to make the world safe for democracy" just ended, *Fit to Win* was advertised as "The Opening Shot in the Big Battle to Make the World Clean and Safe for Posterity" (ad for *Fit to Win*). In April 1919, Public Health Films ran a trade ad, reproducing a letter from Assistant Surgeon General C. C. Pierce, addressed to state and municipal boards of health.

> In carrying forward this campaign throughout civilian life, the United States Public Health Service asks the co-operation of State and Municipal governments and requests the abrogation or suspension of such censorships as might impede this very essential missionary work. "Fit to Win" will be shown to both men and women, but always separate screenings except where audiences may be absolutely segregated according to sex. Children under the age of sixteen will be rigorously excluded. (Ad for *Fit to Win*)

The letter indicates a suspicion that some censorship might be attempted. Moreover, the letter sets out exhibition strategies that were to become standard for exploitation films as they matured in the 1920s—screenings segregated by sex and age limits of about sixteen.[6]

The new films prompted far more caution on the part of reviewers. "Is 'Fit to Win' fit to be shown is the first question that an exhibitor wants answered," suggested the *Moving Picture World*. The journal concluded that under the proper circumstances benefits could result, but that "it does not belong in a family theater to be shown to a mixed audience of men and women" (Weitzel, *Fit to Win*). *Exhibitor's Trade Review* directed theater owners' attention to the prologue, which offered "actual views of diseased men and women with the ugly sores open to view" (review of *Fit to Win*, ETR). One writer speculated that *Fit to Fight* "may have to be shown in the city dump" ("*Fit to Fight* Sheared"). Still, the films were apparently very popular with audiences. In May 1919, *Fit to Win* along with *The End of the Road* was "playing to capacity in the fifth week of a 12-week run" at the Grand opera house in Brooklyn ("*Fit to Win* Allowed"). *The End of the Road*'s opening in a Syracuse theater drew 1,500 "at top dollar price" and did almost $9,000 in one week at a Philadelphia theater "with two shows a day and a 25 to one dollar scale" ("Disapproved Film"; "*End of the Road* Barred").

The *Mutual v. Ohio* decision, handed down by the Supreme Court in 1915, had left motion pictures without First Amendment armor. In spite of efforts to stave off any legal troubles with its ploy of segregated audiences and cautionary reviews, *Fit to Win* and its two companion films were particularly vulnerable to censorship pressure. In Dallas, censors deferred action while a team of physicians passed judgment: "Nauseating close-ups showing ravages of venereal disease on the human body will be lopped out of the film. So will the section that deals with the squalor of the vice district. This was too raw for the medicos, even though they did look at it from a scientific viewpoint" (*"Fit to Fight* Sheared"). In New York City *Fit to Win* was the subject of litigation when the city license commissioner, John Gilchrist, threatened to revoke the license of any theater showing the film ("U.S. Circuit Court"). In court, Gilchrist claimed, "I believe that any film or picture dealing with the social evil, particularly with diseases arising out of the social evil are improper to present before mixed audiences." The commissioner had acted after a letter that was critical of the film appeared in the *Brooklyn Eagle* ("Court Ruling"). After several months in the courts, the commissioner's authority to ban the film was upheld by the U.S. Circuit Court of Appeals ("U.S. Circuit Court"). *The End of the Road* was barred in Pennsylvania and was the subject of a vigorous campaign, instigated by the National Association of the Moving Picture Industry (NAMPI), to have it blocked in Chicago. The Providence, Rhode Island, Police Commission labeled the films "an attempt to 'commercialize vice' " ("End of the Road Barred"; "End of the Road to Be Stopped"; "Providence Police").

Why were the three government films subjected to such harsh censorship when the earlier hygiene films had not been? The most obvious reason for increased censorship seems to have been the graphic footage of the effects of venereal disease. In discussing the success of a British version of *Damaged Goods* (1919), apparently not released in the United States, Annette Kuhn comments, "The film was regarded at the time it was made as lacking in the qualities which would make it good cinema . . . precisely because, in its refusal to construct VD as a spectacle, it failed to capitalize on cinema's potential as a visual medium" (65). The shots in *Fit to Win* described by the Dallas doctors as "too raw" were one likely cause of much of the vocal criticism about the films in the United States. And, in fact, it was the construction of the forbidden-as-spectacle that would come to serve as one of the major points of divergence between mainstream cinema and exploitation films.

Beyond the unpleasant spectacle of disease-ravaged bodies, a study of the psychological effects of *Fit to Win* conducted at Johns Hopkins University by Lashley and Watson, published in 1921, identified a series of criticisms of the films which suggest other possible reasons for the widespread censorship. Two of the criticisms enumerated in Lashley and Watson's analysis seem to have a direct bearing on the change in the public's attitude about the films.

172

First, the government-produced movies emphasized the importance of chemical prophylaxis, something earlier films did not do. As Brandt points out, "The more conservative social hygienists and purity activists centered their attack on the film's advocacy of chemical prophylaxis: 'If you can't be moral, be careful' " (124). Information about prophylaxis was thought to counter messages about continence, thereby increasing immorality. Second, "the picture shows as a characteristic of the young men described in it a carelessness and lack of moral responsibility in sex matters which casts an unmerited reflection upon the decency of the average American home and of the Army" (Lashley and Watson 205).

Furthermore, not only did the films pose prophylaxis as an alternative to continence, *Fit to Fight, Fit to Win*, and *The End of the Road* did not locate the source of venereal diseases in the lower classes as had the earlier films. The five characters at the center of *Fit to Fight/Win*, who face the specter of venereal disease, were not as a group bourgeois but instead a mix of classes. Billy Hale and Chick Carlton are college boys, Kid McCarthy a boxer, Hank Simpson a country bumpkin, and Jack Garvin a cigar salesman. Thus, rather than invading a bourgeois home, venereal disease affects the egalitarian world of the military camp—members of all classes are equally at risk. *The End of the Road* tells the story of venereal disease having the same impact on the bourgeoisie and the working class. No longer are the poor ruining middle-class lives through the transmission of venereal infections and leaving them to face the possibility of race suicide. In the government-made films, syphilis and gonorrhea are equal opportunity diseases.

Unlike the earlier hygiene films such as *Damaged Goods*, the government films presented alternative representations of class. By placing middle-class protagonists on the same level as poorer victims of the disease, class differences were not perpetuated but were broken down. As military training films, the pictures were designed to promote cooperation and a sense of shared experience so energies and efforts could be directed toward winning the war by "keeping fit to fight." But following the war, with the status quo reaffirmed and the class lines that had been obscured by the leveling experience of military life redrawn, the films fell under attack. It should also be noted that in the wake of the war, "un-American" themes were frowned on to such an extent that NAMPI passed a resolution stating the industry's "determination to maintain 100% Americanism upon the screens of this country as scrupulously as during the late emergency" ("American Screens"). While NAMPI was urging 100% Americanism, it was also engaged in an effort to rid the nation's screens of hygiene films.

Finally, the CTCA films were criticized because they were part of a glut of sex hygiene films released in 1919. All of the films previously mentioned (with the possible exception of *A Victim of Sin*) were in release in 1919, along with three others: *Open Your Eyes, The Solitary Sin*, and *Wild Oats*. *Open Your Eyes*, one of the early films produced by the Warner brothers, followed

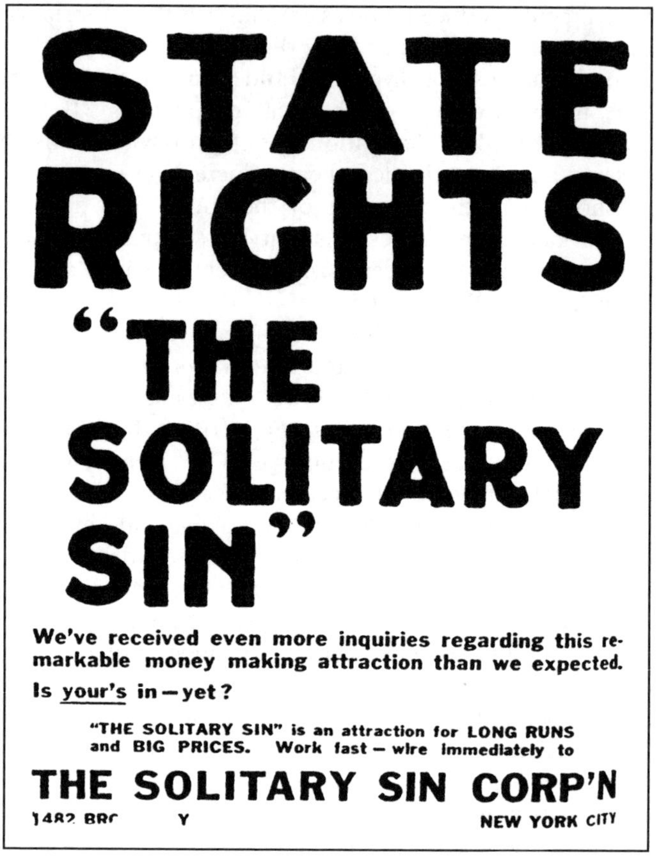

STATE RIGHTS
"THE SOLITARY SIN"

We've received even more inquiries regarding this re-markable money making attraction than we expected.

Is your's in — yet?

"THE SOLITARY SIN" is an attraction for LONG RUNS and BIG PRICES. Work fast — wire immediately to

THE SOLITARY SIN CORP'N
1482 BRC   Y   NEW YORK CITY

Figure 3 The Solitary Sin (1919) was the only film of this period to deal with the subject of masturbation. Like the government-produced venereal disease films, *The Solitary Sin* was censored as part of the backlash against sex hygiene films. (From the collection of the author.)

the familiar formula—syphilis rising from the lower class to attack the bour-geoisie (copyright records, *Open Your Eyes*). *The Solitary Sin*, the only film of the period to deal with the subject of masturbation, is difficult to judge on the basis of the limited plot information available. *Wild Oats* offers another more democratic view of victims and potential victims of syphilis with its rich city dweller/poor country cousin dichotomy (copyright records, *Wild Oats*). Reviews of *Open Your Eyes* were positive, but those for *The Solitary Sin* and *Wild Oats* were less so. *Moving Picture World* criticized *The Solitary Sin* because "it does not succeed in keeping a pleasant side uppermost, as many of its predecessors have done" (McElravy, *The Solitary Sin*). *Wild Oats* was damned for its "coating of vulgar humor" (Weitzel, *Wild Oats*). Whatever the individual merits of these films, they were lumped with the

CTCA films, which represented what seemed to be an abundance of morbidly prurient motion pictures.

The general reaction to these sex hygiene films paralleled the attitude toward the CTCA films—an unfavorable, and in some cases hostile, response that went beyond negative reviews. Like the government films, they were censored. *Open Your Eyes* and *The Solitary Sin* were lumped in with *Fit to Win* and *The End of the Road* and barred in Providence, Rhode Island ("Providence Police"). In Connecticut, a state law was enacted which provided that

> no person shall exhibit, or advertise to be exhibited, in any theater, hall or other place of public amusement or entertainment, any stereopticon views or motion pictures in any way relating to the subject of venereal diseases without first securing a written permit from the state commissioner of health; and no person shall permit the exhibition of any such stereopticon views or motion pictures in any such building owned or controlled by him until such permit has been secured. ("Providence Police")

Violation of the Connecticut law was punishable by a $500 fine, a six-month prison term, or both. The Pennsylvania State Board of Censors banned any film that dealt with venereal disease ("Decision"). With the final decision in the New York City *Fit to Win* case in July 1919 came an editorial in *Exhibitor's Trade Review* which claimed to support sex hygiene campaigns but added, "We part company with those who believe that the desired result will be gained by promiscuous exhibition of such pictures throughout the country." The editors went on to predict "a new storm" of censorship legislation and a crippling of the motion picture's propaganda potential if the hygiene films continued ("Decision").

Following its attempt to have *The End of the Road* barred in May, NAMPI gathered for its annual meeting in Rochester, New York, in August 1919. At that meeting a resolution was passed "unanimously declaring war to the bitter end on anyone making or showing salacious pictures and obligating themselves to submit every film to the National Board of Review" (Priest). *Exhibitor's Trade Review* labeled the resolution "The Death Knell of Legalized Censorship and the 'Educational' Sex Film" ("Death Knell"). In the September 6 edition of the same publication a letter from Surgeon General Rupert Blue was published, referring to an ad for *Some Wild Oats* (alternate title for *Wild Oats*) which had appeared a month earlier ("To Whom"; ad for *Some Wild Oats*). The ad had claimed that the film was "Approved by the Surgeon Generals of the Army and Navy, and the Public Health Department," a fact refuted by Blue. Beneath the letter, the magazine ran a notice that it would no longer accept advertising for or review sex hygiene films ("To Whom").

In the September 20 issue of the *Moving Picture World* a notice from Surgeon General Blue was printed: "This is to inform you that the Public Health Service has withdrawn its indorsement [*sic*] of the films, 'Fit to Win,' 'End of the Road' and 'Open Your Eyes,' and all other pictures dealing with venereal diseases that have been shown or are to be shown commercially" ("Public Health Bureau Withdraws"). The surgeon general's somewhat ironic attack on films the government itself had only recently been using for educational purposes demonstrates that by the end of 1919, the welcome that had greeted *Damaged Goods* in 1914 had turned into almost uniformly sour denunciations. Public health officials, critics, censors, and the leaders of the motion picture industry now attempted to dissociate themselves completely from the sex hygiene feature. A schism occurred in the production community with most producers choosing to toe the industry line by rejecting "salacious pictures." Industry self-censorship, which resulted in "clean" movies, became an imperative as the costs, both economically and in terms of public relations, for striking prints to conform to the whims of individual censor boards became too great. But independents like Samuel Cummins, producer of *Wild Oats*, continued to pursue the profit potential in exploitations.[7] These suddenly disreputable films thus helped set the stage for the disreputable business of exploitation, an industry that would produce hundreds of films at Hollywood's fringe over the next four decades.

Notes

The author would like to thank Eithne Johnson and Janet Staiger for their suggestions and contributions to this paper.

1 "Exploitation movie" as a term likely derives from "exploitation" as a practice that reaches beyond standard advertising and promotion to include stunts and displays (Gaines 31). Exploitation as a promotional practice—such as use of elaborately decorated marquees, lurid lobby displays, and ploys such as adults-only showings—was integral in the success of exploitation films. Exploitation was recognized as a distinct class of motion pictures during the 1920s under the name "blues" or "Main Street movies." Such films were called exploitation movies at least as early as the mid-thirties (review of *She Devil Island*: review of *Wajan*). Under the broad heading of exploitation films fall a number of subcategories, usually defined by the forbidden topic they exploited—the narcotics film, the nudist film, the vice film, the burlesque film, and the sex hygiene film being among the most often produced. The designation was later modified to indicate what was being exploited (i.e., "sexploitation" of the sixties and seventies, "blaxploitation" of the seventies, etc.). Today the term *exploitation film* is applied to most low-budget genre movies.

2 The productive capacity of censorship has been touched on by a number of scholars, with Annette Kuhn's *Cinema, Censorship and Sexuality, 1909–1925* (Routledge, 1988) being perhaps the most recent and thorough example. While the sex hygiene films were the obvious target of the 1919 crackdown, other types of films were swept out of Hollywood's stable of potential topics—birth control movies, white slave films, and those motion pictures that advocated sex education.

Narcotics films, which had been prominent in the mid-teens, also disappeared as a mainstream topic by 1919. The sole exception was *Human Wreckage* (Ince, 1923), Hollywood's penance for matinée idol Wallace Reid's drug death. The production was made with a special dispensation from the Hays Office (Brownlow 109).

3 The reader will note strong similarities between Progressive era discourse on venereal disease and contemporary discourses on AIDS, most notably in the location of the origins of the disease in groups that lack economic and/or political clout—groups that can be pegged as "other."

4 Race suicide was the topic of other sex hygiene films during this period. Motion pictures such as *Race Suicide* (mfr. unknown, 1916, director undetermined), *The Unborn* (Kulee Features, Inc., 1916, dir. undetermined), *Where Are My Children?* (Universal, 1917, dirs. Lois Weber and Philips Smalley), *The Curse of Eve* (Corona Cinema, 1917, dir. Frank Beal), and *Will You Marry Me?* (Major Films, 1917, dir. undetermined) dealt with the subject of abortion as a method of birth control. Weber's 1917 film about a socially prominent woman who undergoes abortions so she can maintain her carefree lifestyle, eventually resulting in her sterility, was typical of the race suicide film.

5 The Progressive's muckraking tendency of revealing an evil in order to combat it—exemplified by the exposés of Chicago's stockyards and prostitution industry by Upton Sinclair and George Kibbe Turner, respectively—was later appropriated by exploitation filmmakers. As exploitation films developed in the 1920s they adopted a pose which claimed that although the subject of the films was unsavory, the exposure of the problem was necessary in order to combat it. This posture of high moral purpose was known as the "square-up." Square-ups, under the legend "forward" or "introduction," usually appeared in a crawl at the beginning of the film. The practice of including a square-up at the beginning of an exploitation movie continued into the 1950s. See Karr for a full discussion of this tactic.

6 Screenings segregated by age and sex were not uncommon in the years leading up to 1919. For example, Chicago's censorship board instituted its "pink permit" in 1914, which forbade children from entering and effectively created a class of "adults only" motion pictures (de Grazia and Newman 9). In 1915 *The Twilight Sleep*, a short film about a "painless childbirth" drug, was limited to "women only" (review of *Twilight Sleep*). After 1920 virtually all theatrical motion pictures segregated by sex were sex hygiene exploitation films. With the exception of some foreign films, I am unaware of any "adults only" movies that played in theaters from 1920 through the 1950s that do not fall under the heading of exploitation. Indeed, the "adults only" label became an important marketing tool and point of differentiation for the exploitation industry.

7 Cummins went on to make and import dozens of exploitation films, including the twenties hygiene hit *The Naked Truth, Ecstasy*, with its fabled nude scenes of Hedy Lamarr, and *Love Life of a Gorilla*.

Works cited

"American Screens for American Ideas." *Exhibitor's Trade Review*, 16 August 1919: 874.

Brandt, Alan M. *No Magic Bullet: A Social History of Venereal Disease in the United States since 1880*. (Rev. ed.) New York: Oxford, 1987.

"Brieux Play Acted." *New York Times*, 15 March 1913: 13.

Brownlow, Kevin. *Behind the Mask of Innocence*. New York: Knopf, 1990.

Clark, J. Bayard. *The Control of Sex Infections*. New York: Macmillan, 1921.

"Court Ruling Upholding Showing of *Fit to Win* Is Foreshadowed as Trial Ends in U.S. Court." *Exhibitor's Trade Review*, 14 June 1919: 104.

"*Damaged Goods* Suit." *Moving Picture World*, 30 October 1915: 1002.

Rev. of *Damaged Goods*, play by Eugene Brieux. *Dial*, 1 April 1913: 288.

Rev. of *Damaged Goods*, play by Eugene Brieux. *Hearst's Magazine* (May 1913): 805–6.

Rev. of *Damaged Goods*, play by Eugene Brieux. *Outlook*, 31 May 1913: 226.

Rev. of *Damaged Goods*. *Moving Picture World*, 2 October 1915: 90–91.

Rev. of *Damaged Goods*. *Variety*, 26 September 1914: 22.

Rev. of *Damaged Goods*. *Variety*, 1 October 1915: 18.

"The Death Knell of Legalized Censorship and the 'Educational' Sex Film." *Exhibitor's Trade Review*, 16 August 1919: 874.

"The Decision in the *Fit to Win* Case." *Exhibitor's Trade Review*, 26 July 1919: 607.

de Grazia, Edward, and Roger K. Newman. *Banned Films: Movies, Censors and the First Amendment*. New York: Bowker, 1982.

"Disapproved War Dept. Film." *Variety*, 21 February 1919: 71.

Doherty, Thomas. *Teenagers and Teenpics: The Juvenilization of American Movies in the 1950s*. Boston: Unwin Hyman, 1988.

"*The End of the Road* to Be Stopped Showing Here." *Moving Picture World*, 24 May 1919: 1167.

"*End of the Road* Barred." *Variety*, 18 July 1919: 46.

"Eugenics Play Indorsed." *New York Times*, 27 February 1913: 8.

"*Fit to Fight* Will Be Heavily Sheared in Dallas." *Moving Picture World*, 28 June 1919: 1954.

Ad for *Fit to Win*. *Moving Picture World*, 12 April 1919: 164.

Rev. of *Fit to Win*. *Exhibitor's Trade Review*, 2 April 1919: 1437.

"*Fit to Win* Allowed to Run." *Variety*, 2 May 1919: 66.

Gaines, Jane. "From Elephants to Lux Soap: The Programming and 'Flow' of Early Motion Picture Exploitation." *The Velvet Light Trap* 25 (1990): 29–43.

Hamilton, James Shelley. "The Sex-Tangled Drama." *Everybody's Magazine* (November 1913): 676–79.

Karr, Kathleen. "The Long Square-up: Exploitation Trends in the Silent Film." *Journal of Popular Film* 3 (1974): 107–29.

Kuhn, Annette. *Cinema, Censorship and Sexuality, 1909–1925*. New York: Routledge, 1988.

Lashley, Karl S., and John B. Watson. "A Psychological Study of Motion Pictures in Relation to Venereal Disease Campaigns." *Social Hygiene* 7 (1921): 180–219.

Levin, R. *Tragedy: Plays, Theory, and Criticism*. New York: Harcourt, Brace, 1960.

McElravy, Robert C. Rev. of *The Solitary Sin*. *Moving Picture World*, 5 July 1919: 112.

——. Rev. of *The Spreading Evil*. *Moving Picture World*, 30 November 1918: 987.

Rev. of *Open Your Eyes*. *New York Times*, 30 June 1919: 16.

Rev. of *Open Your Eyes*. *Variety*, 4 July 1919: 42.

Priest, Janet. "Better Film Fight Won!" *Photoplay* (November 1919): 92 +.

"Providence Police Officials Place Ban on Four Films." *Variety*, 30 May 1919: 82.

"Public Health Bureau Withdraws Indorsement." *Moving Picture World*, 20 September 1919: 1832.

Ramsaye, Terry. Letter. *New York Times*, 2 March 1952: n.p.

Ad for *The Scarlet Trail*. *Moving Picture World*, 11 January 1919: 166.

Rev. of *The Scarlet Trail. Exhibitor's Trade Review*, 4 January 1919: 421.

Rev. of *The Scarlet Trail. New York Times*, 30 December 1918: 17.

Shapiro, Thomas M. *Population Control Politics: Women, Sterilization, and Reproductive Choice*. Philadelphia: Temple UP, 1985.

Rev. of *She Devil Island. Film Daily*, 29 August 1936: n.p.

Ad for *Some Wild Oats. Exhibitor's Trade Review*, 2 August 1919: 682.

Rev. of *S.O.S., Exhibitor's Trade Review*, 2 June 1917: 1824.

Rev. of *The Spreading Evil. Variety*, 22 November 1918: 46.

Sydenstricker, Edgar. "Economic Pressure as a Factor in Venereal Disease." In *Proceedings of the National Conference of Social Work, at the Forty-Sixth Annual Session Held in Atlantic City, New Jersey, June 1–8 1919*. Chicago: n.p., 1920, 208–211.

"That Moral Play." Editorial. *New York Times*, 2 March 1913: sec. 3, 6.

Ad for "To Whom It May Concern." *Exhibitor's Trade Review*, 6 September 1919: 1193.

Rev. of *The Twilight Sleep. Variety*, 27 August 1915: n.p.

"Use Play as a Pulpit to Preach Strong Medical Sermon." *New York Times*, 6 April 1913: V9.

"United States Circuit Court of Appeals Bars *Fit to Win* Showing in New York City." *Exhibitor's Trade Review*, 26 July 1919: 610.

Rev. of *Wajan. Motion Picture Daily*, 21 April 1938: n.p.

Weitzel, Edward. Rev. of *Fit to Win. Moving Picture World*, 12 April 1919: 276.

——. Rev. of *Open Your Eyes. Moving Picture World*, 2 August 1919: 713–14.

——. Rev. of *The Scarlet Trail. Moving Picture World*, 11 January 1919: 246.

——. Rev. of *Wild Oats. Moving Picture World*, 9 August 1919: 882.

Motion pictures

Damaged Goods, Dir. Thomas Ricketts. American Film Manufacturing Company. Mutual, 1914.

The End of the Road. Dir. Edward H. Griffith. U.S. War Department Commission on Training Camp Activities. Public Health Films, 1919.

Fit to Fight. Dir. Edward H. Griffith. U.S. War Department Commission on Training Camp Activities. Public Health Films, 1919.

Fit to Win. Dir. Edward H. Griffith. U.S. War Department Commission on Training Camp Activities. Public Health Films, 1919.

Open Your Eyes. Dir. Gilbert P. Hamilton (Sam and Jack Warner, uncredited). Warner Brothers. Warner Brothers, 1919.

The Scarlet Trail. Dir. John S. Lawrence. G&L Features. A states' rights release, 1919.

The Solitary Sin. Dir. Fred Sullivan. The Solitary Sin Corporation. A states' rights release, 1919.

S.O.S. Dir. William Buckley. American Standard. A states' rights release, 1917.

The Spreading Evil. Dir. James Keane. Mfr. James Keane. A states' rights release, 1918.

A Victim of Sin. Dir. undetermined. Mfr. unknown. Bell Film Exchange, 1913.

Wild Oats (aka *Some Wild Oats* and *Know Thy Husband*). Dir. C. J. Williams. Social Hygiene Films of America. A states' rights release, 1919.

Other records

U.S. Copyright Records, *Fit to Win*, 1919 (LU 14210)
U.S. Copyright Records, *The End of the Road*, 1919 (LU 13332)
U.S. Copyright Records, *Open Your Eyes*, 1919 (LU 13765)
U.S. Copyright Records, *The Scarlet Trail*, 1919 (LU 13451)
U.S. Copyright Records, *Some Wild Oats*, 1919 (LU 15239)
U.S. Copyright Records, *The Spreading Evil*, 1918 (LU 13209)
U.S. Copyright Records, *A Victim of Sin*, 1913 (LU 1053)
U.S. Copyright Records, *Wild Oats*, 1919 (LU 13957)

9

HOLLYWOOD'S SEMI-INDEPENDENT PRODUCTION

Matthew Bernstein

Source: *Cinema Journal* 32(3) (Spring 1993): 41–54.

An independent producer in movies is as much of a free soul as the individual in other lines of work who sets up his own shop or store. He's motivated by the same reasons. He wants to do things in his own way in his own sweet time and at his own cost. He faces the same hazards too. He must buck the "big interests" — or, if he goes along with them, he can do it only by sharing the profits. Nevertheless, because he often gambles on things the entrepreneurial interests won't touch, he boldly helps everyone concerned.

Louella Parsons, *Cosmopolitan*, March 1947

Hollywood's independent production is a messy phenomenon. "Independent production" is an umbrella term, defined negatively, to denote any production practice that is not under the aegis of the major studios of a given period. From the era of the Motion Picture Patents Company through the 1990s, there have always been many types of "independence." Within Hollywood alone low-budget independents like Tiffany-Stahl and Mascot are distinct from their top-budget counterparts like Samuel Goldwyn, David O. Selznick, Sam Spiegel, and Walter Wanger, all of whom released films through United Artists at some point.

Thus any discussion of independence must first delimit its precise object. My focus here is the most visible and commonly understood version of the phenomenon: the procedure by which major Hollywood talents from the 1910s onward form their own companies, hire their own artists and technicians, and deliver a completed, high-budget negative to a national distributor. In her essential study of the Hollywood mode of production, Janet Staiger calls this "commercial independent production," and she has noted that the industry understood it to refer to "a small company with no corporate relationship to a distribution firm."[1] For reasons I will advance below, I believe that further distinctions need to be made and that it is more precise to call this phenomenon Hollywood's "semi-independent production."

Whatever we call it, this practice provides a compelling instance for considering the economic and social determination of the movies. Certainly, as Louella Parsons's comments indicate, talents in Hollywood who undertook "independent" production made several assumptions about its effect on their films. The fact that funds for production could be raised from banks or financing institutions outside of the dominant studios was presumed to grant the producers/directors/screenwriters/actors greater creative autonomy from the scrutiny and authority of studio executives. It also was supposed to give these above-the-line talents the potential to work in multiple positions, short-circuiting the studio system's division of labor. Independence, in short, could facilitate not only profit sharing but individualistic and innovative approaches to narrative structure, plot resolution, and film style.[2]

American film history is sprinkled with pertinent examples that seem to bear out these assumptions. Charles Chaplin was wealthy and popular enough to hire his own technicians at his own studios and produce films that remained immune to contemporary refinements in film style and content. In 1934 King Vidor made the collectivist romance *Our Daily Bread*, which no major studio would finance; in 1937 Fritz Lang's independently produced *You Only Live Once* violated several norms of Hollywood narration. In the 1950s Otto Preminger's *Moon Is Blue* (1953) and *The Man with the Golden Arm* (1955) effectively weakened the Production Code by ignoring it.

Yet, as film critics and scholars have noted since the early 1960s, such films were exceptional. They were hardly representative of the bulk of independent work undertaken in American film, which largely conformed to major studio movies. Instead, as Richard Dyer MacCann noted in 1962, "the departure from the old studio system is more apparent than real. . . . Producers are still only as free as their producing-distributing deals let them be."[3]

Why should this be? In recent years film historians and theorists have questioned the assumption that independent film production in Hollywood had any consistent impact on filmmaking that would distinguish it from dominant studio films.[4] In particular, Janet Staiger's work indicates that the prevalent model of independent production—in which stars, screenwriters, directors, and producers form a corporation; put together a package on an individualized, film-by-film basis; take out bank loans; and turn over a negative to a distributor—represents not a shift in the mode of production but a modification of industry structure, in which an increasing number of firms operate. The independents copied the majors' approach to dividing labor and to their norms of film form and style.[5]

Staiger has persuasively argued that Hollywood's independent production developed as it did because independent producers were, after the 1930s, an elaboration on the unit system of organizing production that was prevalent in Hollywood from 1931 onward. The unit system enabled several producers at each studio to establish a core of talents and technicians to coalesce around a star, director, or genre. The units produced films more efficiently since the producer closely monitored their progress. Unit-produced films were also distinctive from other studio films, since they were believed to reflect the sensibilities of the dominant talents of that unit. Hence, independent production merely took unit production one step further, by separating the production unit on a corporate basis from the major studios and by bringing together the talents of a unit on a short-term, film-by-film basis.[6]

Staiger's work provides us with an invaluable, theoretically informed framework for situating any form of filmmaking in Hollywood throughout the studio system's history. Yet because it is a framework with great descriptive power at a general level, it cannot within reasonable space limitations explore certain nuances of the immediate context by which unit production developed into independent production. More specifically, there is evidence that Staiger's successive stages of management systems (central producer, unit producer, package unit producer) progressed in a less linear fashion than Staiger implies. Her already highly nuanced paradigm for the mode of production in Hollywood thus requires some modification to emphasize further the varieties of production practices.

In describing the advent of unit production, Staiger notes, paraphrasing Howard Lewis's *Motion Picture Industry* (1933), that in 1926 one studio "considered" switching to a system of production in which the studio merely financed the work of several different producers. According to Lewis the firm was inspired by declining attendance that year, and it never acted upon this idea because the advent of sound film production intervened. Staiger's account places the innovation of unit production in 1931. At that time David O. Selznick at RKO and other production executives called for a shift in producing methods in response to declining audience attendance.[7]

In fact unit production was not just "considered" before the advent of sound; it was inaugurated in the 1925–1926 season at the largest production company, Paramount. For example, at the company's Hollywood studio in July 1926, Hector Turnbull supervised *Casey at the Bat* and Lucien Hubbard oversaw *Wings*. The system continued to thrive with eight supervisors (of Clara Bow, Wallace Beery, Esther Ralston, and George Bancroft films). By early 1928, before the studios elected to convert to sound, it was firmly in place at other studios as well.[8]

Paramount, then called Famous Players–Lasky, had implemented the unit production system in mid-1926. It was partly in response to the enormous success of M-G-M's first season under Louis B. Mayer and Irving G. Thalberg, which included Fred Niblo's *Ben-Hur* (1926), Erich von Stroheim's *Merry Widow* (1925), King Vidor's *Big Parade* (1925), and Lon Chaney and Tod

Browning's *Unholy Three* (1925). Jesse Lasky, Famous Players–Lasky's vice-president in charge of production, admitted to *Variety* that M-G-M was "outdistancing [Paramount] on the quality of product during the year past."[9] To compete, Lasky's studio in late 1925 inaugurated an increasing number of roadshow specials such as James Cruze's *Old Ironsides*, Herbert Brenon's *Beau Geste*, and D. W. Griffith's *Sorrows of Satan* (all 1926).

Lasky and his associates also inaugurated unit production to enhance their competitive edge with M-G-M. *Variety* characterized the shift as part of "a radical change in the organization" of the studio, one that was first tried out at the Astoria, Long Island, studio. In conceiving their new system of production, the Famous Players–Lasky executives had in mind previous instances of unit production such as those used by Mack Sennett, D. W. Griffith, and Thomas Ince at Triangle in the mid-teens.

An even more pertinent model, however, was that of previous independent producers. There was no shortage of examples to follow. In the late teens alone, Mary Pickford (and other stars) had an independent company at Famous Players–Lasky's own Paramount Artcraft before creating a new firm to produce for United Artists release. Then there was First National, the association of exhibitors formed in 1917, which typically took funds collected from exhibitors in advance and offered them to producers (like Charlie Chaplin) who were then required to turn over completed films to the distributor-exhibitor. In fact, *Variety* reported, "the distribution branch" of Famous Players–Lasky's, like the distributors and exhibitors at First National, had come up with the plan and had "outlined and dictated" the reorganization of the studio to the company's production arm.[10]

Moreover, the unit plan at Famous Players–Lasky had been preceded by an experiment in late November 1925, whereby Hollywood studio chief Ben P. Schulberg and his associate Hector Turnbull functioned in Hollywood as virtual independents: "It is said there will be no interference from the home office or studio executives during the making of the pictures, that the distribution organization will only be interested in handling the commercial negatives turned over and the producers will be permitted to charge the cost of their productions as they see fit."[11] Thus unit production at Famous Players–Lasky in the mid-1920s (and at several additional studios subsequently) arose largely from an independent model, reversing the development of independent production from unit production in the thirties and after.

Equally striking about the advent of unit production in the mid-twenties is its similarity on paper to independent production. At Famous Players–Lasky it included "special and star units and individual producing companies. The latter group includes those making pictures on the outside for the company such as Harold Lloyd, Douglas MacLean, Eric Von Stroheim, Marshall Neilan, etc. In the case of the special units and star units, each will have its own workers, with latitude in assignments which will allow transfers from one unit to another as occasion requires."[12]

Significantly, *Variety* lumps together two essentially different kinds of "units." The article acknowledges no substantial difference between the "studio" units like those centered on studio contractee Pola Negri and other stars and "independents" like Harold Lloyd. Although they corresponded to different corporate and contractual arrangements, the different terms "unit" and "independent" production actually denoted differences in degrees of autonomy rather than differences in kind. In practice, from the mid-1920s onward unit production and independent production for major studio distribution were interchangeable.

As Staiger (and Lewis) assert, the innovation of the sound film, the consequent decrease in the volume of production, and the escalation of costs effected a reversion to central producer control through 1931. When David O. Selznick revived unit production in August 1931, virtually all the studios except M-G-M endorsed the idea, and *Variety* announced that "one-man control [of studio production] is deemed doomed and of the past."[13] As Staiger observes, the studios renewed unit production for greater cost control and for diversity of output in a period of box office decline.[14] But they also returned to the unit organization because of the revival of double features under way by 1931.

From that year onward, because of rising production costs after the innovation of sound and Depression-era production slowdowns, the majors found it increasingly difficult to meet the continuing demand from their distribution arms and from exhibitors for a high volume of feature films. The revival of double features stabilized the market for low-budget producers, who were also gaining a limited foothold in the first-run market of independent theaters.[15] Through the mid-1930s the major producer-distributor-exhibitors argued against the double-feature temptation, arguing that two films for one tended to downgrade the value of all films and theaters. But even Paramount Publix executives, managing the largest and most widely flung chains, found that in markets like Toledo, where nothing else seemed to lure people into the theaters, double features worked in their first-run houses. By the end of 1931 the Hays office had estimated that 8000 cities used them.[16]

In response, the majors kept trying to stop double features and to control first-run independent theater bookings. In the spring and early summer of 1931, studio executives considered producing the typical $300,000 regular film plus a second, $75,000 feature which they would distribute at the standard flat rate to impinge on Poverty Row's market. They also considered the production of serials and shorts and "four-reelers" that could be sold as a lengthy package which countered the double bill. But spending more money to produce more films was unpalatable to studio executives facing diminished ticket sales and corporate receiverships in the early 1930s.[17]

While Staiger notes the role of double features in stabilizing the market for low-budget independents, she neglects to acknowledge its significance for the revival of unit production.[18] All the major producers except M-G-M turned to unit and A-scale independent production as a remedy to the demand for more films (and after 1932 M-G-M's associate producer system was a de facto unit system). The independents were especially welcome. Their films cost the major studios less—or nothing—because the majors invested in only a portion of the independent's negative costs. But again, the two modes—unit and independent production—held more basic similarities than differences from the perspective of studio protocols.

At RKO David O. Selznick, the champion of the revitalized unit system, signed independent companies to produce for RKO release in May 1932. But while the new independents supplied half of their films' negative costs, they were otherwise virtually identical to the units already at the studio. They were subject to the approval of studio management on stories, casts, technicians, budgets (of $100- to $200,000), and they shot their films at the recently purchased, underused Pathe studio lot. RKO paid its half of the film's negative cost only upon delivery of the completed film, in exchange for a fifty-fifty sharing of profits.[19]

Paramount had revived the unit system in late 1930, asking its producers (including, for a time, Lewis Milestone) to oversee units expected to produce four to five films yearly averaging $300,000. Certain highly valued producers —Cecil B. De Mille, King Vidor, and former Hollywood studio head Ben Schulberg (who produced Sylvia Sidney vehicles)—were completely financed by Paramount in a system that resembled RKO's. The unit leader was paid a flat salary plus 25 to 50 percent of the profits; the costs of the film were borne by Paramount. Like Selznick at RKO, production head Emmanuel Cohen approved the production's preparation in all its particulars, but unlike Selznick he allowed the principal photography to proceed without interference. By late 1932 Cohen counted on unit production to supply half of the year's films.[20]

The success of this program at Paramount encouraged studio executives to expand it in early 1933 to include former supervisors (such as Louis D. Lighton, in charge of family films like *Huckleberry Finn* and *Skippy*; and Lloyd Sheldon, in charge of musicals like *Here Is My Heart* and *Murder at the Vanities*).[21] Yet, Arthur Ungar, in a survey of the unit system in early 1933, noted that Paramount's production executives kept a close eye on the work of the units: "Story must be approved by the story board, production by the production board, casting and direction by [Emmanuel] Cohen, with the end that the so-called bugaboo the unit producer tries to get away from confronts these unit and individual producers who are unable to make the individual headway granted along the best unit plan."[22]

With such strictures in place, the majors' hospitality to independent producers continued into 1934. That March Paramount, while seeking films to pick up from independents outside the studio, made plans to distribute titles produced by Charles Rogers, William LeBaron (Mae West's *Belle of the*

Nineties), and B. P. Schulberg at the Pathe lot on a semi-independent, profit-sharing basis by which Paramount would finance the films entirely.[23] In August 1934 the National Recovery Act's Code Authority ruled that the major studios could not dictate to theater managers the terms for exhibiting their films—i.e., they could not stipulate in contracts whether or not their films should be placed in single or double billings. The "feeling most prevalent in major ranks since the NRA stand," *Variety* reported, "is that producers will have to turn out what the market demands—which from indications right now, means more and cheaper pictures."[24] The scramble for additional product at lower cost was intensified, and unit and independent production provided it. There was, in fact, a small explosion of independent companies on the A-scale.

After the revitalization of unit production, the most pertinent prototype for the independent firms at Paramount and elsewhere was the Screen Guild Company, created by former Paramount supervisor Mike Levee in April 1932, who had ties to the prestigious Theater Guild in New York. Levee raised one million dollars by selling stock in his private corporation hoping in this way to maintain "as much independence as possible." He planned to keep his negative costs low by deferring salaries for actors, writers, and directors in exchange for fifty percent of his films' profits. Anticipating independent production practices of the late 1930s, he supplemented the stock capitalization funds with bank loans secured with the negatives of finished productions.[25] The entire arrangement also promised Levee greater shares of the profits of his films than a studio contract could afford.

In April 1932 Levee's scheme "radically depart[ed] from orthodox organizational methods in film production," but almost immediately Levee had company. Because of studio receiverships and executive upheavals, many producers had been recently dismissed from their studios or had had their contracts renegotiated. These producers were able to line up investors in their ventures. In 1931 *Variety* explained, "Producers with former big studio affiliations figure that their reps will command attention from eastern money and first line releases."[26]

In 1931 they figured wrong, as producers like Selznick could not find investors for independent ventures. But by the following year, investors were easier to find. In May 1932 Benny Zeidman secured financing for independent companies from Joseph Brandt, who was one million dollars richer after selling his Columbia stock to Harry Cohn.[27] Darryl F. Zanuck, quitting Warner Bros., got United Artists president Joseph Schenck and other industry insiders to finance his Twentieth Century Pictures in the spring of 1933. The following year multimillionaires Jock and Cornelius Vanderbilt Whitney financed Merian Cooper and Ernest Schoedsack's Pioneer Pictures, which exploited Technicolor's recently perfected three-strip color process and produced *Becky Sharp*. In the summer of 1934, Jay Paley, uncle of CBS radio network head William Paley, underwrote Walter Wanger Productions, Inc., which produced films for Paramount release. In 1935 Jock Whitney and his relatives agreed to finance Selznick International for David O. Selznick.[28]

These financiers who contributed to stock capitalizations were encouraged not only by a stabilizing national economy but by the hospitality that United Artists and the major studios offered potential A-scale independents. In the case of Ben Hecht and Charles MacArthur, who scripted and directed a quartet of films at Paramount's New York studios in Astoria, film financiers were joined by various service organizations (independent studios, sound licensing companies, and processing laboratories) who also financed B-scale independents.[29]

Those producers who distributed their films through United Artists were a case apart, insofar as their production work could not possibly be confused with that of studio contractees at the other seven major studios. For the latter, however, the equation of unit production and independent production that existed in 1926 remained constant in trade discussions in the early thirties. In early 1933 Emmanuel Cohen testily affirmed that independents were different in degree rather than kind from their unit counterparts: "Every one of our producers on the Paramount lot is a unit. We have nine—not two. They are all under my supervision. Not one of them is independently operated." He called " 'independent production units' on a major lot a 'misnomer.' "[30]

In his survey account of the unit system, Arthur Ungar casually made such equations in phrases like "the unit producer, if figured as an independent, cannot be burdened with unnecessary or excess overhead charges." He noted that Paramount had a "unit plan" with Charles Rogers "who is wholly indie from studio management control and general overhead charges." He observed that both independents and unit producers at Paramount "all must go through the same routine," the system of approvals quoted above. His article concluded that the "best unit plan" was the "independent" plan—such as that enjoyed by Harold Lloyd and Charles Rogers, who financed their own productions and shot them off the lot—because it minimized executive meddling after principal photography began, because it freed the independent of major studio overhead, and it enabled the producer to work on a single project basis.[31]

Thus far I have argued, first, that unit and independent production practices had a spiraling, mutual influence on each other, whereby independent production of the teens and twenties inspires the unit organization at Famous Players–Lasky in 1926, and unit production in 1931 responds to B-scale independence and engenders a burst of A-scale independents. Second, I have noted a discursive confusion of unit and independent production in the trade reports of them. Both of these phenomena demonstrate how, in 1933 as in 1926, independent production for distribution through the majors was considered the equivalent of unit production. There were many reasons for this to be the case: for one thing, independent production at the majors fulfilled the same functions within the studio as unit production—lower cost, higher quality, and a better means of competing with other producers than pre-existing systems afforded.

Then, too, independence could be considered a form of unit production because it served a comparable function in terms of market share and structure. The former studio executives—such as Jesse Lasky, William Le Baron, Ben P. Schulberg, David O. Selznick, Walter Wanger, and Darryl F. Zanuck—who decided to go into business for themselves in the early 1930s did so to make more money than their studio salaries and bonuses would allow. But there were additional reasons: they disagreed with specific management policies (Zanuck at Warner Bros.), they found the studio system itself alienating (Selznick at Paramount), or they felt independence held the promise of enabling them to produce films on subjects that couldn't otherwise be approved (both Selznick and Wanger at Paramount and M-G-M). And as former studio executives they felt entitled to complete control over their films.

In spite of their feeling of rebellion, these executives were, from the very first, electing to produce films on a basis that was tolerated and even encouraged by the system they rejected. The major distributors used these independents at United Artists and especially those on their own studio lots to quash the competition of low-budget independents by distributing their films to hungry exhibitors. Hence, to call Selznick, Twentieth Century Pictures, Wanger, Schulberg, Le Baron, Cohen—and others who produced A-scale pictures for major distribution in the thirties and forties—"independent producers" is entirely misleading. For these independents were in the long term cooperating with the studio-distributors they intended to defy in the short term. The contingent, competitive situations in which the unit system was articulated were the very premise of their cooperation with the distributors. For this reason we should modify our terminology, describing the A-scale producers who delivered films to national distributors as Hollywood's semi-independent producers.

The term "semi-independent production" reminds us that such independence was ambivalently positioned between the absolute independents on the B scale (Monogram, Republic, etc.) on the one hand and the major studio units on the other. The term "semi-independent" also acknowledges that the independent's separate corporate status—the basis Staiger cites for industry definitions of independent production—could prove meaningless in practice. Box office failure quickly depleted the small companies' sparse production monies and could force the semi-independents to revert to studio contractee status. For example, after Paramount independent Walter Wanger produced two films, their dismal grosses compelled him to become a unit producer financed entirely by Paramount in 1935. (While reporting the change in Wanger's financing arrangements *Variety* did not acknowledge the change in his status from independent to unit producer.[32])

Then, too, even if they enjoyed some financial success, the semi-independents could find their boards of directors compromising their goals and production plans. If the boards of directors were agreeable and not interfering, the semi-independents had to contend with the idiosyncracies of the hosting studio managements. These in turn responded to changing business conditions with production and management policies that dictated greater or lesser autonomy for the independents. The actual degree of control over filmmaking enjoyed by any semi-independent depended on such historical contingencies. Then, if all the conditions surrounding the semi-independent were favorable, there was the question of whether the specific producer involved was ready and interested in capitalizing on what semi-independent production had to offer.[33]

That we still continue to distinguish between independent production and unit production only testifies to Janet Staiger's suggestion that both these categories serve the necessary function of reinforcing the ideology of creative individualism that accompanied the Hollywood studio system and that in turn reinforced the persistence of unit and independent work. We can see Staiger's point illustrated in the remarks of Louella Parsons and of Donald Nelson, president of the Society of the Independent Motion Picture Producers, who argued in 1947 that the independents represented the triumph of the small businessman in Hollywood. To the extent that independents did the bidding of their major hosts, this anomaly emerges clearly as a contradiction between the industrial practices of the industry and one of its fundamental ideological tenets.[34]

The equation of unit and semi-independent production in major studio thinking encourages us to review and revise the history of Hollywood's approach to organizing production. Janet Staiger is admirably circumspect in acknowledging that historical processes are mixed and that her research — describing successive and distinct production systems that increased the division of labor in Hollywood — concerns dominant practices only. Yet while Staiger's paradigm for Hollywood's mode of production remains crucial, ongoing research on American filmmaking modifies its historical specificity.

Recently, for example, Charles Musser has challenged Staiger's model of successive organizations of filmmaking in the first two decades of this century. Where Staiger argues for a progression toward increased division of labor, from the "director" system (beginning in 1907) to a "director-unit" system (1909) to "central producer" (1914) systems, Musser finds one shift, from a "collaborative" system of filmmaking prevalent before 1907 to the central producer method, which Musser dates five to seven years earlier than Staiger does. The central producer system was inaugurated to meet the dramatically increased demand for films after the advent of the nickelodeon rather than to facilitate the production of fiction films. Once begun, the central producer system was utilized with greater flexibility than previously recognized: producers could grant directors enormous autonomy (as in those cases Staiger cited as employing the director-unit system) or they could supervise their directors' work very closely.[35]

Similarly, I have argued here to revise Staiger's periodization of the shift from the central producer to the unit producer systems and to explore the relationship between unit and semi-independent producer systems. All three methods co-existed in American filmmaking since the teens. The factors of cost control, efficiency, and individualistic quality which favored the unit and semi-independent methods became especially dear to the major studios in periods of the industry's history when they perceived threats to their market share and their oligopolistic market structure: the twenties and the early thirties. In short, in different periods of the first four decades of this century, each method came to be preferred — rather than innovated — by the dominant studios. When the studios chose to employ them, each mode was flexible enough to tolerate a variety of methods, as the examples of Paramount and RKO's operations indicate. And when the United States government ordered the dismantling of the majors' oligopoly in the late forties, the major's pre-eminence in distribution meant that even the "package unit" independents, like their predecessors, helped the majors maintain their market share.

What bearing then did unit or independent production have on filmmaking in Hollywood's studio era? Like a studio's choice of system for organizing production, this depended on historical circumstance. With a few exceptions (such as those cited earlier), it had very little impact. Though they operated autonomous companies with no major studio financing, Zanuck, Selznick, and Samuel Goldwyn followed the major studios' mode of production and stylistic norms to produce the same genre films that held sway at the majors. Pioneer Pictures did likewise, with the difference that it used its autonomy to innovate new technologies the studios hesitated to employ.

On the other hand, distinctive and transgressive films did on occasion emerge from the unit and independents' ranks, such as at Paramount in the early 1930s. There, former studio executive William Le Baron oversaw the Mae West unit from 1932's *Night after Night* through *Klondike Annie* in 1936. During this period Herman Mankiewicz oversaw the anarchic comedies of the Marx Bros. unit like *Horse Feathers* (1932) and *Duck Soup* (1933).[36] In late 1934 and early 1935 Walter Wanger independently produced *The President Vanishes*, a political melodrama that showed various industrial and political leaders joining forces to lead America into war for greater profits, and *Private Worlds* (1935), a melodrama set, for the first time, in a mental hospital.

But while Mae West, the Marx Brothers, and Wanger's subsequent productions in the decade are less provocative, it is difficult to argue that it was unit or independent production that made their first films crucially different. There is a considerable array of more pertinent factors, such as Paramount's comparatively tolerant management policies and the talents of each unit involved. The Marx Brothers did not require the unit system to realize their outrageous routines on film, as evidenced by their first films, *Coconuts* (1929) and *Animal Crackers* (1930). Similarly, Walter Wanger favored exploiting contemporary social issues to make distinctive films. As a pseudo-unit producer at M-G-M in 1933, he had produced *Gabriel over the White House*, a virtual rehearsal for *The President Vanishes*; both films engendered lengthy meetings between officials from his studio and from the Motion Picture Producers and Distributors Association to discuss their transgressive elements in relation to the Production Code.

In other words, Hollywood's unit and semi-independent production guaranteed the producer nothing. It offered only the *potential* for procedural autonomy and distinctive filmmaking, if the right historical circumstances — the conjunction of studio management, independent boards of directors, and the individual producer — enhanced that potential. Thus, as examples of economically and socially determined practices, the semi-independents are no more revealing than their studio counterparts. This is why the semi-independents' departure from the studio system "is more apparent than real." It is also the reason why we should henceforth distinguish them from their counterparts within Hollywood (the low-budget producers) and without.

Notes

I thank my two anonymous readers, and especially Charles Musser, for encouragement and invaluable suggestions for revisions.

1 Janet Staiger, in David Bordwell, Janet Staiger and Kristin Thompson, *The Classical Hollywood Cinema: Film Style and Mode of Production from 1917 to 1960* (New York: Columbia University Press, 1985), 317.
2 Ibid., 320–21.
3 Richard Dyer MacCann, "Independence with a Vengeance," *Film Quarterly* 15, no. 4 (1962): 14, 19, quoted in Tino Balio, "When Is an Independent Producer Independent? The Case of United Artists after 1948," *The Velvet Light Trap*, 22 (1986): 53.
4 Tino Balio has fleshed out Richard Dyer MacCann's observations by a detailed look at the workings of United Artists and its relation with independent producers. See Tino Balio, *United Artists: The Company Built by the Stars* (Madison, Wis.: University of Wisconsin Press, 1975), and *United Artists: The Company That Changed the Film Industry* (Madison, Wis.: University of Wisconsin Press, 1989). See also, in *The Velvet Light Trap* 22 (1986) on "Hollywood Independents," Kevin Hagopian, "Declarations of Independence: A History of Cagney Productions," 16–32; Matthew Bernstein, "Fritz Lang, Incorporated," 33–52; and Ed Lowry, "Dimension Pictures: Portrait of a Seventies Independent," 65–74. All of these essays provide case studies on the subject to show how James Cagney, Fritz Lang, and low-budget independents tried to produce independently in Hollywood and how their efforts were ultimately compromised.
5 Janet Staiger, "The Package Unit System," in *Classical Hollywood Cinema*, 330–35; see also her "Individualism Versus Collectivism," *Screen* 24, nos. 4–5 (July-October 1983): 68–69.
6 Staiger, in *Classical Hollywood Cinema*, 330.

7 Ibid., 320.
8 "Famous Coast Production Clean Up; Schulberg Is Head, Subject to Lasky," *Variety*, 21 July 1926, 4; "F. P.'s Producing Lay-Out," *Variety*, 28 July 1926, 8; "Par's Supers Assigned," *Variety*, 25 January 1928, 14; "Studios' Unit System," *Variety*, 4 April 1928, 11.
   Variety is highly sympathetic to the dominant film producers and distributors (as opposed to exhibitors and low-budget independents) in its reports on industry developments, and this is precisely its strength as a source for historical research, particularly insofar as it expresses and chronicles studio producers' and executives' concerns.
9 "Present Picture Leaders," *Variety*, 5 January 1926, 8, 18.
10 "Famous Coast Production Clean Up."
11 "F.P. Treating New Producers as Ind.," *Variety*, 25 November 1925, 27.
12 "Famous Coast Production Clean Up."
13 "Par's Unit System Adds Mankiewicz and Heath," *Variety*, 25 Aug. 1931, 7; "Selznick Splits Costs with Radio on Pictures," *Variety*, 27 October 1931, 5.
14 Staiger, in *Classical Hollywood Cinema*, 320–21.
15 For a comprehensive overview of the B-studios during the transition to sound, see Paul Seale, "A Host of Others: Towards a Nonlinear History of Poverty Row and the Coming of Sound," *Wide Angle* 13, no. 1 (1990): 72–103. For contemporary accounts of the double-feature phenomenon, see also "Double Feature Playing More Plentiful and Spreading, Good Only for Distribs; 2d Run Block," *Variety*, 8 October 1930, 4; "Claim Poor Films, Not Depression, Accountable for 20% to 25% Drop in Grosses — 3 Cities Show 14% Off," *Variety*, 13 May 1931, 5; "Indies and Twin Bills Out; Major Firms' Double Attack," *Variety*, 14 June 1932, 5; "New Financing Ups Monogram Budgets," *Variety*, 8 November 1932, 12. In the first article *Variety* reported that roughly forty percent of the theaters still in business were using the double-feature format and that "Indies [i.e., independent producers] right down the line admit that from 50 to 75% of their accounts are with theatres playing double bills."
16 For evidence of the debate on double features, see "Double Feature Programs Are Not Favored for Best Theatres by Big Circuits — Only Necessity Playing," *Variety*, 1 April 1931, 6; "Double Feature Dangers: Many Sides Over 2-For-1 Program," *Variety*, 8 April 1931: 11; "8,000 Cities Use Dual Features," *Variety*, 8 December 1931, 9; "Chains Want 4-Reelers as Dual Feature Offset; Urge Studios to Start before Indies Take Tip," *Variety*, 12 July 1932, 5.
17 "Double Bills and Rentals; Effect Felt at Par Convention"; "Film Shortage Problem; Par. May Jump Program to 100," *Variety*, 29 April 1931, 3; "Two Production Cost Films; $75,000 for Low to $300,000 High," *Variety*, 20 May 1931, 3; "Ousting Double Features; Serials, Shorts Is One Way Out," *Variety*, 23 February 1932, 7.
18 Staiger in *Classical Hollywood Cinema*, 318.
19 "Radio's 12 from Indies Mostly at $100,000," *Variety*, 10 May 1932, 4; "Rogers' Par Deal for 8," *Variety*, 15 March 1932, 4; "Radio's Indie Unit Plan; To Split Profits and Costs 50–50," *Variety*, 15 March 1932, 5; "Schnitzer, Ascher, Lloyd and Fineman Probably Producers in Radio's Unit Plan at Pathe Lot," *Variety*, 22 March 1932, 5; "Inside Stuff — Pictures," *Variety*, 19 April 1932, 6.
20 "Par's Unit System Adds Mankiewicz and Heath," 7; "Schulberg's 8 Films for Par," *Variety*, 23 August 1932, 5; "Par Favors Program Cut to 45; Katz, in Taking on Added Duties, Looks Like Genl. Mgr. of Company," *Variety*, 15 March 1932, 5; "Par Solicits Indies For Program Fillers" *Variety*, 22 March 1932, 5; "Par's Unit Production Plan; Financing for Outsiders On Percentage," *Variety*, 11 October 1932, 5.

21 "Studios Can Cut to $175,000 Cost, Claims E. Cohen—Tells a Few Things," *Variety*, 17 January 1933, 2.
22 Arthur Ungar, "Unit Production as Out?" *Variety*, 3 January 1933, 5.
23 "Par Studio May Go All-Unit; 5 or 6 Producers," *Variety*, 6 March 1934, 5.
24 "Dualism Issue Has Indie Exhibs and Indie Producers Wrought Up; Majors and MPTOA Are against It," *Variety*, 21 August 1934, 4.
25 "Levee, Pomeroy Set Indie Plans," *Variety*, 5 April 1932, 4.
26 "Unit Producing Plan Grows on Coast," *Variety*, 11 August 1931, 5.
27 "Brandt's Indie Deal with Goldberg Puzzle," *Variety*, 10 May 1932, 4.
28 "Jock Whitney Laying $7,000,000 on Line for Nine Technicolors, Merian Cooper Joining In Later," *Variety*, 6 November 1934, 4.
29 "Par's Eastern Prod. Is on a Rental from ERPI to Help Pay Off $1,900,000," *Variety*, 8 May 1934, 3, notes that ERPI (Electronic Research Products, Inc.), one of the studio's major creditors, was financing half of the negative costs for films shot at Paramount's Astoria, New York, studio.
30 "Studios Can Cut to $175,000 Cost."
31 Lloyd and Rogers's arrangements are outlined in "Lasky–Chas. McCarthy Join Fox; Both Men Await Par Settlements," *Variety*, 18 October 1932, 5.
32 "Par Financing Wanger, Jay Paley Out," *Variety*, 20 March 1935, 5.
33 My *Walter Wanger, Hollywood "Independent"* (University of California Press, forthcoming) details the varying historical contingencies that Wanger struggled with—and took advantage of—in his lengthy career as a semi-independent producer.
34 Staiger, "Individualism versus Collectivism," 69; Donald M. Nelson, "The Independent Producer," *Annals of the American Academy of Political and Social Sciences* (1947): 49–57.
35 Charles Musser, "Pre-Classical American Cinema: Its Changing Modes of Production," *Persistence of Vision* 9 (1991): 46–65; see especially 50–55. To Musser the transition from collaborative to central producer methods corresponds both to the industry's shift from small business capitalism (using the partnership method) to industrial and corporate capitalism (with elaborated management hierarchies) and to the preliminary articulation of the classical Hollywood style.
36 Herman Mankiewicz quit the production of *Duck Soup* midway through principal photography.
    For Emmanuel Cohen's business dealings with Mae West, see Ramona Curry, "Mae West as Censored Commodity: The Case of *Klondike Annie*," *Cinema Journal* 31, no. 1 (Fall 1991): 57–84.
    In many ways, the revolving door of studio and independent producing arrangements that thrive in Hollywood and the television industry today are prefigured by the revolving doors at the studios in the 1930s. Walter Wanger, B. P. Schulberg, William Le Baron, and Emmanuel Cohen (who left Paramount in 1936 and produced two films with Mae West for Paramount release later in the decade) were all former executives who returned to Paramount with unit or independent deals.

Part 3

POSTWAR TRANSFORMATION: HOLLYWOOD IN THE AGE OF TELEVISION

10

THE DECLINE OF AN INSTITUTION

Garth Jowett

Source: Garth Jowett, *Film: The Democratic Art*, Boston, Mass.: Little, Brown & Co., 1976, pp. 333–363.

When the fighting ended in 1945, there was widespread anxiety that the cessation of war spending would bring about the economic hardships of the Depression all over again. Fortunately, this was not the case, and in the immediate postwar period, the United States experienced the greatest and most sustained economic growth in its history. Not that the domestic scene was untroubled, for labor difficulties, inflation and shortages, a housing crisis, and increasing social unrest were all features of "peaceful" America. In particular, the inconsistencies in the outdated segregationist policies which pervaded all aspects of American life became conspicuous, and a source of irritation for many — both black and white — who had risked their lives for "democracy."

The war had ended with the explosion of the atomic bomb, and coupled with the increasing political polarization between the Communists and the "free world," the knowledge that man now had weapons capable of destroying the world created a mood of fear and suspicion which would manifest itself in many facets of social as well as political life. In particular, those powerful agencies capable of molding public opinion — the mass media — would themselves be under attack from all sides, as the ideological battle among left, right and center dominated the period 1946–1960. The motion picture industry was especially hard hit and affected by this troubled domestic scene, for it had to contend not only with an irreversible decline in audience due to shifting leisure patterns, but also with an unprecedented political attack, this time aimed more at the people who made the movies, and less at the actual films they produced.

The broken promise

The war had once again brought into sharper focus the issue of the "proper social and cultural role" for the motion picture. All through the Depression, and especially during the war, the motion picture had proved its worth, if not as an "information medium," then certainly as an indispensable form of recreation and diversionary entertainment. The surprising loyalty which the American public had demonstrated for this medium only served to make both the movies' devotees and its critics wish that its tremendous powers were being put to use for some higher purpose than mere entertainment. This view had persisted for fifty years, and the motion picture was no nearer defining its role in 1946 than it had been in 1896.

In 1944, James T. Farrell, the author of the *Studs Lonigan* trilogy and a noted social critic, examined "The Language of Hollywood" in the *Saturday Review of Literature*, and attacked the "tremendous commercial culture [which] has developed as a kind of substitute for a genuinely popular, a genuinely democratic culture, which would recreate and communicate how the mass of the people live, how they feel about working, loving, enjoying, suffering, and dying."[1] What Farrell really objected to was the fact that the tremendous influence of all the mass media, and the motion picture in particular, was determined by "business considerations." This fact of economic necessity denied the writer the opportunity to work free of restrictions, and those who wrote for the screen "reveal a retrogression in consciousness."[2] According to Farrell, the Hollywood "commodity" failed to "fulfill the real cultural needs of the masses of the people," because the movies as a cultural influence did not "help to create those states of consciousness, of awareness of oneself, of others, and of the world, which aid in making people better, and in preparing them to make the world better. Hollywood films usually have the precisely opposite effect; most of them make people less aware, or else falsely aware."[3]

Farrell's attack on commercialization of culture was merciless, and although overstated, his basic premise was sound. However, he did acknowledge that the movies were more the end product of long-noticed tendencies in American society than the cause, although the medium was now so powerful an influence that Hollywood's demands threatened all forms of creative writing.[4]

As was noted in the previous chapter, the motion picture industry had the biggest year in its history in 1946. However, after this blaze of glory, the industry went into a fairly steady economic decline from which it has never recovered. This was not what the industry or its devotees had envisaged in late 1945, when, buoyed by the public's response to the movies' contribution to the war effort, they foresaw a new "golden age" for the medium. It was especially hoped that the war experience would revitalize Hollywood, and that, having learned something about making documentary films, it would

198

infuse the commercial product with a "greater realism." Philip Dunne, who had been chief of production with the O.W.I. overseas branch, suggested that documentary film makers and Hollywood producers had much to offer each other, but this would not be a fruitful exchange "as long as some in Hollywood persist in looking on the documentary as a poor relation of 'The Industry'; as long as so many in that 'Industry' continue to consider the typical documentarian a long-haired crank, his mind cluttered with impracticalities."[5] Dunne noted that many of Hollywood's finest films had dealt with material usually considered purely documentary, movies such as *Fury* (1936), *The Grapes of Wrath* (1940), and the very recent masterpiece *Citizen Kane* (1941). He hoped that more producers would "grasp the enormous responsibility" facing the movie industry "in the critical years ahead," which could best be achieved if their preparation "be not only spiritual but technical . . . by closely observing the methods, and sometimes absorbing the personnel, of the documentary field."[6]

Producer and critic Kenneth MacGowan also noted a trend toward "new techniques" as evidence of the documentary influence in the films released in late 1945. He singled out *The House on 92nd Street, The Story of G.I. Joe, The Pride of the Marines* and the Academy Award-winning *The Lost Weekend* as examples of this trend. MacGowan, however, observed with regret Hollywood's continued reliance on books and plays as the source of its best material, indicating a fear within the film industry not to attempt anything the least bit controversial, unless it had proved publicly acceptable in another medium.[7]

Unfortunately, this hoped-for amalgam between documentary and entertainment was seldom achieved, although the late 1940s was a particularly rich period for creativity in the American film.[8] The problem really stemmed from the inability of the movies' critics (even those who wished to be constructive in their criticism) to understand the power of entertainment to "influence" as much as any documentary. It was precisely this failure to equate entertainment with ideas which had led to the acceptance of control over the movies (and in some cases the same philosophy had affected radio). Nevertheless, the long history of the motion picture had demonstrated over and over again that "entertainment" was capable of exerting a powerful influence on its audience.[9]

Still, the movies were continually criticized for failing to make the most of their potential as an educational influence. As an example, in January, 1947, an editorial in the *Christian Century* complained that, "as one of the three principal media of mass information and education, the motion picture is notably failing to do its share in instructing the American people concerning their responsibilities as citizens of the atomic age . . . the millions who attend the movies each week find there little or nothing to awake them to the possibilities for good or evil of this new dimension of power." The problem, the editorial suggested, lay in the "provincialism" of those who controlled the movie industry, and whose dictum was, "Let others instruct. Our job is entertainment." Thus the movies were abrogating their responsibility and "drugging the national consciousness into slumber." The editorial concluded by noting that nothing would be done about this misused potential "until it is recognized that under its present owners the motion picture industry is supplying the opiate which keeps the people lethargic when they should be aroused as never before."[10]

The movies had achieved some recognition in the hierarchy of American arts in 1935, when the Museum of Modern Art Film Library was opened in New York. Between 1935 and 1945, the museum had done a creditable job of collecting prints and negatives, and now owned the best collection in the United States. Nevertheless, cooperation from Hollywood in this venture had been inconsistent, and Iris Barry, one of the founders of the film library and the current curator, suggested that "now was the time for Hollywood and its technicians to join with the Film Library in a collaboration that would once and for all give precise information to students about . . . the achievements that have carried the motion picture from its celebrated infancy to near maturity and made it indeed an art (as well as an industry) with which one can truly be proud to be connected."[11] Unfortunately, this cooperation was slow in developing, and the film industry continued along its commercial path oblivious to its wider responsibilities. Clara Beranger, a screenwriter and instructor in film, noted that in order to develop new technical talent for the screen, students needed greater practical experience because "the art was so closely tied to its technology." Here too, Hollywood did not seem anxious to encourage such cooperative training ventures.[12]

By 1947, the American film industry was still struggling to come to terms with its potential in the educational field, but here the educators were still partly to blame, because they had not yet discovered the key to the successful utilization of in-the-classroom film instruction. Charles Palmer, writing in *Hollywood Quarterly*, called for a greater effort of co-operation on the part of educators and the film industry to make films which would be integrated into the current curriculum. Such films would be "bought, rather than rented, and bought in large enough numbers to justify the use of top talents and facilities of the motion picture industry."[13] Edgar Dale disagreed with Palmer's call for more "entertainment" in educational films, and suggested in turn that the remedy was "to have more teachers understand what a good film is, and to have producers of these films understand what teaching is." It was obvious that Dale was suspicious of the "entertainment" film which had no obligation to "start a train of thinking."[14] However, Palmer got in the last word in reply to Dale, and reiterated Hollywood's enormous potential, and suggested further that "this potential contribution should not be barred through unjustified prejudice, not be resented as an intrusion on a private reserve."[15] Palmer had made his point — the movies were too important to leave to well-meaning amateurs.

In 1948, the MPAA (the MPPDA had altered its name to the Motion Picture Association of America in 1945) set up a project known as the Children's Film Library, consisting of twenty-eight feature films which were reissues of favorites with juvenile audiences in the past. According to reports in the trade press, the exhibitors, the studios and distributors stood to make very little money from this venture. Sondra Gorney, examining the nature of children's cinema in the United States, commented on the selected films that "one thing is certain: they were never produced with the young audience in mind."[16] She also noted the recent revival of censorship activity aimed directly at movies for children, and which threatened the industry with the loss of almost 20 percent of its audience.[17] The development of special children's films was always an unfulfilled dream for concerned educators, parents, teachers, psychologists and social workers. The eternal question was, "If the MPAA could see some merit in selecting reissues for children's viewing, why could it see no value in making new films exclusively for this audience?" The children of 1948 were to be the adult audiences of 1958; but then Hollywood had never been able to think of the future.

It remained for film director Irving Pichel to sum up the unkept promise of the movies in the postwar period. The war had been an exhilarating experience for those in the film industry who "were able to put the medium . . . to the most effective use it had ever, in their experience, served."[18] By 1948, however, the industry had been "caponized." While Americans had fought for the survival of democracy, he noted, in reality many of the "great issues were left unresolved and their residue constitutes the most derisive factor in our social, economic and political life today." Pichel attacked the film industry for turning its back on the important domestic issues facing America in the late 1940s. He suggested that it was clearly the function of "the art of fiction," including "the dramatic film," to examine and depict the "antagonisms, the aggressions, the strains," in society. However, the movies were being limited in their ability to contribute to an understanding "of those sources of strain which have the greatest contemporary interest for us." Pichel's anger was directed at those politicians who continued to attack "message" films, and also at the "industrial organization" of the film industry which prevented anything "sensitive" from reaching the screen. Thus, Pichel reasoned, "the screen remains a medium but is not a voice. . . . The screen is asked to ignore the antagonisms most current among us, most productive of disruption in the contemporary scene, most dramatic in their threat to our social and political present and future. . . ."[19]

He was making an important point. Because the film industry depended upon such large audiences, it could not afford to antagonize any section of it, and therefore movie content was largely limited to examining problems about which the studios, and the censors, believed that the American public had reached something close to unanimity. Thus the screenplay was seldom able to give the audience wholly new viewpoints. As long as

Hollywood was constrained by a rigid form of ideological and political censorship, dependent upon the mentality of "big business," and threatened with extinction by a small box in the living room, this philosophy would prevail.

The audience examined

After the glorious year in 1946 when close to 1.7 billion dollars was paid by movie patrons to see their favorite entertainment, the fortunes of the American motion picture went steadily downhill, with only the odd year in which this decline has been momentarily halted. In the fourteen-year period between 1946 and 1960, the average weekly attendance dropped from ninety million to forty million. More important, the expenditures declined even more sharply, from one-fifth to less than one-tenth of the available recreational dollars. It was quite obvious to those inside and outside the motion picture industry that for a variety of reasons, the intense love affair between the mass of the American public and their movies was coming to an end. While the movies would continue as a major entertainment medium, by the early 1950s it could no longer claim to be the *major* source of commercial recreation.

At precisely the time that the audience started to decline, Hollywood started to show some curiosity about the nature and taste preferences of its patrons. Earlier, in 1933, Howard T. Lewis had commented on the industry's inability to predict success or to produce films to meet the requirements of "particular classes of audiences," and he pointed out that no satisfactory methods of prediction had been developed, and that "experiment, reliance upon hunches, or blind guess seems to be the usual practice."[20] In 1947, Ernest Borneman, writing in *Harper's* about "The Public Opinion Myth," examined the increasing use of public opinion polls, and suggested that such research went far beyond merely statistical or psychological investigation, but was "essentially tied to the economic structure of the entertainment industry."[21] Borneman questioned whether such "market research" practices were adaptable to the "cultural field," and suggested that the danger lay in the industry's placing far too much reliance on the pollster's findings. So far, according to Borneman, this trend toward "scientific" analysis of the market for movies had been disastrous, for

> . . . the closer they came to a definition of today's demand, the further they found themselves moving away from the creation of an active and continuing market for tomorrow. The perpetual application of consumer analyses to the cultural market had turned that market into a sterile, glutted, and intractable thing . . . Surrendering the job of firing the public mind to new horizons of adventure, the showmen followed the pollsters so deeply into the morass of the

lowest common denominator that their birthright as entertainers and artists got stuck somewhere along the road.[22]

Of course, not everyone agreed with Borneman, and earlier, in 1945, Bosley Crowther had looked at the same phenomenon, and while he made no qualitative judgment, the tone of his article suggests approval for any method which would assist the movie industry in developing a product to meet the wide variety of tastes exhibited by the movie-going public. To demonstrate this "general predisposition of preference," Crowther included a table which had been compiled by the Audience Research Institute (A.R.I.), a subsidiary of the Gallup Poll organization. This table of preference proportions was calculated against an index of 100; the total exceeds 100 because respondents were allowed to make more than one choice:

Table 18 Film Content Preferences, 1945

Type	Males	Females
Musicals	35	49
Light comedy	35	42
Serious drama	23	42
Excitement, adventure	39	25
Slapstick comedy	43	18
Army, navy, aviation	40	23
Detective, mystery	36	24
Romance, mystery	9	32
Westerns	16	7

Source: Bosley Crowther, "It's the Fans Who Make the Films," in the *New York Times Magazine*, June 24, 1945, p. 14.

A.R.I. was busy developing new methods of audience research which included the calculation of the "want to see" or "expectancy level" of a film, which was determined by asking people their opinion of a verbally outlined plot. (Borneman had quoted the famed British film maker Sir Alexander Korda, producer of *The Private Life of Henry VIII*, as saying, "How would you react if someone stopped you on the street, or rang your doorbell, and asked, 'Would you like to see a picture about a sixteenth century English king and his several wives?' ")[23] The tests on completed films were more sophisticated, and utilized specially devised electronic equipment which charted the "enjoyment" level throughout a film by averaging out individual responses. If the "enjoyment level" was lower than the "expectancy level" the trick was to exhibit such films as fast as possible to take advantage of the "want to see" impulse. However, if the reverse was true, then the film had to be carefully "marketed" while the "want to see" was increased by advertising and other forms of exploitation, especially "word of mouth."[24]

The development of these new techniques was part of a desperate bid by Hollywood to minimize any losses. There were two big reasons for such action. One was the rapidly increasing production costs — up 70 percent since 1941. The second was the continued threat of the antitrust action which was bound to cause drastic alterations in movie distribution. If distributors were forced to deal with single films, and not blocks, then each film would have to be sold on its own merits. Naturally, producers wanted each production to be potentially profitable, and were therefore willing to use any technique they could to ensure this.

In a series of articles which culminated in an important book, Dr. Leo A. Handel, the man responsible for MGM's audience research, examined these new techniques in some detail, and concluded that, in fact, such research was far behind audience research for the other mass media. Handel noted that "Hollywood, by and large, resisted the development of high-level audience research. In the race between intuition and the IBM machine the latter came in a poor second."[25] One example of the myths which such haphazard methods had perpetuated was that regarding the sexual composition of the film audience, which supposedly was heavily weighted toward women. Handel pointed out that several independent studies in the 1940s had shown that the audience was, in fact, evenly split between men and women.[26] (This of course, does not take into account the possibility of a historical shift in audience composition between the 1920s and the 1940s — but why this would have happened is uncertain.) Handel also noted after the initial flurry, there was a decrease in the use of general audience research in the late 1940s, and that A.R.I. lost many of its clients in spite of the valuable service the organization had rendered. He suggested that A.R.I.'s own psychological approach to the traditionally reticent film industry was partly to blame, for, "instead of advising what decisions might be taken as a result of the audience studies, they often told the industry executives what to do."[27] This surely would have been the "kiss of death" in Hollywood!

The main thrust of all Handel's writings was that the motion picture industry was "the only major business in the United States which has never made a serious attempt to study its potential market."[28] The reliance on intuition was dangerous, and in any case, different industry luminaries had different intuitions. Thus, at a crucial period in its history, the film industry ignored all the warning signs and continued to use outdated business methods from a previous, and more predictable, period in its past. Not that the industry was alone in its ignorance; even an "expert" like Leo Handel was unable to predict the disastrous effects of television in his 1950 book, *Hollywood Looks At Its Audience*.[29]

Eric Johnston, who had taken over from Will Hays as president of the Motion Picture Association of America (MPAA) in 1945, was a fact-minded man who almost immediately established a research department for the industry. This ambitious research program was to be governed by a committee of audience research consisting of key members of the industry, but in spite of Johnston's urging them to procure sound statistical data about America's moviegoers, the member companies of the MPAA were never happy with the project. After sponsoring some minor inter-industry statistical studies, the research committee discontinued its activities.[30]

Because of the heavy reliance on intuition, and the very haphazard attempts made to understand its audience, the motion picture industry placed a great deal of faith in the persuasive ability of its advertising campaigns to attract patrons into movie theaters. The advertising associated with the movies had always been severely criticized, and had proved to be beyond the control of the Hays Office. Toned down somewhat during the happier days of booming wartime attendance, movie advertising returned to "normal" after 1946. John Elliot Williams, an advertising executive with wide experience in the field of movie publicity, noted that "no form of advertising is more extravagant, more misleading, more mendacious, and sometimes more vicious than the printed matter which exploits the motion picture." Williams continued his devastating, and well-chronicled, attack on movie advertising, pointing out that most campaigns totally and consciously misled the public as to the true nature of the film's content. The independent theaters were particularly guilty of such questionable tactics, although the chains were not without blame. He concluded by suggesting that "film advertising today seems a typical product of those forces which have made the motion picture not only the most timorous of industries . . . but also the most inconstant, slothful and supine."[31]

Movie critic Jay E. Gordon also examined the "dishonest" advertising methods of the film industry and suggested that instead of relying on the studio publicity department, the industry use "specialists" to promote its products, that is, advertising agencies. This practice, Gordon felt, would mean greater honesty, more precise campaigns aimed at specific audiences, and greater benefits for the studios and the public. "Every motion picture produced is a thing apart, a separate and distinguishable entity, an isolated artistic creation . . . [and] . . . should be sold as a separate article of commerce, advertised in accordance with its own merits . . ."[32]

Among the many suggestions made by Jay Gordon was one to "discourage movie gossip columns both in public prints [sic] and on radio and television."[33] This was not an easy, or, for the studios, a desirable thing to do, for the Hollywood gossip columnist had become an indispensable cog in studio publicity machinery. All through the forties and fifties Hollywood continued to be a prime source for news which was dispatched to media outlets all over the globe. In 1954, there were still 411 men and women accredited to the studios by the Johnston office as Hollywood reporters.[34] This group comprised one of the world's largest permanent congregations of journalistic talent and effort, and no other industry came close to achieving this intensity of coverage.

The top Hollywood reporter was, without doubt, Louella Parsons, who had started as a syndicated gossip columnist in 1925. By 1954, she was featured in 625 newspapers throughout the world, with close to 40 million readers. A close second was Hedda Hopper, featured in 70 newspapers, with a circulation of 32 million, and she and Louella had conducted a long-lasting, and publicity garnering, feud, which had finally been settled in 1948.[35] Behind these front-line columnists were the hundreds of independent press agents watching for every opportunity to "plant" an "item" about a client, and the studio publicity men paid to provide the insatiable public with information about their favorite stars, which might eventually lead to another sale at the box office. All of this was necessary for an industry which could only survive by creating illusion to feed the public's fantasies.

The state of the industry, 1946–1950

In 1949, a screenwriter named Herbert Clyde Lewis was quoted as saying, "The swimming pools are drying up all over Hollywood. I do not think I shall see them filled in my generation."[36] Lewis's witticism was supported by the current state of the film industry, for by 1949, it was obvious that making movies was no longer the profitable business it had once been. While the economics of the movie industry have always been complex, the sudden shift from wartime boom to postwar recession, even before the introduction of television, can clearly be attributed to a combination of several factors. The first was the decline in audience which has already been noted, and although Hollywood attempted to reverse this trend, the task proved too difficult. Essentially, the difficulty lay in capturing the "Lost Audience"—that group between the ages of thirty one and sixty who comprised only 35 percent of movie patrons. A survey estimated that if all the people in this age group went to the movies only once a week, the box-office receipts after tax would rise by $800 million a year.[37] While the number of paid admissions had exceeded four billion according to industry statistics, this in fact was broken down into a probable thirty million separate moviegoers, mainly under thirty, and who went several times a week. A further refinement revealed that a mere thirteen to fifteen million individuals actually saw the basic Hollywood staple—the "A" feature film.[38]

The real problem was how to attract the older adults without alienating the under-nineteen group. The movies could not really compete with radio when it came to providing fare for fragmented audiences, and the cost structure was quite different. Therefore, the film industry should have made a more conscientious effort to find out why this large potential group shunned the industry's offerings, but this was never done. Gilbert Seldes began his important book *The Great Audience* (1950) by noting:

Except for the makers of baby foods, no industry in the United States has been so indifferent to the steady falling away of its customers as the movies have been ... The parallel with strained foods breaks down in one detail: the foods would be worthless if the customer didn't outgrow them, and the manufacturer virtually guarantees that they will become unecessary in time and give way to other, more varied nourishment; the makers of movies pretend that what they offer is a balanced ration for adults also. But the reason the customer stops buying the product is the same; in each case the formula no longer satisfies.[39]

What were the reasons for this youthful concentration in the film audience? Certainly content was a major factor, but there were other reasons, as Paul Lazarsfeld pointed out:

The decline of frequent movie attendance with increasing age is very sharp. No other mass medium shows a comparable trend. This is probably due to a variety of factors. Movie-going is essentially a social activity ... and young people are more likely to band together for the purpose of entertainment. Then, for some movies one has to leave the house, which probably becomes more distasteful as one grows older. Finally, radio programs and reading material offer a variety of choices, and each age group can select from these media items that interest them.

The supply of movies, however, is much smaller and the variety more limited, and they are patterned to the tastes of younger people.[40]

Whatever the reasons, the fact remained that movie audiences were declining long before television became a major competitor on the American entertainment scene. This was particularly obvious in the face of the rise in gross national product and disposable income, and the increase in expenditures on recreation. Also, the population of the United States had increased by 8 percent between 1940 and 1950. An examination of all these statistics together could point to only one thing — the movie industry was in trouble.

One reason may have been the public's reaction to the postwar Hollywood product. A survey conducted by *Fortune* magazine in late 1948 found that movie audiences were not overenthusiastic about the quality of the films of that period. When asked, "How do 1948 movies compare to those of two or three years ago?," 23 percent thought that there were "more good ones"; 30 percent felt that they were "the same"; 38 percent thought that there were "fewer good ones"; and 9 percent had no opinion. This particular *Fortune* survey was most revealing in that the results indicated that audiences were beginning to find alternatives to movie-going, and 50 percent of the movie-goers who "are going less often" indicated that they were "too busy, or have other things to do"; 33 percent "did not like any of the current selections"; 16 percent "could not afford them"; and 14 percent gave "other reasons."[41]

The other important reasons for the audience decline can be attributed to the increasing growth of alternative spectator amusements, including professional sports, theater and even opera. Automobiles also enjoyed a healthy postwar sales boom; while the expected rise in the birthrate kept many young couples home. There was a shift in expenditure patterns away from amusement toward more materialistic acquisitions, and movies were unfortunately caught in the squeeze. The motion picture was shown to be not as indispensable a part of American social life as many had thought; all that was now required to diminish the power of the entertainment monolith was to provide a "functional alternative." This is precisely what television was able to do.

The other major problem faced by the movie industry in the period 1946–1950 was that of sharply declining profits, caused by a combination of financial factors over which the industry had very little control. The first was the dramatic rise in production costs, which threatened to destroy profits altogether.[42] The second was the continued difficulty in extracting profits earned out of foreign markets, as most governments were not anxious to submit to continued Hollywood domination of the international motion picture market.[43] Third, and in the long run the most damaging, was the final divorcement of exhibition from the production and distribution functions.[44]

The final victory by the Justice Department, and the enforcement of the divestiture decree, while perfectly legal and philosophically in keeping with Rooseveltian liberal thinking, had a disastrous effect on the film industry, and ultimately on the whole structure of movie-going in America. Charles Higham examined these effects and suggested:

> For confidence in a product, the feeling that it could flow out along guaranteed lines of distribution, was what gave Hollywood films before 1948 their superb attack and vigor. Also, the block-booking custom, evil though it may have been, ensured that many obscure, personal, and fascinating movies could be made and released, feather-bedded by the system and underwritten by more conventional ventures.[45]

The exhibition segment had always been the most profitable part of the motion picture business, and in the postwar period this was even more obvious. Theater operating costs did not rise as fast as production costs, and the box-office split gave a decided advantage to the exhibitor in the initial weeks of a run. Finally, the independent sources of revenue, such as screen advertising and the sale of candy, were quite considerable and highly profitable. For these reasons, once the theaters were separated from the studios, it became extremely difficult for the film industry to show continuous profits; and it would take several years to transfer some of the exhibitor's profits back into production and distribution. In the meantime Hollywood's financial and political woes indicated that there was indeed "panic in Paradise" as studios desperately began to cut back on salaries and production budgets.[46]

Economist Simon N. Whitney noted that the final decree, known as the "*Paramount* decision," represented the most important experiment in vertical "disintegration" ever achieved under the Sherman Antitrust Act.[47] However, the decision was by no means universally popular, and the Department of Justice received more complaints against this decree than any other in history, and the Senate Small Business Committee held extensive and inconclusive hearings on the decision in 1953.

As a result of the 1948 decision by the Supreme Court, Loew's Paramount, RKO, Twentieth Century-Fox, and Warners were ordered to dispose of their theaters, and these five plus Columbia, Universal, and United Artists were forbidden to engage in certain monopolistic practices, including rental to theaters on a circuit-wide basis and block-booking. As a consequence, each of the integrated companies between 1948 and 1954 split into two, with a successor production-distribution company and a divorced theater circuit.

The divorcement, coming as it did during a period of economic hardship for the motion picture industry, was blamed for many of the ills besetting the movies in the early fifties. The decree was seen as the cause of the reduced number of productions released by member studios of the MPAA, but this was, in fact, a trend which had been predicted in 1954, when domestic releases declined by more than 20 percent. This drop was the result of a general cutback in major studio output, but in that year many of the smaller studios turned permanently to manufacturing shorter films (the old "Grade B's") for television. Movie theaters compensated by filling their screen time with independent and foreign films and reissues, and by giving some of the top features a longer playing time.

Table 19 Features Released in the U.S. Market

Date	U.S. Produced	Imported	Total
1946	378	89	467
1947	369	118	487
1948	366	93	459
1949	356	123	479
1950	383	239	622
1951	391	263	654
1952	324	139	463
1953	344	190	534
1954	253	174	427
1955	254	138	392
1956	272	207	479

Source: Various issues of *Film Daily Yearbook*.

The decree's effects were mixed, and it did not take the exhibitors very long to see that many of the hoped-for benefits were not going to materialize. Rental costs for films increased, while some of the big producers, now no longer owning their own theaters, demanded exorbitant fees for "block-busters" such as *The Robe* and *The Caine Mutiny*. Independent theaters were forced to outbid each other for "first runs" and this helped to drive the price for films up even further. (At one point an exhibitors' chain, the Allied States Association, after vainly demanding that rentals be made subject to arbitration, turned to a proposal that the movie industry be declared a *public utility* and its wholesale, not retail, prices be regulated by the Federal Trade Commission.)[48] Also, many exhibitors now belatedly realized the virtues of block-booking, and the time and cost which this practice had saved the independent operator.

In the long run the divorcement decree was but one of several social and economic factors which together caused a total shift in the pattern of motion picture attendance in the postwar period. However, it is worthy of note that the requirement that the motion picture industry disintegrate was against the trends then apparent in the American economy. While Hollywood was being asked to finally comply with a legal decision which had its antecedents in a period nearly forty years earlier, other industries were busy participating in one of the most remarkable merger movements in U.S. economic history.[49] It would not be until the mid-sixties that film companies themselves became prime properties for mergers with such unrelated industries as shoe manufacturing, hotel chains, distilleries and parking lots.[50]

Television and the motion picture industry

It was in 1948 that television became a true mass medium in the United States, when for the first time the television industry was able to expand with a solid technological base. During this year the number of stations on the air increased from seventeen to forty-one, and the number of cities with television transmission from eight to twenty-three. The number of sets sold exceeded the 1947 total by 500 percent, and by 1951 even exceeded the sales of radio sets for that year. Also in 1948, the first attempts at network service started, and immediately attracted important, large national advertisers.[51]

However, by late 1948, the FCC became concerned over the nature of channel allocation and the technical arguments which surrounded the problem of color transmission, and therefore stopped processing new license applications on September 29. This was the famous television "freeze" which allowed existing stations to continue operation, but deferred all other applications pending further study of the technical problems. The number of stations allowed to operate was frozen at 108, but even then the number of sets in use continued to rise from 250,000 to over 15 million between 1948 and 1952.

After the expected initial losses, the television industry began to show enormous profit potential as early as 1951. In that same year, by use of coaxial cable and microwave links, the East Coast and West Coast were joined by a national network service which soon reached 40 percent of all American homes. After the freeze was lifted in 1952, the FCC was flooded with applications for station licenses; this further stimulated the sales of television sets. There was no holding the medium back after this artificial slow-down, and by the mid-1960s television had almost reached total saturation in American homes. A new entertainment favorite had emerged and the motion picture industry would never be the same again!

Table 20 The Growth of Television, 1946–1956

Date	Families with Television Sets[a] (thousands)	No. of Commercial TV Stations[b]	Average Weekly Motion Picture Attendance[c] (millions)
1946	8	6	90
1947	14	7	90
1948	172	17	90
1949	940	50	70
1950	3,875	97	60
1951	10,320	107	54
1952	15,300	108	51
1953	20,400	125	46
1954	26,000	349	49
1955	30,700	411	46
1956	34,900	442	47

[a] *Source: Historical Statistics of the United States,* Series R.98, p. 491.
[b] *Source: Ibid.,* Series R.93, p. 491.
[c] *Source: Ibid.,* Series H.522, p. 225.

It was noted in an earlier chapter that one of the reasons the motion picture industry was so unprepared for the introduction of television was that the experience with radio had left the studios complacent. This attitude was understandable, for although radio had acquired vastly greater audiences, there had been no visible influence on attendance at the movies. Television was seen by the film industry as a form of "visual radio" and not "movies in the home"; and while this was true from a technical and regulatory point of view, operationally the medium utilized the techniques and dramatic effects of motion pictures.

There were a few farsighted individuals who were able to see that television posed a serious threat to the motion picture industry, but even as late as the mid-fifties, most industry executives were still claiming that the movies would "make a comeback." In 1946, Harry P. Warner, a well-known specialist in communications law, warned Hollywood that "television constitutes a long-range threat to the motion picture business." But even he felt that "the day-by-day television product would not compete with the grade 'A' Hollywood production."[52] Once again, the radio experience was used as the criterion, as Warner doubted "whether the interest of the television audience in the home can be maintained for an hour and a half or two hours."[53]

There were several other reasons advanced by movie executives for not taking the television threat too seriously. The immediate decline in movie attendance in those areas where television was available was attributed to the desire on the part of the new viewer to realize the full value from his expensive purchase. Many in the movie industry hoped that once the television set had been paid for, then audiences would begin to return to the movies. This rationalization was coupled with a whole series of subrationalizations related to mankind's supposed gregariousness, which would eventually lead to a desire to return to the social interaction of the movie house. Thus people would tire of "individualized" and "commercial" entertainment in the home; women who were home all day would demand to be taken out at night; and television would not be able to satisfy the basic human demand to "get out and be entertained." Finally, and perhaps the most-often-voiced of all the rationalizations, was that television could never hope to achieve the same "quality" of production as the movies. This last point was the most accurate, but unfortunately quality did not appear to make much difference to the growing television audience, who seemed prepared to watch any- and everything. By 1956, the average daily viewing time per television household in the United States was over five hours![54]

One of the very few movie industry executives who grasped the potential impact of television was Samuel Goldwyn, who in 1950 suggested that after the silent period, and the sound era, Hollywood was now about to enter the third stage of its development — the "Television Age." He further predicted that "within just a few years a great many Hollywood producers, directors, writers and actors who are still coasting on reputations built up in the past are going to wonder what hit them." Goldwyn's solution was to get rid of the "deadwood of the present . . . [and] . . . the faded glories of the past," so that once again it would "take brains instead of just money to make pictures."[55] He also accurately foresaw that full-length feature films would become staple programming fare for television screens, and that Hollywood would eventually become the prime production center for television.

What really separated Goldwyn's evaluation from those of most other movie executives was his clear insight into the intrinsic nature of television — "a form of entertainment in which all the best features of radio, the theater, and motion pictures may be combined."[56] He was also able to identify the solution — movies had to be substantially superior to anything available on the home screen to bring the public out of their homes:

> A factor on our side is that people will always go out to be entertained because human beings are naturally gregarious. But before the

movie-goer of the future arranges for a baby sitter, hurries through dinner, drives several miles, and has to find a place to park, just for the pleasure of stepping up to the box office to *buy* a pair of tickets, he will want to be certain that what he pays for is worth that much more than what he could be seeing at home without any inconvenience at all.[57]

Goldwyn's point about the "organization" required to get out of the house and go to a movie was a valid one. With the "baby boom" just after the war, many of the movies' best customers in the under-thirty-five group were also parents of young children. One father described what going to the movies required of his household:

There was a movie my wife and I wanted to see. Then we began to add up the price. Two tickets at 60¢ each — that's not so bad. But then there was the baby-sitter. Three hours at 50¢ an hour plus car fare is $1.70. Parking the car — that would be another 50¢. Figuring gas and oil would be another 50¢. Add a coke or something afterward, say another 25¢. That's over $4.00. So we stayed home.[58]

With the introduction of television, the motion picture industry now found itself in the same position that the live theater had been in at the turn of the century. Only now it was movie-going that was seen as requiring more formal preparation, whereas watching television made few, if any, social demands of its audience.

The impact of television: a statistical analysis

What was the actual effect on the motion picture industry of the introduction of television? In a remarkable examination of the economic and social impact of television on movie-going, Fredric Stuart provided precise data to substantiate the theory that the introduction of the new medium was the *principal* reason for the decline in movie audiences in the period 1948–1956.[59] Stuart began by examining and comparing the introduction of television in specific geographic areas. From this comparison he established a strong statistical correlation ($r = 0.91$) between television's introduction and the drop in movie attendance. In fact, Stuart concluded, "The evidence suggests that in the absence of television competition there might have been a substantial increase in motion picture revenues between 1948 and 1954."[60]

Before 1948, per capita expenditures on motion pictures were predictable on the basis of per capita income. After the introduction of television, however, this correlation was no longer valid. If the additional independent variable of percent of households with television sets was also considered, then the equation, once again, provided a strong correlation. Thus Stuart clearly demonstrated that density of television penetration in any region was the *major* cause of loss of motion picture revenues.[61]

As part of his analysis Stuart also examined the closing of motion picture theaters. Between 1948 and 1954, the number of movie houses operating in the United States had declined from 18,631 to 18,491. While this does not appear to be a large drop, during this same period the population increased from 146 million to 161 million. Also, this net decrease of 140 theaters was actually made up of a net decrease of 3,095 conventional indoor movie houses, and a net increase of 2,955 drive-in theaters. Stuart's statistical analysis revealed an obvious relationship between dwindling receipts and the closing of movie houses. Surprisingly, and significantly, he found that there was *little* relationship between the opening up of drive-ins and the decline of the conventional four-walled theater. The choice between drive-ins and indoor theaters depended upon other factors, principally weather and the degree of population concentration. He noted: "This [evidence] indicates that Drive-In theaters have *not* appeared as direct replacements for closed indoor theaters."[62]

One of the many interesting points raised by Stuart's work was the seasonal shift in movie attendance patterns. He calculated the quarterly seasonal indices for the two five-year periods, 1943–1948, and 1952–1957, for a comparison of the pre- and post-television patterns. The results were as follows:

Table 21 Quarterly Seasonal Indices for Motion Picture Attendance

	I Winter	II Spring	III Summer	IV Fall
Seasonal index				
1943–1948	102	95	102	101
1952–1957	99	92	107	102

Source: Fredric Stuart, "The Effects of Television on the Motion Picture and Radio Industries," p. 45.

Quarterly variation in attendance had become much more pronounced, and Stuart concluded that these data supported his hypothesis that television was the major cause of changes in motion picture attendance. These seasonal shifts were significant because the movies' largest increase came in the summer quarter, when television viewing was at its weakest, while television had in turn kept audiences at home during the colder months.[63] The increase in summer attendance was, of course, also a reflection of the growing importance of the drive-in movie theater as a permanent fixture on the American landscape.

The drive-in theater

The introduction of the open-air drive-in theater was a significant postwar phenomenon, which was by far the most promising development for the movie industry during this difficult period. Numbering only 100 at the end of the war, by 1956 there were more than 5,000 operating drive-ins in the United States. The drive-in was the invention of Richard M. Hollingshead, Jr., who began in 1933 by combining the two luxuries which he felt that people in a depression would give up last — automobiles and movies.[64]

Hollingshead had once held a patent on the ramp idea used at drive-ins, but after a series of court battles it was finally ruled that ramps were just landscape architecture and not patentable. After this court decision there was a dramatic increase in drive-in construction all over the United States and Canada. By 1951, the drive-in represented 15 percent of the total number of movie houses, but, more important, they accounted for nearly 20 percent of total theater receipts.

In the early years, when the industry could afford to be more selective, outdoor theater operators had great difficulty in renting anything more than old "A" films, "B's" and Westerns. However, in the early fifties when the importance of drive-ins became obvious, and after the *Paramount* decree forbade such practices, the better first-run features began to find their way into drive-in exhibition. Still, many studios were reluctant to rent their top features for first-runs at these "ozone theaters."

The drive-in represented an attempt to simplify those problems which young couples with families encountered by providing an opportunity for the whole family to go out together, with a minimum of fuss and formality. But they also attracted other groups — "young people with aged parents, people with dogs they won't leave at home, teen-agers, and college kids." Owners of these theaters cooperated with family clientele by offering free admission for children, entertainment parks, and even free laundry service for harried housewives who wanted a night out at the movies but were reluctant to leave their housework. In the early days before in-car heaters allowed year-round attendance in the colder regions, some operators offered a free gallon of gasoline so that patrons could keep their engines idling![65]

During its formative stage the drive-in theater had quite justifiably acquired the reputation as a "passion-pit," where young couples could steal a few private moments in the darkened confines of an automobile. It was for this reason that the Province of Quebec banned the construction of outdoor theaters until sometime in the sixties, but Quebec was not alone in its objections. In the early years of their growth, drive-in theaters faced a variety of problems such as municipal zoning regulations, charges of being traffic hazards, and convictions under antinoise bylaws. However, their biggest difficult by far was gaining acceptance and recognition by the motion picture industry itself. Once this was achieved, the drive-in became an important weapon in the industry's vain attempt to regain its former glories.

The industry fights back

The years between 1948 and 1957 were possibly the most important years in the history of the motion picture industry, for it was during this period that the full impact of television was felt, and in the end it was the movies which had to make the adjustment to the acknowledged supremacy of the newer medium. While Hollywood tried many different approaches to entice audiences back into theaters, this was not the most important issue in the battle between the movies and television. The large audiences of the previous thirty years were gone forever; there was nothing that the movie industry could do to bring them back. However, television was permanent and all-pervasive; the issue was how best to integrate the existing framework of film production into the emerging superstructure of television production. Thus, while the public's attention was kept focused on the new technical innovations which the movie industry introduced from time to time, Hollywood was busy behind the scenes transforming itself from a film town into the major television production center. This was, of course, a totally natural transition, but it took a long time for many movie industry executives to accept the necessity of this move. Many have not yet accepted it.

By 1949, the industry was beginning to feel the economic effects of the introduction of television, in combination with the other social reasons which had led to the decline of audiences. In that year only 370 stars were under regular contract to studios, compared with over 750 in 1946. Writers under contract had fallen from 600 in 1946 to below 450. While the big-name performers still received enormous salaries, studios could no longer afford to carry a large stable of contract artists or writers.[66] Even at this early stage, it was quite obvious to many in the industry that salvation for Hollywood lay in cooperation and integration with the television industry, and not in futile, and financially dangerous, all-out competition.

One method of bringing about an amalgamation of movies and television which was widely discussed in the early fifties was the development of a viable form of "theater television." This would have involved offering special features to patrons in color on large screens; thus a technically superior product, surrounded by the atmosphere of the theater and accompanied by "regular" motion pictures. While several such experiments were tried, there was little evidence of long-range economic viability. At one point the movie industry even discussed with the FCC the possibility of reserving certain television frequencies for future exclusive use by theaters.[67] In the long run the only programs which seemed to successfully lend themselves to this form of exhibition were sporting events, especially prizefights; but even such

216

minor triumphs were enough to encourage movie executives to seriously consider large-scale use of theater television.

It was also obvious that the closing of a vast number of smaller movie houses did not really concern the studios, because traditionally 65 to 70 percent of the film rental income came from about 20 percent of the movie houses — from the large downtown theaters in the big cities. The growth of drive-ins more than made up for the rental loss from the smaller suburban theaters. Of the existing older theaters, many were in the rundown sections of cities, and marginal even at the best of times, so Hollywood was not sorry to see them go. Many producers suggested the elimination of all but the modern, well-run houses, where "the new, better movies could be appreciated in worthy surroundings."[68]

In the rush to cut costs, Hollywood studios drastically reduced the number of their productions, with the "B" film — the old second-feature staple — almost entirely eliminated. Particularly hard hit were those studios such as Republic and Monogram, which specialized in producing such films. It was therefore only natural that these hard-pressed studios would open their film vaults to feed the voracious appetite of television programming. However, the members of the MPAA (except Republic) continued to fight the sale of their films to television on the theory that the two media were directly competitive, and if TV wanted the best talent and stories, it could go into the marketplace and bid for them. In the long run such an attitude was counterproductive, and it was inevitable that sooner or later the studios would be forced to sell their libraries to television. In the meantime some studios began to set up separate television production units, which were kept carefully segregated from the movie production facilities. Some studios even contractually forbade their stars to appear on television.

Eventually, antitrust action again forced the studios to make their products available for television use, and the sale or lease of pre-1949 features was a primary source of income for distributors and producers. By 1958, an estimated 3,700 feature films had been sold or leased for television for an estimated $220 million.[69] The use of motion pictures on television proved to be an unexpected boom for many small distributors who held the rights to long-forgotten movies. One aging cowboy star — Hopalong Cassidy (William Boyd was his real name) — had wisely secured the television rights to sixty-six of his old films, and this made him a millionaire overnight. Other cowboy stars such as Roy Rogers and Gene Autry also successfully made the jump from "B" films to television stardom.

Whether it can be attributed to "novelty effect" is difficult to say, but in the period 1948–1952, the American public was obviously more content to stay home and watch old movies for free, than pay to see newer ones. This fact surprised the television industry as much as it did Hollywood.

Once the studios realized that there was money to be made by releasing older films for television distribution, there was a sudden flood of these on the home screen. A special report prepared by Sindlinger and Company for the Theater Owners of America indicated how important old movies were to television stations. The report noted that in the last quarter of 1957, old movies constituted almost one-quarter of the total television viewing time.[70] It was also no coincidence that 1957 was a year in which the movie audience declined quite sharply.

By 1957, Hollywood had already become a "TV town," and *Time* noted that "a single Hollywood TV show, NBC's daily *Matinee Theater*, hires 2,400 actors a year for speaking parts — 50% more than the players used by Warner and Paramount combined in all their 1956 movies. The show uses as many scripts — 250 a year — as all the studios put together."[71] Television was now by far the biggest money-maker and earner for the Hollywood community, with production companies such as Desilu turning out more footage than the combined output of the five major studios.

The pecking order in the community itself was being gradually altered to take into account the newfound status of television stars, but not without some reluctance on the part of the old guard. Social arbiter Mike Romanoff, the owner of one of Hollywood's most famous and prestigious restaurants, scoffed at the "dirty shirt" school which was becoming prevalent in Hollywood in the mid-fifties, and said: "The TV actors can afford to eat here, but they haven't progressed beyond the drugstore counter. They think differently, behave differently, live differently. The dirty shirt is a form of snobbery."[72] From all reports the television crowd in Hollywood took themselves too seriously — "too many men in empty grey flannel suits and expressions" — but what they lacked in glamour they made up in the youth and vitality they brought to the dying film capital, and this attitude was somewhat reminiscent of the early days of Hollywood. Where the old-time film director sported jodhpurs and riding crop, this new breed sported blue jeans and sneakers; but they got impressive results working to production schedules which would have terrified veteran movie makers. Eventually many of these younger men, who received their starts in television, would be at the forefront of the creative renaissance in the American film industry.

There were other indications of the movie industry's acceptance of the power of television with the increasing use of the home medium to advertise new feature films at local theaters, and the trend in the mid-fifties to turn TV plays into movies, using the TV shows as publicity buildups. Some of these were very successful, including Academy Award-winners *Marty* (1954), and *On the Waterfront* (1954), while popular programs such as *Dragnet* (1954) also made a successful transition to the motion picture screen. The success of these films, and others, indicated that the public would still pay for superior entertainment if it was available only in the movie theater. With the closing of many small-profit theaters, and the cutback in production, Hollywood now very deliberately began to turn its attention to providing entertainment which could not be found on the home screen.

Epics, wide-screen and 3-D

In order to present the public with a form of entertainment which would drag them away from their TV sets, the motion picture industry invested a great deal of money and effort in technological innovation designed to improve the visual and auditory (and even the olfactory) quality of realism associated with the movies. In many ways this could be seen as the logical extension of the move toward "realism" which had originally helped spawn the motion picture at the turn of the century. Only now the motion picture was being asked to provide an "experience" which was superior to that available, at no cost, in the privacy and comfort of the home.

Many film historians have pointed out that there was nothing new about the use of wide screens or three-dimensional movies; in 1900, 20,000 to 25,000 people at a time were able to view Lumiere's giant 70-by-53-foot screen in Paris;[73] and William Friese-Green had patented a three-dimensional movie process before 1900.[74] Nevertheless, such processes had always remained in the novelty category until, in a desperate bid to provide something different in answer to the television threat, Hollywood rediscovered them, gave them new names, and risked a great deal of money in promoting them to a curious public.

It was, in fact, two groups of independent producers who gave Hollywood the idea of making the movie screen look different from the television screen. In September, 1952, the newscaster Lowell Thomas, his friend Merian C. Cooper, a Hollywood veteran who had made the immortal *King Kong*, and the inventor of the process, Fred Waller, presented *This Is Cinerama* to astonished New York audiences.[75] The showing at the Broadway Theater was an enormous success as audiences screamed in masochistic delight as they were sent plunging down a Coney Island roller coaster, or flying through the Grand Canyon. The critics were almost unanimous in their praise for the new process that used three projectors and a curved screen, which in the original New York engagement was twenty-five feet high and fifty-one feet wide. Stereophonic sound was an additional refinement which greatly enhanced the illusion of depth. Cinerama gave the viewer the feeling of actually being involved "inside" the screen image, rather than being just an observer of a flat screen.

The technical requirements for Cinerama were such that few theaters could be converted to show these films. The result was that Cinerama spawned a whole new concept of marketing Hollywood motion pictures, which saw the invention of the "road show" movie designed to run in the larger urban centers for long periods of time, sometimes exceeding a year or more. (*This Is Cinerama* had a remarkable run of 122 weeks in New York, played to 2,471,538 people, and took in $4,707,688 at the box office. It subsequently played in eleven other cities in the United States, and five major cities abroad. On February 7, 1955, a new show replaced it for another series of long runs — *Cinerama Holiday*.)[76] While the Cinerama process still had quite annoying technical problems, such as obvious lines where the three images joined, the enthusiasm of the crowds convinced the motion picture industry that such innovations could lure patrons back into movie houses. Whatever the technical difficulties, and the eventual content deficiencies of future Cinerama productions (almost no dramatic productions have been made using the full process), the importance of this innovation should not be overlooked.[77]

While Cinerama was the first, and technically the most "realistic," of the wide-screen processes, the most widely used and promoted was Twentieth Century-Fox's Cinemascope. This utilized an anamorphic lens which spread out the image to give it more width than the ordinary motion picture image ratio of 1.33:1. The new ratio was now 2.55:1 (eventually settling down at 2.35:1), almost doubling the width of the screen, and with a slight curve it appeared as a smaller version of the Cinerama process. The important difference, however, was that conversion to accommodate the Cinemascope screen was less costly and therefore more acceptable to operators of movie theaters. After the initial success of the first Cinemascope production, *The Robe* in 1953, by the middle of 1954 production plans had been announced for seventy-five films using the new process. Fox had leased the process to other major studios, and by the middle of 1955, over twenty thousand theaters throughout the world could show Cinemascope films.

Several wide-screen anamorphic processes, such as Warnerscope, Vistarama, Superscope, Naturama and others, were tried and eventually discarded in favor of the Fox system. Other wide-screen techniques involving larger film stock than the standard 35 mm met with more success. The first of these was Todd-AO, which used 65 mm film; the second was Paramount Studios' VistaVision, which ran the film through the camera sideways to produce the "golden ratio" of 1.85:1. Technically VistaVision was the best of all the wide-screen processes, winning an Academy Award for its developers in 1956.[78]

Perhaps the most publicity sensitive, and at the same time the most insignificant technical innovation, was the use of three-dimensional or stereoscopic optical techniques to make "3-D" motion pictures for theatrical presentation.[79] This process had, in fact, already had a long and unsuccessful history as a movie "gimmick." However, the success of Cinerama prompted a new look at the possibilities of the stereoscopic phenomenon. In the late 1940s a young man named Milton Gunzberg obtained the rights to a three-dimensional process which he called Natural Vision.[80] In order for the viewer to actually see the film on the screen in three dimensions, he had to use special Polaroid glasses. Gunzberg had some difficulty in selling his patented process to the large studios, but eventually an absolutely dreadful film, *Bwana Devil*, was released in "3-D" in late 1952. To everyone's surprise, including Gunzberg, the film broke box-office records all over the country although it had virtually nothing to offer but the illusion of depth. The public was annoyed at having to wear the special glasses, and yet they were still willing to leave the comfort of their homes to sit and stare at lions jumping out of the screen, or spears flying over their heads.

Immediately after this unexpected development, almost all the major studios announced their intention to make some films in 3-D; and in the next three years the movie-going public was periodically treated to such films as *The Charge at Feather River* (which symbolically saw a character spit into the patron's face), *Hondo*, and the best of all, *House of Wax*. Alfred Hitchcock shot one of his best thrillers, *Dial M for Murder*, in 3-D, but eventually decided to release it in a "flat" version. However, by 1955, it was quite obvious that this was not the permanent answer to the movie industry's difficulties, and the added success of the various wide-screen processes meant the death of 3-D. The really important point about all of these technical innovations or "gimmicks" was that Hollywood was revitalized for a short period between 1953 and 1956, as the increased publicity activity succeeded in attracting more people into movie theaters.[81] While there were many who were optimistic about the movies' future, others in the industry were more skeptical, and there is no evidence that any movie executive ever saw a permanent place for 3-D in feature films. Actress Gloria Swanson said bluntly: "Three-D will be a flash in the pan. . . . The only real future for films is in developing some kind of box to collect money for movies on TV." Producer Jerry Wald was more realistic: "I'm enthusiastic about anything that calls attention to Hollywood — 3-D, three colors, two legs or Marilyn Monroe."[82] London movie critic Dilys Powell had perhaps the best comment about the use of three-dimensional techniques: "If I must be placed in the position of a firing-squad victim . . . I want my eyes bandaged."[83]

No examination of the technical innovations used to combat television would be complete without mention of the two films which utilized smells to increase the audience's sense of realism. The film *Behind the Great Wall* opened in New York in December, 1959, and featured a process called AromaRama which released heavy oriental smells to coincide with scenes on the screen. By all accounts the film itself was an excellent documentary, but the scent-yielding process was considered to be "a good commercial one-shot gimmick."[84] Another film, *Scent of Mystery*, used the Smell-O-Vision process which pumped odors to each individual patron by means of a small tube on the back of the seat. Again the film was fairly well accepted, and the smells formed an essential plot element, but the process was considered to be nothing more than a passing novelty.

Besides wide-screen, three-dimensional projection and "smellies," Hollywood developed another plan of attack in the battle with television. Ever since the earliest days of the motion picture industry certain films had been designated "blockbusters" — movies which were singled out because of their production cost, their length, or even their theme, and subjected to special promotional treatment. In the thirties, and forties, with a guaranteed audience of avid movie goers willing to consume most of the studios' output, the production of such films and their costly promotional campaigns had fallen out of favor. One notable exception was the incomparable promotion of David O. Selznick's *Gone With the Wind* in 1939, and this film went on to become one of the greatest money-makers of all time.[85] Only producer-director Cecil B. De Mille was able to continuously turn out such "epic" films. Now, given the opportunity to work with a much larger screen, Hollywood began to turn out these special films with monotonous regularity. De Mille himself started the postwar trend with *Samson and Delilah* (1949), which was still shot in the regular 35 mm format, but all during the fifties studios invested vast sums of money in these spectaculars. After the success of *The Robe* biblical epics were very much in vogue, culminating in the $15 million remake of *Ben Hur* by MGM in 1959. This cycle of "toga epics" came to a sudden end with the fiasco surrounding the failure of Twentieth Century-Fox's *Cleopatra* in the early sixties. This film was reported to have cost more than $40 million, and almost totally wrecked the studio.[86] Nevertheless, forced into providing an obvious alternative to television, the motion picture industry has had to resort to these "road shows" to attract audiences. Sometimes this ploy succeeded, often it failed. But in spite of the inroads made by television in the fifties, at the end of the decade the motion picture industry still survived, although it was a different industry from that of the halcyon days of the thirties and forties, and it would have to change even more if it was going to survive into the seventies.

Notes

1 James T. Farrell, "The Language of Hollywood," *Saturday Review of Literature*, August 5, 1944, p. 29.
2 *Ibid.*, p. 30.
3 *Ibid.*, p. 31.
4 Farrell noted: "This entire structure can be metaphorically described as a grandiose Luna Park of capitalism. And if the serious artist enters it, he well may quote these words from Dante: 'All hope abandon, ye who enter here' " (p. 32).
5 Philip Dunne, "The Documentary and Hollywood," *Hollywood Quarterly*, vol. 1 (1946), p. 166.
6 *Ibid.*, p. 171.
7 Kenneth MacGowan, "A Change of Pattern," *Hollywood Quarterly*, vol. 1 (1946), pp. 148–153.
8 For a detailed examination of films in this period see Charles Higham and Joel Greenberg, *Hollywood in the Forties* (New York: A. S. Barnes and Co., 1968). A refreshing "revisionist" viewpoint is offered in Mark Bergman, "Hollywood in the Forties Revisited," *Velvet Light Trap*, no. 5 (Summer, 1972), pp. 2–5.
9 Gilbert Seldes, astute as ever, understood this fact, and he called for a closer examination of such entertainment "propaganda" in the mass media. This would make the public aware of "the prejudices which dominate radio and the movies," and underscore the fact that entertainment was not "pure." Gilbert Seldes, "Law, Pressure and Public Opinion," *Hollywood Quarterly*, vol. 1 (1946), p. 426.

10 "Are Movies the Opium of the People?," *Christian Century*, no. 64 (January 8, 1947), p. 36.

11 Iris Barry, "Why Wait for Posterity?," *Hollywood Quarterly*, vol. 1 (1946), p. 136.

12 Clara Beranger, "The Cinema is Ready for College," *Theater Arts*, vol. 31, no. 1 (January, 1947), pp. 61–63.

13 Charles Palmer, "Miracles Come C.O.D.," *Hollywood Quarterly*, vol. 2 (1948), p. 387.

14 Edgar Dale, "On Miracles Come C.O.D.," *Hollywood Quarterly*, vol. 3 (1948), p. 84.

15 Charles Palmer, "Reply to a Critic," *Hollywood Quarterly*, vol. 3 (1948), p. 87.

16 Sondra Gorney, "On Children's Cinema: America and Britain," *Hollywood Quarterly*, vol. 3 (1948), p. 57.

17 Miss Gorney noted that in Connecticut a bill was introduced which would have created a special board to approve movies for children under the age of fourteen, while Maryland introduced a bill especially to approve Saturday matinee films (p. 58).

18 Irving Pichel, "Areas of Silence," *Hollywood Quarterly*, vol. 3 (1948), p. 51.

19 *Ibid.*, pp. 52–53.

20 Lewis, *Motion Picture Industry*, p. 83.

21 Ernest Borneman, "The Public Opinion Myth," *Harper's*, vol. 195 (May, 1945), p. 33. This is an extremely useful examination of a "state of mind" in the motion picture industry in the immediate postwar period.

22 *Ibid.*, p. 40.

23 *Ibid.*, p. 31.

24 Bosley Crowther, "It's the Fans Who Make the Films," *New York Times Magazine*, June 24, 1945, p. 29.

25 Leo A. Handel, "Hollywood Market Research," *Quarterly of Film, Radio and Television*, vol. 7 (1953), p. 304. Other useful articles which discuss the nature of motion picture market research are: Marjorie Fiske and Leo A. Handel, "Motion Picture Research: Content and Audience Analysis," *Journal of Marketing*, vol. 11, no. 2 (October, 1946), pp. 129–134; "Motion Picture Research: Response Analysis," in *ibid.*, vol. 11, no. 3 (January, 1947), pp. 273–280; "New Techniques for Studying the Effectiveness of Films," in *ibid.*, vol. 11, no. 4 (April, 1947), pp. 390–393. The final product of Handel's written work was *Hollywood Looks At Its Audience* (Urbana: University of Illinois Press, 1950).

26 Handel, "Hollywood Market Research," p. 305.

27 *Ibid.*, p. 309.

28 *Ibid.*, p. 308. For one of the most detailed examinations of the motion picture audience see Paul F. Lazarsfeld, "Audience Research in the Movie Field," *Annals of the American Academy of Political and Social Science*, vol. 254 (November, 1947), pp. 160–168.

29 Handel, *Hollywood Looks At Its Audience*, p. 98. Handel quotes from a 20th Century Fund study conducted in 1948, which "indicated an enlargement of the domestic market for films because of the growth of population, continued reduction of the work week, wider distribution of national income, and changes in the spending pattern of the average family, with a greater proportion of expenditures going into recreation." Motion pictures were considered to be one of the "insensitive industries."

30 *Ibid.*, p. 308. For details of this MPAA committee see Chambers, "Need For Statistical Research."

31 John Elliot Williams, "They Stopped at Nothing," *Hollywood Quarterly*, vol. 1 (1946), p. 270.

32 Jay E. Gordon, "There's Really No Business Like Show Business," *Quarterly of Film, Radio and Television*, vol. 6 (1951), p. 181.
33 *Ibid.*, p. 183.
34 Of the 411, 32 represented the industry trade press; 13 covered the wire services; 66 worked for magazines (23 for "fan" magazines); 82 were classed as foreign correspondents; and 49 were photographers. The remainder were those who wrote occasional articles or books on the movies. "Hollywood's Press: Why the Stars Are in Your Eyes," *Newsweek*, no. 43 (February 22, 1954), p. 62.
35 For details of the famous feud between Louella Parsons and her arch rival Hedda Hopper, see George Eells, *Hedda and Louella* (New York: G. P. Putman's Sons, 1972).
36 Quoted in Thomas A. Brady, "This Is Where the Money Went," *New Republic*, January 31, 1949, p. 12.
37 Kenneth MacGowan, "And So Into the Sunset . . ." *New Republic*, January 31, 1949, p. 23.
38 Gilbert Seldes, *The Great Audience* (New York: Viking Press, 1950), p. 13.
39 *Ibid.*, pp. 9–10.
40 Lazarsfeld, "Audience Research," pp. 162–163.
41 "The Fortune Survey," *Fortune*, vol. 39, no. 3 (March, 1949), pp. 39–40.
42 For more details of the increasing cost of production see Brady, pp. 12–15.
43 Paul Jarrico, "They Are Not So Innocent Abroad," *New Republic*, January 31, 1949, pp. 17–19. This particular issue of the *New Republic* contains a wealth of information on the current state of the film industry.
44 The "divorcement issue" was extremely complex, and has been subject to varying interpretations. The best discussions are found in Conant, pp. 107–153, and Higham, *Hollywood at Sunset*, 18–32.
45 Higham, *Hollywood at Sunset*, p. 31.
46 "Panic in Paradise," *Time*, no. 50 (September 22, 1947), p. 97.
47 Simon N. Whitney, "The Impact of Anti-Trust Laws: Vertical Disintegration in the Motion Picture Industry," *American Economic Review*, May, 1955, p. 492.
48 *Ibid.*, p. 495.
49 For an embittered attack on the decree see Irving Bernstein, "Hollywood at the Crossroads: An Economic Study of the Motion Picture Industry," study prepared for the Hollywood A.F.L. Film Council, December, 1957.
50 For more information on the motion picture industry's absorption into conglomerates see Domenico Meccoli, "Conglomerates Gobble Up Movies," *Successo*, vol. 12 (March, 1970), pp. 90–95.
51 A sound introduction to this topic is Sydney W. Head, *Broadcasting in America* (Boston: Houghton Mifflin Company, 1972), p. 194.
52 Harry P. Warner, "Television and the Motion Picture Industry," *Hollywood Quarterly*, vol. 2 (1946), p. 16.
53 *Ibid.*, p. 14.
54 Fredric Stuart, *The Effects of Television on the Motion Picture and Radio Industries* (New York: Arno Press, 1975), p. 6.
55 Samuel Goldwyn, "Hollywood in the Television Age," *Hollywood Quarterly*, vol. 4 (1950), p. 145.
56 *Ibid.*, p. 146.
57 *Ibid.*, p. 147.
58 Robert Coughlan, "Now It Is Trouble that Is Supercolossal in Hollywood," *Life*, vol. 31 (August 13, 1951), p. 102. This is an excellent examination of the topic.
59 Stuart, *The Effects of Television*.
60 *Ibid.*, p. 28.

61 *Ibid.*, p. 31. The 1948 relationship between per capita motion picture receipts and per capita personal income indicated a correlation coefficient of 0.77. The interference of television with this relationship was evident with the decline of this coefficient to 0.38, when the same two-variable analysis was applied to 1954 data. When percent of households with television sets was added in a multiple correlation, the correlation coefficient was brought up to the 1948 level (0.78).

62 Stuart, p. 37. The coefficient of partial correlation between the net changes in both theater types by state was 0.14 when the influence of population was removed.

63 Stuart had not included drive-in attendance in his data, taken from *Variety* magazine. This tended to accentuate the change in seasonal attendance brought about just by television. Stuart, p. 47.

64 For details on early drive-ins see *Time*, no. 38 (July 14, 1941), p. 66.

65 Frank J. Taylor, "Big Boom in Outdoor Movies," *Saturday Evening Post*, vol. 229 (September 15, 1956), p. 101. This article contains very useful information on the various services which were being offered by drive-ins during the fifties.

66 These statistics are taken from "Television: Movies' Friend or Foe?," *U.S. News and World Report*, no. 26 (January 7, 1949), p. 24.

67 For further details on the early attempts to counter the threat of television see Rodney Luther, "Television and the Future of Motion Picture Exhibition," *Quarterly of Film, Radio and Television*, vol. 5 (1951), pp. 164–177. Another useful three-part series is Milton MacKaye, "The Big Brawl: Hollywood vs. Television," in *Saturday Evening Post*, vol. 224 (January 19, pp. 17–19; January 26, p. 30; February 2, 1952, p. 30).

68 Coughlan, p. 108.

69 *Wall Street Journal*, February 10, 1958, p. 3.

70 *New York Times*, January 27, 1958, pp. 1, 23.

71 "The New Hollywood," *Time*, no. 69 (May 13, 1957), p. 43.

72 *Ibid.*, p. 44.

73 Kenneth MacGowan, "The Screen's New Look — Wider and Deeper," *Film Quarterly*, vol. 11 (1956), p. 109.

74 Limbacher, *Four Faces of the Film*, p. 104.

75 For more details on the Cinerama process see Limbacher, pp. 91–134; and Higham, *Hollywood at Sunset*, pp. 90–103.

76 MacGowan, "Screen's New Look," p. 111.

77 Film historian James L. Limbacher, in his detailed history of technical developments in the movies, has noted: "Whatever Cinerama's future might be, its past cannot be overlooked. It was Cinerama which started the widescreen revolution and re-interested the public in going to the movies again. It made stereophonic sound something which captured the public's fancy. It caused groups of people to drive as far as 300 miles to see Cinerama. It caused a boom in the tourist business, especially the places where Cinerama had filmed its productions" (p. 98).

78 The permanent move to wide-screen created problems for television projection which still plagues viewers, because the shape of the television screen is quite different from those of the various wide-screen processes.

79 For details on 3-D see Limbacher, pp. 139–192.

80 The story of Gunzberg is dramatically retold in Higham, *Hollywood at Sunset*, pp. 82–89.

81 One enthusiastic screenwriter noted: "Hollywood is hopeful again. After four years of indecisive competition with television . . . the industry has emerged with new courage and confidence . . ." Richard C. Hawkins, "Perspective on 3-D," *Quarterly of Film, Radio and Television*, vol. 7 (1952), p. 325.

82 "Flash in the Pan?," *Time*, no. 61 (March 2, 1953), p. 90.

83 "The New Industry," *Time*, no. 61 (May 4, 1953), p. 102.

84 *Variety*, vol. 217 (December 16, 1959), p. 6.
85 For details on the fascinating story behind this film see Gavin Lambert, *The Making of "Gone With the Wind"* (Boston: Atlantic–Little, Brown, 1973).
86 For more details on the problems of making this film see Walter Wanger and Joe Hyams, *My Life with Cleopatra* (New York: Bantam Books, 1963). The authors aptly describe how a pampered star and lax studio control can combine to cause such immense economic chaos.

11

TELEVISION AND HOLLYWOOD IN THE 1940s

Christopher Anderson

Source: Thomas Schatz (ed.), *History of the American Cinema, Volume 6: Boom and Bust: American Cinema in the 1940s*, Berkeley, Calif.: University of California Press, 1997, pp. 422–444, 521–524.

Television enchanted Hollywood in 1940, but in that regard Hollywood was no different from the rest of the country. Heralded by stories of scientific breakthroughs and by occasional demonstrations of the technology, television's arrival as a popular medium had been anticipated for more than a decade by 1940. As early as 1928, the chairman of RCA, David Sarnoff, had predicted that within five years television would become "as much a part of our life" as radio. Executives in the movie industry may have questioned Sarnoff's time frame, but few ignored his prediction, since press reports throughout the 1930s assumed that television loomed just over the technological horizon. The motion picture trade press certainly fueled speculation, as when the *Hollywood Reporter* announced in November 1934 that commercial TV sets would hit the market by January of the following year. "Television Is Ready," the headline brashly—and prematurely—reported. Los Angeles was also the site of one of the country's most active experimental television stations, Don Lee's W6XAO, which conducted numerous demonstrations over the course of the decade. By the time *Business Week* assured executives that 1939, at last, would be the breakthrough "Television Year," the climate of prophecy had nurtured an intense public fascination with television—in Hollywood as in the rest of the country.[1]

American television made its long-awaited public debut in April 1939, when NBC launched regular service with its coverage of the opening ceremonies of the New York World's Fair. Subsequent broadcasts by NBC and CBS were conducted only on an experimental basis, beamed to a few thousand receivers in the New York area, and yet public awareness of television continued to grow during 1939, fueled by clever publicity campaigns that featured exhibitions of the technology at trade shows and in department stores.[2] Valuable publicity came also from televised events, which had few viewers but captured public attention through accounts in newspapers and magazines.

The motion picture industry participated in one of these televised events when NBC broadcast the Atlanta premiere of GONE WITH THE WIND in December 1939. Perhaps more than any single event, that premiere marked the pinnacle of the movie industry's influence in American culture. With the attention of the national press focused on Atlanta, NBC seized the opportunity for self-promotion, stationing four video cameras near the theater marquee and using them to transmit the first televised movie premiere to its small audience in New York.[3] It was a technical feat that served both the movie industry and the nascent TV business, and the experimental broadcast gained stature by paying homage to the country's preeminent form of popular culture.

This early broadcast offered Hollywood a tantalizing glimpse of the future. Though staged mainly for publicity, it appeared at the time to presage an almost certain bond between the movie and television industries. From the earliest days of commercial radio, the studios had explored the field of broadcasting; many had made unsuccessful bids to form their own radio networks. Now as the new decade dawned, it seemed logical, if not inevitable, that Hollywood would play a key role in shaping American television. Even the Federal Communications Commission (FCC), the government agency responsible for regulating the country's airwaves, hoped that Hollywood studios would apply their particular acumen to the challenge of forming a viable television industry. In August 1940, the FCC chairman, James L. Fly, paid a diplomatic visit to Hollywood, touring the production facilities at Warner Bros., Paramount, and RKO. Before leaving he invited the major studios to seek licenses for television stations and to stake their claim as television producers.[4]

Studio executives, however, were not satisfied merely to experiment in a medium controlled by the existing radio networks; they wanted to *command* the television industry just as they dominated the movie industry, by controlling the channels of distribution. Consequently, Hollywood approached broadcasting with two goals. First, studios or their parent companies invested directly in stations, networks, and electronics manufacturers as part of their general strategies for corporate diversification. Second, the studios sought to influence the development of television technology, which they anticipated would become a revolutionary new mode of distribution and exhibition for motion pictures.

The networks had developed a particular model of broadcasting based on transmitting commercially sponsored programs to home receivers. The studios, on the other hand, envisioned alternative uses for the technology, uses that would conform more closely to the economic exchange of the theatrical box office. These included theater television, in which programs would be transmitted to theaters and shown on movie screens, and subscription television, in which home viewers would pay directly for the opportunity to view exclusive, commercial-free programming. By recognizing these ambitions, the historian Michele Hilmes argues, "a new picture emerges of Hollywood as an active experimenter with the new technology, presenting a serious challenge to the established broadcasting interests."[5]

Entering the 1940s, the Hollywood studios were eager to explore television, and the federal government endorsed their ambitions. Yet the radio networks, which quickly adapted radio's economic practices and program forms, exerted a far greater influence over television's development as a national medium. Given Hollywood's expressed interests, why didn't the movie industry play a larger role in the development of television during the 1940s? Why did the television industry come to be controlled by the radio networks instead of the studios? And why have so many subsequent stories testified to the hostility of studio executives, who were often said to have despised television during its early years?

This chapter explores the history of television in Hollywood during the 1940s in order to understand how the conditions and events of that decade combined to thwart the ambitions of the major studios. Because American television was suspended during the war and did not really develop as a popular medium until the networks introduced regular prime-time programming in 1948, television during much of this decade existed in an inchoate form, more a projection of social and commercial fantasies than a public institution. Television gradually achieved definition during this period of anticipation and experimentation, publicity and policy making, demonstration and debate. Under these circumstances, Hollywood tried to ensure that television would never be strictly defined as a domestic medium aimed at individual homes, nor as the logical domain of the radio networks, but that it would be equally viable as an extension of the studio system, perhaps even as a public medium based in movie theaters.

Launching television, 1939–1942

From the time of NBC's inaugural telecast in 1939 until World War II forced the suspension of consumer electronics manufacturing in 1942, Americans witnessed a flurry of activity surrounding television, including a series of debates over proposed technical standards, the beginning of commercial broadcasts, and the first demonstrations of theater television. The period was dominated by RCA, which pushed hard to see its technology adopted as the technical standard for the entire industry. For RCA, according to the historian J. Fred MacDonald,

> the launching of television in 1939 was a double-edged business enterprise intended to sell TV sets to the public and impose RCA

technical standards on the industry. If RCA/NBC could develop, produce, and market receivers as well as programs, the corporation could establish itself as the technological, manufacturing, commercial, and programming giant of television. With such an advantage it could monopolize the emerging industry from the outset. (J. Fred MacDonald, *One Nation Under Television: The Rise and Decline of Network TV* [New York: Pantheon, 1990], p. 14)

The motion picture industry, however, did not concede control of television to RCA. For years the Hollywood community had monitored technological developments in the field described initially by the trade journals as "visual broadcasting."[6] Because the major studios had extensive experience in radio, they eagerly awaited the moment when it would be feasible to diversify into television. The Motion Picture Producers and Distributors of America (MPPDA), the industry trade organization, prepared several studies of television for the studios during the 1920s and 1930s.[7]

Individual studios and independent producers sought their own advantage in television during the 1930s. Warner Bros. carefully monitored television patents filed by Theodor Nakken, Ludwig Silberstein, and others. Rumors in the trade press even claimed that Warner Bros. attempted to lure the television research pioneer Vladimir Zworykin away from RCA during this period.[8] Contracts negotiated by studios and independent producers began to contain clauses governing television rights. Indeed, television played a central role in Walt Disney's decision in 1936 not to renew his distribution contract with United Artists. When United Artists refused to grant Disney the television rights to his feature films, he abandoned the company and signed with RKO—a decision that paid huge dividends for the producer in years to come.[9] Hollywood's fascination with television in the years leading up to its commercial introduction can be seen in a remark by the producer David O. Selznick after he had attended a demonstration of the technology in the laboratory of the inventor Philo T. Farnsworth in 1937. "I do not believe that television can be stopped," he reported to his board of directors. "Some day, it will undoubtedly have a future so stupendous that we cannot even foresee its possibilities."[10]

The first major studio to move beyond enthusiastic endorsements and actually invest in television was Paramount, which had forged an initial alliance with the broadcasting industry by purchasing a substantial interest in the CBS radio network during the late 1920s. Although Paramount liquidated its CBS investment by 1932, the studio continued to seek opportunities in broadcasting once it had begun to recover from the effects of the Depression.[11] In July 1938, Paramount paid $164,000 for a 25 percent interest in DuMont Laboratories, a television manufacturing firm founded by the inventor Allen B. DuMont. According to Paul Raibourn, the studio executive in charge of television, Paramount made the investment to ensure that the movie industry would not be squeezed out of TV by the radio networks and to direct DuMont research toward theater television.[12] For the second time in less than a decade, Paramount asserted its leadership in broadcasting, setting a precedent that was recognized immediately in the movie industry.

The MPPDA's 1939 study of television, the latest in a series of reports by the industry's trade organization, expressed the belief that television could be shaped to the major studios' advantage, particularly if the studios committed themselves to developing theater television. Courtland Smith, the report's author, advised the studios to follow Paramount's lead and seek greater influence in the medium—by participating in experimental broadcasts and by lobbying the FCC as it considered technical standards. The timing would never be better for the movie industry to control distribution by establishing their own networks. "Television needs us, and very badly," he reported. "Most television people hope to relegate film to a minor position and bring the direct pick-up [live broadcast] into all programs. In fact, if networks were now possible they might adopt the policy of excluding film. . . . There being no networks, film will start unopposed and as an essential factor."[13]

Though Smith encouraged the studios to participate in the market that would develop around home TV receivers, he argued that Hollywood's success in television would rest ultimately on its ability to foster the growth of theater TV, since video projection technology promised benefits for both the studios and theater owners. In part, this meant fighting a rhetorical battle against established radio interests in an effort to influence the FCC, which already seemed predisposed to view television as primarily a domestic medium like radio. "We never should let the idea become generally accepted that television means pictures in the home *instead* of pictures in the theater," Smith argued. "It would seem to be wise to combat the idea at once. It seems obvious now that television, as it affects the motion picture industry, is not only a matter of film production for the home but also of a new type of show for the motion picture theaters. It may well be at the box office of the motion picture theater that television will make its first profit."[14]

The historian Michele Hilmes has noted that the movie industry, by conceiving of theater television as a viable alternative to home receivers, proposed not only to develop a mode of reception for television that differed from radio but also to create an alternative to the economics of commercial broadcasting, one that substituted the direct revenue from theater attendance for the indirect revenue of advertising.[15] Instead of waiting for advertisers to shift to television only after the medium had attracted a critical mass of viewers, the movie industry could hasten the adoption of television by using box-office admissions as the medium's economic foundation. Theater TV, speculated one industry reporter, offered an obvious solution to the cost of TV production: "Many television programs will probably be so expensive to produce that they will not be sent over the air free to anyone who has a receiver in his home but to theaters by special wires or on a separate wavelength which cannot be received on home sets."[16]

Private demonstrations of television projection systems had been conducted in research laboratories since 1930, but the technology was not presented to the public until 1939, when the British companies Baird Television and Scophony Ltd. equipped several London theaters, making it possible for movie patrons to view live broadcasts of prizefights and horse races. The first public demonstrations in the United States took place at the New York World's Fair, where Baird and RCA introduced their systems. RCA quickly became the leader in theater TV research, developing an electronic system that used a cathode-ray tube similar to that in home TV sets in order to project a video image directly onto a theater screen. RCA staged private demonstrations for FCC commissioners in February 1940 and for stockholders in April.[17]

The first full-scale public screening took place at the New Yorker Theater in New York City during January 1941. This initial telecast, presented to representatives of the FCC, advertising agencies, and the movie industry, consisted of a one-act play and performances of ballet, opera, and vaudeville. In May, RCA arranged a second demonstration specifically for movie industry distributors and exhibitors, who would be the target audience for the company's imminent marketing campaign. Executives from the studios' New York offices joined a standing-room-only crowd of 1,500 people to view a live program transmitted from the NBC studios. The program featured a variety of live events, including a news report by NBC's Lowell Thomas, a roundtable discussion concerning the potential for covering sporting events via theater TV, a prizefight taking place in Madison Square Garden, and a dramatic sketch staged in the NBC studios. Able to project an image of 15 × 20 feet at a cost of $30,000 per unit, the RCA system offered adequate sound and visual quality but did not measure up to the standards of a Hollywood feature. The critic Terry Ramsaye, who attended the event as a reporter for the *Motion Picture Herald*, was generally unimpressed by the technical quality. "If theatre television proves to be an art," he reported shortly afterwards, "it was the first art to be born in the doghouse."[18]

According to Ralph Beal, the head of television research at RCA, the electronics manufacturer assumed that American television ultimately would consist of two separate services, one directed at home receivers and the other at movie theaters. As a manufacturer of radio and TV receivers, and as the parent company of NBC, RCA believed that television should be targeted primarily at audiences in the home. Television, according to its chairman David Sarnoff, was destined to be a "vital element" in a culture increasingly centered on the family home.[19] On the other hand, RCA was also the leader in developing the technology for theater television, for which it made equally definitive claims. "Theater television has great promise," stated one RCA brochure. "It heralds the linking of playhouses in the nation into television networks that can transform every village theater into a Madison Square Garden or a Metropolitan Opera House."[20]

These types of statements began to define a potential relationship between home and theater television: theater TV would serve as a forum for public events and performances, while home television would incorporate the programming strategies of radio, relying on advertiser-sponsored series. RCA concentrated on the market for home receivers but also envisioned theater TV as the "public" form of television, the ideal technology for screens located in hotels, cafés, small newsreel theaters, and regular movie theaters. The movie industry also encouraged the notion that theater television would provide moviegoers with privileged access to public events. For instance, a 1940 Paramount short subject, "Ted Husing's Television Revue," introduced theater patrons to the notion of theater TV and extolled the virtue of witnessing live events, suggesting that theater TV would connect the movie theater to the public sphere. "No longer will you have to stay at home from the movies just to hear what's going on in the world," the narrator explained. "Come to the movies to see and hear."[21] Paramount's president, Barney Balaban, used a similar rationale in explaining his company's investment in theater TV. "Instead of being competition, television may be an asset to the theater business," Balaban said. "On nights when a big fight is being held, or perhaps the President is making an important address, imagine how much more business could be obtained by televising the event. Instead of a patron sitting at home and hearing an audible broadcast, he will be able to come to our theaters and not only hear the broadcast but see the entire show on the television screen."[22]

As these comments indicate, RCA and the movie industry shared complementary visions of a dual television system able to serve both home and theater with separate types of programming. Since RCA needed to market its video projection technology to theaters, many of which were controlled by the studios, it initially had a strong incentive to ally itself with the movie industry in calling for the development of theater TV. But once the studios began venturing further into television, conflicts arose between RCA and Hollywood, primarily because RCA opposed any form of competition that threatened its dominance over the television industry or its hopes for seeing its own technology adopted as the industrywide standard.

Paramount's investment in DuMont created tensions between the movie and broadcasting industries because Paramount immediately emerged as a rival to RCA, just as it had during its brief partnership with CBS in the early 1930s. The tone of this renewed rivalry was set during the FCC's 1940 hearings over television's technical standards when DuMont, along with other electronics manufacturers, challenged RCA's proposed standards. DuMont asked the FCC to support competition and not to freeze technological development by accepting RCA's proposals. The FCC, according to

MacDonald, "wavered between reluctant support for the bullying enterprise of Sarnoff and RCA, the desire to keep the new industry open to competition, and the desire to protect consumers from buying TV sets that would become obsolete quickly."[23]

In February 1940, the FCC announced that commercial broadcasting would begin in September, although the commission had not yet established technical standards. Following the announcement, RCA launched an energetic marketing campaign in order to flood the market with its own receivers and perhaps establish the *de facto* industry standard. To prevent consumers from purchasing sets that might soon be obsolete, the FCC reacted by postponing the introduction of commercial broadcasts and calling for new hearings in April 1940.[24]

At these hearings, RCA went on the offensive against its competitors, explicitly accusing Paramount of inhibiting the development of television through its investment in DuMont. In a brief filed with the FCC, RCA claimed, "The motion picture interests which are financing DuMont Laboratories have a much greater financial stake in the movie industry than they have in television. Their recent interest in television is primarily for the purpose of 'protecting' their larger interest in the movie and theater industry and not to develop the new art of television. Therefore, they desire the adoption of systems and methods that would make television inferior rather than superior to motion pictures."[25] By leveling such charges against Paramount, RCA introduced two ideas that would come to influence the government's response to the movie industry's increased presence in television. First, RCA implied that the movie industry would exploit television solely for commercial gain, whereas the experienced radio networks recognized the responsibility of broadcasters to serve the "public interest," as policy mandated. Second, it suggested that the movie studios were masking their true motives, which were not to promote television but to slow its growth in order to protect their theaters.[26]

On the contrary, Paramount had moved aggressively into television following its 1938 investment in DuMont. In July 1939, the studio formed a television subsidiary, Television Productions, Inc. And in spite of RCA's aspersions, the FCC granted Paramount and its related companies four experimental television permits, while giving RCA only three. Paramount capitalized on this opportunity by announcing that it had purchased a vehicle for use as a mobile television unit capable of feeding live remote telecasts to DuMont and its experimental stations. Paramount also began using television as a lure for its movie theaters, installing DuMont TV sets in the lobbies of its Chicago-based Balaban & Katz theaters, with the sets tuned to the theater circuit's own experimental TV station, W9XBK.[27]

RCA's accusations about Paramount had little immediate influence on the FCC; in fact, it was shortly after the hearings that FCC Chairman Fly visited Hollywood with an invitation for the studios to participate more actively in developing television. But over the next few years—as the studios faced new charges of antitrust violations—the FCC began to have its own doubts about allowing the Hollywood studios to play a major role in the television industry.

The war years, 1942–1945

The FCC approved technical standards for television in April 1941 and authorized commercial broadcasts beginning in July 1941. With manufacturers prepared to market TV receivers, American television appeared to be on the verge of fulfilling the predictions of the previous decade. But World War II intervened, and television's development came to a halt by mid-1942 as manufacturers ceased producing consumer electronics and turned instead to making equipment for the military. Ten commercial stations were broadcasting in mid-1942, and six remained on the air throughout the war. As advertisers drifted away, these stations reduced their schedules to a token four hours per week, transmitting to the roughly ten thousand TV sets in the United States mainly concentrated in New York, Chicago, and Los Angeles.

Commercial television was suspended for the duration of the war, but the federal government was eager to pave the way for a quick launch once the war ended. "During the postwar period," FCC Chairman Fly predicted, "television will be one of the first industries arising to serve as a cushion against unemployment and depression."[28] During 1944–1945, the FCC conducted hearings to establish spectrum allocation for television, and many historians believe that these hearings were the single most important event in determining the eventual structure of American television. The critical issue at these hearings was whether television broadcasting should remain in the VHF band of the electromagnetic spectrum (as advocated by RCA), thus restricting its channel capacity, or whether it should be moved to the UHF band, which had a much greater capacity. These hearings were a turning point because they offered the last opportunity to shift U.S. broadcasting to the UHF band without severely disrupting manufacturers and consumers.[29]

In May 1945, however, the FCC approved a system of thirteen-channel VHF broadcasting and encouraged the use of UHF solely for experimental broadcasts. By restricting the number of available channels, the FCC created an artificial scarcity that guaranteed fierce competition in the television industry. As J. Fred MacDonald has written, "To make channels so scarce effectively guaranteed that U.S. television would be broadcast TV, dominated by those few corporations able to afford stations in the largest cities, provide attractive programs, attract national advertisers, and quickly build a chain of affiliates eager to appeal to the mass audience."[30] In other words, the high demand for a limited number of channels meant that radio's mode of commercial network broadcasting was likely to dominate television as well; there would be no opportunity to explore alternative forms of television. As a result of the FCC's decision, small networks and independent stations—like those envisioned by the studios—were placed at a competitive disadvantage in relation to NBC and CBS, which were prepared to sign affiliates as soon as commercial broadcasting resumed after the war.

During the war, the major studios still assumed that they would be competitive in the television industry. As the movie industry prospered, the major studios jockeyed for position in television because they recognized that commercial television would be launched almost immediately after the war ended. At the same time, however, the studios were aware that conditions in the movie industry—a new round of antitrust litigation, an uncertain international market, and a rise in independent production—would necessitate changes in the studio system. Eager to stake out the future of distribution and exhibition through television, each of the studios made substantial investments in station ownership and theater TV. The studios were not alone in pursuing these investments: a 1945 survey reported that 50 percent of exhibitors intended to operate TV stations, while nearly 60 percent planned to install theater TV systems.[31]

In late 1943 the studios began applying for station licenses and developing plans for production. MGM in December 1943 assigned Nat Wolf to form a television department, and Wolf subsequently hired the radio writers George Wells and Norman Corwin, assigning them to write screenplays until they could be used in actual television production. MGM's parent company, Loew's, subsequently applied for permits to construct stations in New York, Los Angeles, and Washington, D.C.[32] RKO hired Ralph Austrian from NBC, giving him responsibility for exploring all phases of television. In June 1944, Austrian helped form RKO Television Corporation, a subsidiary that would produce TV news and entertainment. RKO became the first major studio to produce for television with the telecast of "Talk Fast, Mister," a one-hour drama filmed at RKO-Pathé studios in New York and broadcast by DuMont's New York station in December 1944. Later RKO created a series of ten-minute short subjects for TV by recycling stock footage to create a quiz show titled *Do You Know?* and a nostalgia series titled *Ten Years Ago Today*.[33] Warner Bros. in 1944 filed an application for a Hollywood television station to be operated by its radio station, KFWB, and purchased seventeen acres on Mulholland Drive to be used for constructing the station. Twentieth Century-Fox, through its theater circuits, filed applications in Los Angeles, New York, Boston, Seattle, Kansas City, and St. Louis. Even the independent producer Walt Disney anticipated the future growth of television by applying for a permit to construct a station at the Disney studio.[34]

Paramount continued to set the pace for the integration of television into the movie industry. Its subsidiary Television Productions, Inc., launched a Los Angeles experimental station, W6XYZ, in February 1943. The Balaban & Katz station in Chicago, WBKB, became a commercial station in

October 1943. Many of the studio's theater circuits prepared station applications across the country, in New England, Michigan, Texas, Pennsylvania, and Florida. Paramount also kept pace with RCA by joining with British Scophony and General Precision Equipment (the single largest shareholder of 20th Century-Fox) in 1943 to form the Scophony Corporation of America, a U.S. subsidiary of Britain's leader in theater TV research.[35]

Of course, technological innovation alone could not ensure the success of theater TV; studios also had to devise a system for producing and distributing the necessary programming. The studios stressed the need to create networks of theaters in order to cover the expense of production. "All that theatre television needs to become a reality," claimed RKO's Ralph B. Austrian, "is a means of interconnecting a chain of theatres. . . . It is not beyond the bounds of possibilities to visualize a nationwide chain of theatres reaching out for home television personalities as fast as they are developed, and paying them enough to make it worth their while to perform for theatres only, rather than for the home audience." *Variety* reported that some in the movie industry even wanted to create streamlined theaters devoted exclusively to television, relying on programming transmitted from a central network source. In 1944, Paramount asked the FCC to approve two microwave relay networks that would connect the studio's stations and theaters in just such a network. Indeed, frequency allocation would prove to be a crucial factor in determining the eventual success or failure of theater TV. In 1945, the Society of Motion Picture Engineers (SMPE) testified before the FCC that theater TV would not be able to exist without the allocation of special frequencies reserved exclusively for the studios to transmit programming to theaters. In response, the FCC agreed to set aside several frequencies for experimental applications of theater TV but chose not to allocate channels for its commercial development.[36]

As this decision suggests, during the war years the federal government became increasingly skeptical of the movie industry's role in television and seldom encouraged further expansion by the studios. Although the FCC welcomed the studios in 1940, the atmosphere in Washington had changed dramatically by 1945, when FCC Chairman Paul A. Porter addressed a meeting of industry leaders in Hollywood and warned them that the movie industry should not expect a significant role in television after the war; his agency would see to it that television would not become a "Hollywood bauble."[37]

This surprising shift occurred because Washington had become increasingly concerned about the threat of monopolies forming in the television industry. The FCC's 1938 hearings on network monopoly in radio broadcasting had led to its 1941 *Report on Chain Broadcasting*. The FCC concluded that NBC and CBS had restricted competition in radio by exercising inordinate control over affiliated stations and that NBC should be forced to divest one of its two radio networks in order to foster competition. In October 1943, after the courts had upheld the FCC's findings, NBC sold its Blue network to Edward H. Noble, who later changed the name to the American Broadcasting Company.

The major studios increasingly fell under a cloud of suspicion as they once again faced antitrust allegations in charges filed by the Justice Department in August 1944. While these antitrust proceedings moved through the courts. Washington scrutinized the movie industry more carefully. In December 1945, for instance, the Justice Department filed suit against American Scophony, charging that Paramount and its associates had monopolistic control over theater TV patents and had delayed the technology's development for fear that theater TV would undermine the movie business.[38] These charges, which obviously echoed RCA's previous allegations about Paramount, signaled a dramatic change in the relationship between Washington and Hollywood. The FCC's commitment to VHF virtually guaranteed that a precious few networks would exert enormous influence over television. It was becoming apparent that these networks were likely to be formed by the radio networks and not by the studios.

Thwarted ambitions of the major studios, 1946–1950

In spite of the intense expectations that surrounded television by the end of World War II, commercial television was slow to develop after the war. The FCC had received 116 license applications from 50 cities by the end of 1945, but two years later there were still only 16 stations on the air and fewer than 200,000 TV sets in the country. Of course, television was solely a metropolitan phenomenon, with stations and viewers concentrated mainly along the East Coast and in Chicago and Los Angeles. The electronics industry needed time to retool for consumer markets, but lingering uncertainty over technical standards also made manufacturers and consumers wary about moving forward. Those interested in television awaited a definitive ruling about which of the competing color standards—a mechanical system developed by CBS or an electronic system advocated by RCA—would receive the FCC's approval. In March 1947, the FCC rejected the CBS color system, which was incompatible with existing technology, and this decision launched the expansion of American television because it established that, for the foreseeable future, television would be broadcast in black-and-white.[39]

Following the war, the major studios continued to lay the groundwork for the eventual role of television in the studio system. Faced with a pending antitrust ruling that threatened to disrupt the movie industry, the studios had an unusually strong incentive for exploring opportunities for diversification. Warner Bros. and Paramount were the most aggressive studios attempting to diversify into television.

To compete with Paramount, Warner Bros. in 1947 joined 20th Century-Fox and RCA in a project to develop and market RCA's technology for theater TV. This collaborative research led to a public screening of the Joe

Louis–Jersey Joe Walcott heavyweight prizefight at the Fox-Philadelphia Theater in June 1948 and to demonstrations on the studio's Burbank lot in late 1948 and early 1949.[40] In April 1948, Warner Bros. also filed an application for a Chicago TV station and prepared applications in five other cities. Two months later, Warner Bros. asked the FCC to allow the studio to purchase two radio stations and Los Angeles TV station KLAC from Dorothy Thackery, former publisher of the *New York Post*.[41] For Warner Bros., these investments represented the first steps in organizing a broadcast network that would support an expansion into television.

It is no coincidence that Warner Bros. stepped up its TV-related activities in 1948, a year in which studio executives faced the worst destabilization of the studio system since the Depression. After the industry's peak year of 1946, nationwide box-office attendance had declined steadily, while foreign revenue also diminished as a result of protectionist legislation enacted by European countries.[42] The *Paramount* decision threatened to curtail another source of revenue by eliminating the steady profits delivered by studio-controlled theaters once the studios divested themselves of their theater circuits. Under these conditions, Warner Bros. virtually ceased studio operations from November 1948 to February 1949. When the trade press interpreted the shutdown as a distress signal, Jack Warner denied the rumors; the studio's temporary inactivity was not a shutdown per se, he claimed, but an opportunity for "appraisal, analysis, and planning for the future."[43]

As a result of this reflection, Warner Bros. executives devised a new production strategy that promised to salvage aspects of the studio system by integrating film and television production. Harry Warner declared in January 1949 that Warner Bros. would introduce television production at its Burbank studios as soon as the FCC approved the purchase of the Thackery stations. Planning to use owned-and-operated stations as the cornerstone for expansion into further station ownership or the development of a network, the company would produce programming both for broadcast television and for theater TV. Jack Warner would continue to supervise the production of theatrical features, while Harry would assume responsibility for the television division.[44] This decision marked the origins at Warner Bros. of the policy that ultimately would lead the studio system into the television age. Increasingly, theatrical features would be produced individually by independent units, while the studio's traditional mode of production would be dedicated to serving the television market. The studio would balance the shift toward unique, expensive films with a standardized product that served the same function as had its more routine features during much of the studio era.

Paramount continued to pursue an even wider range of interests in television. Its experimental Los Angeles station began commercial broadcasts in 1947 as KTLA, the first commercial station west of the Mississippi. In 1948, Television Productions, Inc., formed the Paramount Television Network to distribute filmed programs produced at KTLA. This was not a true broadcast network but an alternative source of programming using film distribution instead of live broadcasts to supply local stations. Through American Scophony, Paramount also began to explore the potential for subscription TV, an early precursor of pay cable that used wired transmissions to bypass broadcasters altogether. This technology was being developed in the late 1940s but was not tested in actual markets until the 1950s. In general, however, Paramount's interest in American Scophony diminished following the antitrust suit filed by the Justice Department in 1945. Paramount and General Precision eventually signed a consent decree in January 1949, agreeing to divest all stock interest in Scophony, but Paramount already had begun to develop its own version of theater television even before leaving Scophony.[45]

Unlike the electronic systems developed by RCA and Scophony, which projected a video image directly onto a movie screen, Paramount's theater TV employed an "intermediate film system": in the theater, a video image was filmed from a TV monitor, the footage developed immediately, and the film projected through a normal projector; the entire process took about one minute. Paramount's intermediate film system made its public debut in April 1948 by presenting live coverage of a boxing match to three thousand people in New York's Paramount Theater. The studio assumed that its TV stations, WBKB in Chicago and KTLA in Los Angeles, would function as centers for networks of TV-equipped theaters. By February 1949, the equipment had been installed in theaters in both cities; in June, Paramount launched theater TV telecasts at the Balaban & Katz flagship Chicago Theater. Subsequent telecasts at the Chicago Theater and at other Balaban & Katz theaters in the Chicago area continued to use theater TV for covering special live events, especially sports (boxing matches, Big Ten football, the 1949 World Series) and occasional news events (such as speeches by Dwight Eisenhower and Douglas MacArthur).[46]

All plans for expanding into station ownership and theater television were dashed, however, when the FCC stepped in following the *Paramount* ruling to investigate whether the major studios legitimately had the right to own television stations. Senator Edwin C. Johnson, chairman of the Senate Interstate Commerce Committee, which monitored the broadcasting industries, decried the fact that "interests who have accepted consent decrees stand defiantly at the counter demanding the right to get into television." The Communications Act of 1934 had authorized the FCC to refuse station licenses to any individual or organization convicted of monopolistic practices, and the commission was now prepared to decide whether this provision should be applied to the movie studios whose collusion had precipitated the *Paramount* decision. FCC Chairman Wayne Coy even asked the Justice Department to determine whether the studios' activities in television constituted further violations of antitrust laws.[47]

The FCC never actually delivered a ruling on this question because the station application process was abruptly suspended in September 1948 when the commission declared a freeze on the licensing of TV stations, postponing decisions on all pending applications until solutions had been found for various technical problems that still plagued television, including lingering questions about spectrum allocation, signal interference, and color standards. The station application freeze began as a six-month moratorium to allow the FCC to reevaluate television policy, but the issues involved were too complicated to untangle in such a short period; the freeze ultimately lasted four years, until the commission delivered its *Sixth Report and Order* in May 1952.

Still, American television was hardly frozen during this four-year period. As stations approved before the freeze went on the air, advertisers and the public were drawn to the new medium. The number of stations rose from 50 in 1948 to 108 in 1952, and the number of sets in U.S. homes increased from 1.2 million to 15 million. Historians have argued that because of this growth the freeze actually gave NBC and CBS an insurmountable advantage in the television industry, enabling them to solidify their positions in local markets during a period of limited competition.[48] With the tacit support of the FCC, the radio networks extended their power into the TV industry by establishing owned-and-operated stations in major cities and by signing affiliate contracts with the vast majority of these early stations—which were owned primarily by radio broadcasters who were accustomed to the network structure. Allen B. DuMont, who had launched his own ill-fated network, complained that "the freeze reserved to two networks the almost exclusive right to broadcast in all but 12 of the 63 markets which had television service. It meant that [DuMont and ABC] did not have . . . an opportunity to get programs into the markets so necessary . . . to attract advertisers."[49]

The government's role in excluding the major studios from owning television stations during this period was critical in determining the eventual structure of the television industry. As Douglas Gomery has noted, the *Paramount* decision not only broke up the studio system but "guaranteed that the majors would not secure a significant place in the ownership of U.S. television networks and stations. The radio industry was able to secure a hold which continues to the present day."[50] Hollywood's major studios watched helplessly during the freeze as their plans for television disintegrated. Hoping to force a decision by the FCC, a frustrated 20th Century-Fox petitioned the Justice Department in March 1949 for a ruling on whether the studios should be eligible for broadcast licenses. Meanwhile, Warner Bros. dismissed its Chicago station application in May 1949, after a studio survey concluded that the first year of operation in Chicago—if that year ever came—would cost nearly $800,000. Ultimately, the Thackery TV interests grew tired of waiting for the FCC to approve Warner Bros.' purchase of their Los Angeles stations and pulled out of the deal.[51] With all licensing decisions delayed indefinitely by the freeze, the other studios dismissed their remaining applications as well.

Even as the *Paramount* decision was used by the government to thwart the studios' plans to establish their own stations and networks, the FCC's reluctance to support alternative technologies by allocating frequencies for their use also made theater TV financially untenable. As Michele Hilmes explains, "Through a tendency to protect established interests against innovative competition . . . and [in] what is surely one of the worst examples of regulatory foot-dragging in history, the FCC managed to delay, avert, and handicap testing and operation of these systems to the point that the companies involved could no longer support their efforts."[52]

Although Warner Bros. had planned an initial network of twenty-five theaters equipped with video projection, it would install television systems in only thirteen of its theaters in the coming years.[53] Paramount was also unable to make a profit on theater television and withdrew the systems from its Chicago theaters in 1951. Theater television expanded briefly in the early 1950s, though it never achieved any sort of widespread acceptance. In 1950, ten theaters in the United States were equipped for video projection, and the number peaked in 1952 with seventy-five theaters in thirty-seven cities.[54]

As many in the industry had predicted, theater television failed in part because the FCC would not assign broadcast frequencies exclusively for theater use. Because the studios were unable to acquire stations, they also found it impossible to form a network capable of linking theaters across the country; consequently, the cost of theater TV broadcasts fell on individual theaters and could not be subsidized by a network structure. By the early 1950s, television had become overwhelmingly oriented toward the family home. Not even a single theater added video projection in 1953, and the system slowly disappeared, replaced in theaters by new exhibition technologies like CinemaScope and 3-D.

In spite of their clear designs on the television business, most of the major studios found themselves in the late 1940s with no substantial connections to the new medium and no incentive to forge ahead (the exception being Paramount, which still owned Los Angeles TV station KTLA and an interest in DuMont). Because the major studios had been thwarted from gaining control of distribution, the integration of television in Hollywood occurred through television production, which originated as the domain of independent producers with razor-thin profit margins and little stake in the studio system.

Television production in Hollywood, 1946–1950

The major studios clearly saw promise in television during the 1940s, but they were not blinded by ambition; they proceeded cautiously by the end of the decade because they were reluctant to take any action that would leave them subservient to the existing radio networks. Yet even though the major studios withdrew from television, Hollywood's engagement with the medium continued apace, fueled by independent producers who rushed forward to supply the new medium's demand for programming.

As small-scale entrepreneurs, Hollywood's first television producers experienced few of the reservations that deterred the movie industry's major powers. They had grown accustomed to squeezing themselves into the cracks and crevices of the studio system—operating on tiny budgets, surviving on minimal profits, designing products that earned money in the neglected areas of a market defined by larger companies. Independent producers and small studios, like Monogram and Republic, typically filled the exhibitors' need for such products as B features, short subjects, serials, and travelogues, the less prestigious and profitable entertainment that completed a theater's daily program, but that the major companies produced with less frequency after the early 1940s. Adaptability was the key to survival in a market that discriminated against any small producer. By necessity, then, independent producers worked with a much broader definition of filmed entertainment, considering many formats that strayed from the major studios' dominant feature-length narratives. Unburdened by commitment to any particular system of distribution or exhibition, to a certain conception of the producer's autonomy and authority, or to any particular definition of the cinematic text, these producers were less devoted to a single medium than to exploiting the potential of any market and any product that promised a return on their investment.

The television industry during the late 1940s and early 1950s was not an ideal alternative to the studio system, since the networks were beginning to monopolize the nation's TV stations as effectively as the studios had controlled theaters. By comparison, however, the market for TV programming was relatively open. Though the majority of network programs were produced for live broadcast by such New York-based advertising agencies as J. Walter Thompson and Young and Rubicam, Hollywood producers discovered a welcome market; the successful ones, like William "Hopalong Cassidy" Boyd or Hal Roach, were able to license filmed programming to networks and local stations or to national, regional, and local sponsors who would then purchase broadcast time. Early television offered meager financial rewards, but it opened new channels of distribution outside the influence of the major studios, providing refuge to producers whose movies traditionally had languished in tiny neighborhood or rural theaters.

An entrepreneur like Jerry Fairbanks epitomized the spirit of the early telefilm pioneers. A producer of short subjects at Paramount for many years, Fairbanks chased the lure of television riches in 1946 when he opened his own telefilm production company in a small studio at the heart of Sunset Boulevard's Poverty Row studios. Inspired by the general corporate culture at Paramount, the studio most committed to television, and by the ingenuity of the studio's short-subject division, Fairbanks envisioned TV production as his opportunity to surpass the studio system. Although there were only a dozen TV stations broadcasting at the time, Fairbanks believed the most optimistic forecasts that more than a thousand stations would bombard the nation's airwaves by 1953. While many of these thousand stations would be network affiliates broadcasting live programs from New York, Fairbanks and others speculated that they would have an insatiable appetite for filmed programming because they would quickly exhaust the network's ability to supply new programs. Although TV production did not promise to be immediately profitable, Fairbanks imagined this imminent demand and saw no ceiling on the potential value of filmed TV programs, which could be circulated indefinitely among the country's new TV stations.

Fairbanks was a tinkerer and a cut-rate visionary; he relished the challenge of adapting studio system production techniques to the demanding economies of television during an era when a half-hour television program, like his 1948 series *Public Prosecutor*, could not count on more than a $20,000 budget. During the late 1940s, in the trade journals and popular press, Fairbanks touted his "Multicam" production system, which adapted live TV's three-camera shooting technique for film production. While there were precedents for multi-camera shooting in the film industry, Fairbanks used 16mm Mitchell cameras mounted on tripod dollies to approximate video's capacity for quick, continuous shooting while creating a product—a motion picture print—that was durable, reproducible, and transportable; moreover, its visual quality surpassed that of live TV's kinescopes, which were filmed off the screen of TV monitors airing the live production.

Because of his limited budget, Fairbanks could not afford to duplicate video's practice of running all three cameras simultaneously. To economize on film stock, much of the editing was completed "in-camera," with only one designated camera running at any given moment. This technique necessitated rigorous preproduction planning in which lighting, camera angles, editing decisions, and the movement of cameras and performers had to be orchestrated precisely before the cameras rolled. Cables and banks of 300-watt reflector lights were suspended from the ceiling so that they would not impede the movement of actors or cameras. Newly developed zoom lenses were fitted onto the cameras to facilitate rapid shifts in focus or changes in composition. Fairbanks registered a number of patents related to this process, including the tripod dollies, an electronic method for marking synchronization among all three cameras and the sound recorder, and a device for following focus on the Mitchell camera's parallax viewer. At a time when other filmed half-hour episodes had production schedules of two or three days, Fairbanks could shoot an episode in a matter of hours. Production costs were kept so low that the single most expensive item in the budget was the film stock and processing, which accounted for only 3 percent of a feature film budget but was 25 to 30 percent of the budget for any Fairbanks program.[55]

In 1948, NBC contracted Fairbanks to produce the first filmed series for network TV, *Public Prosecutor*, starring John Howard. The program looks primitive by the standards of contemporary feature film production. Narrated by Howard, who addresses the camera throughout much of the story, the bare-bones mystery plots are condensed to fit into fifteen-minute segments modeled after the format of radio episodes. The verbal exposition is so insistent that the images begin to seem redundant; the episodes truly resemble radio with pictures. Sets are often undecorated. Actors appear distracted, if not anguished, as they try to hit their marks consistently in the first take. In spite of the opportunities for shot selection offered by the Multicam system, the camera work consists mainly of single-take medium shots or simple over-the-shoulder dialogue sequences. In promoting his Multicam system, Fairbanks claimed that his minimum length per take was five minutes, with the average take lasting between seven and eight minutes. Although this may be true of other Fairbanks programs, an episode of *Public Prosecutor* contains frequent, seemingly unnecessary editing within any given sequence. The network-financed budget for the series was $8,800 per episode. Still, the network could not find sponsors—even after reducing the asking price to $5,000 per episode. With each episode's production costs exceeding $10,000, Fairbanks discontinued production before completing a season's worth of episodes.[56] Fairbanks's company survived the setback, going on to produce series such as *Silver Theater* (1950) and *Front Page Detective* (1951–1953), but it certainly was not an impressive debut for filmed programming on the networks.

Many other independent producers joined Fairbanks in this first speculative period of telefilm production, which extended from 1946 through the 1951–1952 TV season. "Everybody who could buy or borrow a little drug-store movie camera announced himself as a TV-film producer," Fairbanks claimed in describing these early days.[57] News accounts during this period estimated that over eight hundred producers sought telefilm riches in the years prior to 1952. As a result, over two thousand unsold pilots languished on storage shelves or rotted in trash bins, having failed to attract a sponsor for network broadcast or syndication. Neglected studios, empty warehouses, supermarkets, and family garages were transformed into temporary soundstages; 16mm cameras disappeared from stores; personal savings accounts were drained—all in the frantic gold rush years of the early telefilm industry.

The most visible producers to emerge in telefilm production during the late 1940s were the B-movie cowboys, who quickly became icons of the early video age: William "Hopalong Cassidy" Boyd, Gene Autry, and Roy Rogers. Boyd provided the telefilm industry's first unabashed success story, fueling every independent producer's wildest fantasies about deliverance from the studio system. During the 1940s, he had shrewdly invested $350,000 to acquire the television rights to the series of Hopalong Cassidy feature films in which he had starred since 1935; in addition, he acquired the rights to use the Hopalong Cassidy character in other media, including television, and in character merchandising. After marketing the features to local stations during the late 1940s, Boyd produced a *Hopalong Cassidy* TV series for NBC beginning in 1949.

By tapping into the growing postwar youth market and by taking advantage of television's emergent position at the center of an expanding popular culture marketplace, Boyd founded a Hopalong Cassidy industry that within only a few years included a radio series, a comic strip, comic books, a popular fan club, and a dazzling array of licensed merchandise—with an estimated total value of $200 million.[58] Spurred by Boyd's canny reincarnation, Autry and Rogers also revived moribund careers and earned fantastic wealth, beginning in the late 1940s, by producing television Westerns on the same dusty backlots that once had provided the settings for their B Westerns.

From the pack of fly-by-night producers that surrounded these cowboy heroes in the early telefilm business, five significant production companies emerged: Fairbanks, the Hal Roach Studios, Bing Crosby Enterprises, Ziv Television Programs, Inc., and Louis Snader Productions. The varied backgrounds of these producers give some sense of the many career routes that delivered early entrepreneurs to the telefilm industry.[59]

The Hal Roach Studios arrived in television as an established Poverty Row movie studio. After years at the margins of the movie industry, the Roach studio was familiar with the many low-budget alternatives to standard narrative features. The studio itself was virtually dormant in 1949 when Hal Roach Jr., after years of kicking around the industry, joined the company and convinced his father to rent space to telefilm producers and to form their own TV production unit. Roach produced situation comedies such as *The Stu Erwin Show* (1950–1955) and *My Little Margie* (1952–1955), and crime dramas like *Racket Squad* (1950–1953). As the studio increased its output, Hal Jr. became one of the early influential figures in the telefilm business, helping to found both the Television Film Producers' Association and the Academy of Television Arts and Sciences.

Bing Crosby was a performer and shrewd businessman, who always had moved easily between movies, radio, recordings, and live performances. Under the guidance of Basil Grillo and Crosby's brother Everett, Bing Crosby Enterprises during the 1940s had diversified into a number of unrelated businesses, producing orange juice, ice cream, sport shirts, and a wide variety of endorsed merchandise. An early proponent of the shift from live radio broadcast to transcribed performances, Crosby also was a chief investor in Ampex's development of videotape. As a result of these investments, Crosby was probably the most reputable and highly capitalized of the early telefilm producers. Crosby's company during its early years focused primarily on anthology series like *Fireside Theater* (1950–1958) and *Rebound* (1952).

Frederick Ziv, a syndicator of radio transcriptions to local stations, viewed telefilm production as an obvious extension of his existing business—an alternative to live broadcasting that provided local radio stations with some autonomy from the networks. Ziv Television Programs, Inc., packaged fifteen-minute sports and news programs for TV beginning in 1948. In 1949, his company began production on *The Cisco Kid* (1950–1956), its first dramatic TV series. By shooting the series in color when all other producers were using black-and-white film, Ziv ensured the residual value of the series for decades. Ziv's subsequent work consisted primarily of action series with male heroes, such as *Boston Blackie* (1951–1953) and *Dangerous Assignment* (1951–1952).

Louis Snader, an ex-musician and real estate tycoon, was probably the least likely member of this group, and his success was the shortest-lived. Louis Snader Productions produced the television version of *Dick Tracy* in 1950, but Snader hoped to make his real mark through his introduction in 1949 of "Telescriptions," three-minute filmed musical performances featuring stars like Peggy Lee, Mel Torme, and the Jordanaires. Producing twelve per day at a cost of $2,500 each, Snader imagined that his short films could be programmed flexibly into the daily schedule of local stations. Snader anticipated that Telescriptions would be hosted by TV jockeys who would become as influential as radio's newly celebrated disk jockeys.[60] Snader's peculiar contribution to the early telefilm—imagining TV mimicking radio's new recorded-music format and unwittingly anticipating the form of music videos—gives some idea of the flexibility of these producers, of their willingness to explore the options made possible by TV.

Only two of Hollywood's major studios attempted to move into television production during the late 1940s, and these were two of the least profitable studios in the studio system: Universal-International and Columbia. At first glance, it seems ironic that Universal and Columbia were the first studio system pioneers in TV production since they traditionally had demonstrated the least interest in broadcasting. But in fact Universal and Columbia were best equipped to adapt to the programming demands and economic relations of television. While the five largest studios jockeyed for position—buying radio stations, investing in television research, applying for TV station licenses—Universal and Columbia never had the investment capital to diversify into broadcasting. Along with United Artists, Universal and Columbia did not own the revenue-generating theater chains that provided the major studios with the financial security to consider diversification. Universal and Columbia saw their relationship to the TV industry as an extension of their subordinate status in the studio system: they were prepared to supply product to a market beyond their control.

Universal first began television production in 1947 as one measure in a desperate attempt to put the brakes on runaway financial losses that had piled up following the box-office failure of a number of prestige independent productions financed and distributed by the studio starting in 1946.[61] Universal turned to the production of TV commercials as a side venture of its New York-based subsidiary United World Films, the world's largest distributor of 8mm and 16mm film. The company immediately established itself by producing for clients such as Lever's Lux Soap, General Electric, and Gulf Oil. By 1949, the company had moved its TV operations to Los Angeles in hopes of expanding into the production of documentaries and other types of programming. Since the TV division's net profits for the first year were less than $40,000, the studio probably did not intend for TV production to boost its profits so much as to buy time by paying for facilities and labor at a time when lack of funds even forced the studio temporarily to shut its doors.[62] Universal staked its eventual movie comeback on a series of low-budget, proto-situation comedies featuring Ma and Pa Kettle and Francis the Talking Mule, but it never sold a television series and consequently remained in TV solely as a producer of commercials.

Although Columbia initially entered television under much the same circumstances as Universal, its rapid diversification beyond commercials made it more successful. In the spring of 1949, Columbia's president, Harry Cohn, hired his nephew Ralph, the son of the studio cofounder Jack Cohn, to conduct a preliminary study of Columbia's immediate and long-range prospects in the field of television. For the previous two years. Ralph Cohn had acquired a firsthand knowledge of television while running a two-man organization, Pioneer Television, which produced TV commercials in New York. Cohn presented a fifty-page analysis in which he advised that Columbia immediately assemble an organization to produce TV commercials and, ultimately, filmed programs for both network and local broadcast.[63]

In June 1949, Columbia formed a television production subsidiary through Screen Gems, the former animation company that had produced the studio's short subjects since the Cohns purchased it from Charles Mintz in 1934. During its first two years. Screen Gems produced only commercials, delivering more than two hundred for such clients as American Tobacco, Hamilton Watch, and BVD.[64] Soon thereafter, Screen Gems began producing television series, and within a few years its success with series like *Father Knows Best* (1954–1960) would elevate it into the ranks of Hollywood's major powers.

Created under severe economic constraints, Hollywood's earliest filmed television programs scarcely affected the movie industry's major studios. During the first stage of television production in Hollywood, roughly 1946 until 1951, telefilm production took place on the distant fringes of the studio system. The province of Hollywood outsiders and castoffs, telefilm's underfinanced, uncoordinated early ventures merited little attention from industry leaders. Gradually, however, the market for telefilm production solidified as sponsors and the networks looked to Hollywood for programming and as more established independent producers turned to television in hopes of reaping profits through syndication and merchandising. As early as 1951, these producers began to leave their mark on the medium. During the fall of that year, Desi Arnaz and Lucille Ball premiered *I Love Lucy* (1951–1957), the first filmed situation comedy to have a national impact. Jack Webb followed later that season with *Dragnet* (1952–1959), the first successful

248

crime series shot on film. Within a year, *I Love Lucy* and *Dragnet*, two filmed series produced in Hollywood, stood atop the network ratings as the most popular series on TV.

Conclusion

Jack Warner's legendary antagonism toward television was not evident until the end of the 1940s. Considering his studio's long-term commitment to television, it was a significant departure from Warner Bros. tradition when he announced in early 1950 that "the only screens which will carry Warner Bros. products will be the screens of motion picture theaters the world over."[65] Warner's hostility to television has sometimes seemed like the natural result of competition between the movie industry and an upstart rival; in fact, it might never have existed were it not for FCC actions that prevented the studio from forming its own network or seeing its investment in theater TV pan out. Judging by the plans that Warner Bros. unveiled in 1949, the studio executives conceived of television as a central component of the postwar studio system, a new source of income in an unpredictable economic environment.

For much of the 1940s, it was possible for Hollywood's major studios to imagine that they would play a significant role in shaping American television, that television under their influence might not simply duplicate the model of broadcasting established during the radio era. They envisioned two complementary forms of television which would feature different types of programming, one designed for home audiences and the other for theaters. By the dawn of national television service in the late 1940s, however, it was already clear from the FCC's actions that American television would follow the radio model: television would be an advertiser-supported medium dominated by the established broadcast networks, with programming transmitted almost solely to home receivers.

The FCC's growing distrust of the studios may have seemed gratuitous, perhaps even willfully biased in favor of the radio networks, but the antitrust charges of the 1940s cast grave doubts on the worthiness of the studios to hold broadcast licenses. Michele Hilmes has shown that the FCC's suspicion echoed more general public criticism of the movie industry following the *Paramount* decision. An article in the February 1949 *Consumer Reports*, for instance, forecast dire problems for the future of television should the studios, with their acknowledged record of monopolistic practices, find a foothold in the medium. Given power in both the movie and television industries, these oppressors of independent theater owners might be tempted to commit any number of abuses; most important, as RCA warned in 1940, they could slow the development of television to protect the movie business or erode broadcating's public service standards in their quest for profits.[66]

According to Hilmes, the *Paramount* decision helped to foster the contrasting images that justified the FCC's discrimination between the movie and broadcast industries: Hollywood appeared to be a potential public menace, while the radio networks—which had themselves engaged in a host of monopolistic practices—posed as beneficent public servants. Supported by public sentiment, the FCC's inquiries into Hollywood antitrust violations and general reluctance to support technological or economic alternatives to the broadcast networks blocked virtually every plan for television that originated in Hollywood.

During the 1940s, even Paramount, the studio that diversified most aggressively into television, could not succeed beyond its interest in DuMont and its ownership of local stations in Los Angeles and Chicago. Blocked from owning individual stations, building networks, or developing theater TV, Hollywood's leaders recognized at the end of the decade that they had lost the opportunity to compete with the broadcast networks, which became firmly entrenched during the freeze. Producing for television without controlling distribution was an unthinkable compromise for the studios. Doubtless the studio system would have to adapt in order to survive the postwar era, but the studios were not yet prepared to create a product that they would neither distribute nor exhibit; distribution was still the key to a studio's power and self-determination. Therefore, while the major studios other than Paramount retreated from television at the end of the 1940s, independent film producers began to integrate television into the movie industry. The history of television in the studio era is a chronicle of thwarted ambitions. The full-scale integration of television in Hollywood would not occur until the 1950s, when the major studios themselves would begin to produce for television.

Notes

1 J. Fred MacDonald, *One Nation Under Television: The Rise and Decline of Network TV* (New York: Pantheon, 1990), p. 8; "Television Is Ready," *Hollywood Reporter*, 28 November 1934, p. 1; Joseph H. Udelson, *The Great Television Race: A History of the American Television Industry, 1925–1941* (Tuscaloosa: University of Alabama Press, 1982); "1939—Television Year," *Business Week*, 1 December 1938, pp. 17–31. See also Garth Jowett, "Dangling the Dream? The Presentation of Television to the American Public, 1928–1952," *Historical Journal of Film, Radio and Television* 14, no. 2 (1994), pp. 121–145. According to Jowett, the climate of prophecy surrounding television also sowed considerable skepticism among a public that had witnessed many premature predictions and lackluster demonstrations during the 1930s.

2 MacDonald, *One Nation Under Television*, pp. 19–20.

3 Ronald Haver, *David O. Selznick's Hollywood* (New York: Bonanza Books, 1980), p. 304; "Television for 'GWTW' Premiere," *Hollywood Reporter*, 12 December 1939, p. 1.

4 "Fly Sees Hollywood as Source of Television Program Supply," *Motion Picture Herald*, 31 August 1940, p. 59; "Fly Impressed by Tour of Movie Lots," *Broadcasting*, 1 September 1940, p. 40.

5 Michele Hilmes, *Hollywood and Broadcasting From Radio to Cable* (Champaign: University of Illinois Press, 1990), p. 8.

6 "Warner Seeking MBS Interest but Rejection of Offer Is Seen," *Broadcasting*, 1 May 1936, p. 8.

7 "Film Industry Advised to Grab Television," *Broadcasting*, 15 June 1937, p. 7, quoted in David Alan Larson, "Integration and Attempted Integration Between the Motion Picture and Television Industries" (Ph.D. diss., Ohio University, 1979), p. 31. For more on the movie industry's consideration of television during the 1930s, see Eric Smoodin, "Motion Pictures and Television, 1930–1945: A Pre-History of Relations Between the Two Media," *Journal of the University Film and Video Association* 34, no. 3 (Summer 1982), pp. 3–8. For a more detailed discussion of Hollywood's role in radio, see Richard B. Jewell, "Hollywood and Radio: Competition and Partnership in the 1930s," *Historical Journal of Film, Radio, and Television* 4, no. 2 (1984), pp. 125–141, and Hilmes, *Hollywood and Broadcasting*, pp. 53–74.

8 Warner Bros. Pictures, general television file, 1930–1936, Warner Bros. Pictures Collection, Department of Special Collections, Doheny Library, University of Southern California; Lawrence Bergreen, *Look Now, Pay Later: The Rise of Network Broadcasting* (New York: New American Library, 1980), p. 121.

9 Tino Balio, *United Artists: The Company Built by the Stars* (Madison: University of Wisconsin Press, 1976), pp. 136–138.

10 Selznick to John Hay Whitney, 17 November 1937; Selznick to John Wharton, 24 November 1937; both in Selznick Collection, UT.

11 For more on the CBS-Paramount merger, see Jonathan Buchsbaum, "Zukor Buys Protection: The Paramount Stock Purchase of 1929," *Cine-Tracts* 2 (Summer-Fall 1979), pp. 49–62; Douglas Gomery, *The Hollywood Studio System* (New York: St. Martin's Press, 1986), pp. 124–132; Hilmes, *Hollywood and Broadcasting*, pp. 36–46.

12 "Paul Raibourn of Par Stresses Why Film Co. Bought into DuMont," *Variety*, 1 May 1940, p. 4. For a more complete account of Paramount's investment in DuMont, see Timothy R. White, "Hollywood's Attempt at Appropriating Television: The Case of Paramount Pictures," in Tino Balio, ed., *Hollywood in the Age of Television* (Boston: Unwin Hyman, 1990), pp. 145–163; and Timothy R. White, "Hollywood on (Re)Trial: The American Broadcasting-United Paramount Merger Hearing," *Cinema Journal* 31, no. 3 (Spring 1992), pp. 19–36.

13 "Television vs. Theatre," *Variety*, 3 May 1939, p. 1, 30.

14 *Ibid.*

15 Hilmes, *Hollywood and Broadcasting*, p. 117.

16 "Television Comes to That Corner Again," *Motion Picture Herald*, 11 January 1941, p. 27.

17 "Prize Fight's Telecasting Irks Exhibs," *Variety*, 1 March 1939, p. 1: "Noncommercial BBC Embarrassed by Runaway Theatre Television," *Variety*, 8 March 1939, p. 1; "Baird Vision to Enter U.S. During N.Y. Fair," *Variety*, 1 March 1939, p. 2; "RCA Shows Wide-Screen Television for Theaters to Its Stockholders," *Motion Picture Herald*, 11 May 1940, p. 5.

18 "Television Brought to Theatre by RCA Large Screen Showing," *Motion Picture Herald*, 1 February 1941, pp. 30–31; "Theatre Television," *Motion Picture Herald*, 10 May 1941, p. 9; Terry Ramsaye, "Wired Television Makes Debut," *Motion Picture Herald*, 17 May 1941, p. 15. Movie industry executives in attendance included Paramount's Barney Balaban, Columbia's Jack Cohn, Loew's Nicholas Schenck, 20th Century-Fox's Spyros Skouras, and Warner Bros.'s Albert Warner.

19 "Paramount First Film Studio to Turn to Production," *Motion Picture Herald*, 14 September 1940, p. 19; "Television a Home Element, Says Sarnoff," *Motion Picture Herald*, 1 July 1939, p. 33.

20 Quoted in William Boddy, *Fifties Television: The Industry and Its Critics* (Champaign: University of Illinois Press, 1990), p. 23.

21 Douglas Gomery, "Failed Opportunities: The Integration of the U.S. Motion Picture and Television Industries," *Quarterly Review of Film Studies* 9, no. 3 (Summer 1984), p. 221; "Paramount Produces a Film to Show Advantages of Television," *Motion Picture Herald*, 16 March 1940, p. 29.

22 "Balaban Stresses Television Value," *Motion Picture Herald*, 1 February 1941, p. 32.

23 MacDonald, *One Nation Under Television*, p. 18.

24 "Commercial Television Is Delayed," *Motion Picture Herald*, 30 March 1940, p. 31.

25 "Paramount in Television, First Active Film Tieup," *Motion Picture Herald*, 20 April 1940, p. 14; "Motion Picture Industry Accused by RCA of Trying to Hamstring Television," *Motion Picture Herald*, 11 May 1940, p. 41.

26 See White, "Hollywood's Attempt at Appropriating Television," pp. 146–147; Hilmes, *Hollywood and Broadcasting*, p. 134.

27 "Paramount's Television Victory," *Variety*, 24 April 1940, p. 3; "FCC Gives Paramount Group Four Telecast Permits," *Motion Picture Herald*, 29 June 1940, p. 24; "Paramount First Film Studio to Turn to Television Production," *Motion Picture Herald*, 14 September 1940, p. 19; "B & K Will Telecast to Chicago Theatres Within Three Months," *Motion Picture Herald*, 18 January 1941, p. 29. DuMont introduced stations in New York and Washington, D.C.; the studio's Balaban & Katz theater circuit began broadcasting from a station in Chicago; and Television Productions, Inc., was given a permit for a station in Los Angeles. RCA, meanwhile, received permits for stations in New York, Chicago, and Washington, D.C.

28 MacDonald, *One Nation Under Television*, p. 34.

29 Boddy, *Fifties Television*, p. 44.

30 MacDonald, *One Nation Under Television*, p. 38.

31 Al Steen, "Television Developments," *1946 Film Daily Year Book*, p. 75.

32 "Majors Bolster Stake in Postwar Television," *Motion Picture Herald*, 5 June 1943, p. 31; "Hollywood Eyes Television as Postwar Customer," *Motion Picture Herald*, 25 December 1943, p. 25; Al Steen, "Television in 1943," *1944 Film Daily Year Book*, p. 685; "Television for Leo," *Motion Picture Herald*, 2 December 1944, p. 9.

33 "Hollywood Eyes Television as Postwar Customer," *Motion Picture Herald*, 25 December 1943, p. 25; "Television Group to See First Film Made for Medium," *Motion Picture Herald*, 9 December 1944, p. 15; Al Steen, "Television Developments of 1944," *1945 Film Daily Year Book*, p. 722; "RKO Unwraps Pix Package for Tele," *Variety*, 20 March 1946, 3.

34 "Warners Buys Station Site," *Motion Picture Herald*, 23 September 1944, p. 32; "Hollywood Digs In," *Business Week*, 24 March 1945, pp. 94–95; Ralph Wilk, "Television in Hollywood," *1946 Film Daily Year Book*, p. 742.

35 "Trade Plans for Postwar Boom in Television," *Motion Picture Herald*, 27 February 1943, p. 23; "Majors Bolster Stake in Postwar Television," *Motion Picture Herald*, 5 June 1943, p. 31.

36 Larson, "Integration and Attempted Integration," pp. 57–58; "Tele Theaters in All Keys," *Variety*, 12 January 1944, p. 5; Gomery, "Failed Opportunities," p. 224; "Theatre Television's Slice of the Spectrum Must Wait," *Motion Picture Herald*, 20 January 1945, p. 35; "Theatre Television Battles Again for Spectrum Space," *Motion Picture Herald*, 10 March 1945, p. 27.

37 "Closed Circuit," *Broadcasting*, 9 April 1945, p. 4, quoted in Larson, "Integration and Attempted Integration," p. 65.

38 "U.S. Suit Charges Film Cartel Bars Theatre Television," *Motion Picture Herald*, 22 December 1945, p. 23; "Release Video Patents Is Answer of Justice Dept. to Par," *Variety*, 26 December 1945, 3.

39 MacDonald, *One Nation Under Television*, p. 42; Boddy, *Fifties Television*, pp. 47–48.

40 "Link Warners to NBC Television," *Variety*, 30 January 1946, p. 1; "Warner-RCA Deal Unlocks Theatre Television Gate," *Motion Picture Herald*, 19 July 1947, p. 17; "RCA, 20th-Fox in Television Pact," *Motion Picture Herald*, 13 September 1947, p. 44; "Infant Theater Television Stuck with Diaper Pins," *Motion Picture Herald*, 3 July 1948, 13.

41 "Warners Buys Station Site," *Motion Picture Herald*, 23 September 1944, p. 32; "Hollywood Digs In," *Business Week*, 24 March 1945, pp. 94–95; Larson, "Integration and Attempted Integration," pp. 59, 73–74; Gomery, "Failed Opportunities," pp. 221, 225; Thomas F. Brady, "Warners to Make Television Films," *New York Times*, 4 January 1949, p. 21: "Suit Against Warner Holds up Radio Deal," *New York Times*, 18 February 1949, p. 37.

42 For a more detailed account of these conditions, see Douglas Gomery, "The Coming of Television and the 'Lost' Motion Picture Audience," *Journal of Film and Video* 38 (Summer 1985), pp. 5–11; and Thomas H. Guback, "Hollywood's International Market," in Tino Balio, ed., *The American Film Industry*, rev. ed. (Madison: University of Wisconsin Press, 1985), pp. 470–475.

43 Thomas F. Brady, "Hollywood Studio in Contract Field," *New York Times*, 22 November 1948, p. 29.

44 Thomas F. Brady, "New Hollywood Enterprise," *New York Times*, 9 January 1949, sect. 2, p. 5.

45 White, "Hollywood's Attempt at Appropriating Television," p. 148; Gomery, "Failed Opportunities," pp. 225–226.

46 Gomery, "Failed Opportunities," pp. 221–223.

47 "Par Under Fire for Its TV Plans," *Variety*, 27 April 1949, p. 6; "Quiz Justice Dept. on Legality of Pix Entry into Video," *Variety*, 1 December 1948, p. 3.

48 Boddy, *Fifties Television*, pp. 50–52; MacDonald, *One Nation Under Television*, pp. 60–61.

49 MacDonald, *One Nation Under Television*, pp. 60–61.

50 Gomery, "Failed Opportunities," p. 227.

51 "Film Cos. Stymied Till FCC Rules Whether They're Anti-trust Violators," *Variety*, 16 March 1949, p. 26; "Suit Against Warners Holds up Radio Deal," p. 37.

52 Hilmes, *Hollywood and Broadcasting*, p. 130.

53 "Warners Wants out on Chi TV, but Assures FCC on Coast Aspirations," *Variety*, 11 May 1949, p. 26; "FCC Okays WINS, KLAC-TV Sales, Approves Other Transfers," *Variety*, 30 December 1953, p. 33.

54 Gomery, "Failed Opportunities," p. 223.

55 Jerry Fairbanks, "New Low-Cost TV Film Technique," *Television*, November 1949, pp. 23, 28; Jerry Fairbanks, "Multiple-Camera Techniques for Making Films," *American Cinematographer*, July 1950, pp. 238, 244.

56 Mary Gannon, "Hollywood and Television Try New Financial Patterns," *Television*, November 1948, p. 32.

57 "Film for '52," *Newsweek*, 11 August 1952, p. 54.

58 See J. Fred MacDonald, *Who Shot the Sheriff? The Rise and Fall of the TV Western* (New York: Praeger, 1987), pp. 20–24.

59 Much of this information is taken from "The Men Who Make and Sell TV Film," *Television*, July 1953, pp. 19–21. See also Barbara Moore, "The Cisco Kid and Friends: The Syndication of Television Series from 1948 to 1952," *Journal of Popular Film and Television* 8 (Spring 1980), pp. 26–33.

60 "Hollywood Can Grind out Film Fare for TV," *Business Week*, 24 November 1951, pp. 122–126.
61 Gomery, *The Hollywood Studio System*, pp. 148, 157.
62 "The Feature Is the Commercial," *Broadcasting*, 13 January 1958, p. 46.
63 "Screen Gems Has New Iron in Fire," *Broadcasting*, 13 April 1958, p. 76.
64 Albert R. Kroeger, "Steady as She Goes—Upward," *Television*, December 1965, p. 52; "Screen Gems Has New Iron," *Broadcasting*, 13 April 1958, p. 76.
65 "No Warners Films on Video, Jack L. Tells Sales Chiefs," *Los Angeles Daily News*, 14 July 1950, p. 27.
66 Hilmes, *Hollywood and Broadcasting*, p. 136.

12

THE STUDIOS MOVE INTO PRIME TIME

Hollywood and the television industry in the 1950s

William Boddy

Source: *Cinema Journal* 24(4) (Summer 1985): 23–37.

Contemporary observers and historians of both the motion-picture industry and the network television industry portray the decade of the 1950s as a period of traumatic change. In traditional film histories, the period represents the site of convergent crises: the divorcement of the major studios from their theaters, the loss of a major part of the film audience, the political blacklist. In such accounts, the rise of network television becomes another unwelcome external intrusion. No longer able to ignore television, the studios belatedly recognize the electronic market and leap into prime-time programming in 1955, simultaneously selling off their feature libraries to the hungry new medium.

The mid-1950s were even more disorienting to contemporary observers of the television industry, marked by the precipitious fall from the self-proclaimed heights of television's "Golden Age" of live anthology drama of the early and mid-1950s to the "vast wasteland" many of the same critics diagnosed and denounced a few years later. For these partisans of live drama, it was Hollywood which destroyed the aesthetic promise of television with the studio-produced action-adventure series of the late 1950s.

It is clear that the mid-1950s witnessed a new configuration of the motion-picture and television industries with the release of pre-1948 features to television and the entrance of major studios in the television series market. But our understanding of the economic shifts within and between the two industries is still imperfect. There seems to be little communication between historians of the motion-picture industry and those of network television;

traditionally, different sources and fields of competence have defined the two areas, and the broadcast historian's territory of radio manufacturing and networking, national advertising, and federal regulation is still foreign to most film historians exploring the intersections of Hollywood and television. Even in the specialized literature, one side of the relation will often be slighted, one industry's trade press and primary source material neglected. I would like here to clear up several misconceptions about the relations between Hollywood and the television industry in the 1950s: that the major studios closed their eyes to television until the mid-1950s in hopes that it would go away, and that ABC President, Leonard Goldenson, with his motion-picture background and contacts, was personally responsible for inaugurating what was then derisively called "Hollywood television" in the mid-1950s.

It is difficult to find a period in television history when the major Hollywood studios did not take an active interest in the industry. Paramount, for example, by 1944 owned and operated television stations in Los Angeles and Chicago; controlled a theater-television firm, American Scophony; held a twenty-nine percent interest in DuMont Laboratories, a television manufacturer and network operator; and controlled significant patents on the cathode ray tube.[1] Paramount executive Paul Railborn sat on the boards of directors of American Scophony and DuMont Television Network; by 1951 Paramount's Los Angeles station was syndicating programming to forty-three stations, and the studio subsequently acquired a fifty percent interest in a subscription-television firm.

Significant in the list of investments and activities by this single Hollywood studio in early television is the extent to which motion-picture producers remained frustrated in their attempts to exploit non-broadcast television. Paramount's and the other studios' repeated defeats at the Federal Communications Commission regarding Paramount's interest in DuMont, and the application for allocations for theater television and subscription television describe a clear pattern of administrative bias, not directed against Paramount or the motion-picture industry, but reflecting the Commission's loyalty to the established interests in radio manufacturing and broadcasting. Almost by default, then, the terms of confrontation and exchange between Hollywood and the television industry would be set from the positions of program supplier and network customer, and moreover, within an industry defined by the networks' powerful economic position with their affiliates and their advertisers. The historical question remains: if the studios were frustrated in the 1950s in their attempts to exploit alternative uses of television, such as theater television or subscription television, and in their attempts at other forms of entry into network television, such as chain ownership of stations, television manufacturing, and network operation, what accounts for the economic relations which did emerge in the 1950s between the studios as program providers and the three networks?

The studios had two types of product to sell to television: their libraries of existing feature films, and original series programs, or telefilms. To understand the history of Hollywood as a program supplier to the television industry there must be an appreciation of the distinct and changing interests *within* each industry in the 1950s. In Hollywood, for example, the calculations of the studios regarding television as a market were affected by the series of consent decrees which separated the producers/distributors from their theaters. While the first of the decrees was signed in 1948, divorcement was not completed until 1959, and the still-integrated major studios looked at television from the points of view of exhibitors and producers through much of the 1950s. Throughout the period, the trade press noted consistent pressure from independent exhibitors on motion-picture producers, including threats of boycotts against any studio which released theatrical films to television or moved too precipitously into telefilm production. Both Columbia and Universal-International used separate, non-theatrical crews and casts when they set up telefilm subsidiaries in the early 1950s, reportedly in part to shield the studios from such exhibitor reprisals.[2] Producer concern over exhibitors' reaction to studio moves into television was signalled in a 1944, pre-divorcement statement by the head of RKO, who attempted to reassure theater owners:

> Motion picture exhibitors are the customers and the only customers of the major distribution companies. Exhibitor interests come first and must be protected in every way possible, but this cannot be done simply by ignoring this new medium of entertainment. To turn our backs on television would be a disservice to the exhibitor.
>
> We believe that the most suitable types of television programs . . . will be far different in character from the feature motion pictures created in Hollywood for theatrical exhibition . . .
>
> Rather than stand aside while others pre-empt the field, it would seem to be in the best interests of the entire motion picture industry that production-distribution companies should participate in television, not only to protect themselves but exhibitors as well, by directing television programming into fields which would be far removed from feature films created for the theatre. Unless this is done, there will be a tendency for television to become dependent upon the showing of feature pictures made primarily for theatrical exhibition.[3]

Despite such studio protestations, film producers and exhibitors viewed television's prospects quite differently, and the structural changes within the motion-picture industry in the early 1950s shifted the balance of power between the two groups. When the industry began to recover from its post-War economic slump in 1953, the new prosperity was not equally shared by producers and exhibitors. The feature film industry which emerged in the

257

mid-1950s was significantly different in structure from that of the pre-War years: studios slashed fixed costs and contract talent, picked up more independently-produced projects, and produced fewer, more expensive films with higher promotion budgets (including spending for television advertising). The growing use of pre-sold material and the new widescreen adventure and spectacle films brought large revenues to the studios: between 1953 and 1956, thirty CinemaScope features each earned more than $5,000,000 at the box office, an amount that only 100 films had captured before 1953.[4] Twentieth Century-Fox, the studio with the largest commitment to widescreen, earned $8,000,000 net revenues from 32 films in 1953; in 1954, it received $16,000,000 from only 13 films. The new good fortune of the studios, however, was not shared by many exhibitors; in part as a result of the restructuring of the industry following divorcement and the new supply and marketing practices, exhibitors saw an increasing percentage of their costs committed to film rentals.[5] In 1954 it was estimated that only thirty-two percent of theaters were breaking even on box-office revenues alone.[6] The cumulative effect of these changes within the theatrical film industry in the early 1950s was a shift of power from exhibition to production-distribution, and the implications for the studios' interests in the television market included the fading force of exhibitor anti-television pressure and boycott threats.

A more powerful disincentive for the major studios to enter early telefilm production were the low prices offered for television programming through the early 1950s. The 1940s witnessed a prolonged debate over the prospects of advertiser-supported television being able to support Hollywood production costs. Of some comfort perhaps was the argument proposed by an author in *Harper's* in 1948: "People will look at and listen to television programs for the same reason that they now listen to the radio: the television set is placed where it will form a part of the living habits of the American people. They will accept a much poorer level of entertainment in their homes than they will demand if they have to leave the house or apartment to attend a public performance."[7] Despite such assurances of lowered expectations of the home audience, many early observers were fearful that the per-minute production costs of even low-budget Hollywood filmmaking would be too rich for the television market. A popular book on television in 1940 argued: "The expense to be faced is almost terrifying. Translated into terms of running time on the screen, a motion picture play may cost from $1,000 to $35,000 a minute, with $1,000 representing about the worst that the public will tolerate. If we are to have every day a new television comedy and tragedy lasting an hour and a half, the studio incurs an outlay that dwarfes anything with which producers are familiar."[8]

While by 1952 Columbia (Screen Gems), Universal (United World Films), and Monogram (Interstate Television) were involved in telefilm production, *Business Week* that year described the mood among the major studios as one of "watchful waiting." The studios "probably can't make shorts for commercial sponsorship profitable now," the magazine concluded. "They will have to slash costs first."[9]

What kept telefilm prices and budgets low through the mid-1950s was not merely the lack of sufficient audience circulation to bid up advertising fees, but the hostility of the two dominant networks, NBC and CBS, to prime-time film programming. While film programming was an important part of local television schedules, especially before the completion of transcontinental coaxial cable for live network interconnection and for new stations which often lacked full facilities for live production, the networks resisted the use of telefilm on two grounds. First, the networks were fearful of jeopardizing their dual role as suppliers of programming to affiliates and as station sales agents for national advertisers. Film programs, the networks feared, would allow individual stations to make their own arrangements with program producers on the one hand and with sponsors on the other, bypassing the networks completely. In addition, reflecting on the experience of network radio, where a majority of sponsored programs were produced by or licensed to a sponsor or advertising agency, the network merely selling time, both CBS and NBC in the early 1950s were determined to prevent a similar situation in television. In the first years of network television, following the pattern of network radio, the sponsor and advertising agency did play a large role in program production and licensing; in 1949, for example, five of the ten top shows were produced in-house by a single advertising agency, Young and Rubicam.[10] The networks' first strategy to assert network control over program production and scheduling included a growing emphasis on self-production, often live. Both CBS and NBC constructed extensive production facilities in Los Angeles in 1951. (Stock analyst Robert Gilbert called CBS's new Television City "a factory to produce lower cost shows.")[11] CBS entered long-term television contracts with several radio and motion-picture stars, and NBC reported that fifty-nine percent of its overall schedule in 1952 was self-produced.[12]

The constraints of film industry structure and low program prices did not prevent independent producers from entering the telefilm market in the late 1940s and early 1950s. F. W. Ziv, the nation's largest syndicator of radio programs, joined independent film producers such as Jerry Fairbanks, William Pine and William Thomas, and Hal Roach, Jr. Other entrepreneurs entered the television market with re-edited theatrical films, such as the successful *Hopalong Cassidy*. The independent telefilm market was highly competitive and unstable; since the networks resisted film programs and controlled virtually all of prime time in most television markets, telefilm syndicators were restricted to non-network fringe time, when audiences and advertising fees were much smaller. Distribution costs of syndicated film programs to markets on a station-by-station basis were much higher than network interconnection costs. Telefilm producers complained that Eastern advertiser agencies were hostile to film programming, fearing the loss of the agency's 15 percent commission with a ceding of a direct production role. Until 1952, commercial banks accustomed to working with theatrical producers were unwilling to finance telefilm production, and while producers frequently faced sponsor demands for thirteen or twenty-six completed episodes before a series sale, without a network sale producers faced a payback period of at least two or three years.[13]

Meanwhile the telefilm market was flooded with unsold thirty-minute pilots produced on speculation; one observer estimated that there were over 200 unpurchased pilots in Hollywood in 1951, and telefilm producer Jerry Fairbanks complained of a gold-rush atmosphere when "everyone who could buy or borrow a little drugstore movie camera announced himself as a TV-film producer." *Time* magazine reported in 1954 that of 500 telefilm companies recently established in Hollywood, only 46 survived beyond one-shot projects and only 6 firms made substantial profits.[14]

Faced with a competitive market and low program fees, the early independent telefilm producers specialized in thirty-minute, low-budget, action-adventure series (crime and suspense, Westerns, science fiction) and situation comedies, rather than the more prestigious anthology drama programs like those produced live in New York. A 1951 *Business Week* article entitled "Hollywood Cameras Grind Out Film Fare for TV," suggested the production conditions for such early film programs: one telefilm producer created sixty-minute episodes on one and one-half to three day shooting schedules; thirty-minute programs reached stations five days after shooting was completed; and a single performer would shoot seven short subjects for television in the morning and five more in the afternoon of a single day. Successful telefilm producer Frederick Ziv later recalled: "In the early days of television, we had to produce these things cheap. There's just no question about it, and cheap is the word. Not inexpensive, but cheap."[15]

The re-packaging of the marginal Hollywood features available for television in the early 1950s was controlled by the same imperatives; a 1950 trade article entitled "How to Use TV Films Effectively" advised station managers and sponsors how to prepare existing feature films for broadcast: "Far from ruining a picture, expert editing can make it even better for TV. Obviously, twenty-five minutes hacked indiscriminately from any film will leave viewers confused and annoyed. How do you snip out thirty per cent of a carefully made product and still have it make sense? First eliminate all dark scenes that won't show up on a TV tube, and then all the long shots in which distant objects get lost. . . ."[16] *Sponsor* magazine in 1953 noted the unhappy experiences of some advertising agencies which went to Hollywood in the early 1950s in search of film programming: "These top agencies somehow got the idea that they had bought what constituted Hollywood. And then came the disillusionment. They found out that what they had bought in the main were a lot of out of work producers, directors and writers—not the real genius that had made Hollywood a world by-word in entertainment."[17]

Given the financial constraints and management attitudes in the early telefilm industry, it is small wonder that the critical reputation of such programs suffered in comparison with the big-budget, sixty-minute anthology drama programs and network spectaculars originating from New York. The critical split was reinforced by the aesthetic claims of television critics that the medium was in its essence a live one. In a 1952 *New York Times* article, "A Plea for Live Video," critic Jack Gould denounced the "dogeared films that Hollywood is turning out for television, the pedestrian little half-hour quickies that are cluttering up the facilities of even the best of networks."[18] In 1956 critic Gilbert Seldes decried what he called the "oil slick of Hollywood's" influence on the medium; such critical scorn was seconded and hyperbolized by executives of the two dominant networks in the mid-1950s.[19] Eager to defend themselves against charges of illegal business practices in their treatment of program producers and television advertisers, the networks painted themselves as allies of the critical defenders of the aesthetically-privileged nationwide live dramatic broadcast—a network monopoly—against the designs of Hollywood film producers. Responding to testimony accusing the networks of violations of anti-trust laws, NBC President Robert Sarnoff first read *New York Times* critic Jack Gould's praises of live television into the *Congressional Record* and then argued: "Today, television broadcasting is at a crossroads: one fork has color signposts and points to programming created for the medium itself. The other fork follows a detour to a reservoir of motion picture film, built over the past twenty years."[20] Elsewhere in its testimony NBC denounced its critics as a conspiracy of Hollywood film interests eager to unload a flood of film programs and feature films on the medium, thereby reducing network television programming to "the lowest common Hollywood denominator . . . a continuing flow of stale and stereotyped film product." NBC warned the Senate Committee of the prospect of surrendering television to what it called the "film-come-latelys or the promoters with Hollywood backlogs in their portfolios"; "the accumulated product in Hollywood's vaults—most of it musty and outdated—would hit television with the impact of a tidal wave. The American people would literally drown in a celluloid sea."[21]

Striking about such stirring network defenses of live television in 1955 and 1956 is how misleading Sarnoff's color-coded signposts are as markers to paths the networks were already following. The proportion of live prime-time programming on all three networks fell from 50 to 30 percent in 1955–56, and the number of live drama programs in prime time on the three networks fell from fourteen in 1955 to seven in 1957 to one in 1959.[22] The precipitous decline of the New York live anthology drama programs and their replacement by Hollywood telefilms were not the results of a single network's strategy, a product of ABC's Goldenson's film industry background and associations, but represented a fundamental re-calculation by the networks of their relations with affiliates, program producers, and advertisers.

The move to telefilm programming by the dominant networks and the entrance of the major part of the Hollywood industry into telefilm production were both responses to the growing profit potential of telefilms in the mid-1950s. TV film's increasing value was due not merely to television's growing audiences and advertising fees, but also to other fundamental changes in the nature of television advertising and the ancillary markets for telefilm. By the mid-1950s film programs had demonstrated their ability to generate revenues subsequent to their original television release in reruns, subsidiary rights, and foreign sales. Conventional wisdom in the earlier speculation and experience in film programming was that such programs would have little re-use value. A 1939 commentator argued: "Rarely does a moviegoer see a film more than once. There is little reason to believe that a looker will consent to see a telecine transmission more frequently. Afterwards, the film must be relegated to the vaults."[23] As late as 1952, in an article entitled "Is the Rush to Film Shows Economically Sound?," *Sponsor* magazine cited a sponsor's cancellation of *Amos and Andy* reruns due to audience protest and noted an industry consensus that audiences perceived reruns as unwelcome and unacceptable.[24] However, by 1954 the magazine reported that the ratings of reruns could exceed those of the episodes' original broadcast, and in 1955 a telefilm producer argued that a successful series could be reissued in endless three-year cycles.[25]

By the mid-1950s the potential profits from merchandising spin-offs and other subsidiary rights of television series had also been demonstrated; the merchandising revenues in 1953 from just two successful TV series, *Hopalong Cassidy* and *Howdy Doody*, amounted to $1,500,000. By the middle of the decade revenues from the foreign licensing of telefilms began to climb, with the introduction of commercial television in Great Britain and new television markets in other countries. Like domestic syndication of reruns, foreign syndication, merchandising, and other subsidiary revenues could amount to almost pure profit to the series's owner, since production costs were generally recouped in initial release.[26]

The economic value of film programming was also affected by the changing composition and strategies of television advertisers, in turn responding to larger shifts in American manufacturing, retailing, and demographics. In 1950, the largest television network, NBC, reported that the top ten TV advertisers included Ford, General Motors, RCA, Philco, and the Mohawk Carpet Company; low-ticket goods manufacturer General Mills was ranked twenty-nine and Procter and Gamble twenty-four. Procter and Gamble's television budget moved from $7,000,000 in 1951 to $14,000,000 in 1952 to $24,000,000 in 1953, when it became television's largest advertiser. By 1957 the company was responsible for one dollar of every eleven spent on network television. In the mid-1950s there was an emphatic shift in network advertising to firms manufacturing small-ticket consumer goods; by 1955 the top six product categories (food products, toiletries, automobiles, household equipment, tobacco products, and soaps) constituted 78 percent of network billings. For these makers of inexpensive consumer goods of low product differentiation, television sponsorship was useful not for corporate identification, but solely for product advertising. Large advertisers favored telefilm series for their consistency and purchased programs on the basis of their ratings history in "formula" buying patterns. In 1952 Procter and Gamble led other large manufacturers of inexpensive consumer products into national advertising in daytime and other fringe hours; their favored program vehicle was the proven off-network film series that could be striped across the week. These sponsors, less concerned with the corporate image advertising typical of the prestige live anthology programs, reinforced a trend in network television away from single-sponsor programs to a pattern of multiple sponsorship, with advertising insertions scattered across several shows. From the 1955–56 to 1961–62 seasons the number of single-sponsor programs on all three networks fell from seventy-five to twenty-six while those sponsored by three or more advertisers rose from ten to forty-seven.[27]

The move of ABC to "Hollywood television" in the mid-1950s can be seen as a rational response to the new economic prospects of telefilm and the new structure of television advertising, as well as to problems unique to its status as the distant, number three network. Through the television station license "freeze" of 1948–52 both DuMont and ABC had serious difficulties clearing their live programs against the two dominant networks; through the mid-1950s many television markets were served by only one or two stations which split affiliation but favored the programs of CBS and NBC. In 1953 ABC had a live clearance rate of only 34 percent. Through the rest of the decade ABC held a smaller affiliate roster than its two network rivals, and one made up disproportionately of post-freeze stations, including the financially precarious UHF licensees. ABC's dependence on delayed broadcasts, given its problems with live clearance, made film programming more attractive than the use of visually degraded kinescope transcriptions of live shows.[28]

FCC approval of the ABC-UPT merger in 1953 brought the network the promise of $30,000,000 in program development funds from the cash-rich theater chain (in part due to the Paramount consent decree which ordered the chain to sell nearly two-thirds of its theaters in five years). Avoiding the bidding contests of the east coast network spectaculars of the other two networks, ABC looked to Hollywood for new programming. Its telefilm procurement policies also reflected another problem specific to ABC's last-place status: when the network did carry a successful advertiser-supplied program, it often watched helplessly as the sponsor moved the show to one of the stronger networks. The key to the network's film strategy, therefore, was not the earlier NBC and CBS policy of self-production, but network licensing of independently produced programs. A prototype of the new procurement pol-icy was ABC's 1953 agreement with independent producer Hal Roach, Jr.: in exchange for the network's contribution to pilot and series production costs, ABC acquired a profit share and syndication rights to the program and assumed licensing and scheduling control. The landmark in the new procurement pattern, however, came with ABC's *Disneyland* in 1954. The program (like *The Mickey Mouse Club* the following year) was unprecedented in both the number of reruns per season, the number of commercial breaks per hour, and the amount of each program devoted to direct promotion of Disney's feature films, comic books, trademark mer-chandise, and new amusement park. *Television* magazine wrote in 1955 that Disney turned to television more for such promotion than for program exhibition, and noted that one-fifth to one-third of the sixty-minute *Disney-land* was dedicated to studio promotion. The show was also very profitable for ABC, contributing almost half of the network's revenues in 1954, and it made 1955 the first profitable year for the network.[29]

The major studios which followed Disney's lead into telefilm production in 1955 repeated the heavy promotional quality of *Disneyland*, including extended promotion of current theatrical product also designed to placate theater owners. The new studio telefilm series of 1955–56 devoted nine to fifteen minutes of each hour to studio interviews and "looks behind the scenes" at the studios' feature activity. One new program, the thirty-minute *MGM Parade*, was an entirely promotional compilation produced by the studio's trailer department. A 1955 *Sponsor* magazine article, "Should Hollywood Get it for Free?," objected to the saturated promotional quality of the new studio shows, and with the exception of one of the spun-off studio properties of *Warner Brothers Presents, Cheyenne*, the shows per-formed poorly in the ratings and were jettisoned in favor of conventional action-adventure series formats.[30]

ABC's new program procurement policies were consonant with television advertisers' changing strategies and demographic targets. In his thesis on ABC's programming strategies of the 1950s, Fred Silverman argued: "Syn-onymous with the development of 'bread and butter' programming was the network's recognition of the young post-War families with small chil-dren. . . . In fact, practically all of the programs developed and/or acquired by ABC between 1954 and 1956 were geared to these families."[31] In a 1959 profile of the network, *Forbes* magazine explained: "Unlike the other net-works, who claim to supply something for everybody, Goldenson and Treyz [ABC's program head] don't even pretend to that goal. 'We're after a specific audience,' explains Goldenson, 'the young housewife—one cut above the teenager—with two to four kids, who has to buy the clothing, the food, the soaps, the home remedies.' "[32] As *Forbes* hints, by the end of the 1950s the differences between ABC and the two more established networks regard-ing program philosophy and advertising strategy were cosmetic. While for many contemporary lamenters of the demise of live drama ABC played the villain of the piece—a role reinforced by the protestations of the other networks of their commitment to live drama and program balance—marked differences in the program schedules of the three networks by 1960 are difficult to discern. By 1958, ABC alumni had moved into positions as program heads at NBC and CBS. Thus, the widely-held personalist accounts which credit ABC's Goldenson's Hollywood background or connections with the new procurement practices are misleading. The function of specific network executives as public image markers of largely spurious product differentiation among the three networks is suggested when, during the quiz show scandals and widespread critical complaints of program mediocrity of 1958–60, CBS program head James Aubrey explained his relationship to industry scholar-statesman Dr. Frank Stanton, CBS President: "Stanton is acknowledged to be the symbol of the respectable broadcaster. You have to maintain respectability though it's difficult and costly. At the same time you have to maintain leadership in audience. Competition is fierce. The egg-heads, they criticize no matter what, because in general they just don't like television. I'm a businessman. I have to be."[33]

The growing potential profits from telefilm syndication and subsidiary revenues and the network success of *Disneyland* brought about a rapid consolidation of the telefilm industry. The major studios entered or expanded in the telefilm market, often through acquisition, and independent producers merged into larger firms. According to *Variety* the rush of the major studios into telefilm production after the success of *Disneyland* created "awe and fear" among independent producers of telefilms.[34] An historian of television syndication concluded that by 1956 "few small syndicators were left."[35]

A final note should be made about the terms negotiated between the major-studio suppliers of telefilm programs and the three networks. Here the studios' two products, feature films and original telefilms, occasioned very different bargaining situations. The reason network executives in the mid-1950s were so exercised by the prospect of the "musty and out-dated" features being released to television was the considerable market power those who controlled such feature packages brought to negotiations over their television use. The revenues from feature release to television were considerable: C&C Cola, which started the full-scale release of pre-1948 features to television, made $25,000,000 from its package of 740 RKO films in individual station deals in less than twelve months. Columbia reported revenues from feature leases to television of $9,700,000 in 1956; Warner Bros. reported $15,000,000 in similar income the same year. Upsetting to the networks were the novel financial arrangements often made between the studios or feature packagers and individual stations, including C&C's bartering of station advertising time for feature films, Twentieth Century-Fox's exchange of its feature library for a 50 percent interest in a national feature film "network" of 128 stations clearing sixty minutes a week for national advertisers, and

MGM's swapping of features for an ownership interest in seven television stations. Though the alternative network of feature films did not succeed, feature films did boost the ratings of independent stations competing against network affiliates in local markets and did bring the studios tremendous revenues. Despite CBS's presentation of *The Wizard of Oz* as a recurring network special, the networks boycotted feature films in prime time until the 1960s, and the effect of features in the 1950s was largely to displace local live programming, not network telefilm.[36]

Network resistance to feature films was rooted in the unique conditions of the network program procurement market. Unlike the pattern established in the mid-1950s telefilm market, where the network would typically exchange a financial contribution to pilot or series production costs for long-term licensing rights, a share in the profits and subsidiary and syndication rights at an early stage of a series project—at treatment, script or pilot—when the program was untested and difficult to appraise, feature films came with box-office records which were good rating predictors. Furthermore, the supply of feature films of proven appeal is limited, the sellers are few, and desirable films are often tied to less desirable ones in a package. Indeed, the eventual introduction of features into network prime time in the 1960s did bring about a bidding war among the three networks, raising fees for feature films much faster than those for telefilm programming; partly in an attempt to hold down feature costs, all three networks turned to the made-for-TV movie by the second half of the 1960s.[37]

In entering the telefilm market in the mid-1950s, even the major studios were forced to negotiate with the three networks on largely network terms. The prospect of the major studios needing development money from the networks to finance series production, the rationale of the networks' "risk" and justification for network profit participation and control of subsidiary and syndication rights, struck many observers as dubious if not absurd and was denounced as a fig leaf covering the abuse of the networks' extraordinary power as monopsonistic buyers of prime time programming. By 1953 both CBS and NBC had repudiated their earlier attempts to gain network control over program procurement and scheduling through self-production of a major part of their prime-time schedules, and reconsidered their earlier fears of film programming. The revised network strategy was based on a new confidence in the networks' powerful market position in relation to their affiliates (especially when the lifting of the station freeze improved the split-affiliation and clearance problems) and their national advertisers. The root of the economic power of the networks in dealings with both television sponsors and program producers—including the major studios—rested in network dominance of the affiliates' prime-time schedules. The oligopolistic three-firm structure of the networks as buyers of programs and sellers of advertising time is a product of the allocation and licensing policies of the FCC, especially those of the 1940s and the 1952 *Sixth Report and Order*. The

FCC's decision to locate television in the inadequate VHF band and its version of localism in station licensing limited by technical necessity the number of large-market stations necessary to support wider network competition, and the three networks transferred this monopoly power into their negotiations with program suppliers. In the years since the establishment of modern network procurement and sponsorship policies in the mid-1950s disturbances in the market structure have been minor, such as the emergence of feature films in network prime time in the early 1960s or the rise of the made-for-TV movie later in the decade. More fundamental in design and effect were the 1971 FCC financial and syndication rules which stemmed from House, Senate, Justice Department, and Commission investigations going back to the mid-1950s, which attempted to restrain network advantage in the program procurement process. It is only in the past ten years, with the rise of VHF and UHF independent stations, satellite distribution, and the growth of cable and pay-per-view services that the procurement practices of the three networks, and with them the chief determinants of television's relations with the motion picture industry, have been fundamentally challenged.

Notes

1 "Box Office Job," *Business Week*, no. 772 (17 June 1944): 94.
2 "California As a Program Source," *Television* 8, no. 4 (April 1951): 38.
3 *Radio Daily—Television Daily*, 15 June 1944, 5, 7; quoted in Alan David Larson, "Integration and Attempted Integration Between the Motion Picture and Television Industries Through 1956" (Ph.D., diss., Ohio University, 1979), 60–61.
4 Larson, *Radio Daily—Television Daily*, 204; Lawrence L. Murray, "Complacency, Competition and Cooperation: The Film Industry Responds to the Challenge of Television," *Journal of Popular Film* 6, no. 1 (Winter 1977–78): 56; see also Janet Staiger, "Individualism versus Collectivism," *Screen* 24, no. 3 (July–August 1983): 68–79.
5 Freeman Lincoln, "Comeback of the Movies," *Fortune* 51, no. 2 (February 1955): 130; see also Michael Conant, *Antitrust in the Motion-Picture Industry: Economic and Legal Aspects* (Berkeley: University of California Press, 1960): 172; Ernest Borneman, "United States versus Hollywood: The Case Study of an Antitrust Suit," in Tino Balio, ed., *The American Film Industry* (Madison: University of Wisconsin Press, 1976): 320, 343, 361.
6 Murray, "Complacency, Competition and Cooperation," 51.
7 Bernard B. Smith, "Television—There Ought to be a Law," *Harper's Magazine* 197, no. 1180 (Sept. 1948): 37.
8 John Porterfield and Kay Reynolds, eds., *We Present Television* (New York: Norton, 1940): 29.
9 "Hollywood Learns to Live with TV," *Business Week* no. 1197 (9 Aug. 1952): 46–47.
10 *Television* 6, no. 2 (Feb. 1949): 4.
11 Ronald Gilbert, "Television 1953—Wall Street," *Television* 10, no. 1 (Jan. 1953): 36.
12 U.S. Congress, House, Committee on Interstate and Foreign Commerce, *Investigation of Radio and Television Programs, Hearings* before the Communications

Subcommittee of the Committee on Interstate and Foreign Commerce, House of Representatives on HR 278, 82d Cong., 2d sess., 1952, 268.

13 Milton MacKaye, "The Big Brawl: Hollywood vs. Television," *The Saturday Evening Post*, 26 Jan. 1952, 119; Frederick Kugel, "The Economics of Film," *Television* 8, no. 7 (July 1951): 13, 45; "California as a Program Source," *Television* 8, no. 4 (April 1951): 38; "Filmed TV," *Newsweek*, 12 Feb. 1952, 78.

14 MacKaye, "The Big Brawl," 119; "Film for '52," *Newsweek* 11 Aug. 1952, 137; "Film vs. Live Shows," *Time*, 29 March 1954, 77.

15 "Hollywood Cameras Grind Out Film Fare for TV," *Business Week* no. 1160 (24 Nov. 1951): 124; Ziv quoted in Morleen Getz Rouse, "A History of the F.W. Ziv Radio and Television Syndication Companies, 1930–1960" (Ph.D. diss., University of Michigan, 1976), 79.

16 "How to Use TV Films Effectively," *Sponsor* 4, no. 13 (19 June 1950): 33.

17 "Have TV Costs Reached Their Ceiling?" *Sponsor* 7, no. 19 (21 Sept. 1953): 106.

18 Jack Gould, "A Plea for Live Video," *New York Times*, 7 Dec. 1952, II, 17.

19 Gilbert Seldes, *The Public Arts* (New York: Simon and Schuster, 1956): 184.

20 U.S. Congress, Senate, Committee on Interstate and Foreign Commerce, *The Television Inquiry, Vol. 4: Network Practices, Hearings* before the Committee on Interstate and Foreign Commerce, Senate, 84th Cong., 2d sess., 1956, 1715.

21 Ibid., 2279.

22 "Sponsor Scope," *Sponsor* 11, no. 17 (27 April 1957): 10; Frank Henry Jakes, "A Study of Standards Imposed by Four Leading Television Critics With Respect to Live Television Drama" (Ph.D. diss., Ohio State University, 1960): 9.

23 John Western, "Television Girds for Battle," *Public Opinion Quarterly* 3, no. 4 (Oct. 1939): 558.

24 "Is the Rush to Film Shows Economically Sound?" *Sponsor* 6, no. 15 (28 July 1952): 69.

25 "Film Basics," *Sponsor* 8, no. 14 (12 July 1954): 186; Don Sharpe, "TV Film: Will Economics Stifle Creativity?," *Television* 12, no. 4 (April 1955): 81.

26 George Bauer, "Government Regulation of Television" (New York: New York University Graduate School of Public Administration, 1956, mimeograph): 360; "Film's $100,000,000 Year," *Sponsor* 10, no. 2 (23 January 1956): 31.

27 NBC, *Research Bulletin* no. 8 (1950); NBC, *Sales Facts Bulletin* no. 21 (3 April 1953); NBC, *Bulletin Research and Planning*, 15 July 1955; NBC, *Research and Planning Bulletin*, 8 Nov. 1955, 4; NBC, *Research Bulletin*, 30 April 1958, 1, 4; U.S., Federal Communications Commission, Office of Network Study, *Interim Report: Responsibility for Broadcast Matter*, Docket no. 12782 (Washington D.C.: Government Printing Office, 1960), 139; U.S., Federal Communications Commission, Office of Network Study, *Second Interim Report: Television Network Program Procurement*, Docket no. 12782 (Washington, D.C.: Government Printing Office, 1965), 497–528; "As the Film Men See It," *Sponsor* 10, no. 2 (23 Jan. 1956): 31.

28 Martin Meyer, "ABC: Portrait of a Network," *Show* 1, no. 1 (Sept. 1961): 59; Fred Silverman, "An Analysis of ABC Television Network Programming From February 1953 to October 1959" (Master's thesis, Ohio State University, 1959), 8.

29 "AB-PT's 'Full Speed Ahead' Sets in Motion '$30,000,000 Agenda', " *Variety*, 11 Feb. 1953, 1; quoted in Larson, "Integration," 211; Silverman, "An Analysis," 64; Robert Cuniff, "Selznick Talks About Television," *Television* 12, no. 2 (Feb. 1955); 67; Frank Orme, "TV's Most Important Show," *Television* 12, no. 6 (June 1955): 32.

30 Silverman, "An Analysis," 154; Charles Sinclair, "Should Hollywood Get it for Free?" *Sponsor* 9, no. 16 (8 Aug. 1955): 31.

31 Silverman, "An Analysis," 154.

32 "abc of ABC," *Forbes* 83, no. 12 (15 June 1959): 17.

33 Quoted in John Bartlow Martin, "Television USA: Wasteland or Wonderland?" Part II, *Saturday Evening Post*, 28 Oct. 1961, 60.

34 "Majors Worry Syndicators," *Variety*, 11 May 1955, 39; quoted in Larson, "Integration," 237.

35 Barbara Ann Moore, "Syndication of First-Run Television Programming: Its Development and Current Status" (Ph.D. diss., Ohio University, 1979), 39.

36 Abby Rand, "2500 Films—How Will They Change TV?" *Television* 13, no. 7 (July 1956): 64; "That Tom . . . He Makes Money!" *Television* 12, no. 9 (Sept. 1955): 25–26; Amy Schnapper, "The Distribution of Theatrical Films to Television" (Ph.D. diss., University of Wisconsin-Madison, 1975), 88–89.

37 Barry Litman, "The Economics of the Television Market for Theatrical Movies," *Journal of Communication* 29, no. 4 (Autumn 1979): 20–33.

13

INTRODUCTION TO *A CINEMA* *OF LONELINESS*

Phillip Robert Kolker

Source: Phillip Robert Kolker, *A Cinema of Loneliness: Penn, Kubrick, Scorsese, Spielberg, Altman*, New York: Oxford University Press, 1980, pp. 3–16, 407–408.

When the studios, as independent corporate bodies, fell apart in the late fifties and early sixties, assembly-line film production ended. Previously each of the major studios was a self-contained filmmaking factory with its own labor pool of producers, directors, writers, players, and technicians, turning out many films a month during the years of peak production. This self-containment and mass production created mediocrity to be sure, as well as an arrogance that comes with security of product and market. But out of the arrogance and the mediocrity came also a body of work of formal skill and contextual complexity unmatched by the cinema of any other country. If the films produced were not intended to be taken seriously as enduring examples of individual artistic worth, they often enough overcame the intent of their makers to stand as enduring examples of *filmmaking*, and all the collective energy that implies. They came as well to stand for the collectivity of film viewers; they created the images in which a culture consented to see itself.

The studios were places where support and security were offered to those who could work within their restraints, and when they fell that security and assuredness fell with them. The reasons for their fall were many and varied. Television, of course, was a major cause. In the late forties and early fifties, population patterns shifted. People moved to the suburbs and watched television rather than going out to the movies once or twice a week. Indeed, television now shares with film the major work of producing narratives for the culture. But even before the impact of television was fully felt, movie attendance began falling from its 1946 peak. Studio executives met this falling-off by tightening budgets, firing production staff (mainly in their story and publicity departments), and in general lessening the production values of their films. An attitude of self-defeat seemed to be in operation, an attitude that was reinforced by two other events that occurred between 1947 and 1949, which in fact initiated the studios' change and ultimate collapse. The hearings of the House Committee on Un-American Activities made production heads fearful and timid, uncertain as to what kind of content might be branded as subversive, what kind of creative person—director, writer, player—would be frowned upon as un-American. HUAC and Hollywood's self-imposed blacklist managed to damage irrevocably any courage the old studios might have had. The courts managed to damage their economic power. The divestiture rulings of the late forties separated the studios from the theaters they had previously owned. They could no longer count upon a guaranteed market for their films and had to seek out exhibition outlets on an individual basis. On top of this, foreign markets began placing quotas on American film. The confidence and self-sufficiency that had supported the studios since the twenties fell apart.

Uncertain as to what they could say in their films, uncertain as to whom they could say it, the studios floundered. They squandered their efforts on technical experiments—Cinerama, CinemaScope, 3D—and on overblown biblical and Roman epics. This is not to say that important films were not made in the fifties—they were, and it is a decade of films as rich in ideological contradictions as the eighties—only that the focal point of Hollywood filmmaking became diffuse, and by the end of the decade the "product," once controlled by a studio from inception to exhibition, was controlled and executed by different hands, from different sources, and for different ends.

The studios still exist, of course, but the physical means of production are no longer as centralized as they were during the decades from the twenties to the early fifties; the studios do not have their own in-house players and technicians, nor do they have strong individual identities (during the thirties and forties, each of the studios had developed a style and approach, a stock company of players, and even typical story subjects which made their films quickly recognizable). On the contrary, they are without identity and homogeneous. Whereas individuals such as Louis B. Mayer at Metro-Goldwyn-Mayer, Darryl F. Zanuck at Twentieth Century-Fox, Jack L. Warner at Warner Brothers, Harry Cohn at Columbia guided their studios with dictatorial power for years, now production executives move from one studio to another, trading past successes on recent failures and the promise of future blockbusters.

The studios through which these individuals move are no longer independent entities (perhaps "independence" is a relative term, for in their original incarnation the studios were quite dependent upon their financial officers on the East Coast and the banks who backed their films). Now they are either part of some larger, diversified corporation or owned by individuals whose function—and this is the major point of difference—is not making film, but amassing media outlets for various ideological reasons, the most important of which is the production of profit from the dissemination of news and fiction. The "product," more than before, is a means to this end. From an assembly line product made to service the mass entertainment market, film (and its reincarnation on videotape) is now part of a large structure of ownership and distribution. The studios of the past appear to be small businesses by comparison.

The effect of all this on the films that are made has already been noted. Homogeneity of production results in homogeneity of product. Filmmakers of imagination no longer have a centralized community of administrators and craftsmen who can be drawn upon to support them from production to production. Each project has first to be accepted by a corporate administrator, developed, financed, and produced as part of a major "deal." To be accepted and secured it must satisfy requirements, stated and unstated, of conventionality, easy legibility, sentimentality or brutality. Instead of the studio producer reigning over a production, the corporate executive, accountant, and talent broker have powerful control. The deal and the contract loom over the production, affecting it perhaps more perniciously than any boorish old studio head ever could.[1]

Huge amounts of money are spent (or promised) in hopes of making huge amounts of money. The shaky independence originally gained by some filmmakers when the old studio structure fell is now thoroughly compromised by the fact that many films are made as part of a complex economic structure that is created with the expectation that the individual film and its eventual appearance on videotape will spawn not only large financial returns, but offspring that will further those returns even more. The phantom promise of "artistic freedom" offered when the old Hollywood structure collapsed has turned into something of an economic nightmare where costs, salaries, profits, and reputations are juggled and manipulated, with the film itself all but disappearing in a mass of contracts and bookkeeping.

That small group of filmmakers who emerged in the late sixties and early seventies and were able to take brief advantage of the transitional state of the studios, using their talents in critical, self-conscious ways, examining the assumptions and forms of commercial narrative cinema, had a difficult task. They were without community or security. The corporate community that rapidly re-formed around them limited and compromised their small efforts, and they must now more than ever deal with the fact that without profitable returns on their work, they could not work at all. "Studio interference" has merely changed its complexion and complexity, incorporating not only economic pressures, but the individual filmmaker's own judgment and fears.

Those filmmakers have survived or succumbed to the changes in production in various ways. Robert Altman and Stanley Kubrick continue to accommodate themselves to the situation. During the seventies, Altman created his own mini-studio within which he could work with a minimum of interference. He seemed able to get backing for his films on his own terms, even though he had not had a commercial hit since *M.A.S.H.* in 1969. In

1980, after a number of his films failed commercially, Twentieth Century-Fox refused to distribute *Health*. Even though the enormous production of *Popeye* did do well, Altman decided to withdraw completely from mainstream production and sold his studio. He has since continued his career with inexpensively filmed versions of works originally written and produced for theater. Paris is now his center of operations. Kubrick divorced himself from the chaos of contemporary American production in the early sixties. He works in England, and his films have been successful enough so that he can command both money and independence. He followed his demanding and uncommercial film *Barry Lyndon* with the commercially oriented adaptation of a Stephen King novel, *The Shining*, thereby re-establishing his financial viability. Arthur Penn seemed able to work happily within the confusing bounds of post-studio production in the mid- and late sixties. His films were popular, though their popularity derived from an inherent sense of defeat that seems to have undone their creator. As a filmmaker, Penn has just barely survived into the eighties, and that survival has come with a decline in formal control and an increase in reactionary content. Martin Scorsese has survived well by making films for modest amounts of money and modest returns. Though his recent films are less formally adventurous than his seventies work, they continue (with the exception of *The Color of Money*) to be thoughtfully constructed, inquiring deeply into the nature of cinematic and cultural perception. Unlike Scorsese, Spielberg has rapidly become the master of the enormous budget and enormous project; he has formed his own production company and oversees the work of other directors. Where Coppola's imagination seemed to shrivel under the heat of large production, Spielberg's has flourished. But it is a peculiar kind of flourishing, in which imagination is put at the service of placation and manipulation. Spielberg's energy and ability to accommodate his audience make him, for the moment, the most significant figure of the "new" Hollywood and its economic demands.

But we must be careful. Dwelling upon economic realities works only to a point, after which the critic runs the risk of getting caught up in a self-defeating cycle in which the film's existence as a commodity makes serious discussion of its form and content impossible. Other realities must be attended to. In American filmmaking (and not only in American filmmaking) the economic situation is only one of many factors that determine what a film will be. The sense of defeat alluded to in regard to Arthur Penn's work is not only a problem of film finance, but of the way Penn views, and communicates his view of, American culture. The fact that his recent films have moved to the right may be the result of a confluence of personal, ideological, and economic pressure, but it is not a move dictated only by that last item. That Coppola got himself caught up in enormous projects, with a concomitant failure of narrative and structural control, while Scorsese is content with smaller, more experimental works, is as much a matter of personal inclination and emotional response as anything else. Spielberg has thrived on the big-budget, special effects film; but he is able to spend huge sums because the narrative structure and ideological energy of his films bring large audiences who are moved by them. Ideological assent generates money, not the other way around. What Spielberg has to say in *E.T.* or *The Color Purple* and Scorsese in *Taxi Driver* or *The King of Comedy* is indeed determined by the economic necessities of filmmaking, but it is determined as well by the very different ways these filmmakers perceive and respond to the culture, the ways film has delineated that culture, and the response of the culture to film.[2]

To understand this more clearly, let me repeat the fact that the initial period of transition during the late fifties and early sixties permitted a certain freedom of inquiry, which, no matter how compromised, continues to leave a small mark on most of the filmmakers who concern us here. Most of them remain, despite other problems, delighted with film and its formal properties, curious about what they can do with their medium. Their roots go back to the burst of cinematic enthusiasm and creative energy in Europe in the late fifties, where young filmmakers re-examined traditions and conventions in ways that had an enormous influence on the Americans who followed them.

The French, and Europeans in general, never had a studio system comparable to America's. At the same time, they never had an intellectual condescension toward film comparable to America's. Unlike their American counterparts, French intellectuals have not considered film a substandard form of entertainment, but rather a form of expression to be taken seriously. They have loved film, and American film in particular, both intellectually and emotionally. In the fifties, a particularly obsessed group of Frenchmen, among them Jean-Luc Godard, François Truffaut, Claude Chabrol, Eric Rohmer, and Jacques Rivette, formed a group around Henri Langlois's Paris Cinémathèque and André Bazin's journal *Cahiers du Cinéma*. They glorified American film to the detriment of French film; they perceived the ability of the individual filmmaker to rise above studio uniformity. They recognized the visual strength of American film (partly because, knowing little English and seeing unsubtitled prints, they were unencumbered by dialogue), and they recognized the strength of American film's generic patterns. They used their understanding to fashion an approach both to their own and to American cinema in a concerted critical effort. They reevaluated the role of the screenwriter and the director, they explored film genres; in short, they celebrated and analyzed film as a special narrative form with a voice, a text, and an audience deeply interrelated.[3] Their critical perceptions were passed on to American film scholars. They themselves turned to filmmaking, with an organized knowledge of what they wished to do. Their films were small, personal, and inexpensive. Early on they worked together (for *Breathless*, Truffaut supplied the story, Chabrol the technical assistance, and Godard, of course, the direction), and at least briefly after they went their own ways a sense of communal origins, and certainly a sense of commitment to cinema, continued.[4]

The influence of the French New Wave on both American film criticism and filmmaking is important and still visible, if now somewhat perfunctory (Truffaut appears as the scientist Lacombe in Spielberg's *Close Encounters of the Third Kind* and his film *Wild Child* is alluded to in *The Color Purple*; a sign in a Paris café that reads "Don't Shoot the Piano Player Anymore" is visible in Penn's *Target*). Despite the influence, no "new wave" in America occurred, no movement. That brief freedom I have been discussing was really a freedom to be alone within a structure that momentarily entertained some experimentation. The experiments that were undertaken, based upon some things the New Wave was doing, were very much on an individual basis and made within the tradition of Hollywood film. The filmmakers discussed here used those traditions and the basic patterns of American filmmaking as a point of interrogation, foregrounding them, bringing them to consciousness, attempting to determine their further usefulness as narrative tools. They tried in various ways to come to terms with narrative itself, the story and its telling, and to realize the possibilities inherent in refusing the classical American approach to film, which is to make the formal structure of a work erase itself as it creates its content. These directors, especially in their late sixties and seventies work, delighted in making the viewer aware of the act of watching a film, revealing it as an artifice, something made in special ways, to be perceived in special ways. Even Steven Spielberg, younger than the others and deeply committed to commercial narrative conventions, continues the New Wave tradition of playful allusiveness to other films within his own work.

The paradoxes and the contradictions inherent in all this are painful. Influenced by a group of French intellectuals, some American filmmakers became thoughtful about their films. But, unlike their French colleagues, the films they made rarely explored ideas and rarely explored their own larger ramifications. As delighted as they were (and in some instances still are) in the formal possibilities of their medium, as conscious as they were of the genres they emulated or attacked, they did not go very far beyond the tradition and never presented real alternatives to that tradition (in Spielberg's films, especially, the knowledge of form and structure is used to reinforce traditional response and whole hearted assent). Although their films sometimes carry on an ideological debate with the culture that breeds them, they never confront that culture with another ideology, with other ways of seeing itself, with social and political possibilities that are new or challenging. These are films made in isolation and, with few exceptions, about isolation. For without challenging the ideology many of them find abhorrent, they only perpetuate the passivity and aloneness that has become their central image.

A critical approach to these films gets caught up in the conflicts and contradictions. These filmmakers have created a body of exciting work, formally adventurous, carefully thought out, and often structurally challenging. But for all the challenge and adventure, their films speak to a continual impotence in the world, an inability to change and to create change. When they do depict action, it is invariably performed by lone heroes in an enormously destructive and anti-social manner, further affirming that actual change, collectively undertaken, is impossible. The only way to deal with them, therefore, is by examining the contradictions, keeping them present, in the foreground, confronting the films formally and contextually, aware that, no matter how much separation is made for the sake of discussion, form and content are inseparable.

To this end, this study will attempt to address the filmmakers and their works from a variety of perspectives. It will not constitute a complete history of recent American film, nor an economic survey, though both history and economics will support the discussions. There will not be a film-by-film analysis of each director's output. Not all films are of equal interest or of equal worth, and where a filmmaker's output is large it is impractical to give every film equal attention. I have attempted to avoid, wherever possible, the director's own analysis of his work. The interview, while a useful tool in film studies, seems to me too often to serve as a means of getting closer to the creator of a work rather than to the creation. My preference is to concentrate on the film itself, that organized series of images and sounds that have meaning, that exist in a carefully delimited time and space that is created when they are projected on a screen and perceived by a viewer. Films are initiated by individuals, who put the images and sounds together in specific ways, and who are influenced by their own perceptions of the world and by previous films. The films are perceived (and it is the act of perceiving that completes them) by individuals who are also influenced by their perceptions of the world and by previous films. This complex of relationships is my major subject.

The process of discussing these films will be, partly, a process of demystification (and demythification as well). There are no assumptions that what constitutes a film is merely a story with interesting and well-motivated characters that either succeeds or fails to entertain us for a few hours. On the contrary, the "story" is constituted by the formal structure of the film, which is in turn constituted by other films and the history of responses to them. Given the fact that the filmmakers under discussion already know this, one of my tasks will be to extend that knowledge further, to explain how they put it to use and how the spectator then uses it or is used by it. For this reason there will be digressions along the way, detours into the past of American cinema, discussions of its genres, some of its major directors and their influences, some of the formal attributes of film that the directors under discussion perpetuate, reflect upon, or change.

The major questions to be raised and, hopefully, answered in this study are "How?" and "Why?" How and why do filmmakers construct their works the way they do? How and why does a viewer react to them? In answering these questions I must reaffirm the fact that film, by virtue of the popularity and the immediacy of its fictions, by the nature of its means of production and consumption, is profoundly tied up with the cultural, social, and political being of the viewer. In other words, the examination of a film cannot be restricted only to the formal and thematic elements of its text or genre. Films are seen and understood (in various ways) by a great many people. They have an effect, calculated or uncalculated; the conventions and myths they have built and continue to build go beyond them and are deeply embedded in the culture.

Film is a major carrier of our ideology. To define more precisely what I mean by this, it is necessary to back up and recover some ground. American film, from its beginnings, has attempted to hide itself, to make invisible the telling of its stories and to downplay or deny the ways in which it supports, reinforces, and even sometimes subverts the major cultural, political, and social attitudes that surround and penetrate it. Film is "only" entertainment. Film is "realistic," true to life. These contradictory statements have supported American film throughout its history, hiding some basic facts about its existence. American film, like all fiction, is a carefully crafted lie: make-believe. Film processes "reality" into the forms of fiction (or, more accurately, uses its forms to create cinematic realities) which allude to, evoke, substitute for, and alter external "reality." Film is a representation, a mediation.

This processing or representation involves the active creation of ideas, feelings, attitudes, points of view, fears, and aspirations that are formed by images, gestures, and events that the viewer either assents to or opposes. Any given film is an organization, on the level of fictional narrative, of aspects of the self and the world. That narrative substitutes for ordinary experience characters and action in a cinematically determined space and time. This organization is not innocent (not since the early part of the century, at least). Choices are made as to subject and as to the way that subject will be realized, manifested—created, ultimately—in the forms of cinema. When it is decided that those forms are to be invisible, that the act of substitution or representation will not appear to be an act of substitution or representation, that the form of the fiction will recede behind the fiction itself and therefore create the illusion that the fiction is somehow "real" and unmediated, then a very specific relationship is set up with the audience. This relationship is based upon the assumption and assertion that what is seen is "real" and cannot be questioned.[5] There are enormous implications to this phenomenon, implications that some of the filmmakers discussed here are aware of and respond to in their own work. As indicated, they have begun to take cognizance of the cinematic forms at their disposal and make that cognizance apparent. With the exception of Spielberg, they began by questioning the ideology, both formal and contextual, of their cinematic heritage, and making their questions visible.

Yet I imagine many of them would hesitate if they were told they were involved in an explicit ideological endeavor, for the term itself is fraught with connotations of manipulation, of single-mindedness, of unyielding adherence to a political point of view. In our culture, it is often demanded by critics and artists alike that art be free of any specific political attitudes. But film, of any period, by any filmmaker, speaks to an audience about specific things in specific ways. Its form and content, its fictional mode and the ways in which it is read, are part of and reflect the larger social, cultural, psychological, and political structure. That structure is itself determined by the way individuals alone or collectively perceive themselves and their existence in the world. This is what I mean by "ideology": the complex of images and ideas individuals have of themselves, the ways they assent to or deny their time, place, class, the political structure of their society. ". . . Ideology is not a slogan under which political and economic interest of a class presents itself," write Rosalind Coward and John Ellis. "It is the way in which the individual actively lives his or her role within the social totality; it therefore participates in the construction of that individual so that he or she can act." The authors quote the French philosopher Louis Althusser, who offers a definition remarkable for its use of a cinematic metaphor: "*ideologies* are complex formations of montages of notions—representations—images on the one hand, and of montages of behaviours—conducts—attitudes—gestures on the other. . . ." Elsewhere, Althusser defines ideology as "the 'lived' relation between men [and women] and their world, or a reflected form of this unconscious relation. . . ."[6] Expanding upon this, Terry Eagleton writes that ideology "is the very medium in which I 'live out' my relation to society, the realm of signs and social practices which binds me to the social structure and lends me a sense of coherent purpose and identity." He goes on to point out that ideology is "the link or nexus between discourses and power," the way an individual is represented in and to the world and the way the world represents itself to an individual. Ideology constructs the very image of the individual and his or her potency or impotence in the world.[7]

Every culture has a dominant ideology, and as far as individuals assent to it, the ideology becomes part of the means of interpreting the self in the world and is seen reflected continually in the popular media, in politics, religion, education. But an ideology is never, anywhere, monolithic. It is full of contradictions, perpetually shifting and modifying itself as struggles within the culture continue and as contradictions and conflicts develop. American film is both the carrier of the dominant ideology and a reflector, occasionally even an arbitrator, of the changes and shifts within it.[8] Film tends to support the dominant ideology when it presents itself as unmediated reality, entertaining the viewer while reinforcing accepted notions of love, heroism, domesticity, class structure, sexuality, history. During the late sixties and early seventies, some film questioned assumptions, as some directors became more independent and more in control of their work. In the eighties, American film once again became a great affirming force and, in some instances, went beyond affirmation to the active creation of ideological images and attitudes, forming discourses of power for the powerless. In the discussions that follow, I will attempt to define and account for both events.

The essential point for the analysis that follows is that narrative film is *fiction*, not reality. It substitutes images and sounds for "real" experience, and with those images and sounds communicates to us and manipulates particular feelings, ideas, and perspectives on reality. Film is not innocent, not *merely* entertainment, and most especially not divorced from the culture out of which it comes and into which it feeds. This is why I find it impossible to talk about the events and the characters of films as if they had an existence separate from the formal apparatus that creates the fiction they inhabit. While I will discuss conventional notions of motivation and character psychology, these discussions should always be seen in the context of the various structures and conventions of the cinematic fiction and the viewer's perception of them. The nature of conventional fiction is to present a clean and concentrated view of life. Even if this view is made to include ambiguities and questions, it is always neater than anything perceived in the loose and open narratives that constitute daily life. I want to return the fiction to its proper place as artifice, as something made, and to reduce the emotional aura that most American film narratives create in the viewer, in an attempt to understand the sources of that aura.

A few further things by way of methodology. Most of the films discussed here have been viewed, closely, on an editing table or VCR. I have therefore been able to look at them somewhat in the manner of reading a book, stopping, starting, going back and forth at will. This is, of course, not the way the films are generally seen by an audience. One of the many powers the film narrative exercises over the viewer is the inexorability of its telling. But because of videotape, more and more viewers are able to counter this power and re-create the privileged viewing situation once the reserve of filmmakers or critics with access to archives (though there are major problems created by the poor resolution of the videotaped image and the inaccurate rendering of screen width). To give one's self over to the controlling spell of a film narrative is now more an expression of desire rather than necessity. Some readers may wish to use this new access to material along with the book in order to discover the mechanisms of the films.

One thing that will be discovered is that, despite the greater availibility of the image, the ability to create an accurate verbal rendering of it remains elusive. At best, the descriptions may recall or allude to what exists in the film for the purposes of analysis; they may occasionally evoke; they will never take the place of the images themselves. The verbal description is always tenuous and subject to correction.

There are two textual components of film that do not receive here the attention they should. One is music; the other is film acting. The reason for their slight treatment is, frankly, a feeling of inadequacy on my part to deal with them in any but a cursory way. Film criticism has yet to develop an analytic vocabulary appropriate to the complexity of music's interaction with the narrative, or its function in helping to create the narrative. (Eisenstein made a start many years ago, but certainly the difficulties involved in learning music theory have prevented film critics from carrying his work forward.) While it is difficult to analyze the relationships between music and narrative within a particular film, one can comment on larger trends in film music: the return of the symphonic score in the late seventies; the domination of the synthesizer in the eighties. Nor is there a vocabulary adequate to an accurate and objective discussion about film acting: what it is and how it affects the film and its audience, how an individual creates a presence on the screen, what that presence is, and what the viewer's relationship is to it. Part of the problem lies in the difficulty of overcoming the Hollywood cult of personality. The serious critic may talk about the director, but the publicist and reviewer still sell the picture by the star. This phenomenon tends to pull attention away from the film itself and focus attention on the individual—who, more often than not, is a person built up by the accretion of his or her roles and publicity (Humphrey Bogart, John Wayne, Marilyn Monroe are examples)—rather than look closely at what is being created within the particular film under discussion. When critical examination is given to character in the particular film, the tendency is to fall into the trap of psychological realism I noted earlier and begin discussing the character as if he or she had an existence rather than a function within the total narrative structure. Between these extremes fall the adjectives: such and such a player gave an "edgy" or "nervous" performance, was "brilliant," was "absorbed" in the role. And, that final refuge of unexamined assumptions, was "believable."

I have few alternatives to these problems except to emphasize the fact that performance is one part of the film's structure and most interesting when integrated within the total design. I will be examining a few actors who move through more than one film under discussion: Gene Hackman appears in *Bonnie and Clyde, Night Moves, Target*, and *The Conversation*; Warren Beatty in *Mickey One, Bonnie and Clyde*, and *McCabe and Mrs. Miller*; Robert De Niro in *Mean Streets, Taxi Driver, New York, New York, Raging Bull*, and *The King of Comedy*. Discussion of the characters they play may give some indication of their style and through this some indication of the changing forms of acting styles in recent film and how the relationship between actor and director is drawn. But much work remains to be done in this area.[9]

Finally, all of the filmmakers given major attention in this study are still working. Their careers are in progress and their future films will continue to prove or deny what is said about their work to date. Because of this I have avoided anything like a grand summary or an overall evaluation of what they have done. This book is deeply opinionated, but hardly final.

Notes

1 Some of the ideas for the decline of Hollywood production values and shifts in studio personnel during the late forties were developed with David Parker. An excellent summary of the changes in Hollywood from the late forties through the sixties—from which much of the information in this section is drawn—can be found in Robert Sklar, *Movie-Made America: A Cultural History of American Movies* (New York: Vintage Books, 1994), 249–304. See also Gordon Gow, *Hollywood in the Fifties* (New York: A. S. Barnes, 1971); John Baxter, *Hollywood in the Sixties* (New York: A. S. Barnes, 1972); Axel Madsen, *The New Hollywood: American Movies in the Seventies* (New York: Crowell, 1975); William Paul, "Hollywood Harakiri," *Film Comment* 13 (March–April 1977); Stephen M. Silverman, "Hollywood Cloning: Sequels, Prequels, Remakes, and Spinoffs," *American Film* 3 (July–August 1978), 24–30. For an excellent study of the financial character of the studios, see Douglas Gomery, "The American Film Industry of the 1970s: Stasis in the 'New Hollywood'," *Wide Angle* 5, No. 4 (1983), 52–59. More recent studies of Hollywood economics include Justin Wyatt, *High Concept: Movies and Marketing in Hollywood* (Austin: University of Texas Press, 1994); Steve Neale and Murray Smith, eds., *Contemporary Hollywood Cinema* (New York and London: Routledge, 1998) and Jon Lewis, ed., *The New American Cinema* (Durham, N.C., and London: Duke University Press, 1998).
2 See James Monaco, *The New Wave* (New York: Oxford University Press, 1976), 3–12. Monaco's remains the best study of the French movement and has served as something of a model for this book.
3 In recent years, filmmaking in France has fallen on hard times. The initial cohesion is gone, and while critical commitment remained strong—at least until the early eighties—production has reverted to the classical, linear style. Many French films are now made with an American audience in mind. See David L. Overby, "France: The Newest Wave," *Sight and Sound* 47 (Spring 1978), 86–90; Annette Insdorf, "French Films American Style," *New York Times* (July 28, 1985), H16.
4 Many people have examined the phenomenon of film's effacing its existence as film. Two out of many possible references are Colin MacCabe, "Realism and the Cinema: Notes on Some Brechtian Theses," *Tracking the Signifier* (Minneapolis: University of Minnesota Press, 1985), 33–57; Christian Metz, *The Imaginary Signifier*, trans. Celia Britton, Annwyl Williams, Ben Brewster, Alfred Guzzetti (Bloomington: Indiana University Press, 1982), 3–68. For the idea of fiction as lie and substitution, see Umberto Eco, *A Theory of Semiotics* (Bloomington and London: Indiana University Press, 1976), 6–7.
5 Louis Althusser, *Language and Materialism* (London: Routledge & Kegan Paul, 1977), 67. The second quotation from Althusser comes from *For Marx*, trans. Ben Brewster (New York: Random House, Vintage Books, 1970), 252. For a direct application of ideological theory to cinema studies, see Jean-Louis Comolli and Jean Narboni, "Cinema/Ideology/Criticism," in Bill Nichols, ed., *Movies and Methods*, Vol. I (Berkeley and Los Angeles: University of California Press, 1976), 23–30; Editors of *Cahiers du Cinéma*, "John Ford's *Young Mr. Lincoln*," in *Movies and Methods* I, 493–529. The April 1978 issue of *Jump Cut* (No. 17) has an excellent series of essays summarizing the subject. See also Bill Nichols, *Ideology and the Image* (Bloomington: Indiana University Press, 1981).

6 Terry Eagleton, *Literary Theory* (Minneapolis: University of Minnesota Press, 1983), 172, 210.
7 See Michael Rosenthal, "Ideology, Determinism and Relative Autonomy," *Jump Cut*, No. 17 (April 1978), 19–22.
8 Some recent work on film music includes Kathryn Kalinak, *Settling the Score: Music and the Classical Hollywood Film* (Madison: University of Wisconsin Press, 1992) and Caryl Flinn, *Strains of Utopia: Gender, Nostalgia, and Hollywood Film Music* (Princeton, N.J.: Princeton University Press, 1992).
9 One of the first serious discussions of acting is Richard Dyer, *Stars* (London: The British Film Institute, 1979). Some more recent attempts to open up a serious discourse on acting include James Naremore's *Acting in the Cinema* (Berkeley and Los Angeles: University of California Press, 1988) and Christine Gledhill, ed., *Stardom: Industry of Desire* (London and New York: Routledge, 1991).

Part 4

THE NEW HOLLYWOOD

14

THE NEW HOLLYWOOD

Thomas Schatz

Source: Jim Collins, Hillary Radner and Ava Preacher Collins (eds), *Film Theory Goes to the Movies*, New York: Routledge, 1993, pp. 8–36, 265–268.

Among the more curious and confounding terms in media studies is "the New Hollywood." In its broadest historical sense the term applies to the American cinema after World War II, when Hollywood's entrenched "studio system" collapsed and commercial television began to sweep the newly sub-urbanized national landscape. That marked the end of Hollywood's "classical" era of the 1920s, 1930s, and early 1940s, when movies were mass produced by a cartel of studios for a virtually guaranteed market. All that changed in the postwar decade, as motion pictures came to be produced and sold on a film-by-film basis and as "watching TV" rapidly replaced "going to the movies" as America's preferred ritual of habituated, mass-mediated narrative entertainment.[1]

Ensuing pronouncements of the "death of Hollywood" proved to be greatly exaggerated, however; the industry not only survived but flourished in a changing media marketplace. Among the more remarkable developments in recent media history, in fact, is the staying power of the major studios (Paramount, MGM, Warners, et al.) and of the movie itself—that is, the theatrically released feature film—in an increasingly vast and complex "entertainment industry." This is no small feat, considering the changes Hollywood has faced since the late 1940s. The industry adjusted to those changes, and in the process its ways of doing business and of making movies changed as well—and thus the difficulty in defining the New Hollywood, which has meant something different from one period of adjustment to another.

The key to Hollywood's survival and the one abiding aspect of its postwar transformation has been the steady rise of the movie blockbuster. In terms of budgets, production values, and market strategy, Hollywood has been increasingly hit-driven since the early 1950s. This marks a significant departure from the classical era, when the studios turned out a few "prestige"

285

pictures each year and relished the occasional runaway box-office hit, but relied primarily on routine A-class features to generate revenues. The exceptional became the rule in postwar Hollywood, as the occasional hit gave way to the calculated blockbuster.

The most obvious measure of this blockbuster syndrome is box-office revenues, which have indeed surged over the past forty years.[2] In 1983, *Variety* commissioned a study of the industry's all-time commercial hits in "constant dollars"—that is, in figures adjusted for inflation—which placed only two films made before 1950, *Gone With the Wind* (1939) and *Snow White and the Seven Dwarfs* (1937), in the top 75.[3] In other words, of the 7,000 or so Hollywood features released before 1950, only two enjoyed the kind of success that has become routine since then—and particularly in the past two decades. According to *Variety's* most recent (January, 1992) update of the all-time "film rental champs," 90 of the top 100 hits have been produced since 1970, and all of the top 20 since *Jaws* in 1975.[4]

The blockbuster syndrome went into high gear in the mid-1970s, despite (and in some ways because of) the concurrent emergence of competing media technologies and new delivery systems, notably pay-cable TV and home video (VCRs). This was the first period of sustained economic vitality and industry stability since the classical era. Thus this post-1975 era best warrants the term "the New Hollywood," and for essentially the same reasons associated the "classical" era. Both terms connote not only specific historical periods, but also characteristic qualities of the movie industry at the time—particularly its economic and institutional structure, its mode of production, and its system of narrative conventions.

This is not to say that the New Hollywood is as stable or well integrated as the classical Hollywood, however. As we will see, the government's postwar dismantling of the "vertically integrated" studio system ensured a more competitive movie marketplace, and a more fundamentally disintegrated industry as well. The marketplace became even more fragmented and uncertain with the emergence of TV and other media industries, and with the massive changes in lifestyle accompanying suburban migration and the related family/housing/baby boom. In one sense the mid-1970s ascent of the New Hollywood marks the studios' eventual coming-to-terms with an increasingly fragmented entertainment industry—with its demographics and target audiences, its diversified "multimedia" conglomerates, its global(ized) markets and new delivery systems. And equally fragmented, perhaps, are the movies themselves, especially the high-cost, high-tech, high-stakes block-busters, those multi-purpose entertainment machines that breed music videos and soundtrack albums, TV series and videocassettes, video games and theme park rides, novelizations and comic books.

Hollywood's mid-1970s restabilization came after some thirty years of uncertainty and disarray. I would suggest, in fact, that the movie industry underwent three fairly distinct decade-long phases after the War—from 1946 to 1955, from 1956 to 1965, and from 1966 to 1975. These phases were distinguished by various developments both inside and outside the industry, and four in particular: the shift to independent motion picture production, the changing role of the studios, the emergence of commercial TV, and changes in American lifestyle and patterns of media consumption. The key markers in these phases were huge hits like *The Ten Commandments* in 1956, *The Sound of Music* in 1965, and *Jaws* in 1975 which redefined the nature, scope, and profit potential of the blockbuster movie, and which lay the foundation for the films and filmmaking practices of the New Hollywood.

To understand the New Hollywood, we need to chart these postwar phases and the concurrent emergence of the blockbuster syndrome in American filmmaking. Our ultimate focus, though, will be on the post-1975 New Hollywood and its complex interplay of economic, aesthetic, and technological forces. If recent studies of classical Hollywood have taught us anything, it is that we cannot consider either the filmmaking process or films themselves in isolation from their economic, technological, and industrial context. As we will see, this interplay of forces is in many ways even more complex in the New Hollywood, especially when blockbusters are involved. In today's media marketplace, it has become virtually impossible to identify or isolate the "text" itself, or to distinguish a film's aesthetic or narrative quality from its commercial imperatives. As Eileen Meehan suggests in a perceptive study of *Batman*, to analyze contemporary movies "we must be able to understand them as always and simultaneously text and commodity, intertext and product line."[5]

The goal of this essay is to situate that "understanding" historically, tracing the emergence and the complex workings of the New Hollywood. The emphasis throughout will be on the high-cost, high-tech, high-stakes productions that have driven the postwar movie industry—and that now drive the global multimedia marketplace at large. While one crucial dimension of the New Hollywood is the "space" that has been opened for independent and alternative cinema, the fact is that these mainstream hits are where stars, genres, and cinematic innovations invariably are established, where the "grammar" of cinema is most likely to be refined, and where the essential qualities of the medium—its popular and commercial character—are most evident. These blockbuster hits are, for better or worse, what the New Hollywood is about, and thus are the necessary starting point for any analysis of contemporary American cinema.

Hollywood in transition

The year 1946 marked the culmination of a five-year "war boom" for Hollywood, with record revenues of over $1.5 billion and weekly ticket sales of 90 to 100 million.[6] The two biggest hits in 1946 were "major independent" productions: Sam Goldwyn's *The Best Years of Our Lives* and David O.

Selznick's *Duel in the Sun*. Both returned $11.3 million in rentals, a huge sum at the time, and signaled important changes in the industry—though Selznick's *Duel* was the more telling of the two.[7] Like his *Gone With the Wind*, it was a prototype New Hollywood blockbuster: a "pre-sold" spectacle (based on a popular historical novel) with top stars, an excessive budget, a sprawling story, and state-of-the-art production values. Selznick himself termed *Duel* "an exercise in making a big-grossing film," gambling on a nationwide promotion-and-release campaign after weak sneak previews.[8] When the gamble paid off, he proclaimed it a "tremendous milestone in motion picture merchandising and exhibition."[9]

That proved to be prophetic, given Hollywood's wholesale postwar transformation, which was actually well under way in 1946. The Justice Department's pursuit of Hollywood's major powers for antitrust practices began to show results in the courts that year, and culminated in the Supreme Court's May 1948 *Paramount* decree, which forced the major studios to divest their theater chains and to cease various tactics which had enabled them to control the market. Without the cash flow from their theaters and a guaranteed outlet for their product, the established studio system was effectively finished. The studios gradually fired their contract personnel and phased out active production, and began leasing their facilities for independent projects, generally providing co-financing and distribution as well. This shift to "one-film deals" also affected the established relations of power, with top talent (and their agents and attorneys) gaining more authority over production.[10]

The studios' new role as financing-and-distribution entities also jibed with other industry developments. The war boom had ended rather suddenly in 1947 as the economy slumped and, more importantly, as millions of couples married, settled down, and started families—many of them moving to the suburbs and away from urban centers, where movie business thrived. Declining attendance at home was complemented by a decline in international trade in 1947–1948, notably in the newly reopened European markets where "protectionist" policies were initiated to foster domestic production and to restrict the revenues that could be taken out of the country. This encouraged the studios to enter into co-financing and co-production deals overseas, which complemented the changing strategy at home and fueled the general postwar rise in motion picture imports as well as independent production.

Another crucial factor on the domestic front was, of course, television. Early on, the major studios had met the competition head on with efforts to differentiate movies from TV programs. There was a marked increase in historical spectacles, Westerns, and biblical epics, invariably designed for a global market and shot on location with international casts. These were enhanced by the increased use of Technicolor and by innovations in technology, notably widescreen formats and 3-D. These efforts soon began paying off despite TV's continued growth, as *Fortune*'s Freeman Lincoln pointed out in a 1955 piece aptly titled, "The Comeback of the Movies." Lincoln noted that, traditionally, "any picture that topped $5 million worldwide was a smash hit," and he estimated that only about 100 Hollywood releases had ever reached that total. "In September, 1953, 20th Century-Fox released *The Robe*, which has since grossed better than $20 million around the world and is expected to surpass $30 million," wrote Lincoln, and pointed out that "in the 17 months since *The Robe* was turned loose nearly 30 pictures have grossed more than the previously magic $5 million."[11]

As Hollywood's blockbuster mentality took hold in 1955, the majors finally ventured into television. MGM, Warners, and Fox, taking a cue from Disney and the lesser Hollywood powers already involved in "telefilm" series production, began producing filmed series of their own in the Fall of 1955.[12] And late that year the majors also began to sell or lease their pre-1948 features to TV syndicators. In 1956 alone, some 3,000 feature films went into syndication; by 1958, all of the majors had unloaded hundreds of pre-1948 films.[13] In 1960, the studios and talent guilds agreed on residual payments for post-1948 films, leading to another wave of movie syndication and to Hollywood movies being scheduled in regular prime-time. Telefilm production was also on the rise in the late 1950s, as the studios relied increasingly on TV series to keep their facilities in constant operation, since more and more feature films were shot on location. The studios also had begun realizing sizable profits from the syndication of hit TV series, both as reruns in the U.S. and as first-run series abroad. As the studios upgraded series production and as the preferred programming format shifted from live video to telefilm—despite the introduction of videotape in 1957—the networks steadily shifted their production operations from New York to Los Angeles. By 1960 virtually all prime-time fictional series were produced on film in Hollywood, with the traditional studio powers dominating this trend.

Meanwhile the blockbuster mentality intensified. Lincoln had suggested in his 1955 *Fortune* piece, "The beauty of the big picture nowadays is, of course, that there seems to be no limit to what the box office return may be."[14] The ensuing decade bore this out with a vengeance, bracketed by two colossal hits: *The Ten Commandments* in 1956, with domestic rentals of $43 million (versus *The Robe*'s $17.5 million), and *The Sound of Music* in 1965, with rentals of $79.9 million. Other top hits from the decade included similarly "big" all-star projects, most of them shot on location for an international market:

Around the World in 80 Days (1956; $23 million in rentals)
The Bridge on the River Kwai (1957; $17.2 million)
South Pacific (1958; $17.5 million)
Ben-Hur (1959; $36.5 million)
Lawrence of Arabia (1962; $17.7 million)
The Longest Day (1962; $17.6 million)
Cleopatra (1963; $26 million)

Goldfinger (1964; $23 million)
Thunderball (1965; $28.5 million)
Dr. Zhivago (1965; $46.5 million)

While these mega-hits dominated the high end of Hollywood's output, the studios looked for ways beyond TV series production to diversify their media interests. Besides the need to hedge their bets on high-stakes blockbusters, this impulse to diversify was a response to the postwar boom in entertainment and leisure activities, the increasing segmentation of media audiences in a period of general prosperity and population growth, and the sophisticated new advertising and marketing strategies used to measure and attract those audiences. MCA was the clear industry leader in terms of diversification, having expanded from a music booking and talent agency in the 1930s and 1940s into telefilm production and syndication in the 1950s, eventually buying Decca Records and then Universal Pictures in the early 1960s.

The 1950s and 1960s also saw diversified, segmented moviegoing trends, most of them keyed to the immense, emergent "youth market." With the baby boom generation reaching active consumer status and developing distinctive interests and tastes, there was a marked surge in drive-in moviegoing, itself a phenomenon directly associated with post-war suburbanization and the family boom. With the emergent youth market, drive-in viewing fare turned increasingly to low-budget "teenpics" and "exploitation" films. The "art cinema" and foreign film movements also took off in the late 1950s and early 1960s, as neighborhood movie houses and campus film societies screened alternatives to mainstream Hollywood and as film courses began springing up on college campuses. These indicated a more "cine-literate" generation—with that literacy actually enhanced by TV, which had become a veritable archive of American film history.

While the exploitation and art cinema movements produced a few commercial hits—Hitchcock's *Psycho* and Fellini's *La Dolce Vita* in 1960, for instance—the box office was dominated well into the 1960s by much the same blockbuster mentality as in previous decades. Indeed, the biopics, historical and biblical epics, literary adaptations, and transplanted stage musicals of the 1950s and 1960s differed from the prestige pictures of the classical era only in their oversized budgets, casts, running times, and screen width. If the emergent youth culture and increasingly diversified media marketplace were danger signs, they were lost on the studios—particularly after the huge commercial success of two very traditional mainstream films in 1965, *The Sound of Music* and *Dr. Zhivago*.

Actually, Hollywood was on the verge of its worst economic slump since the War—fueled to a degree by those two 1965 hits, because they led to a cycle of expensive, heavily promoted commercial flops. Fox, for instance, went on a blockbuster musical binge in an effort to replicate its success with *The Sound of Music*, and the results were disastrous: losses of $11 million on

Dr. Dolittle in 1967, $15 million on *Star!* in 1968, and $16 million in 1969 on *Hello Dolly*, at the time the most expensive film ever made.[15] Fox then tightened its belt, avoiding bankruptcy thanks to two relatively inexpensive, offbeat films: *Butch Cassidy and the Sundance Kid* (1969; $46 million in rentals), and *MASH* (1970; $36.7 million).

Those two hits were significant for a number of reasons besides the reversal of Fox's fortunes, reasons which signaled changes of aesthetic as well as economic direction in late-1960s Hollywood. With the blockbuster strategy stalled, the industry saw a period of widespread and unprecedented innovation, due largely to a new "generation" of Hollywood filmmakers like Robert Altman, Arthur Penn, Mike Nichols, and Bob Rafelson, who were turning out films that had as much in common with the European art cinema as with classical Hollywood. There was also a growing contingent of international auteurs—Bergman, Fellini, Truffaut, Bertolucci, Polanski, Kubrick—who, in the wake of the 1966 success of Antonioni's *Blow-Up* and Claude Lelouch's *A Man and a Woman*, developed a quasi-independent rapport with Hollywood, making films for a Euro-American market and bringing art cinema into the mainstream.

Thus an "American film renaissance" of sorts was induced by a succession of big-budget flops and successful imports. Its key constituency was the American youth, by now the most dependable segment of regular moviegoers as attendance continued to fall despite the overall increase in population. Younger viewers contributed heavily to the success of sizable hits like *Bonnie and Clyde* (1967; rentals of $22.8 million), *2001: A Space Odyssey* (1968; $25.5 million), and *The Graduate* (1968; $43 million), and they were almost solely responsible for modest hits like *Easy Rider* (1969; $19 million) and *Woodstock* (1970; $16.4 million). As these films suggest, the older baby boomers were reaching critical mass as a target market and were something of a countercultural force as well, caught up in the antiwar movement, civil rights, the sexual revolution, and so on. And with the 1966 breakdown of Hollywood's Production Code and the emergence in 1968 of the new ratings system—itself a further indication of the segmented movie audiences— filmmakers were experimenting with more politically subversive, sexually explicit, and/or graphically violent material.

As one might suspect. Hollywood's cultivation of the youth market and penchant for innovation in the late 1960s and early 1970s scarcely indicated a favorable market climate. On the contrary, they reflected the studios' uncertainty and growing desperation. Film historian Tino Balio has written about "the Recession of 1969" and its aftermath, when "Hollywood nearly collapsed."[16] *Variety* at the time pegged combined industry losses for 1969–1971 at $600 million, and according to an economic study by Joseph Dominick, studio profits fell from an average of $64 million in the five-year span from 1964 to 1968, to $13 million from 1969 to 1973.[17] Market conditions rendered the studios ripe for takeover, and in fact a number of the studios were absorbed in a post-1965 conglomerate wave. Paramount was taken over by Gulf & Western in 1966, United Artists by Transamerica in 1967, and Warner Bros. by Kinney National Services in 1969, the same year MGM was bought out by real-estate tycoon Kirk Kerkorian. This trend proved to be a mixed blessing for the studios. The cash-rich parent company relieved much of the financial pressures and spurred diversification, but the new owners knew little about the movie business and, as the market worsened, tended to view their Hollywood subsidiaries as troublesome tax write-offs.

One bright spot during this period was the surge in network prices paid for hit movies. Back in 1961, NBC had paid Fox an average of $180,000 for each feature shown on *Saturday Night at the Movies*; that year 45 features were broadcast in prime time. By 1970, the average price tag per feature was up to $800,000, with the networks spending $65 million on a total of 166 feature films. That total jumped to 227 for the 1971–1972 season, when movies comprised over one quarter of all prime-time programming. The average price went up as well, due largely to ABC's paying $50 million in the Summer of 1971 for a package of blockbusters, including $5 million for *Lawrence of Arabia*, $3 million for the 1970 hit, *Love Story*, and $2.5 million each for seven James Bond films.[18] Significantly enough, however, these big payoffs were going only to top Hollywood hits as all three networks began producing their own TV-movies. Hollywood features comprised only half of the movies shown on network TV in the 1971–1972 season, and that percentage declined further in subsequent years, as made-for-TV movie production increased.

The network payoff for top movie hits scarcely reversed the late-sixties downturn, as *The Graduate* in 1968 was the only release between 1965 and 1969 to surpass even $30 million in rentals. *Butch Cassidy, Airport*, and *Love Story* in 1969–1970 all earned $45 to $50 million, carrying much of the freight in those otherwise bleak economic years. *Airport* was especially important in that it generated a cycle of successful "disaster pictures" like *The Poseidon Adventure, The Towering Inferno*, and *Earthquake*, all solid performers in the $40 to $50 million range, though they were fairly expensive to produce and not quite the breakaway hits that the industry so desperately needed.

The first real sign of a reversal of the industry's sagging fortunes came with *The Godfather*, a 1972 Paramount release that returned over $86 million. *The Godfather* was that rarest of movies, a critical and commercial smash with widespread appeal, drawing art cinema connoisseurs and disaffected youth as well as mainstream moviegoers. Adapted from Mario Puzo's novel while it was still in galleys, the project was scarcely mounted as a surefire hit. Director Francis Ford Coppola was a debt-ridden film school product with far more success as a writer, and star Marlon Brando hadn't had a hit in over a decade. The huge sales of the novel, published while the film was in production, generated interest, as did well-publicized stories of problems on the set, cost overruns, and protests from Italian-American groups. By the time of its release, *The Godfather* had attained "event" status, and audiences responded to Coppola's stylish and highly stylized hybrid of the gangster genre and family melodrama. Like so many 1970s films, *The Godfather* had a strong nostalgic quality, invoking the male ethos and patriarchal order of a bygone era—and putting its three male co-stars, Al Pacino, James Caan, and Robert Duvall, on the industry map.

The Godfather also did well in the international market, thus spurring an upturn in the overseas as well as the domestic market. Domestic theater admissions in 1972 were up roughly 20 percent over 1971, reversing a 7-year slide, and total box-office revenues surged from the $1 billion range, where they had stagnated for several years, to $1.64 billion. While *The Godfather* alone accounted for nearly 10 percent of those gross proceeds, other films clearly were contributing; revenues for the top ten box-office hits of 1972 were up nearly 70 percent over the previous year. That momentum held through 1973 and then the market surged again in 1974, nearing the $2 billion mark—and thus finally surpassing Hollywood's postwar box-office peak. Key to the upturn were the now-predictable spate of disaster films, though these were far outdistanced by three hits which, in different ways, were sure signs of a changing industry.

One was *American Graffiti*, a surprise Summer 1973 hit written and directed by Coppola protégé George Lucas. A coming-of-age film with strong commercial tie-ins to both TV and rock music, the story's 1962 setting enabled Lucas to circumvent (or rather to predate) the current socio-political climate and broadened its appeal to older viewers. Two even bigger hits were late-1973 releases, *The Sting* and *The Exorcist* ($78 million and $86 million, respectively). *The Sting* was yet another nostalgia piece, a 1930s-era gangster/buddy/caper hybrid, reprising the Newman-Redford pairing of five years earlier—something like "Butch and Sundance meet the Godfather." The nostalgia and studied innocence of both *The Sting* and *American Graffiti* were hardly evident in *The Exorcist*, William Friedkin's kinetic, gut-wrenching, effects-laden exercise in screen violence and horror. While *Psycho* and *Rosemary's Baby* had proved that horror thrillers could attain hit status, *The Exorcist* pushed the logic and limits of the genre (and the viewer's capacity for masochistic pleasure) to new extremes, resulting in a truly monstrous hit and perhaps the clearest indication of the emergent New Hollywood.

Jaws and the New Hollywood

If any single film marked the arrival of the New Hollywood, it was *Jaws*, the Spielberg-directed thriller that recalibrated the profit potential of the Hollywood hit, and redefined its status as a marketable commodity and cultural phenomenon as well. The film brought an emphatic end to

Hollywood's five-year recession, while ushering in an era of high-cost, high-tech, high-speed thrillers. *Jaws'* release also happened to coincide with developments both inside and outside the movie industry in the mid-1970s which, while having little or nothing to do with that particular film, were equally important to the emergent New Hollywood.

Jaws, like *Love Story, The Godfather, The Exorcist*, and several other recent hits, was presold via a current best-selling novel. And like *The Godfather*, movie rights to the novel were purchased before it was published, and publicity from the deal and from the subsequent production helped spur the initial book sales—of a reported 7.6 million copies before the film's release in this case—which in turn fueled public interest in the film.[19] The *Jaws* deal was packaged by International Creative Management (ICM), which represented author Peter Benchley and handled the sale of the movie rights. ICM also represented the producing team of Richard Zanuck and David Brown, whose recent hits included *Butch Cassidy* and *The Sting*, and who worked with ICM to put together the movie project with MCA/Universal and *wunderkind* director Steven Spielberg.[20]

Initially budgeted at $3.5 million, *Jaws* was expensive by contemporary standards (average production costs in 1975 were $2.5 million), but it was scarcely a big-ticket project in that age of $10 million musicals and $20 million disaster epics.[21] The budget did steadily escalate due to logistical problems and Spielberg's ever-expanding vision and confidence; in fact problems with the mechanical shark pushed the effects budget alone to over $3 million. The producers managed to parlay those problems into positive publicity, however, and continued to hype the film during post-production. The movie was planned for a Summer 1975 release due to its subject matter, even though in those years most calculated hits were released during the Christmas holidays. Zanuck and Brown compensated by spending $2.5 million on promotion, much of it invested in a media blitz during the week before the film's 464-screen opening.[22]

The print campaign featured a poster depicting a huge shark rising through the water toward an unsuspecting swimmer, while the radio and TV ads exploited John Williams's now-famous "Jaws theme." The provocative poster art and Williams's pulsating, foreboding theme conveyed the essence of the film experience and worked their way into the national consciousness, setting new standards for motion picture promotion. With the public's appetite sufficiently whetted, *Jaws'* release set off a feeding frenzy as 25 million tickets were sold in the film's first 38 days of release. After this quick start, the shark proved to have "good legs" at the box office, running strong throughout the summer en route to a record $102.5 million in rentals in 1975. In the process, *Jaws* became a veritable sub-industry unto itself via commercial tie-ins and merchandising ploys. But hype and promotion aside, *Jaws'* success ultimately centered on the appeal of the film itself; one enduring verity in the movie business is that, whatever the marketing efforts, only positive audience response and favorable word-of-mouth can propel a film to genuine hit status.

Jaws was essentially an action film and a thriller, of course, though it effectively melded various genres and story types. It tapped into the monster movie tradition with a revenge-of-nature subtext (like *King Kong, The Birds*, et al.), and in the film's latter stages the shark begins to take on supernatural, even Satanic, qualities à la *Rosemary's Baby* and *The Exorcist*. And given the fact that the initial victims are women and children, *Jaws* also had ties to the high-gore "slasher" film, which had been given considerable impetus a year earlier by *The Texas Chainsaw Massacre*. The seagoing chase in the latter half is also a buddy film and a male initiation story, with Brodie the cop, Hooper the scientist, and Quint the sea captain providing different strategies for dealing with the shark and different takes on male heroic behavior.

Technically, *Jaws* is an adept "chase film" that takes the viewer on an emotional roller coaster, first in awaiting the subsequent (and increasingly graphic) shark attacks, then in the actual pursuit of the shark. The narrative is precise and effectively paced, with each stage building to a climactic peak, then dissipating, then building again until the explosive finale. The performances, camera work, and editing are all crucial to this effect, as is John Williams's score. This was in fact the breakthrough film for Williams, the first in a run of huge hits that he scored (including *Star Wars, Close Encounters of the Third Kind, Raiders of the Lost Ark*, and *E.T.*) whose music is absolutely essential to the emotional impact of the film.

Many critics disparaged that impact, dismissing *Jaws* as an utterly mechanical (if technically flawless) exercise in viewer manipulation. James Monaco cites *Jaws* itself as the basis for the "Bruce aesthetic" (named after the film crew's pet name for the marauding robotic shark), whose ultimate cinematic effect is "visceral—mechanical rather than human." More exciting than interesting, more style than substance, *Jaws* and its myriad offspring, argues Monaco, are mere "machines of entertainment, precisely calculated to achieve their effect."[23] Others have argued, however, that *Jaws* is redeemed by several factors, notably the political critique in the film's first half, the essential humanity of Brodie, and the growing camaraderie of the three pursuers.

Critical debate aside, *Jaws* was a social, industrial, and economic phenomenon of the first order, a cinematic idea and cultural commodity whose time had come. In many ways, the film simply confirmed or consolidated various existing industry trends and practices. In terms of marketing, *Jaws*' nationwide release and concurrent ad campaign underscored the value of saturation booking and advertising, which placed increased importance on a film's box-office performance in its opening weeks of release. "Frontloading" the audience became a widespread marketing ploy, since it maximized a movie's event status while diminishing the potential damage done to weak pictures by negative reviews and poor word of mouth. *Jaws* also confirmed the viability of the "summer hit," indicating an adjustment in seasonal release tactics and a few other new moviegoing trends as well. One involved the composition and industry conceptualization of the youth market, which was shifting from the politically hip, cineliterate viewers of a few years earlier to even younger viewers with more conservative tastes and sensibilities. Demographically, this trend reflected the aging of the front-end baby boomers and the ascendence not only of their younger siblings but of their children as well—a new generation with time and spending money and a penchant for wandering suburban shopping malls and for repeated viewings of their favorite films.

This signaled a crucial shift in moviegoing and exhibition that accompanied the rise of the modern "shopping center." Until the mid-1970s, despite suburbanization and the rise of the drive-in, movie exhibition still was dominated by a select group of so-called "key run" bookings in major markets. According to Axel Madsen's 1975 study of the industry, over 60 percent of box-office revenues were generated by 1,000 key-run indoor theaters—out of a total of roughly 11,500 indoor and 3,500 outdoor theaters in the U.S.[24] Though Madsen scarcely saw it at the time, this was about to change dramatically. Between 1965 and 1970, the number of shopping malls in the U.S. increased from about 1,500 to 12,500; by 1980 the number would reach 22,500.[25] The number of indoor theaters, which had held remarkably steady from 1965 to 1974 at just over 10,000, began to increase sharply in 1975 and reached a total of 22,750 by 1990, due largely to the surge of mall-based "multi-plex" theaters.[26]

With the shifting market patterns and changing conception of youth culture, the mid-1970s also saw the rapid decline of the art cinema movement as a significant industry force. A number of films in 1974–1975 marked both the peak and, as it turned out, the waning of the Hollywood renaissance— Altman's *Nashville*, Penn's *Night Moves*, Polanski's *Chinatown*, and most notably perhaps, Coppola's *The Conversation*. The consummate American auteur and "godfather" to a generation of film-makers, Coppola's own artistic bent and maverick filmmaking left him oddly out of step with the times. While Coppola was in the Philippines filming *Apocalypse Now*, a brilliant though self-indulgent, self-destructive venture of Wellesian proportions, his protégés Lucas and Spielberg were busy refining the New Hollywood's Bruce aesthetic (via *Star Wars* and *Close Encounters*), while replacing the director-as-author with a director-as-superstar ethos.

The emergence of star directors like Lucas and Spielberg evinced not only the growing salaries and leverage of top talent, but also the increasing influence of Hollywood's top agents and talent agencies. The kind of packaging done by ICM on *Jaws* was fast becoming the rule on high-stakes projects, with ICM and another powerful agency, Creative Artists Associates (CAA), relying on aggressive packaging to compete with the venerable William Morris Agency. Interestingly enough, both ICM and CAA were created in

1974—ICM via merger and CAA by five young agents who bolted William Morris and, led by Michael Ovitz, set out to revamp the industry and upgrade the power and status of the agent-packager. For the most part they succeeded, and consequently top agents, most often from CAA or ICM, became even more important than studio executives in putting together movie projects. And not surprisingly, given this shift in the power structure, an increasing number of top studio executives after the mid-1970s came from the agency ranks.

Yet another significant mid-1970s industry trend was the elimination of tax loopholes and write-offs which had provided incentives for investors, especially those financing independent films. This cut down the number of innovative and offbeat films, although by now the critical mass of cinephiles and art cinema theaters was sufficient to sustain a vigorous alternative cinema. This conservative turn coincided with an upswing in defensive market tactics, notably an increase in sequels, series, reissues, and remakes. From 1964 to 1968, sequels and reissues combined accounted for just under five percent of all Hollywood releases. From 1974 to 1978, they comprised 17.5 percent. *Jaws*, for instance, was reissued in 1976 (as was *The Exorcist*), generating another $16 million in rentals, and in 1978 the first of several sequels, *Jaws 2*, was released, returning $49.3 million in rentals and clearly securing the Jaws "franchise."[27]

Another crucial dimension of the New Hollywood's mid-1970s emergence was the relationship between cinema and television, which was redefined altogether by three distinct developments. The first involved TV advertising which, incredibly enough, had not been an important factor in movie marketing up to that time. A breakthrough of sorts occurred in 1974 with the reissue of a low-budget independent 1971 feature, *Billy Jack*, whose director and star, Tom Laughlin, successfully sued Warner Bros. for not sufficiently promoting the film on its initial release. For the 1974 reissue, according to *Variety*, "Laughlin compelled Warners to try what was then a revolutionary marketing tactic: 'Billy Jack' received massive amounts of tv advertising support, an unheard of practice at the time."[28] The film went on to earn $32.5 million in rentals, after generating only $4 million in its initial release. This tactic gained further credibility with the *Jaws* campaign and others, soon becoming standard practice and taking motion picture marketing into a new era.

A second crucial development grew out of the FCC's 1972 Report and Order on Cable Television and the 1975 launch of SATCOM I, which effectively ended the three-network stranglehold over commercial television.[29] Pay-cable services started slowly after the 1972 ruling, but the launching of America's first commercially available geo-stationary orbit satellite—and the August 1975 decision by Home Box Office (HBO) to go onto SATCOM—changed all that. HBO immediately became a truly nationwide "movie channel" and a key player in the ancillary movie market. Cable TV proved to be a boon to Hollywood in another way as well, thanks to the FCC's "Must Carry" and "Prime Time Access" rules which increased the demand for syndicated series and movies. That in turn sent syndication prices soaring, providing another windfall for those studios producing TV series.

An even more radical change in Hollywood's relationship with television came with the introduction in 1975 of Sony's Betamax videotape recorder, thus initiating the "home-video revolution." In 1977 Matsushita, the Japanese parent company of Pioneer, JVC, and other consumer electronics companies, introduced its "video home system" (VHS), setting off a battle for the home-video market. Matsushita's VHS format prevailed for several reasons: VHS was less expensive (though technically inferior), more flexible and efficient in off-the-air recording, and Matsushita was more savvy and aggressive in acquiring "software" (i.e., the rights to movie titles) as a means of pushing its hardware.[30]

While Hollywood's initial response to the "Japanese threat" was predictably (and characteristically) negative, it became increasingly evident that the key home-video commodity was the Hollywood film—and particularly the blockbuster hit with its vast multi-media potential. And there was plenty to drive these new media industries, as Hollywood's blockbuster mentality reestablished itself with a vengeance in 1977–1978. Total domestic grosses, which had reached $2 billion for the first time in 1975, surged to $2.65 billion in 1977 and $2.8 billion in 1978, a 40 percent climb in only three years, with hits like *Star Wars, Grease, Close Encounters, Superman*, and *Saturday Night Fever* doing record business. From *The Sound of Music* in 1965 through 1976, only seven pictures (including *Jaws*) had returned $50 million in rentals; in 1977–1978 nine films surpassed that mark.

While *Star Wars* was the top hit of the period, doing $127 million in rentals in 1977 and then another $38 million as a reissue in 1978, *Saturday Night Fever* was, in its own way, an equally significant and symptomatic New Hollywood blockbuster. The film did well at the box office ($74 million in rentals) and signaled both the erosion of various industry barriers and also the multimedia potential of movie hits. The film starred TV sitcom star John Travolta, the first of many "cross-over" stars of the late-seventies and eighties. The Bee Gees soundtrack dominated the pop charts and album sales, and along with the film helped spur the "disco craze" in the club scene and recording industry. *Saturday Night Fever* also keyed the shift from the traditional Hollywood musical to the "music movie," a dominant eighties form, and was an obvious precursor to MTV.

In terms of story, *Saturday Night Fever* was yet another male coming-of-age film, centering on the Travolta character's quest for freedom, self-expression, and the Big Time as a dancer on Broadway. The age-old male initiation rite had found new life in Hollywood with the success of *The Graduate* and the emergent youth market, and proved exceptionally well suited to changes in the industry and the marketplace during the 1970s. One measure of its adaptability and appeal was *Star Wars*, which charts Luke Skywalker's initiation into manhood in altogether different terms—though here too the coming-of-age story, while providing the spine of the film, is developed in remarkably superficial terms. Indeed, *Star Wars* is so fast-paced ("breathtaking," in movie ad-speak) and resolutely plot-driven that character depth and development are scarcely on the narrative agenda.

This emphasis on plot over character marks a significant departure from classical Hollywood films, including *The Godfather* and even *Jaws*, wherein plot tended to emerge more organically as a function of the drives, desires, motivations, and goals of the central characters. In *Star Wars* and its myriad successors, however, particularly male action-adventure films, characters (even "the hero") are essentially plot functions. *The Godfather* and *Star Wars*, for example, are in many ways quite similar but ultimately very different kinds of stories. Like *Star Wars, The Godfather* is itself a male action film, a drama of succession, and a coming-of-age story centering on Michael's ascension to warrior status by fighting the "gang wars." Both films have a mythic dimension, and are in fact variations on the Arthurian legend. But where *Star Wars* is so obviously and inexorably plot-driven, *The Godfather* develops its story in terms of character—initially Don Corleone, then sons Sonny and Michael, and finally Michael alone—whose decisions and actions define the narrative trajectory of the film.

This is not to say that *Star Wars* does not "work" as a narrative, but that the way it works may indicate a shift in the nature of film narrative. From *The Godfather* to *Jaws* to *Star Wars*, we see films that are increasingly plot-driven, increasingly visceral, kinetic, and fast-paced, increasingly reliant on special effects, increasingly "fantastic" (and thus apolitical), and increasingly targeted at younger audiences. And significantly enough, the lack of complex characters or plot in *Star Wars* opens the film to other possibilities, notably its radical amalgamation of genre conventions and its elaborate play of cinematic references. The film, as J. Hoberman has said, "pioneered the genre pastiche—synthesizing a methodology so soulless that its most human characters were a pair of robots."[31] The hell-bent narrative careers from one genre-coded episode to another—from Western to war film to vine-swinging adventure—and also effectively melds different styles and genres in individual sequences. The bar scene early on which introduces Han Solo's character, for instance, is an inspired amalgam of Western, film noir, hardboiled detective, and sci fi. Thus the seemingly one-dimensional characters and ruthlessly linear chase-film plotting are offset by a purposeful incoherence which actually "opens" the film to different readings (and readers), allowing for multiple interpretive strategies and thus broadening the potential audience appeal. This is reinforced by the film's oddly nostalgic quality, due mainly to its evocations of old movie serials and TV series (*Flash Gordon*, *Captain Video*, and so on), references that undoubtedly are lost on younger viewers but relished by their cineliterate parents and senior siblings.

Like *Jaws*, Lucas's space epic is a masterwork of narrative technique and film technology. It too features an excessive John Williams score and signature musical theme, and Lucas's general attention to sound and audio effects was as widely praised as the visuals. Indeed, while the film was shut out in its major Oscar nominations (best picture, director, and screenplay), it won Academy Awards for editing, art direction, costume design, visual effects, and musical score, along with a special achievement award for sound effects editing. And although *Star Wars* was the twenty-first feature to be released with a Dolby soundtrack, it was the first to induce theater owners to install Dolby sound systems.[32] There were countless commercial tie-ins, as well as a multi-billion dollar licensing and merchandising bonanza. And strictly as a movie franchise it had tremendous legs, as this inventory of its first decade well indicates:

May 1977 *Star Wars* released
July 1978 *Star Wars* reissue #1
May 1979 *Star Wars* reissue #2
May 1980 *Star Wars* sequel #1: *The Empire Strikes Back*
Apr 1981 *Star Wars* reissue #3
May 1982 *Star Wars* available on videocassette
Aug 1982 *Star Wars* reissue #4
Feb 1983 *Star Wars* appears on pay-cable TV
May 1983 *Star Wars* sequel #2: *Return of the Jedi*
Feb 1984 *Star Wars* on network TV
Mar 1985 *Star Wars* trilogy screened in 8 cities
Jan 1987 "Star Tours" opens at Disneyland[33]

The promise of *Jaws* was confirmed by *Star Wars*, the only other film at the time to surpass $100 million in rentals. *Star Wars* also secured Lucas's place with Spielberg as charter member of "Hollywood's delayed New Wave," as J. Hoberman put it, a group of brash young filmmakers (Brian DePalma, John Landis, Lawrence Kasdan, John Carpenter, et al.) steeped in movie lore whose "cult blockbusters" and genre hybrids elevated "the most vital and disreputable genres of their youth . . . to cosmic heights."[34] Perhaps inevitably, Lucas and Spielberg decided to join forces—a decision they made, as legend has it, while vacationing in Hawaii in May 1977, a week before the release of *Star Wars*, and during a break between the shooting and editing of *Close Encounters*. Lucas was mulling over an idea for a movie serial about the exploits of an adventurer-anthropologist; Spielberg loved the idea, and he convinced Lucas to write and produce the first installment, and to let him direct.[35]

The result, of course, was *Raiders of the Lost Ark*, the huge 1981 hit that established the billion-dollar Indiana Jones franchise and further solidified the two filmmakers in the New Hollywood pantheon. Indeed, whether working together or on their own projects—notably Spielberg on *E.T.* and Lucas on the *Star Wars* sequels—the two virtually rewrote the box-office record books in the late 1970s and 1980s. With the release of their third Indiana Jones collaboration in 1989, Lucas and Spielberg could claim eight of the ten biggest hits in movie history, all of them surpassing $100 million in rentals.[36] Seven of those hits came out in the decade following the release of *Jaws*, a period that Hoberman has aptly termed "ten years that shook the world" of cinema, and that A.D. Murphy calls "the modern era of super-blockbuster films."[37]

Into the 1980s

The importance of the Lucas and Spielberg super-blockbusters can hardly be overstated, considering their impact on theatrical and video markets in the U.S., which along with the rapidly expanding global entertainment market went into overdrive in the 1980s. After surpassing $2 billion in 1975, Hollywood's domestic theatrical revenues climbed steadily from $2.75 billion in 1980 to $5 billion in both 1989 and 1990. And remarkably enough, this steady theatrical growth throughout the 1980s was outpaced rather dramatically by various "secondary markets," particularly pay-cable and home video. During the 1980s, the number of U.S. households with VCRs climbed from 1.85 million (one home in 40) to 62 million (two-thirds of all homes). Pre-recorded videocassette sales rose from only three million in 1980 to 220 million in 1990—an increase of 6,500 percent—while the number of cable households rose from 19.6 million in 1980 to 55 million in 1990, with pay subscriptions increasing from 9 million to 42 million during the decade.[38]

This growth has been a tremendous windfall for Hollywood, since both the pay-cable and home-video industries have been driven primarily by feature films, and in fact have been as hit-driven as the theatrical market. Through all the changes during the 1980s, domestic theatrical release remained the launching pad for blockbuster hits, and it established a movie's value in virtually all other secondary or ancillary markets. Yet even with the record-setting box-office revenues throughout the 1980s, the portion of the Hollywood majors' income from theater rentals actually, declined, while total revenues have soared. According to Robert Levin, president of international motion picture marketing for Disney, the domestic box office in 1978 comprised just over half (54 percent) of the majors' overall income, with a mere 4 percent coming from pay-cable and home video combined. By 1986, box-office revenues comprised barely one quarter (28 percent) of the majors' total, with pay-cable and home video combining for over half (12 percent and 40 percent respectively).[39] Home-video revenues actually exceeded worldwide theatrical revenues that year, 1986, and by decade's end cassette revenues alone actually doubled domestic box-office revenues.[40]

Another crucial secondary market for Hollywood has been the box office overseas, particularly in Europe. While the overseas pay-TV and home-video markets are still taking shape, European theatrical began surging in 1985 and reached record levels in 1990, when a number of top hits—including *Pretty Woman, Total Recall, The Little Mermaid*, and *Dances With Wolves*— actually did better box office in Europe than in the U.S.[41] And *Forbes* magazine has estimated that the European theatrical market will double by 1995, as multiplexing picks up in Western Europe and as new markets open in Eastern Europe.[42]

With the astounding growth of both theatrical and video markets and the continued stature of the Hollywood-produced feature, the American movie industry has become increasingly stable in the late 1980s. What's more, the blockbuster mentality seems to have leveled off somewhat. In the early 1980s, one or two huge hits tended to dominate the marketplace, doing well over $100 million and far outdistancing other top hits. From 1986–1990, however, the number of super-blockbuster hits dropped while the number of mid-range hits earning $10 million or more in rentals increased significantly, as did the number returning $50 million or more—still the measure of block-buster-hit status. From 1975 to 1985 ten films earned $100 million or more in rentals; there have been only four since. Meanwhile, the number of films earning $50 million or more has climbed considerably. From 1965 to 1975, only six reached this mark; from 1976 to 1980 there were 13; from 1981 to 1985 there were 17. From 1986 to 1990, 30 films surpassed $50 million in rentals.

As the economic stakes have risen so have production and marketing costs. The average "negative cost" (i.e., money spent to complete the actual film) on all major studio releases climbed from $9.4 million in 1980 to $26.8 million in 1990. Over the same period, average costs for prints and advertising rose from $4.3 million per film in 1980 to $11.6 million in 1990.[43] The rise in production costs is due largely to two dominant factors: an increased reliance on special effects and the soaring salaries paid to top talent, especially stars. The rise in marketing costs reflects Hollywood's deepening commitment to saturation booking and advertising, which has grown more expensive with the continued multiplex phenomenon and the increased ad opportunities due to cable and VCRs. The number of indoor theaters in the U.S. increased from about 14,000 in 1980 to over 22,000 in 1990, which meant that widespread nationwide release required anywhere from 1,000 to 2,700 prints, at roughly $2,500 per print. But the primary reason for rising marketing costs is TV advertising, particularly for high-stakes blockbusters. In 1990, for example, well over $20 million was spent on TV ads alone for *Dick Tracy, Total Recall*, and *Die Hard 2*.[44]

While this may seem like fiscal madness, there is method in it. Consider the performance of the three top hits of the "blockbuster Summer" in 1989, Hollywood's single biggest season ever. In a four-week span beginning

Memorial Day weekend, *Indiana Jones and the Last Crusade, Ghostbusters II*, and *Batman* enjoyed successive weekend releases in at least 2,300 theaters in the U.S. and Canada after heavy TV advertising. Each of these pre-sold entertainment machines set a new box-office record for its opening weekend, culminating in *Batman's* three-day ticket sales of $40.5 million. In an era when $100 million in gross revenues is one measure of a blockbuster hit, it took *Indiana Jones* just 19 days to reach that total; it took *Batman* 11. And like so many recent hits, all three underwent a "fast burn" at the box office. Compare these week-to-week box-office revenues on Hollywood's two all-time summer hits, *E.T.* (1982) and *Batman*, which well indicate certain crucial 1980s market trends.[45]

	wk 1	2	3	4	5	6	7	8	9	10
E.T.	$22m	22	26	24	23	23	19	19	16	15
Batman	70	52	30	24	18	13	11	8	5	4

E.T. earned another $100 million at the box office, which in 1982 was its only serious source of domestic income, while *Batman* was pulled from domestic theatrical for the home-video market—where it generated another $179 million in revenues.[46] Few recent films match *Batman's* home-video performance, and for that matter, few match its box-office legs, either. In 1990, no saturation summer releases except *Ghost* and *Pretty Woman* had any real pull beyond five weeks, although a number of films (*Total Recall, Die Hard 2, Dick Tracy*) grossed over $100 million at the box office.

The three top hits of 1990, *Home Alone, Ghost,* and *Pretty Woman*, bucked the calculated blockbuster trend and demonstrated why Hollywood relies on a steady output of "smaller" (i.e., less expensive) films which, mainly via word of mouth rather than massive pre-selling and promotion, might emerge as surprise hits. Such "sleepers" are most welcome, of course, even in this age of high-cost, high-tech, high-volume behemoths, and they invariably are well exploited once they begin to take off—as were those three surprise hits of 1990. And each undoubtedly will spawn a sequel of calculated blockbuster proportions, with the studio hoping not only for a profitable follow-up but for the kind of success that MGM/UA had with *Rocky*, a modest, offbeat sleeper in 1976 that became a billion-dollar entertainment franchise.

Many have touted the three 1990 hits as a return to reason in Hollywood filmmaking, including Disney production chief Jeffrey Katzenberg in a now legendary interoffice memo of January 1991. Katzenberg warned of "the 'blockbuster mentality' that has gripped our industry," and encouraged a return to "the kind of modest, story-driven movie we tended to make in our salad days."[47] The memo was leaked to the press and caused quite a stir, but scarcely signaled any real change at Disney or anywhere else. *Variety* subtly underscored this point by running excerpts from the memo directly below an even more prominent story with the banner headline, "Megabudgets Boom Despite Talk of Doom." That story inventoried the numerous high-cost Hollywood films "still being greenlighted," including several at Disney.[48]

In one sense, Katzenberg's memo was a rationale for *Dick Tracy*, the 1990 Disney blockbuster that cost $46 million to produce and another $55 million to market and release, with $44 million spent on advertising and promotion alone. Those figures were disclosed some two months before Katzenberg's memo and startled many industry observers, since by then the film had run its theatrical course and returned only about $60 million to Disney in rentals. But Hollywood insiders (including Katzenberg, no doubt) well understood the logic, given today's entertainment marketplace. As one competing executive told the *New York Times*, Disney had to "build awareness" of the Tracy story and character not simply to sell the film, but to establish "the value of a new character in the Disney family . . . so that it could be brought back in a sequel and used in Disney's theme parks."[49]

The future of the Tracy franchise remains to be seen, but one can hardly fault Disney for making the investment. Lip service to scaled-down movie-making aside, Hollywood's blockbuster mentality is more entrenched now than ever, the industry is more secure, and certain rules of the movie marketplace are virtually set in stone. The first is William Goldman's 1983 axiom, "nobody knows anything," which is quoted with increasing frequency these years as it grows ever more evident that, despite all the market studies and promotional strategies, the kind of public response that generates a bona fide hit simply cannot be manufactured, calculated, or predicted.[50] The studios have learned to hedge their bets and increase the odds, however, and thus these other rules—all designed not only to complement but to counter the Goldman Rule.

The most basic of these rules is that only star vehicles with solid production values have any real chance at the box office (and thus in secondary markets as well). Such films nowadays cost $20 to $30 million, and will push $50 million if top stars, special effects, and/or logistical difficulties are involved. The next rule concerns what is termed the "reward risk" factor, and holds that reaping the potential benefits of a hit requires heavy up-front spending on marketing as well as production. A corollary to this is that risk can be minimized via pre-sold pictures, and today the most effective pre-selling involves previous movie hits or other familiar media products (TV series, pop songs, comic books). An aesthetic corollary holds that films with minimal character complexity or development and by-the-numbers plotting (especially male action pictures) are the most readily reformulated and thus the most likely to be parlayed into a full-blown franchise.

Another cardinal rule is that a film's theatrical release, with its attendant media exposure, creates a cultural commodity that might be regenerated in any number of media forms: Perhaps in pop music, and not only as a hit single or musical score; note that *Batman* had two soundtrack albums and *Dick Tracy* had three. Perhaps as an arcade game, a $7 billion industry in 1990; note that *Hook* and *Terminator 2* both were released simultaneously as movies and video games. Perhaps as a theme park ride; note that Disney earns far more on its theme parks than on motion pictures and television, and that the hottest new Disney World attraction is "Toon Town," adapted from *Who Framed Roger Rabbit?*[51] Perhaps as a comic book or related item; note that the Advance Comics Special Batlist offered 214 separate pieces of *Batman*-related paraphernalia.[52] Perhaps in "novelized" form, with print (and audiocassette) versions of movie hits regularly becoming worldwide best-sellers; note that Simon and Schuster, a Paramount subdivision and the nation's largest bookseller, has devoted an entire division to its Star Trek publications.

These rules are evident not only in today's multimedia worldwide blockbusters, but also in the structure and operations of international corporate giants that produce and market them. Competing successfully in today's high-stakes entertainment marketplace requires an operation that is not only well financed and productive, but also diversified and well coordinated. John Mickelthwait of the *Economist* has written that an entertainment company "needs financial muscle to produce enough software to give itself a decent chance for bringing in a hit, and marketing muscle to make the most of that hit when it happens."[53] Thus there has been a trend toward "tight diversification" and "synergy" in the recent merger-and-acquisitions wave, bringing movie studios into direct play with television production companies, network and cable TV, music and recording companies, and book, magazine, and newspaper publishers, and possibly even with games, toys, theme parks, and electronics hardware manufacturers as well.

So obviously enough, diversification and conglomeration remain key factors in the entertainment industry, though today's media empires are much different than those of the 1960s and 1970s like Gulf & Western, Kinney, and Transamerica. Those top-heavy, widely diversified conglomerates sold out, "downsized," or otherwise regrouped to achieve tighter diversification. Gulf & Western, for instance, sold all but its media holdings by the late 1980s and changed its corporate name to Paramount Communications. Kinney created a media subsidiary in Warner Communications, which also downsized in the early 1980s—only to expand via a $13 billion marriage with Time in 1989 (to avoid a hostile $12 billion takeover by Paramount), thereby creating Time Warner, the world's largest multimedia company and a model of synergy, with holdings in movies, TV production, cable, records, and book and magazine publishing. Because movies drive the global multimedia marketplace, a key holding for any media conglomerate is a motion picture studio; but there is no typical media conglomerate these days due to the widening range of entertainment markets and rapid changes in media technology.

Conglomeration has taken on another new dimension in that several studios have been purchased by foreign media companies: Fox by Rupert Murdoch's News Corporation in 1985, Columbia by Sony in 1989, and MCA/Universal by Matsushita in 1990. The Fox purchase may have greater implications for TV than cinema, given the creation of a "fourth network" in America and its expansion into Europe. The Sony and Matsushita buyouts take the cinema-television synergy in yet another direction, since this time the two consumer electronics giants are battling over domination of the multi-billion-dollar high definition television (HDTV) market. Columbia and MCA gave the two firms sizable media libraries and active production companies, which may well give them an edge in the race not only to develop but to sell HDTV.

The Sony-Columbia and Matsushita-MCA deals are significant in terms of "talent" as well. Beyond the $3.5 billion Sony paid for Columbia, the company also spent roughly $750 million for the services of Peter Guber and Jon Peters, two successful producers (*Batman, Rain Man*, et al.) then under contact to Warners. This underscored the importance of corporate and studio management in the diversified, globalized, synergized marketplace. Indeed, the most successful companies in the mid-to-late 1980s— Paramount, Disney, Warners, and Universal—all enjoyed consistent, capable executive leadership. Successful studio management involves not only positioning movies in a global multimedia market, but also dealing effectively with top talent and their agents, which introduces other human factors into the New Hollywood equation. These factors were best indicated by the role of Michael Ovitz in both the Sony and Matsushita deals. Co-founder and chief executive of CAA, Ovitz is the most powerful agent in Hollywood's premiere agency. He was a key advisor in the Sony-Columbia deal, and in fact he packaged *Rain Man* during the negotiations and later helped arrange the Guber-Peters transaction. And Ovitz quite literally brokered the Matsushita-MCA deal, acting as the sole go-between during the year-long negotiations.[54]

Ovitz's rise to power in the New Hollywood has been due to various factors: CAA's steadily expanding client list, its packaging of top talent in highly desirable movie packages, and its capacity to secure favorable terms for its clients when cutting movie deals. In perhaps no other industry is the "art of the deal" so important, and in that regard Ovitz is Hollywood's consummate artist. He also is a master at managing relationships—whether interpersonal, institutional, or corporate, as the Columbia and MCA deals both demonstrate. And more than any other single factor, Ovitz's and CAA's success has hinged on the increasingly hit-driven nature of the entertainment industry, and in turn on the star-driven nature of top industry products.

The "star system" is as old as the movie industry itself, of course. "Marquee value," "bankable" talent, and "star vehicles" have always been vital to Hollywood's market strategy, just as the "star persona" has keyed both the narrative and production economies of moviemaking. In the classical era, in fact, studios built their entire production and marketing operations around a few prime star-genre formulas. In the New Hollywood, however, where fewer films carry much wider commercial and cultural impact, and where personas are prone to multimedia reincarnation, the star's commercial value, cultural cache, and creative clout have increased enormously. The most obvious indication of this is the rampant escalation of star salaries during the 1980s—a phenomenon often traced to Sylvester Stallone's $15 million paycheck in 1983 for *Rocky IV*.[55] Interestingly enough, many (if not most) of the seminal New Hollywood blockbusters were not star-driven; in fact many secured stardom for their lead actors. But as the blockbuster sequels and multimedia markets coalesced in the early 1980s, both the salary scale and narrative agency of top stars rose dramatically—to a point where Stallone, Arnold Schwarzenegger, Bruce Willis, Michael Douglas, Eddie Murphy, Sean Connery, and Kevin Costner earn seven or even eight figures per film, having become not only genres but franchises unto themselves, and where "star vehicles" are often simply that: stylish, careening machines designed for their star-drivers which, in terms of plot and character development, tend to go nowhere fast.

Not surprisingly, the studios bemoan their dwindling profit margins due to increased talent costs while top talent demand—and often get— "participation" deals on potential blockbusters. CAA's package for *Hook* gave Dustin Hoffman, Robin Williams, and Steven Spielberg a reported 40 percent of the box-office take, and Jack Nicholson's escalating 15 to 20 percent of the gross on *Batman* paid him upwards of $50 million.[56] While studio laments about narrowing margins are understandable, so too are agency efforts to secure a piece of the box-office take for their clients, particularly in light of the limited payoff for stars and other talent in ancillary markets and in licensing and merchandising deals. And given the potential long-term payoff of a franchise-scale blockbuster, the stars' demands are as inevitable as the studios' grudging willingness to accommodate them. As Geraldine Fabrikant suggests in a *New York Times* piece on soaring production costs: "Some studios can more easily justify paying higher prices for talent these days because, with the consolidation of the media industry and the rise of integrated entertainment conglomerates that distribute movies, books, recordings, television programming and magazines, they have more outlets through which to recoup their investments."[57]

The economics and aesthetics of the New Hollywood

This brings us back, yet again, to the New Hollywood blockbuster's peculiar status as what Eileen Meehan has aptly termed a "commercial intertext." As Meehan suggests, today's conglomerates "view every project as a multimedia production line," and thus *Batman* "is best understood as a multimedia, multimarket sales campaign."[58] Others have noted the increased interplay of moviemaking and advertising, notably Mark Crispin Miller in a cover story for the *Atlantic*, "Hollywood: The Ad." Miller opens with an indictment of the "product placement" trend in movies (a means of offsetting production costs which, as he suggests, often brings the narrative to a dead halt), and he goes on to discuss other areas where movies and advertising—especially TV advertising—have begun to merge. Like TV ads, says Miller, movies today aspire to a total "look" and seem more designed than directed, often by filmmakers segueing from studio to ad agency. And now that movies are more likely to be seen on a VCR than a theater screen, cinematic technique is adjusted accordingly, conforming with the small screen's "most hypnotic images," its ads. Visual and spatial scale are downsized, action is repetitiously foregrounded and centered, pace and transitions are quicker, music and montage are more prevalent, and slick production values and special effects abound.[59]

While Miller's view of the cinema as the last bastion of high culture under siege by the twin evils of TV and advertising displays a rather limited understanding of the contemporary culture industries, there is no question but that movie and ad techniques are intermingling. In fact, one might argue that the New Hollywood's calculated blockbusters are themselves massive advertisements for their product lines—a notion that places a very different value on their one-dimensional characters, mechanical plots, and high-gloss style. This evokes that New Hollywood buzzword, "high concept," a term best defined perhaps by its chief progenitor, Steven Spielberg, in an interview back in 1978: "What interests me more than anything else is the idea. If a person can tell me the idea in twenty-five words or less, it's going to be a good movie."[60] And a pretty good ad campaign as well—whether condensed into a 30-second movie trailer or as a feature-length plug for any number of multimedia reiterations.

This paradoxical reduction and reiteration of blockbuster movie narratives points up the central, governing contradiction in contemporary cinema. On the one hand, the seemingly infinite capacity for multimedia reiteration of a movie hit redefines textual boundaries, creates a dynamic commercial intertext that is more process than product, and involves the audience(s) in the creative process—not only as multimarket consumers but also as mediators in the play of narrative signification. On the other hand, the actual movie "itself," if indeed it can be isolated and understood as such (which is questionable at best), often has been reduced and stylized to a point where, for some observers, it scarcely even qualifies as a narrative.

Critic Richard Schickel, for instance, has stated: "In the best of all possible marketing worlds the movie will inspire some simple summarizing graphic treatment, adaptable to all media, by which it can be instantly recognized the world over, even by subliterates."[61] The assembly-line process in the studio era demanded that story ideas be progressively refined into a classical three-act structure of exposition, complication, and resolution. But now-adays, says Schickel, "Hollywood seems to have lost or abandoned the art of narrative. . . . [Filmmakers] are generally not refining stories at all, they are spicing up 'concepts' (as they like to call them), refining gimmicks, making sure there are no complexities to fur our tongues when it comes time to spread the word of mouth." Schickel argues that all genres have merged into two meta-categories, comedies and action-adventure films, both of which offer "a succession of undifferentiated sensations, lucky or unlucky acci-dents, that have little or nothing to do with whatever went before or is about to come next," with a mere "illusion of forward motion" created via music and editing.[62]

Schickel excuses his "geriatric grumble" while demeaning "youthful" moviegoers for their lack of "very sophisticated tastes or expectations when it comes to narrative," and his nod to audience fragmentation along gener-ational lines raises a few important issues.[63] To begin with, younger viewers—despite "grownup" biases about limited attention spans, depth of feeling, and intellectual development—are far more likely to be active multimedia players, consumers, and semioticians, and thus to gauge a movie in intertex-tual terms and to appreciate in it a richness and complexity that may well be lost on middle-aged movie critics. In fact, given the penchant these years to pre-sell movies via other popular culture products (rock songs, comic books, TV series, etc.), chances are that younger, media-literate viewers encounter a movie in an already-activated narrative process. The size, scope, and emo-tional charge of the movie and its concurrent ad campaign certainly privilege the big screen "version" of the story, but the movie itself scarcely begins or ends the textual cycle.

This in turn raises the issue of narrative "integrity," which in classical Hollywood was a textual feature directly related to the integrity of both the "art form" and the system of production. While movies during the studio era certainly had their intertextual qualities, these were incidental and rarely undermined the internal coherence of the narrative itself. While many (per-haps most) New Hollywood films still aspire to this kind of narrative integ-rity, the blockbuster tends to be intertextual and purposefully incoherent—virtually of necessity, given the current conditions of cultural production and consumption. Put another way, the vertical integration of classical Hollywood, which ensured a closed industrial system and coherent narrative, has given way to "horizontal integration" of the New Hollywood's tightly diversified media conglomerates, which favors texts strategically "open" to multiple readings and multimedia reiteration.

These calculated blockbusters utterly dominate the movie industry, but they also promote alternative films and filmmaking practices in a number of ways. Because the majors' high-cost, high-stakes projects require a concen-tration of resources and limit overall output, they tend to foster product demand. This demand is satisfied, for the most part, by moderately priced star vehicles financed and distributed by the majors, which may emerge as surprise hits but essentially serve to keep the industry machinery running, to develop new talent, and to maintain a steady supply of dependable main-stream products. Complementing these routine features, and far more inter-esting from a critical and cultural perspective, are the low-cost films from independent outfits like Mirimax and New Line Cinema. In fact, the very market fragmentation which the studios' franchise projects are designed to exploit and overcome, these independents are exploiting in a very different way via their small-is-beautiful, market-niche approach.

Mirimax, for instance, has carved out a niche by financing or buying and then distributing low-budget art films and imports like *sex, lies and videotape, My Left Foot, Cinema Paradiso*, and *Tie Me Up, Tie Me Down* to a fairly consistent art film crowd. New Line's strategy is more wide-ranging, target-ing an array of demographic groups and taste cultures from art film aficion-ados and environmentalists to born-again Christians and wrestling fans. If any one of New Line's products takes off at the box office, it's liable to be a teen pic like *Teenage Mutant Ninja Turtles*, which returned $67 million in rentals in 1990. While fully exploiting that hit was a real challenge for a company like New Line, an even bigger challenge, no doubt, was resisting the urge to expand their operations, upgrade their product, and compete with the majors—an impulse that proved disastrous for many independent com-panies during the 1980s.[64]

Thus we might see the New Hollywood as producing three different classes of movie: the calculated blockbuster designed with the multimedia market-place and franchise status in mind, the mainstream A-class star vehicle with sleeper-hit potential, and the low-cost independent feature targeted for a specific market and with little chance of anything more than "cult film" status. These three classes of movie have corresponding ranks of auteurs, from the superstar directors at the "high end" like Spielberg and Lucas, whose knack for engineering hits has transformed their names into virtual trademarks, to those filmmakers on the margins like Gus Van Sant, John Sayles, and the Coen brothers, whose creative control and personal style are considerably less constrained by commercial imperatives. And then there are the established genre auteurs like Jonathan Demme, Martin Scorsese, David Lynch, and Woody Allen who, like Ford and Hitchcock and the other top studio directors of old, are the most perplexing and intriguing cases—each of them part visionary cineaste and part commercial hack, whose best films flirt with hit status and critique the very genres (and audiences) they exploit.

Despite its stratification, the New Hollywood is scarcely a balkanized or rigidly class-bound system. On the contrary, these classes of films and film-makers are in a state of dynamic tension with one another and continually intermingle. Consider, for instance, the two recent forays into that most con-temptible of genres, the psycho-killer/stalk-and-slash film, by Jonathan Demme in *The Silence of the Lambs* and Martin Scorsese in *Cape Fear*. Each film took the genre into uncharted narrative and thematic territory; each was a cinematic tour-de-force, enhancing both the aesthetic and commercial value of the form; and each thoroughly terrified audiences, thereby reinforcing the genre's capacity to explore the dark recesses of the collective American psyche and underscoring the cinema's vital contact with its public.

Besides winning the Oscar for "Best Picture of 1991," *Silence of the Lambs* emerged as a solid international hit, indicating the potential global currency of the genre while raising some interesting questions about the New Hollywood's high-end products vis-à-vis the American cultural experience. With the rapid development of multiplex theaters and home video in Europe and the Far East, and the concurrent advances in advertising and marketing, one can readily foresee the "global release" of calculated blockbusters far beyond the scale of a *Batman* or *Terminator 2*, let alone a surprise hit like *The Silence of the Lambs*. This may require a very different kind of product, effectively segregating the calculated blockbuster from the studios' other feature output and redefining the Hollywood cinema as an American culture industry. But it's much more likely that the New Hollywood and its characteristic blockbuster product will endure, given the social and economic development in the major overseas markets, the survival instincts and overall economic stability of the Hollywood studios, and the established global appeal of its products.

Notes

1 Recent studies of "classical" Hollywood and the "studio system" include *The Classical Hollywood Cinema: Film Style and Mode of Production to 1960*. David Bordwell, Janet Staiger, and Kristin Thompson (New York: Columbia University Press, 1985); *The Hollywood Studio System*, Douglas Gomery (New York: St. Martin, 1986); and *The Genius of the System: Hollywood Filmmaking in the Studio Era*, Thomas Schatz (New York: Pantheon, 1988).

2 Here and throughout this essay, I will be referring to *"rentals"* (or "rental receipts") and also to *"gross revenues"* (or "box-office revenues"). This is a crucial distinction, since the gross revenues indicate the amount of money actually spent at the box office, whereas rental receipts refer, as *Variety* puts it, to "actual amounts received by the distributor"—i.e., to the moneys returned by theaters to the company (usually a "studio") that released the movie. Unless otherwise indicated, both the rentals and gross revenues involve only the "domestic box office"—i.e., theatrical release in the U.S. and Canada.

   All of the references to box-office performance and rental receipts in this article are taken from *Variety*, most of them from its most recent (January 11–17, 1989; pp. 28–74) survey of "All-Time Film Rental Champs," which includes all motion pictures returning at least $4 million in rentals. Because this survey is continually updated, the totals include reissues and thus may be considerably higher than the rentals from initial release. In these cases I try to use figures from earlier *Variety* surveys for purposes of accuracy.

3 " 'Gone With the Wind' Again Tops All-Time List," *Variety* (May 4, 1983), p. 15.

4 "Top 100 All-Time Film Rental Champs," *Variety* (January 6, 1992), p. 86.

5 Eileen R. Meehan, " 'Holy Commodity Fetish, Batman!': The Political Economy of a Commercial Intertext," in *The Many Lives of the Batman*, Roberta E. Pearson and William Uricchio, eds. (New York: BFI-Routledge, 1991), p. 62.

6 Christopher H. Sterling and Timothy R. Haight, *The Mass Media: Aspen Institute Guide to Communications Industry Trends* (New York: Praeger, 1978), pp. 187 and 352. Unless otherwise noted, the statistics on attendance, ticket sales, etc., are from this reliable compendium of statistical data on the movie industry.

7 "All-Time Film Rental Champs," *Variety* (January 11–17, 1989), pp. 28–74.

8 Personal correspondence from Selznick to Louis B. Mayer, September 16, 1953; David O. Selznick Collection, Humanities Research Center, University of Texas at Austin.

9 Rudy Behlmer, ed., *Memo from David O. Selznick* (New York: Viking, 1972), p. 373.

10 See Janet Staiger, "Individualism Versus Collectivism," *Screen* 24 (July–October, 1983), pp. 68–79.

11 Freeman Lincoln, "The Comeback of the Movies," *Fortune* (February, 1955), p. 127.

12 See Robert Vianello, "The Rise of the Telefilm and the Networks' Hegemony Over the Motion Picture Industry," *Quarterly Review of Film Studies* (Summer, 1984) pp. 204–18.

13 See William Lafferty, "Feature Films on Prime-Time Television," in *Hollywood in the Age of Television*, Tino Balio, ed. (Boston: Unwin Hyman, 1990), pp. 235–256.

14 Lincoln, "Comeback," p. 131.

15 Stephen M. Silverman, *The Fox That Got Away* (Secaucus, N.J.: Lyle Stuart Inc., 1988), pp. 323–329.

16 Tino Balio, "Introduction to Part II" of *Hollywood in the Age of Television*, pp. 259–260.

17 Joseph R. Dominick, "Film Economics and Film Content: 1964–1983," in *Current Research in Film* (Norwood, N.J.: Ablex, 1987), p. 144.

18 Lafferty, "Feature Films," pp. 245–248.

19 Michael Pye and Lynda Myles, *The Movie Brats* (New York: Holt, Rinehart and Winston, 1979), p. 236.

20 Carl Gottlieb, *The Jaws Log* (New York: Dell, 1975), pp. 15–19. Note that Dell is a subdivision of MCA.

21 Gottlieb, *Jaws Log*, p. 62.

22 Pye and Myles, *Movie Brats*, p. 232.

23 James Monaco, *American Film Now* (New York: New American Library, 1979), p. 50.

24 Axel Madsen, *The New Hollywood* (New York: Thomas Y. Crowell, 1975), p. 94.

25 Balio, "Introduction to Part I," *Hollywood in the Age of Television*, p. 29.

26 "Theatrical Data" section in "1990 U.S. Economic Review" (New York: Motion Picture Association of America, 1991), p. 3.

27 Dominick, "Film Economics," p. 146.

28 Jennifer Pendleton, "Fast Forward, Reverse," *Daily Variety* (58th Anniversary Issue, "Focus on Entertainment Marketing," October, 1991), p. 14.

29 Michelle Hilmes, "Breaking the Broadcast Bottleneck," in Balio, *Hollywood*, pp. 299–300.

30 See Hilmes, "Breaking," and also Bruce A. Austin, "Home Video: The Second-Run 'Theater' of the 1990s," in Balio, *Hollywood*, pp. 319–349.

31 J. Hoberman, "Ten Years That Shook the World," *American Film* 10 (June, 1985); p. 42.

32 Jim McCullaugh, "*Star Wars* Hikes Demand for Dolby," *Billboard* (July 9, 1977), p. 4.

33 *"Star Wars:* A Cultural Phenomenon," *Box Office* (July, 1987), pp. 36–38.
34 Hoberman, "Ten Years," pp. 36–37.
35 "Behind the Scenes on *Raiders of the Lost Ark," American Cinematographer* (November, 1981), p. 1096. See also Tony Crawley, *The Steven Spielberg Story* (New York: Quill, 1983), p. 90.
36 "Top 100 All-Time Film Rental Champs," *Variety* (January 11–17, 1989), p. 26.
37 Hoberman, "Ten Years," and A. D. Murphy, "Twenty Years of Weekly Film Ticket Sales in U.S. Theaters," *Variety* (March 15–21, 1989), p. 26.
38 Figures from "Theatrical Data" and "VCR and Cable" sections in MPAA's "1990 U.S. Economic Review."
39 Robert B. Levin and John H. Murphy, unpublished case study of Walt Disney Pictures' 1986 marketing strategies, for use in an advertising course taught by Professor Murphy.
40 Richard Natale, "Hollywood's 'new math': Does it still add up?," *Variety* (September 23, 1991), pp. 1, 95.
41 Terry Ilott, "Yank pix flex pecs in new Euro arena," *Variety* (August 19, 1991), pp. 1, 60.
42 John Marcon, Jr., "Dream Factory to the World," *Forbes* (April 29, 1991), p. 100.
43 Figures from "Prints and Advertising Costs of New Features" in MPAA's "1990 U.S. Economic Review."
44 Charles Fleming, "Pitching costs out of ballpark: Record pic-spending spells windfall for tv," *Variety* (June 27, 1990), p. 1.
45 "Week-by-week domestic b.o. gross," *Variety* (January 7, 1991), p. 10.
46 "Video and Theatrical Revenues," *Variety* (September 24, 1990), p. 108.
47 "The Teachings of Chairman Jeff," *Variety* (February 4, 1991), p. 24. Article contains excerpts of the January 11 memo.
48 Charles Fleming, "Megabudgets Boom Despite Talk of Doom," *Variety* (February 4, 1991), pp. 5ff.
49 Geraldine Fabrikant, "In Land of Big Bucks, Even Bigger Bucks," *New York Times* (October 18, 1990), p. C5.
50 William Goldman, *Adventures in the Screen Trade* (New York: Warner Books, 1983), p. 39.
51 "Disney's profits in park: Off 23%," *The Hollywood Reporter* (November 15, 1991), pp. 1, 6.
52 Meehan, " 'Holy Commodity," p. 47.
53 John Mickelthwait, "A Survey of the Entertainment Industry," *The Economist* (December 23, 1989), p. 5.
54 For an excellent overview of both the Sony and Matsushita deals, and Ovitz's role in each, see Connie Bruck, "Leap of Faith," *New Yorker* (September 9, 1991), pp. 38–74.
55 Lawrence Cohn, "Stars' Rocketing Salaries Keep Pushing Envelope," *Variety* (September 24, 1990), p. 3.
56 Spielberg/Hoffman/Williams deal reported in Geraldine Fabrikant, "The Hole in Hollywood's Pocket," *New York Times* (December 10, 1990), p. C7. Nicholson deal in Ben Stein, "Holy Bat-Debt!," *Entertainment Weekly* (April 26, 1991), p. 12.
57 Fabrikant, "The Hole in Hollywood's Pocket," p. C7.
58 Meehan, " 'Holy Commodity," p. 52.
59 Mark Crispin Miller, "Hollywood: The Ad." *Atlantic Monthly* (April, 1990), pp. 49–52.
60 Quoted in Hoberman, "Ten Years," p. 36.
61 Richard Schickel, "The Crisis in Movie Narrative," *Gannett Center Journal* 3 (Summer, 1989), p. 2.
62 Schickel, "Crisis," pp. 3–4.

63 Schickel, "Crisis," p. 3.
64 See Joshua Hammer, " 'Small Is Beautiful,' " *Newsweek* (November 26, 1990), pp. 52–53, and William Grimes, "Film Maker's Secret Is Knowing What's Not for Everyone," *New York Times* (December 2, 1991), pp. B1+.

15

1975–1985

Ten years that shook the world

J. Hoberman

Source: *American Film* (June 1985): 34–59.

For American movies, the decade between 1975 and 1985 was as momentous as any since the end of World War II—offering not simply an unprecedented succession of megahits and an explosion of new technologies, but the spectacle of a new generation swimming with, and in some cases against, a powerful conservative tide.

The cultural upheavals of the late sixties spawned a cinema of genre criticism and directorial nonconformity; the retrenchment of the mid-seventies brought the waning days and ultimate reversal of the *Bonnie and Clyde–Easy Rider*, small-and-weird-can-be-beautiful revolution. The past decade marked the decline and fall of the maverick genre revisionists (Robert Altman, Sam Peckinpah, Arthur Penn) as well as the diminished fortunes of those radical individualists (Stanley Kubrick, Bob Rafelson, John Cassavetes, Dennis Hopper, Hal Ashby) who had flourished, after a fashion, in the late sixties and early seventies.

For Hollywood, June 1975 offered a vision of things to come. Only six weeks after the fall of Saigon, this historic month saw the release of two key movies, both in their ways brilliant modifications of the current disaster cycle that had had its real-world equivalents in Vietnam and Watergate. The multistar, mounting-doom, intersecting-plot format of *Earthquake* and *The Towering Inferno* was elaborated and politicized by *Nashville*, the film widely regarded as Robert Altman's masterpiece. Preceded by Pauline Kael's influential and notorious rave in the *New Yorker*—she saw Altman's rough cut two months before the film's release and declared it "an orgy for movie lovers"—*Nashville* achieved considerable critical and even modest financial success. But if *Nashville* could be said to have deconstructed the disaster film, Steven Spielberg's *Jaws* gave the cycle a second lease on life.

315

Where *Nashville* exploded the genre, *Jaws* imploded it. The twenty-eight-year-old Spielberg stripped the disaster film down, trimmed the flab, and turned it into a pure mechanism. Where *Nashville* offered a glibly pessimistic view of American life, predicting the rise of a politics as meretricious and authoritarian as the mass culture industry, *Jaws* was bravely optimistic: The film's hero—a family man as well as a cop—triumphed over brute nature and mendacious politicians alike, defeating the giant shark where ivory-tower oceanographers and lower-class fishermen failed. Opening simultaneously at five hundred theaters on a wave of saturation television advertising, *Jaws* went on to become the top-grossing movie of all time. At least until 1977.

If, as Robert Evans, then Paramount's head of production, told *Time* magazine in 1974, "the making of a blockbuster is the newest art form of the 20th century," Steven Spielberg was a budding Michelangelo. And if the history of Hollywood can be read as a history of genres and directors, then the trends of the past ten years are illuminated by the contrasting fates of *Nashville* and *Jaws*, Altman and Spielberg. Altman—who worked in (and disassembled) every genre from sci-fi and war films through musicals and *noir* to the Western and the gangster film—may have been, as *Film Comment* quixotically asserted in its end-of-the-seventies roundup, "the director of the seventies," but he didn't have a single solid commercial hit between *M*A*S*H* (1970) and *Popeye* (1980). Spielberg—who specialized in putting genres back together—became the most bankable director who ever lived.

In pre-*Jaws* Hollywood, talent agents had reigned supreme. The buzzword was "packaging." Two superstars, a proven writer, and a hot director were supposed to guarantee a hit. The theory was undone by flops like *Lucky Lady* (1975), *The Missouri Breaks* (1976), and *New York, New York* (1977). *Jaws* was something else: Its presold property and media-blitz saturation release pattern heralded the rise of marketing men and "high concept." Spielberg virtually defined the latter's mystical quality in a 1978 *American Film* "Dialogue on Film" when he declared: "What interests me more than anything else is the idea. If a person can tell me the idea in twenty-five words or less, it's going to make a pretty good movie. I like ideas, especially movie ideas, that you can hold in your hand."

As Hollywood passed mid-decade, nostalgia was in the air; minority tastes were swept aside by a new cinema of consensus. Fittingly, the movie that anticipated this development was George Lucas's 1973 *American Graffiti*, the first film to periodicize the sixties, and itself a small, unheralded sleeper. But the possibility of making such small pictures diminished as costs dramatically escalated. In 1975, the average combined cost to make and market a film was $3.1 million. A film had to sell more than five million tickets to break even. In 1984, the cost to make and release an average film had escalated to $14.4 million, and the number of tickets sold to reach the break-even point had risen to fifteen million. The tax shelters that had financed twenty percent of all movie starts between 1973 and 1976 were eliminated. Although the number of studio releases declined steadily throughout the seventies, the audience share of the ten top-grossing films tripled the growth rate of the film audience as a whole. As James Monaco, who calculated this discrepancy in *American Film Now*, observed: "Increasingly, we are all going to see the same ten movies."

Altman, Peckinpah, Kubrick, and company were succeeded by the generation of television-bred (and, in some cases, trained), film school—educated directors known as the "movie brats." These included such consummate formula artists as Spielberg and Lucas (and later Lawrence Kasdan, John Landis, John Carpenter, and Joe Dante), as well as more subversive, less monumentally successful directors like Brian De Palma and Martin Scorsese. With Francis Coppola as their avatar and *Jaws* as proof of their Manifest Destiny, the movie brats (many of whom got their first break with Roger Corman) elevated drive-in monster movies, Abbott and Costello-style slapstick, rock 'n' roll musicals, Saturday-morning science fiction—the most vital and disreputable genres of their youth—to cosmic heights.

In a certain sense, the movie brats were Hollywood's delayed New Wave—as ambitious, self-confident, and steeped in cinema as the movie-crazed French boys who haunted the Cinémathèque Française during the fifties. The movie brats were inspired by this example; their triumph supports the notion that although he's never managed to make a movie in Hollywood, the most influential film personality of the past twenty-five years has been Jean-Luc Godard. Juxtaposing Hollywood genres with Picasso, mixing documentary and fiction (and later experimenting with video), Godard was the model sixties cineast. One can see his influence on a slightly older contemporary like Altman, but Godard's real impact—as well as that of other New Wave directors, such as François Truffaut (to whom Spielberg paid homage in *Close Encounters of the Third Kind*) and Claude Chabrol—was felt by the generation (in West Germany as well as America) who spent the sixties in film school.

Godard was among the first to understand that the period of classic cinema was over, or—put another way—to see film history as a text. The American version of this realization took the form of the genre parodies spawned by Mel Brooks's *Blazing Saddles* (1974) and *Young Frankenstein* (1974), diluted by his epigones (Gene Wilder and Marty Feldman) and others, culminating with blockbuster flourish in last year's megasmash *Ghostbusters*. Like Altman before him, Brooks recognized that the Hollywood of his childhood was long gone—giving him license to play with spent genres as though they were tin soldiers. But the recognition of childhood's end that characterized the films of older directors like Altman and Brooks gave way in the next generation to a widespread yearning for the lost "innocence" of childhood or adolescence.

Following Godard, the movie brats brought an unprecedented degree of celluloid erudition to their creations. Films swarmed with allusions to *Psycho* and *The Searchers*, not to mention *Rebel Without a Cause*, *Forbidden Planet*, and *The Wizard of Oz*. Unlike Godard, however, the young American directors did not see this sort of intertextuality as part of a larger cultural critique. Rather than deconstruct the Hollywood system, their most successful movies strove to resurrect its greatest triumphs. As Marx did to Hegel, they stood Godard on his head.

Where Altman's *The Long Goodbye* (1973) exposed the contradictions in the myth of the saintly private eye through a canny juxtaposition of the forties and the seventies, Lawrence Kasdan's *Body Heat* eight years later, also set in the present, used the plot devices, lighting, and compositional clichés of forties *noir*, as well as nostalgic forties costumes, to fabricate a museum waxwork of a passé Hollywood style. So powerful was the urge to duplicate past triumphs that sequelitis ran rampant during the late seventies and early eighties (including belated addenda to *Psycho* and *2001: A Space Odyssey*), while long-running series like the James Bond and *Pink Panther* movies profited from a new burst of popularity.

As the seventies wore on, it became apparent that the overarching impulse was less an attempt to revise genres than to revive them. How else to explain the incredible recycling of retired mixed-media figures (Buck Rogers, Flash Gordon, Popeye, Superman, Supergirl, Sheena, Little Orphan Annie, Tarzan, the Lone Ranger, and Conan the Barbarian) that followed in *Star Wars'* wake? The 1975–77 television season, which spawned Wonder Woman and the Hulk, was a harbinger of this recycling, which soon grew to encompass entire television series (*Star Trek*, *The Twilight Zone*) and even comic books (*Creepshow*). By 1984, everything old had already been new again.

So far as Hollywood was concerned, 1976 was the sixties' last hurrah. Amazingly, *One Flew Over the Cuckoo's Nest* was not only an Oscar-winning Best Picture, but also the year's biggest hit. Just as significantly, 1976 saw a dip in box-office figures. But that was only momentary: Grosses took off over the next few years as the zeitgeist came home to roost.

The period between November 1976 and November 1978 proved to be a watershed for the themes and trends of the next half-dozen years. The cycles of the early seventies—blaxploitation and upscale porn, the urban Western and the disaster epic, buddy, caper, and vigilante films, the road movie—expired as new tendencies took their place. In 1977 and 1978, remakes, redneck and slapstick comedies, space operas, slasher flicks, post-sixties youth films, and a few self-consciously "grown-up" movies came to dominate the scene.

Rocky was as nearly unhyped a small picture as *American Graffiti*—and as much a function of one man's belief. Released in late 1976, Sylvester Stallone's self-generated vehicle resurrected the sports inspirational and canonized the white ethnic in the shamelessly manipulative terms of a stone-age nickelodeon. Rocky was the first working-class movie icon to capture the public imagination in the half-dozen years since the hardhat Joe opened fire on the hippie spawn of the degenerate middle class. (Interestingly, *Joe* had been the maiden effort of *Rocky*'s director, John Avildsen.) But although Stallone espoused a populism so primitive it would have embarrassed D. W. Griffith, his timing was nothing short of miraculous. Not only did *Rocky* benefit from the Bicentennial (which it cannily exploited) and the recent Olympics, but the film virtually divined Jimmy Carter's long-shot presidential campaign. Like the born-again Christianity that Carter helped popularize, the passion of Stallone's burned-out palooka was predicated on the grace of a second chance.

Rocky also profited from a nasty white backlash against the black gains of the sixties, even as it implicitly celebrated the rise of Italian directors and actors—Francis Coppola, Martin Scorsese, Al Pacino, Robert De Niro—in the new Hollywood. Stallone's Horatio Alger story inspired a few other serious working-class, white-ethnic films, including *Blue Collar* (1978), *Bloodbrothers* (1978), *F.I.S.T.* (1978), and *The Deer Hunter* (1978)—not to mention a liberal, female *Rocky*, *Norma Rae* (1979). But with the notable exceptions of *Rocky*'s two sequels, none of these had nearly the same impact. Indeed, save for *The Deer Hunter*, none of them seemed to grasp the secret of *Rocky*'s success. Aggressively innocent and proudly upbeat, Stallone declared that movies were about making the audience feel good about itself (and America). Increasingly, the fantasy of realizing an impossible dream against all odds had become a Hollywood staple.

Six months later, the industry was rocked by an even bigger bombshell. *Star Wars*, which opened in May 1977, was not just the highest-grossing film before *E.T.*, but arguably the quintessential Hollywood product. (*Time* called *Star Wars* "a subliminal history of movies, wrapped in a riveting tale of suspense and adventure.") Drawing on the Western and the war film, borrowing motifs from fantasies as varied as *The Wizard of Oz* and *Triumph of the Will*, George Lucas pioneered the genre pastiche—synthesizing a mythology so soulless that its most human characters were a pair of robots. As recondite in its way as *The Rocky Horror Picture Show* (which also exploded as a cult phenomenon in 1977), *Star Wars* was the first and greatest cult blockbuster.

In genre terms, Lucas's newfangled space opera had the same relation to the futurist dystopias of the early and mid-seventies as *Rocky* did to the urban realism of *Taxi Driver* or *Dog Day Afternoon*. As spectacle, *Star Wars* replaced the fading disaster film with the sci-fi extravaganza. Moreover, in preempting the following year's Nam and anti-Nam cycle, *Star Wars* effectively made the screen safe for militarism, opening the way for the various service comedies, dramas, and romances of the early eighties. Lucas's crypto-war film even seemed to leap beyond movies into the realm of video games.

Not since *2001* had any science fiction film attracted so much attention. According to Lucas biographer Dale Pollock, the director had studied *2001* carefully. He was "in awe of Kubrick's technical craftsmanship, but the movie was too obscure and downbeat for his tastes." Lucas preferred a Capralike enthusiasm and moral simplicity—and a religious faith that countered high technology with the mystic "Force." After *Star Wars*, science fiction (and by implication all genre filmmaking) was born again, bigger and better than ever, without doubt or deconstruction. "There's a whole generation growing up without any kind of fairy tales," Lucas explained.

Opening later that year, Spielberg's *Close Encounters of the Third Kind*—at once resurrecting the fifties flying-saucer film and inverting its alarmist theme—amalgamated *Rocky*'s feel-good ethos and Lucas's born-again sci-fi. But *Saturday Night Fever*, released for Christmas 1977, was an even more crucial trendsetter. The first post-sixties youth film set in the present, *Saturday Night Fever* addressed a new generation of filmgoers. "The film has new subject matter," Pauline Kael observed in her review; it's about "how the financially pinched seventies generation that grew up on TV attempts to find its own forms of beauty and release."

Seconding *Rocky*'s idealization of white ethnics—John Avildsen was the original director, before being replaced by John Badham—*Saturday Night Fever* similarly tempered urban grit with the inspirational show biz of a backstage musical. Cashing in on the current disco craze with a sensational sound track album tie-in, the film established the contemporary dance musical. In this last sense, however, *Saturday Night Fever* was ahead of its time. Alan Parker's *Fame* was an obvious spin-off, but not until the early eighties did *Saturday Night Fever*'s true successors—*Flashdance*, *Footloose*, and *Purple Rain* (not to mention the Stallone-directed sequel *Stayin' Alive*)—emerge. As *Star Wars* forecast the video game, *Saturday Night Fever* anticipated the rise of the music video, which was itself scarcely more than a presold star and images synced to ready-made sound track—a new symbiosis between rock and film. By 1984, the year's five best-selling pop singles were all from movies.

Production schedules being what they are, it generally takes two years for an innovation to make itself felt. *Jaws* had little impact on the 1976 movie season. But, always quicker to respond to shifts in the national mood, television was already in the midst of a wholesale overhaul. Instituted in late 1974, the so-called "family hour" spelled the beginning of the end of the hard-action cop shows ("Cannon," "Kojak," "Police Story") which, born of Nam-era tumult, saturated the airwaves during Richard Nixon's second term. In March 1975, ABC commissioned a psychographic study revealing that, after Vietnam and Watergate, viewers wanted a return to traditional values. Soon period sit-coms and costumed superheros—the same ones that anticipated Hollywood's subsequent interest in comic books and pulp—reigned supreme.

320

No television genre during the past decade proved more resilient than the situation comedy. From the retreat of the cop show in 1975 through the ascendancy of the prime-time soap in 1983, there were never less than a half-dozen sit-coms in the ten top-rated television shows. In 1975, Norman Lear was the unchallenged ruler of the airwaves with seven sit-coms—"All in the Family," "Sanford and Son," "Maude," "The Jeffersons," "Good Times," "Hot L Baltimore," and "One Day at a Time" (the first show with a single, divorced heroine)—online, three of them in the top ten.

Unlike everything else on television, Lear's work was actually taken seriously. Not only had he brought a new frankness (sexual and otherwise) to television comedy but, as Michael Arlen observed in the *New Yorker* in 1975, his comedies were innovative in their dependence "on the new contemporary consciousness of 'media'. . . . The basis of the Lear programs is not so much the family and its problems as it is the commonality that seems to have been created largely by television itself." A year after Arlen's piece appeared, Lear brought forth his masterpiece, "Mary Hartman, Mary Hartman," a program so reflexive that the eponymous heroine had her climactic nervous breakdown on another television show (namely David Susskind's).

Although Lear's sit-coms thrived on sexual, racial, and class conflict (and their facile resolution), his media consciousness was not in itself political— the "commonality" he explored was just another way to define "American." During the late seventies there emerged a new breed of baby-boom television comics whose humor eschewed social issues in favor of a near total dependence on intertextuality, an intricate knowledge of contemporary television, movies, music, and sports. "Saturday Night Live" had its peak years between 1977 and 1979 (after Chevy Chase went to Hollywood but before John Belushi and Dan Aykroyd followed him) and was succeeded, in the early eighties, by "SCTV"—a Canadian show that went even further to effect an epic synthesis of every television genre.

Lear was superseded on other fronts as well. With "Happy Days" and its spin-offs, "Laverne and Shirley" (a vehicle for *American Graffiti* star Cindy Williams) and "Mork & Mindy" (whose spaceman angle was inspired by *Star Wars*), the Lucasoid Garry Marshall eclipsed the Altmanlike Lear as the sultan of sit-com. In 1977, "All in the Family" was succeeded by "Laverne and Shirley" as America's most-watched television program.

Just as Scorsese and Lumet forged a new sort of urban filmmaking that *Rocky* and *Saturday Night Fever* would blandly appropriate, so Lear's "All in the Family" and "Sanford and Son" brought back the working-class sit-com only to have Marshall sanitize it. And just as Marshall brought back the fifties, the sexual "revolution" of the sixties was introduced and denatured by network television in such smarmy offerings as "Charlie's Angels," "Three's Company," "The Love Boat," and "Soap"—all of which appeared on ABC during 1977.

Of course, television was scarcely monolithic. Liberal blockbusters like *Roots* (1977), *Holocaust* (1978), and *The Day After* (1983) were among the most-watched television events of the decade. Lear and "M*A*S*H" continued to transmit the sixties values of social tolerance and antimilitarism while, as pioneered by "The Mary Tyler Moore Show," workplace and single-woman sit-coms proliferated throughout the seventies. Other MTM productions—notably "Lou Grant," "Hill Street Blues," and "St. Elsewhere"—continued a tradition of quality television. They were, in fact, the sort of programs a proto-Yuppie like Mary Richards would watch. But as the seventies waned, interest shifted from the lives of "average" Americans like Archie Bunker or Laverne and Shirley to the escapades of the super-rich and ultrapowerful. "Dallas"—America's favorite show during the Reagan administration's first thousand days—begat "Dynasty" and "Falcon Crest" (the latter starring the president's ex-wife, Jane Wyman) to join it in the 1983 top ten. The badly titled "Lifestyles of the Rich and Famous" became a syndicated smash.

Almost in spite of itself, beleaguered PBS functioned as a kind of unpaid R&D outfit for the networks. The documentary series "An American Family" and the BBC pickup "Upstairs, Downstairs" (both of which were first telecast in 1973) anticipated the mixture of miniseries, prime-time soap, and grotesque family sit-com that has characterized network television from the mid-seventies through the mid-eighties.

A 1977 survey revealed that although only thirteen percent of all movie tickets were bought by patrons more than forty years old (a figure that has scarcely changed since), a whopping fifty-seven percent were purchased by those under twenty-five. (Over the next two years, the youngest part of the audience grew even more dominant—twelve- to twenty-year-old admissions were up eight percent, mainly at the expense of those twenty-one to thirty-nine.) A massive youth market had emerged, for whom *The Graduate* and *Easy Rider* were ancient history. The time was right for a bubble gum blockbuster and *Saturday Night Fever* was followed in the summer of 1978 by two other epochal youth pix: *Grease* and *Animal House*.

Although adapted from a long-running Broadway show, *Grease* was a sequel to *Saturday Night Fever* in star (John Travolta), production company (Robert Stigwood), and merchandising (an adroitly coordinated blitz of radio spots, record tie-ins, and personality posters). "Danny, in *Grease*, could almost be the big Broadway role that *Saturday Night Fever*'s Tony was born to play," observed critic Dave Kehr. *Grease* continued the erasure of the sixties by reveling in fifties chic.

A prime example of the movies' symbiotic relationship with television, *Grease* picked up on the success of "Happy Days" (itself influenced by *American Graffiti*). Elevating the Fonz to a universal principle—Henry Winkler was in fact Stigwood's first choice for the role that went to Travolta—*Grease* reversed family-film sterotypes by making high school hoods into good guys and "grease" a sacrament rather than an epithet. Even more than *Saturday Night Fever*, *Grease* affirmed the new post-sixties youth market. Its success assured a steady flow of teen pix, ranging from arty adaptations of S. E. Hinton to the frankly incendiary to the merely prurient clones of Bob Clark's monumental *American Graffiti* vulgarization: *Porky's*.

But the anarchistic, superficially antiauthoritarian *Porky's* had another progenitor: John Landis's *Animal House*, which, up until *Tootsie*, was the highest-grossing comedy ever made. Like *Grease*, *Animal House* was set in a more innocent age—the same pre-Nam sixties as *American Graffiti*. Its key attraction, though, was raunchy slapstick founded on male-group bonding, a regressive celebration of adolescent sexual humor, and the use of a particular institution as a dramatic locus. Further, *Animal House* introduced John Belushi as the point man for the new breed of television clown who would come to dominate screen comedy.

Anticipated by the mid-seventies television sit-com boom and fueled by the stars who began rolling off the "Saturday Night Live" assembly line, comedy proved the most universal mode of the past decade. In 1981, with the exception of *Raiders of the Lost Ark*, *Superman II*, and the latest James Bond flick (hardly models of sobriety themselves), everything else in the ten top-grossing films was strictly for laughs. In 1980, half of the ten top grossers (*The Jerk*, *Airplane!*, *Smokey and the Bandit II*, *Private Benjamin*, and *The Blues Brothers*) were comedies.

A second wave broke with *Tootsie* and Eddie Murphy. If not quite a white man in blackface—as superfeminist Dorothy Michaels was literally a man in skirts—Murphy was a less threatening black star than Richard Pryor, as well as one who had exploited a consensus target group: homosexuals. Murphy's *Beverly Hills Cop* swamped the competition when it was released for Christmas 1984, grossing $58 million in less than a month to finish fourth for the year behind *Ghostbusters*, *Indiana Jones and the Temple of Doom*, and *Gremlins*.

If Mel Brooks and Woody Allen were the reigning comedy directors of the mid-seventies, the end of the decade found them overshadowed by such relative nonentities as ex-stunt-man Hal Needham, who pioneered redneck comedy with *Smokey and the Bandit* and *The Cannonball Run*, and *Animal House* producer Ivan Reitman, who, better than anyone else (even Landis), reproduced the formula of *Animal House* with the highly successful *Meatballs*, *Stripes*, and, finally, *Ghostbusters*. The highest-grossing comedy ever made—a film that ruled American movie screens during the summer of 1984 as absolutely as Ronald Reagan dominated American politics—*Ghostbusters* brought *Animal House*-style humor and the "Saturday Night Live" gang to bear on the post-*Star Wars* high-tech spectacle, wrapping the package in the probusiness, socially conservative attitudes of the mid-eighties.

Bill Murray—with Dan Aykroyd, Chevy Chase, and Jane Curtin running as distant seconds—proved to be the strongest survivor of the first "Saturday

Night Live" generation. Along with John Hurt and Kurt Russell, as well as the explosion of white-bread teen stars, came the general eclipse of older ethnic actors like George Segal, Elliott Gould, and Al Pacino. Of the younger ones, Sylvester Stallone has been mondo box office only when playing Rocky (with the possible exception of *First Blood*), while John Travolta has yet to live up to the heat generated by his remarkable one-two combination, *Saturday Night Fever* and *Grease*. Waspy Harrison Ford, more consistent if less charismatic, established himself in the early eighties less as a luminary in his own right than as the perfect specimen of homo Lucasus, although *Witness* may prove a swifter rocket to superstardom than the rickety craft he piloted in *Star Wars*. Among the comics, Woody Allen attained his maximum appeal as an icon until the late seventies, before relinquishing the title of America's greatest nebbish to the less complicated (and less ethnic) Dudley Moore.

The corollary to the youth film was the new grown-up movie, so termed by Stephen Farber in *American Film* in 1981. Paul Mazursky, Robert Benton, Alan Alda, Mark Rydell, and occasionally Herbert Ross were grown-up auteurs, with Woody Allen and (between bouts with the *Pink Panther* series) Blake Edwards providing comic relief. The sensibility was at least as much New York as Los Angeles. The popularity of PBS's "Masterpiece Theatre" demonstrated the appeal of genteel drama while the Australian cinema, and later the new British cinema, provided foreign support. Although *Chariots of Fire* managed the Herculean task of refitting *Rocky* as a grown-up film, the trend's most significant achievement was in improving the status of women in Hollywood movies.

"From a woman's point of view, the ten years from, say, 1962 or 1963 to 1973 have been the most disheartening in screen history," wrote Molly Haskell in *From Reverence to Rape* (perhaps the most influential film book of the mid-seventies). With the exception of independent films produced by the feminist wing of the newsreel movement, and isolated failures like *Diary of a Mad Housewife* or *Up the Sandbox*, women were celluloid prisoners of their sex. John Cassavetes's *A Woman Under the Influence* (1974) and Martin Scorsese's *Alice Doesn't Live Here Anymore* (1975) were avatars of the sudden flurry of new women's films in 1977 and 1978: *Julia*, *The Turning Point*, *An Unmarried Woman*, *Coming Home*, and the independent *Girlfriends*.

Nevertheless, women seem increasingly marooned. Barbra Streisand and Jane Fonda, the most consistently popular female stars of the past decade, are both creatures of the sixties. So, too, is Goldie Hawn, a star of the second rank, who like Streisand and Fonda, has maintained her visibility by functioning as a producer. (The example appears not to have been lost on Jessica Lange, one of the more gifted new stars of the eighties.)

The resilience that carried Fonda from a Hollywood childhood through a stint as a European sex toy and political militant to universal respect as an actress even enabled her to become a home-video star, demonstrating that very quality of energetic fortitude in the best-selling *Jane Fonda's Workout*. Fonda's example has not necessarily helped others, however. The resistance, if not outright ridicule, that greeted Streisand's directorial debut with *Yentl* underscored the difficulty women have had in actually making movies, despite the qualified success of a new crop of promising women directors, including Susan Seidelman, Amy Heckerling, Martha Coolidge, and Gillian Armstrong.

Moreover, as Molly Haskell observed in a 1979 interview, a further aspect of the grown-up movie has been the appropriation of female issues by male characters. Thus child care became the cross Dustin Hoffman had to bear in *Kramer vs. Kramer*, Burt Reynolds survived a divorce in *Starting Over*, Dudley Moore coped with menopause in *10* and with pregnancy in *Micki & Maude*. The apotheosis of this trend, *Tootsie*, demonstrated that the best women are really men and sexism is something most effectively fought by Dustin Hoffman in drag. Only in the light of ferocious backlash could *Tootsie* be perceived as a feminist film.

John Carpenter's *Halloween*, released in October 1978, went *Jaws* several degrees better as a dehumanized shock machine to become the most profitable independent film ever made. *Halloween* detonated a massive horror explosion between 1979 and 1981. If, as *From Reverence to Rape* suggested, the early seventies obsession with such ultimate macho men as the Mafia and Nazis can in fact be construed as an antifeminist backlash, the post-*Halloween* "slasher" film was a volcanic eruption of blatant misogyny, with nubile girls typically being stabbed to death immediately after engaging in intercourse. Along with herpes and the Moral Majority, the cycle appeared as a cosmic retribution against the sexual acting out of the sixties and early seventies.

While the cop and vigilante films of the early seventies emphasized the superego, the horror flicks that replaced them as the movies' preeminent morality play identified with the id. So long as the Vietnam War lasted, America could imagine itself a tough cop with a dirty job to do; once the war ended, however, murderous impulses were delegitimized and driven underground. Post-*Halloween* horror films were nightmares where creatures as implacable as Dirty Harry became killers, and no summer camp or high school prom was safe. Indeed, Clint Eastwood's revisionist *Tightrope* explicitly acknowledged the relationship between its vigilante cop protagonist and *Halloween*'s psycho.

Like *Halloween*, its successors were often set in blandest suburbia, a conceit that reached its apogee with the Spielberg-presented *Poltergeist* and *Gremlins*. The 1980–81 werewolf cycle was akin, if somewhat classier, in revealing the horror lurking within the soul of ordinary Americans. Given the upbeat tone of most Hollywood films, it fell to sleazy slasher flicks to express the darker side of the "Happy Days" cosmos.

By 1975 it was apparent that the extraordinary period that saw the formation of an indigenous avant-garde, the so-called New American Cinema, was finally over. The Anthology Film Archives in New York had established a canon of classics (effectively closing the books on the period of frantic activity that began in 1958 with Stan Brakhage's *Anticipation of the Night*), and Jonas Mekas was forced from the *Village Voice*, where, for more than fifteen years, he had criticized and exhorted avant-garde filmmakers.

Like their contemporary Godard, American underground filmmakers such as Kenneth Anger, Jack Smith, Ken Jacobs, Ron Rice, and the Kuchar brothers took the movies as their subject matter—effecting a comic, brutal, and defiantly low-budget demystification of Hollywood mythology. A second wave of avant-gardists, commonly known as the structuralists, were even more reflexive, addressing the phenomenon of film itself. The success of these two tendencies (as well as the "first-person" cinema pioneered by Stan Brakhage and others) seemed to preempt further development. Although every major avant-garde filmmaker of the sixties inspired a plethora of second- and third-rate imitators during the seventies, there were few figures who broke new ground.

Three exceptions to the general malaise were Yvonne Rainer, James Benning, and Mark Rappaport. All were profoundly influenced by the New American Cinema without being part of it; all set off in new narrative directions. (The Belgian director Chantal Akerman, who lived in New York during the early seventies and was heavily influenced by the avant-garde films she saw there, is a related figure—and an arguably more important one.) In working with narrative in a feature format, Rainer, Rappaport, and Benning built a bridge between the New American Cinema and the burgeoning American independent movement. The Super-8 sound camera went on the market in 1974; within four years it became the basic tool of a whole new underground—defined largely in opposition to the anthologized avant-garde of the sixties and early seventies. An entire movement of Super-8 punk movies was born, flourished, and declined between 1977 and 1982 on New York's Lower East Side.

If Super-8 supplied the technology for a reaction against the established avant-garde, video extended the New American Cinema by other means. Super-8 sound arrived at a time of cultural stasis and economic stagflation. Video, which appeared at the height of the sixties counterculture, was born with more grandiose expectations than any other media. Exceptions like Nam June Paik aside, many of the first practitioners were the utopian, McLuhanized, mainly documentary video communes of the late sixties and early seventies, along with the cutting edge of conceptual or post-object artists. The latter managed to hold on longer. *Radical Software*, the influential visionary video journal published by the Raindance Collective, folded in 1974. The same year, a conference on the future of television held at the

Museum of Modern Art was dominated by the tapes and presentations of established gallery artists.

In retrospect, 1975 appears to have been the key year in the recognition of video as video, the replacement of "artists' video" by video art. "Video Art," the first comprehensive survey of the field, was organized by the Institute of Contemporary Art at the University of Pennsylvania. Meanwhile, in New York, the Museum of Modern Art began to acquire video for its permanent collection. The Whitney Museum of American Art included sixteen video artists in its "1985 Biennial Exhibition." WNET Thirteen, New York's PBS affiliate, has begun an ongoing broadcast series of independently produced videotapes. Strengthened by this new and varied institutional base, a new generation of younger, television-bred video artists has moved to the fore, some—like Bill Viola and Barbara Buckner—with marked affinities to the "visionary" filmmakers of the New American Cinema.

As in Hollywood, the 1976–78 period was something of a watershed for independents. The art world saw the comeback of figurative painting and the rise of neo-expressionism; in pop music and youth culture, 1978–1979 was the heyday of punk rock. Both developments would profoundly affect avant-garde and independent films. The phenomenal success of *The Rocky Horror Picture Show* as a midnight attraction reaffirmed the existence of a grass-roots movie audience apart from Hollywood, just as Barbara Kopple's 1977 *Harlan County U.S.A.* sparked a new American independent movement.

With few exceptions, the leading American documentary filmmakers of the sixties and early seventies—Ricky Leacock, D. A. Pennebaker, Frederick Wiseman, the Maysles brothers—were identified with cinema verité. Both as a style and a philosophy, verité had a profound influence on film culture. If the "rockumentary" has been its most popular legacy, verité also inspired the similarly spontaneous (but more politically structured) guerrilla newsreels of the late sixties and early seventies. At the same time, films like *David Holzman's Diary* by Jim McBride used the notion of cinema verité as a kind of metaphor for the new "postliterate" film culture. The notion of "truth twenty-four times per second" was so identified with the politics of the period, it seems appropriate that Robert Kramer and John Douglas's ambitious three-hour *Milestones*—a kind of countercultural *Nashville*, also released in 1975—should have appropriated the verité style to fictionalize a generation's passion.

As *Milestones* marked the end of one movement, *Harlan County* signaled the birth of another one, although—given the subsequent eclipse of the sixties' cinema verité and newsreel-style agitprop—it's ironic that the first example of the new American documentary should be a "direct cinema"-style account of a prolonged and bloody miners' strike. But *Harlan County*'s innovation had more to do with how it was made than what it showed. During the four years it took her to complete it, Kopple explored virtually every avenue of existent foundation funding, receiving aid from a number of organizations, including the AFI. Until she made a successful application to the National Endowment for the Arts (NEA) for assistance in 1974, the agency had never plowed major money into topical films. *Harlan County*'s high profile at the 1976 New York Film Festival and subsequent Oscar put the funding of feature documentaries squarely on the public arts agenda.

Aided by the NEA and its sister agency, the National Endowment for the Humanities, and stimulated by the growth of state arts agencies and public television (as well as the new ethnicity of the mid-seventies), a regional cinema began to develop: the Cine Manifest group in North Dakota, Victor Nuñez in Florida, Eagle Pennell in Texas, Les Blank emerged as a major American documentarian with his celebrations of regional and ethnic subcultures. Other subcultures ignored by Hollywood provided subject matter (and, to a degree, audiences) for films like *El Super*, *Northern Lights*, *Heartland*, *Chan Is Missing*, and *El Norte*.

By the end of the seventies, many independent films had proved to be surprising commercial hits—for example, John Sayles's epochal *Return of the Secaucus Seven*, which dealt with the aging of the sixties generation in far less glamorous terms than did *Milestones*, and provided Lawrence Kasdan with the premise for *The Big Chill*. Although only a handful of independent directors (including Susan Seidelman, Martha Coolidge, Claudia Weill, and Richard Pearce) have crossed over to Hollywood, the movement left its mark on the industry. Projects as varied as *Norma Rae*, *The China Syndrome*, *Reds*, *Zelig*, *Swing Shift*, *Yentl*, *Under Fire*, *Country*, and *Alamo Bay*, not to mention "Hill Street Blues," were, in one sense or another, either anticipated or inspired by independents.

The early eighties also saw the punk Super-8 film converge with several other styles to create a New York school. Several of the original Super-8 filmmakers went on to produce more elaborate (and conventional) films, while others picked up the look and subject matter of the punk movies— *Smithereens*, *Liquid Sky*, and *Stranger Than Paradise* popularized aspects of the earlier films and became commerical hits. Although David Lynch's *Eraserhead* was the last of the midnight blockbusters, there is no more eloquent proof of the triumph of the midnight aesthetic than that such prototypical midnight movies as *Liquid Sky*, *Repo Man*, and *Stranger Than Paradise* have all enjoyed considerable success doing business at normal hours.

In general, the seventies was the period when the cultural tendencies of the sixties attempted to institutionalize themselves. Midnight movies were one example, but there were other, more formal ones. Founded in 1974, the Association of Independent Video and Filmmakers (AIVF) was the first of several self-help groups organized by documentary filmmakers to protect their interests, and it proved a successful pressure group in Washington and elsewhere. Filmmakers organized self-distribution companies like New Day

Films and First Run Features. The Film Fund, whose purpose is to funnel money to social-change films, was organized in 1977, and the Independent Feature Project, which performs a variety of services for filmmakers, was initially funded in 1979.

Throughout the Carter years, the NEA and NEH, as well as state agencies like the New York State Council for the Arts, became increasingly important in supporting the work of American independent filmmakers. Indeed, it would not be too much to say that an entire documentary style developed in response to this new situation.

Like Barbara Kopple, many of the new documentarians had a background of political activism, and, like *Harlan County*, most of their films focused on labor or left-wing issues. Unlike *Harlan County*, however, virtually all of these documentaries—like *Union Maids* (1976), which treated the forging of the CIO, and *Hollywood on Trial* (1976), which dealt with the Cold War blacklist—were set in the past. A related documentary tendency, partially inspired by the compilation films of Emile de Antonio, made extensive use of archival footage.

In one sense, the new, public-funded documentary was a form of "visual" oral history. In another—no less than *Rocky*, *Star Wars*, or *Grease*—it was, with few exceptions, an expression of nostalgia for a simpler world, one more symptom of self-consciousness and cultural exhaustion.

The single most consistent tendency in the movies of the past ten years (Hollywood, avant-garde, documentary) has been their escalating reflexiveness. Most movies are now more about other movies than they are about life. Perhaps this was always the case, but, if so, pains were taken to naturalize them. Today, the degree of mannerism is unprecedented. The image of an old movie on television, a sign of hipness in the early seventies, has become one of Hollywood's hoariest clichés.

Although the continual replay of movie history may suggest the life of a drowning man flashing before his eyes, this high level of self-consciousness is part of the logic of film history, as well as a trend within the entire media system. For Americanness (and Americanization) can virtually be defined by one's familiarity with the particular nexus of popular music, moves, television programs, sports events, and weekly newsmagazines we term "the media." Even the long-overdue push to preserve and restore films—The American Film Institute declared 1983–1993 the Decade of Preservation, and reconstructed versions of *Napoleon*, *A Star Is Born*, *Becky Sharp*, and *Way Down East* debuted—can be seen, at least in part, as another manifestation of this cultural self-consciousness.

This was all very much in the air by the early seventies, but at first, in a characteristically solipsistic misunderstanding, perhaps prompted by the 1974 success of *That's Entertainment!*, Hollywood confused the trend toward reflexivity with a nostalgia for its own golden age. The mid-seventies saw an unprecedented and largely unsuccessful slew of movies about Hollywood history (mainly the twenties and thirties). Nor did failure dam the flood of remakes that began as a trickle with *Farewell, My Lovely* in 1975 and soon became a deluge—encompassing everything from Hollywood landmarks and classic comedies to cultish B-movies, vintage *noir*, and even (appropriately enough) films of the French New Wave.

Indeed, Hollywood filmmaking has become almost alchemical in its search for the perfect formula: *Star Wars* + product familiarity = *Star Trek* (1979, 1982, 1984); *Star Wars* + product familiarity + *Rocky* = *Superman* (1978, 1980, 1983); *Star Wars* + *Rocky* + *Animal House* = *Raiders of the Lost Ark* (1981, 1984); and *Animal House* + *Grease* + redneck comedies = *Porky's* (1982, 1983, 1985)—to name only those films that themselves inspired sequels. Of the one-shots: *Star Wars* + *Halloween* = *Alien* (1979); *Saturday Night Fever* + *Rocky* = *Flashdance* (1983); *Animal House* + *Halloween* + *E.T.* = *Gremlins* (1984); *Star Wars* + *Animal House* + genre comedies = *Ghostbusters* (1984).

Pastiche, repetition, the blending of high and popular art are all characteristic of what has come to be called postmodernism. In film, these tendencies were anticipated by the underground movies of the sixties (just as the reflexiveness of the seventies was preceded by the modernist avant-garde concern with the irreducible properties of cinema), but they are now more typical of video. The same tapes are equally at home in museums, on broadcast television, in rock clubs and media centers. Nothing says more about the health of video as a medium than the variety of venues that purvey video art.

Slowly building momentum from the mid-seventies on, the music video burst upon the scene as a cultural force when Warner Amex's all-rock-video cable station, MTV, went online in 1981. (The ultimate magpie form, rock videos are even more crammed with media allusions than the films of hardcore movie brats like Spielberg and Scorsese.) Within two years, rock videos rejuvenated the moribund record industry (saving it from the threat of video games) and made the leap to network television. The often derided MTV aesthetic has already spawned two Hollywood blockbusters (*Flashdance* and *Purple Rain*) as well as at least one network television series ("Miami Vice"), and a number of rock video's more flamboyant directing talents, notably Russell Mulcahy and Steve Barron, have gone on to make commercial features.

If nothing else, the events of the past ten years demonstrate the cyclical nature of American popular culture. The cop shows that disappeared in the mid-seventies are back in the mid-eighties, albeit in a new form. The black stars and themes that faded away around the same time have also returned, just as the sci-fi spectacle and perhaps even the youth film seemed, in early 1985, marked for decline. Small films and sleepers are again in evidence—although these, for the most part, are produced outside Hollywood. One cannot be too surprised that Robert Altman and Martin Scorsese, arguably the most original directors of their respective generations, are currently working on independent projects.

Reliant as they have been on public funding, the independent movement and, to a lesser degree, the avant-garde, face a problematic future. The NEA's Media Arts budget peaked at $13.2 million in 1981. It has been reduced by approximately twenty-two percent under the Reagan administration and more cuts can be expected.

Hollywood's ten top-grossing films have all been released since 1975. And even if one adjusts the figures to compensate for the dollar's reduced purchasing power—seven of the all-time dozen blockbusters were still made between 1975 and 1985. Filmmakers not yet forty have achieved success unimaginable to the classic directors they emulated—and, what's more, they did it their way. Moreover, the movies remain the preeminent metaphor maker of American culture. The 1984 presidential campaign, for example, was dominated by their buzzwords and catch phrases ("star wars," "the evil empire," "temple of doom"). If the mechanical nature of film itself is beginning to appear anachronistic in the electronic age, the movie industry has never seemed more harmoniously integrated with television and pop music—using both as a ready-made pool of new stars and a source of themes. Yet perhaps this united front is only the last of the movie's illusions.

The rise of a Steven Spielberg or the triumph of one or two *Ghostbusters* each year can hardly prevent the earthquake that threatens to rock Hollywood. Although 1984 was the first $4 billion year in industry history, it's difficult to be sanguine about the future of movies. *E.T.* or no *E.T.*, Hollywood faces its greatest crisis since 1948, when, fresh from the years of its largest audiences, the movie moguls sought to meet the simultaneous challenges of divestiture and television.

According to the A. C. Nielsen Company, it was during the Marshall-dominated 1976–1977 and 1977–78 seasons that network television achieved its maximum audience share. Thereafter, ABC-CBS-NBC began to suffer viewer attrition under the combined assault of cable systems, video games, and videocassette recorders. When Sony introduced the Betamax in 1975, the machine carried a price tag of $1,400—almost three times the present average price. Ten years later, one out of every seven American households has a VCR and video-rental outlets are as common as Laundromats.

Last year's Supreme Court ruling that home taping of television shows did not constitute a violation of copyright laws seems to have been the final validation; an astonishing forty percent of the nation's seventeen million VCRs were purchased during 1984. If television gave every home its own personal repertory house, the VCR has the potential to equip every viewer with the equivalent of a Moviola or Steenbeck. The appreciation thus engendered for fragmented (or fetishized) bits of film will likely have as profound an effect on the film culture of the eighties and nineties as television

331

had on that of the fifties, sixties, and seventies. So, too, will the fragmentation of the movie audience that VCRs will bring in their wake.

Along with VCRs, the growth of pay television has threatened Hollywood in a number of unforeseen ways. Not only have the cable networks begun to produce their own films, but their voracious appetite for Hollywood movies threatens to jeopardize the network rentals, which help subsidize production. Both Hollywood and the networks are preparing to deal with the challenge of the various home video systems—and that's the shake-out that will determine the shape of the next ten years in American film.

16

PAY TELEVISION

Breaking the broadcast bottleneck

Michele Hilmes

Source: Tino Balio (ed.), *Hollywood in the Age of Television*, Boston, Mass.: Unwin Hyman, 1990, pp. 297–318.

For most of its history, the U.S. system of broadcasting has built upon and profited from a distribution bottleneck: the network structure, which effectively limited the number of national channels in most markets to two or three. Though the economics of broadcasting alone might not have allowed more than three stations to thrive in most local markets, it is a technological rather than a purely economic factor that both created and supported the network system during most of its early years. This technology consists of the very backbone of networking itself: the web of wires owned and operated by the American Telephone and Telegraph company (AT&T), with which first NBC, then CBS, and finally the spun-off NBC blue network that became ABC strung together their affiliates across the country, and through which their programming was distributed. Though radio, and later television, might have been "broadcast" technologies at the local end—using the publicly owned airwaves to carry their signals from the local stations into the living rooms of the community—they remained wire-transmitted technologies at heart. From the networks' central transmission points to the local stations, broadcasting relied on a government-regulated but privately owned system of long lines controlled by AT&T.

AT&T's monopoly over wire transmission and the mutually beneficial series of agreements reached with RCA in the mid-1920s made the entry of others into the broadcasting field difficult. Out of all other applicants for national network lines after 1926, only CBS was granted access to AT&T wires. This bottleneck affected the film industry as well. Both Paramount and MGM attempted to start networks in the late 1920s, and although the reasons for their withdrawal are complex, one factor seems to have been the unavailability of AT&T lines.[1] However, it is with the arrival of television in the late 1940s that the situation became acute, both for the film industry, whose ready supply of film programming stood poised to find a new broadcast outlet, and for the viewers at home. Not until 1975 does a truly viable alternative to the AT&T system emerge. But early efforts to circumvent the limitations of the network system took place on two fronts: by the film industry, in the form of over-the-air subscription television; and by home market entrepreneurs, in the form of cable television. These two concepts would later come together, with the help of a new transmission technology, to produce "pay television"—referred to variously as "pay cable" or PTV[2]— leading to the successful integration of film and cable that we see today.

To begin with the situation on the consumer end, radio's relatively low costs and greater carrying power had made operation and reception of local radio stations fairly widespread. Television stations were much more expensive to put on the air, and television signals were subject to greater interference and degradation over distance than those of AM radio. These factors, combined with the FCC "freeze" on the granting of broadcasting licenses in the early 1950s, left many U.S. communities with no available television service well into that decade. Communities isolated by geography or distance often found themselves unable to receive even one television signal, as the rest of the country moved into the television age. Local entrepreneurs acted to correct that situation, and by doing so drove in the initial wedge that eventually would split apart the three-network system and usher in the age of cable.

Across the country, in Pennsylvania, Colorado, Utah, and other remote and rugged locations, local businessmen erected large antennas on the highest available ground and strung cables to the homes of the town's residents, usually charging them not only a connection fee but a small amount monthly. These early "community antennas" provided no original programming, but merely relayed the signals of the closest existing stations. Though at first the nearby broadcasters encouraged cable connection as an additional market for their advertising, they soon raised objections to having their local market invaded by signals brought in from distant locations, as the community antennas allowed the cable operators to do. Appealing to the FCC for protection, broadcasters were able to keep cable's growth to a minimum through the sixties and early seventies. As long as cable had to rely on existing broadcast programming, distributed primarily through the existing system of AT&T long lines and subject to FCC regulation designed to protect the interests of broadcasters, cable remained a limited technology firmly ancillary to broadcast television.

The film industry, meanwhile, found itself locked out of television network operations and limited in its attempts to own and operate television stations as well. A few of the larger studios responded by investigating the possibilities of an alternative technology: subscription television, an early form of PTV, which used UHF frequencies (or various forms of non-AT&T wire connection) to transmit scrambled movies to paying customers. Several systems were developed, ranging from Paramount's 'Telemeter', a type of "coin box" operation that allowed customers to drop money into a box on top of the TV to unscramble the movie signal, to the Zenith Phonevision system, which first used telephone lines to transmit its signal but later adapted to a broadcast, punch card operation. The combined objections of broadcasters and theater owners, again appealing to the FCC, inhibited development of these systems. By the time the FCC authorized the subscription television interests to so much as test their alternative technology, 13 years had elapsed and cable television had already begun to look like a promising, ready-made substitute for over-the-air technologies.

However, in the early 1960s the FCC, finally subsuming cable operations under its full authority, began to lay down a system of guidelines for cable that, while at least allowing for its continued operation and growth, placed heavy restrictions on the new medium. Through rulings on importation of distant signals, must-carry legislation, and program-by-program consent from broadcasters for cable transmission, the FCC made it clear that cable television existed as a distribution service distinctly subservient to television broadcasting, limited in the amount of original or nonbroadcast material it would be allowed to supply. As long as the slowly but persistently increasing network of local cable lines continued to be dependent on over-the-air programming, the network bottleneck still remained, simply carried over onto the technology of cable—itself not really a new technology, but a makeshift, cobbled-together system of wires under new decentralized ownership. This state of affairs is reflected in cable TV subscription figures, which grew slowly during the 1960s and early 1970s. At the end of 1971, only 9.6 percent of U.S. TV homes subscribed to cable, through almost three thousand local cable systems.[3]

The first step in freeing cable from its restricted status came with the FCC's 1972 *Report and Order on Cable Television*. While maintaining strict controls over potential "siphoning off" of broadcast programming, this new set of rules did respond to increasing interest in the possibilities presented by cable by encouraging local franchises to make more creative use of vacant channel space. Though the FCC seems to have envisioned locally originated programs on these channels, it also allowed the systems to lease channel space to outside program providers. Soon after the 1972 ruling, the first pay cable services made their appearance. One of the earliest was a small subsidiary of media conglomerate Time Inc. called Home Box Office (HBO), operating initially over a cable system in Wilkes-Barre, Pennsylvania. HBO supplied programming unavailable over regular broadcast channels, mainly live sports and theatrical films, for a monthly fee, using a combination of microwave connection and physical transportation of videotape as its network expanded to cable systems in other pay TV locations. During the early to mid-1970s, a few other pay TV services were cautiously originated, including Viacom's Showtime service and one operated by Warner Communications that would later evolve into The Movie Channel. Pay cable grew slowly, reaching only 3 percent of cable subscribers by the middle of 1975.[4]

Breakthrough

The first real crack in the bottleneck occurs in 1975, perhaps unforeseen by those who made it possible. The launching of SATCOM I, the first commercially available geostationary orbit satellite, marks the beginning of a new era in communications that would eventually affect all aspects of the media industries—but perhaps none with more impact than cable television. Satellite transmission capability finally began to transform television into a true "broadcast" medium, loosening its dependence on the nineteenth-century technology of wired transmission and giving it the ability to offer an almost limitless variety of channels and services. Cable interests were not slow to perceive the possibilities in this new medium. One of these was HBO, which on September 30, 1975 began offering 12 hours of pay programming daily via two transponders leased by its parent company on SATCOM I. Satellite transmission allowed HBO to create the first "pay network," transmitting to cable systems across the country simultaneously, without awkward relays or distance-sensitive costs.

HBO differentiated its programming from that available on the broadcast networks by bidding more for exclusive or first rights to new theatrical films and major sports events and showing them uninterrupted by advertising. Cable customers proved willing to pay for this alternative programming, and a "two tier" system of cable arose, with a growing number of subscribers paying their basic monthly charge for a combination of local stations, superstations, and basic cable networks (those supported by advertising), plus a monthly fee for their "premium" HBO service. The local cable operator kept a portion of this premium—usually around half—with the balance going back to HBO. Though the FCC at first attempted to place restrictions similar to those in effect for broadcast programming on this new service, by 1978 a series of appeals and rulings had invalidated most rules on pay cable, leaving an open field.

As satellite distribution opened up new possibilities to the cable field, another trend began to emerge. In 1978 HBO's parent, Time Inc., purchased the American Television and Communications Corporation (ATC), a cable multiple systems operator (MSO) owning 98 cable systems serving over 675,000 subscribers. Time Inc. thus became overnight the second largest MSO in the country. Vertical integration had begun. That same year Viacom, another MSO, also became vertically integrated when it placed its subscription service on satellite. This new premium channel, Showtime, became HBO's main competitor and remains so today, throughout many ownership changes and mergers. The first jolt of competition hit HBO immediately

336

when later that year the Teleprompter Corporation, the nation's largest MSO with over 1 million subscribers and heretofore one of HBO's best customers, purchased a 50 percent interest in Showtime. This caused a drop in HBO's subscriber rate of approximately 250,000, as Teleprompter's local operations dropped HBO from their channel line-up and switched to the new service.

Indeed, cable operators were not slow to take full advantage of their ability to control access to PTV services within their franchises. According to statistics compiled in 1980, 87 percent of ATC's pay television customers subscribed to HBO, leaving only 3 percent for Showtime and 1 percent to a third competitor, The Movie Channel; 75 percent of Teleprompter's customers subscribed to Showtime; and of Warner Amex Cable subscribers fully 79 percent received the Warner Amex premium service, The Movie Channel.[5] In other words, cable systems tended to promote their own vertically integrated premium services almost exclusively; very few systems even carried those of their competitors, and of those that did, the competing service's subscriber numbers were substantially smaller. HBO's dominance of the total market can be seen in overall PTV figures. By 1980 fully 4 million, or 60 percent, of the nation's 7 million PTV subscribers belonged to HBO. Showtime came in a distant second, with 20 percent of the market or 1.5 million subscribers.

Between 1978 and 1980 several other pay television services began satellite distribution, including Warner Communication's The Movie Channel, HBO's supplemental all-movie service Cinemax, and a few more specialized or regional services; basic cable channels proliferated at an alarming rate. Movie release patterns, which had remained basically the same for years— first run, second domestic run, foreign run, network TV, and finally syndication, over a period that might take as long as 14 years—began to change. By 1983 that pattern had shifted to incorporate videocassette release immediately after, or even during, first run, with PTV exhibition following, sometimes within the same year. This virtually eliminated second-run houses and made broadcast network showings distinctly less profitable. In compensation to the studios, ancillary rights to these new outlets provided revenues that more than made up for the loss of traditional income. However, dependence on PTV in particular had its price.[6]

HBO's position as the dominant PTV service gave it considerable leverage in bargaining for program rights. While studios split box office profits 50/50 with theater owners, PTV revenues are divided three ways. For each $9.00 charged to an HBO customer, the cable operator keeps approximately $5.00 and HBO itself receives the balance, out of which $1.50 to $1.75 goes to the studios for films. This leaves producers only a 16 percent to 20 percent share of PTV profits, with HBO in control. In addition, HBO had begun as early as 1976 to finance theatrical films, in exchange for guaranteed PTV rights; by June 12, 1983, the *New York Times Magazine* could report, "Time Inc. has become, by far, Hollywood's largest financier of movies." HBO's increasing involvement in film financing affected the studios' hegemony in the field. It gave independent filmmakers another source of backing for their productions, often resulting in the sale of ancillary PTV rights to HBO prior to making a theatrical distribution with one of the studios.

This type of "pre-buy" arrangement limited the extent of profits a studio could possibly receive from picking up an independent project; previously, a film that bombed at the box office could at least break even through sale of PTV and broadcast rights. In the words of Richard Frank, a Paramount Pictures executive, "Most movies lose money on their theatrical run. Therefore, if the producer sells off exclusive pay rights to HBO before the project comes to a studio for financing, the studio has lost a key element in offsetting its risk."[7] Deprived of this fail-safe, studios became reluctant to risk backing independent projects, increasing the independents' dependence on HBO and consequently HBO's influence on the movie business. With its pay cable market assured, and a voracious schedule to fill up with films of nearly any description, HBO could afford to take risks where the studios could not. "When the studios make a movie, they don't know if anybody's going to show up. . . . We don't live or die on any individual movie," according to Frank Biondi, president of HBO. HBO and its parent company, Time Inc., soon became an important force in Hollywood, sparking a rise in independent film production backed by HBO.[8]

Thus a situation comparable to the film industry's predivestiture arrangement took shape, as large companies such as Time Inc., Teleprompter, and Viacom both financed and distributed programming, with an assured outlet in wholly owned cable systems nationwide. The film industry began to feel the squeeze. HBO's dominance in the pay TV business allowed it to exert considerable pressure on its film suppliers, especially since its acquisition in 1976 of Telemation Program Services, a distribution company that bought pay television rights to films and other properties for sale to "stand-alone" cable systems—those not affiliated with an MSO, the equivalent of an "independent" broadcast station. These developments put the film studios, in the words of one movie executive, at a disadvantage in the market on these levels:

> one in terms of the local monopolies . . . the second in terms of MSO's and the projection that MSO's would increasingly constitute the bulk of the marketplace. And the third that HBO in particular, in terms of its control of the universe of subscribers, put the individual movie companies into a noncompetitive, untenable position.[9]

Another industry analyst claimed that, "The power exerted by the duopoly of HBO and Showtime has enabled them to keep down the fees paid to the studios," as the financial return on licensing agreements shrank from $16 per subscriber a few years before to about $7 as of 1980.[10]

Again in the view of film industry sources, HBO in particular did not hesitate to use its position in the market to drive film prices down. According to an official of MCA/Universal, one of the first companies to license films to HBO,

> We had numerous meetings with HBO representatives who indicated that they only had a need for five studios' product and there were seven studios, or words to that effect. And that if I didn't get on the wagon soon, it would leave without me.

In another case, it is reported that when Twentieth Century–Fox refused HBO's bid for its hit film *Breaking Away*, choosing instead to sell to NBC, no Fox films appeared on HBO for a year in retaliation.[11]

To the film industry, the situation appeared depressingly familiar: discouraged from radio broadcasting, blocked from offering movies over subscription television, then virtually excluded from the major network schedules, history seemed to be repeating itself as the 1970s drew to a close. Starting in 1978, executives from the major film studios began to meet, formally and informally, to discuss a workable scheme that could compete successfully with the PTV giants.

> Our goals are basically the same. To erode HBO's ever increasing leverage and eliminate outside middlemen from our business. We know from the network television business what can happen to us and we don't want it to happen again. We cannot sit idly by watching HBO gobbling up the market with our product. The revenue potential is staggering.[12]

Film industry response

For a variety of reasons—including its past experience with subscription TV, failed negotiations with Showtime and The Movie Channel, and the knowledge that to compete effectively with the entrenched services, a response involving more than one studio would be necessary—the film industry waited until 1980 to attempt to remedy this situation. In a series of meetings held in the latter half of 1979, representatives from Columbia, Paramount, MCA, and Twentieth Century–Fox reached an agreement to form a new pay TV service, to be called Premiere. A fifth partner was the Getty Oil Corporation, whose transponder on the COMSTAR satellite would provide distribution for the service. Premiere would be an all-movie service, operating only during evening hours and showing three films each night, Monday through Thursday, with four films on Friday, Saturday, and Sunday. About half of the approximately 150 films per year needed to meet this schedule would come from the four partners, with the rest from other producers on a nonexclusive basis. The primary concern of those involved in Premiere was to differentiate the service sufficiently from HBO to persuade cable systems to make room on their limited cable space for the new PTV channel. Since none of the Premiere partners were MSO's, they, unlike HBO, would be unable to enforce Premiere's inclusion at the local level and would have to make up the difference in product differentiation and aggressive marketing.

This insistence of differentiation led to the joint venture's downfall through the infamous "nine-month window" provision, designed to provide the service with exclusive programming. For nine months after the release of each film licensed to Premiere—and this would include the total theatrical output (except for X-rated films) of each of the four studios—they would belong exclusively to Premiere; no other service or outlet would be allowed to purchase rights or exhibit these films. With exclusive contract to over half of the total Hollywood output, Premiere could market itself as *the* Hollywood PTV network, virtually ensuring itself a space on any cable system. To placate the cable operator worried about losing HBO subscribers should 70 percent of its movies suddenly be cut, Premiere claimed that its nine-month exclusivity would eliminate the kind of duplication that currently existed on HBO/Showtime/TMC schedules. In other words, said the Premiere marketing literature, the subscriber will want at least two services: Premiere for movies, and HBO or Showtime for sports, specials, and other programming.[13]

Though Premiere's reasoning might have been valid, it should have come as no surprise that objections would be raised to such a plan; indeed, at the urging of HBO and Showtime, the Justice Department began an investigation in April 1980 and filed a civil antitrust suit in August of the same year, charging Premiere with violation of the Sherman Antitrust Act. Showtime representatives called Premiere "an illegal conspiracy" involving "price fixing and attempted monopoly," while HBO spokesmen noted, "it's simply illegal for companies to get together, to set up a mechanism of pricing and to boycott competitors."[14] Despite the studios' reply that the Premiere scheme merely responded to an existing market imbalance, the courts found against Premiere. In the colorful words of one MCA executive, "We may also control a number of toilets in Orange Country. The relevant place to look at is the market we're trying to get into."[15] On December 31, 1980, Judge Gerald L. Goettel issued an injunction against the service, which had been scheduled to start on January 1.[16] One of Judge Goettel's reasons for this action was that initiation of the new service might have the effect of driving HBO's only two existing competitors, Showtime and The Movie Channel, out of business, thus reducing the overall number of pay channel competitors. Though the matter never came to trial, the Premiere partners were advised that a trial would probably lead to a decision against them. Plans for Premiere were formally abandoned early in 1981.

Post Premiere

However, even this severe and costly blow did not deter the movie industry from seeking another foothold in the PTV business. In the months following the Premiere debacle, Columbia Pictures took one route: tacitly abandoning the idea of an ownership position in cable, it decided to accept the current situation by becoming the first major studio to sign an exclusive five-year contract to supply pictures to HBO. In return, HBO agreed to invest up front in Columbia's films, besides paying a fee based on per-film theatrical revenues. Two of the other Premiere partners took a different approach, making one more attempt at ownership of a cable channel. In November 1982 Paramount and Universal began discussions with Warner Communications and American Express, owners of The Movie Channel, to purchase a partnership in that service. Before these plans had been finalized, Showtime's parent company, Viacom, became interested in the project, finally agreeing to merge Showtime and The Movie Channel under the joint ownership of Paramount, Universal, Warners, and itself. Each of these four companies would own 22.58 percent of the new service, with American Express holding the remaining 9.68 percent.[17]

But the Justice Department proved no more willing to condone this sort of cooperation between supplier and distributor than it had with Premiere. Contending that not only would substantial vertical integration result from this plan, but the merger of two secondary PTV services would again reduce the number of competitors in the pay television field, the Justice Department decided that this proposal was anticompetitive, objecting particularly to the involvement of the two movie studios in the venture. Paramount and Universal then withdrew from the proposal, and the Justice Department agreed to withdraw its objections. A merger of the two services was completed in August 1983 under the joint ownership of Viacom, Warners, and American Express. Warners and American Express later sold their interest to Viacom, which now wholly owns the merged Showtime/The Movie Channel service.[18]

This second indication on the part of the Justice Department that vertical integration between program supplier and distributor/exhibitor would not be allowed seems to have convinced the major studios that these tactics could not succeed. In their place, the film industry has pursued three major strategies for adapting to the new satellite-distributed marketplace: cross-ownership, in which film studios, PTV services, and even broadcast networks jointly produce, distribute, and exhibit films; package deals like Columbia's, whereby the film studios enter into exclusive or nonexclusive contract with one or another of the established PTV services; and investment in other aspects of cable distribution, especially basic cable services.

The most remarkable example of the first strategy was the creation in 1983 of the "first new major film studio since the 1940s," as it was billed by its owners. This was Tri-Star studios, formed by a partnership between

341

Columbia Pictures, HBO, and the CBS television network. Tri-Star released 15 films in its first two years of operation, including such hits as *The Natural* and *Rambo*, all produced by Columbia, reserved for HBO pay television viewing, and finally aired on CBS. However, other pressures caused this unique partnership to dissolve after its two-year honeymoon. Originally owned by the three partners at 25 percent each, with the remaining 25 percent sold publicly, CBS sold its shares to Columbia in 1985. One reason for Columbia's purchase was the prospect of also producing shows for television, which Tri-Star was prohibited from doing as long as it was partially owned by a network.[19] In 1986, Time Inc. sold half its shares to Columbia, subsequently forming its own production house, HBO Pictures. This left Columbia 43 percent owner of Tri-Star, with another 43 percent of shares publicly held and the remaining 14 percent retained by Time. By the end of 1987, Tri-Star had indeed expanded into production both for network and syndication, in addition to ownership of the Loew's theater chain. Plans were announced late in 1987 for the merger of Tri-Star and the Coca-Cola Company's entertainment divisions through a stock purchase agreement. Besides Columbia Pictures, Coca-Cola also owned, as of the end of 1987, Embassy Communications and Merv Griffin Enterprises, both television production houses, and was part owner of RCA/Columbia Home Video and the Weintraub Entertainment Group. In 1988, all of Coca-Cola's production ventures, including Tri-Star, were subsumed under a new subsidiary called Columbia Pictures Entertainment.[20] Another film studio partially owned by PTV interests is Orion Pictures, in which both HBO and Showtime have purchased a small equity through financing arrangements.

The second strategic option, the signing of distribution agreements with PTV services, was selected by Paramount Pictures in the aftermath of the failed Showtime/TMC venture. Paramount signed a five-year exclusive contract with the new combined pay service in December 1983, agreeing to release all of its films to Showtime/TMC after theatrical distribution and videocassette release. This agreement affected about 75 Paramount films over the five-year term and involved only pay cable distribution, with no investment on the pay channel's part in the production of the films. The distribution pattern consisted of release on videocassette about six months after the theatrical run, with exhibition on Showtime/The Movie Channel possible after a further six months. Widely heralded as the potential savior of the troubled second-place service, Paramount's films did indeed help Showtime/The Movie Channel to gain subscribers during the 1983 to 1988 period. However, when the agreement expired in 1988, Paramount surprised industry analysts by switching to a nonexclusive agreement with HBO for another five years. HBO also retains an agreement with Columbia, since that studio's original 1981 agreement was extended to last until 1990 by subsequent negotiation. Other studios currently under nonexclusive contract with HBO included MCA/Universal, Warner Bros., Orion, and Twentieth Century–Fox, with Fox also agreeing to handle theatrical distribution of HBO-produced films.

The issue of concern for film studios in the late 1980s in their relations with the two major PTV services centers on exclusivity. By offering only nonexclusive contracts, HBO can pay the film studios less for their product, while leaving open the possibility that they may simultaneously market their films elsewhere. However, given HBO's dominance of the PTV market, it is unlikely that any competitor would be willing to pay any substantial amount to duplicate programming already available on HBO. So HBO's nonexclusive agreements become defacto exclusives; the only difference lies in the amount paid to the studios for this right. Showtime/TMC, on the other hand, prefers exclusive agreements because of its fear that HBO could come in with high offers for the most attractive films, cutting out any advantage Showtime/TMC could offer its customers. By mid-1988 Showtime counted only Cannon Pictures, Atlantic Releasing, The De Laurentiis Entertainment Group, and Disney's Touchstone Pictures among its exclusive suppliers. A change in management in mid-1987, when National Amusements Inc. bought Showtime/TMC's parent Viacom, could bring about some changes in the PTV contract system.[21]

The third option, ownership interests of another sort in cable, are becoming the rule rather than the exception in film industry/cable relations in the 1980s. One of the more visible success stories is Disney Corporation's The Disney Channel, which debuted in September 1983 under the sole ownership of Disney Studios, backed by an arrangement with Westinghouse, then the owner of MSO Group W Cable. Disney's venture avoided problems with the Justice Department and has met with considerable commercial success, due to the unique characteristics of the studio and the service. Since only one studio was involved rather than a possible "price-fixing" consortium, as in the Premiere case, the Justice Department could not object on antitrust grounds; this ability to form a one-studio PTV service in turn rests on the fact that Disney films in themselves are sufficiently differentiated from the bulk of film programming as to make the service easy to identify and sell. By the end of 1987 Disney had 3.2 million subscribers nationwide, making it the fourth-rated PTV service.

Other studios have invested in basic cable services. Paramount and MCA jointly own and operate the USA Network, an advertiser-supported entertainment and sports channel founded in 1980 and reaching over 39 million homes as of 1988. MCA also owns WOR, a broadcast/cable "superstation" operating out of New York with the potential of reaching over 9.5 million homes nationwide. Warner Communications, a diversified media company built on the foundations of the former studio, started early in cable. By 1988 its subsidiary Warner Cable operated 101 systems across the United States. In 1979 it formed Warner Amex Satellite Entertainment Company, with American Express as a partner. The new company, Warner Amex, took an interest in innovative uses of basic cable programming, purchasing the highly original and influential Music Television (MTV) channel and its adult-oriented spin-off Video Hits I (VH-1), as well as the nation's top children's cable channel, Nickelodeon. Warner Amex at one time also owned the merged Showtime/TMC, as mentioned above, but following heavy losses in its cable system division and from its Atari subsidiary in 1986, Warner sold its interest in The Movie Channel, along with all of its basic cable services, to Viacom. However, in 1987 Warner Communications—now divorced from American Express—purchased a part interest in the Turner Broadcasting System, as did United Artists Communications, Viacom, and several other cable companies, in the wake of Ted Turner's financial crisis following his aborted 1985 takeover of the CBS television network. CBS had previously purchased the MGM/UA film library (prompting the current "colorization" controversy), which forms the backbone of yet another basic cable channel, the TNT network, a 1988 entry into the basic cable sweepstakes. As for Warner, its 1989 announcement of a merger with media conglomerate and HBO parent Time Inc. promises the start of yet another phase of media industry economics, as will be discussed below.

While all of these ventures and agreements represent the most visible aspects of the film industry's response to the new era in cable communications, pay cable's effect on the film industry exceeds simple marketing and cross-ownership considerations. The emergence of cable, and particularly of satellite-distributed pay systems, had a far-ranging impact on all aspects of the media business, including the traditional broadcast networks and stations. Some of these, in turn, crept around through the back door of existing relations with the film industry to create new markets for traditional studio output, as well as opportunities to create new types of programs. For instance, the proliferation of cable systems after 1978—spurred by the growth of pay cable—had a side effect of boosting the viability of the former stepchildren of the broadcasting structure: independent television stations. FCC must-carry legislation mandated that cable systems carry any over-the-air station in their market, even the puniest UHF operation; cable carriage, in turn, brought new audiences to the small independents, enabling them to compete more effectively in the local broadcast market. The independents' new visibility sparked a need for more and better programming than their former diet of network reruns and old movies. Into this breach stepped the film studios and their television subsidiaries, with syndicated film packages and so-called "first-run syndication" programming, produced specifically with this new market in mind.

Most remarkably, the new strength of these independents produced the birth of the first new broadcast network in 30 years, as the former studio Twentieth Century–Fox, purchased by media magnate Rupert Murdoch's News Corporation in 1985, launched the Fox Broadcasting Network in October 1986. Fox began on a small scale, providing just one night of prime-time programming a week to unaffiliated stations across the country. By 1988 it had expanded to two, with a third forthcoming in 1989. A drop in overall network ratings in 1987—based in part on the new Nielsen "peoplemeter" system—has led some critics to question the viability of a fourth broadcast network at this time. Partially in response to this, Fox's Monday night schedule will consist of "The Fox Movie of the Week," to be supplied by Fox Film Corporation.[22] Though future prospects are still uncertain, its corporate affiliation with Metromedia, a broadcasting and television production company also owned by Murdoch, with several of the nation's largest independent stations in its stable, should contribute to the new network's success.

Beyond pay cable

Besides distribution directly related to cable, three other new technologies have had a considerable impact on film production and release in the late 1980s. One of these is the rapid growth of the home videocassette recorder, which is discussed in detail in another chapter of this book. Videocassettes have become a permanent and highly profitable step in the film distribution chain, traditionally occurring immediately after theatrical release and before pay cable exhibition. In 1986 videocassette revenues exceeded traditional box office income for the first time in history; in 1987 home video accounted for 30 percent of total consumer electronic media spending, against 19 percent at the box office and 18 percent for pay cable.[23]

The second "new" technology, pay-per-view, bears striking resemblance to the subscription television systems advocated by film interests in the 1940s, though it is based upon a far more sophisticated technology. Pay-per-view, or PPV, in the 1980s relies upon addressable converter devices, which have a two-way communication ability to allow a customer at home to select whichever film the PPV service is offering at a given time and be billed only for the cost of that film rather than at a monthly rate, as with PTV. The nation's largest PPV network, Request Television, is owned by Reiss Media Enterprises, but owes its existence to an investment of over $40 million over the last five years by several film companies: Columbia, Disney, Lorimar, MGM-UA, New World, Paramount, Fox, Universal, and Warner. Request currently serves 3.7 million homes, offering two to four movies per week along with special events such as sports and concerts. Other PPV operations include Viewer's Choice, owned by Viacom, second largest at 3.5 million addressable homes; Playboy; Home Premiere TV; Jerrold's Cable Video Store; and Graff PPV.

PPV networks operate virtually as middlemen between studios and cable operators. Viewer's Choice splits its revenues three ways, with 50 percent of subscriber fees going directly back to the studios, 40 percent to the cable operators, and a 10 percent "fee" to the PPV service. Request Television goes even further by simply selling transponder time to studios, which they may program as they please. The PPV service then takes a smaller percentage of revenues, as the studio and cable operator divide profits 45/55. After five years of slow growth, PPV subscribership jumped 24 percent in 1988, due in part to a resolution of release-pattern difficulties. Previously, PPV release came immediately after theatrical run, before videocassette distribution, which in turn occurred before pay cable release. Pay cable operators such as HBO and Showtime originally regarded PPV as an "offensive weapon" against videocassette competition, since PPV exposure allowed newly released movies to be taped at home, thus weakening video sales and rentals and speeding up release to the pay cable networks. This situation changed dramatically with the 1988 shift in distribution patterns; now films are released to PPV after, rather than before, videocassette distribution, at once relieving video retailers, opposition to the medium and contributing to the downturn in pay cable subscribership. This is clearly a move in the direction of more control over posttheatrical release on the part of the movie studios, now that ownership of pay cable has been ruled out. In addition, the gradual dissemination of more sophisticated addressable converters in newly deregulated cable systems makes the spread of PPV possible; new, easier-to-use decoders also allow PPV consumers to make ordering decisions more impulsively, thus boosting sales.[24]

Of equal, and potentially related, significance is the 1980s boom in direct satellite distribution of all of the above cable, broadcast, and pay offerings, called DBS. Across the country, satellite receive-only dishes have blossomed in backyards and pastures, especially in rural areas unserved by cable. Though confusion over whether or not to scramble these signals, previously received for free by dish owners, disrupted dish purchase trends in 1986 and 1987, 1988 saw the figures climbing again. In March 1987 Viacom began offering a package of 12 cable channels—including Showtime/TMC, CNN, ESPN, Lifetime, and Nickelodeon—for a monthly fee of $17.95, and the Video Cipher II descrambling technology has become a standard part of the home satellite package. Currently, five companies have applied to the FCC to launch a total of ten satellites to be dedicated to DBS service, each capable of carrying up to 16 channels of programming developed specifically for the new medium. With development of new, higher-frequency KU band satellites, the size of the receiving dish has begun to diminish as well. In mid-1988 COMSAT and Matsushita jointly introduced a 15-inch flat plate antenna that could be mounted on a wall or sit near a door or window inside the house. For the film industry, the most important development in DBS may be the recently announced plans of Touchstone Video Network, backed by Uniden, the telephone and satellite company, for a PPV service to be delivered via direct broadcast satellite. Beginning in 1989, subscribers would be able to select from among ten simultaneously and continuously transmitted films, paying only for the one they select, to be received over their backyard or living room dish, with the charges appearing on their monthly telephone bill.[25]

As receiving dishes become more manageable and affordable, and with previous ordering and billing difficulties smoothed out by new decoders and telephone company involvement, DBS could become the primary method of reception for all those signals currently picked up through a combination of broadcast, microwave, and cable transmission, without the former technologies' limitations on channel space. Though it is hard to predict the combined effects of technology, regulation, and economics on the ultimate resolution of this service, it has the potential for finally freeing television completely from its restrictive roots in nineteenth-century wired transmission, thus opening up the number of potential channels to the almost limitless capacity of high-frequency broadcasting. If yet another new technology, high-definition television (HDTV), is to survive and prosper in the 1990s, KU band satellite transmission will be necessary to provide sufficient band width for the improved television pictures it promises to supply.[26]

High-definition television, still in its early stages of development in this country, is a technology for improving the resolution of the television picture by doubling the number of times each TV picture is "scanned," or read by the camera. Developed by laboratories both in the United States and Japan, several competing systems are currently in experimental use. Two factors have worked to slow adoption of this improved broadcast standard: First, as mentioned above, the doubled signals would require significantly more band width for transmission than current signals, and given the already crowded conditions in the normal broadcast spectrum, another means of distribution, such as DBS, would need to be cleared. Second, television sets employing the current 525-line picture would be incapable of receiving HDTV's 1125-line signal, requiring HDTV providers to offer duplicate services well into the future, or else requiring a considerable investment in new technology on the part of the consumer.

What does this mean for the movie companies? HDTV could finally bring a picture quality to the home screen to rival that of the theater. In fact, during 1988 a French movie distributor, Videac, announced plans to distribute films to movie theaters via HDTV, using France's TELECOM I satellite to reach cinemas in small towns across the country. With satellite distribution simultaneously, and at long last, removing the channel "scarcity" upon which so much of our current broadcast and cable economics and regulations are based, and with PPV technology bringing the direct sale economics of the box office into the home as well, the home may become the movie theater of tomorrow. Certainly an increasing number of channels of distribution implies an increasing need for programming, and so far the film companies have proved themselves more than adequate in retaining their hold on the supply end of the business.

347

Through investment in pay television, television production, syndication, basic cable, and videocassettes, alongside regular and increasing theatrical production, the film studios of today exist in a high-demand market. With the broadcast bottleneck finally broken, and the restrictive regulatory conditions of scarcity removed, they may be able to move more freely into the highly competitive distribution market of the satellite era. The success of videocassette sales and rentals in the 1980s, compared to the relative slump in PTV subscriptions and overall broadcast ratings, indicates that the consumer enjoys films above almost any other type of electronic entertainment and prefers to be able to select from a wide variety of alternatives rather than a limited menu, to be viewed at a time of his or her own choosing. This seems to be precisely what the current situation stands poised to deliver, to the ultimate benefit of the production companies.

Furthermore, evidence suggests that Hollywood may be succeeding in a sort of "pincer play" on its rivals. With pay-per-view and videocassette release capturing the posttheatrical market before PTV can get to it, earlier basic cable play dates, plus more original production, on studio-owned basic cable services, combined with deregulation-inspired hikes in cable subscription rates by local cable operators, PTV may find itself squeezed out of the market by studio-controlled alternatives. Thus, despite earlier defeats, the ultimate effect of the challenge of PTV may be to leave the studios in a more diversified position than ever before.

A new era

As the 1980s draw to a close, yet another era in film/television/cable industry relations seems to be emerging, based in large part on the expanding international distribution structure. Developments in European broadcasting systems in particular promise to open up a vast new market for U.S.-produced programming, as well as opportunities for investment and competition on a new international scale. Besides the increased commercialization of broadcast networks and stations across Europe and the loosening of restrictions and quotas on foreign import programs,[27] the advent of direct broadcast satellite systems in England and across the continent strengthens the demand for American-produced programming. Rupert Murdoch's Sky Television began operation of five DBS channels across Europe in early 1989; a competitor, the British Satellite Broadcasting Company (BSB), announced plans to launch three channels of its own in the fall of 1989. Both of these, have aggressively pursued Hollywood studios for exclusive contracts. Sky Television, through Murdoch's cross-ownership, has access to the Twentieth Century–Fox catalogue and Orion films. BSB, owned by a consortium of Australian, British, and French media companies, includes MCA/Universal, Paramount, Columbia/TriStar, MGM/UA, and several independents in its stable of producers. This new European DBS market, combined with the ever-expanding number of terrestrial outlets in the United Kingdom, Italy, and West Germany in particular, provides a fortuitous source of additional revenue to American studios: "However it comes down, it's a major add-on to the U.S. revenue flow. Unlike cable in the U.S., which ate into network revenues, it's new money," according to MGM/UA chairman Norman Horowitz. European distribution will add one more step to the American film release chain, probably occurring about 12 months after videocassette release.[28]

Perhaps partly in anticipation of these events, and partly in response to the growing size of media conglomerates in the international media market, another visible characteristic of the media industry of the 1990s promises to be merger and consolidation on a large scale. The acquisition of Warner Communications by Time Inc. brings a U.S.-based company into line with other global media powers, companies which combine interests in all or most aspects of the media field. The deal has made Time-Warner the largest media corporation in the world, with interests in book and magazine publishing, film and television programming, broadcasting, cable systems, and the music industry. It can now compete worldwide with such integrated corporations as Bertelsmann A.G. of West Germany, Murdoch's Australian-based News Corporation, and Hachette S.A. of France, along with Capital Cities/ABC at home. According to *The Wall Street Journal*, "The leading media companies see the world dominated by a few giant concerns by the end of the century, each company controlling a vast empire of media and entertainment properties that amounts to a global distribution system for advertising and promotion dollars."[29] Already the global merger trend has sparked acquisitions in the U.S. market. Just a few weeks after Time-Warner, MGM/UA announced its partial purchase by Australian-based Qintex Corporation, owner of one of the Australian broadcast networks. Though this fell through, in October 1989 an acquisition of even larger import occurred when the Sony Corporation of Japan purchased Columbia Pictures, effectively adding another level to its vertically integrated empire in the communications industry. Meanwhile, rumors of a possible merger of MSO and program distributor Viacom with either Gulf+Western or MCA began to circulate, as U.S. media company stocks rose dramatically. This activity, combined with speculation that other major international corporations such as Sony are also looking for U.S. media investments, makes the future for Hollywood appear bright, as the words of one far-seeing Hollywood executive indicate:

When television started in the 1950's, there was a strong view that that was the end of Hollywood. When cable came, we thought that would kill our sales to the networks. None of these things happened. Every time the market expands, the combination is greater than before. After all, it should be immaterial to Hollywood how people see its product so long as they pay.[30]

Notes

1 Michele Hilmes, *Hollywood and Broadcasting* (Champaign: University of Illinois Press, forthcoming). Though regional and cooperative networks such as the Mutual Broadcasting System, founded in 1934 by four powerful independent stations (WOR New York, WGN Chicago, WXYZ Detroit, and WLW Cincinnati), managed to survive into the 1940s, their success was hindered by the policies and rate structures then in use by AT&T, which gave precedence and more favorable rates to heavy users and prohibited interconnection of its lines with those of other wire providers. Occasional or part-time networks found themselves forced to contract for time on the wires far in excess of that which they could actually use—or find advertisers to pay for; the interconnection policy prevented them from contracting with another provider. See Committee on Interstate and Foreign Commerce, *Investigation of the Telephone Industry in the United States*, 76th Cong., 1st sess., House Document No. 340, 1939.

2 I will use the term "pay television" synonymously with "pay cable" throughout most of this chapter. Though pay television can include such related noncable distribution channels as over-the-air subscription TV or satellite master antennae services, such as those in hotels, it has come to refer primarily to its most visible and widely accessible component, pay cable, and I will be using the term in this sense except where otherwise specified.

3 Christopher Sterling, "Cable and Pay Television," in Benjamin M. Compaine, ed., *Who Owns the Media?* (White Plains, N.Y.: Knowledge Industry Publications, 1979), p. 295.

4 Sterling, "Cable and Pay Television," p. 311.

5 Christopher Sterling, "Cable and Pay Television," in Benjamin M. Compaine, Christopher Sterling, Thomas Guback, and J. Kendrick Noble, eds., *Who Owns the Media?* 2nd Edition (White Plains, N.Y.: Knowledge Industry Publications, 1982), p. 434.

6 "How TV Is Revolutionizing Hollywood," *Business Week*, February 21, 1983, pp. 78–79.

7 Tony Schwartz, "Hollywood Debates HBO Role in Film Financing," *New York Times*, July 7, 1982.

8 Robert Lindsey, "Home Box Office Moves In On Hollywood," *New York Times Magazine*, June 12, 1983, pp. 31 ff.

9 Lawrence B. Hilford, "Deposition taken in *United States of America v. Columbia Pictures Industries, Inc.; Getty Oil Company; MCA Inc.; Paramount Pictures Corporation; and Twentieth Century–Fox Film Corporation.*" Civil Action #8-Civ. 4438, United States District Court for the Southern District of New York, September 9, 1980, p. 62.

10 "Hollywood Battles for New Markets," *Dun's Review* (June 1980) p. 75.

11 Quote from Fred Dawson, "Waiting for Goettel," *Cablevision*, December 1, 1980, pp. 88–96; Jane Mayer, "Hard Bargainer: Show Buyer for HBO Is a Power in Pay TV, A 'Pain' in Hollywood," *Wall Street Journal*, August 15, 1983, p. 1:1; Pamela G. Hollie, "Hollywood Offers Pay-TV Challenge," *New York Times*, April 29, 1980, p. D1; Tony Schwartz, "New Pay TV Network to Offer Box-Office Hits," *New York Times*, May 19, 1980, D1:4.

12 Tony Schwartz, "Pay Cable Is Fighting for Movies," *New York Times*, August 22, 1981, p. C24:1.

13 Premiere publicity package, 1980.

14 "Time Inc. to Oppose Getty TV-Film Deal," *New York Times*, April 24, 1980, p. D4:1; "Getty's Pay TV Venture Is Sued By Justice Unit," *Wall Street Journal*,

August 5, 1980, p. 5:1; *Broadcasting*, April 28, 1980, pp. 22, 23; "Hollywood Challenges HBO Clout In Lucrative Cable-Movie Business," *Wall Street Journal*, August 11, 1980, p. 15:4.

15 Tony Schwartz, "New Pay-TV Service to Offer Box-Office Hits," *New York Times*, May 19, 1980, pp. D1, 10.

16 "U.S. Says 5 Companies Broke Law in Plan to Limit Movies on Pay TV," *New York Times*, August 5, 1980, p. 1:1; "Getty's Man on Pay TV," *New York Times*, August 7, 1980, p. D2:5.

17 Jack Banks, "A Survey of the Pay Cable Industry: Concentration and Integration in a Stagnant Video Market" (unpublished paper presented to the Regional Conference of the Union for Democratic Communications in Eagle Creek, California, October 23–25, 1987), pp. 16, 17.

18 "Justice Agency Approves Pay-TV Merge After 2 Distributors Removed As Investors," *Wall Street Journal*, August 15, 1983, p. 8:1.

19 Laura Landro, "Coke's Columbia May Increase Its Stake in Tri-Star; Sale of CBS's Share Is Seen," *Wall Street Journal*, November 14, 1985, p. 7:1.

20 *Broadcasting*, April 28, 1980, pp. 22–23; *View* (June 1983); *Channels 1988 Field Guide to the Electronic Environment* (December 1987), p. 47.

21 "Great Expectations: One More Time," *Channels 1988 Field Guide to the Electronic Environment* (December 1987), p. 117.

22 Fox Revamps Saturday, Will Expand with Movies," *Broadcasting*, May 23, 1988.

23 "At the Crossroads," *Channels 1988 Field Guide to the Electronic Environment* (December 1988), p. 102.

24 "Forcing Open a New Window," *Channels 1987 Field Guide to the Electronic Environment* (December 1987), p. 82; "Waging the Battle for Ultimate Consumer Comfort," *Channels 1988 Field Guide to the Electronic Environment* (December 1987), p. 121; "At the Crossroads," p. 102.

25 "The Birds Fly Low," *Channels 1988 Field Guide to the Electronic Environment* (December 1988), p. 122.

26 "The Dish Crowd Fights for a Pipeline in the Sky," *Channels 1988 Field Guide to the Electronic Media* (December 1987), p. 99; Stephen Brookes, "After Signals Get Scrambled, Home-Satellite Firms Adjust," *Insight*, September 26, 1988, pp. 38–40.

27 "Media Markets Around the World," *Electronic Media*, May 1, 1989, p. 46 ff.

28 Kevin Pearce, "Hollywood Reaps a Windfall From Television's Richest Endeavor," *Channels* (March 1989), p. 9.

29 "Plenty of Fish in Pond Time-Warner Wants to Swim In," *The Wall Street Journal*, March 7, 1989, p. B1.

30 *The Economist*, July 30, 1983, p. 73.

Suggestions for further reading

Channels Field Guide to the Electronic Environment. New York: C.C. Publishing: Yearly summary of activities published as December issue each year.

Drummond, Philip, and Richard Patterson, eds. *Television in Transition*. London: British Film Institute, 1985.

Hilmes, Michele. *Hollywood and Broadcasting: A History of Economic and Structural Interaction from Radio to Cable*. Champaign: University of Illinois Press (forthcoming).

Hollins, Timothy. *Beyond Broadcasting: Into the Cable Age*. Champaign: University of Illinois Press, 1984.

LeDuc, Don R. *Cable Television and the FCC: A Crisis in Media Control*. Philadelphia: Temple University Press, 1973.

Mosco, Vincent. *Broadcasting in the United States: Innovative Challenge and Organizational Control.* New York: Ablex, 1979.

Negrine, Ralph M., ed. *Cable Television and the Future of Broadcasting.* New York: St. Martin's Press, 1985.

Noam, Eli M., ed. *Video Media Competition: Regulation, Economics, and Technology.* New York: Columbia University Press, 1985.

Sterling, Christopher, "Cable and Pay Television," in Benjamin M. Compaine, Christopher Sterling, Thomas Guback, and J. Kendrick Noble, eds. *Who Owns the Media?* White Plains, N.Y.: Knowledge Industry Publications, 1982.

Tydeman, John, and Ellen J. Kelm, *New Media in Europe: Satellite, Cable, VCR's and Videotex.* New York: McGraw-Hill, 1988.

17

THE MULTIPLEX

The modern American motion picture theater as message

Gary Edgerton

Source: *Journal of Popular Film and Television* IX(4) (1982): 158–165.

Motion picture theater design has changed along with what the movie-going experience itself has meant to Americans throughout the twentieth century. The nickelodeon, the movie palace, the studio chain theater and the multiplex have dominated domestic exhibition during their respective eras. Each phase has defined customer, product and architectural contingencies, such as who makes up the movie-going public, what movie content eventually gets national exposure, and how theater design contributes to the overall meaning of going to the movies. Most times these questions are left unasked, as the answers themselves lie hidden in the socio-cultural subtext of the film viewing experience. Still, how and where the ritual of movie-going in America is held inevitably reflects both the business ethos that motivates the exhibition arm of the industry, as well as some of the cultural inclinations of contemporary Americans and how they have evolved in the last eighty-five years.

In retrospect, American film forged the beginnings of an identity between 1896 and 1912, struggling for a visibility beyond the automata or lower billings in vaudeville. In fact, as early as the late 1890s, make-shift storefront theaters holding little more than seats, a screen, and a projector began appearing. Significantly, these operations were designed specifically for presenting movies, as film form evolved from mere reproduction to a storyline, and then gained added narrative sophistication. Additionally, as film producers were stumbling through the trial and error process of developing film art, early exhibitors were equally oblivious to how one should best exploit this new product. Exhibitor strategies would actually develop slower than aesthetics, primarily because priorities in retailing are characteristically subject to changes in product quality and/or output.

By 1905, the age of the nickelodeon had arrived as the number of store-front theaters nationwide exceeded one thousand for the first time.[1] This figure would multiply more than ten times by 1913, as movies were becoming big business complete with antitrust litigations, numerous state and municipal censorship laws, and the beginnings of multi-reel storytelling. Occurring concurrently with these developments, the era of the movie palace was also beginning with the opening of the Regent in New York in 1913,[2] and later this period came to full fruition during the first few years following the end of World War I.

The story of the age of the movie palace, approximately 1913 to 1931, is covered most aptly by Ben M. Hall in *The Best Remaining Seats*.[3] These movie houses were structures which were substantially more than just theaters. Decorated with the most expensive rugs, furniture and fixtures available, these dream palaces were both part of the show and indices of a more general aspiration for achieving the "good life" which millions of Americans paid money week after week to share collectively. As Hall recalls,

> The United States in the twenties was dotted with a thousand Xanadus. Decreed by some local (or chain-owing) Kubla Khan, these pleasure domes gave expression to the most secret and polychrome dreams of a whole group of architects who might have otherwise gone through life doomed to turning out churches, hotels, banks and high schools. The architecture of the movie palace was a triumph of suppressed desire and its practitioners ranged in style from the purely classic to a widely abandoned eclectic.[4]

The widespread proliferation of these movie palaces throughout the teens and early 1920s demonstrates that these "most secret and polychrome dreams" must have struck a responsive chord with America's movie-going public. As has never before or since been the case with motion picture exhibition, the architectural designs and furnishings of America's motion picture theaters were blatantly alive with the country's materialistic ethos leaving the movie palaces themselves to function as a new cultural form expressing an older, mythic content of how Americans felt about their country and themselves. It was almost as if the dream spilled off the screen and embellished the walls, the statues, the domed ceilings and the army of attendants. In a sense, the entire movie-going experience was an opportunity to enter a new and exciting cultural phenomenon ripe with mythic messages in which the environment itself signalled loudly that it was time to dream, even before the lights went out. Unfortunately, movie palaces were also an indication of a culture running blindly into a realization of its own excesses. The stock market crash would make society, as a whole, stop and think in 1929, while exhibitors, in turn, found dream palace upkeep and overhead an expensive burden as the American movie industry began to feel the backlash from the great Depression in 1932.

The next phase in American motion picture exhibition began in 1932 and ended in 1948 with the Paramount Decision.[5] During this era the most successful theater type was the studio chain theater, corporative and operating en bloc in order to corner as large a portion of the marketplace as possible.[6] The economic realities of the Depression changed the tendency in American film exhibition from house extravagance, to methods of booking, bookkeeping and promotion conducted more in line with the rationality of a company policy. More significantly, however, was exhibition's evolving attitude toward retail strategy. With the substantial drop in movie attendance in the early 1930s,[7] "the 'double feature' . . . games, cash prizes and other inducements were . . . added by exhibitors to the regular movie program in an attempt to prop up sagging box office receipts."[8] Added to these retail gimmicks, concessions were also introduced into the film viewing experience for the first time. Initially candy, and then ice cream were provided as convenience items, and also as a means of attracting additional revenues by increasing the number of admissions. By 1948, however, concessions had become money-making ends unto themselves, and this point would become all the more significant as domestic exhibition entered its mature phase.

In the mature state of an industry, businessmen maximize profits rather than volume. Specifically, prices increase faster than unit volume, new product development slows, and competitive industries capture market share at the older industry's expense.[9]

Actually, it is inaccurate to presume that exhibition sprung right into its mature phase in 1948. Still, as Phillip Lowe, current president of the National Association of Concessionaires points out, the process toward exhibitor maturation was identifiably set in motion directly subsequent to the Paramount Decision.

What happened was that really, when television came in, that was in the early fifties, that was the beginning of the mature stage . . . in fact that was when film production started going down. So for historical precedent probably the fifties, but it really didn't impact until the seventies.[10]

Therefore, in the fifteen years following the Paramount case, the major distributors literally curtailed their total number of releases by one-half, 448 to 223,[11] as both a reaction against dwindling admissions and as a method of keeping demand high and, in turn, maintaining their oligopolistic control over the domestic marketplace. Competition from television also entered into the equation that lowered supply by cutting movie attendance even further.

Consequently, major product for the movie retailer diminished substantially leaving exhibitors with few alternatives as a result. In addition, domestic theater owners had to either compromise their role as showmen even further by devising new means of generating capital, or leave the business of exhibiting films altogether.

Whether by force or choice, the latter alternative had more takers than expected. Over 20 percent of the domestic four-wall theaters closed by 1953.[12] On the other hand, the number of drive-ins nationwide increased from 820 in 1948 to a peak of 4,063 in 1958,[13] while concurrently concession sales for outdoor theaters also grew, as did menu size. In addition, hard-top exhibitors followed suit as they too became increasingly conscious of concessions in the early 1950s. "In 1948, concession sales accounted for 7.8 percent of all receipts, in 1954 for 20.8 percent, in 1958 for 16 percent, and in 1963 for 15 percent."[14] Table 1 indicates how from 1954 through 1972 "monies per customer" spent on concessions grew from 12.8 cents to 26.3 cents for four-wall and drive-in theaters combined. By 1977, this figure would double again breaking "the magical 50 cents per person barrier," a highwater mark that Phillip Lowe calls "the four minute mile for Concessionaires."[15]

In the past three decades, selling concessions itself has become a much more sophisticated business evolving its own unique retail strategies. Since 1948, as the major distributors have come to demand a higher share of box-office revenues from the exhibitor,[16] the emphasis in exhibition has switched from projecting films to selling concessions, and exhibitors have simultaneously passed on as much of this cost as possible to their merchandising of secondary products. In the 1970s, the squeeze from the distributor's split of box-office revenues has risen to such an alarming proportion in fact, that theater owners have responded by retailing concessions at a 60 percent profit margin.[17] Consequently, industry estimates gauge that increased pricing has alienated movie-goers to a point where only one in six now buys concessions.[18] Nevertheless, Phillip Lowe suggests that the present state of high pricing is really more beneficial to exhibitors

Table 1 Concession Outlay per Customer Average

	Receipts from Concessions (in thousands)	*Number of Admissions (in millions)*	*Concession Revenues per Customer*
1954	$290,805.2	2,270.4	12.8¢
1958	185,711.76	1,553.8	12.0¢
1963	158,586.83	1,093.4	14.5¢
1967	164,067.53	926.5	17.7¢
1972	245,438.11	934.4	26.3¢
1977	n.a.	n.a.	50.0¢

Source: Computed from U.S. Department of Commerce, *1972 Census of Selected Service Industries*, Motion Picture Industry, pp. 3–4; and MPAA Statistics.

than the option of lowering prices in the hopes of attracting a few more customers.

> The concept of how to sell refreshments to a captive audience is an interesting one because in that point in time they are locked in for all intents and purposes. Now the question then is, for call it one hundred people in your theater, will more, depending on whether you have high pricing or low pricing, if you have low pricing will that many more on an incremental analysis basis buy? We're talking about will refreshment price merchandising to a captive audience increase with unit elasticity? The answer is no. What that means is if you sell a candy bar for fifty cents or a dollar . . . you will not sell twice as many at fifty cents as you will at a dollar, and therefore, you might as well extract the highest possible price that you can from people in that type of captive environment.[19]

Consistently, the above quote has wider implications for the American motion picture industry at large. Customers are being treated by exhibitors in much the same way that exhibitors are being concurrently manipulated by the major distributors. With the oligopolistic market structure that exists, domestic exhibitors are the distributors' captive audience. In turn, the major distributors "extract the highest possible price" from the exhibition arm of the industry.

Phillip Lowe also elaborates on other ways that the theater owner/movie-goer relationship has changed in the 1970s.

> Theater owners are constantly looking at other ways of maximizing income. One of the things that they're doing is they're putting pinball machines and electronic game machines in their lobbies . . . it's become an accepted national strategy . . . Prints, artwork T-shirts, all kinds of stuff. This is quite successful . . . no it doesn't alienate customers, quite the opposite. It's voluntary so it can't alienate customers. It's a way of offering them a total entertainment experience, or stated another way, it's a way of maximizing a theater owner's revenue.[20]

Therefore, in the mature phase of motion picture exhibition, the biggest development is the changing emphasis from movies to secondary products. Industrial consensus across the board agrees that if a theater owner is to make money and stay in business, his profits must come from concessions and other ancillary merchandise. Exhibitors in the 1970s generate only an estimated 1.5 percent profit on box-office revenues,[21] and consequently this figure would allow inflation alone to sound the death knell for domestic motion picture theaters if movies were their only source of income.

In addition, this shift in emphasis from merchandising feature films to selling concessions also shows up in contemporary motion picture theater design. The message implicit in the decor and surroundings of the modern theater is no longer "to dream." Its function, color and design communicate to the movie-goer an entirely different signal. Today, the most progressive type of theater, and the most characteristic of its era, the multiplex,[22] tells its occupants it is time "to buy."

The first multiplex in America was built in Kansas City by the American Multi-Cinema Corporation in 1963. Multiplexing has since proven itself to be a major stimulant, enabling a handful of chains to grow gradually at first, then meteorically over the subsequent two decades.[23] Table 2 suggests the industry-wide growth of multiplexing during the decade of the 1970s. Back during the 1963 national Theatre Owners of America (TOA) Convention, however, Drew Eberson, whose family had been in the business of constructing domestic theaters for over forty years, accurately forecasted the future of theater design in a speech entitled, "A Look Ahead at Theater Trends."

Table 2 U.S. Motion Picture Theaters (end of year)

	1939 (Census)	1948 (Census)		
Indoor	n.a.	17,811		
Drive-In	n.a.	820		
Total	15,115	18,631		

	1954 (Census)	1958 (Census)	1963 (Census)	1967 (Census)
Indoor	14,716	12,291	9,150	8,803
Drive-In	3,775	4,063	3,502	3,384
Total	18,491	16,354	12,652	12,187

	1972 (Census)	Est. Screens	1974 (Census)	Est. Screens
Indoor	9,209	10,694	9,645	11,612
Drive-In	3,490	3,734	3,519	3,772
Total	12,699	14,428	13,164	15,384

	1975 (Census)	Est. Screens	1979 (Census)	Est. Screens
Indoor	9,857	12,168	9,021	13,331
Drive-In	3,535	3,801	3,197	3,570
Total	13,392	15,969	12,218	16,901

Source: U.S. Department of Commerce, *Bureau of Census*, and MPAA Statistics.

During the 1920s the boom was on. We were designing and opening at least one theater a month. The seating capacities were between 2,000 and 5,000 seats. The "golden age" of the motion picture palace was with us. Cost budgets were not too important—get it done— have it bigger, grander, more ornate and more palacelike . . .

Then came the depression and from then on there were peaks and valleys in theater construction. During the 30s and 40s . . . the watchword was economy. High cost of certain types of labor ruled out ornamental plaster, iron work and bronze. We then created a theater by using extremely simple lines and a great deal of color splashes—so-called "modernistic" . . .

And now the boom is on again! But what a different theater! The modern design of course has eliminated the heavy ornamentation, the rising orchestra pit and the elaborate playrooms of the past. The theaters of the 30s with their loud, crass, vulgar colors are gone . . .

My theme is the theater of tomorrow, an auditorium functional in design, a comfortable seat with plenty of leg room and sufficient lighting to prevent groping and tripping; a lobby and foyer with attractive eye appeal, colors harmoniously blended to sooth and yet be admired and a sales area with a head-on shot and equipment which blends with the architectural design and with no unsightly bulges . . .[24]

This ability to "blend with the architectural design . . . with no unsightly bulges" is exactly what sets the multiplex apart from older theater models and makes it the characteristic movie-house of today. In 1965, theater architect Robert W. Kahn put it another way when explaining the appeal of the shopping center theater. "In recent decades motion picture theaters have gone from wild rococo to dullest soap box. Today good design calls for a practical, economical theater that is comfortable and pleasurable to attend, and that will stay attractive beyond the life of any fad or current style."[25] In other words, Kahn is alluding to the fact that in being "beyond . . . any fad," theater design today is either a style for all seasons, or no fashion at all depending upon one's perspective. The atomism of the 1920s which set the Roxy in New York City apart from the Midland in Kansas City, or Radio City Music Hall, has given way to an unprecedented move toward homogeneity where an AMC theater in Missouri looks much the same as one does in New York. In addition, an AMC multiplex anywhere strikingly resembles a respective General Cinema complex, which both conjure up hints of recognition when comparing design, format and color scheme to the neighborhood mall stores and fast food outlets.

The entrepreneural spirit which enlivened the movie palace of yesterday and was reflected in the individuality and audacity of its design has now been replaced by the efficiency and corporate rationality which, in turn, invigorates the decor of the multiplex. As a result, the dream palace way of doing business has today been grounded in the dollar and cents realities of streamlining and increasing profitability to equity invested. Put another way, the exhibitor as merchant has won out over those psycho-social regions of the mind that are usually exercised by the exhibitor as shaman or showman. Consequently, the contemporary movie theater is no longer an exclusive showcase for dreams, but a combination projector/screen and retail outlet. In like manner, an exhibitor's role today has about as much to do with promoting movies as art, or pop art, as a manager at McDonald's concerns himself with nutrition and dietetics. The decor for each of these establishments reflects their common intent of transmitting a simple, yet effective message to the prospective consumer. The evolving language of American commercialese communicates: bright colors, vinyl and laminated covered furnishings, plastic panel art, sloping wall and ceiling design and glaring lights highlighting a centrally located concession area, and an imitation brick linoleum walkway leading to air conditioned auditoriums I, II, III and IV.

Services that immediately gratify are the modes of making money today, and motion picture exhibition is no different than any other sector of the American marketplace. Let the customer relax, make him both responsive and compliant, and above all manipulate the environment so it will be easy for him to spend money. After all, a comfortable consumer is an uncritical buyer, a message implicit in Phillip Lowe's explanation of the advantages of a circular, centrally located concession area as opposed to the traditional backbar, freestanding counter.

> They have the capacity of having more people. If you look at the circumference of that circle versus the front space at a counter, you can just get more people around that circle, and they all think they're going to be next. If you're the third person in line, or the third row of persons waiting to be served, it takes a lot more patience. So we can get more people around a circular stand than you could three or four deep in a back-bar stand.[26]

Therefore, the evolution of theater design from movie palace to multiplex is a switch in emphasis from consumer dreaming to buying. No longer is the imagination meant to be titillated, as much as the senses soothed. Robert L. Beacher, president of the Forest Bay Construction, comments on these strategies.

> The primary objective of the designer is to create an innovative lobby effect by removing the standee wall and enclosing the inner lobby for a friendly living room atmosphere . . . the secret in effective redesign

and twinning of existing theaters depends upon the utilization and retention of a portion of the "old look" to allow the more conservative film-goer a sense of both newness and familiarity. At the same time a mood of comfort and warmth is created.[27]

Ultimately, the relationship between the exhibitor/theatrical environment and the movie-goer has always been a vital supplement to the more obvious dynamic between the audience and the filmmakers in determining what the movie-going experience means to those who attend films. Today, movie theater architects are fundamentally concerned with establishing "a mood of comfort and warmth." In turn, contemporary motion picture theater design both maintains and reflects this ever growing stress on tactile concerns, quite unlike the movie palace's emphasis on the imagination. On a practical level, this switch is consistent with the fact that developments in the contemporary movie business now make it essential that today's exhibitors increasingly earn their livelihoods from the sale of goods in their concession areas, rather than from box-office receipts. Consequently, American theater owners must exert maximum effort in order to corner the captive movie audience before it retreats into the darkened auditorium. These exhibitors hope to sooth, calm, mollify and placate the senses of as many compliant customers as possible. After all, that is what their retail and environmental strategems are designed to accomplish.

On the other hand, many American movie-goers today do, in fact, go to the movies to be viscerally manipulated. Although beyond the scope of this particular essay, both Pauline Kael[28] and James Monaco[29] have recently argued that this manipulator/manipulated paradigm is also the characteristic relationship between contemporary filmmakers and the American audience. Monaco calls the blockbuster films of the 1970s, "entertainment machines." He notes that America is now in an era of filmmaking when "visceral action sells best."[30] Likewise, Kael makes reference to "feelies," which are movies that are "more gripping than entertaining. . . . It [*Alien*] reached out, grabbed you, and squeezed your stomach."[31] Again, tactile effects appear to take precedence. Still, drawing connections between the modern American motion picture theater on one hand, and the evolving nature of contemporary film form on the other, is certainly an elusive pursuit. Nevertheless, it can be firmly established that both film content and the environment in which the movie is seen always affect one another in some way. How, and to what extent these factors work in tandem, however, must for the time being at least, remain the concern of future research.

Notes

1 Kenneth MacGowan, *Behind the Screen, The History and Techniques of the Motion Picture* (New York: Dell Publishing, 1965), p. 129.
2 Ben M. Hall, *The Best Remaining Seats* (New York: Bramhall House, 1961), p. 30.

3 Hall.

4 Hall, p. 93.

5 In 1948, the Supreme Court upheld a lower court's decision that the eight Paramount defendants had violated antitrust laws according to the Sherman Act. According to the Paramount Decision, Paramount, MGM/Loew's, RKO, Twentieth Century-Fox and Warner's were considered "majors" because of their size and the fact that they owned theaters. Three smaller yet dominant companies, Universal, United Artists and Columbia, were also implicated in the litigation. Eventually, the "majors" were forced to divest themselves of their theater holdings.

6 The theater chains linked to the five major studios were: Paramount Pictures, Inc., Twentieth Century-Fox, Warner Brothers, Loew's, Inc. and RKO Corporation. Actually during the 1930s and early 1940s, these five major companies, along with Universal, United Artists and Columbia, also formulated preferential deals with the remaining large-sized independent theater chains nationwide. Consequently, theater circuits solely owned by the five major studios, jointly owned between the major studios, or owned by compliant large-sized independent theater chains had cornered the motion picture marketplace in virtually all major American municipalities, states and/or regions.

7 The *U.S. Department of Commerce, Social and Economic Statistics Administration, Bureau of Economic Analysis* (*Survey of Current Business*) lists U.S. Motion Picture Box Office Receipts (in $ millions) from 1930 through 1935 as follows: 1930—732; 1931—719; 1932—527; 1933—482; 1934—518; and 1935—556.

8 Robert H. Stanley, *The Celluloid Empire: A History of the American Movie Industry* (New York: Hastings House, 1978), pp. 84 and 85.

9 Phillip M. Lowe, "The Beginning of the End," in National Association of Theatre Owners, *Encyclopedia of Exhibition*, 1979, p. 18.

10 Interview with Phillip M. Lowe, July 30, 1980.

11 National Association of Theatre Owners, *Encyclopedia of Exhibition*, 1979, p. 58.

12 *Problems of Independent Motion Picture Exhibitors Relating to Distribution Trade Practices*, hearings before a subcommittee of the Select Committee on Small Business, U.S. Senate, 83rd Congress, 1st Session (Washington, D.C.: Government Printing Office, 1953), p. 947.

13 U.S. Department of Commerce, Bureau of Census, and National Association of Theatre Owners, *Encyclopedia of Exhibition*, 1979, p. 42.

14 Robert D. Lamson, "Motion Picture Exhibition: An Economic Analysis of Quality, Output and Productivity," Unpublished Ph.D. dissertation, University of Washington, 1968, p. 56.

15 Phillip M. Lowe, "Don't Bite the Hand That Feeds You," in National Association of Theatre Owners, *Encyclopedia of Exhibition*, 1979, p. 120.

16 The estimated split of the domestic box-office dollar earned by America's film distributors was 26.9 percent in 1948; 34.4 percent in 1958; 36 percent in 1964; 31.6 percent in 1972; 39 percent in 1977; and over 40 percent in 1980. The 1948, 1958 and 1964 figures were computed from data in *Film Daily Year Book* by Robert D. Lamson, "Motion Picture Exhibition: An Economic Analysis of Quality, Output and Productivity," unpublished Ph.D. dissertation, University of Washington, 1968. The percentages for the 1970s were computed from data received from Warner Communication, the MPAA and found in *Boxoffice* by David J. Londoner, "The Changing Economics of Entertainment," report written for Wertheim & Co., Inc., 1978, p. 21.

17 John Larmett, Elias Savada and Frederic Schwartz, Jr., *Analysis and Conclusions of the Washington Task Force of the Motion Picture Industry* (Washington, D.C.: 1978), p. 16.

18 Lowe, "The Beginning of the End," p. 21.
19 Interview with Phillip M. Lowe, July 30, 1980.
20 Interview with Phillip M. Lowe, July 30, 1980.
21 Larmett et al., *Washington Task Force*, p. 14.
22 Multiplexing is the practice of housing two or more screens under one roof, thus maximizing audience size while essentially paying building and management overhead costs, employees' salaries, etc., for only one structure.
23 By early 1980, the top four theater circuits boasted 2,719 screens, a concentration of 16 percent of the domestic total. Since 1970, the General Cinema Corporation has grown from 233 screens to 894; the United Artists Theater Circuit from 390 to 773; and the American Multi-Cinema Corporation from 147 to 552. In addition, Plitt, a circuit that increased its size substantially when it bought ABC Theaters, had grown to 530 screens by early 1980.
      During the past two decades these four circuits also did substantial multiplexing, which along with the easing of corporate emphasis on the drive-in theater, a willingness to diversify into other business pursuits, a corporate policy of centralization and persistent growth, and an exploitation of the suburban market, were the major policy positions that separated the successful motion picture theater circuits in America from the also-rans.
      Computed from data in the *1965 International Motion Picture Almanac* (ed.) Charles S. Aaronson (New York: Quigley Publications, 1965), pp. 510–522 and the *1980 International Motion Picture Almanac* (ed.) Richard Gertner (New York: Quigley Publications, 1980), pp. 497–523, the General Cinema Corporation increased the number of sites it multiplexed from 5.4 percent in 1963 to 81.9 percent in 1978. Over that same time period, the United Artists Theater Circuit increased the percentage of sites it multiplexed from 0 to 43.1 percent, while the American Multi-Cinema went from 8.3 percent to 97.7 percent. Comparable data on Plitt and ABC Theaters is not available.
24 Drew Eberson, excerpts from the speech, "A Look Ahead at Theatre Trends," *1963 Theatre Owners of America Convention Program*, p. Speech 13.
25 Robert W. Kahn, "What's Playing at the Shopping Center?" *1965 Theatre Owners of America Convention Program*, p. 41.
26 Interview with Phillip M. Lowe, July 30, 1980.
27 Robert L. Beacher, "A New Look in Twin Theatre Design," in the National Association of Theatre Owners, *Encyclopedia of Exhibition*, 1976, p. 110.
28 Pauline Kael, "Why Are Movies So Bad? or the Numbers," *The New Yorker*, June 23, 1980, pp. 82–93.
29 James Monaco, *American Film Now* (New York: New American Library, 1979) pp. 49–80.
30 Monaco, p. 52.
31 Kael, p. 93.

18

IS HOLLYWOOD AMERICA?

The trans-nationalization of the American film industry*

Frederick Wasser

Source: *Critical Studies in Mass Communication* 12(4) (1995): 423–437.

The American film industry no longer addresses a national audience. Hollywood's domination of international trade has altered its relationship with the domestic market. This study locates and elaborates a postwar disassociation between films and the domestic audience in changing finance and marketing practices. The development in the nineteen seventies of pre-selling *unproduced films to worldwide territories eroded the previous classic Hollywood emphasis on the American viewer. The economic history of this trans-nationalization is an important clue to the problem of why American films contribute so little to the social fabric.*

The relationship between the mass media and national culture is undergoing a dramatic evolution. Mass media hegemony, once a matter of one national culture dominating another, can no longer explain the national character of the institutions of mass media. Instead, deracinated transnational media now dominate all national audiences. This shift is still obscure, particularly in film and television where the institutions producing and distributing culture are still the direct descendants of traditional Hollywood film companies such as Time-Warner, Sony Pictures, Fox, Disney and others. However, the current strategies of these companies no longer privilege a special relationship with the national American audience. I describe the recent history of one medium, cinema, in order to uncover the conditions under which the dominant Hollywood studios ceased to be primarily American, ceased to be institutions of national culture.

* Frederick Wasser thanks Professors Thomas Guback and Sandra Braman and his anonymous reviewers.

Trans-nationalization is an economic/cultural phenomenon. It is difficult to study for precisely that reason. However, by concentrating on the financing of American films (the act which initiates the cycle of production, distribution and reception) the history of Hollywood transnationalization can be isolated. This history provides another important tool with which to engage current policy debates over the cultural importance of global filmmaking.[1]

The rupture between audience and producers has reached the acceleration stage of an ongoing fifty-year transformation. In the beginning, American film was organized on a national basis. It was a leisure activity that actively sought to cross local boundaries of class, and regional loyalties. Although priced for the working class, American films—in their content and marketing—constantly reached out to and soon captured the middle class. It was an industry shaped by immigrants, both as producers and as audience, conveying a strong assimilationist message. Films, by and large, either ignored or treated as picturesque the regional and class conflicts that fractured 19th century America. Distribution exchanges encouraged producers to appeal to a wide national audience rather than to more local ones. These patterns, set in the first decades of the industry, motivated film makers to present themselves as American artists, responding to the domestic audience and extolling their product over imported films representing foreign suspect values (Uricchio and Pearson, 1993, p. 52).

When the American film triumphed on the international market eighty years ago, a metaphor developed of America sharing its culture with the rest of the world. This metaphor assumed the paradigm of national cinemas created for national audiences. However the transnationalization of Hollywood film production shows the breakdown of this metaphor. Transnationalization is not to be observed in the export of film products but in the relationship of the film industry with the national audience. Traditionally the American film audience has had a rhetorical importance for the American film industry that exceeded the domestic size of the market (ranging from 50 to 75 percent for a major film release). The financing and distribution of films were premised on first finding success here before seeking further profits overseas. Now the domestic primacy is being reduced. On a per capita basis the American viewer is of no more importance than any other member of the global audience.

This paper will describe the development of economic practices of the post war years that led to the audience shift. The key moment occurred in the seventies with the international financing innovations of the film producer Dino DeLaurentiis and the banker Frans Afman. They pioneered the present landscape where funds from everywhere, intermingle and merge in Los Angeles to finance films for the world. Their legacy is not only important as an organizing principle of film history but also as an example of how globalization determines patterns even within the "dominant" culture of the United States.

Transnationalization and complementary communication

In order to evaluate the trajectory of this history, we need to review two modeling terms: Sepstrups' transnationalization and Deutsch's complementaries of communication. The Danish media scholar Preben Sepstrup recently suggested some precise definitions in the globalization of culture vocabulary (Sepstrup, 1990, chs. 4–5). His review of the literature on media imperialism showed the need for a distinction between "international flow" and "transnationalization." International flow is the movement of messages across national boundaries that also mark the boundaries between two or more cultural systems. Transnationalization is the first order effect of the international flow on the production, supply and consumption of the messages. This first order effect, in turn, creates second level effects on the production and reproduction of culture and ideology. Transnationalization analysis examines the various institutions promoted or destroyed by the export surplus of American mass media. Debates about the first order effects focus on Hollywood's domination of international trade and its devastation of other national film production centers. The second order level debates occur over the extent to which an international audience adopts American values because of their increased exposure to American mass media.

Although these levels intermingle, it is useful to distinguish between the various levels of debate. By making these distinctions it is possible to see that the relationships between the various levels are not transparent or necessarily intuitive. For example, several writers have argued that, despite trade dominance, audiences have reinterpreted American media products according to their own needs and have resisted the importation of American values (Tracey, 1988; Liebes and Katz, 1991). In another context the health of a national media industry does not mean that local values are being promulgated. Brazil's telenovelas are as successful in the global market as most American television shows. However, as Omar Souki Oliveira has complained, this does not mean those telenovelas are serving Brazilian cultural needs or exporting Brazilian values. The shows are situated in a fantasy of developed affluence and feature stars whose looks tend towards a European model. Despite their popularity with the Brazilian audience, telenovelas undermine the autonomy of their own national culture (Oliveira, 1992, p. 128).

The Brazilian example demonstrates that although domestic productions may be popular with domestic audiences, domestic producers are not necessarily in dialogue with their national culture. The conditions for such a national dialogue have been elaborated by Karl Deutsch in his notion of the complementaries of communication. He begins with the question of what constitutes a "people" and quickly eliminates such physical tests as a shared space, a shared language, or even a shared history (Deutsch, 1966, ch. 4). Rather, the answer is to be found in the exchange of information. If information is shared according to common codes albeit among different classes and different subcultures, then we may refer to the "complementary habits and facilities of communication we may call a people" (p. 96).

The complementary does not erase the differences of a stratified society but does suggest that the various strata of society have more information flow among themselves than with external groups. Deutsch (1966, p. 101) warns that if a ruling group's "main interests and ties lie elsewhere, perhaps outside the country, or if it has accepted alien speech, habits, or religion, or if, finally, it has come to care only for its own group interests in a quite narrow manner, then the national and social leadership may devolve upon the next class below it . . ."

I find this operational definition of national communications of greater use in examining the Hollywood film industry than more interpretative frameworks regarding the imagined "nation." This imagination must necessarily be examined based either on the self-reports of the national audience or on the interpretations of analysts dangerously assuming the position of the implied audience. This kind of audience analysis has to presuppose that the audience has autonomy over its culture. Otherwise the site of analysis would have to relocate to that group possessing such autonomy. But the subject of the study of international cinema is a study of the loss of that autonomy. Therefore, reliance on audience analysis can obscure the loss of audience autonomy. In the Brazilian example cited above, the popularity of the Brazilian telenovela is not a mark of its complementariness within Brazil. If we look at the flow of information we see that the telenovela is designed for a small domestic audience capable of buying the consumer products advertised on the episodes and for an international consumerist audience. Its popularity among those Brazilians who cannot participate in the consumer market is of far less objective importance to the producers. They become an accidental audience despite their own avowed enthusiasm for the programs.

Complementary communication in the mass media is observable on the institutional level. Institutional agents—producers, distributors, exhibitors— make visible decisions about their markets. The meanings of these decisions are embedded in the rise and fall and transformations of companies as they seek to survive and to thrive. It is here that the full cycle of communication from transmission to reception to feedback can be observed and evaluated for its social importance, not in direct measurements of the audience.

Since I wish to distinguish the international hegemony of the U.S. film industry from its transnationalization, I will now describe the early history of Hollywood and the nature of its global dominance before moving on to the nature of global presales and financing.

The ups and downs of Hollywood

The film industry reached a mature stage during the First World War when Hollywood obtained its domination of the global market (Thompson, 1985, pp. 88–89). A group of men, remarkably similar to each other in their position within the national culture, facilitated the maturing process. They were immigrants successfully expanding film from an urban working class amusement to a mainstream entertainment playing simultaneously to the entire nation.

This group was trying to market film "culture" to both an audience that they felt comfortable with and a more rooted middle class to which they aspired. Neal Gabler has written convincingly of the link between the class aspirations of the Jewish movie moguls and their specific strategies in the exhibition and production of films. They bought theaters that they upgraded in order to attract a "respectable" audience. They were the first American distributors to insist on longer length films. These longer films presented narratives attractive to the American middle class. As their formulas proved successful, they reinvested their returns into an integrated production center feeding theaters that they owned throughout the country. The vertical integration of the film studio was a direct reflection of Adolph Zukor's, William Fox's, Sam Katz's and the other moguls' will to construct an American film audience. They tailored their product to first capture this vast audience and only secondarily to be distributed overseas.[2]

During these formative decades, studio spokespeople often expressed their concern for the cultural needs of the American public and how films contributed to the nation. These pronouncements are of rhetorical interest. A more definite demonstration of the national character of the Hollywood film industry occurred when the studios began using domestic profits from national theater chains to maintain world-wide dominance after the First World War. American distributors debated whether to demand European circuits pay in dollars or in the war-weakened local currencies. Responding to the threat of falling foreign earnings, Carl Laemmle (1920, p. 11), the influential president of Universal Film Company, wrote an opinion piece suggesting that each segment of the global market had to support its fair share of Hollywood's production costs. In other words each national audience had to pay on the same per capita basis in dollars.[3] Other distributors and film executives ignored his advice. P. A. Powers (1920, p. 1201), vice president at Universal, a senior independent producer and rival of Laemmle, wrote in *Moving Picture World*, that Hollywood should budget its films so that negative costs could be recovered in the domestic market. Films were to be exported at whatever level the overseas market could bear to pay. The film historian, Kristin Thompson more recently concluded that the industry historically followed Powers' advice, whether through inertia or design, and charged so little for American films in foreign markets that local producers complained that Hollywood distributors were "dumping" their product overseas (Thompson, 1985, p. 104).

Powers was not necessarily advocating dumping. The actual thrust of his remarks was to reduce what he termed "the colossal salaries to artists and the phenomenal prices [paid] to authors" (Powers, 1920, p. 1201). However, huge domestic exhibitors wanted the big pictures and costly talent. Various theater chains, most notably Balaban and Katz, were being organized on a national scale (Gomery, 1992, pp. 40–43). These national film theater chains could support the high cost of filmmaking in the twenties without the help of overseas revenues. Exhibitors had achieved advantages of efficient distribution and reliable returns, in part by emulating the new national food store chains such as Atlantic & Pacific (Gomery, 1979; Allen, 1980). During the mid-twenties, several national theater chains merged with the large production companies to control their source of programming. Production and distribution were now firmly under the control of men whose rise to power was through domestic exhibition. This large scale vertical integration tightened the relationship between the film industry and the national audience.

The size of the American audience almost doubled in response to the sound revolution of 1927.[4] The domestic box office and Wall Street investments financed the increase in production costs and the expansion of the industry. The adoption of sound eliminated the last vestiges of regional differences between theaters since live presentations featuring local talent were eliminated in favor of nationally distributed short films to play between feature presentations.

These are the years when nationally based cinema dominated national culture, not only here but elsewhere. Martin-Barbero (1993, p. 158) has stated that mass entertainment, especially film, had an important role in constructing the national identity of the newly urbanized masses of Argentina and Mexico. In this aspect, a vertically integrated American film industry played a role more similar to the popular cinema of Latin America than it did to European film-making. Both north and south American cinemas appealed to the masses flocking to the urban centers and seeking new national identities to replace the traditional ones of the village or the old world. By contrast, European films addressed audiences more secure in their national identity and more wary of massification.

Domestic upheavals after 1946

1946 was the best year ever for Hollywood. A record number of Americans attended the movie theaters and American films came back to Europe after its war time absence. However, in the next few years American attendance dropped rapidly—by 32 percent from 1949 to 1950 and approximately 5 percent each of the subsequent years until it stabilized in 1958 at one half of its 1945–1948 average (Vogel, 1990, p. 359). The middle class was changing its lifestyle and was devoting its leisure time to television and other pursuits rather than attending centralized movie theaters. Also, in 1948 the Justice Department and the Federal court forced the five major studios (Paramount et al.) to divest their theater holdings since control of both production and exhibition facilitated the Paramount defendants' pooling of profits and other monopolistic conspiracies (Conant, 1960, ch. 4).

The "complementaries of communication" between the movie industry and America was eroding. Exhibitors had previously assumed a loyal audience. They boasted in 1929 that, "You don't need to know what's playing at a Publix house [a Paramount theater]. It's bound to be the best show in town" (Gomery, 1979, p. 35). But the 1948 separation of the studios from the theater chains forced production executives into a new way of thinking about the audience. "Mr. Zukor [was, at this time, chairman of Paramount] declared in the middle of 1949 . . . 'The public is just not going to a theater for the sake of seeing any picture.' " (Seldes, 1951, p. 41). Pictures had to be targeted to a market, not to a nation. Distributors tried to appeal to different demographic groups, in particular, youth. Gilbert Seldes (1951, p. 13), the noted media critic of the day, was already complaining in 1951, that movies were made for those under twenty. This tendency accelerated during the subsequent decades, culminating in the complete obsession with youth culture after the runaway success of *Easy Rider*. This 1969 ground breaker earned $19 million for the distributor. Of course if films were designed for youth, the international and domestic audiences became unified in the producer's mind, because age stratification crosses borders.

An entire generation of international youth had received a crash course in appreciating American movies when the distributors released the backlog of films after the war. These movies portrayed a country that had escaped devastation and defeated fascism. They celebrated an American concern with the enjoyment of life. This early exposure nurtured future global players in the transnationalized cinema. David Puttnam, the Oscar winning British film producer, recalled "I was brought up on movies . . . and for the most part, they were American movies. . . . I was one among millions of young people who basked in the benign, positive and powerful aura of post-Marshall plan, concerned and responsible America" (Yule, 1989, pp. 196–197).

Throughout the fifties Hollywood threw money at the screen in an attempt to buy back its decimated domestic audience with visual splendor that differentiated its product from the prosaic television fare. The studios had the cash to do so from the good years and from the sale of domestic theaters. In an attempt to make the money go even further by escaping the high costs of Los Angeles film crews and cast, producers used blocked funds to shoot overseas (Guback, 1985, p. 120). Peter Lev chronicles such efforts as *To Catch a Thief* (1954) shot in France, *Alexander the Great* (1955) shot in Spain, *The Ten Commandments* (1956) filmed in various countries (Lev, 1993). This trend accelerated up through 1963 and then leveled off. Particularly in Italy, and throughout Europe, a new generation of experienced film workers and studio facilities was financed by this cycle of overseas Hollywood productions. Of course the money they earned gave them the flexibility to also work on local "art" films. This influx of American movie money made possible the careers of Frederico Fellini, Francois Truffaut and even Jean-Luc Godard, among others.

The European film renaissance of the sixties found an audience in the United States. Bergman, Antonioni, Vilgot (*I am Curious-Yellow* [1967]) Sjoman, Bertolucci, and others inspired a new generation of American filmmakers to address the sexual revolution. This "sophisticated" theme further stratified the audience by demographic rather than national criteria. Increasingly, American film makers acknowledged the stylistic influences of European and Japanese films. The international cross-fertilization of styles and themes set the context for a new approach to film financing and distribution. It is not surprising, in this setting, that foreign marketing techniques should filter back into Hollywood. The career of DeLaurentiis shows this shift from domestic to global marketing in the seventies.

Foreign presales

Dino DeLaurentiis introduced global thinking to American film financing. He had started out in his native southern Italy right before World War II. He was able in a rather mysterious way to produce films despite the postwar devastation. The 1950 production of *Bitter Rice* put him on the map and his production of Fellini's *La Strada* (1951) gave DeLaurentiis a place in cinema history. He worked on a wide variety of films in Italy, from the serious to the sexy. He produced Fellini's *Nights of Cabiria* in 1952 but parted company with the director over *La Dolce Vita*. It is interesting that subsequently DeLaurentiis and Fellini tried to reunite but that partnership fell apart when Fellini refused to shoot in English (Greenberg, 1975, p. 91). DeLaurentiis also collaborated on eighty productions with Carlo Ponti but they split up in 1957 when DeLaurentiis claimed Ponti resisted his global marketing decisions for their co-productions (Brenner, 1973, p. 53).

In the next decade DeLaurentiis was successful enough to build a studio on the southern outskirts of Rome, with government subsidies. But a string of disappointing releases through the late nineteen sixties placed DeLaurentiis at risk, particularly after the flop of his Soviet co-production of *Waterloo*. He was committed to the international market and was annoyed at the Italian government's insistence that his movies had to have Italian principals, which he felt limited his global opportunities. In 1972 he jump-started his career by moving to America and he never looked back to his native film industry.

He arrived in the United States at a key moment—five years after Jack Warner sold Warner Brothers and a few years before the death of Adolph Zukor, markers of the passing of the first film generation. He arrived at a historic low point in domestic theatrical box office earnings, a little bit before the technologies of video and cable developed into new markets. When he arrived, DeLaurentiis resisted going to work for the conglomerates of

Hollywood. He would not become just another producer on a major studio lot. He wished to maintain a more general and allocative control over his films. Also, unlike his rival American film producers, DeLaurentiis was not interested in building his power by entering into a dialogue with the American audience. He had already made big films pay for themselves with the global audience. During the Italian phase of his career, he had accumulated relations with different distributors around the world. Now, he insisted on maintaining these relations by selling his productions directly to these distributors. The only equity he would give to a Hollywood distributor was the North American territory. In return, he sought fifty percent funding. The other fifty percent would come in piece-by-piece as he sold off pieces of the world market to the individual distributors. A Walter Reade executive exclaimed at the time that "Dino is the only producer who thinks of the United States as just another territory" (Brenner, 1993, p. 52).

A fellow European, the ex-Austrian Charles Bluhdorn, was the CEO of the conglomerate Gulf and Western that controlled Paramount. DeLaurentiis entered into partnership with this studio. The arrangement paid off with a string of hits such as *Serpico* (1973), *Death Wish* (1974), and *Three Days of the Condor* (1975).[5]

The domestic "complementaries of communication" was being widened to a worldwide box office. Indeed, the fact that *Death Wish* was a hit in America was an irrelevant surprise to DeLaurentiis. He had budgeted the film by counting on the star status of Charles Bronson overseas. The turn around in the perceptions of the importance of the American audience was also mirrored by a reversal in the source of financing. Because DeLaurentiis sought funding in advance of production from his overseas distributors, his films are the first instance since World War I of American films being made with foreign investments. Financing through "presales" was greatly assisted when in 1973, Bluhdorn introduced DeLaurentiis to Frans Afman, a banker from the Slavenburg bank of Rotterdam, who was in America to investigate possibilities of doing business here. Afman and DeLaurentiis went on to develop the global presales technique. The bank advanced cash against the distributors' written guarantees.

DeLaurentiis was very protective about his presales network. It gave him the power to say no. He even turned down an offer from Barry Diller—at that time at Paramount—for global rights on *King Kong* (1976) when that production got into trouble. He felt his personal relations with distributors around the world had to be honored, particularly when he was under the pressure of producing a blockbuster. Afman covered DeLaurentiis as costs escalated from ten to twenty-four million dollars (Murphy, 1976, p. 32). The film eventually earned nearly $75 million for the distributors (DeLaurentiis, 1986, p. 14).

Presales was also a source of weakness. By selling off exhibition rights in the film before it was made, DeLaurentiis diminished his ability to participate in profits if the film became a hit. He was unable to take full advantage of his successes and had to continue to go back to his distributors for new guarantees on every production. Of course, it was hard to anticipate the market for an unmade film. Therefore, it was imperative to put together a film package that resembled previous successes as much as possible. This meant a heavy reliance on action genres and big stars. DeLaurentiis was quite willing to pay huge fees in order to obtain stars whose presence would facilitate the preselling (Kent, 1991, p. 83). It was difficult to judge whether the pressure of preselling was driving the explosion in talent fees, but established American studios were quick to blame DeLaurentiis for driving up the price of major movie stars.

The most important thing about preselling was that it allowed foreign film producers to come to Hollywood and make "Hollywood" pictures independent of the American companies and of American financing. Frans Afman had been increasing his entertainment portfolio when the French bank Crédit Lyonnais took over the failing Slavenberg bank in 1981 (d'Aubert, 1993, p. 183). The irony was that Crédit Lyonnais, owned by the French government encouraged Afman's Hollywood activities even as the French Ministry of Culture worried about the "Americanization" of French movie screens. Afman's clients now included many producers of different nationalities united in their orientation towards the global audience. Because of his activities, Crédit Lyonnais would eventually claim to be the number one bank in film financing.[6] It was involved with production companies such as Carolco, Cannon, Castle Rock, Cinergi, DeLaurentiis Entertainment Group, Empire, Epic, Hemdale, Largo, Morgan Creek, Nelson Entertainment, New World, Sovereign, Trans World Entertainment and others. It provided key loans to such films as *Dances with Wolves*, *Crimes of the Heart*, *Blue Velvet*, *Salvador*, *Platoon*, *Hoosier*, *A Room with a View*, *Superman I and II* and many, many others. A number of these studios, especially Cannon films, became important enough to be dubbed by the trade journals as "Mini-majors" to signify their challenge to the major studios. In a 1986 prospectus, DeLaurentiis (1986, p. 16) divided the motion picture industry into "Majors" (owning their own production studios and worldwide distribution systems), "Mini-Majors" (similar to the majors but not owning production studios and concentrating on lower budgeted films), and "Independents" (producers not releasing films on a continual pattern). Crédit Lyonnais' willingness to underwrite global presales caused "Minis" and "Independents" to proliferate, as did the introduction of new technologies of distribution.

The adoption of the Video Cassette Recorder (VCR) had a double effect overseas during the early eighties. First, movies could now be marketed to an audience who preferred to stay at home. Second, VCR usage, satellites, and terrestrial cable networks placed tremendous pressure on state controlled broadcasting systems to increase the variety and "entertainment" portion of their programming (Blumler and Hoffman-Riem, 1992, p. 21). Governments responded by either allowing the creation of alternative commercial channels and/or redirecting the mandate of the state-controlled television system to include more entertainment. In all these cases, the opportunity for selling films to global television vastly expanded through the eighties up until the present.

The expansion of the market through home video rentals and global television sales had the effect of encouraging the "Mini-majors" to expand even further and to over-extend. 1987 became a turning point down for the two largest, DeLaurentiis and Cannon. Both had acquired studios and theater chains and had turned into public corporations offering stock. But they were not producing particularly successful movies and their presales techniques eliminated their ability to build up a cash reserve from the few popular movies that they did produce.

The original global presellers had run out of money by the end of the eighties. DeLaurentiis went out of business and sold off his film library in 1990. Cannon, Hemdale, and other low budget filmmakers ended the decade with a series of forced mergers and liquidations that effectively eliminated their independence as film producers. Crédit Lyonnais became involved with Giancarlo Parretti's "byzantine" takeover of MGM studios. The deals he had put together to buy MGM turned out to be less than realistic and the French bank had to take over the ailing studio in May 1992 ("The bank," 1993). This was an unhappy ending to the bank's decade long venture in film financing. The various entertainment division officers of the bank have been replaced by the current conservative French government. But the "Mini-majors" did not fade away before they demonstrated it was possible for distributors to make more money overseas than in the domestic markets (Yule, 1987, p. 118).

DeLaurentiis' legacy

The transnationalization that DeLaurentiis pioneered (of bringing foreign money to Hollywood to make films for the global audience) is expanding today. Peter Bart, former studio executive and long time editorial director of the movie's industry bible, *Variety*, wrote recently about the importance of foreign film producers in contemporary Hollywood. He cites Mario Kassar, Arnon Milchan and Andy Vajna who have financed a combination of big films costing a total of $500 to $600 million. Vajna is associated with the *Die Hard* series. Kassar (CEO of Carolco Pictures) has produced a string of Schwarzenegger and Stallone hits and Milchan has bankrolled several Oliver Stone films, to name only a few of their high profile projects. They are successfully following the path laid out by DeLaurentiis when he first decided to treat the "United States as just another territory." They are global film producers, savvy about the international audience and raising money all over the world in order to make "event" films. These are huge budget films that are expected to gross upwards of a hundred million dollars.

Such large grosses can only be obtained when the film does very well in both the domestic and foreign markets. Sam Kitt, a current Universal executive, confirms that all the major studios consider the global audience, before launching a more expensive than average movie ($27 million or more in negative costs) (personal interview, July 30, 1993). The consideration of the global audience has paid off. *Variety* stated that "in 1994, for the first time, offshore rentals [rentals are that portion of the box office revenues that are returned to the distributor which is almost always a major Hollywood studio] surpassed North American figures." ("Worldwide rentals," 1995, p. 28) The big blockbuster producers have taken the advice of Carl Laemmle albeit some seventy years later. They are produced in anticipation that every part of the globe will pay its share of the revenues. From 1985 to 1990, production costs rose from $16.8 million to $26.8 million, an increase of 63 percent. Domestic revenues from all markets (theatrical, video and television) went from $5.3 billion to $8.2 billion and foreign revenues went from $1.5 billion to $5.2 billion in the same time period (Hoffman, 1992, chart A). The domestic market remains vital but the 247 percent increase in foreign earnings—both a measure of the weakness of the dollar and the increased sales of U.S. films—is driving the exponential increase in total revenues and the willingness to pay ever more money for the biggest films.

The global audience's influence goes beyond the aggregate figures. If one merely looks at the returns then the only change has been quantitative, as the foreign returns increase from the 30 percent characteristic of the twenties and thirties (Donahue, 1987, p. 145) to the current level of 51 percent. But the transnationalization is a much more profound change that is reflected in the foreign media companies investing heavily in Hollywood films. Milchan, Vajna, Kassar and others are able to put together big investments because they work with large foreign programmers, the most prominent being Canal Plus. Canal Plus is a French pay TV/production group with 1993 revenues of $1.7 billion ("Data Box," 1994, p. 240). Just like the American film theater chains of the teens and twenties, Canal Plus wants to participate in film productions in order to gain leverage over film seller's price demands. ("Euros learn biz," 1994, p. 82). Some of the other foreign companies involved in production deals are Italy's RCS, Holland's Polygram, Japan's Pioneer, U.K.'s Rank and Germany's Capella (Dawtrey, 1994, p. 75).

I have not emphasized the high profile take overs of Columbia and MCA/Universal by the Japanese electronic firms of Sony and Matsushita respectively. This is because the new owners have been relatively passive and have not yet visibly re-oriented marketing decisions away from the domestic audience. The bulk of the electronic firms' business is selling machines, not programming. Indeed Matsushita has sold MCA/Universal to Seagram this year, obviously regretting its venture into programming equity. Transnationalization is more evident among media companies trying to construct a global audience with internationally financed programming.

Conclusion

I have used Sepstrup's differentiation between the transnationalization of national film industries and the effects it may have on audience meaning-making to uncover the moment that global film financing became influential in Hollywood film production. The following remarks will associate this economic history with attempts to understand the new landscape of world-wide movie viewing. The development of global film financing is implicitly at the heart of a new line of investigation about film and culture. This investigation takes the old question about the effect that American film dominance has had on foreign audiences and turns it around. Now it asks what effect this dominance has had on the role of film in American culture.

One answer lies in the way film style has changed and Timothy Corrigan's notion that the current multi-group audience is too much for any one film to address with old standards of coherence. He observes that there is "a larger pattern of illegibility in the international [Hollywood?] movie industry as it responds to widespread changes in production and distribution of film texts whereby viewing becomes an odd combination of distraction and appropriation" (Corrigan, 1991, p. 77). The old "realism" codes of Hollywood are not evolving but are breaking down as producers design films for a global audience. Shekhar Kapur (the director of the Hindu film *The Bandit Queen*) joked that one of the biggest box office American films of last year *True Lies* copies the conventions of the Indian film industry in its use of the fantastic.[7]

Kapur was not celebrating *True Lies* as an innovative hybrid of a global film culture but was suggesting that the Hollywood blockbuster misappropriated the Hindu film style. Other critics have more clearly denounced the negative effects of the American film industry directing its focus toward the global audience. The global audience is too infinite to be knowable. Therefore, attempts to appeal to such an audience are bound to be crude and to be overly reductive. Michael Medved and the media scholar, George Gerbner, have linked the rise in irresponsible depictions of violence in film to the need to service a global audience with easy-to-understand action movies (Medved, 1992, p. 290). David Puttnam used his brief term as studio chief of Columbia Pictures (1987–1988) to argue that the film industry has to develop a greater sense of community responsibility (Yule, 1989, p. 198). Certainly this is even harder to do with a global market than it was when the perceived market was national.

In my conversations with American film executives,[8] it was obvious that they perceive the world wide market as desiring a certain image of America to be featured in the movies. Each executive may have differing and changing notions of the desired image—one season it may be hedonist consumers on the open road with fast cars—the next season it may be the American ethic of an individual hero struggling against all corrupt collectives. The point is not whether international viewers are actually seduced by such images but that film producers set for themselves the task of portraying an "America" that is a dreamscape for "universal" desires rather than a historic reality. They differ from a previous generation of producers who engaged in the task of presenting myth as reality to the American public. At least mythmaking contained some possibility of artistic engagement with historic concerns and problems. The trend line is not absolute but the economic circumstances of current production determines that fewer and fewer films will address a specific community or the national audience in a profound way.

Ralph Waldo Emerson (1940, pp. 62–63) warned us in 1834 that "We have listened too long to the courtly muses of Europe. . . . See already the tragic consequence. The mind of this country, taught to aim at low objects, eats upon itself." His remarks, although in another context, are apt. Our cinema, by disengaging from a national dialogue, portrays a country aimed at low objects. American film makers have only sporadically addressed the American audience with artistic integrity. It will now be even more difficult to address the global audience in such a manner.

Notes

1 Richard Frank (the former president of Walt Disney Studios) told a congressional hearing that, "We should not focus exclusively on matters of economics. This issue [export of US films] involves not just entertainment, but also ideas. American films and TV shows are just that, American. They show our country, and what it stands for, from our highest ideals to our gravest challenges" (U.S. Congress, 1990, p. 51). The irony is that Disney is well known for lifting stories out of cultural context, whether local or national. It is precisely to challenge Frank's bland assertion that his product exemplifies American ideals that it is important to study the phenomenon of transnationalization. At this point, I cannot see that Frank has any greater claim to cultural importance than the extreme global profitability of Disney products.
2 Carl Laemmle (1920, p. 11) (the founder and president of Universal Film) referred to the export market as "velvet," "unexpected money."
3 Is it not coincidental that Laemmle had already shown that he was the most European oriented of the studio heads? He often went for sentimental visits and gave a great deal of money to his German birthplace. Neal Gabler has described his general lack of concern over his immigrant status in American society.
4 It went from 50 million per week in 1926 to 95 million per week in 1929 (Vogel, 1990, p. 359).
5 Frederic Jameson (1992, pp. 13–15) used *Three Days of the Condor* in his description of a postmodern paranoid style. I don't think it was a causal relationship but an instructive coincidence that this film was produced with money from DeLaurentiis' international network.
6 Personal interview with Fred Spar, CL's American spokesperson, January 11, 1993.

7 As heard on David Darcy's report on Indian Cinema at the Toronto Film Festival, broadcast on Morning Edition, National Public Radio Network, September 22, 1994.
8 This includes Sam Kitt (mentioned above), Peter Weatherall of Full Moon, Castle Rock, Mark Borde and other mid-level distribution people.

References

Allen, J. T. (1980). The film viewer as consumer. *Quarterly Review of Film Studies*, 5(4): 481–499.

d'Aubert, F. (1993). *L'Argent Sale: Enquête sur un krach retentissant*. Paris: Plon.

The bank, the studio, the mogul and the lawyers. (1993, January 23). *The Economist*, p. 71.

Bart, P. (1993, November 1). Euromavens take control. *Variety*, pp. 4, 54.

Blumler, J. G. & Hoffman-Riem, W. (1992). New roles for public television in western Europe: Challenges and prospects. *Journal of Communication*, 42(1): 20–35.

Brenner, M. (1973, October 21). Dino DeLaurentiis conquers America. *New York*, pp. 51–55.

Conant, M. (1960). *Antitrust in the motion picture industry: Economic and legal analysis*. Berkeley: University of California Press.

Corrigan, T. (1991). *A cinema without walls: Movies and culture after Vietnam*. New Brunswick, NJ: Rutgers University Press.

Data box. (1994, October). *Screen Digest*, p. 240.

Dawtrey, A. (1994, March 7). Eurobucks back megapix. *Variety*, pp. 1, 75.

De Laurentiis entertainment group inc. (1986, May 30). *Prospectus*. New York: Paine Webber, Inc.

Deutsch, K. (1966). *Nationalism and social communication: An inquiry into the foundations of nationality* (2nd ed.). Cambridge, MA: MIT Press.

Donahue, S. M. (1987). *American film distribution: The changing marketplace*. Ann Arbor, MI: UMI Research Press.

Emerson, R. W. (1940). *The complete essays and other writings of Ralph Waldo Emerson*. New York: Random House.

Euros learn biz from the U.S. (1994, October 10). *Variety*, pp. 53, 82.

Gabler, N. (1988). *An empire of their own: How the Jews invented Hollywood*. New York: Crown Publishers.

Gomery, D. (1979). The movies become big business: Public theatres and the chain store strategy. *Cinema Journal*, 18(2): 26–40.

Gomery, D. (1992). *Shared pleasures: A history of movie presentation in the United States*. Madison: The University of Wisconsin Press.

Greenberg, A. (1975, May). Dino DeLaurentis. *Film International*, pp. 91–92.

Guback, T. (1985). Nonmarket factors in the international distribution of American films. In B. Austin (Ed.), *Current research in film: Audiences, economics and law* (vol. 1) (pp. 111–126). Norwood, NJ: Ablex Publishing.

Hoffman, P. (1992, May). L'Affaire de cinema Aujourd' Hui. Address at Cannes Film Festival, France.

Jameson, F. (1993). *The geopolitical aesthetic: Cinema and space in the world system*. Bloomington: Indiana University Press.

Kent, N. (1991). *Naked Hollywood: Money and power in the movies today*. New York: St. Martin's Press.

Knoedelseder, W. K., Jr. (1987, August 30). DeLaurentiis: Producer's picture darkens. *Los Angeles Times*, pt. 4, pp. 1–2.

Laemmle, C. (1920, January 1). The higher cost of films. *The Bioscope*, p. 11.

Lev, P. (1993). *The Euro-American cinema*. Austin: University of Texas Press.

Liebes, T. & Katz, E. (1991). *The export of meaning*. Oxford, NY: Oxford University Press.

Martin-Barbero, J. (1993). *Communication, culture and hegemony: From the media to meditations*. Newbury Park, CA: Sage Publications.

Medved, M. (1992). *Hollywood vs. America: Popular culture and the war on traditional values*. New York: HarperCollins.

Murphy, M. (1976, December 20). The Kong papers: Ten days in Dino's palm. *New West*, pp. 26–37.

Oliveira, O. S. (1992). Brazilian soaps outshine Hollywood: Is cultural imperialism fading out? In K. Nordenstreng & H. Schiller (eds.), *Beyond national sovereignty: International communication in the 1990s*. Norwood, NJ: Ablex Publishing.

Powers, P. A. (1920, February 21). Huge salaries, foreign exchange and competition imperil industry. *The Moving Picture World*, p. 1201.

Schiller, H. (1989). Disney, Dallas and electronic data flows: The transnationalization of culture. In C. Thomsen (Ed.), *Cultural transfer or electronic imperialism?* (pp. 33–44). Heidelberg, Germany: Carl Winter Universitätsverlag.

Seldes, G. (1951). *The great audience*. New York: Viking Press.

Sepstrup, P. (1990). *Transnationalization of television in Western Europe*. London: John Libbey & Co.

Thompson, K. (1985). *Exporting entertainment: America in the world film market 1907–1934*. London: BFI Press.

Tracey, M. (1988). Popular culture and the economics of global television. *Intermedia*, 16(2): 8–25.

Uricchio, W. & Pearson, R. E. (1993). *Reframing culture: The case of the vitagraph quality films*. Princeton, NJ: Princeton University Press.

U.S. Congress. (1990). Television broadcasting and the European community. Hearing before the Subcommittee on Telecommunications and Finance on July 26, 1989. Washington, DC: Government Printing Office.

Vogel, H. L. (1990). *Entertainment industry economics: A guide for financial analysis* (2nd ed.). New York: Cambridge University Press.

"Worldwide rentals beat domestic take." (1995, February 13). *Variety*, p. 28.

Yule, A. (1987). *Hollywood a go-go: An account of the Cannon phenomenon*. London: Sphere Books Ltd.

Yule, A. (1989). *Fast fade: David Puttnam, Columbia Pictures and the battle for Hollywood*. New York: Delacourte Press.

19

SEX, LIES AND MARKETING

Miramax and the development of the quality indie blockbuster

Alisa Perren

Source: *Film Quarterly* 55(2) (2001): 30–39.

> The origins of an *American Beauty* are in 1989 with Steven Soderbergh doing that kind of movie.
>
> —Harvey Weinstein, 2000[1]

In 1989, the world of independent distribution was in disarray. While the appearance of the video market in the 1980s had helped spur the emergence and expansion of a number of independent distributors, by the end of the decade several of these same companies—including Vestron, Island, and Cinecom—had overextended themselves by investing heavily in larger budget, in-house productions. Consequently, by 1989, many within the industry were predicting the death of the independent distributor. However, what seemed to be the decline of independent distribution was actually an "independent shakedown," a label presciently attached to the period by *Los Angeles Times* writer Daniel Cerone in June 1989.[2] Cerone saw that it was a transitional time within the independent world. While the vast majority of independent distributors who had thrived in the 80s were forced to declare bankruptcy by the end of the decade, a few companies were positioned to make a significant mark on the industrial structure and aesthetics of low-budget filmmaking in the 90s. At the head of the pack was Miramax.

The August 1989 release of *sex, lies and videotape* by Miramax marked a turning point in American independent cinema. In fact, the film should be perceived as central to the development of New Hollywood aesthetics, economics, and structure.[3] *sex, lies and videotape* ushered in the era of the "indie blockbusters"—films that, on a smaller scale, replicate the exploitation marketing and box-office performance of the major studio high-concept event pictures.[4] On a cost-to-earning ratio, Steven Soderbergh's creation—with its $1.1 million dollar budget and $24 million plus in North American box office—was a better investment than *Batman*, which—at an investment of $50 million—returned $250 million in domestic box office.[5]

These figures begin to suggest how *sex, lies and videotape* helped to set the standard for low-budget, niche-based distribution in the 90s and to lay the groundwork for a bifurcation within the entertainment industry.[6] In the ten years following the release of *sex, lies and videotape*, each major studio or media conglomerate created or purchased at least one specialty division. These divisions generally operated relatively autonomously from the studio in terms of production and distribution. In the wake of Disney's April 1993 purchase of Miramax, a number of studio-based niche operations emerged, including Universal Focus, Paramount Classics, and Fox Searchlight. The studios focused predominantly on the distribution of big-budget spectacles, while studio-based subsidiaries (which Miramax became in 1993, when Disney purchased the company) focused predominantly on smaller-scale quality pictures that centered on the foibles of well-developed characters.[7] While the majors favored projects such as *The Rock* (1996), *Con Air* (1997), and *Enemy of the State* (1998), studio subsidiaries developed such films as *Shine* (1996), *Good Will Hunting* (1997), and *The Cider House Rules* (1999). But it was *sex, lies and videotape*, in the skillful hands of Miramax, that redefined the label of "independence" as it was used by the press and the entertainment industry. During the years that followed its release, a number of films would replicate its financial success and media attention. And the vast majority of these would be theatrically distributed in the U.S. by Miramax.

Miramax in the 1980s

Founded in downtown Buffalo, New York, in 1979 by brothers Harvey and Robert (Bob) Weinstein, Miramax began, like many low-budget distributors of the late 70s and early 80s, by booking live rock-and-roll acts as well as exhibiting classic films and concert movies. But the Weinsteins soon branched out, first with film festivals that screened cult favorites and foreign-language films, and then by moving into production and distribution. They made the kinds of movies that the studios weren't interested in but that had developed into profitable ventures by virtue of the emergence of the home video market. As they slowly expanded during the course of the 80s, the Weinsteins and their staff grew increasingly adept at selling positive images of themselves and their company along with their films. They became known for employing exploitation marketing tactics to promote their movies, with publicity stunts ranging from encouraging *Erendira* (1983) actress Claudia Ohana to pose for *Playboy* to setting up actor Daniel Day-Lewis, who portrayed cerebral palsy sufferer Christy Brown in *My Left Foot* (1989), to testify before Congress on behalf of the Americans With Disabilities Act.

Because the company's executives were so skilled at selling positive images of themselves and their films (including *sex, lies and videotape*), reconstructing a history of Miramax becomes a complicated task. It is often hard to distinguish legitimate claims from exaggeration. Yet in spite of Miramax's effective integration of myth and fact, a number of details about the contours of the company's development can be untangled from the mix.

During the 80s, Miramax consistently released three to four films per year. Except for a few failed efforts in production, including the 1986 co-directorial effort *Playing for Keeps* (released through Universal), the company focused mainly on acquiring and distributing films produced by outside companies. Miramax was interested in a range of documentary, foreign-language, and art house-oriented films, basing their choices on three criteria. First, they selected movies that could be promoted as quality pictures—films that aspired to the status of "art" in terms of style and narrative construction. These movies were often promoted at least in part on the merits of their director's unique vision. Such films—examples are Lizzie Borden's *Working Girls* (1987), Bille August's *Pelle the Conquerer* (1987), and Errol Morris's *The Thin Blue Line* (1988)—had the potential for garnering critical support from the outset, a crucial component for distributors working with limited advertising budgets. Second, Miramax selected nonclassical films that focused on unconventional subjects and styles: *Working Girls* was a hard-edged critique of prostitution, while *The Thin Blue Line* was a documentary about a man on death row whom Morris proved to be wrongly accused. Both films' documentary aesthetic also set them apart from most slick, glossy Hollywood product. Third, Miramax found marketing hooks that could help the films transition from the art house to the multiplex. With *Working Girls*, for example, the Weinsteins "determined how to sell the sex in a film that was utterly, demonstrably unsexy," while with *The Thin Blue Line* Harvey Weinstein pledged, "Never has Miramax had a movie where a man's life hangs in the balance."[8]

Thus, by appealing to multiple niches and using sex, violence, and controversy as sales strategies, the Weinsteins gained a foothold in an increasingly competitive marketplace and attracted the attention of producers and financiers looking for a distributor. As much as Miramax's success can be interpreted as an accident or side effect of a more broadly shifting industrial structure, such an interpretation must be balanced by attention to the business savvy and acute judgment of Miramax executives, led by the Weinstein brothers. Other strategies developed by the Weinsteins throughout the late 80s further aided the company's growth even as most other independent distributors failed. The Weinsteins limited their spending, opted for continuing in acquisitions rather than producing their own films, and restricted their release schedule. The factor that finally motivated the brothers to go into production was an infusion of money in 1988 from Midland Montague Ventures, an arm of the London-based Midland Bank. With a $25 million debt/equity package, the brothers moved from acquiring and distributing films to producing them. Their first in-house production through this arrangement was the aptly titled *Scandal* (1989), a film about British defense minister John Profumo's affair with teenager Christine Keeler. The controversy, with its rumors of the betrayal of state secrets, may have contributed to the fall of the Conservative government in 1963, but it helped Miramax produce a hit. Costing $7 million in a co-venture with Britain's Palace Pictures, the film grossed $30 million worldwide, in part due to a poster that featured a nude Joanne Whalley-Kilmer as Keeler provocatively straddling a chair, and in part due to a promotional/talk-show tour by Keeler herself.

With the success of *Scandal* and the help of good reviews, shrewd marketing, strong festival screenings, and extensive promotions, Miramax began a string of hits that peaked with *Cinema Paradiso, My Left Foot*, and, of course, *sex, lies and videotape*, which played a particularly important role in redefining low-budget filmmaking and marketing. The company rapidly rose from being a mid-level independent distributor to become one of the few surviving independent distributors of the 80s. Even as companies such as Orion, MCEG, and Vestron disappeared from the film scene, Miramax thrived, turning the very label of independent into a sign of distinction. In this process of differentiation, independent films earned more money—and gained more interest from the studios.

sex, lies and videotape: the beginning of the indie boom

It is notable that Miramax played no role in the initial development of *sex, lies and videotape*. In fact, the company did not have any involvement with the movie until it premiered at the U.S. Film Festival (later renamed the Sundance Film Festival) in 1989. The film was co-financed by RCA/Columbia Home Video and Virgin; RCA/Columbia obtained domestic video rights while Virgin retained foreign video. The producers were free to seek a theatrical distributor if RCA/Columbia rejected it upon "first look." This expectation of earning the investment back by video sales and rentals was a holdover from the early 80s, before the consolidation of the video rental industry.

Although the financiers expected to make back their money through rentals, this did not imply that they approved of the presence of the word "videotape" in the film's title. Even before they saw it, according to Soderbergh, the marketing people at RCA/Columbia had asked for a change, believing that "the vendors would *say* that the buying public would *think* that the film was shot on videotape."[9] The film's marketers—even before Miramax—obviously believed that an independent movie carried connotations bearing specific "qualities," but although these qualities may have included the more controversial (and hence salable) elements of sex and lies, they did not include the suggested "low-quality" appearance of videotape.

The use of the word in the title was, however, probably more of a boon than a bane. As producer John Pierson explains, the word resonated symbolically: "By using videotape in the title . . . and in the film itself, Soderbergh almost literally ushered in the new era of the video-educated filmmaker."[10] Thus a film in which women confess their sexual histories and anxieties on videotape to help a central male character satisfy himself sexually was marked as timely and distinct for both technological and social reasons. The themes of impotence and sexual paranoia rang true in the late 80s, when AIDS panics were leading the news.

The film gained in popularity throughout the festival (which at this time had 30,000 visitors and was a much more low-profile event than would be the case in later years), screening in front of sold-out audiences and receiving rave reviews. Soderbergh more modestly observed that the "praise is getting out of hand,"[11] but *sex, lies and videotape* left the festival with the Dramatic Competition Audience Award and theatrical distribution offers from several independent distributors as well as one major studio. Yet in spite of extensive praise lavished on the film by the press and festival-goers alike, North American theatrical rights for *sex, lies and videotape* were not sold until a few weeks later, when Miramax purchased them at the American Film Market in Los Angeles. According to Soderbergh, Harvey Weinstein said that he would not go back to New York until he had the movie.[12] By 1989, Miramax had already established a reputation for outbidding the rest of the independent distributors. Yet when Miramax later reflected on how they "won" the rights to *sex, lies and videotape*, "the Weinsteins maintain[ed] that their marketing plan was as crucial as their cash advance."[13]

It is because marketing is as significant as content in the building of the quality independent blockbuster that Miramax's role can be seen as crucial in determining the film's box-office success. Ultimately, the interest created in the film as a result of Miramax's skillful distribution cannot be distinguished from the interest created in it by virtue of its subject matter and storyline. The company played up *sex, lies and videotape* to the press in ways that helped the film move out of the so-called art-house ghetto. In the process of marketing *sex, lies and videotape* as a quality independent as opposed to an art-house entity, Miramax also played itself up to the press in ways that helped to construct the company as the primary force in the film's development and financial success.

The marketing of the film began months before its August opening. According to Bob Weinstein, Miramax started to develop the pre-release buzz for *sex, lies and videotape* at the Cannes Film Festival in May 1989.[14] The film was initially screened for the main competition, but it was rejected and subsequently placed in the Director's Fortnight, the venue for new films from up-and-coming directors. However, a last-minute cancellation from another American film placed *sex, lies and videotape* back in the main competition. Soderbergh worried about the movie being lost in the shuffle, particularly as it was competing against Spike Lee's high-profile *Do the Right Thing*. Yet his film ended up playing to standing ovations and shutting out Lee's film for awards. By the conclusion of the Cannes festival, *sex, lies and videotape* had won the prestigious Palme d'Or, given Soderbergh and his film enormous free publicity, and added to the cachet of festivals as valuable sites for building word of mouth.

Cannes marked just the beginning of the summer marketing blitz initiated by Miramax. The original 1989 press kit for *sex, lies and videotape* hints at the image the company tried to craft to the press and public: "The Weinstein brothers built their company with an aggressive marketing and distribution strategy, individually tailoring each film's release to suit its particular strengths." The very notion of "tailoring" a film on the basis of its strengths reveals the company's dependence on niche marketing. "Marketing is not a dirty word," Harvey Weinstein told the *Los Angeles Times* in May 1989. He continued, in what may be seen as a shorthand manifesto for Miramax as well as a more emphatic articulation of previous conceptions of quality independents:

> Although we market artistic films, we don't use the starving-artist mentality in our releases. Other distributors slap out a movie, put an ad in the newspaper—usually not a very good one—and hope that the audience will find it by a miracle. And most often they don't. It's the distributors' responsibility to find the audience.[15]

For *sex, lies and videotape*, this amounted to an attempt to give the film the specialized attention that Soderbergh so desired, packaged as if it was a major studio release. Just one of the means by which Miramax accomplished this was by tapping into the high concept in even the lowest-budgeted film.[16] Thus when Soderbergh developed his own trailer, Miramax quickly rejected it, telling him it was "arthouse death." Although Soderbergh saw his trailer containing "a mood perfectly emulat[ing] the mood of the film . . . [and] not like other trailer [he'd] ever seen," Miramax demurred. Soderbergh finally reached a compromise with Miramax in which the company used its own trailer, but also filled in some additional footage shot by Soderbergh as a transitional device.

All this suggests that although Miramax may have sold each film on its merits, the company nonetheless had certain ideas about what worked in promoting niche films. Clearly avant-garde trailers were not part of the company's conception of good marketing. An analysis of one of the print advertisements for *sex, lies and videotape* reveals several characteristics of Miramax marketing. In the one-sheet for the film's domestic theatrical distribution, Miramax tried to appeal to several markets simultaneously. First they pursued the art-house audience—a group consisting of cine-literate baby boomers who had grown up on a blend of international art cinema and New

American Cinema. This niche, which was presumed to be knowledgeable of the status of festivals as sites for the celebration of global cinema, was sought through the text of the advertisement. At the top of the one-sheet, the most significant festival honors bestowed on the film were listed. Below the list of awards, a number of positive press responses were listed, including opinions from some of the best-known reviewers from the *New York Times*, the *Chicago Sun-Times*, and *Time* magazine.

The second niche targeted by Miramax was the youth audience—college students and twentysomethings. The largest print in the ad, aside from the film's title, came from two critics' statements that constructed two different visions of the film. The first comment, "One of the Best of 1989," associated the movie with the kinds of films that usually receive kudos, such as dramas. Meanwhile, the second comment, "An Edgy, Intense Comedy," suggested a lighter movie well suited for the August release date. The movie was thus differentiated as being more serious than its summer blockbuster counterparts even as it was drawn closer to studio product by its association with comedy. Meanwhile, the images depicted in the advertisement—of multiple couples embracing and kissing—contributed to the film's edgy mystique. Along with the film's title, these images conveyed raciness, excitement, something more adult—and not coincidentally, something more commercial. These images also conformed to the "exploitation" marketing tactics so characteristic of the company at this point in its development. As one reporter observed of Miramax's effective print ads, the company eagerly hinted at sexual desires that were not necessarily apparent in the films themselves.[17]

To many within the industry, Miramax's attempts to find the high concept in low-budget films—while still targeting specific niches in the market—was a welcome approach to a then-struggling independent film scene. As one public relations spokesman stated, in a manner that summed up the sentiments of many, "The marketers of quality independent films aren't doing as effective a job as they might be doing."[18] Hence the logic of Bob Weinstein declaring that "Some guys run from controversy, we run toward it."[19] By establishing this renegade image, Miramax differentiated itself within the marketplace.

The Weinsteins may have penetrated multiplexes in 1989, but they nonetheless remained aware of their position relative to the studios. Specifically, they recognized that their films had to complement rather than compete with the studios' product. They had no illusions that they could match the studios in terms of either financial investment or marketing scale. Thus they relied heavily on free publicity, word of mouth, and counter-programming strategies.[20] While they eventually released *sex, lies and videotape* on about 350 screens, they opened it slowly and let it build on positive reviews and reactions over more than six months. They scheduled a platform release for the film, opening it first only in Los Angeles and New York, and then later moving it into nationwide release by the end of the month. Thus *sex, lies and videotape* had its broadest opening in the time period when the studio block-busters were fading and quality product was in short supply.

Press and industry discourse on *sex, lies and videotape*

To Steven Soderbergh, the overall impact of his film was jarring. In 1990, he returned to Sundance to find a far different scene, one to which he responded negatively. "I'm a little concerned by what *sex, lies* might have wrought here," Soderbergh told the Associated Press, adding, "this can become more of a film market than a film festival." Soderbergh's opinion seemed to be in the minority, however. Many more of those working for independents, as well as those writing about them, looked favorably at the mutually beneficial relationship developing between independents and festivals. Few could have anticipated that this relationship would evolve to the point where the per-vasive attitude at Sundance 2000 would be described as "Buy low, *but buy, dammit*. Fail to snap up a certain movie and you might miss out on the next $140 million dollar cash cow. Turn up your nose at a trend and the future might pass you by."[21]

What is apparent in retrospect is that the "small is beautiful" mentality that was beginning to become omnipresent at festivals as well as for promo-tional purposes was, in fact, the beginning of a larger industrial shift. Rather than *Batman* and *sex, lies and videotape* representing anomalies at both the mass-market and niche levels respectively, they were signals of broader struc-tural and aesthetic changes afoot in New Hollywood. Even as the studios were reviving the same high-concept formulas with such 1990 releases as *Rocky V, Predator 2, Back to the Future III*, and *Days of Thunder*, the independents seemed comparatively fresh and cutting-edge with such films as *Longtime Companion, Pump Up the Volume, Henry V*, and *The Grifters*. The dichotomy between these two types of films indicates the widening split in the kinds of films being produced. The movies that were starting to return the most profits with the smallest risks were either the high-budget, high-concept franchises that had broad international appeal, or low-budget independents that could be targeted to a number of audiences and promoted relatively inexpensively through festivals, word of mouth, and positive crit-ical response.

Thus, although independent releases were down 15 percent in 1989 from the previous year, and box-office receipts were down 7 percent, the slump was short-lived. The continuing global expansion of the industry, rather than contributing to what many predicted would be the demise of independent and/or low-budget filmmaking, actually contributed to their growth. The conditions of social diversity, along with a post-Fordist markets structure, similarly led to the development of niche markets as byproducts of the film industry's ever-expanding global orientation. At the same time that many industry analysts predicted the inevitable demise of all but the high-concept blockbuster, then-Cinecom president Amir Malin explained more precisely why niche films would remain attractive culturally and economically:

> Just because someone sees *Indiana Jones* doesn't mean they won't want to see a sophisticated film like *sex, lies and videotape* or *Scenes from the Class Struggle [of Beverly Hills]*. The fallout will occur with the standard studio fare that cannot compete with the *Raiders, Ghostbusters* and *Batmans*.[22]

Malin's comments were prescient for two reasons. First, on the level of industrial structure, he suggests why standard studio fare (or the so-called middle-class films) would be the least cost-effective. Such movies, which at the time of *sex, lies and videotape* included thrillers such as *Pacific Heights* (1990) and romances such as *Joe Versus the Volcano* (1990), based their appeal primarily on their stories or their stars. The studios' event films, conversely, based their appeal on action, special effects, superstars, and simple marketing hooks.[23] Event pictures drove up the marketing, production, and distribution costs of all studio films. However, from the mid-70s onward, the studios increasingly viewed them as worthwhile because of their broader international appeal and synergistic potential.

To a growing number of industry executives, middle-level films did not offer the same global opportunities as event films. If event films failed at home, they could still make money abroad; a Stallone film—typically an event due to his superstar presence—could easily be translated across the globe, guaranteeing international box-office success even if its fate was uncertain in the U.S. If middle-level films failed at home, they were not likely to perform any better abroad, since they had neither the effects and action nor the simple marketing hooks that were the high-concept foundations of the globally oriented Hollywood product. With Disney estimating that by 1996, 60 percent of studio revenues were coming from abroad, and with many executives predicting that the international box office could increase to 80 percent of total entertainment revenues by the first decade of the millennium, event films continued to become more desirable. Meanwhile, middle-level star-genre vehicles—the types of films that were the staple of the Hollywood studio era—continued to lose value.

The second reason for the foresight in Malin's comments comes from his exploitation of the rhetoric of quality. In using the label "sophisticated" to describe *sex, lies and videotape*, Malin employed language in a manner similar to the Weinsteins. In other words, he depicted these movies as special films rather than as industry products. More important than the actual industrial circumstances within which a movie such as *sex, lies and videotape* was produced is the manner in which it was constructed by its marketing team and the press. Companies such as Miramax could take terms such as "independent," "quality," "specialty," and "sophisticated" and use them as points of distinction, helped by the fact that in the late 80s the studios were frequently portrayed in the media as ever-expanding monoliths cranking out cookie-cutter sequels with excessive action and minimal plots.

Miramax's rapid growth stemmed largely from making itself and its films favorites of the press with its emphasis on how films such as *sex, lies and videotape* were different from Hollywood product. Yet at the same time, the company broadened the audience of these same movies by portraying them as what Hollywood had to offer *and more*: full of sex, violence, and risky content.[24] This marketing sleight of hand, in which the films were at once similar and different from Hollywood, helped Miramax and other low-budget distributors carve out an often financially lucrative and aesthetically viable space for independent cinema from the late 80s and into the 90s.

The $24 million earned by *sex, lies and videotape* in its U.S. theatrical release was, however, a small sum compared to the $80 million-plus earned by the quality indie blockbuster hits released later in the decade—movies that included *Pulp Fiction* (1994), *Good Will Hunting*, and *The Talented Mr. Ripley* (1999). Artisan's *The Blair Witch Project*, released almost exactly ten years after *sex, lies and videotape*, represented the culmination of the 1990s independent blockbuster trend. In its cost-to-profit ratio, its application of exploitation marketing tactics, its cinéma-vérité aesthetic, and its use of the discourse of independence to differentiate itself, *The Blair Witch Project* could be considered the cinematic descendant of Soderbergh's 1989 film.

If a strict structural definition of quality indie blockbusters were to apply, then very few independent films would qualify for it. Clearly, from an industrial standpoint, *Pulp Fiction, Good Will Hunting*, and *The Talented Mr. Ripley* are not independent; aesthetically, their independence is also questionable. In the New Hollywood as it evolved in the age of Miramax, indie films increasingly employed established stars and featured classical filmmaking and scripts from established talent. In other words, 1990s indies—if such Miramax movies as *Citizen Ruth* (1996), *Copland* (1997), and *Rounders* (1998) are included—could be considered a hybrid of the studio system's A picture and the post-studio-era exploitation film. This suggests the extent to which "independence" (or its hip offspring, "indie") served as a discursive tool employed by the press and the industry. In addition, such indie examples provide further proof that, by the late 90s, the industry's focus was divided between two types of films: niche-targeted and high-concept. Within this context, the niche arena functioned as the key site in which new styles and modes of storytelling were blended to varying degrees; all the while, established talent merged with newer, up-and-coming actors, writers, and directors.

Thus a term that was introduced by the press during the late 80s as a descriptive label to explain structural and aesthetic changes afoot in the New Hollywood morphed in the next decade into a publicity tool for

Miramax and its many imitators. The surprising fact was that even though by the mid-90s the label no longer held any definitional value, the press continued to celebrate the companies and the films as if they were guerrillas and renegades fighting Evil Hollywood. The most blatant example of this came from the consistent declaration by the mainstream press that "Independents Day" was afoot during the 1995 Oscar nominations. In this oft-titled "Year of the Independents," four low-budget indies—*The English Patient* (Miramax/Disney), *Breaking the Waves* (October/Universal), *Fargo* (Gramercy/Polygram), and *Shine* (Fine Line/Time Warner)—allegedly trounced the studios, which could only muster up one nominee, *Jerry Maguire* (Columbia). The irony was that all of these independents were released by subsidiaries owned by major media corporations. Yet attention to this shift came much more slowly. During most of the 90s, the main-stream press continued to depict the relationship between independents and majors in terms of conflict and opposition. It was not until Miramax tried to promote *Shakespeare in Love* (1998) as an independent that the tide truly started to turn. It was at this point that a significant portion of the press began to question the use of the label of independence by specialty divi-sions—and by themselves.

sex, lies and videotape: the template for the distribution of the 90s niche film

The critical and financial success of *sex, lies and videotape* not only served as an initial step in Miramax's ascendance to the status of top specialty dis-tributor of the 90s, it was also an indication of a changing industry. The bifurcation of the industry came with some repercussions. First, the two Hollywoods each developed interrelated but fundamentally distinct aesthet-ics. While superstars and super explosions defined the high-concept films, quality independents became defined by well-known actors working for scale because of their belief in the script's explosive subject matter. If high-concept films became known primarily for their glossy look and high production values, quality independents were distinguished by virtue of their gritty look or edgy content. Following in the tradition established by *sex, lies and videotape*, independents of the 90s often stood out either because of an excessiveness in style, sex, and violence, or because of a minimalist aesthetic that emphasizes dialogue over camerawork.

Second, as these films developed in the hands of studio-based specialty divisions, they needed to have a clearly defined niche—whether it was teens, African-Americans, Latinos, women, or the art-house audience. In the pro-cess, there was a decline not only in the types of low-budget films that attained distribution, but also in the production of the so-called middle-range product—the standard star-genre formulations that were the bread and butter of the studio system. By the late 90s, such films were typically only placed into production based on the influence wielded by such powerful stars as Jim Carrey, Tom Hanks, and Julia Roberts.

At the beginning of the new millennium, Miramax—as well as the independent scene that it fostered—has changed dramatically. After years of financial support from Disney, the company has grown from an independent to an industry powerhouse in its own right. Miramax regularly releases more than 25 films a year. Films like *Scary Movie, Scream,* and *Chocolat* help the company bring in over $500,000,000 at the box office annually. Occasionally Miramax acquires smaller, independently produced pictures like *Human Traffic* and *Committed*; however, such films are no longer a priority for the company's executives, nor are they the focus of its marketing muscle. Miramax now focuses on developing its own stable of talent—writers, producers, and filmmakers with whom the company had nurtured relationships during the 1990s. Many of these people, including Quentin Tarantino, Kevin Williamson, Robert Rodriguez, Wes Craven, Anthony Minghella, and John Madden, have seen their careers blossom in large part due to Miramax's support.

The company, as well as much of the talent it has supported, has long since moved beyond the boundaries of the independent film world. The styles, subjects, and talent that defined the quality indie scene of the early 90s have now been incorporated into the Hollywood system. Films that earlier might have been labeled quality indies are now regularly produced by studio subsidiaries such as Fox Searchlight, Fine Line Pictures, and of course, Miramax. The content and distribution of *Boys Don't Cry, Dancer in the Dark*, and Soderbergh's own *Traffic* replicate that of *sex, lies and videotape*. And, as Harvey Weinstein observes, *American Beauty* is a direct cinematic descendant of *sex, lies and videotape*. These films continue the tradition established by Miramax in the late 80s and early 90s: aesthetically and topically challenging films can be commercially successful with skillful marketing.

The future, however, does not seem quite so bright for many newer filmmakers and independent distributors struggling to find a space in today's marketplace. With the industry now dominated by a combination of studios releasing big-budget films and specialty distributors handling niche films, independent distributors such as Cowboy Booking International, Winstar, and New Yorker Films are fighting to acquire films and secure available screens. Meanwhile, several of the most influential independent distributors, including Trimark and The Shooting Gallery, have succumbed to today's market pressures and ceased to exist. All of this translates into a much more competitive and uncertain terrain for filmmakers working outside of the studio environment. While Miramax led the way in transforming Hollywood aesthetics, economics, and structure during the 90s, the company has now become a crucial part of the system. It remains to be seen what the next *sex, lies and videotape* will be—and what as yet unidentified company will help drive its success.

Notes

1 Jeff Gordinier, "Defy and Conquer," *Entertainment Weekly Special Edition: Our 10th Anniversary*, Spring 2000, p. 31.
2 Daniel Cerone, "Independent Film Makers, Marketers, Confront Box-Office Crisis," *Los Angeles Times*, 15 September, 1989, sec. 6, p. 4.
3 I employ the New Hollywood label as it is used by Thomas Schatz, "The New Hollywood," in *Film Theory Goes to the Movies*, ed. Jim Collins, Hillary Radner, and Ava Preacher Collins (New York: Routledge, 1998), pp. 25–32. For an extensive discussion of the intersection of aesthetics and marketing of big-budget Hollywood films, see Justin Wyatt, *High Concept: Movies and Marketing in Hollywood* (Austin, TX: University of Texas Press, 1994).
4 The term "indie" has been widely used by trade journalists to include films from studio specialty and niche subsidiaries such as Miramax, Fine Line, and Paramount Classics.
5 Paul D. Colford, "Movies Are Their Game; Miramax Steers Small Films into the Public Consciousness," *Newsday*, 20 February, 1990, part II, p. 8.
6 Scholars and journalists have acknowledged that there has been a split within the industry in recent years between low-budget niche films and high-concept event films, but in general, scholarly work on the emergence of independents and specialty houses has been limited. The majority of attention has been on the evolution of the high-concept blockbuster and big-budget product of the major studios. For examples, see Tino Balio, " 'A Major Presence in All the World's Important Markets': The Globalization of Hollywood in the 1990s," in *Contemporary Hollywood Cinema*, ed. Steve Neale and Murray Smith (London: Routledge, 1993), pp. 8–36, and Schatz, "The Return of the Hollywood Studio System," in *Conglomerates and the Media*, ed. Erik Barnouw (New York: The New York Press, 1997), pp. 73–106. While Balio, Schatz, and others have addressed the growth of specialty houses to an extent, Justin Wyatt has done the majority of work on low-budget product. For examples, see his discussions of Miramax and New Line in "Economic Constraints/Economic Opportunities: Robert Altman as Auteur," *The Velvet Light Trap* 38 (Fall 1996), pp. 51–67; "The Formation of the 'Major Independent': Miramax, New Line and the New Hollywood," in *Contemporary Hollywood Cinema*, pp. 74–90; and "From Roadshowing to Saturation Release: Majors, Independents and Marketing/Distribution Innovations," in *The New American Cinema*, ed. Jon Lewis (Durham, N.C.: Duke University Press, 1998), pp. 64–86.
7 I use the word "quality" throughout in much the same way it is used by Jane Feuer, Paul Kerr, and Tise Vahimagi in *MTM 'Quality Television'* (London: BFI, 1984). In "The MTM Style," Feuer, for example, writes that "The very concept of 'quality' is itself ideological. In interpreting an MTM programme as a quality programme, the quality audience is permitted to enjoy a form of television which is seen as more literate, more stylistically complex and more psychologically 'deep' than ordinary fare. The quality audience gets to separate itself from the mass audience and can watch TV without guilt, and without realising that the double-edged discourse that they are getting is also ordinary TV" (56). Quality independent films functioned in a similar sense for theatrical features released in the hands of Miramax.
8 John Pierson, *Spike, Mike, Slackers and Dykes: A Guided Tour Across a Decade of Independent American Cinema* (New York: Hyperion/Miramax Books, 1995), pp. 84, 87.
9 Steven Soderbergh, *sex, lies and videotape* (New York: Harper & Row, 1990), p. 21.

In the decade between the release of *sex, lies and videotape* and *The Blair Witch Project* (1999), this attitude shifted to a certain extent. By the end of the 1990s, it often became a means of product differentiation that a movie was shot on digital video.

10 Pierson, p. 131.

11 Aljean Harmetz, "Independent Films Get Bigger but Go Begging," *New York Times*, 1 February, 1989, p. C17.

12 Soderbergh, p. 225.

13 Colford, p. 8.

14 Ibid.

15 Cerone, "Taking an Independent Path," *Los Angeles Times*, 3 May, 1989, part 6, p. 1.

16 I apply the label "high concept" in much the same manner as it is applied by Wyatt in *High Concept*. He writes: "High concept can be conceived . . . as a product differentiated through the emphasis on style in production and through the integration of the film with their marketing" (23).

17 Colford, p. 8.

18 Cerone, "Independent Film Makers, Marketers Confront Box-Office Crisis," p. 4.

19 Cerone, "Taking an Independent Path, p. 1.

20 These tactics would change significantly by the late 90s as Miramax became the prominent studio subsidiary with a solid stable of prominent talent such as Quentin Tarantino, Wes Craven, and Kevin Williamson. At this point, both their product as well as their financial output altered somewhat, as vast sums of money were directed at marketing more commercially viable genre films such as *Scream* (1996), *Jackie Brown* (1997), and *The Faculty* (1998). Yet in terms of quality independents, Miramax's strategies remained remarkably stable during the 90s, altering only to the extent that the company had more capital to invest in production and marketing.

21 Jeff Gordinier and Chris Nashawaty, "Film's Next Frontier," *Entertainment Weekly*, 11 February, 2000, p. 20.

22 Cerone, "Smaller Films Seek a Summer Place," p. 1.

23 See Wyatt, *High Concept*, chapter 1.

24 The tension between presenting something "different" from the majors—and yet also more of the same—was a crucial element in Miramax's rise and its attractiveness to Disney. Yet paradoxically, it has also been the source of much consternation between Disney and Miramax as well as between Miramax and the press. The subsidiary and its parent have been repeatedly forced to test the threshold of what the public could handle in terms of risky and controversial subject matter on numerous occasions, including most dramatically *Kids* (1994), *Dogma* (1999), and *O* (2001). With both *Kids* and *Dogma*, the public outcry over Disney's relationship to these films compelled Miramax to sell the rights to both projects. With *O*, which portrayed racial conflict and violence in an American high school, Miramax kept the project shelved in the wake of the Columbine incident. There was scarcely any media outcry about Miramax handling this film; rather, the company pre-empted any such public conversation by continually pushing the film's release back until finally independent distributor Lion's Gate took over the film's theatrical distribution. This is just one further example of the way that a corporate parent has played a role in shifting the content and marketing strategies of Miramax in recent years. The same story could easily be told with other studio subsidiaries as well.